EUI — Series A — 2.1.3
Cappelletti/Seccombe/Weiler (Gen. Eds.)
Integration Through Law
Vol. 1: Cappelletti/Seccombe/Weiler (Eds.),
Methods, Tools and Institutions
Book 3: Forces and Potential for a European Identity

European University Institute
Institut Universitaire Européen
Europäisches Hochschulinstitut
Istituto Universitario Europeo

Series A

Law/Droit/Recht/Diritto

2.1.3

Badia Fiesolana — Firenze

Integration Through Law

Europe and the American Federal Experience

A Series under the General Editorship of

Mauro Cappelletti · Monica Seccombe · Joseph Weiler

Volume 1

Methods, Tools and Institutions

Book 3

Forces and Potential for a European Identity

edited by

Mauro Cappelletti · Monica Seccombe · Joseph Weiler

1986

Walter de Gruyter · Berlin · New York

Library of Congress Cataloging-in-Publication Data

Main entry under title:

Integration through law.

(Series A, Law / European University Institute = Series A, Droit / Institute Universitaire Européen ; 2.1.-)

Includes index.

Contents: v. 1. Methods, tools, and institutions. bk. 1. A political, legal, and economic overview. bk. 2. Political organs, integration techniques, and judicial process. bk. 3. Forces and potential for a European identity -- v. 2. Environmental protection policy / E. Rehbinder and R. Stewart.

1. Law--European Economic Community countries. 2. Law--United States. 3. Federal government.

I. Cappelletti, Mauro. II. Seccombe, Monica. III. Weiler, Joseph, 1951- . IV. Series: Series A--Law ; 2.1, etc.

KJE5075.I58 1985 340'.2 85-16320

ISBN 0-89925-111-0 (U.S. : v. 1.3) 342

CIP-Kurztitelaufnahme der Deutschen Bibliothek

Integration through law : Europe and the American federal experience / a ser. under the general editorship of Mauro Cappelletti ... – Berlin ; New York : de Gruyter

(European University Institute : Ser. A, Law ; 2)

NE: Cappelletti, Mauro [Hrsg.]; Istituto Universitario Europeo ⟨Fiesole⟩: European University Institute / A

Vol. 1. Methods, tools and institutions.

Book 3. Forces and potential for a European identity / ed. by Mauro Cappelletti ... – 1985.

ISBN 3-11-010332-X

Dust Cover Design: Rudolf Hübler, Berlin. — Setting: Satz-Rechen-Zentrum, Berlin.

Printing: H. Heenemann GmbH & Co., Berlin.

Binding: Verlagsbuchbinderei Dieter Mikolai, Berlin.

Printed in Germany.

Preface

The Florence Integration Through Law Series is the product of a research project centered in the Law Department of the European University Institute, and as such it reflects the research interests of the Department: it is a contextual examination of European legal developments in comparative perspective. In the general introduction to the Series (published in Book One of this volume), we explained fully the philosophy, methodology and scope of the Project. Here we wish merely to recapitulate some of the principal themes in this volume and to explain its relation to the entire Project.

The European Legal Integration Project set out to examine the role of law in, and the legal impact of, integration in Europe, using the United States federal system as a comparative point of reference. The Project was conceived and executed in two parts. In Part One (published in Volume I) a number of teams of American and European scholars examined a wide range of legal techniques and mechanisms for integration and undertook an overall general analysis of law and integration. The first book of Volume I ("A Political, Legal, and Economic Overview") establishes the comparative and interdisciplinary context, providing background studies on the political, legal and economic implications of integration in Europe and America and including studies on other federal systems (Australia, Canada, Germany and Switzerland) to add comparative perspective. The second book ("Political Organs, Integration Techniques, and Judicial Process") analyzes the pre- and post-normative stages of the legal process, examining the decision-making and implementation problems, and the role of political and judicial organs therein, and describing the various forms of normative techniques available in a federal or supranational context.

In this, the third and final book of Volume I, the contributors focus on how the law can be harnessed to promote the governmental or integrational objectives of union. They isolate for consideration some substantive goals (foreign policy, free movement of goods and persons, human rights protection and legal education), in order to elucidate the ways in which law has been or can be used to promote substantive objectives. This approach is more fully developed in the studies in Part Two of the Project which deals in greater detail with substantive areas of federal/transnational policy and is open-ended. To date monographs have been planned in the following five areas: environmental protection, consumer protection, harmonization of corporation law and capital markets, energy policy, and regional policy. It is hoped that further studies may be undertaken in the future.

Florence, December 1984 *M. C., M. S., J. W.*

Acknowledgements

This is one of several volumes on "Integration Through Law: Europe and the American Federal Experience" being published under the joint sponsorship of the European University Institute and the Ford Foundation, which together funded an international research project on "Methods, Tools and Potential for European Legal Integration in Light of the American Federal Experience" co-directed by Professors Mauro Cappelletti and Joseph Weiler. The Project, headquartered at the European University Institute in Florence, involved the participation of over forty scholars mostly from Europe and America. In addition to thanking the European University Institute and the Ford Foundation which were the principal sponsors, the Project Directors would like to express their gratitude to the Institutions of the European Communities, particularly the Commission, whose contribution has been most encouraging. A special acknowledgement is due to Professor Martin Shapiro of the University of California at Berkeley, who coordinated the American contributions to the Project, and also to the following law graduates who acted as Associate Editors:

Robert Helm
Gwendolyn Griffith
Deborah McIntyre
Betty Meshack
Bruno de Witte
Karen Burke
Grayson McCouch
William Skrzyniarz
Robert Wise
Christopher Bertics

Finally we acknowledge our debt to the Project secretaries: Evie Valerio, Marie-Ange Catotti and Lisa Alisi.

Summary Table of Contents

Table of Contents

Part I
The International Dimension

Towards a European Foreign Policy? — The European Foreign Affairs System from the Perspective of the United States Constitution
by Eric Stein *in collaboration with* Louis Henkin

Part II
The Social and Economic Dimension

Migrant Workers and Rights of Mobility in the European Community and the United States: A Study of Law, Community, and Citizenship in the Welfare State

by Bryant Garth

Legal Integration and the Free Movement of Goods: The American and European Experience
by Donald Kommers *and* Michel Waelbroeck

Part III
The Moral and Cultural Dimension

The Protection of Fundamental Human Rights as a Vehicle of Integration
by Jochen Abr. Frowein, Stephen Schulhofer *and* Martin Shapiro

A List of Abbreviations is to be found in Book 1

Table of Cases

European Court of Justice

European Commission of Human Rights

European Court of Human Rights

International Court of Justice

National Courts

France

Conseil d'Etat

Germany, Federal Republic of

Bundesverfassungsgericht (Constitutional Court)

Verwaltungsgericht, Neustadt a/d Weinstrasse

United Kingdom

United States of America

Part I

The International Dimension

Towards a European Foreign Policy? The European Foreign Affairs System from the Perspective of the United States Constitution

ERIC STEIN*

in collaboration with

LOUIS HENKIN**

I. Introduction

A. Purpose of the Study

This study will describe the constitutional and institutional arrangements for the conduct of foreign relations in the United States and in the Europe of the Ten, identifying the differences and their consequences. It will consider what features of the United States system and experience were important in achieving a unified, national posture in foreign affairs and it will explore

* Hessel E. Yntema Professor of Law, University of Michigan Law School.

I am indebted to Professor Louis Henkin of Columbia University Law School for his invaluable advice; I drew heavily on his writings, particularly on his classic *Foreign Affairs and the Constitution.* I also appreciate greatly the assistance of Mr Hermann da Fonseca-Wollheim, Deputy Head of Delegation of the Commission of the EC, Washington, D.C., and Mr Per Lachmann, Chief Legal Advisor on Common Market Law, Ministry of Foreign Affairs, Copenhagen, Denmark, visiting scholar, University of Michigan Law School.

I have received helpful comments from Dr C.-D. Ehlermann, Director General, Legal Service of the Commission of the EC, and from Mr J. Bourgeois of his staff; from Professor H. G. Schermers of Leiden University, the Netherlands; and from the participants in the conference held at the European University Institute, Florence, Italy, in December 1981. Herbert Glaser, Philippe Jambrun, Jeffrey Lehman, Jacqueline Letzler-Kuster, Paul van Leeuwen, Mitri Najjar and Yves Quintin, students at the University of Michigan Law School, assisted me in the research. However, I alone, am responsible for the opinions expressed in the paper.

I completed the final draft of this article at the Max-Planck Institut für ausländisches öffentliches Recht und Völkerrecht in Heidelberg, with the support of the Alexander von Humboldt Stiftung which is gratefully acknowledged.

** University Professor, Columbia University.

whether, despite the crucial differences, the federal experience may offer helpful insights to European decision-makers. Consideration will be given to the trends affecting the institutions of the European Community and the European Political Cooperation mechanism which militate for or against Europe speaking with a single voice in the international arena.

This introductory part will set forth definitions of the basic concepts and the pattern for analysis employed in the study, and it will highlight the salient differences between the foreign affairs structures in the United States and in the Europe of the Ten.

B. The "Foreign Affairs Powers": A Definition and a Pattern for Analysis

States, the classic "persons" in international law, wield the full panoply of foreign affairs powers. International organizations may also have an "international personality" and possess certain foreign affairs powers. Federal states and international organizations are archetypes of divided power systems. We are concerned with the scope and modalities of foreign affairs powers in two divided power systems, a federal state and the Community, a *sui generis* divided power system (a "new legal order in international law"[1]), placed on a continuum somewhere between a traditional inter-governmental organization and a federal state, exercising more extensive foreign affairs powers than any other international organization.

1. States: Foreign Affairs Powers

In the international political system, the government of a state has the following principal capacities, rights and duties: (a) to communicate with other governments (and other "persons" in international law) through a variety of formal and informal means ("diplomacy," active and passive right of legation); (b) to determine national policies affecting other states (authority within the territory and maritime and air space, foreign economic policy, security and defense policy, communication and transportation, regulation of aliens, or of nationals abroad); (c) to make treaties and participate in the formation of customary international law and to participate in international organizations; (d) to carry out obligations under international law and agreements, and to pursue remedies for violations of obligations by others; and to extend diplomatic protection and advance international claims on behalf of its nationals and to respond to international claims.[2]

[1] Case 26/62, Van Gend en Loos v. Nederlandse Administratie der Belastingen, [1963] ECR 1, 12.

[2] *See, e. g.*, Pescatore, *Les relations extérieures des Communautés européennes*, [1961] II Rec. des Cours Acad. dr. int. 1, 19–20.

2. International Organizations

Pursuant to different theories, international organizations have: (a) only such "personality," capacity, rights and duties in the international system as are specifically attributed in their charter; (b) all such powers as are needed to achieve the charter purposes as determined by the appropriate interpretation of the charter; (c) certain "inherent" powers, not necessarily derived from the charter but recognized by international law as applicable to international organizations generally.[3]

3. Divided Power Systems: Allocation of Powers

In divided power systems all powers are allocated between the composite entity and its component parts. The allocation is grounded in the constitutive documents which may take the form of a constitution or a treaty. As a treaty-based system becomes more intimately integrated, important questions arise whether the provisions relating to the allocation of powers are to be interpreted in accordance with international institutional law or in a constitutional mode, germane to internal public law.

In divided-power systems, two principles of allocation of powers may be examined: (a) allocation between the central authority and the component units; and (b) allocation between the institutions of the central authority (in a federation: legislative, executive, judiciary; in the Community: inter-governmental law-and-policy-making, executive, judiciary, parliament).[4]

The allocations vary over time. Tension may develop, due either to power competition or disagreement on the merit of an action, either between the central authority and the component units (problems of "federalism"); or, between the institutions of the central authority itself (problems of "separation of powers," "checks and balances").

Allocation apart, there may be limitations on the government's exercise of power in foreign relations because some powers are in principle withheld by the constitution or charter or because general limitations on delegated authority exist, for instance the limitations embodied in a "Bill of Rights" or based on general principles for the protection of human rights.

4. Foreign Affairs Powers and Foreign Policy

Effective foreign policy postulates a communications network assuring a flow of information, establishing and reviewing objectives on a hierarchic scale of priorities, strategic planning of action and implementation through diplomacy and through foreign economic, financial, cultural, and military instrumentalities. In modern pluralist systems, the process is "democratized" with parlia-

[3] E. Stein, P. Hay & M. Waelbroeck, European Community Law and Institutions in Perspective 927–29 (Indianapolis/New York, Bobbs-Merrill, 1976).

[4] Is the foreign relations power "executive," "legislative," or "federative"? *See,* Q. Wright, The Control of American Foreign Relations 134 ff (New York, MacMillan, 1922).

mentary bodies, political parties and cultural-scientific-special interest groups claiming greater voice. In particular, even where the component states as such are excluded from any *participation* in foreign policy process, they may *impinge* on the process. Moreover, foreign affairs cannot be separated from domestic affairs: above all in economic life, they are inseparably mixed.[5]

C. United States and European Systems Contrasted: The Relevance of a Comparison

Despite basic systemic and contextual differences, comparison in certain "internal" fields (*e.g.*, interstate commerce in the United States and free movement of goods within the EEC) has clearly proved of interest to both Americans and Europeans.[6] However, in the foreign affairs field the institutional differences are even more pronounced so as to raise the question whether a comparison can be meaningful.

1. Some Differences

a) Unitary Authority v. Divided Power

With respect to foreign affairs the United States is, in effect, a unitary state with exclusive federal foreign affairs power, a national diplomatic establishment and a national army. Under the United States Constitution, the component states are excluded from participation in foreign affairs but their activities and laws often impinge on federal policy and activities.[7] In the Community, on the other hand, there is a complex division of foreign affairs powers between the Member States and the Community institutions. The Member States remain sovereign nation-states, they retain full control of their armies, defense policies and foreign "political" policies (subject to an extra-Community consultative mechanism, the European Political Cooperation).[8] In the economic and monetary fields, the Members share their authority with the Community. However, even

[5] In seeking to identify the variables that enhance or inhibit integration in foreign affairs the paradigms evolved by the various doctrines (functionalist, neo-functionalist, federalist, security-Community, etc.) may be helpful. For a discussion and further references *see* Elazar & Greilsammer, *The Federal Democracy: The U.S.A. and Europe Compared — A Political Science Perspective, supra* this vol., Bk. 1, at § II.A.3.b.

[6] *See, e.g.*, Stein & Sandalow, *On the Two Systems: An Overview*, in COURTS AND FREE MARKETS: PERSPECTIVES FROM THE UNITED STATES AND EUROPE 3, 3–4 (T. Sandalow & E. Stein eds., Oxford/New York, Clarendon Press, 1982) [hereinafter cited as COURTS AND FREE MARKETS].

[7] In foreign affairs, states are "deaf and dumb" according to King, as quoted in 1 FARRAND, THE RECORDS OF THE FEDERAL CONVENTION OF 1787, at 323 (New Haven, Yale U.P., 1937). *See* L. HENKIN, FOREIGN AFFAIRS AND THE CONSTITUTION 336 n.71 (New York, Foundation Press, 1972).

[8] For discussion of the European Political Cooperation mechanism, *see infra* notes 244–308 and accompanying text.

in the areas within the exclusive power of the Community, the Member States, unlike the American states, *participate* in the policy-making as a result of their role in the central Community organ, the Council of Ministers.

The foreign affairs power of the Federal Government in the United States has been exclusive of the states since its inception by virtue first of the Articles of Confederation and then of the Constitution. The President and the Congress have been the primary actors and whatever constitutional controversy there has been has related to allocation between President and Congress, not between federal and state authority. "Federalism," on the whole, has not been an issue in foreign relations. In general, any controversy between states of the Union about the foreign policy of the United States has centered on the content of the policy, *e.g.* free trade or protectionism, rather than on its constitutional underpinning, although the arguments have sometimes been dressed in a constitutional mode. In comparison with "domestic" constitutional law, the changes in foreign relations constitutional law have not been radical. The courts have not played a crucial role in foreign affairs law, and scholars, accustomed to dealing principally in case law, have neglected the field.[9]

Allocation of power within the Community generally continues to evolve. The Community foreign affairs power, too, has been subject to evolution, since the Community itself is conceived as a *dynamic* progression. The Community institutions are expected to assume new powers as economic and political integration advances. As a result, the "federalism" issue – the tension between Member States ("assembled in the Council of Ministers")[10] and the Community (represented by the independent executive Commission) – has been at the center of the foreign relations debate, and the Court of Justice has performed the task of umpire. In contrast with the United States, the case law of the Court of Justice is essential and legal literature is more than abundant. The Community's "parliamentary" organ, the European Parliament, on the other hand, has played but a limited advisory role, although, particularly since it has been chosen by direct election, it has been increasingly vocal in demanding more meaningful participation in foreign affairs.

b) Relations Among Constituent States

In the United States, relations among the states of the Union are "internal" relations and they are governed exclusively by "domestic" (principally

[9] L. HENKIN, *supra* note 7, at 5–6. More recently, scholarly output has been increasing because of the increased number of litigations with foreign affairs aspects.

[10] I have used the phrase "assembled in the Council of Ministers" to stress the intergovernmental nature of the Council. "The Representatives of the Member States meeting in the Council" are, of course, an entirely different matter. *See* P.S.R.F. MATHIJSEN, A GUIDE TO EUROPEAN COMMUNITY LAW § 5–12, at 243–44 (2nd ed., London/New York, Sweet & Maxwell/M. Bender, 1975). *Cf.* the phrase "United States, in Congress assembled" in the Articles of Confederation, *e.g.* in Art. V: "In determining questions in the United States, in Congress assembled, each State shall have one vote."

constitutional and federal) law.[11] In the Community, major sectors of relations among Member States are not governed by Community law, but continue to be determined by international law or appropriate Member State law.

c) Citizenship

In the United States, the Constitution itself provided the foundation for a single national citizenship and federal control of immigration. Federal citizenship is primary, state citizenship is of minor importance and of none in foreign affairs. A citizen of the United States is ipso facto citizen of the state of his domicile.[12]

In Europe, however, there is no Community citizenship, only Member State citizenship, and each state retains its own alien control regime, subject only to the Treaty rights of Member State nationals to move freely within the Community for specific economic purposes. By a special agreement the Benelux countries maintain a common control over aliens.

2. The Relevance of a Comparison

Considering these vital differences, one may ask whether a comparison may be useful only for highlighting and better comprehending the characteristics of each system, or whether the federal experience and method may also be relevant for the European decision-makers. The question is particularly appropriate in view of the different methods employed by American federalism in domestic and foreign affairs. In the domestic field states continue to have considerable scope in pursuing their domestic policies but no such suppleness and flexibility exist in dealing with foreign nations.

Pescatore rightly rejects any effort to attribute any specific foreign relations power to the Community by analogy with the powers of a nation-state, unitary or federal; he is nevertheless convinced that "federalist interpretation of the

[11] The Supreme Court occasionally draws on customary international law in deciding disputes between states, especially in matters analogous to international disputes, *e.g.*, boundaries. *See, e.g.*, Arkansas v. Tennessee, 246 U.S. 158, 170 (1918) and 310 U.S. 563, 570 (1940).

[12] Congressional power over naturalization is exclusive of the individual states. The Constitutional foundation was solidified by the post-Civil War fourteenth amendment which provided in sec. 1: "All persons born or naturalized in the United States, and subject to the jurisdiction thereof, are citizens of the United States and of the state wherein they reside." Under the Articles of Confederation, "the free inhabitants" of each state (not including paupers, vagabonds and fugitives from justice) were "entitled to all privileges and immunities of free citizens in the several States" (Art. IV), but it was left to each state individually to prescribe the terms upon which it would admit foreigners to citizenship. Thus, a lax policy of naturalization in one state could frustrate the stricter policies of the other states. According to Roger Sherman, the Constitution gave Congress the power to establish a uniform rule of naturalization (art. I, sec. 8, cl. 4), in order "to prevent particular States receiving citizens, and forcing them upon others." Quoted in E. Dumbauld, The Constitution of the United States 139 (Norman, Okla., U. Okla. P., 1964).

European Treaties is particularly fruitful; ... it is really in the thought, in the methods and in the historical experience of federalism that the future builders of Europe should seek their inspiration, much more than in the domain of international relations."[13]

II. The Formal Allocation of Powers in the United States and in the European Community

A. The Impact of Foreign Affairs Concerns on the Allocation of Powers in Both Systems

"Foreign affairs" played an important role at the inception of the American Republic and of the Community: both emerged from a war which loosened the established order and called for innovating structures. The necessity of presenting a united front to the rest of the world has had far-reaching implications for both. However, interesting as this juxtaposition may be, the egregious contextual differences call into question any facile comparison.

1. Post-Revolution America

In America, it was the 1776 War of Independence that severed the centralizing tie between the colonies and their mother country, Britain. Under the "Articles of Confederation and Perpetual Union" the foreign affairs powers were vested in "the United States, in Congress assembled" with each of the thirteen states wielding one vote; major foreign affairs issues were to be decided by a majority of nine of the thirteen votes.[14] There was no provision for an executive. Despite the decisive contextual differences, the analogy in institutional terms between "the United States, in Congress assembled," and the ten Member States of the Community, "assembled" in the EC Council of Ministers (and deciding in effect by consensus) is tempting, but the existence of the executive Commission, and its role in foreign affairs, bear testimony that in this respect the Community is more effectively organized than was the Confederation.

The inadequacies of the Confederation for coping with foreign affairs supplied a significant impulse for the federal Constitution. In the first place, the proceeding whereby Congress conducted diplomacy and negotiated treaties through its agents "suffered from the want of secrecy and dispatch"[15] so as to

[13] Pescatore, *supra* note 2, at 21.

[14] M. Jensen, The Articles of Confederation – An Interpretation of the Social Constitutional History of the American Revolution 1774–1781, at 143–45 (Madison, Wis., U. Wis. P., 1940).

[15] The Federalist No. 64, at 393 (J. Jay) (C. C. Rossiter ed., New York, The New American Library, 1961). The Congress was not in continuous session, it was rent by bitter disagreements; absenteeism often caused lack of a quorum and it was frequently embroiled in trivialities. E. Dumbauld, *supra* note 12, at 32–33.

seriously impair the international position of the young republic. The efforts to build up the office of the Congress' secretary for foreign affairs from that of a glorified clerk met with only a qualified success due to Congress' jurisdictional jealousy.[16] One is reminded of the checkered history of the attempts – thus far similarly unsuccessful – to establish a permanent secretariat for the European Political Cooperation mechanism.[17] While confederate diplomatic activity lagged, contrary to specific prohibitions in the Articles individual states engaged in diplomatic negotiations with foreign nations, concluded agreements, outfitted their own armies and navies, imposed embargoes, engaged in war with the Indians and formed compacts with each other.[18] The Congress' lack of independent power to raise troops and impose taxes for their support resulted in the nation being forced to endure incursions on its territorial sovereignty.[19] The chaotic situation which undermined the credibility of the Confederation was compounded by the inability of the Congress to force recalcitrant states into compliance with treaties concluded by the Congress with European nations.[20] The lack of power in the Congress to regulate foreign commerce[21] made effective trade negotiations impossible, and when the British imposed an embargo on the crucial American trade in the West Indies, the Congress was in no position to retaliate. The young Republic was frustrated in its attempts to establish a "new international economic order" based on equitable commercial relations.[22]

The prominence of foreign relations concerns in the Constitutional Convention and in the subsequent ratification debates confirms the influence the external environment exerted toward a radical reshaping of the central government in the federal pattern.

2. Post-War Europe

In Europe, the upheaval caused by "the greatest civil war in history" loosened the traditional attachments to state sovereignty enough to allow for a modest

[16] On the first secretary, Robert R. Livingston, *see* L.S. Kaplan, Colonies into Nation: American Diplomacy 1763–1801, at 151 (New York, MacMillan, 1972); on John Jay's tenure, *see id.* at 155.

[17] *See infra* text accompanying note 264.

[18] W.P. Murphy, The Triumph of Nationalism 38 (Chicago, Quadrangle Books, 1967); F.W. Marks, Independence on Trial 3–4 (Baton Rouge, La. State U.P., 1973); Van Tyne, *Sovereignty in the American Revolution: A Historical Study,* 12 Am. Hist. Rev. 529, 540–41 (1907).

[19] F.W. Marks, *supra* note 18, at 15, 47. Under the Articles, the Congress had only the power to agree upon the number of troops to be raised but the men were recruited by the states, although at Continental expense.

[20] T. Bailey, A Diplomatic History of the American People, ch. 5 (8th ed., New York, Appleton-Century-Crofts (Meredith), 1969).

[21] *See* Art. VI as read with Art. IX of the Articles of Confederation.

[22] F.W. Marks, *supra* note 18, at 54–56, 68. *See also, generally,* P.A. Varg, Foreign Policies of the Founding Fathers 51–53 (Lansing, Mich., Mich. State U.P., 1963).

transfer of power in pursuance of the Monnet model of progressive integration by sectors.[23] In 1951, the Community, in its first incarnation, became reality in the coal and steel sector because, at a critical moment, it offered an urgently needed solution for dealing with the defeated Germany.[24] The inexorable American pressure for German rearmament arising from the Korean War forced the temporary abandonment of Monnet's priority for integration in the economic and monetary sectors and brought forth, in the early 1950's, the abortive draft for the European Defense Community, with the concommittant European Political Community.[25] "I have never believed," wrote Monnet, "that we should tackle the problem of Europe via defense. Although this would no doubt be one task for the future federation, it seemed to me by no means the most powerful or compelling motive for unity. ... [W]e were forced to take short cuts."[26]

It is illuminating for an understanding of the European Political Cooperation mechanism as it has developed since 1969 that, although the Defense Community had envisaged an integration of armed forces and military budgets and other steps toward a federal structure, the Political Community did not call for additional transfer of national powers; a common foreign policy was to evolve through coordination of national policies by the member states.[27] In 1954, the two schemes (both of which were of French origin, as was the European Coal and Steel Community) fell victim to a change of the French Government and its reversion to the policy of a "French Europe." As a result, instead of a European controlled army, France had to accept the most dreaded of alternatives, the reconstitution of a German national army in a "feebly coordinated structure" of a military alliance.[28] This marked the end of the attempt to create a European army as an instrument of a common foreign policy and defense.

With France having lost the initiative, it was left to Belgian and Dutch statesmen to restore the sectoral integration process on the basis of Monnet's priorities. The result was the European Economic Community and the Euratom Treaties. It is difficult to identify or to measure the weight of the discrete variables motivating a major historic movement but it is probably accurate to say that foreign affairs concerns played a less prominent role in the

23 For further discussion of the process of integration after World War II, *see* Elazar & Greilsammer, *supra* note 5, at § II.A.3.b.

24 J. Monnet, Memoirs 288–317, 340 (New York, Doubleday & Co., 1978).

25 The European Defense Community Treaty, Paris, 27 May 1952, Cmd. No. 9127 (London, H.M.S.O., 1952); J. Legaret & E. Martin-Dumesnil, La Communauté Européenne de Défense – Etude analytique du traité du 27 mai 1952 (Paris, Lib. J. Vrin, 1953); Ad hoc Assembly, Draft Treaty embodying the Statute of the European Community presented to the Assembly by the Constitutional Committee, Doc. 12, 2nd Part, Paris, 26 Feb. 1953.

26 J. Monnet, *supra* note 24, at 338, 343.

27 *Id.* at 394.

28 *Id.* at 395, 398.

impulse toward these two treaties than was the case with the ECSC.[29] However, the Suez Canal imbroglio may have eased the passage of the Rome Treaties through national parliaments.[30] Moreover, it is beyond question that particularly during the early history, the perceived threat from the East and American power in the West favored significantly the integration process.[31] Generally, the Community's foreign relations have developed to a great extent in response to outside pressures and demands.[32] In responding to these outside stimuli the Commission has often acted not only in the interest of Community foreign policy but also in furtherance of its own authority and of the integrity of the Community's independent personality.

B. The Allocation of Powers in the Constituent Documents

Unlike some modern national constitutions[33] neither the United States Constitution nor the Community Treaties allocate in bulk "power to conduct foreign relations." Instead, on their face they adopt the pattern of "enumerated powers" or "*compétence d'attribution*" by attributing specific powers to particular central authorities. More specifically, in the Constitution provisions scattered in three articles vest certain powers in Congress, others in the President (alone or jointly with the Senate),[34] and in one article states are expressly denied a role in the important aspects of foreign affairs.[35] The Constitution is

[29] The important *Spaak Report* which served as a foundation for the two treaties devotes a single page – on "unification of the commercial policy" – out of a total of 135 pp. to a foreign affairs subject. Comité Intergouvernemental créé par la Conférence de Messine, Rapport des Chefs de Délégation aux Ministres des Affaires Etrangères 75 (Brussels, Secrétariat, 21 Apr. 1956).

[30] Monnet quotes Armand as suggesting "that we erect a statue to Nasser, the federator of Europe. It was a joke." J. Monnet, *supra* note 24, at 422.

[31] The intensity of American power – and its impact – have varied. For instance, Secretary Dulles' pressure in support of the European Defense Community is said to have contributed to its defeat in France, but Secretary Kissinger's counterproductive "Year of Europe" campaign may have stimulated the debate over "European identity."

[32] *See infra* note 165 and accompanying text.

[33] *See, e.g.*, Grundgesetz (GG] art. 32 (W.Ger.). *See also id.* art. 59.

[34] U.S. Const. art. I, § 8, cls. 1–5, 10–16; art. II, § 2, cls. 1–2, § 3; art. VI, § 2. On judicial power, *see* art. III, § 2, cls. 1–2; § 3, cl. 1.

[35] U.S. Const. art. 1, § 10 provides:

> 1. No State shall enter into any treaty, alliance, or confederation; grant letters of marque and reprisal....
>
> 2. No State shall, without the consent of the Congress, lay any imposts or duties on imports or exports, except what may be absolutely necessary for executing its inspection laws: and the net produce of all duties and imposts, laid by any State on imports or exports, shall be for the use of the treasury of the United States; and all such laws shall be subject to the revision and control of the Congress.

silent on many other foreign affairs powers. Similarly, the Treaties contain attributions to the Commission and the Council of specific powers in a series of articles[36] but, in contrast with the Constitution, there is no express denial of a Member States' role in foreign affairs. However, the argument that the absence alone of such denial preserved Member State power has been rejected by the Court of Justice.[37] It is left to the central authorities to deal with the "silences and gaps" in the constitutive instrument.

1. Specific Attributions of Foreign Affairs Powers - An Overview

a) In the United States Constitution

As mentioned earlier,[38] the dissatisfaction with making war and conducting diplomacy by the collective "United States, in Congress assembled," was a major impetus for the decision to convene the Constitutional Convention and seek a "more perfect union." The same painful experience impelled the Founders to create the office of President and vest it with "executive powers." The sparse clauses in the Constitution pertaining to his role in foreign affairs (shared in some instances by the Senate) provide:

Article II:

Section 2. 1. The President shall be commander-in-chief of the army and navy of the United States, and of the militia of the several States, when called into the actual service of the United States. ...

2. He shall have power, by and with the advice and consent of the Senate, to make treaties, provided two thirds of the senators present concur; and he shall nominate, and by and with the advice and consent of the Senate, shall appoint ambassadors, other public ministers and consuls. ...

3. The President shall have power to fill up all vacancies that may happen during the recess of the Senate, by granting commissions which shall expire at the end of their next session.

Section 3. ... [H]e shall receive ambassadors and other public ministers; he shall take care that the laws be faithfully executed, and shall commission all the officers of the United States.[39]

However, on the face of the Constitution at any rate, the principal policy powers in foreign (as in domestic) affairs were assigned to Congress. Article I, section 8 provides in pertinent part:

3. No State shall, without the consent of Congress, lay any duty of tonnage, keep troops, or ships of war in time of peace, enter into any agreement or compact with another State, or with a foreign power, or engage in war, unless actually invaded, or in such imminent danger as will not admit of delay.

See also art. I, § 9, cls. 5 & 6.

36 EEC Treaty arts. 28, 111–14, 228–31, 237–38.

37 *See infra* text accompanying note 207.

38 *See supra* notes 14–22 and accompanying text.

39 Art. II, cls. 1 & 2, § 3. *See* E.S. Corwin, The President's Control of Foreign Relations 3 (Princeton, Princeton U.P., 1917).

The Congress shall have the power

1. To lay and collect taxes, duties, imposts, and excises, to pay the debts and provide for the common defense and general welfare of the United States. ...

...

3. To regulate commerce with foreign nations. ...

4. To establish an uniform rule of naturalization. ...

...

10. To define and punish piracies and felonies committed on the high seas, and offenses against the law of nations;

11. To declare war, grant letters of marque and reprisal, and make rules concerning captures on land and water;

12. To raise and support armies, but no appropriation of money to that use shall be for a longer term than two years;

13. To provide and maintain a navy. ...

...

18. To make all laws which shall be necessary and proper for carrying into execution the foregoing powers, and all other powers vested by this Constitution in the government of the United States, or any department or officer thereof.

There is, as I have already suggested, more to foreign affairs than can be accounted for by the laconic allocations of the Constitution. Although Congress' enumerated grants are much more generous – since they include "all legislative powers," war power, the power of the purse and regulation of commerce – powers not expressly delegated in the Constitution have largely flowed to the President who has become the predominant actor in foreign affairs. The President and Congress share the *total* and *exclusive* foreign affairs power of the United States but the distribution between them corresponds only in some measure to the classic separation of legislative from executive functions in domestic affairs. The competition for power between the two branches has constituted "the dominant, least-tractable constitutional issue of American foreign relations."[40]

b) In the EEC Treaty

The specific attributions of foreign affairs powers to the Community center on foreign commercial policy which is implemented through "autonomous" Community acts, international agreements and interaction with international organizations. Except perhaps for the power to enact common commercial policy there are no general grants such as we encountered in the Constitution.

The attributed powers are shared between the independent Commission, "the conscience of the Community," and the "Member States assembled in Council," with the Council holding the preponderant authority of final decision. In specified instances, (but not, for example, in the important tariff and trade negotiations) the European Parliament must be consulted, but its opinions are advisory only and its budgetary power is very limited. The traditional structure of three separate and equal branches – the executive, legislative and judicial – obviously has no application in the foreign affairs area any more than in the domestic affairs.

[40] L. Henkin, *supra* note 7, at 90.

The Commission is given the exclusive right of initiative which, with respect to "autonomous acts," such as modifications of the Common Customs Tariff, it exercises by making a formal proposal to the Council; the Council cannot act without such proposal and cannot modify it except by a unanimous vote.[41] However, in the process of making commercial agreements the Commission can only recommend opening the negotiations but it alone negotiates under the direction of the Council which in turn "concludes" the resulting agreement.[42]

Outside the commercial policy chapter, the Treaty part dealing with general and final provisions is headed by article 210 which affirms the Community's "legal personality."[43] Other provisions lay down the general treaty-making procedure;[44] authorize the Community to enter into agreements of "association" of an undetermined content with third countries or international bodies;[45] direct the Commission to enter into appropriate relationships with specified international organizations;[46] and regulate the conditions of accession to Community membership of "any European State" which may apply.[47]

41 EEC Treaty arts. 28, 113(1)–(2) & 149.

42 EEC Treaty arts. 111 and 112: tariff negotiations and harmonization of national policies during the transitional period; arts. 113 and 114: negotiation and conclusion of tariff and trade agreements with third countries. *See also* art. 115: protective measures against deflections of trade; art. 116: Member States to proceed "only by common action" within international organizations.

43 Discussed *infra* text accompanying note 69.

44 Art. 228 provides:

> 1. Where this Treaty provides for the conclusion of agreements between the Community and one or more States or an international organisation, such agreements shall be negotiated by the Commission. Subject to the powers vested in the Commission in this field, such agreements shall be concluded by the Council, after consulting the Assembly where required by this Treaty.
>
> The Council, the Commission or a Member State may obtain beforehand the opinion of the Court of Justice as to whether an agreement envisaged is compatible with the provisions of this Treaty. Where the opinion of the Court of Justice is adverse, the agreement may enter into force only in accordance with Article 236.
>
> 2. Agreements concluded under these conditions shall be binding on the institutions of the Community and on Member States.

45 Art. 238 provides:

> The Community may conclude with a third State, a union of States or an international organisation agreements establishing an association involving reciprocal rights and obligations, common action and special procedures.
>
> These agreements shall be concluded by the Council, acting unanimously after consulting the Assembly.
>
> Where such agreements call for amendments to this Treaty, these amendments shall first be adopted in accordance with the procedure laid down in Article 236.

46 EEC Treaty arts. 229, 230, 231. Part Four on association of the overseas countries and territories is of limited importance today.

47 EEC Treaty art. 237.

In the United States, where the monopoly in foreign affairs of the Federal Government has been accepted from the inception, the courts were left with the task of inventing a plausible doctrine.[48] In Europe, although the Commission with the Council are called upon in the first instance to draw a line between the Member State and Community foreign affairs powers, the complex and controversial task of fashioning a coherent doctrine from the handful of Treaty attributions fell to the Court of Justice.

2. Methodology of Constituent Documents – Interpretation

a) Gaps in the United States Constitution and How They Are Filled

In the United States, no explanation of the lacunae and no interpretive method for filling them has been universally accepted, but under all the doctrines, foreign affairs remain exclusively federal.[49] Henkin lists several attempts to fill the missing powers by traditional methods of constitutional interpretation and construction:

> Traditional interpreters of the Constitution have attempted to find the missing powers by traditional doctrines of constitutional construction. Foreign affairs powers expressly granted have been held to imply others: for example, the power to make treaties implies the power to terminate or break them. And some powers taken together have been found to "result" in others: for example, the power to appoint ambassadors and the power to receive foreign ambassadors "result" in the power to do other things involved in maintaining relations with a foreign country. Foreign affairs powers ... have been spun also from general grants of power and from designations read as grants, for example, the power of Congress to do what is "necessary and proper" to carry out other powers (Art. I, sec. 8), or the provision vesting in the President "the executive Power" (Art. II, sec. 1). Additional powers for the federal government might be inferred from their express denial to the States.[50]

Neither these methods nor the extrapolation from "the Constitution as a whole," while serving their purpose in specific instances, have been accepted as sufficient and exclusive. In 1889, in the *Chinese Exclusion Case*,[51] the Supreme Court embraced a more radical interpretation, when it held that in addition to the enumerated powers and their derivatives, the Constitution vests in the Federal Government powers inherent in the United States as an independent and sovereign state.[52] But it did not explain where in the Constitution one can find such a grant and how it can be justified in the face of the tenth amendment which lays down the rule of "enumerated powers," namely that powers not

[48] *See infra* text accompanying notes 49–64. Those who reject *Curtiss-Wright* (*see infra* note 54) would say that the federal monopoly is on the face of the Constitution, the missing powers being there but hidden in other clauses and the exclusion of the states complete in art. I, § 10.

[49] L. Henkin, *supra* note 7, at 16. For this section, and throughout this essay, I rely heavily on his classic study.

[50] *Id.* at 17.

[51] 130 U.S. 581 (1889).

[52] *Id.* at 603–04.

delegated to the Federal Government are reserved to the states.[53] Finally, in the celebrated *Curtiss-Wright* case,[54] decided in 1936, the Court concluded that the federal foreign affairs powers do not depend on the Constitution (or on the Constitution alone) but are inherent in the national "external sovereignty." Although some of these powers are mentioned in the Constitution, they – unlike federal domestic powers – are not reserved to the states if not enumerated. Instead one must look to international law and practice to determine their full array.[55] Thus, the status of the United States as a subject of international law (its "international personality") determines not only the scope and reach of its inherent foreign affairs powers in relation to other nations but also – and this is the remarkable implication of Justice Sutherland's doctrine – the allocation of all these powers to the federal authorities to the exclusion of the states. One is reminded in this context of the ambiguous reference by the Court of Justice to "the international personality" of the Community as a source of its "capacity" in international relations.[56]

Justice Sutherland supported his doctrine by a historical argument. The thirteen American colonies, he argued, upon independence became a sovereign nation, the "external sovereignty" passing directly from the Crown not to the colonies severally but to them "in their collective and corporate capacity as the United States of America." Powers of "internal sovereignty," however, remained in the individual states. Even before the Declaration of Independence the Continental Congress exercised the power of war and peace, and thereafter foreign affairs powers were assumed by the Confederation as the "sole possessor of external sovereignty" and subsequently under the Constitution they passed to the Federal Government.[57] Yet in contrast to this view of history, there is evidence that after the Declaration of Independence at least some of the former colonies considered themselves sovereign states and even under the Articles of Confederation it is not entirely clear whether "the United States, in Congress assembled" were a sovereign state rather than a league of states in Vattel's sense, acting together through the agency of the Congress.[58] Justice Sutherland's historical perception by no means goes unchallenged[59] but

53 The tenth amendment came into force two years after the Constitution and is commonly considered to be one of the "Bill of Rights" amendments (the first ten amendments).

54 United States v. Curtiss-Wright Export Corp., 299 U.S. 304 (1936). The question was whether the Congress had the authority to delegate to the President broad discretionary power to impose an arms embargo on countries embroiled in the Chaco war.

55 *See* L. Henkin's lucid summary, *supra* note 7, at 22–23.

56 Discussed *infra* text accompanying notes 69–74.

57 United States v. Curtiss-Wright Export Corp., 299 U.S. 304, 316–18 (1936).

58 For references in support of this view, *see* Morris, *The Forging of the Union Reconsidered: A Historical Refutation of State Sovereignty over Seabeds*, 74 Colum. L. Rev. 1056, 1066 (1974).

59 Levitan, *The Foreign Relations Power: An Analysis of Mr. Justice Sutherland's Theory*, 55 Yale L.J. 467, 478 (1946).

it has received considerable support.[60] The *Curtiss-Wright* opinion has been cited with approval in later cases and has never been rejected by the Supreme Court. However, subsequent cases discreetly avoid specific reference to Sutherland's "extra-Constitutional underpinning"[61] and the courts usually appear satisfied with inferring the federal power from the explicit or implied powers of the President or Congress.

The sharp distinction between the limitations on domestic and foreign affairs power which is at the core of the *Curtiss-Wright* doctrine has lost most of its practical cogency after the mid-1930's, as a result of the dramatic expansion of the Federal Government's domestic powers, particularly under the broad construction of the Commerce Clause.[62] Although the Supreme Court continues to pay lip-service to the theory of enumerated powers, its decisions since 1937 in practical effect sanction virtually plenary Congressional authority in the domestic economic sphere and nearly plenary authority beyond that sphere.[63] Subject to a few thus far isolated exceptions in the domestic area, the Constitution "has largely ceased to limit powers delegated to the Federal Government in domestic as in foreign affairs and federalism, as a limitation on national power, survives only by grace of the Federal Government and the political forces it reflects."[64] Thus the limitations on the Federal Government's powers in the foreign as in the domestic fields are generally determined not on the basis of the tenth amendment but by reference to specific prohibitions in the Consti-

[60] L. Henkin, *supra* note 7, lists the authorities at 289–91 n.10. He concludes that there is perhaps no disagreement that under the Articles of Confederation the states retained no external sovereignty but it is not agreed whether the states had sovereignty before the Articles; whether under the Articles they could have gained (or regained) sovereignty at will; and whether the sovereignty passed directly from the United States under the Articles, to the United States under the Constitution. *Id.* at 291. Also, Sutherland's view need not depend on whether the Constitution was a compact among the states or among the peoples of the states. *Id.* at 289 n.8. For an effort to show that "challenging his history does not necessarily destroy" Sutherland's doctrine, *see id.* at 23–24.

[61] *See* Justice Jackson's concurring opinion in Youngstown Sheet & Tube Co. v. Sawyer, 343 U.S. 579, 635–36 n.2 (1952) referring to Sutherland's discussion as a "dictum." For the support and criticism (prior to *Curtiss-Wright*) of the "general theory of sovereign powers which would vest in the national government all [foreign affairs] powers not expressly prohibited" by the constitutional document *see* Q. Wright, *supra* note 4, at 131.

[62] *See* Sandalow, *The Expansion of Federal Legislative Authority;* Linde, *Transportation and State Laws Under the United States Constitution: The Evolution of Judicial Doctrine;* and Blasi, *Constitutional Limitations on the Power of States to Regulate the Movement of Goods in Interstate Commerce,* in Courts and Free Markets, *supra* note 6, at 49, 139 & 174, respectively.

[63] *See* Stein & Sandalow, *supra* note 6, at 18.

[64] L. Henkin, *supra* note 7, at 26. The two cases indicating the exceptions are Oregon v. Mitchell, 400 U.S. 112 (1970) and National League of Cities v. Usery, 426 U.S. 833 (1976), *overruled,* Garcia v. San Antonio Metropolitan Transit Authority *et al.,* 105 S. Ct. 1005 (1985).

tution, particularly the Bill of Rights or implied prohibitions derived from the fundamental nature of the governmental structure established by the Constitution. However, despite the removal of the "federalism" issue as the ground for constitutional controversy, tension in foreign affairs continues because of the contest for power and disagreement over policy between the legislative and executive branches of the Federal Government itself.

b) Gaps in the Community Treaties and How They Are Filled

In sharp contrast with the situation in the United States, there can be no dispute over the continuing "external sovereignty" of the Member States of the Community, considering their exclusive power over their respective armies and national defense and foreign policies; only in the foreign economic sphere where the Members share their powers with the Community does the "federalism" issue of power allocation arise. In that sphere the Court of Justice was asked – not unlike the American Supreme Court in a comparable situation – to rule whether the Community had the authority to exercise specific foreign affairs powers which were not expressly listed among its "enumerated powers."

Early in its history, when faced with the question of the limitations on the Community power in the *domestic* economic field, the Court of Justice applied the traditional implied powers doctrine according to which international treaty norms "imply those norms without which the first mentioned norms make no sense or could not be applied in a reasonable and useful manner."[65] Subsequently it broadened the formula by adding the teleological concept of "*effet utile*" and the more elaborate articulation looking to "the spirit, general scheme and the wording of the Treaty" (*esprit, économie, texte*).[66] It was primarily the last mentioned interpretive device on which the Court relied in the landmark *ERTA* case[67] to reach a remarkable conclusion that would do away for all practical purposes with the "enumerated powers" principle as applied to foreign affairs. The Community foreign affairs power, the Court held, does not depend on the limited specific Treaty attributions but may be found in the general provisions as viewed in the over-all Treaty system. Thus, the Community has the power to enter into international agreements with third countries on

65 *See, e.g.*, Case 8/55, Fédération Charbonnière de Belgique v. High Authority, [1954–6] ECR 245; Case 20/59, Italy v. High Authority, [1960] ECR 325; Case 25/59, The Netherlands v. High Authority, [1960] ECR 355. *See also, generally*, Ganshof van der Meersch, *L'ordre juridique des Communautés Européennes et le droit international*, [1975] V Rec. des Cours Acad. dr. int. 1; Sasse & Yourow, *The Growth of Legislative Power of the European Communities*, in Courts and Free Markets, *supra* note 6, at 92, 94.

66 Stein & Sandalow, *supra* note 6, at 16 ff, emphasizing the analogy to Justice Marshall's approach in McCulloch v. Maryland, 17 U.S. (4 Wheat.) 316 (1819).

67 Case 22/70, Commission v. Council, [1971] ECR 263 *[ERTA]* (the case involved the European Road Transport Agreement, referred to as ERTA). *See infra* text accompanying note 183.

any matter which falls within its internal competence if such agreement is necessary for the achievement of a Community objective.[68] As in the United States, the need for the Member States to speak with a single voice in international economic relations has been held to require a broad Community power.

To buttress its novel doctrine, the Court referred to the "international personality" of the Community which it found emplanted in article 210.[69] It interpreted the article to mean that "in its external relations the Community enjoys the capacity to establish contractual [*i.e.* treaty] links with third countries over the whole field of objectives defined" in the Treaty part on "Principles" and in its general and final provisions.[70] If the Court meant to say that the Community may derive foreign affairs powers from its status as a person in international law it would have – *mutatis mutandis* – applied to the Community the Supreme Court's rationale in the *Chinese Exclusion Case*, if not in the *Curtiss-Wright* case.[71] It is more likely, however, that the *ERTA* Court had in mind simply but-

[68] Also discussed *infra* text accompanying notes 182–88. EEC Treaty art. 4(1) ("Each institution shall act within the limits of the powers conferred on it by this Treaty") is often cited as a basis for the "enumerated powers" principle. But, as Pescatore points out, this provision "lays down the idea of 'separation of powers' [between the Community institutions], but says nothing about the question of the power relationships between the Community and its Member States." P. PESCATORE, THE LAW OF INTEGRATION 37 n.19 (Leiden, Sijthoff, 1974).

[69] EEC Treaty art. 210: "The Community shall have legal personality."

[70] Case 22/70, *ERTA*, [1971] ECR 263, 274; and Joined Cases 3, 4 & 6/76, Cornelis Kramer and Others, [1976] ECR 1279, 1308.

[71] *See supra* notes 51 and 54. Most writers agree that in the passage quoted *supra*, text accompanying note 70, the Court purports to say that "international personality" provides the general capacity to enter into international agreements but that any specific treaty-power must be found in the Treaty. Kovar, *L'affaire de l'A.E.T.R. devant la Cour de justice des Communautés européennes et la compétence internationale de la C.E.E.*, 17 A.F.D.I. 386, 391 (1971); Ganshof van der Meersch, *Les relations extérieures de la C.E.E. dans le domaine des politiques communes et l'arrêt de la Cour de Justice du 31 mars 1971*, 8 C.D.E. 127, 137 ff (1972). But some question the need for or logic of the passage as so interpreted.

I was able to find only one writer who interprets the ECJ case law to mean the Community may fill the lacunae in the Treaty grants of foreign relations powers directly from public international law, *i.e.*, Bleckmann, who argues that the Court, "in the *Kramer* case, expressed an opinion which we might indeed generalize: the Community, in the limits of its competence for agriculture, traffic *[sic]* and so on, might execute all competences which public international law attributes to States . . . "; and, more generally, that, contrary to the prevailing opinion in literature, "certain competences might be directly deduced from public international law" (a proposition reminiscent of the *Curtiss-Wright* rationale adjusted to the partially integrated nature of the Community). Bleckmann, *The Competence of the E.E.C.*, in DIVISION OF POWERS BETWEEN THE EUROPEAN COMMUNITIES AND THEIR MEMBER STATES IN THE FIELD OF EXTERNAL RELATIONS 3, 13–14 (C.W. Timmermans & E.L.M. Völker eds., Deventer (N.L.), Kluwer, 1981) [hereinafter cited as DIVISION OF POWERS]. *See also* Bleckmann, *Zur Verbindlichkeit des allgemeinen Völkerrechts für internationale Organisationen*, 37 ZAÖRV 107 (1977). In *Kramer* (also discussed *infra* text accompanying note 185) – a

tressing its broad systemic construction of the Treaty and rejecting the fanciful doctrine that only states – and not international organizations or groupings – can possess an international personality,[72] and that in particular the Community itself, being devoid of any functional personality, is nothing more than an agency, "a common organ in the hands of States."[73] "This theoretical construction," observed extra-judicially one of the judges who participated in the *ERTA* case, "expresses quite realistically the attitude taken in practice by some Member States who tend to consider the Community as a convenient tool for furthering their interest in some respect, but who at the same time would reserve the possibility of resuming at will their own prerogatives whenever it fits their national interests."[74]

It deserves particular attention that the *ERTA* Court went out of the way to declare (in what may be viewed as a dictum) that the "necessary and proper" powers provision in article 235 of the EEC Treaty applied not only to domestic powers but to foreign affairs powers as well.[75] In fact, the Council has invoked the article as a supplementary authority when enacting certain regulations concerning foreign commerce[76] and as an exclusive source in concluding trea-

progeny of *ERTA* applying the "internal/external parallelism" doctrine – at issue was the power of the EC to enter into international commitments for the conservation of fishing resources of the sea. Having determined that the pre-condition (existence of "internal" powers *re* conservation measures) was satisfied and holding that the Council in fact had such power, the Court had to decide whether this power was limited to the fishing zones of the Member States or if it extended to also allow regulation of high sea fishing by fishermen from the Member States. The Court found, on the basis of art. 102 of the Act of Accession as well as art. 1 of Council Reg. (EEC) No. 2142/70 (JO No. L 236, 27 Oct. 1970, p.5; [1970] OJ (spec. Eng. ed.) at 707) and "the very nature of things," that "the rule-making authority of the Community *ratione materiae* also extends – in so far as the Member States have similar authority under public international law – to fishing on the high seas." Joined Cases 3, 4, & 6/76, *Kramer*, [1976] ECR 1279, 1309.

72 *See especially* Quadri, *La personnalité internationale de la Communauté*, in LES RELATIONS EXTÉRIEURES DE LA COMMUNAUTÉ EUROPÉENNE UNIFIÉE 41, 41–42, 47 (M. Melchior ed., Univ. of Liège, Institut d'Etudes Juridiques Européennes, 1969) and sources cited therein at 41 & 42 n.2.

73 A. GIARDINA, COMUNITÀ EUROPEE E STATI TERZI 115, 160, 167 (Naples, Jovene, 1964).

74 Pescatore, in DIVISION OF POWERS, *supra* note 71, at 69, 75. In the United States, the states could not "regain" anything that the Federal Government has except by constitutional amendment, and the amendment process is not within the exclusive control of the states since an amendment usually requires prior approval of two-thirds of both Houses of Congress.

75 Case 22/70, *ERTA*, [1971] ECR 263, 283.

76 *See, e.g.*, Council Reg. (EEC) No. 802/68 of 27 June 1968, on the Common Definition of the Concept of the Origin of Goods, JO No. L 148, 20 June 1969, p. 1 ([1968–69] II OJ (spec. Eng. ed.) at 165) and Council Reg. (EEC) No. 1318/71 of 21 June 1971 amending Reg. (EEC) No. 802/68, OJ No. L 139, 25 June 1971, p. 6 (referring to EEC Treaty arts. 111, 113, 155, 227 & 235).

ties dealing with objectives not specifically included among the objectives enumerated in the Treaty such as the protection of the environment.[77]

In domestic affairs, the Court of Justice, without specifically rejecting the "enumerated powers" doctrine, has also employed the teleological, system-conditioned formula discussed above, to reduce legal restraints on the Community law-maker in the economic field to a minimum – and in this respect the situation is not dissimilar to the virtually unfettered powers pursuant to the Commerce Clause of the United States Congress after 1937. There are of course important political constraints on Congress. The political constraints on the Community institutions have been formidable indeed, particularly in the last few years when the Community has been prevented by Member States "assembled in the Council" from progressing even in areas clearly within its exclusive powers.[78]

In foreign affairs, as we have seen, the Court of Justice begins its Treaty analysis with the same teleological formula but ends with the controversial "internal/external parallelism" doctrine which in effect lifts the "enumerated powers" restraints. Thus – as in the United States – the ways of identifying "constitutional limitations" differ in domestic and foreign affairs. Unlike in the United States, however, where the "federalism" issue has ceased to be a limiting factor, the power allocation between the Member States and the Community (represented by the Commission), has been the principal cause of tension.

It should not come as a surprise that Community power – like American federal power – is limited by specific prohibitions in the Treaty; by the basic institutional structure;[79] and, last but not least, by norms protecting fundamental

[77] Mastellone, *The External Relations of the E.E.C. in the Field of Environment Protection*, 30 I.C.L.Q. 104, 111 ff (1981). U.S. Const. art. I, § 8, cl. 18 empowers Congress to "make all laws which shall be necessary and proper for carrying into execution the foregoing powers, and all other powers vested by this Constitution in the government of the United States," whereas EEC Treaty art. 235 authorizes powers necessary "to attain, in the course of the operation of the common market, one of the objectives of the Community." Thus in the United States, in theory, an implied power can be derived only from a power enumerated in the Constitution, whereas in the Community it must be related to one of its "objectives," obviously a broader concept than "powers." Yet early in its history, Chief Justice Marshall's Supreme Court turned "powers" into "objectives" to reach a broad definition of federal legislative powers. *See* McCulloch v. Maryland, 17 U.S. (4 Wheat.) 316 (1819) and comment by Sandalow, *supra* note 62, at 59. As in *ERTA*, in *McCulloch* Marshall upheld federal power without relying solely on the "necessary and proper" clause, but he nevertheless expatiated on it at length. As for foreign affairs powers, it may be argued under *Curtiss-Wright* that Congress can carry out all powers of the United States inherent in its sovereignty.

[78] *See, generally,* Krislov, Ehlermann & Weiler, *Political Organs and the Decision-Making Process in the United States and the European Communities, supra* this vol., Bk. 2.

[79] *See infra* text accompanying notes 203–11.

human rights, written and unwritten,[80] which the Court derives from the general principles common to the national legal orders of the Members and from the European Convention on Human Rights since all Members have ratified it.

III. The Reality of Foreign Affairs Powers

This part will investigate the nature and the actual working of the mechanisms for the exercise of the foreign affairs powers in both the United States and the European systems, illustrating the institutional tensions rooted in the constituent documents. In respect of each of the foreign affairs powers, as defined earlier, the first section examines the provisions which have been made for the division of powers, both between the central authority and the constituent states, and between the institutions of the central authority, concentrating primarily on the manner in which the centralized authority executes its functions. The second part focusses on the foreign affairs powers retained by the Member States, and in particular on one important device, the European Political Cooperation mechanism, through which the Member States seek to coordinate the exercise of certain non-delegated powers outside the Community framework.

A. The Division of Powers and Arrangements for the Exercise of the Foreign Affairs Powers

1. Communication and Diplomacy

a) In the United States

From the beginning, the President has been the "sole organ of the nation in its external relations, and its sole representative with foreign nations."[81] He directs a huge "foreign affairs establishment" in Washington which is linked to more than a hundred American diplomatic missions abroad and maintains contact with a host of local foreign embassies. The President has a near-monopoly of information and expert advice although professional staffs of the Congressional Committees dealing with foreign affairs have recently been "the fastest growing bureaucracy" on the Capitol.[82] The President, with

80 *See, e.g.*, right to equal pay for men and women in EEC Treaty art. 119 and Case 43/75, Defrenne v. Sabena, [1976] ECR 455; and Case 44/79, Hauer v. Land Rheinland-Pfalz, [1979] ECR 3727.

81 John Marshall's statement in the House of Representatives, 10 Annals of Cong. 613 (1800), *reprinted in* 18 U.S. (5 Wheat.) Appendix at 26 n.1 (1820).

82 Rovine, *Congressional-Executive Relations and United States Foreign Policy*, 17 Willamette L. Rev. 41, 48 (1980). *See also* Weiss Fagen, *U.S. Foreign Policy and Human Rights: The Role of Congress*, in Parliamentary Control Over Foreign Policy:

Senate consent, appoints American ambassadors and receives foreign ambassadors;[83] in addition, that he has the power to appoint personal representatives for foreign assignments without Senate's concurrence is now firmly established, although this was challenged in the Senate in the early years.[84] In fact, the President has often appointed members of Congress to United States negotiating teams[85] as a means of "coopting" them and marshalling congressional support for his policies. On the other hand, Congress by legislation has at times purported to impose Congressional representation on the President.[86] Moreover, Congress has acquired substantial control over the foreign service by detailed legislation on the number, qualifications, and organization of the personnel[87] and it has also vested foreign affairs functions in administrative agencies which have enjoyed considerable independence of the President, such as the International Trade Commission.[88]

b) In the Community

In the Community, there is no "sole organ" to do business with the outside world even though the Commission aspires to this function and, despite its collective character, is perhaps best organized for it. The Commission has its own expert "foreign establishment" in Brussels, centered in the Directorates General for External Relations (DG I) and for Development (DG VIII), and comprising other specialized units dealing with the customs union, financing, agricultural exports, international environment, etc. Outside its headquarters, the Commission maintains over sixty "delegations," missions, and press and information offices in foreign capitals and at the seat of major international organizations, where they enjoy diplomatic or functional immunities. The delegations at the major world centers perform tasks of information and liaison similar to traditional diplomatic functions. The other missions have predominantly technical duties and assignments under cooperative agreements

LEGAL ESSAYS 111 (A. Cassese ed., Alphen a/d Rijn/Germantown, Md., Sijthoff & Noordhoff, 1980); Kohl, *Congressional Foreign Affairs Committees in the United States of America*, in PARLIAMENTARY FOREIGN AFFAIRS COMMITTEES: THE NATIONAL SETTING 285 (A. Cassese ed., Padua/New York, CEDAM/Oceana Pubs., 1982).

[83] U.S. CONST. art. II, § 2, cl. 2 and art. II, § 3. The Senate consents to or rejects the appointment; it probably cannot consent with conditions. E.S. CORWIN, THE PRESIDENT: OFFICE AND POWERS 1787–1957, at 78 (New York, N.Y.U.P., 1957).

[84] H.M. WRISTON, EXECUTIVE AGENTS IN AMERICAN FOREIGN RELATIONS (Baltimore, Johns Hopkins Press, 1929).

[85] This despite the apparent prohibition in U.S. CONST. art. I, § 6, cl. 2.

[86] *See, e.g.*, Trade Act of 1974, ch. VI, § 161(a), Pub. L. No. 93–618, 88 Stat. 2008, 19 U.S.C. § 2211(a) (1975). In the Community the Council often "imposes" its representatives on the Commission. *See infra* text accompanying notes 170 & 180.

[87] To what extent can Congress impose duties on an executive officer? Kendall v. United States, 37 U.S. (12 Pet.) 524, 610 (1838).

[88] Formerly called the Tariff Commission. *See* the Trade Act of 1974, § 171(a), 19 U.S.C. § 2231(a).

between the Community and the host states.[89] In Brussels, more than one hundred foreign missions are accredited to the Community[90] (not to the Commission) and provide the Commission with information and the opportunity for day-to-day contacts.

The Treaty is silent on the active or passive right of legation, although some authors point to a provision in the supplementary protocol on privileges and immunities which assumes the presence of third-party missions at the seat of the Community.[91] Others would rely on the Community's "inherent powers" or its "international personality" as the appropriate source of the right of legation.[92] The more convincing approach is to imply the necessary Community power from its power to enter into treaties; and the Commission's authority from its role in treaty negotiations, its general executive authority to provide for its own organization,[93] and, last but not least, at this juncture, from the ample reservoir of "subsequent practice," a legitimate index of interpretation.

The division of powers and functions between the Commission and the Council has proved particularly controversial, because of the sensitivities and idiosyncrasies of the Member Governments with respect to diplomatic contacts and representation. The Member Governments keep an eagle's eye on, and tight control over, the Commission's activities. The Commissioners are appointed by "common agreement" of the ten Governments. Although the Commission appoints its employees, their number and status is governed by Council regulations and the budget requires concurrence by the Council. The Commission seeks the Council's consent before opening a permanent delegation abroad and the accreditation of a foreign state representative to the Community is considered to require unanimous agreement in the Council. Thus

89 12 J. Mégret, J.V. Louis, D. Vignes, M. Waelbroeck, J. Deworst & P. Brückner, Le Droit de la Communauté économique européenne, Commentaire du Traité et de textes pris pour son application 6–8 (Brussels, Institut d'études Européennes, Ed. de l'Univ. de Bruxelles, 1970–) [hereinafter cited as Brussels Commentary]; G. Sjöstedt, The External Role of the European Community 107 (Westmead, U.K., Saxonhouse, 1977).

90 Bull. EC 1–1981, point 2.2.35. The Protocol on the Privileges and Immunities of the European Communities of 8 Apr. 1965, art. 17 provides that the "Member State in whose territory the Communities have their seat shall accord the customary diplomatic immunities and privileges to missions of third countries accredited to the Communities." The Protocol, along with the Merger Treaty, became part of Belgian domestic law. *See* Salmon, *Les représentations et missions permanentes auprès de la CEE et de l'Euratom*, in 1 Les Missions permanentes auprès des organisations internationales 561, 718 ff (M. Virally, P. Gerbet & J. Salmon eds., Brussels, Bruylant, 1971).

91 Protocol on the Privileges and Immunities of the European Communities of 8 Apr. 1965, art. 17. *See supra* note 90.

92 *See* authors listed in Salmon, *supra* note 90, at 718 n.l.

93 EEC Treaty arts. 155 & 228. *See* Sauvignon, *Les Communautés européennes et le droit de legation actif*, [1978] R.M.C. 176, 180. *See generally*, 2 H.G. Schermers, International Institutional Law 733 (Leiden, Sijthoff, 1972); 12 Brussels Commentary, *supra* note 89, at 8.

France in 1964 blocked the establishment of relations with Taiwan and delayed the acceptance of a representative from Fiji because he had criticized French nuclear tests.[94] The complex procedure for "establishing relations" with a foreign government and accreditation of its ambassador involves both the Commission and the Council through the Committee of Permanent Representatives. Until 1966, following diplomatic usage, the foreign representative presented his credentials in a formal champagne ceremony to the President of the Commission exclusively but, after an outburst of the Gaullist Government's outrage at such pretension, the ceremony was dropped and since then the credentials are submitted to the President of the Council as well as to the Commission's President.[95]

In foreign capitals, the Commission's missions parallel the national embassies of the Member States. Moreover, as a part of the European Political Cooperation scheme, heads of these embassies meet in groups chaired by the ambassador whose state holds the rotating "Presidency" of the Council, to discuss political issues of common interest.[96] The line dividing the respective competences of the Commission's delegations and the national embassies is to follow the division between Community and national jurisdictions. It takes little imagination to fathom the problems of coordination and friction to which I shall return.[97]

2. Power to "Make" and to "Implement" Foreign Policy by "Autonomous Acts"

Foreign policy is made and implemented[98] by "autonomous" (unilateral) acts, such as declarations, resolutions, instructions to representatives, assertions of claims, appropriation of funds and legislation; and by "conventional acts," that is, international agreements, bilateral or multilateral.

a) In the United States

i) The President's ascendancy in formulating policy

From the inception tension has existed between the President and Congress over which institution should be supreme in formulating foreign policy, but over the years the President has gained the ascendancy. Because of the President's exclusive charge of relations with other nations and his control of the channels of communications, and because Congress was not always in session, successive Presidents began to make not only small decisions in daily intercourse but larger policy determinations as well. For instance, by implication from the power to appoint and receive ambassadors, the President asserted,

[94] 12 BRUSSELS COMMENTARY, *supra* note 89, at 10–11.

[95] The new procedure was included in the "Luxembourg Compromise" following the French boycott of the Community. BULL. EC 3–1966, at pp. 8–9.

[96] *See infra* notes 262–63 and accompanying text.

[97] *See infra* text accompanying notes 270–78.

[98] There can be no meaningful distinction between making and implementing foreign policy.

against some early opposition by Congress, the exclusive power to recognize or not to recognize new states, governments or foreign annexations of territory.[99] As a result, the President is now able to set prospective policy committing the United States to future action, for example, in influential doctrines such as the Monroe, Open-Door, Truman, or Nixon doctrines, while the legislative branch has been relegated to merely adopting "sense of Congress resolutions," which have no legal effect and often have little political impact.[100]

Although it is the Congress that provides for defense and declares war,[101] the President has independent powers as a Commander-in-Chief,[102] including the controversial right to send troops abroad. This right, although established by repeated exercise, has been limited by the War Powers Resolution of 1973.[103]

ii) Congress' role in formulating policy

Congress' power to regulate foreign commerce[104] has been a crucial instrument of American foreign policy and it has grown, incident to "the explosion" of the

99 In the early 20th century Congress pretended to some part in the recognition of new states. 1 G. Hackworth, Digest of International Law 162–63 (Washington, Dep't. of State Pubs., U.S. Gov't Print. Off., 1960); L. Henkin, *supra* note 7, at 82, & 335 n.65.

100 *See, e.g.*, 26 Cong. Rec. 2001–2002 (1894) (a resolution of the House of Representatives condemning a U.S. minister for illegally aiding in overthrowing the government of the Hawaiian Islands); S. Res. 327, 69th Cong., 2nd Sess., 68 Cong. Rec. 2233 (1927) (favoring arbitration of an oil dispute with Mexico); H. J. Res. 1145, 78 Stat. 384 (1964) (Gulf of Tonkin Resolution).

101 U.S. Const. art. I, § 8, cls. 1, 11–14.

102 U.S. Const. art. II, § 2, cl. 1.

103 In the War Powers Resolution of 1973 the Congress denied that the President had authority to commit U.S. forces into hostilities on his own authority unless there had been an attack on the U.S. or its armed forces. The Resolution requires the President to consult with Congress "in every possible instance" before introducing U.S. forces into hostilities. The President must terminate hostilities within 60 days unless Congress authorizes him to continue, and Congress may direct him to terminate hostilities at any time by concurrent resolution (not subject to the President's veto). Pub. L. No. 93–148, 87 Stat. 555 (codified at 50 U.S.C. § 1541–48 (1976 & Supp. IV 1980) (H.R.J. Res. 542, adopted over a Presidential veto on 7 Nov. 1973). The Constitutionality of this Resolution has been questioned. *See generally* A. Van W. Thomas & A.J. Thomas, Jr., The War-Making Powers of the President – Constitutional and International Law Aspects (Dallas, SMU Press, 1982); W.T. Reveley, III, War Powers of the President and Congress – Who Holds the Arrows and Olive Branch? (Charlottesville, U.P. of Va., 1981). In view of the broad language in the *Chadha* case, *infra* note 114, the "legislative veto" feature of the Resolution must probably be considered unconstitutional unless the war power is viewed as particularly "legislative." Although President Washington alone proclaimed neutrality, thereafter Congress asserted this authority. The President can occupy territory but annexation can be done only by Congress or a treaty approved by the Senate. Hawaii and Texas became states by an agreement concluded by the President and approved by both Houses of Congress.

104 U.S. Const. art. I, § 8, cl. 3.

power to regulate interstate commerce. The commerce power supports virtually any federal legislation relating to foreign relations including trade, shipping, aviation, communications, trade marks, and travel abroad.[105] In the vital field of trade, Congress provided for a federal tariff structure[106] and related customs law as well as extensive protective legislation on antidumping, countervailing duties, economic sanctions, etc.[107] "Statutory" tariff rates, set by Congress, are modified pursuant to bilateral or multilateral agreements negotiated by the President upon Congressional authorization periodically extended under elaborate safeguards.[108] The extensive federal international finance and banking legislation is based on the commerce and "money" power,[109] foreign aid is supported by the "spending power,"[110] and the power of Congress to regulate gambling and narcotics trade is founded on its power to tax.[111]

Congressional legislation regulating entry, status and exclusion of aliens and immigration, originally based on the commerce power, was later justified on the power "inherent in sovereignty" or on the "foreign affairs" power, the latter supporting also statutes governing the conduct of Americans abroad.[112]

Only relatively recently did the Congress undertake to legislate on two foreign affairs issues that until then had been within the exclusive province of the

[105] Patent and copyright legislation is based on a specific grant in art. I, § 8, cl. 8. Trade marks are regulated under the commerce power, art. I, § 8, cl. 3.

[106] *See* U.S. CONST. art. I, § 8, cl. 1.

[107] *See, e.g.*, Tariff Act of 1930, ch. 497, 46 Stat. 590 (1930) (codified *as amended* at 19 U.S.C. §§ 1202–1677(g) (1976 & Supp. IV, 1980)). Customs Simplification Act of 1956, ch. 887, § 2(a), 70 Stat. 943, 19 U.S.C. § 1401(a) (1976 & Supp. IV 1980) (adding new § 402 to the Tariff Act of 1930), *as amended by* Pub. L. No. 96–39, title II, § 201(a), 93 Stat. 194 (1979), and Pub. L. No. 96–490, § 2, 94 Stat. 2556 (1980) (Valuation). International Emergency Economic Powers Act, Pub. L. No. 95–223, title II, § 202, 91 Stat. 1626, 50 U.S.C. §§ 1701–1706 (1976 & Supp. IV, 1980). Trade Agreements Act of 1979, Pub. L. No. 96–39, 93 Stat. 144, 19 U.S.C. §§ 1671–1677(g) (1976 & Supp. IV, 1980) (Countervailing and Antidumping Duties).

[108] The Tariff Act of 1930 sets the tariff structure and rates which are amended from time to time. The tariff schedules of the U.S. show in one column the "most-favored-nation" ("proclaimed" or "modified") rates and in the other the "statutory rates." A column marked "LDDC" states the rates for least developed developing countries. *See* Tariff Schedules of the United States, Annotated 1111 (Wash. D.C., U.S. Int'l Trade Comm'n Pubs., 1981).

[109] U.S. CONST. § 8, cl. 2: "To borrow money on the credit of the United States."

[110] U.S. CONST. art. I, § 8, cl. 1.

[111] U.S. CONST. art. I, § 8, cl. 1.

[112] *See* L. HENKIN, *supra* note 7, at 74–76. On the power to extradite aliens or U.S. citizens, *see id.* at 326 n.40. U.S. CONST. art. I, § 8, cl. 4 gives Congress the power "[t]o establish an uniform rule of naturalization." The "necessary and proper clause" has also played a significant role in Congressional action affecting foreign affairs. L. HENKIN, *supra* note 7, at 78.

Department of State and the courts: the rules governing "acts of state" and sovereign immunity of foreign governments.[113]

The Congress has delegated extensive powers to the President, thus contributing to the growth of his authority. In many instances, however, the Congress has subjected the delegation to elaborate devices designed to scrutinize and recoup the delegated authority. The favorite instrumentality has been the so-called legislative veto.[114]

In international trade legislation the Congress has mandated complex administrative procedures of a quasi-judicial character, involving several executive departments and independent agencies, with a recourse to judicial review. Some view this trend as an excessive "judicialization" of a field where at least the major problems affecting national economy may call for high level governmental decisions and a flexible approach rather than formalized adversary procedures.[115]

b) In the Community

As we have seen, the foreign affairs powers of the Community lie primarily in the field of external economic relations, with the Member States determining policy in other areas. The Community institutions, invoking article 103 and the

113 The Supreme Court has "federalized" the "act of state" doctrine and possibly other rules of customary international law as well, in Banco Nacional de Cuba v. Sabbatino, 376 U.S. 398 (1964) (although some believe that the act of state doctrine has always been viewed as federal); but Congress reduced the scope of the doctrine as laid down by the Court in the "Sabbatino Amendment" to the Foreign Assistance Act of 1964, 78 Stat. 1013 (*as amended* and codified in 22 U.S.C. § 2370e). The Foreign Sovereign Immunities Act was adopted on 21 Oct. 1976, Pub. L. No. 94–583, 90 Stat. 2891, 28 U.S.C. §§ 1602–11 (1976).

As contemplated in EEC Treaty art. 220, the Member States concluded treaties among themselves "federalizing" (*i.e.* turning into Community law) rules on jurisdiction and recognition of their national courts' judgments, on recognition of companies and on Community patent. Presumably, in an advanced state of integration, this process could be employed to provide Community law rules on issues pertaining to foreign affairs, such as the two issues mentioned above, extradition, etc.

114 An agreement negotiated by the President pursuant to a delegated authority must be brought before the Congress and the President is authorized to conclude it unless, within a set period of time, both Houses of Congress, and in some instances either House alone, disapprove it. However, in a sweeping opinion the Supreme Court held a section of the Immigration and Nationality Act authorizing "one–House veto" unconstitutional because a veto by the House of Representatives is essentially legislative and thus subject to the constitutional requirements of passage by a majority of both Houses and presentation to the President. Immigration & Naturalization Serv. v. Chadha, 103 S. Ct. 2764 (1983). In other instances the President may use a delegated authority only if he makes an express finding of a special national interest (*e.g.*, supplying foreign aid or arms to countries violating human rights, exporting nuclear materials to states unwilling to accept safeguards). T.M. FRANCK & E. WEISBAND, FOREIGN POLICY BY CONGRESS 83–115 (Oxford/New York, O.U.P., 1979).

115 Ehrenhaft, *The "Judicialization" of Trade Law*, 56 NOTRE DAME LAW. 595 (1981).

"necessary and proper" clause, article 235, have taken a few hesitant steps toward an economic and monetary union, which – if it should ever become a reality – would have far-reaching foreign affairs implications.[116] These plans have made little progress due to the absence of the proverbial political will of the Governments, rather than to legal-constitutional restraints.

In the foreign trade area, the Community institutions were not granted the broad power "to regulate foreign commerce." However, not unlike the Congress, the Council, drawing on articles 28 and 235, has been able to reenact annually a consolidated Common Customs Tariff (CCT),[117] modify it,[118] and adopt customs related regulations on customs valuation[119] and rules of origin.[120] Other regulations based primarily on article 113 deal with import monitoring systems, goods from state-trading countries, consolidation of the remaining quantitative import restrictions, general preferences for less developed countries and others.[121] The autonomous protective measures enacted by the Council include a regulation against dumping and subsidies.[122] In legislation on agricultural export subsidies, fisheries, and food assistance the Council has relied on its broad Treaty power to fashion common agricultural policy.[123] The Council has delegated substantial implementing functions to the Commission, but invariably has insisted on surrounding it by "management committees" composed of national officials through which the Member Governments have exerted an even tighter control over the Commission's activities than Congress exercises over the President and over the International Trade Commission under the trade legislation. Comparing the scope of the delegated power in the two systems, Bourgeois casts an envious eye at the relatively wide powers granted by Congress to the President to take speedy protective measures. On

[116] *See generally* 6 BRUSSELS COMMENTARY, *supra* note 89, at 29 ff.

[117] 1 H. SMIT & P.E. HERZOG, THE LAW OF THE E.E.C., A COMMENTARY 2–112 (New York, M. Bender, 1976). The CCT shows two columns of rates: "autonomous" and "conventional." *See, e.g.*, Council Reg. (EEC) No. 3000/79 of 20 Dec. 1979, OJ No. L 342, 31 Dec. 1979, p.1.

[118] 1 H. SMIT & P.E. HERZOG, *supra* note 117, at 2–113.

[119] Council Reg. (EEC) No. 1224/80 of 28 May 1980, OJ No. L 134, 31 May 1980, p.1. *See generally* Snyder, *Customs Valuation in the European Economic Community*, 11 GA. J. INT'L & COMP. L. 79 (1981).

[120] Council Reg. (EEC) No. 802/68 of 27 June 1968, JO No. L 148, 20 June 1969, p.1. ([1968–69] II OJ (spec. Eng. ed.) at 165), *amended by* Council Reg. (EEC) No. 1318/71 of 21 June 1971, JO No. L 139, 25 June 1971, p.6 ([1971] OJ (spec. Eng. ed.) at 394) and the Act of Accession, Annex I, point I (1).

[121] 6 BRUSSELS COMMENTARY, *supra* note 89, at 396 ff and 12 *id.* at 178–79; 3 H. SMIT & P.E. HERZOG, *supra* note 117, at 3–671 ff.

[122] Council Reg. (EEC) No. 459/68 on Protection Against Practices of Dumping, Premiums and Subsidies by Non-Member States, JO No. L 931, 17 Apr. 1968, p.1 ([1968–69] II OJ (spec. Eng. ed.) at 80), as amended by Council Reg. (EEC) No. 2011/73, OJ No. L 206, 27 July 1973, p.3; Council Reg. (EEC) No. 3017/79 on Protection Against Dumped and Subsidized Exports, OJ No. L 339, 31 Dec. 1979, p.1.

[123] EEC Treaty arts. 38–48; 12 BRUSSELS COMMENTARY, *supra* note 89, at 179–80.

the other hand he notes (again by comparison with American procedures) the "deficit in legal protection" of individuals injured by Community protective measures, due to the excessively restrictive interpretation of individual access to the Court of Justice.[124]

In addition to the power delegated to it by the Council, the Commission possesses limited autonomous authority. In the exercise of that authority, the Commission determines grants of aid to victims of catastrophies and the opening of a delegation or mission in third countries. Nevertheless, the Commission in fact always seeks prior opinion or agreement from the Council. The Commission's role in certain foreign affairs matters (*e.g.* food aid, aid to non-associated developing countries) has become enmeshed in the dispute between the Council and the Parliament over the responsibility for the implementation of the Community budget.[125]

In contrast with the United States federal power, the Member States retain full authority over citizenship, immigration, and the status of nationals of third countries on Community territory. A suggestion has come from the Members of the European Parliament that certain aspects of the treatment of third country nationals, such as the granting of the right of asylum and the status of alien family members of Community workers, need to be treated in the Community or European Political Cooperation context.[126]

3. Treaty-Making Power

a) In the United States

The unhappy experience with the Confederate Congress undertaking to negotiate treaties and its inability to enforce them against the states[127] motivated the treaty provisions in the Constitution. Thus it is the President who makes treaties but only with "the advice and consent" of two-thirds of the Senators pres-

124 *See* Bourgeois, *The Common Commercial Policy – Scope and Nature of the Powers,* in PROTECTIONISM AND THE EUROPEAN COMMUNITY 1 (E.L. Völker ed., Deventer (NL), Kluwer, 1983). *See* in this connection Case 307/81, Alusuisse Italia SpA. v. Council and Commission, [1982] ECR 3463. *See also supra* text accompanying note 115.

125 *See* Ehlermann, *Conflict in Implementation of Community Law,* in 3 F.I.D.E., REPORTS OF THE NINTH CONGRESS, LONDON, 25–27 SEPT. 1980, at pp. 3.1, 3.10–11, 3.14–15 (London, Sweet & Maxwell, 1980). L'AIDE ALIMENTAIRE DE LA CEE DANS LE NOUVEAU CONTEXTE DES STRATÉGIES ALIMENTAIRES 97–99 (P. Richard ed., Brussells, Prométhée & Agence Europe, 1983); Peter van den Bossche, The Nature of the European Community Food Aid to Developing Countries (Doctorate thesis in progress, European University Institute, Florence, 1983).

126 *See Migrant Workers,* No. 3212 (NS) EUROPE, 23 Sept. 1981, at 16. (Eng. ed., Brussels, Agence Internationale d'Information pour la Presse). "The rules regarding freedom of movement for nationals of the Member States also apply, in part, to members of their families who are not nationals of a Member State. The relevant Community regulations provide that Member States shall provide such persons with all possible facilities in obtaining the necessary visas." Answer by Commissioner Narjes to Written Question No. 2161/80, OJ No. C 165, 6 July 1981, p.18.

127 *See supra* text accompanying note 20; *see also* T. BAILEY, *supra* note 20, at 52–66.

ent.[128] The states are expressly barred from treaty-making and from entering, without the consent of Congress, into "any agreement or compact with another state, or a foreign power."[129] Treaties, along with the Constitution and federal legislation, are given the normative status of "supreme law of the land." This means that state courts must give effect to treaties, even if inconsistent with state law and, in addition, cases arising from treaties are placed within the power of the federal judiciary.[130] These provisions, although clearly a radical break with the Confederate system, have left many questions for later answers.

i) Treaty-making process

The Founders did not wish to make treaty-making unduly easy and – in what has proved to be a vain hope – did not expect the need for many treaties. The House of Representatives was excluded from the procedure because its fluc-

[128] U.S. CONST. art II, § 2, cl. 2.

[129] *See* U.S. CONST. art. I, § 10, cl. 1; "No State shall enter into any treaty, alliance, or confederation. . . . "; and cl. 3: "No State shall, without the consent of Congress . . . enter into any agreement or compact with another State, or with a foreign power. . . ." There is no authoritative determination of the distinction between a "treaty" and an "agreement or compact." In Virginia v. Tennessee, 148 U.S. 503, 519 (1893), involving an interstate (not foreign) compact, the Court held that despite the constitutional language, agreements or compacts require consent of Congress only when they "tend to the increase of political power in the States, which may encroach upon or interfere with the just supremacy of the United States." Whether by so narrowing the constitutional requirement, or because consent was assumed, state and local authorities have in fact entered into agreements and arrangements with foreign counterparts (such as Canadian Provinces or towns) without seeking consent of Congress on such matters as coordination of roads, police cooperation and border control. According to COUNCIL OF STATE GOVERNMENTS, INTERSTATE COMPACTS, 1783–1977 (A Revised Compilation) (Kentucky, Lexington, 1977) (updated), Congress consented or was asked to consent only to 10 compacts with foreign authorities, dealing with an international bridge, a port authority, forest fire prevention, lake basins, tax on fuel in busses, motor vehicle registration, and interpleader (8 with Canadian, one with Mexican and one generally with foreign authorities); in two instances the Congress reserved its decision on foreign participation in an interstate compact and in one case it expressly disapproved it. The Council of State Governments lists 177 interstate compacts. *See generally*, L. HENKIN, *supra* note 7, at 229–34; L. DI MARZO, COMPONENT UNITS OF FEDERAL STATES AND INTERNATIONAL AGREEMENTS 38–42, 82–84, 100–01 *et passim* (Alphen a/d Rijn, Sijthoff & Noordhoff, 1980); Engdahl, *Characterization of Interstate Arrangements: When is a Compact not a Compact?*, 64 MICH. L. REV. 63 (1965); P.T. HARDY, INTERSTATE COMPACTS – THE TIES THAT BIND (Georgia, Univ. of Georgia, Institute of Government, 1982).

Several states of the Union have maintained trade offices in foreign countries with a view to promoting exports of their products.

If Denmark wished to conclude an agreement with Norway on a matter clearly within the treaty power of the Community but of local interest only, could it do so with the consent of the Commission or the Council, without engaging the Community treaty–making machinery?

[130] U.S. CONST. art. VI, § 2; art. III, § 2, cl. 1.

tuating, short-term, large membership would not allow it to act with expertise, speed, or secrecy.[131] On the other hand, the Senate, at that time "a cozy club of twenty-six members," representing particularly state interests and not elected by popular vote, proved more acceptable. Nevertheless, the proposal that the Senate should act by simple majority was defeated, albeit by a single vote.[132]

The "advice" function of the Senate which was intended to enlist senatorial participation in ongoing negotiations, began to "slip" as early as 1794.[133] Gradually, but quite early, the function was virtually abandoned. The President has refrained from consulting the Senate on terms of a treaty before or during the negotiations and the Senate, itself preferring to "pass judgment" rather than to advise, has responded by insisting on changes in the finished texts of agreements as a part of its "consent" function.[134] The restrictions, conditions and understandings that the Senate sought to impose upon already signed and often delicately balanced treaties, such as the Versailles Settlement, SALT I, the Panama Canal Treaty or the British Tax Treaty, have caused acute difficulties with the treaty partners. Although the Senate may not be exactly a "graveyard" for treaties it may be termed, with a touch of poetic license and some exaggeration, their mortuary, considering the host of important treaties gathering dust in the Senate Foreign Relations Committee.[135]

131 L. Henkin, *supra* note 7, at 373 n.4.

132 L. Henkin, *supra* note 7, at 374, *quoting* 2 Farrand, *supra* note 7, at 532–54. The two–thirds majority corresponds roughly to the nine of the thirteen states whose consent was required under Art. IX of the Articles of Confederation.

133 In a widely told story, President Washington actually went to the Senate in 1789 expecting yes–or–no answers on a proposed treaty with Creek Indians, but the Senate referred the matter to a committee; the President, stalking out, muttered that he was damned if he would ever go there again – and he did not – but he continued to seek Senatorial advice by less direct means. The Jay Treaty of 1794 was the first treaty on which the Senate's "advice" in advance was not sought. T.M. Franck & E. Weisband, *supra* note 114, at 135–36. *See also* Franck & Weisband, *Advice and Consent*, N.Y. Times, 28 Feb. 1978, at M35 (commenting on the efforts by individual senators to negotiate with the Panamanian Government on the Canal Treaty).

134 Some 167 treaties were modified and 104 more rejected of the 1046 treaties submitted up to 1944. T.M. Franck & E. Weisband, *supra* note 114, at 136–37.

135 All currently unapproved treaties can be found at Senate Comm. on Foreign Relations, Legislative Calendar No. 3, 97th Cong., 2nd Sess. 7 (1982). *See, e.g.*, the Convention on the Prevention and Punishment of the Crime of Genocide, signed on behalf of the United States on 11 Dec. 1948 (EX. O, 81–1, 16 June 1949); the International Convention on the Elimination of All Forms of Racial Discrimination, signed on behalf of the United States on 23 Sept. 1966 (EX. C, 95–2, 23 Feb. 1978); the International Covenant on Economic, Social and Cultural Rights, signed on behalf of the United States on 5 Oct. 1977 (EX. D, 95–2, 23 Feb. 1978); the International Covenant on Civil and Political Rights, signed on behalf of the United States on 5 Oct. 1977 (EX. E, 95–2, 23 Feb. 1978); the American Convention on Human Rights, signed on behalf of the United States on 1 June 1977 (EX. F, 95–2, 23 Feb. 1978); and Convention No. 105 Concerning Abolition of Forced Labor adopted by the International Labor Organisation at its 40th session at Geneva, 25 June 1957 (EX. K, 88–1, 22 July 1963).

Franck and Weisband give a vivid description of the President's efforts to deal with "senatorial obstructionism" by two devices: by "cooption" – that is by appointing Senators to treaty negotiating delegations and drawing on both Houses for key foreign policy appointments in the Administration; and by "circumvention."[136] The latter tactic involves by-passing Senate opposition by means of an executive agreement concluded by the President alone, or by seeking an approval by simple majorities of both Houses for an executive agreement negotiated (or to be negotiated) by the President. Neither device is mentioned in the Constitution but both have been sanctioned by extensive practice.[137] The employment of executive agreements by the President alone has been responsible for a great deal of friction in the uneasy partnership between the two branches of government.[138]

Despite the congenital deficiencies of the system, there is broad support for the role of the Senate as a necessary "brake" on the "imperial Presidency," and any remedy is invariably sought in improved consultation procedures which would restore and perhaps institutionalize some of the Senate's "advice" function.

ii) Limitations on treaty-making power

Although it is not obvious that the Founders intended to subject treaties to any constitutional limitations and no treaty has ever been held unconstitutional, the treaty-makers have always assumed, and the Supreme Court has made it clear, that such limitations exist.[139] These limitations, however, have different effects than, and they are determined through a different method than that employed in respect of, the limitations on domestic powers of the Federal Government.

(a) Separation of powers. In the first place, limitations derived from the separation of powers between the legislative and executive branches can hardly apply in the traditional way since a treaty may legislate as well as create international obligations although the House is excluded from the process.[140]

[136] T.M. Franck & E. Weisband, *supra* note 114, at 138–45.

[137] *See supra* note 103, last sentence. There is considerable support for the proposition that whatever the President can do by a treaty with the consent of two-thirds of the Senate he can also do by an executive agreement with the approval of the majority of both Houses. In principle, however, the Department of State would not agree with this proposition.

[138] *See infra* text accompanying note 163.

[139] Reid v. Covert, 354 U.S. 1, 16–17 (1957).

[140] L. Henkin, *supra* note 7, at 148–51, 159–60, discusses the arguments in support of limitations on the treaty power based on separation of powers. There is little reality today in these arguments. The Circuit Court of Appeals for the District of Columbia recently held that the Constitution does not prohibit the transfer of U.S. property to Panama through the self-executing Panama Canal Zone Treaty, and the Supreme Court denied certiorari. Edwards v. Carter, 580 F.2d 1055 (D.C. Cir.), *cert. denied*, 436 U.S. 907 (1978). *See* Comment, *Constitutional Law – Treaty Power – Disposal of United States Territories – Panama Canal Treaties*, 1979 Wis. L. Rev. 837.

(b) *Federalism and the tenth amendment.* The federalism argument, that would allow treaty power only in matters already delegated to the Federal Government for legislative regulation, was put to rest in 1920 in the landmark case of *Missouri v. Holland.*[141] The treaty power, acording to Justice Holmes who wrote the opinion in this case, was delegated to the federal treaty-makers in addition to, and independently of, the delegations to Congress, and since the treaty power was so delegated, whatever is within it was not reserved to the states by the tenth amendment or by "some invisible radiation" from its terms. Thus many matters clearly "reserved to the states" as regards domestic legislation (such as inheritance and access to local occupations) may and have been the subject of international treaties. However, "the Constitution probably protects some few states' rights, activities, and properties against any federal invasion, even by treaty."[142] In *Geofroy v. Riggs*[143] the Supreme Court held,

> [i]t would not be contended that [the treaty power] extends so far as to authorize what the Constitution forbids, or a change in the character of the government or in that of one of the States, or a cession of any portion of the territory of the latter, without its consent. . . . But with these exceptions, it is not perceived that there is any limit to the questions which can be adjusted touching any matter which is properly the subject of negotiations with a foreign country.[144]

(c) *The Bill of Rights.* The most important, if not the only real constitutional limitations on the treaty power can clearly be found in the Bill of Rights which prohibits impairment of individual rights by federal authorities.[145]

In the past a much debated question was what the Court had meant in seeming to confine the treaty power to matters "properly the subject of negotiations with a foreign country." The often repeated assertions that the treaty power is barred from "domestic matters" or "matters not of international concern"[146] or "not pertaining to the conduct of international relations" can mean only – although authoritative case law is conspicuously absent – that a treaty must be a bona fide agreement between the United States and another state.[147]

iii) Self-executing and non-self-executing treaties

Although the "supremacy clause" was included in the Constitution primarily to assure treaty compliance by states[148] it was interpreted by Chief Justice Marshall

141 252 U.S. 416 (1920). *See infra* notes 182, 195.

142 L. Henkin, *supra* note 7, at 147.

143 133 U.S. 258 (1890).

144 *Id.* at 267.

145 For other prohibitions in the Constitution *see* art. I, § 9. *See generally* L. H. Tribe, American Constitutional Law (Mineola, Foundation Press, 1978–79).

146 *See, e.g.,* the statement by Charles Evans Hughes (formerly Secretary of State and later Chief Justice of the Supreme Court) in 23 Proc. Am. Soc'y Int'l L. 194–96 (1929).

147 Henkin, *International Concern and the Treaty Power of the United States,* 63 AJIL 272, 276–77 (1969). This view has now been accepted in the revised draft Restatement of Foreign Releations Law § 304 (Tent. Draft No. 1; Philadelphia, A.L.I., 1 Apr. 1980); *see id.,* Reporter's Note 2, at 88.

148 *See supra* text accompanying note 127.

to mean also that treaties may add to, and change, domestic law automatically and directly upon ratification, without any "transformation" by an act of Congress:[149]

A treaty is in its nature a contract between two nations, not a legislative act. It does not generally effect, of itself, the object to be accomplished, especially so far as its operation is infra-territorial; but is carried into execution by the sovereign power of the respective parties to the instrument.

In the United States a different principle is established. Our Constitution declares a treaty to be the law of the land. It is, consequently, to be regarded in courts of justice as equivalent to an act of the legislature, whenever it operates of itself without the aid of any legislative provision.

But when the terms of the stipulation import a contract, when either of the parties engages to perform a particular act, the treaty addresses itself to the political, not the judicial department; and the legislature must execute the contract before it can become a rule for the Court.[150]

Whether a treaty is self-executing or non-self-executing is ultimately a matter of judicial interpretation in a "case or controversy." The courts, however, will accord "great weight" to the interpretation offered by the Department of State, but they will not consider themselves bound by it.[151] The courts have as a rule applied the historic method of interpretation to determine intent on the basis of the text, context and legislative history of the treaty. Yet, unless legislative implementation is specifically provided for or clearly implied, the search for subjective intent is often illusory since the question in fact was not considered by the negotiators. Only more recently, perhaps under the impact of the many multilateral treaties, have the courts inclined toward the objective purpose-oriented method, but they have failed to develop consistent objective criteria by which to decide whether a treaty is to be considered self-executing.[152] It is accepted, however, that a treaty that entails expenditure of funds by the United States or imposes criminal sanctions cannot be executed without an act of Congress; but a treaty apparently can serve as "authorization" legislation supporting subsequent appropriation of funds by Congress.[153] On the other hand, the courts have generally attributed self-executing effect to treaties of friendship, commerce and navigation, often without even discerning the issue.[154]

149 Even a self-executing treaty, however, may not become "law of the land" binding individuals until it is proclaimed by the President so as to give notice to the persons concerned. Haver v. Yaker, 76 U.S. (9 Wall.) 32, 34–35 (1869).

150 Foster v. Neilson, 27 U.S. (2 Pet.) 253, 313–14 (1829).

151 Factor v. Laubenheimer, 290 U.S. 276, 295 (1933).

152 *See generally,* Evans, *Self-Executing Treaties in the United States of America,* 1953 BRIT. Y.B. INT'L L. 178; *see* cases collected in draft RESTATEMENT, *supra* note 147, § 131 at 55–57. *See,* in this context, *infra* note 231, last paragraph.

153 L. HENKIN, *supra* note 7, at 159 n. 98, with a list of authorities.

154 *See, e.g.,* Asakura v. City of Seattle, 265 U.S. 332 (1924). For an analysis of the more recent case law *see* J.S. Hilboldt, The Enforcement of Treaty Rights by American Courts and the Self-Executing Treaty Doctrine (unpublished research paper, Univ. of Michigan, 1981).

iv) Some unanswered questions

(a) Congress' obligation to implement a treaty. Among the problems unresolved by the courts is the question whether Congress is constitutionally obligated to implement a non-self-executing treaty. Congress has accepted the obligation to carry out treaty commitments, although it has not always given the President all he said the treaty called for.[155]

(b) Conflict between a treaty and federal statute. Another question on which the Constitution is silent is how to resolve a conflict between a treaty and a federal statute. The Supreme Court has ruled that although a self-executing treaty supersedes any conflicting state law or constitution, it supersedes only a *prior* inconsistent federal statute (if the two cannot be reconciled), but it is itself superseded as "law of the land" by a subsequent federal statute if Congress clearly intended to legislate against it.[156] Thus although the Congress may legislate against a treaty – and the courts enforce the legislation – internationally the United States remains obligated and in default until the treaty is terminated. This situation, which contrasts with the earlier view of a treaty as a "higher law,"[157] is surely not conducive to reliable partnership or consistent with the modern conception of the effect to be given to international law in domestic legal orders.

(c) Limitations on Presidential power to conclude executive agreements. Although the Supreme Court has upheld, in a few instances, the President's independent power to enter into executive agreements and has also given them effect to modify state law, the limits of this power and the effect on federal law remain largely undefined.[158]

(d) Procedures for termination of treaties. There is no conclusive answer to the question of who can terminate a treaty although a Court of Appeals recently upheld, and the Supreme Court affirmed, the President's decision to end the Mutual Defense Treaty with Taiwan without reference to the Senate or to the Congress.[159]

155 L. HENKIN, *supra* note 7, at 162.

156 *See, e.g.*, Whitney v. Robertson, 124 U.S. 190, 194 (1888).

157 Both Jay and Jefferson (at least initially) assumed that a treaty as "higher law" in the natural law sense would prevail not only over pre-existing but also over later federal law. Jay in THE FEDERALIST No. 64, *supra* note 15, at 394, and Jefferson in 2 J. STORY, COMMENTARIES ON THE CONSTITUTION OF THE UNITED SATES § 1841, at 609 n.1 (M.M. Bigelow ed., 5th ed., Boston, Little, Brown & Co., 1891). The U.S. Supreme Court has chosen a different rule. *See* E. STEIN, P. HAY & M. WAELBROECK, *supra* note 3, at 106–08.

158 United States v. Pink, 315 U.S. 203 (1942); United States v. Belmont, 301 U.S. 324 (1937); Dames & Moore v. Regan, 453 U.S. 654 (1981). *But see* United States v. Guy W. Capps, Inc., 204 F.2d 655 (4th Cir. 1953), *aff'd*, 348 U.S. 296 (1955) (on other grounds).

159 Goldwater v. Carter, 617 F.2d 697 (D.C. Cir. 1979), *aff'd per curiam*, 444 U.S. 996 (1979). *See* Pappas, *The Constitutional Allocation of Competence in the Termination of Treaties*, 13 N.Y.U. J. INT'L L. & POL. 473 (1981); Glennon, *Treaty Process Reform: Saving Constitutionalism Without Destroying Diplomacy*, 52 CIN. L. REV. 84 (1983).

v) Attacks on the existing procedures

The Supreme Court's broad interpretation of the treaty power was at least in some measure responsible for the periodic campaigns in and outside the Congress to impose limitations on the treaty process. In the early 1950's a coalition of Mid-Western Republicans and Southern Democrats in the Senate, disturbed by the United Nations human rights program that they regarded as an attempt at imposed "social engineering" unrelated to international concerns of the United States, launched a massive effort to amend the Constitution. In its extreme form, the Bricker Amendment,[160] although not purporting to limit the federal power to make treaties, would have eliminated the self-executing feature and made all treaties non-self-executing. It would also have barred Congress from implementing treaties by laws which were not within the power of Congress apart from the treaty. This, it was assumed, would prevent the implementation of the human rights and other treaties in the United States.

Although the amendment in a diluted form passed the Senate after a long and acrimonious debate, it was not pressed further.[161] Yet the great constitutional free-for-all has contributed to the Executive Branch's reluctance to sign and urge Senate approval of human rights treaties; and when it has attempted to promote such treaties, it has met with stony silence in the Senate.[162] More recently, disturbed by the Presidential use of executive agreements particularly concerning foreign military bases, Congress has had before it numerous bills to limit or regulate executive agreements. Congress succeeded only in adopting a law requiring the Executive Branch to notify the appropriate Congressional committees within a set deadline of any executive agreements it had concluded.[163] Responding to the continuing pressure from the Congress, the Department of State agreed to extend the notification duty to consultations on the form, although not on the substance, of the proposed agreement.[164]

160 S.J. Res. 1, 83rd Cong. 1st Sess., 99 Cong. Rec. 6773 (1953).

161 *See* the Bricker Hearings before the Senate Subcommittee on the Judiciary, listed in L. Henkin, *supra* note 7, at 384 n.35, 394 n. 69. *See also* W.W. Bishop, Jr., International Law, Cases and Materials 110–12 (3rd ed., Boston/Toronto, Little, Brown & Co., 1971).

162 Of all the modern treaties touching upon human rights, the U.S. became a party to the Treaty on Slavery, the Protocol on the Status of Refugees and the Treaty on the Rights of Women. Of the 140 conventions on uniform labor standards adopted by the ILO, the U.S. has ratified only 7, as compared, for example, with 96 accepted by France, and 68 accepted by the U.K. International Labor Office, International Labor Conventions Chart of Ratifications (Geneva, 1975).

163 The Case–Zablocki Act, Pub. L. No. 92–403, 86 Stat. 619, 1 U.S.C. § 112b (1972), *as amended by* Pub. L. No. 95–5, § 5, 91 Stat. 224 (1977), and Pub. L. No. 95–426, title VII, § 708, 92 Stat. 993 (1978).

164 Franck and Weisband believe that "for the first time in this century, a procedure has been established for getting advice of the Senate Foreign Relations Committee, before and during negotiations," on the form of the agreement. T. M. Franck & E. Weisband, *supra* note 114, at 151. *See also supra* text accompanying notes 133–35.

b) In the Community

Most of the landmark cases decided by the Court of Justice in the foreign affairs area concern the treaty-making authority. In its earliest years the Community was understandably absorbed with the demanding internal task of building the common market, but because the Community was born into an interdependent world economy it was from the outset compelled to deal with third countries and the proliferating international organizations. By the nature of things, the treaty power was the principal instrument for the Community to replace bilateral relationships between its Members and third countries and to create new relationships. After an initial phase during which it reacted to the most insistent outside pressures, the Community has sought to evolve a more comprehensive foreign commercial policy within which to place its treaty-making activities. The Community was virtually thrust into the GATT negotiations as it progressively assumed responsibility for the Common Customs Tariff. Other European states, concerned with the economic and political impact of the emerging new "trade block," insisted on negotiating special "associations" aiming at eventual admission to full membership (Greece and Turkey) or creating industrial free trade areas comprising their and the Community's territories (the European Free Trade Association (EFTA) states). Mediterranean and North African countries, historically within the Member States' orbit, demanded preferential arrangements, and the original Treaty-based tie with former African colonies was expanded into a novel type of treaty partnership – Yaoundé and Lomé Conventions – ultimately including some sixty African, Carribean and Pacific states. The Community has concluded arrangements with almost all the industrialized and third-world states in a bewildering variety of commercial, "association," and "economic cooperation" agreements, dealing with questions of trade, economic development, science and technology, environment, transport, fisheries, food aid, etc. The Community has also established links with a great number of global and regional organizations. Only Japan, and the Soviet Union with most of its allies, remain outside this elaborate treaty-network, bearing evidence of the Community's position as the world's largest trader.[165]

165 The Soviet Union refuses to "recognize" the Community. *See,* however, the Convention on Future Multilateral Cooperation in the North–East Atlantic Fisheries, art. 20 (OJ No. L 227, 12 Aug. 1981, p. 22, at p. 27), which opened the Convention for signature by 12 states including the Soviet Union, and by the EEC. The Convention was "approved" by Council Dec. 81/608 of 13 July 1981, OJ No. L 227, 12 Aug. 1981, p. 21. Of course, joining with the EEC in a multilateral treaty does not by itself imply recognition. *See generally* Wellenstein, *The Relations of the European Communities with Eastern Europe,* in ESSAYS IN EUROPEAN LAW AND INTEGRATION 197–208 (D. O'Keeffe & H.G. Schermers eds., Deventer (NL), Kluwer, 1982). The problem with Japan is simply one of economic considerations. *See generally* K.J. TWITCHETT, EUROPE AND THE WORLD – THE EXTERNAL RELATIONS OF THE COMMON MARKET (London, Europa Pub., 1976); W.J. FELD, THE EUROPEAN COMMUNITY IN WORLD AFFAIRS (New York, Alfred Pub. Co., 1976).

i) Treaty-making process: Who "makes" treaties?

(a) The Community procedure. According to the Treaty provisions[166] the Commission negotiates international agreements under a "mandate" from the Council. The Council, after consulting the European Parliament where the Treaty requires it to do so, "concludes" the agreement. Case law and ample practice, often inspired by accepted international treaty-making procedures has filled in some of the gaps.

(i) The Commission's role: Negotiating under the Council's direction. In principle, the Commission – like the President in the United States – is responsible for handling the negotiations.[167] Although not necessarily required to do so, the Commission does not institute formal negotiations without obtaining an authorization from the Council, and at times it even seeks Council concurrence for exploratory talks.[168] The Commission makes recommendations and the Council issues directives or "mandates" to it at the outset and in the course of the negotiations which the Commission must follow.[169] The Commission's recommendations do not have the status of formal proposals as in the internal law-making procedure and they can be freely changed or disregarded by the Council. In addition, a Council-appointed committee composed of officials from national ministries sits with the Commission negotiator and looks over his shoulders during the negotiations, but its members do not speak. This pattern, prescribed for commercial agreements,[170] has in practice been adopted for other negotiations as well.

For a classification of the various types of agreements concluded by the Community, according to their legal basis, form and content *see* C. FLAESCH–MOUGIN, LES ACCORDS EXTERNES DE LA COMMUNAUTÉ ÉCONOMIQUE EUROPÉENNE – ESSAI D'UNE TYPOLOGIE (Brussels, Ed. de l'Univ. de Bruxelles, 1979).

[166] Essentially EEC Treaty arts. 113, 114, 228–231, 238. *See supra* notes 41–42, 44–46.

[167] For exceptions, particularly where the Community treaty power is contested or in international organizations, *see* 12 BRUSSELS COMMENTARY, *supra* note 89, at 32. As a rule, the negotiations on behalf of the Commission are conducted by an official of the DG for External Relations but other departments have been drawn into the process. *Id.* at 33. *See generally* Mégret, *Conclusion, formes et effets des accords internationaux passés par la CEE,* 1965 R.M.C. 19; Melchior, *La procédure de conclusion des accords externes de la CEE,* 2 REV. BELGE DR. INT. 187 (1966); C. FLAESCH–MOUGIN, *supra* note 165, at 72–75.

[168] EEC Treaty art. 113 does, but the general art. 228 does not, require such prior authorization. The Commission embarked on exploratory talks with Egypt without checking with the Council and that brought the wrath of the Council on its head. On the readiness of the U.S. Department of State to consult with the Senate on the form of the proposed agreement, *see supra* text accompanying note 164.

[169] These Council acts are prepared by COREPER with the Commission's collaboration. On the negotiations generally, *see* U. AYBERK, LE MÉCANISME DE LA PRISE DES DÉCISIONS COMMUNAUTAIRES EN MATIÈRE DE RELATIONS INTERNATIONALES 341 ff (Brussels, Bruylant, 1978); Bot, *Negotiating Community Agreements: Procedure and Practice,* 7 C.M.L. REV. 286 (1970).

[170] EEC Treaty art. 113(3).

As a rule the Council's directives allow the Commission only limited discretion and require references to the Council, where consensus is often elusive. The consequent delays irritate the Commission's partners in the negotiations. One is reminded of the position of an American negotiating team which, in important commercial negotiations, must keep close contact not only with the office of the Representative for Trade Negotiations, the Department of Commerce and the Department of State in Washington which issue the negotiating instructions, but also at times directly with the White House and the appropriate Congressional committees.[171]

The Council directives cannot be kept secret and the publicity handicaps the Commission's negotiating posture. When the negotiation results in an agreed text the Council, if it approves, authorizes a specific official to sign the agreement, subject to final "conclusion." It is after the signature that the European Parliament is consulted.

(ii) *The European Parliament's role: Consultation by the Council prior to "conclusion."* In response to increasingly insistent criticism by the deputies, the Council agreed, first in 1964 with respect to "association" agreements and in 1973 with respect to commercial agreements, to provide information and an opportunity for the Parliament to hold a debate on a proposed negotiation before it is started, to have the Commission advise the appropriate committee of the Parliament on a confidential basis of the substance of the agreement before it is signed, and last, but not least, to make available to the Parliament the text before it is finally "concluded."[172] It is said, however, that the procedure has not increased the Parliament's input to any appreciable degree, and suggestions have been advanced that the Parliament be given formal power to approve or reject an agreement, in line with the corresponding powers of the national parliaments.[173] It is probably correct to say that without such formal power of "consent" the power of "advice" will remain largely illusory.[174]

(iii) *Conclusion of a treaty and the Council's role.* An agreement becomes internationally binding upon the Community when the Council "concludes" it

171 *See generally,* Winham, *Robert Strauss, the MTN, and the Control of Faction,* 14 J. World Trade L. 377 (1980).

172 12 Brussels Commentary, *supra* note 89, at 42–44 (discussing the "Luns" and "Luns–Westerterp" procedures).

173 It is questionable whether this could be done under the "necessary and proper" power, art. 235, as suggested by Seeler, *Das direkt gewählte Europäische Parlament - ein neues Parlament,* 15 EuR 201, 210 (1980). A Treaty amendment would probably be necessary to grant the Parliament such legal power. However, the Parliament could be given such authority in practice by a political understanding with the Council.

174 Discussion with Professor Joseph Weiler, E.U.I., Florence. In the present state of the Community decision-making it is difficult enough to obtain the consensus of the ten Governments; obviously, a requirement of Parliamentary "consent" would add to the complexity of the process. *See generally* Weiler, *The European Parliament and Foreign Affairs: External Relations of the European Economic Community,* in Parliamentary Control Over Foreign Policy, *supra* note 82, at 151.

either by a "regulation," or by a decision *sui generis*, and the instruments of ratification are exchanged with the other party.[175] According to the Treaty, a weighted majority suffices when the Council votes on commercial agreements while unanimity is required for agreements concluded under articles 238 or 235 – a distinction of little practical import as long as the consensus requirement prevails.[176]

In comparison with the American system, the Council performs the Senate's original function of "advice" on ongoing negotiations (albeit with a mandatory effect), the Senate's "consent" role, as well as the President's function of "making" the treaty. Paradoxically, in the United States, the House of Representatives, initially the only popularly elected chamber, is entirely excluded from treaty-making, although it has a part in implementation of treaties and an equal voice in authorizing the President to conclude executive agreements especially on tariffs and trade. In Europe the European Parliament may at least give advice and clamors for additional influence.

(b) *Mixed agreements and areas of Member State competence.* It will come as a surprise to an American lawyer that in a variety of instances an agreement is concluded by both the Community and by the Member States in their individual capacities. This form referred to as "mixed agreements," although viewed by some as of a doubtful constitutional validity, has become established practice and has received the implicit blessing of the Court.[177] Mixed agreements developed when circumstances called for an agreement to include subjects which fell outside the treaty-making power of the Community and could not conveniently be dealt with separately, but they have also been employed where the Community alone should have been the party.[178] In fact, there has been a rapid increase in the number of mixed agreements and they have been extended to cover a variety of subjects with the result that they may be considered to be

[175] Raux & Flaesch-Mougin, *Les accords externes de la C.E.E.*, 11 R.T.D.E. 227, 246–47 (1975). Past practice shows no consistency in the choice between a regulation and a decision. Bebr suggests that "at present" the Council acts by regulation. Bebr, *Agreements Concluded by the Community and Their Possible Direct Effect*, 20 C.M.L. Rev. 35, 39 (1983).

[176] The voting requirements with respect to agreements concluded under other Treaty articles in application of the internal/external parallelisms rule would presumably be determined by the article in question.

In the less formal "short" procedure, the Council directs the President to authorize signing the agreement and the signature constitutes the conclusion binding the Community. On the form of conclusion, *see* Raux & Flaesch-Mougin, *supra* note 175, at 245–51; Raux & Perrot, *Les accords externes de la C.E.E.*, 12 R.T.D.E. 295, 311–13 (1976); Raux, *Les accords externes de la C.E.E.*, 15 R.T.D.E. 664, 666 (1979).

[177] *See especially* Opinion 1/78, given pursuant to Art. 228(1) EEC, (International Agreement on Natural Rubber), [1979] ECR 2871, discussed *infra* text accompanying note 190. On this subject, *see generally* 12 Brussels Commentary, *supra* note 89, at 49–52.

[178] *See* Costonis, *The Association with Nigeria*, in L'Association à la Communauté Economique Européenne 215, 298 (Brussels, Institut d'Etudes Européennes, Presses Univ. de Bruxelles, 1970).

more important than agreements concluded by the Community alone.[179] Although the practice has not been consistent, in principle the Commission alone conducts the negotiations for bilateral "mixed agreements," but in multilateral treaty negotiations or international conferences there are either eleven delegations (ten Members and the Commission), or a "two-headed" delegation of the Commission and the "Presidency" of the Council, or a single combined delegation with the Commission representative more often than not acting as the spokesman on Community matters.[180]

ii) The reach of, and "limitations" on, the Community power – *ERTA* and its progeny[181]

In contrast to the United States, the issue in Europe has been the division between the "delegated" Community power and the broad "reserved" powers of its Members.

As we have seen, the Treaty expressly authorizes the Community only to enter into tariff and trade and "association" agreements (articles 113, 238) and to establish working relationships with international organizations (articles 229 to 231). However, contrary to the prevailing learned opinion, and to the consternation of some Member Governments, the Court of Justice rejected the principle of enumerated powers in favor of the doctrine that Community treaty power should be coextensive with its internal powers (internal/external parallelism).[182]

(a) *Internal and external parallelism: Implied powers.* The main issues in this connection have been whether it is possible for the Community in support of its given internal functions to take measures in the international arena for which no explicit powers exist, and the extent to which the internal functions must

[179] *See generally* MIXED AGREEMENTS (D. O'Keeffe & H.G. Schermers eds., Deventer (NL), Kluwer, 1983), and *especially* Ehlermann, *Mixed Agreements: A List of Problems, id.* at 1.

[180] *See infra* text accompanying note 289, on representation in the EPC system. EEC Treaty art. 116 provides: "Member States shall, in respect of all matters of particular interest to the common market, proceed within the framework of international organizations of an economic character only by common action...." For obvious reasons, the Commission has been down-playing the importance of this provision, and the Court ignored it in *ERTA;* but the Council has relied on it in several instances, as in the International Energy Agency and earlier commodity agreements negotiations. 12 BRUSSELS COMMENTARY, *supra* note 89, at 52.

[181] The extensive literature is listed *inter alia* in Pescatore, *External Relations in the Case-Law of the Court of Justice of the European Communities,* 16 C.M.L.REV. 615, 615–16 n.1 (1979).

[182] *See supra* text accompanying note 68. It has been said that the internal/external parallelism principle is the "exact reverse" of the rule of Missouri v. Holland, 252 U.S. 416 (1920), where the Supreme Court held on the basis of the "necessary and proper" clause that "internal" legislative powers of Congress are coextensive with the federal treaty power. Riesenfeld in 1978 PROC. AM. SOC'Y INT'L L. 185. *But see infra* note 195. *See also supra* text accompanying note 141.

actually have been already undertaken before the external competence may be said to arise. Once external competence has been established, the problem has been to determine whether it is exclusive or concurrent with the competence of the Member States.

In the *ERTA* case[183] the Court was asked by the Commission to rule that the Commission alone had the power to negotiate a multinational road transport agreement within the United Nations Economic Commission for Europe. The Court answered that although the Treaty part on transportation does not expressly confer such power on the Community, its "internal" authority to frame a common policy in the field of transport carries with it treaty power in that field and that a regulation previously adopted by the Council on the same subject covering internal transport "necessarily vested in the Community power to enter into any agreements with third countries relating to the subject-matter governed by that regulation to the exclusion of any concurrent powers of the Member States."[184] Thus although declaring the Community's exclusive power the Court left open the question whether its treaty-making authority is in principle merely potential and inchoate, and must be first activated by a "common rule" to be adopted by the institutions within the internal sphere (such as a regulation) and if so, what sort of a rule would have that effect. Similarly, in the *Kramer* case,[185] the Court found that despite the absence of a specific Treaty grant in the fisheries area, the Community had the authority to enter into a convention on conservation of ocean fishing resources because of its power under the Treaty to frame a common agricultural policy and given the existence of a Council regulation on fisheries conservation in Member States' maritime waters.[186] Not until its *Opinion 1/76*[187] has the Court made it clear that the Community treaty power is not necessarily dependent on a prior internal measure but may flow "by implication" directly from the Treaty provision creating the internal competence, "in so far as the participation of the Community in the international agreement is ... necessary for the attainment of one of the objectives of the Community."[188]

[183] Case 22/70, *ERTA*, [1971] ECR 263. For references to comments on this case, *see* Pescatore, *supra* note 181, at 619 n.6.

[184] Case 22/70, *ERTA*, [1971] ECR 263, 275, 276.

[185] Joined Cases 3, 4 & 6/76, *Kramer*, [1976] ECR 1279. For references to comments, *see also* Pescatore, *supra* note 181, at 620 n. 8.

[186] In addition to the regulation mentioned above the Court referred to art. 102 of the Act of Accession of the United Kingdom, Denmark and Ireland. Joined Cases 3, 4 & 6/76, *Kramer*, [1976] ECR 1279, 1309.

[187] Opinion 1/76, given pursuant to Art. 228(1) EEC, (Draft Agreement establishing a European laying-up fund for inland waterway vessels), [1977] ECR 741. For comments, *see* Groux, *Le parallélisme des compétences internes et externes de la Communauté économique européenne*, 14 C.D.E. 3 (1978); Philip, *A propos de l'avis 1/76 de la Cour de justice des Communautés européennes*, 1978 R.M.C. 55.

[188] Opinion 1/76, [1977] ECR 741, 755. Ruling 1/78, delivered pursuant to Art. 103 EAEC, (Draft Convention of the International Atomic Energy Agency on the Physical Protection of Nuclear Materials, Facilities and Transports), [1978] ECR

(b) *Express treaty-making powers: The field of commercial policy.* In the foreign commercial policy field, where the Community is given expressly the power to make common policy and specifically to negotiate tariff and trade agreements, the principal issues have been to identify the subjects falling within the category of foreign commercial policy and to determine whether the Community treaty-making power is "exclusive," "shared," or concurrent with the powers of the Member States.

The European Court has adopted an expansive approach in delineating the areas of Community competence. For instance, the Court had no difficulty in finding that an "understanding" on export credit standards negotiated in the Organization for Economic Cooperation and Development (OECD) fell within the scope of commercial policy and thus within the Community's treaty power which is not dependent on prior exercise of an internal power[189] and excludes any parallel power on the part of the Members. Most recently, the Court recognized, against the Council's opposition, that the Community's commercial-policy treaty power extends beyond the classic agreements designed to liberalize international trade: it embraces also the modern commodity agreements (specifically the International Agreement on Natural Rubber under negotiation in the United Nations Conference on Trade and Development), despite their essentially regulatory features and complex objectives that impinge upon the development policies and general economic policies which are within the national competence of the Member States.[190]

(c) *Exclusive, shared or concurrent powers? – Pre-emption.* At this juncture, due to the consistent case law of the Court of Justice, the principle of internal/external parallelism is no longer in question, and it is accepted by all the Member Governments. The controversy centers, however, on the bold assertions of the exclusive character of the Community power within the orbit of its competence, to the preclusion of the Member States. In reality, the Court has

2151, may perhaps also be interpreted to support the above cited position, even though the Euratom Treaty provisions differ from those of the EEC.

189 Opinion 1/75, given pursuant to Art. 228(1) of the EEC Treaty, (Understanding on a Local Cost Standard), [1975] ECR 1355.

> A commercial policy is in fact made up by the combination and interaction of internal and external measures, without priority being taken by one over the others. Sometimes agreements are concluded in execution of a policy fixed in advance, sometimes that policy is defined by the agreements themselves.

Id. at 1363. Maas, *The External Powers of the E.E.C. with Regard to Commercial Policy: Comment on Opinion 1/75*, 13 C.M.L. Rev. 379 (1976).

190 Opinion 1/78, (International Agreement on Natural Rubber), [1979] ECR 2871. For comments *see* Brückner, *Quelques observations au sujet de l'avis 1/78 ('caoutchouc') de la Cour de Justice*, 1980 R.M.C. 4; Steenbergen, *La notion de politique commerciale commune après l'avis 1/78 de la Cour de Justice*, 16 C.D.E. 54 (1980). The Court pointed to the clauses in the agreement "concerning technological assistance, research programmes, the maintenance of fair conditions of labour in the rubber industry and consultations relating to national tax policies which may have an effect on the price of rubber." [1979] ECR 2871, 2916.

been more prudent and pragmatic in this respect, balancing the institutional interests of the Community against the concerns of third states and taking into account the practical need for effective action, as well as the political sensibilities of the Member Governments bent on protecting their own foreign affairs power. The Court's practice is reminiscent of the method used by the United States Supreme Court in the *domestic* sphere when it is asked to rule whether a state law is "pre-empted" by an act of Congress. In the absence of clear evidence of "the intent of Congress," the Court in effect must "rely upon its own judgment as to whether, or to what extent, an intelligent legislature would have wished to permit state legislation touching upon the subject-matter of the federal legislation."[191] In particular, the Supreme Court will consider whether the law is non-discriminatory and reflects a legitimate state objective which is consistent with the federal objective.[192]

Thus in the *ERTA* case, although the Court of Justice solemnly proclaimed that the Community alone was competent particularly in view of the "pre-emptive" Council Regulation, the Court nevertheless let the Member States continue the negotiations that they had been carrying on for a number of years, because "[a]t that stage of the negotiations, to have suggested to the third countries concerned that there was now a new distribution of powers within the Community might well have jeopardized the successful outcome."[193]

In *Kramer*[194] the Court again found exclusive Community power over maritime fisheries conservation policy, but it held that the Dutch Government's conservation measures were not "precluded" by prior Community law as long as the Council was unable to agree on what the common policy should be. Yet in other cases the Court disallowed Irish and British "conservation" measures on the ground that they were discriminatory or were enacted in disregard of the agreed consultation procedures.[195]

[191] Stein & Sandalow, *supra* note 6, at 35. In the Community, the pre-emption concept appears to be used also in discussing whether the Treaty directly limits the competence of Member States to enact legislation. *Id.* at 33.

[192] *See generally* Cohen, *Congressional Power to Define State Power to Regulate Commerce: Consent and Pre-Emption*, in COURTS AND FREE MARKETS, *supra* note 6, at 523.

[193] [1971] ECR 263, 282. *See also supra* text accompanying note 183. However, the Members must continue to act "in the interest and on behalf of the Community." Case 22/70, *ERTA*, [1971] ECR 263, 282 at para. 90. When the Court held an agreement incompatible with the Treaty in Opinion 1/76, (inland waterway vessels), [1977] ECR 741, Switzerland was the only non-member party affected.

[194] Joined Cases 3, 4 & 6/76, [1976] ECR 1279. *See supra* text accompanying note 185.

[195] Case 61/77, Commission v. Ireland, [1978] ECR 417; Case 804/79, Commission v. U.K., [1981] ECR 1045. *See also* Case 181/80, Procureur Général près la Cour d'Appel de Pau and Others v. Arbelaiz-Emazabel, [1981] ECR 2961.

It is fairly universally accepted that the Community has exclusive external authority with regard to fisheries. The debate has been rather as to whether the Member States are also excluded from internal competence, that is, whether internal and external fisheries policy is so inter-linked that the exclusivity of the one must be reflected in the other.

In what is perhaps the most striking compromise, (the logic of which has been criticized), in the *International Natural Rubber Agreement* case the Court ruled that although the Agreement was within the Community's exclusive commercial treaty power, nevertheless the Member States were entitled to join as parties, since the anticipated expenses would not necessarily be borne by the Community budget and the Member States might be called upon to assume the burden of financing the proposed buffer stock which the Court considered an "essential feature" of the Agreement.[196] In fact, by a later mutual accommodation between the Commission and the Council all commodity agreements are now dealt with as "mixed agreements."[197]

In the *International Natural Rubber Agreement* case, the Court made it clear that if the funding were to be provided from the Community budget rather than from Member State funds "no problem would arise as regards the exclusive powers of the Community to conclude the agreement."[198] One may assume that if the Community enters into an agreement which falls within its treaty power and provides for financial expenditure to come from the Community budget, then the budgetary authorities, that is the Council with the European Parliament, are obligated not only under international law but also under Community law to make the necessary entry into the budget without further Community legislation.[199] The analogous question in the United States has no truly author-

J. Usher, European Community Law and National Law 66–67 (London, Allen & Unwin, 1981). In this light the issue resembles Missouri v. Holland, 252 U.S. 416 (1920) (discussed *supra* at note 141). There a lower federal court held a Congressional act for the protection of migratory birds unconstitutional on the ground that the Congress impinged on the "states' rights." The Federal Government then entered into a treaty with Canada on the same subject and the Supreme Court upheld the act of Congress on the basis of the "necessary and proper" clause in the Constitution as necessary to implement the treaty. It may thus be said that the President with the Senate could do what Congress alone (at that time) perhaps could not constitutionally do. Thus, it could be said that in the fisheries situation in Europe, the internal/external rule is not applied as "the exact reverse" of the American constitutional practice (*see supra* text accompanying note 182), but in conformity with it.

196 For a criticism, *see, e.g.*, Steenbergen, *supra* note 190, at 67; and Barav, *The Division of External Relations Power Between the EEC and the Member States in the Case-Law of the Court of Justice*, in Division of Powers, *supra* note 71, at 29, 51. ***But see*** the response by Pescatore, *id.* at 69, 71.

197 In 1981 the Council decided on a proposal from the Commission that, "all international commodity agreements will be signed simultaneously by the Community and the Member States which will be parties to such agreements. The negotiations will be conducted by a single delegation; as a general rule the Community's position will be expressed by the Commission representative." Bull. EC 3-1981, p. 55, point 2.2.17. The arrangement has given rise to difficulties in UNCTAD which have not been resolved as yet. Ehlermann, *supra* note 179, at 8.

198 Opinion 1/78, [1979] ECR 2871, 2917–18.

199 On this assumption, could the Commission seek to enforce the obligation against the other institutions in an action before the Court? What would be the European Parliament's authority over this item of the budget?

itative answer from the Supreme Court,[200] but beginning in 1796 Congress has consistently appropriated funds to meet treaty commitments, considering itself morally obligated.

In the commercial policy field, the Court appears to be more insistent than in other areas on enforcing Community pre-emption with respect to both "autonomous" and "conventional" acts.[201] Waelbroeck calls the Court's approach in that field "conceptualist-federalist," as compared with the more lenient, "pragmatic" approach to pre-emption now employed internally in the area of the common agricultural policy.[202]

(d) *General "constitutional" limitations.* In *Opinion 1/76*, where the question before the Court concerned the position of the Community in setting up an international organization by international agreement, the Court held the proposed agreement incompatible with the Treaty because the structure of the international organization it envisaged would "call in question the power of the institutions of the Community and, moreover, alter in a manner inconsistent with the Treaty the relationship between Member States within the context of the Community."[203] One is reminded of the warning by the Supreme Court in *Geofroy v. Riggs*[204] that a treaty purporting to "change the character of the government" would be held unconstitutional[205] although the Supreme Court thus far has had no occasion to hold a treaty unconstitutional on this or any other ground.

In a later opinion, arising under the Euratom Treaty, the Court again manifested its concern lest the adhesion to the proposed international convention on nuclear safety not impair the internal distribution of powers between the Community and its Members.[206] A more significant aspect of this opinion is the ruling that even though the Treaty expressly preserves the Member States' authority to regulate access to nuclear materials by national public safety and

[200] *See supra* text accompanying note 155.

[201] *See* Waelbroeck, *The Emergent Doctrine of Community Pre-Emption — Consent and Re-Delegation,* in COURTS AND FREE MARKETS, *supra* note 6, at 548, 553–54, and the case law cited therein.

[202] *Id.* at 551, 555 ff. *See also* Louis, *Quelques réflexions sur la répartition des compétences entre la Communauté européenne et ses états membres,* [1979] II REV. D'INTÉGRATION EUROPÉENNE/J. EUR. INTEGRATION 355.

[203] Opinion 1/76, (inland waterway vessels), [1977] ECR 741, 757.

[204] 133 U.S. 258 (1890). *See supra* text accompanying note 143.

[205] *See supra* text accompanying note 144. Perhaps the Court had in mind a different type of a change, *e.g.,* from a republican form of government to a monarchy?

[206] Ruling 1/78, [1978] ECR 2151. The Court made it clear, however, that the matter of the distribution of powers between the Community and the Member States was an internal Community question of no concern to the third parties, and need not be spelled out in the convention "particularly as it may change in the course of time." *Id.* at 2180. Note, however, that according to Ehlermann "third countries insist increasingly that the Community and its Member States explain and define the internal distribution of powers." *Supra* note 179, at 8.

health regulations, the Community is not thereby prevented from entering international commitments on the same subject.[207]

The two opinions just discussed illustrate the exercise by the Court of its "preventive" jurisdiction (EEC Treaty article 228(1)) that enables it to rule on the compatibility of an "envisaged" Community agreement with the Treaty before the agreement comes into force. However, the Court has extended its power of "constitutional review" to agreements already in force, even though the Treaty does not specifically sanction such extension. When asked to interpret the Community Association Agreement with Greece, the Court held that as soon as such an agreement enters into force its provisions become "an integral part of Community law" and that as an act of one of the Community institutions the agreement becomes subject to the Court's jurisdiction.[208]

It appears, therefore, that the "constitutionality" of an agreement (or perhaps more specifically of the Community act concluding the agreement) may be tested through the entire gamut of procedures available for contesting the validity of any Community act.[209] Thus a Community agreement, like a treaty concluded by the United States, may be held invalid internally while continuing in force as an international obligation, although thus far in neither system has a treaty actually in force been held "unconstitutional."[210] In reality, it is not unlikely that in the United States a treaty which passed the barrier of a vigilant, conservative Senate could be successfully challenged in the courts,

207 *Id.* at 2172–73.

208 Case 181/73, Haegeman v. Belgium, [1974] ECR 449, 460 [*Haegeman II*]. Louis and Brückner seem to suggest that the Court's ruling has made art. 228(2) superfluous but that the article "gives third states a complete security." 12 BRUSSELS COMMENTARY, *supra* note 89, at 62–63. In a similar vein, *see* Pescatore *Les Communautés en tant que personnes de droit international*, in LES NOUVELLES, DROIT DES COMMUNAUTÉS EUROPÉENNES 107, 119 (W. Ganshof van der Meersch ed., Brussels, Maison F. Larcier, 1969) [hereinafter cited as LES NOUVELLES]. What, in this context, would be the status of a "mixed agreement"? Would only the part within the Communtiy competence become "an integral part of Community law"? *See also infra* note 217.

209 EEC Treaty arts. 173, 175, 177, 184. 12 BRUSSELS COMMENTARY, *supra* note 89, at 184–86. Case 181/73, *Haegeman II*, [1974] ECR 449, involved art. 177 jurisdiction. *See also* Opinion 1/76, [1977] ECR 741, 760. para. 18. However, in *Opinion 1/75* the Court declared that

> the question whether the conclusion of a given agreement is within the power of the Community and whether, in a given case, such power has been exercised in conformity with the provisions of the Treaty is, in principle, a question which may be submitted to the Court of Justice, either directly, under Article 169 or Article 173 of the Treaty, or in accordance with the preliminary procedure.

[1975] ECR 1355, 1361. *See also supra* note 189. On the effects of an "annulment" of a Community agreement, *see* Barav, *supra* note 196, at 32, with further references.

210 The legal basis for the absolute "supremacy" in the Community legal order of the constitutive Treaty over its agreements with third states is apparently derived from the "preventive" control in arts. 228(1) & 238, and from the nature of the Community's treaty power as derived from, and limited by, the EEC Treaty. 12 BRUSSELS COMMENTARY, *supra* note 89, at 181–82.

and the same applies to a Community agreement approved by a consensus of the Member States in the Council.

(e) Extra-legal and political constraints. Owing primarily to outside pressures, treaty-making has been a growth area even during the current period of relative stagnation in other Community activities. However, after *ERTA*, some Member Governments have opposed certain "internal" legislation in the Council on the ground that its adoption may give rise to Community treaty power on the same subject matter. Moreover, there is evidence that, except for agreements falling squarely within the area of commercial policy, the Council has been reluctant to rely on Community powers as declared in the *ERTA* case and in *Opinion 1/76*, preferring instead to invoke the less controversial "necessary and proper" clause of article 235, either exclusively (as in the environmental protection agreements), or in conjunction with article 113 (as in the agreement of cooperation with Canada) or article 43 (as in the United Nations Relief and Works Agency Conventions).[211] Moreover, as to the form

[211] J. Bourgeois, a member of the EC Commission's legal staff dealing with foreign affairs, was able to cite only a single agreement "justified by an implicit but clear reference to *Opinion 1/76,*" *i.e.,* the European Convention for the protection of animals kept for farming purposes, based on arts. 43 (common agricultural policy) and 100 (harmonization of laws), EEC Council Dec. of 19 June 1978, OJ No. L 323, 17 Nov. 1978, p. 12. He suggests that the Community's numerous international agreements on fisheries conservation (*see also supra* notes 71, 195) may also be regarded as based on art. 43 in conformity with the *Opinion 1/76* doctrine, although the Council had previously adopted limited provisions that may be regarded as "common rules" in the *ERTA* sense. Bourgeois states:

> [The] Community has initiated early in 1980 an agreement on international passenger transport by road which ought to be concluded in the course of 1980 by a decision based on *Article 75* [Commission proposal in 1982, OJ No. C 31, 8 Feb. 1982, p.1]. Relying on Article 84(2) the Council set up information on the activities of third countries in the area of maritime transport (Decision of 19 September 1978, OJ No. L 258 of 21. 9. 78, p. 35). Articles 43 and 100 are the legal bases of the Council Decision of 18 July 1977 on the acceptance of Codex alimentarius standards for sugar.
>
> *Article 235* has been relied upon together with *Art. 113* for the EEC/Canada Agreement (OJ No. L 260 of 1976, p.1) and the additional protocol to the EEC/Portugal Agreement (OJ No. L 274 of 1978, p.8). The Council concluded the EEC/ASEAN Agreement on the same bases (OJ No. L 144 of 1980, p.1). The Commission proposes to conclude the Agreement with Brazil also on those bases (OJ No. C 169 of 9. 7. 80, p.3). Article 235 is the (sole) legal basis on which the Council relied to conclude agreements in the field of environmental protection: Bonn Convention of 1976 (OJ No. L 240 of 1977, p.35). Barcelona Convention of 1976 (OJ No. L 240 of 1977, p.1), Paris Convention of 1974 (OJ No. L 194 of 1975, p.5).

Division of Powers, *supra* note 71, at 109 n.4. *Article 235* has been relied upon together with *art. 43* for the conclusion of the Convention between the EEC and the United Nations Relief and Works Agency for Palestine Refugees (UNRWA), Concerning Aid to Refugees in the Countries of the Near–East. *See* Council Dec. 80/444/EEC of 21 Apr. 1980, OJ No. L 108, 26 Apr. 1980, p.5; Council Dec. 81/1071/

in which Community agreements are concluded, apart from the many agreements in the basic commercial policy field which the Community has concluded alone, the Council has clearly favored "mixed agreements" in which the Community is joined by the Member States as parties. Thus the practice confirms the acute sensitivity of the Member Governments when it comes to recognizing the foreign affairs powers of the Community.

iii) Effects of agreements concluded by the Community[212]

The lapidary text in article 228(2),[213] that agreements concluded by the Community are "***binding***" both on its ***institutions and on the Member States***, is the only clue the Treaty offers with respect to the effect of such agreements in international law, in Community law or Member State law. The silence is even more resounding if compared with the explicit statement in the United States Constitution that treaties are "supreme law of the land" and binding on the states.[214] It is said – but this appears to be the minority view – that the paragraph in question deals only with the effect of agreements in the Community legal system and that third states, party to agreements with the Community, acquire international legal rights only as against the Community and not also against the Member States.[215] This interpretation would be consistent with the American federal system because a third state, party to a treaty with the United States, in principle acquires treaty rights only against the United States since

EEC of 21 Dec. 1981, OJ No. L 392, 31 Dec. 1981, p.3; Council Dec. 82/879/EEC of 21 Dec. 1982, OJ No. L 371, 30 Dec. 1982, p.42; Council Dec. 83/518/EEC of 17 Oct. 1983, OJ No. L 293, 25 Oct. 1983, p.17.

See also the Convention on Conservation of Wild Animals and Natural Environment of Europe, approved by Council Decision of 3 Dec. 1981, OJ No. L 38, 10 Feb. 1982, p.1. The Convention is based on art. 235, although the decision preamble mentions the Community action program on the environment and Council Directive 79/409, concerning conservation of wild birds.

On earlier efforts to apply the *ERTA* doctrine, *see* C. FLAESCH–MOUGIN, *supra* note 165, 175–77.

212 On this topic *see especially* 12 BRUSSELS COMMENTARY, *supra* note 89, at 62–63, 181–97; H. KRÜCK, VÖLKERRECHTLICHE VERTRÄGE IM RECHT DER EUROPÄISCHEN GEMEINSCHAFTEN (Berlin/Heidelberg/New York, Springer, 1977); O. JACOT–GUILLARMOD, DROIT COMMUNAUTAIRE ET DROIT INTERNATIONAL PUBLIC (Geneva, Georg–Librairie de l'Université, 1979); Bleckmann, *Der gemischte Vertrag im Europarecht*, 11 EUR 301 (1976); Pescatore, *supra* note 208, at 107; Meessen, *The Application of Rules of Public International Law Within Community Law*, 13 C.M.L. REV. 485, 497 (1976); White, *Effects of International Treaties Within the Community Order*, 1 EUR. L. REV. 102 (1976).

213 *See supra* note 44. *Cf.* the preliminary draft art. 36 *bis* (with a commentary) of the International Law Commission, *Question of Treaties Concluded Between States and International Organizations or Between Two or More International Organizations*, [1978] II Y.B. INT'L L. COMM'N, Part Two, at 123.

214 U.S. CONST. art. VI, § 2. *See supra* text accompanying note 130.

215 H. KRÜCK, *supra* note 212, at 125.

the component states have no international personality. However, unlike the states in the American Federation, Member States have retained their international personality and for this, if for no other reason, the analogy is misleading, despite the fact that the Community has its own international personality. In effect, as reported by d'Orville, the majority of writers takes the view (supported by textual interpretation) that article 228(2) is not just an internal norm: on the contrary, Member States as well as the Community assume obligations toward a third state, party to an agreement with the Community.[216]

(a) Conflict between Community international agreements and acts of the Community or of the Member States. As we have seen, the Court of Justice has taken the view that an international agreement is *an act of one of the institutions* of the Community and as such is open to review in the regular manner before the Court of Justice. However, although the Court has upheld the superiority of the constitutive Treaty over Community agreements with third states, it does view such agreements as a special category of Community acts, partaking of the "higher" rank of international law, and, because of that, superior to both prior and subsequent ordinary Community acts, including Council regulations.[217] Whether or not this significant holding can be derived from positive Treaty law, it is a reasonable application of an evolving modern constitutional practice that

[216] M. D'Orville, *Vertragliche Handelspolitik*, in Die rechtlichen Grundlagen für die gemeinsame Zoll- und Handelspolitik der EWG 57–58 (Cologne, Heymann, 1973). For the authority supporting the minority and majority view, *see id.* at 57 nn.118 & 119 respectively. D'Orville argues along the following lines: Art. 228(2) does not name the obligee of the two obligors, the Community institutions and the Member States; but it is obvious that the obligee must be the same entity and this can be only the third state, party to the agreement with the Community. Community institutions are bound vis-à-vis that party in any case (*i.e.*, presumably even if there were no art. 228(2)). The only other possible alternative to this interpretation would be to view the paragraph as an exclusively internal norm but, considering its text, this is not persuasive. The paragraph strengthens greatly the position of the Community as a treaty partner and this consideration supports the proposition that the EEC founders had intended the above interpretation.

[217] Joined Cases 21 to 24/72, International Fruit Co. NV v. Produktschap voor Groenten en Fruit, [1972] ECR 1219 [*International Fruit*]; Case 9/73, Schlüter v. Hauptzollamt Lörrach, [1973] ECR 1135. *See also* Case 40/72, Schröder v. Federal Republic of Germany, [1973] ECR 125; Case 112/80, Firma Anton Dürbeck v. Hauptzollamt Frankfurt am Main-Flughafen, [1981] ECR 1095; Case 181/80, *Arbelaiz-Emazabel*, [1981] ECR 2961; Joined Cases 180 & 266/80, Crujeiras Tome v. Procureur de la République, and Procureur de la République v. Yurrita, [1981] ECR 2997. One commentator believes that a "mixed agreement" concluded jointly by the Community and the Member States on their behalf, also binds both the Community institutions and the Members in its entirety, unless it provides that certain provisions bind specific parties only. Moreover, in this view, a mixed agreement has the same rank of superiority over national law as does an agreement concluded by the Community alone. Bleckmann, *supra* note 212, at 303. *But see* Lachmann, *EF's Forhold Til Tredjelande*, in Karnovs EF Samling 1028 n.20 (O. Due, O. Lando & W. von Eyben eds., 2nd ed., Copenhagen, Karnovs Forlag, 1979).

recognizes the necessity of granting international commitments superior recognition in domestic law, in the interest of a more stable world order.[218] Regrettably, the United States Supreme Court, without a compelling constitutional reason, has established the contrary rule that in the internal legal order a treaty prevails only over a prior, but not over a subsequent, act of Congress.[219] In any event, in the Community, any act of the institutions that violates a Community agreement with a third state may be brought directly or indirectly before the Court and annulled or declared invalid.[220]

Since international agreements concluded by the Community form an integral part of Community law as soon as they come into force, any violation of such an agreement by *a Member State* constitutes a violation of Community law and may be branded as such in a declaratory judgment of the Court of Justice, in an action instituted in accordance with the normal rules for review by the Commission or another Member State.[221] The Member State violation may also in certain circumstances be brought indirectly before the Court of Justice by means of the preliminary ruling procedure initiated by a private party before a Member State tribunal.[222] In the United States there is some authority in support of the Federal Government's judicial remedy against a state that violates a treaty,[223] but it is very sparse. Generally, a private party must raise the issue in the course of private litigation, and since that may not happen, the foreign state,

218 Such a rule is recognized in the Netherlands, Luxembourg, Belgium, France, and Greece. In the Netherlands, the courts are expressly barred from reviewing treaties for constitutionality. Pescatore believes that since in the Community legal order the Court affirmed the supremacy of Community law over Member State law (including Member States' Constitutions) "it would be inconceivable" not to apply the same rule to the relationship between Community law and international law. Cited in 12 BRUSSELS COMMENTARY, *supra* note 89, at 182.

219 *See supra* text accompanying note 156. In contrast with the Continental system, in the U.S. treaty–making and law–making are not effectively in the same hands. This fact may perhaps be advanced in explanation of the Supreme Court's posture. *See infra* note 305.

220 EEC Treaty arts. 169, 173, 175, 177, 184. The Commission, the Council, or a Member State, and if they can show "direct and individual concern," "any natural or legal person" (regardless of their nationality) may institute a direct action before the Court, but a third state party to the agreement cannot, unless it could qualify as a legal person with a "direct and individual concern." An act of the institutions that violates a Community agreement may also be referred to the Court by a Member State tribunal in accordance with art. 177. *See infra* text accompanying notes 225–32. *And see* Case 40/72, Schröder v. F.R. Germany, [1973] ECR 125.

221 EEC Treaty arts. 169, 170, 171. Again, the third state would most likely not itself have standing.

222 EEC Treaty art. 177. *See, e.g.*, Case 181/73, *Haegeman II*, [1974] ECR 449. As to the circumstances in which such challenges can be raised in Member State courts, *see infra* notes 225–31 and accompanying text.

223 L. HENKIN, *supra* note 7, at 167.

party to the treaty, may find itself without a remedy in the American domestic legal order.[224]

Perhaps the most effective remedy against violations of Community agreements was fashioned in the landmark *International Fruit* case,[225] where the Court extended the concept of the "direct applicability" (or self-execution) of provisions of the constituent Treaty to include Community agreements with third states. At the same time, the Court reserved to itself the final authority to determine whether such an agreement is "directly applicable," and can produce "direct effects," that is whether an individual can derive directly from the agreement a right which Member State courts must enforce, without any implementing action by either the Community institutions or Member States.[226] It is of obvious importance for the uniform application of a Community agreement throughout Community territory (and it accords with the federal pattern) that the Court of Justice's determination bind Member State courts regardless of their national constitutional practices governing the effects of treaties in their internal legal order. To decide whether an agreement is directly applicable and has direct effects, the Court examines "the spirit, general scheme and text" of the agreement in question. This is the same purpose-oriented interpretive formula that the Court employs in deciding which parts of the constitutive Treaty itself are "directly applicable." This test, on its face at any rate, is more liberal than the method generally followed by American courts in deciding the "federal question" whether a treaty accords rights to an individual for which he or she has a direct judicial remedy.[227] Yet in *International Fruit*, the Court of Justice held several GATT articles not to be directly applicable, contrary to the view adopted by American lower courts and doctrine.[228]

[224] *See* the position of the Department of State in its note to the Japanese Government in E. Stein, P. Hay & M. Waelbroeck, *supra* note 3, at 1071. The challenge by a private party assumes of course that the treaty grants private rights to individuals.

[225] Joined Cases 21 to 24/72, [1972] ECR 1219. *See also, e.g.* Case 181/73, *Haegeman II*, [1974] ECR 449 (Association with Greece); Case 87/75, Bresciani v. Amministrazione Italiana, [1976] ECR 129 (Yaoundé Convention); Case 65/77, Razanatsimba, [1977] ECR 2229 (Lomé Convention); Case 52/77, Cayrol v. Rivoira, [1977] ECR 2261 (commercial agreement with Spain).

[226] The individual will sue in the appropriate Member State court that will be expected to refer this "preliminary question" to the Court of Justice pursuant to art. 177.

[227] *See supra* text accompanying note 152.

[228] I agree with Ganshof van der Meersch that the teleological test employed by the Court is *mutatis mutandis* compatible with the rules on treaty interpretation in the Vienna Convention on the Law of Treaties of 1969. Cited in O. Jacot-Guillarmod, *supra* notes 212, at 116. It should be kept in mind, however, that the non-availability of legislative history materials of the Community Treaties and the special nature of integration dynamics necessarily influence the interpretation. In 1972 in *International Fruit* the ECJ found that GATT provisions cannot be considered directly applicable and to have direct effects because of the indeterminacy of the obligations, flexibility and the many derogations, and it has not since departed from that view (Case 266/81, Società Italiana per l'Oleodotto Transalpino (SIOT) v. Ministero delle Finanze dello

Should the Court interpret Community agreements in the same liberal spirit as it has the provisions of the constitutive Treaty itself,[229] individual recourse to the judiciary would prove the most effective of the varied means available for enforcing Community agreements in the Community legal order.[230] It has been suggested, however, that such liberal enforcement of Community agreements may be against Community interests unless a reciprocal treatment in the courts of the Community's partners, parties to such agreements, is assured. In fact, the judgment in the *Polydor* case, rendered in 1982, is a clear signal that the Court will interpret Community agreements with third countries less liberally than it has done with regard to similar, if not identical, provisions of the EEC Treaty.[231]

Stato, [1983] ECR 731; Joined Cases 267–269/81, Amministrazione delle Finanze dello Stato v. Società Petrolifera Italiana SpA & Others, [1983] ECR 801; Joined Cases 290 & 291/81, Compagnia Singer SpA v. Amministrazione delle Finanze dello Stato, [1983] ECR 847). This is also the view taken by German courts but it is contrary to the Italian and United States doctrine. *See* Joined Cases 21 to 24/72, [1972] 1219, 1237–38 (opinion of Mayras, A.G.). For the American cases and view, *see* Jackson, *The GATT in United States Domestic Law,* 66 MICH. L. REV. 249 (1967).

229 *See* cases cited *supra* note 225. The holding on GATT has been criticized. *See* Pescatore, *supra* note 181, at 637 n.42.

230 Individual action in national courts with a reference to the ECJ under art. 177 has been by far the most frequently invoked and the most effective means of enforcing the Treaty and the Community legislation against violations by Member States. In one case, involving the Multifiber Agreement concluded by the Community, this enforcement process proved ineffective because the French *Conseil d'Etat* improperly refused to refer the question of direct applicability to the Court of Justice and itself ruled that the agreement was not directly applicable. C.E. (F), Judgment of 12 Oct. 1979, Syndicat des importateurs de vêtements et de produits artisanaux, [1979] Rec. Leb. 373; 15 R.T.D.E. 730 (1979).

231 *See* Case 270/80, Polydor Ltd. and RSO Records Inc. v. Harlequin Record Shops Ltd. and Simons Records Ltd., [1982] ECR 329. The Free Trade Association Agreement (FTAA) with Portugal contains a prohibition of measures equivalent to quantitative restrictions in terms essentially identical with EEC Treaty arts. 30 and 36. The same prohibitions appear in the other six FTAA's with the other EFTA countries, and practically in the same terms in many other agreements. In *Polydor,* an English owner of a copyright protected by English law sought to prevent importations from Portugal into England by a third party of gramaphone records lawfully manufactured and marketed in Portugal by his licensee. The ECJ has consistently held that similar attempts to prevent importation *from one Member State to another* constitute measures equivalent to quantitative restrictions (a partitioning of the "single market") prohibited by art. 30 in conjunction with art. 36. In *Polydor* it held that despite the identity of the language, the restriction on imports from Portugal was not prohibited by the FTAA because its provisions do

> not have the same purpose as the EEC Treaty inasmuch as the latter ... seeks to create a single market reproducing as closely as possible the conditions of a domestic market.... In the present case such a distinction is all the more necessary inasmuch as the instruments which the Community has at its disposal in order to achieve the uniform application of Community law and the progressive abolition of legislative disparities within the common market have no equivalent in the context of the relations between the Community and Portugal.

Provisions in the Community agreements that are not "directly applicable" may be implemented either by Community legislation or by the Member States

Id. at 349. Contrary to the approach in *International Fruit*, the Court refused to rule on whether the relevant provisions of the FTAA with Portugal were "directly applicable," even though the English court specifically put this question to it and the issue was extensively argued by the parties and by the Commission. The narrowly confined holding leaves open the possibility that other more glaring ("core") restrictions may nevertheless fall within the prohibition of the FTAA's (and may be held "directly applicable"), although the unfortunate reference to the difference in the "instruments," quoted above, if taken literally, would preclude such a nuanced application which was also urged by the Commission. In Case 104/81, Hauptzollamt Mainz v. C.A. Kupferberg, [1982] ECR 3641, the Court interpreted a "core" provision in the FTAA with Portugal (prohibition of fiscal discrimination) as being directly applicable and conferring rights on individuals. However, even though directly effective, the FTAA provision would not be given the same broad interpretation as the corresponding EEC article 95 prohibiting fiscal discrimination within the Community. *See similarly* Case 17/81, Pabst & Richarz KG v. Hauptzollamt Oldenburg, [1982] ECR 1331; Pescatore, *The Doctrine of "Direct Effect": An Infant Disease of Community Law*, 8 Eur. L. Rev. 155, 171–74 (1983). Bebr, *Agreements Concluded by the Community and Their Possible Direct Effect: From* International Fruit Company *to* Kupferberg, 20 C.M.L. Rev. 35 (1983).

On the discussion prior to *Polydor, see* March Hunnings, *Enforceability of the EEC-EFTA Free Trade Agreements*, 2 Eur. L. Rev. 163 (1977); Waelbroeck, *Enforceability of the EEC-EFTA Free Trade Agreements: A. Reply*, 3 Eur. L. Rev. 27 (1978); March Hunnings, *Enforceability of the EEC-EFTA Free Trade Agreements – A Rejoinder, id.* at 278; Mestmäcker, *Die Gewährleistung gerechter Wettbewerbsbedingungen in den Freihandelsabkommen der EG*, in Festschrift für Konrad Zweigert 681 (H. Bernstein, U. Drobnig & H. Kötz eds., Tübingen, Mohr (Siebeck), 1981).

In a different context, involving a multilateral treaty, a lower U.S. court stated:

> The Convention on the High Sea is a multilateral treaty which has been ratified by over fifty nations, some of which do not recognize treaties as self-executing.... It is difficult therefore to ascribe to the language of the treaty any common intent that the treaty should of its own force operate as the domestic law of the ratifying nations. This is not to say that by entering into such a multilatral treaty the United States cannot without legislation execute provisions of it, but one would expect that in these circumstances the United States would make that intention clear. *The lack of mutuality between the United States and countries that do not recognize treaties as self-executing would seem to call for as much.* Here there was no such manifestation.

United States v. Postal, 589 F.2d 862 (5th Cir. 1979) (emphasis added).

For an appropriately critical comment, *see* Riesenfeld, *The Doctrine of Self-Executing Treaties and* U.S. v. Postal: *Win at Any Price?*, 74 AJIL 892 (1980).

In *Polydor*, the Commission's opposition to direct applicability of the FTAA provisions was based, *inter alia*, on concern for "the proper division of powers within the Community legal system between the legislature and the executive on the one hand and the judiciary on the other." [1982] ECR 329, 343. The separation-of-powers consideration is clearly an element to be taken into account by the American court when it ponders whether a treaty is self-executing. *See supra* text accompanying note 148–54.

under Community direction. Bourgeois believes that Member States are obligated to enact the necessary implementing measures by virtue of article 228(2).[232]

(b) *Community succession to multilateral treaty obligations of the Member States.* Another significant conclusion in *International Fruit*, illustrating the integration dynamics, bears upon the problem of "succession" by the Community to the rights and obligations of a multilateral treaty to which the Member States are party, even if the Community itself does not become a party. The Court stated:

> [I]n so far as under the EEC Treaty the Community has assumed the powers previously exercised by Member States in the area governed by the General Agreement [on Tariffs and Trade] the provisions of that agreement have the effect of binding the Community.[233]

To that extent the Community has "replaced the Members."[234]

As a general proposition, Member States are required by Treaty article 234 to bring their international treaty commitments antedating the Community in line with their obligations under the constitutive Treaty through whatever means are available in international intercourse.

4. Power to Protect Citizens Abroad and to Advance International Claims – International Responsibility

a) In the United States

Diplomatic protection and international responsibility are within the exclusive domain of the Federal Government in the United States. The Federal Government alone bears the responsibility for any action by federal or state authorities that violates an international law right of another state or of an individual under modern human rights law.[235]

The Department of State deals with other Governments in these matters. If negotiations do not produce a settlement of a claim, the United States may have recourse to political dispute settlement procedures or international adjudication and ultimately to means of self-help, such as retorsion or retaliation.

232 Bourgeois, *Some Comments on the Practice*, in DIVISION OF POWERS, *supra* note 71, at 97, 107.

233 [1972] ECR 1219, 1227.

234 Case 38/75, Douaneagent der NV Nederlandse Spoorwegen v. Inspecteur der invoerrechten en accijnzen, [1975] ECR 1439, 1450. This case reached the same conclusion with respect to Community succession to the Brussels Nomenclature Convention of 1950. The question of "succession" has also been raised in relation to the European Convention on Human Rights, to which the ECJ has referred as one source for determining the common standards of fundamental human rights that the Community institutions must observe. *See* most recently, Case 44/79, *Hauer*, [1979] ECR 3727, 3745.

235 *See* FOREIGN RELATIONS LAW OF THE UNITED STATES, RESTATEMENT (SECOND) OF THE LAW §§ 164 ff (St. Paul, Minn., ALI Pubs., 1965).

If a settlement is reached, it is incorporated in an agreement concluded either by the President alone in the form of an executive agreement, or by the President with the Senate in the form of a treaty. The settlement would provide for payment of an individual claim or more generally for lump-sum payment for a series of related claims, or for international arbitration. The Congress may prescribe conditions for the settlement, and it has established the International Claims Commission, a federal agency charged with distributing to American claimants funds received from lump-sum settlements. In the absence of Congressional opposition, the courts have consistently uphelp broad Presidential powers to deal with international claims, even where a settlement was challenged on the ground that it was inadequate and not agreed to by the individual claimant and unless compensated by the United States, would deprive the claimant of property without due process of law.[236]

Aliens in the United States depend for their protection primarily on the judiciary. Since the Bill of Rights in principle protects aliens equally with citizens, it generally statisfies the standard required by the law on international responsibility for treatment of aliens.[237]

b) In the Community

There is no "hard law," but there is a great deal of academic discourse about the position of the Community in this field – a question that must be determined by interpretation of the constituent Treaty and customary international law, taking into acount the *sui generis* character of the Community.[238] Several reasons support the position that the Community has the power to press international claims and may be held internationally responsible, not unlike the United States Government. First, despite the pervasive role of the Member States in the Community's life, its institutions have a sufficient degree of autonomy in the areas of its competence, including foreign affairs. Second, the Community is capable of providing relief through its law-making and judicial system, and it has its own financial resources, budgetary procedures and limited borrowing powers to offer material reparation. Third, its international personality has been widely recognized by other states and international organizations. Fourth, particularly because of its control of the import and export regimes, the Community is capable of imposing economic measures of retorsion or retaliation where its rights or interests are disregarded.[239] Finally, by virtue of Com-

[236] *See, e.g.*, United States v. Pink, 315 U.S. 203 (1942); Dames & Moore v. Regan, 453 U.S. 654 (1981).

[237] *See generally* L. HENKIN, *supra* note 7, at 251–70.

[238] *See* authorities cited in 12 BRUSSELS COMMENTARY, *supra* note 89, at 15–19. *But see* Bothe, *Die Stellung der Europäischen Gemeinschaft im Völkerrecht*, 37 ZAÖRV 122 (1977) and authorities cited therein. On the special problems arising from "mixed agreements," *see* Ehlermann, *supra* note 179, at 20.

[239] *See, e.g.*, retaliatory action by the Community against the U.S., Council Decision of 4–5 June 1962, [1962] JO No. 1518, p.62, *reproduced in* E. STEIN & P. HAY, LAW AND INSTITUTIONS IN THE ATLANTIC AREA 384–85 (Indianapolis, Bobbs-Merril, 1967). On the EC power to impose sanctions *see infra* notes 303–04 and accompanying text.

munity law, Community institutions (as well as the Member States in Community matters) are bound to respect international obligations even more firmly than is the Federal Government in the United States.[240]

Accordingly, if a third state violates an agreement it has concluded with the Community, the Community is in a position to demand relief and reparation, both in its own interest and on behalf of a Community citizen concerned. Similarly, in a non-contractual setting, the Community may bring a claim against a third state responsible under customary international law for sub-standard treatment of a Community official, agent or enterprise.[241]

Conversely, the Community may be held internationally responsible by a third state if its institutions or a Member State act against a commitment undertaken by the Community in an international agreement or if the Community institutions treat a third-state national below the international law standard. In the latter case the individual alien is required to exhaust "domestic remedies" under Community law before an international claim may be pressed against the Community. It would presumably be the Commission, acting under a Council mandate, that would conduct the necessary negotiations on behalf of the Community.

If an agreement with a third state fails to provide a dispute settlement procedure, the Community and the third state may resort to the generally available diplomatic and judicial settlement procedures.[242] However, since only states have access to the International Court of Justice or the Permanent Court of Arbitration, a special arbitration tribunal would have to be agreed upon by the parties for adjudication of the dispute. In practice, the burden of satisfying a claim of the third state may ultimately fall upon the Member States. Moreover, Member States could probably be held directly responsible if Community institutions are unable to provide due satisfaction or, of course, if the Community should cease to exist.[243]

240 *See supra* text accompanying note 217.

241 Bleckmann, *The Personal Jurisdiction of the European Community,* 17 C.M.L. REV. 467 (1980). Where the Community advances a claim on behalf of an official or an enterprise, it would no doubt coordinate its action with the Member State of the claimant's nationality. The Community's power to bring an international claim is frequently explained or buttressed by a reference to the opinion of the International Court of Justice on the Reparation for Injuries Suffered in the Service of the United Nations, 1949 I.C.J. REP. 174.

242 Hilf, *Europäische Gemeinschaften und internationale Streitbeilegung,* in VÖLKERRECHT ALS RECHTSORDNUNG, INTERNATIONALE GERICHTSBARKEIT, MENSCHENRECHTE 387 (R. Bernhardt, W.K. Geck, G. Jaenicke, H. Steinberger eds., Berlin/Heidelberg/New York, Springer, 1983).

243 *See also supra* text accompanying note 215–16. Particular problems in this context may arise from "mixed agreements," discussed *supra,* text accompanying notes 177–80.

B. Arrangements for the Coordination of Non-Attributed Powers: "Political" Foreign Policy – European Political Cooperation (EPC) and Its Interaction with the Community

As we have seen, whereas in the United States the totality of foreign affairs powers has been delegated to the Federal Government, in Europe it is only in limited fields that powers have been attributed to the Community. Thus, while the Community has far-reaching powers in the area of external economic relations, areas such as defense and "political" foreign policy remain within the competence of the Member States. The way in which the non-attributed powers are exercised, however, has important implications for the common venture, and it is therefore in the interest of both the Community as a whole and of each of the Member States to coordinate policies even outside the Community framework. A major attempt to meet this need in the "political" foreign policy field has resulted in the development of a new mechanism, known as European Political Cooperation.[244]

1. The EPC: Its Origins, Structure and Scope

The European Political Cooperation (EPC) mechanism began to evolve in 1969. It is as elusive in its mode of operation as in its actual impact on European foreign policies and it must be understood in the light of its antecedents.

a) Origins and Foundation of the EPC

i) The antecedents of the EPC

After his return to the Presidency in 1958, General de Gaulle, no longer hopeful of a membership in the "nuclear power club," concluded that France could recapture its world power status within more intimate forms of cooperation among European sovereign states. But he remained emphatically opposed to

[244] In addition to the works cited *infra* notes 245–306, *see generally* P. DE SCHOUTHEETE, LA COOPÉRATION POLITIQUE EUROPÉENNE (with bibliography at 227–31) (Paris/Brussels, Fernand Nathan/Ed. Labor, 1980); J. MONNET, *supra* note 24; THE UNITED STATES AND WESTERN EUROPE – POLITICAL, ECONOMIC AND STRATEGIC PERSPECTIVES (W.F. Hanrieder ed., Cambridge, Winthrop Publishers, Inc., 1974) (particularly Hoffmann, *Toward a Common European Foreign Policy?*, at 79); W. Wessels, The European Political Cooperation – Model or Nuisance for a New Institutional Equilibrium (mimeo, prepared for "Symposium on: The Community Institutions at the Beginning of the 1980's – In Search of a New Balance," Semaine de Bruges, 1980, College of Europe, Bruges, Belgium, 1980); DIE EUROPÄISCHE POLITISCHE ZUSAMMENARBEIT – LEISTUNGSVERMÖGEN UND STRUKTUR DER EPZ (R. Rummel & W. Wessels eds., Bonn, Europa Union, 1978); AUF DEM WEG ZUR EUROPÄISCHEN UNION – DISKUSSIONSBEITRÄGE ZUM TINDEMANS-BERICHT (H. Schneider & W. Wessels eds., Bonn, Europa Union, 1977); Dolan & Caporaso, *The External Relations of the European Community,* 440 ANNALS AM. ACAD. POL. & SOC. SCI. 135 (1978); von der Gablentz, *Luxembourg Revisited or the Importance of European Political Cooperation,* 16 C.M.L. REV. 685 (1979).

the pattern of integration: "supranationality" was an illusion which would only solidify the division of Europe and strengthen its dependence on the United States. It was in this context that the French Government launched its proposals for a new consultative framework outside the Community institutions.[245]

The major French proposal, the "Fouchet plan" of 1961, called for a "Union of *States*" (in contrast with the "union among the *peoples*" in the EEC Treaty Preamble) which would cover common foreign and defense policies, and beyond that, extend cooperation to science, culture, and human rights. Under the plan, the Heads of Government and Foreign Ministers of the Six would meet regularly in a "Council," and a "European Political Commission" of senior national diplomats, with its seat in Paris (rather than Brussels), would prepare the Council's work.

The Dutch and the Belgians perceived the proposal as a time bomb aimed at NATO and at the foundations of the Community; and they interpreted de Gaulle's opposition to British membership in the Community as further evidence of a design to establish a Franco-German "directorate" without the institutional protection for the smaller members that is offered in the Community. In December 1961, the European Parliament prepared a counterproposal designed to mitigate what were considered the pernicious aspects of the Fouchet Plan.[246] The acrimonious negotiations ended in a deadlock. During the ensuing period of dissension, France embarked on a boycott of the still fragile Community institutions and withdrew from the NATO military structures.[247]

ii) The Foundation of the EPC

The year 1969 marks a turning point and the "birth year" of the EPC. That year the recently installed Pompidou Government lifted the bar on British membership in the Community. In an atmosphere of a revived "European euphoria" a summit meeting of the Six at the Hague directed the Foreign Ministers to study the best way of achieving "political unification, within the context of enlargement," in order to make Europe capable of assuming its world-wide responsibilities. At the same time, the Heads of Government called for a series of concrete measures to advance the Community toward an economic and monetary union.[248]

245 Wood, *Foreign Policy and Defense in the European Community*, 18 VA. J. INT'L L. 389, 399 ff (1978); Stein & Carreau, *Law and Peaceful Change in a Subsystem: "With drawal" of France from the North Atlantic Treaty Organization*, 62 AJIL 577 (1968).

246 For the text of the Fouchet Plan and the Recommendations of the European Parliament, *see* Council of Europe, Consultative Assembly, Political Committee, Doc. No. AS/Pol (13) 69 and AS/Pol (13) 77.

247 P. DE SCHOUTHEETE, *supra* note 244, at 18–26; and Wood, *supra* note 245, at 405.

248 EUROPEAN POLITICAL COOPERATION (EPC) 23–24 (3rd ed., Press and Information Office of the Federal Government, Public Document, Bonn, 1978) [hereinafter cited as EPC Docs.].

The Ministers responded a year later by approving, in Luxembourg, the "Davignon Report"[249] which serves as a foundation for the EPC. The report reverts to the method of governmental cooperation in foreign policy and may be read as implicitly rejecting the idea that a "political Community" could emerge through the integration process.[250] In the post-Gaullist climate the concept of "cooperation," rejected less than a decade earlier, received unanimous acceptance – not as a substitute for the integration process[251] but as a complementary, parallel, but separate process in the foreign affairs area. The two processes were to be transformed "before the end of the present decade ... into a European Union" that would encompass "the whole complex of relations [between the Member States]."[252] In contrast with this undefined ultimate goal, the immediate modest objectives of the cooperation were stated to be, better mutual understanding by the Governments of the "great international problems" through exchanges of information and consultation; harmonization of views; coordination of positions; and, "where it appears possible and desirable, common actions."[253]

There is no normative instrument – only communiqués and "reports" reflecting political undertakings by the Heads of State or Government – no legal obligation of any sort. However, the engagement to consult was extended somewhat in 1973 to include seeking "common policies on practical problems," and on these questions "each State undertakes as a general rule not to take up final positions without prior consultation with its partners."[254] The consultation practice was "codified" and the commitment to consult was reaffirmed in somewhat greater detail in 1981.[255]

[249] BULL. EC 11–1970, at p.9. (The Davignon Report was adopted by the Foreign Ministers of the Six as the *Luxembourg Report of 27 Oct. 1970. See* EPC DOCS., *supra* note 248, at 26.)

[250] H. da Fonseca-Wollheim, Dix ans de Coopération politique européenne 1 (mimeo, EC Commission, 1981). (Also translated into German: *Zehn Jahre Europäische Politische Zusammenarbeit,* 1981 INTEGRATION 47 (No.2, Institut für Europäische Politik, Bonn) [hereinafter *EPZ*]; and into English: Ten Years of European Political Cooperation (mimeo, EC Commission, 1981). The English text became available only after the completion of the present study.)

[251] Some feel that the EPC offers in fact a competing alternative method preferable to the "mistaken" Community pattern. However, the *Hague Communiqué* reaffirmed the support for the Community as a nucleus of European unity. EPC DOCS., *supra* note 248, at 22.

[252] Paris Summit, 1972. *Id.* at 38.

[253] *Luxembourg Report, 1970. Id.* at 29.

[254] *Copenhagen Report, 1973. Id.* at 58–59.

[255] Part I of the *Report on European Political Cooperation* approved by the Foreign Ministers in London on 13 Oct. 1981. The Report provides more specific procedural guidelines for the cooperation process. *Report on European Political Cooperation,* EUROPE, DOCS. No. 1174, 17 Oct. 1981; BULL. EC, SUPP. 3/81, at pp. 14–17 [hereinafter cited as *London Report, 1981]. See also infra* note 267.

b) The Organizational Structure of the EPC

Unlike an international organization, the EPC does not have any institutions of its own since it is entirely in the hands of national officials acting for their respective Governments. This – it is said – is appropriate and necessary in a field that demands the highest degree of mutual trust and respect for the confidentiality of "state secrets."[256] At French insistence, the EPC structures were to be hermetically separated from Community institutions in order to avoid contamination with the insidious Brussels atmosphere of "supranationalism" and "atlanticism."[257] The Community staff also inclined initially toward a separation because it eyed the EPC with a jaundiced eye as still another French device directed against Community power but, as we shall see, in practice this separation has proved difficult to maintain.

i) The high-level, policy-making fora

At the head of the actual EPC mechanism is the "*European Council*," an institutionalized summit of the ten Heads of State or Government accompanied by Foreign Ministers that was to convene initially at least three times a year.[258] As a "common roof," this Council is expected to coordinate the work of the EPC and the Communities.

The principal forum is the formal *Conference of the Foreign Affairs Ministers* meeting on EPC matters. Originally scheduled to take place at least once each six months in the capital of the Council President-in-Office, the meetings have in fact been much more frequent.

In 1973, the French Foreign Minister, M. Jobert, pressed the separateness from the Community to a point of forcing the Ministers to meet in EPC in Copenhagen in the morning, and to assemble the same afternoon in Brussels as a Community Council to deal with Community business. With the change in personnel and atmosphere, however, the EPC ministerial meetings now often take place back to back with the Community Council in Brussels or Luxembourg.

In 1974, the pretended separation was diluted somewhat further at the high level by still another common forum, the "*informal*" *meetings of Foreign Affairs Ministers* to discuss both EPC and EC affairs ("meetings *à la Gymnich*").

256 H. Kramer & R. Rummel, Gemeinschaftsbildung Westeuropas in der Aussenpolitik, Zur Tragfähigkeit der Europäischen Politischen Zusammenarbeit (EPZ) 20 (Baden–Baden, Nomos, 1978).

257 Wallace & Allen, *Political Cooperation: Procedure as a Substitute for Policy,* in Policy–Making in the European Communities 227, 230 (H. Wallace, W. Wallace & C. Webb eds., London, John Wiley & Sons, 1977).

258 Paris Summit, 1974. EPC Docs., *supra* note 248, at 90. *See generally* on the machinery, *Luxembourg Report, 1970,* and *Copenhagen Report, 1973. Id.* at 26 ff, 51 ff.

ii) Advisory bodies, back-up services and mechanisms for the exchange of information

The heads of the political departments in the Ministries of Foreign Affairs meet once a month as a *Political Committee* to prepare ministerial meetings and steer the groups of experts, and more often during the sessions of the U.N. General Assembly and of the Councils. The Committee's function is comparable to the role of the Brussels Committee of Permanent Representatives which prepares the work for the Community Council.

Within each Ministry of Foreign Affairs, a "*European correspondent*" coordinates the EPC work under the supervision of the Political Director. These diplomats constitute a "*group of European correspondents*"[259] which takes care of the procedural and organizational matters and prepares papers for the higher-level meetings.

Also under the direction of the Political Committee are the varied "*groups of experts,*" drawn from Foreign Affairs Ministries and organized according to regions (Africa, Asia, Mediterranean, Middle East, Latin America);[260] international fora (U.N., Conference on Security and Cooperation in Europe (CSCE)); subject matter (U.N.-disarmament); or function (chiefs of protocol, chiefs of communications).[261] Practical considerations forced the creation of the "Group for Coordination of the Arab-European Dialogue," common to the Community and EPC.

Another quasi-institutional element consists of the organized *cooperation of the Ambassadors* of the Member States posted in third states and at the seats of international organizations. They consult daily if necessary, as in time of a crisis (*e.g.* in Teheran or at the U.N.). Occasionally, the Political Committee asks the Ambassadors for a common report on a specific subject but such reports are said to reflect the lowest common denominator.[262] The Ambassador of the Member State holding the Presidency of the Council acts as a spokesman in any demarche or outside contacts. When a Minister receives an important third country visitor or himself returns from a visit to a third country, he provides a briefing, which has now become institutionalized, for the resident Ambassadors of the other members.[263]

A special coded *telex system* ("COREU," "*correspondence européenne*") facilitates continuing contacts, with some 5000 messages exchanged annually.

[259] The name recalls the American "Committees of Correspondence" that organized the American Revolution.

[260] Only North America and the EFTA states are not covered.

[261] There were 12 such groups when this study was written. The "Group of High Officials of Ministries of Justice" deals with judicial cooperation under EPC.

[262] H. da Fonseca-Wollheim, Dix ans de CPE, *supra* note 250, at 5.

[263] This adds a new function for Ambassadors sheared of their traditional importance because of the innumerable direct contacts among the Ministers.

iii) Administration of the EPC

Since there is no permanent secretariat, the *Presidency*, that is the Foreign Minister of the country holding the office of the President in the Community Council of Ministers, with whatever special staff of his own he may have available, is responsible for preparing all the meetings, drafting most of the declarations, reports and conclusions, even responses to questions to be answered in the European Parliament during his term of office. With the increasing business, the burden of the Presidency has become extremely heavy particularly for the smaller Members. During the busy periods the Presidency must organize a multitude of consultation meetings and act as spokesman in a variety of fora.[264] Building upon evolving custom, the Foreign Ministers agreed in 1981 that "the Presidency will be assisted by a small team of officials seconded from preceding and succeeding Presidencies" and assigned to the staff of their Embassies in the Presidency capital; as a further means to alleviate his burden the President may delegate certain tasks to his successor or predecessor.[265]

c) The Scope of the EPC

i) The general scope

In principle, EPC embraces foreign policies of Member States with respect to third states. By this definition, foreign policy problems *between* the Members, such as the Northern Ireland question (or earlier, the status of Algeria), are excluded.[266] More recently, voices have been heard in and outside the European Parliament in support of bringing the Irish question within the EPC, particularly in the context of the violations of basic rights.[267] Also excluded are the economic and monetary aspects of foreign affairs that are within the jurisdiction of the Community – a jurisdiction that cannot be impaired by EPC. Finally, entire geographic regions and certain important aspects of foreign affairs have eluded the EPC process in practice.

ii) Particular exclusions from the EPC scope

(a) *Private and reserved domains.* In deference to certain Members' special interests, particular areas, namely East Berlin, the Maghreb and (until the Chad affair) "francophone" Africa, have been viewed politically as "private

264 *E.g.*, in the seven U.N. General Assembly Committees.

265 *London Report, 1981, supra* note 255, at para. 10. *See also* H. da Fonseca-Wollheim, Dix ans de CPE, *supra* note 250, at 6.

266 Etienne, *Community Integration: The External Environment*, 18 J.C.M. Stud. 289, 290 (1980). It has been suggested that one reason for such exclusion was to avoid adverse repercussions on inter-Member relations.

267 *See European Parliament*, No. 3147 (NS) Europe, 27 May 1981, at 4; Written Question No. 1042/80 by Mr. Ansart to the EPC Foreign Ministers meeting, OJ No. C 60, 19 Mar. 1981, p.1. In their 1981 Report, the Foreign Ministers agreed "to maintain the flexible and pragmatic approach which has made it possible to discuss in Political Cooperation certain important foreign policy questions bearing on the political aspects of security." *London Report, 1981, supra* note 255, at Part I.

domains." Similarly, France and the United Kingdom generally are not prepared to consult on their vote in the U.N. Security Council.

(b) *Special relationships: East-West, EFTA and the U.S.A.* Political East-West relations were exclusively bilateral until the establishment of the common position at the Conference on Security and Cooperation in Europe (CSCE). This was the first successful EPC inroad which was broadened after the Afghanistan affair.

No need has been felt for special political consultations among the Ten on political relations with the EFTA countries. Although the procedural aspects of relations with the United States (the incidence and form of advance consultations) have been considered by the EPC,[268] substantive issues had only rarely been the subject of multilateral deliberations before the Iranian hostage and Afghanistan affairs.

(c) *Defense.* Defense policy is the farthest reaching exclusion, considering its vital role in foreign policy. Ireland and France, a non-member and a "half-member" of NATO, have been insistent on keeping the NATO and EPC fora separate.[269]

2. Coordination and Interaction with the Community[270]

Although the necessity for coordination between the economic decision-making in the Community and the EPC procedures has been recognized from the outset, only a limited progress has been made in establishing a working relationship between the two systems.

[268] Document on the European Identity, Copenhagen, 14 Dec. 1973, in EPC Docs., *supra* note 248, at 72 ff; Press Statement after the 14th EPC Ministerial Meeting, Bonn, 11 June 1974, *id.* at 86 (the *Gymnich* formula for consultation). Detailed consultations with the United States and other allies have taken place in CSCE.

[269] United Kingdom and Denmark, and in part the Federal Republic as well, take the same position to protect NATO. Commissioner Tugendhat argued that since it is difficult to draw a dividing line between industrial policy and defense issues such as equipment procurement, cooperation should not be left exclusively to NATO. "If the commitment to political cooperation were strengthened, it would inevitably spill over into the security field." *Mr. Tugendhat says that there is a Community side to Europe's Defence Problems,* No. 3140 (NS) EUROPE, 16 May 1981, at 3. Other issues not dealt with by EPC are the Law of the Sea negotiations (coordinated within the Community framework), UNESCO items (dealt with in Ministries of Culture), and anti-terrorism measures ("TREVI") (coordinated by Ministries of the Interior and police experts). On "judicial cooperation" *see* H. da Fonseca-Wollheim, Dix ans de CPE, *supra* note 250, at 8–9. *See* Resolution on the European judicial area (extradition) adopted by the European Parliament on 9 July 1982, OJ No. C 238, 13 Sept. 1982, pp. 83–85.

[270] *See especially* Bonvicini, *The Problem of Coordination Between Political Cooperation and Community Activities,* 12 LO SPETTATORE INTERNAZIONALE 55 (1977).

a) Interaction at the Highest Levels

As indicated above, at the highest level the same individuals, the Heads of State or Government in the European Council and the Foreign Ministers, play two roles – one in Community matters and one in EPC – thus assuring a degree of awareness if not coordination. However, different and separate staffs do the preparatory work through different procedures: in the Community, formalized decision-making, initiated by the Commission's proposals, culminates in proposals by the Committee of Permanent Representatives to the Council of Ministers; in the EPC the small national staff in the capital of the Council's President-in-Office, backed up by the committees of national diplomats, prepares the political files through the consensual consultation process.

From an institutional point of view, responsibilities within the two frameworks remain strictly divided. Although the Ministers are no longer obliged to hold the respective meetings at separate times, they maintain the distinction scrupulously. As Bonvicini reports, the degree of the rigidity in the allocation of questions on the agenda depends on the incumbent President's inclination and his ability to persuade his colleagues.[271]

b) The Commission's Participation

The most important step toward coordination has been the admission of the Community Commission to regular participation in EPC work.[272] The President of the Commission and the commissioner responsible for external affairs now participate regularly in the European Council and in the EPC Conference of Foreign Ministers. They speak but do not vote, and their particular role is undefined. This development represented a radical change in the attitudes of both sides. It was due to the greater flexibility of the French President as much as to the positive experience with the Commission's role in the preparation for the CSCE and the realization that Community instrumentalities are useful, if concrete results are to be achieved in foreign policy. For the Commission itself this new activity posed a problem of internal organization and coordination.[273]

At the working level, since 1975 the Commission staff has participated without any restrictions in the meetings of the Political Committee.[274]

271 *Id.* at 58–59.

272 *The Luxembourg Report of 1970* provided that should the work of the Ministers affect activities of the Communities, "the Commission will be invited to make known its views." EPC Docs., *supra* note 248, at 31. The *Copenhagen Report of 1973* noted with satisfaction the expanded practice. *Id.* at 53.

273 General responsibility was given to the Commission President and the General Secretariat who are given support by the Commissioner responsible for external relations and his staff. Bonvicini, *supra* note 270, at 60.

274 H. da Fonseca-Wollheim, Dix ans de CPE, *supra* note 250, at 15 (and also in *EPZ* at 52); Bonvicini, *supra* note 270, at 60. According to Bonvicini, at a low level there is practically no coordination; correspondents, ambassadors, and experts employed by the ad hoc groups work independently with practically no support from Community officials. *Id.* at 64. The accuracy of the reference to ad hoc groups is questioned by H. da Fonseca-Wollheim, letter to Eric Stein (4 Dec. 1981).

Although Community officials take part in most of the EPC groups of experts touching upon Community affairs, until recently they were not allowed to take part in the European Correspondents' Group and thus could not participate in the preparation of the Political Committee's meetings nor, perhaps more importantly, in the follow-up of any decisions taken. The Commission is still denied a direct connection with the COREU telex network, but it receives daily copies of the messages from the Belgian Foreign Affairs Ministry.[275]

The participation of the Commission personnel, "still sporadic and superficial, even if growing" is based on custom and express or tacit invitation. In 1981, the Foreign Ministers agreed that "[w]ithin the framework of the established rules and procedures the Ten attach importance to the Commission of the European Communities being fully associated with Political Cooperation at all levels."[276] Unlike its important role in the Community, the Commission does not have the authority to initiate action.

It is interesting that the Political Committee has emerged as a competing actor not so much for the Commission, as may have been expected, but for the Committee of Permanent Representatives who until the arrival of EPC had the exclusive role of backing up the work of the Ministers and filtering the activities of the Commission. There is no satisfactory working relationship between these two important bodies; the fact that both are staffed predominantly from the same national Foreign Affairs Ministries does not seem to prevent a degree of jealousy and friction.

c) The Interaction Between the European Parliament and the EPC

Under the Community Treaties, the European Parliament has "political" control over the Commission, including the theoretical authority to dismiss the Commission by a vote of no-confidence. It has no such power with respect to EPC, and its functions, broadly defined in the EPC documents,[277] are entirely advisory. This condition appears unpalatable to the deputies who have criticized both the separation of the two systems and the scarcity of information made available to them.[278]

[275] The Commission receives political information from the EPC groups which the economic officials on the COREPER staff may not have because of the separation between the political and economic sections within some of the national ministries. H. da Fonseca–Wollheim, Dix ans de CPE, *supra* note 250, at 15–16, (also in *EPZ* at 52); Bonvicini, *supra* note 270, at 61–62.

[276] *London Report of 1981, supra* note 255, at para. 12.

[277] *See supra* note 248, at 31, 47, 58, 91, 93. A link between the EPC and the European Parliament was envisaged already in the *Luxembourg Report of 27 Oct. 1970,* in the form of a biannual colloquy between the Ministers and the Political Commission of the Parliament to discuss questions within the EPC ambit. On the other hand the Commission was to be invited "to make known its views" only "should the work of the Ministers affect the activities of the European Communities." EPC Docs., *supra* note 248, at 31.

[278] *See, e.g.,* Blumenfeld, *Report on EPC,* 1977–78, E.P. Working Docs., Doc. 427/77 (containing language of the Resolution of the European Parliament of 19 Jan. 1978

Although the Parliament has routinely adopted resolutions on current international political problems,[279] the impact has been indifferent and its link with the EPC perfunctory: The Foreign Minister of the "Presidency" state meets periodically with the Parliament's Political Committee in more or less desultory "colloquia"; and the President-in-Office makes annual reports and answers Parliamentary questions (the number of which has risen substantially since the direct parliamentary elections). The answers require a consensus of the ten Governments, and no information is published on EPC consultations unless and until a consensus is reached. It is not surprising that the answers have been a source of frustration for the Parliamentarians, since any information supplied has invariably already entered the public domain and decisions have already been taken by the Governments.

3. Activities, Accomplishments and Limitations of the EPC

a) *Internal Process: Exchange of Information, Consultation and Harmonization of Positions*

A basic function of the network of national diplomats has been the exchange and pooling of information. The "club atmosphere," it is said, encourages openness and reduces surprises; and the absence of transnational institutions eliminates jurisdictional friction and doctrinal disputes. The working of the Communities has drawn into the European arena large sectors of national bureaucracies in the economic, environmental, scientific and social bureaus. Because of the EPC, this process of "Europeanization" has now reached deeply into the national foreign service establishments, and is producing, the argument continues, a "European reflex" among them that is bringing about a basic change in their outlook.[280] By the same token, the exclusive character of the "club" has added fuel to the charges of elitism and of a lack of genuine

on EPC). The separation is "artificial ... comic division ... more a pretence than a reality," *per* Patijn (EMP), E. Parl. Debates, Sitting of Tuesday, 9 July 1974, OJ Annex, No. 179, p. 89; "utterly false," "fiction," *per* Lord Chelwood (EMP), *id.* at 92. ***But see contra*** Maigaard (EMP), (Danish Socialist People's Party), insisting on keeping the fiction alive to avoid freezing the Iron Curtain and to preserve the limits of Denmark's commitment as defined in the national referendum. *Id.* at 93. ***See generally,*** the report drawn up on behalf of the Political Affairs Committee, REPORT ON EUROPEAN POLITICAL COOPERATION AND THE ROLE OF THE EUROPEAN PARLIAMENT (Rapporteur: Lady Elles) 1981–1982, E.P.WORKING DOCS., Doc. 1–335/81, 30 June 1981 [hereinafter the *Elles Report*]. *See also London Report of 1981, supra* note 255, at para. 11.

279 *See generally* Gaja, *The European Parliament and Foreign Affairs: Political Cooperation Among the Nine,* in PARLIAMENTARY CONTROL OVER FOREIGN POLICY, ***supra*** note 82, at 191, 198 ff.

280 P. DE SCHOUTHEETE, ***supra*** note 244, at 50–53, 118. Schoutheete suggests, at 118, that in the Communities after 1965–66 the movement has been in the direction of "renationalization" of common policies. In his view, the EPC has contributed to a movement in the opposite direction.

democratic control over European institutions. There is also the danger that a consensus reached on a confidential basis among the diplomats may not survive when exposed to the winds of national politics.

Unlike the Community Treaties, the documents establishing the EPC[281] set no concrete objectives, programs of action or deadlines. The hope, however, if not the expectation, is that the consultation process will mature into a customary rule, the breach of which will appear increasingly costly and that it will lead to a definition of common basic conceptions and common planning.[282] Thus far, the EPC has selected the consultation topics – within the arbitrary limits discussed above – episodically, in reaction to international developments, rather than on the basis of overall planning.

The consultation and consensus process has its own costs in efficiency and timeliness, as shown in the Afghan affair and in the Iranian hostage situation.[283] There are physical limitations on the diplomats' capacity to travel to the innumerable meetings and on the number of tasks that can be handled by the "Presidency."[284] Moreover, the much vaunted informality and flexibility of the process is beginning to show signs of bureaucratization. To mitigate the danger of undue delays, the Foreign Ministers agreed in 1981 that the Political Committee, or, if necessary, the Ministers, will convene within forty-eight hours at the request of three Member States.[285]

Although there is no objective way of measuring the impact of the process, there has been a gradual movement toward common positions on Rhodesia, Namibia, Cyprus, human rights violations and, surprisingly, on the Middle East.[286]

b) External Process: "Declaratory" Diplomacy and Common Positions in International Fora

Once a consensus is reached it may take the shape of a declaration following a meeting of the Ministers or the Heads of State or Government; a demarche with a third state; a mandate to the President-in-Office to undertake a diplomatic mission; or an agreement on a common position to be taken at an international

[281] Collected in EPC Docs., *supra* note 248.

[282] Simonet in P. de Schoutheete, *supra* note 244, at 49. The progressive enlargement bringing in new members has not made this harmonization any easier.

[283] After the Soviet entry into Afghanistan on 27 Dec. 1979, it took the Ministers until 15 Jan. 1980 to formulate a common declaration, long after the national governments had stated their positions and the U.N. General Assembly had taken up the matter. *Id.* at 128.

[284] *See supra* text accompanying note 264; P. de Schoutheete, *supra* note 244, at 127.

[285] *London Report of 1981, supra* note 255, at para. 13. The Political Committee is said to constitute a bottle neck. Unlike in the Community, however, where about one third of the personnel works on interpreting and translating in the seven languages, EPC documents are prepared and discussions held in French or English without translation. P. de Schoutheete, *supra* note 244, at 49.

[286] P. de Schoutheete, *supra* note 244, at 48.

conference or in an international organization, or even on a common guidance for nationals (*e.g.*, the code of conduct for national business enterprises working in South Africa).

i) Recognition

Efforts to coordinate and synchronize national acts of recognition of new states or governments – and thus to initiate something akin to a "common recognition" – have proved unsuccessful thus far even with respect to Bangladesh, not to speak of Angola or Mozambique.[287] The European Council has made it clear that "in the present state of European integration, international rules on recognition remain applicable in their entirety and such recognition still lies within the exclusive competence of each State." Thus, although the establishment by Spain of diplomatic relations with Israel is not a prerequisite for Spain's accession to membership in the Community, it "could only facilitate the harmonization of the foreign policies of the Nine [all of whom maintain such relations], which would be in keeping with the objectives of European political cooperation."[288]

ii) International conferences and missions

The common position which the Nine were able to maintain over a period of four years at the thirty-five states' Conference on Security and Cooperation in Europe (CSCE) in Helsinki, catapulted the Nine into a position of leadership in the Atlantic Alliance group. With the U.S. occupied elsewhere, the Nine became the principal spokesman for that group in relation to the Warsaw Pact and the non-aligned groups. Commission officials formed a part of the negotiating team which was led by the "Presidency of the day."[289] The solidarity of the Member States persevered through the Belgrade and Madrid sessions as well. This appears to be one demonstrable accomplishment of the EPC.

On the Arab-Israeli conflict the Member States have reached a significant measure of agreement since 1973, despite initial dramatic differences. Having agreed on a common platform, the Ministers sent the President-in-Office on two exploratory missions that, however, have not produced any noticeable impact. The "Euro-Arab dialogue," initiated by the European Summit in 1973 on a French proposal, led to the establishment of an EPC coordination group which reports both to the EPC Political Committee and to the Committee of the Permanent Representatives of the Community Council. In the General

287 McGeehan & Warnecke, *Europe's Foreign Policies: Economics, Politics or Both?*, 17 ORBIS 1251, 1268 (1974); Wallace, *British External Relations and the European Community: The Changing Context of Foreign Policy-Making*, 12 J.C.M. STUD. 28, 45 (1973); P. DE SCHOUTHEETE, *supra* note 244, at 90.

288 Written Question No. 489/80, OJ No. C 251, 29 Sept. 1980, p. 12. *See* similarly with respect to the level of Member State diplomatic representation, Written Question No. 2047/82, OJ No. C 104, 18 Apr. 1983, p. 21.

289 Aldo Moro signed the final act in his position as Prime Minister of Italy and, expressly, also as President of the Council of the Communities.

Commission of the dialogue, composed of European and Arab delegations at the Ambassadorial level, the Chairman of the EPC coordinating group speaks on political aspects, while a Commission official deals with economic and technical matters.[290] Thus far, however, this laboriously constructed structure has failed to show tangible results.

iii) The U.N. General Assembly

Several months prior to a U.N. General Assembly session the EPC working-group on the United Nations begins to study the agenda items for the benefit of the Political Committee. That Committee meets in New York at the opening of the session. During the three months' session, the permanent representatives to the United Nations, delegates and staff of the Ten meet at the call of the "Presidency" as many as 200 times. The President-in-Office states the common views of the Ten in the general debate.[291]

While the number of subjects covered by the consultations had grown, the percentage of identical voting had remained more or less stable since 1974 at the 80% to 84% level. The statistics, however, do not tell the whole story because the voting has diverged on important resolutions.[292] It has been suggested that despite the divergences, the Ten have acquired in the United Nations a "reputation of a coherent and effective group"[293] but the progression towards common voting seems to have reached a plateau.

Suggestions have come from Belgian Socialist Parliamentarians that Members of the European Parliament be appointed to national delegations of

[290] P. DE SCHOUTHEETE, *supra* note 244, at 82; Allen, *The Euro-Arab Dialogue,* 16 J.C.M. STUD. 323, 330 (1978).

[291] In 1979 a representative of the "Presidency" spoke 82 times to explain the votes of the Nine. P. DE SCHOUTHEETE, *supra* note 244, at 73.

[292] In the 1980 Assembly, there were "three-way split" votes (yes/no/abstention) on decolonization, apartheid, UNCTAD, and legal aspects of the New International Economic Order. Certain progress has been noted in the disappearence of yes-votes by a Member State on resolutions openly critical of another Member. H. da Fonseca-Wollheim, Dix ans de CPE, *supra* note 250, at 28 (also in *EPZ* at 58). P. DE SCHOUTHEETE, *supra* note 244, at 73, offers a more encouraging view of the statistics: in 1978 the Nine voted the same way on two-thirds of resolutions whereas in 1973 the number did not exceed 50%. In the 37th session of the General Assembly (1982) the Ten shared a common position on 270 resolutions (including "Consensuses"), 72% of the total. On resolutions which were put to a vote the Ten voted together on only 41% of the cases. Written Question No. 2125/82, OJ No. C 125, 9 May 1983, p.20. *See also* Written Question No. 687/75, OJ No. C 139, 21 June 1976, pp. 6–8 (on the general activities in New York). For a more detailed analysis and statistics, *see* B. LINDEMANN, EG-STAATEN UND VEREINTE NATIONEN, particularly at 143, 145 (Munich/Vienna, R. Oldenbourg Verlag, 1978); Hurwitz, *The EEC in the United Nations: The Voting Behavior of Eight Countries, 1948–1973,* 12 J.C.M. STUD. 224 (1975); Hansen, *Die Europäische Politische Zusammenarbeit bei den Vereinten Nationen,* 30 EUROPA-ARCHIV 493 (1975).

[293] P. DE SCHOUTHEETE, *supra* note 244, at 73.

the United Nations. This would conform to a consistent United States practice of including Members of the Senate or House of Representatives foreign affairs committees in United States delegations to the United Nations General Assembly.[294]

c) "Common Action": Positive and Negative

Since the EPC system has no instrumentalities for implementing a common position, it must rely on Member States who hold a wide arsenal of such means, and on the Community with its budget and commercial and economic development policies powers.

Occasionally, when the Commission contemplates specific action, it requests an opinion on political aspects directly from the Political Committee or from one of the EPC groups, and at times an EPC group takes up the political implications of a Community activity at its own initiative.[295] Paradoxically, however, neither the important agreement between the Community and the People's Republic of China nor the (now deadlocked) negotiations between the Community and COMECON have appeared on the EPC agenda.[296]

i) Positive action

When in 1975 the existence of the freshly established democratic institutions in Portugal was in danger following the "Revolution of Carnations," the European Council declared its political support of "a pluralist democracy" in that country, but it was the Community's European Investment Bank that provided special credit from the Community budget, and the Commission that opened economic negotiations with the Portuguese Government.[297] Similar interaction between the EPC and the Community led to substantial economic assistance, from both the Community and national budgets, to Indochina refugees in 1979 and, a year later, to the supply to Poland of critical agricultural commodities at favorable prices.

ii) Negative action: The sanctions

Imposition of economic sanctions against a third state has posed particular problems of interaction between the EPC, the Community and the Member

[294] *Elles Report, supra* note 278, at 23.

[295] Examples are the Community negotiations with the Andean Group after the militiary coup in Bolivia, the association agreement with Cyprus, the compatibility with foreign policy objectives of Member States of proposed Community assistance to certain third states. H. da Fonseca-Wollheim, Dix ans de CPE, *supra* note 250, at 26 (also in *EPZ*, at 56–57).

[296] *Id.* at 26–27 (in *EPZ* at 57).

[297] *Id.* at 22–23 (in *EPZ* at 55). It is said that this common action was in fact an ex post facto "Europeanization" of an undertaking by the German Government about which there had been no agreement at the outset and that this was also the case with the French "initiative" in Zaire in 1977 and 1978. De Montbrial, *Gedanken über das politische Europa*, 36 Europa-Archiv 217, 221 (1981).

States. Clearly, the EPC is concerned in view of the exclusively political objective; however, the means invariably fall within the commercial policy which is the exclusive domain of the Community. Yet EEC Treaty article 224 does contemplate that the Member States may act individually in the event of "serious international tension constituting threat of war" or in order to carry out obligations they have accepted for the purpose of maintaining peace and international security, and it calls for consultations if the sanctions may affect the functioning of the Common Market.[298]

(a) When the United Nations Security Council imposed an economic embargo against *Rhodesia* there were consultations within the EPC but the response came exclusively from the individual Member States. Several years later, when the question of compliance with the embargo was raised in the European Parliament, the Council of Ministers took the view that such measures, because of their political objective, were outside the common commercial policy sphere and within the national competence under article 224; although the Community "as a separate entity is not responsible for applying these decisions," nevertheless its regulations must be applied with due consideration to international commitments.[299]

(b) In the *Iranian hostage* case, the resolution on sanctions against Iran was vetoed in the United Nations Security Council by the Soviet Union, but the Foreign Ministers agreed, again in the context of the EPC, to seek necessary legislation in the national Parliaments that would enable the Member States to impose sanctions in accordance with the defeated United Nations resolution.[300]

[298] Art. 225 adds that if the individual Member State measures distort competition the Commission with the Member State concerned shall examine how these measures can be adjusted to Treaty rules.

[299] Written Question 526/75 to the Council, OJ No. C 89, 16 Apr. 1976, p. 6. The Commission agreed that Member States could act under art. 224 but it pointed to U.N. Charter Article 48(2) which obligates the UN members to carry out Security Council decisions "directly and through their action in the appropriate international agencies of which they are members"; because "the Community as such has never been approached by the Security Council [regarding compliance with the embargo] the Commission sees no need to consider the feasibility of applying in its common commercial policy the sanctions," nor did it see any need for consultation. *See* Commission's Answer to Question 527/75, OJ No. C 89, 16 Apr. 1976, p.8. *See generally,* P.J. KUYPER, THE IMPLEMENTATION OF INTERNATIONAL SANCTIONS: THE NETHERLANDS AND RHODESIA (Alphen a/d Rijn, Sijthoff & Noordhoff, 1978); *see also* Kuyper, *Sanctions Against Rhodesia. The EEC and the Implementation of General International Legal Rules,* 12 C.M.L. REV. 231 (1975). In 1977, the U.N. Security Council adopted an arms embargo against the Republic of South Africa. The chairman of the EPC Conference of Foreign Ministers declared the Nine "are resolved to apply the arms embargo." BULL. EC 11–1977, point 3.2.6. Under art. 223(1)b any Member State may act to protect its security interests with respect to arms trade and the arms embargo was apparently handled by the Member States under this provision.

[300] BULL. EC 4–1980, point 1.2.7.

"We ha[d] to resort," reported a Dutch diplomat, "to Articles 224 and 225 because the opportunity to base the operations of the Community on Article 113 has been lost."[301]

(c) Following the Soviet invasion of *Afghanistan*, the EPC Conference of Ministers issued an anodyne declaration reflecting the previously publicized national policy statements, but in this case the Community became directly involved in support of President Carter's wheat embargo. The Commission, with the Council's approval, acted to prevent Community wheat exports replacing American deliveries.[302]

(d) A breakthrough of sorts for Community power occurred in connection with the sanctions against the Soviet Union after the declaration of martial law in *Poland*. In a regulation based specifically on article 113, the Council of Ministers noted that the "interests of the Community" required reduction in the imports from the Soviet Union and imposed a series of minor restrictions on such imports. In a companion regulation the Council exempted Greece from this measure, allegedly because the current state of incomplete integration of that country into the customs union called for special protection of its commerce.[303]

301 Gosses in DIVISION OF POWERS, *supra* note 71, at 127. The Commissioner concerned claimed that "the Commission shares responsibility for the implementation of whatever measures are agreed at the political level." BULL. EC 4–1980, point 1.2.5. For detailed discussion of the sanctions against Iran, *see* Petersmann, *Internationale Wirtschaftssanktionen als Problem des Völkerrechts und des Europarechts*, 1981 ZVGLRWISS 22, 22–26; and Schröder, *infra* note 304. *See generally*, Nicolaysen, *Autonome Handelspolitik der EWG*, in STAATSRECHT – VÖLKERRECHT – EUROPARECHT. FESTSCHRIFT FÜR H.-J. SCHLOCHAUER ZUM 75. GEBURTSTAG, 855, 869 ff (I. von Münch ed., Berlin/New York, Walter de Gruyter, 1981). *See also* DIVISION OF POWERS, *supra* note 71, at 140–142.

302 BULL. EC 1–1980, points 1.1.3, 4, 8 & 2.1.36. The Council also called for examination of other trade measures, including export credit restrictions.

303 Council Regs. (EEC) Nos. 596/82 & 597/82 of 15 March 1982, OJ No. L 72, 16 Mar. 1982, pp. 15–19. Denmark initially opposed Community action, ostensibly on the legal ground that sanctions were beyond Community power. Eventually it abandoned its opposition but the Council greatly reduced the Commission's list of items to be affected by the sanctions. The Regulation was expected to have minimal practical impact and it was viewed as little more than an indication of displeasure with the Soviet role in Poland. *See, EEC Proposes Cuts in Soviet Imports*, Int'l Herald Trib., 26 Feb. 1982, at 2. The exemption of Greece by a special regulation, obviously motivated by the political stance of the Greek Government rather than by serious economic considerations, illustrates the difficulty in Council decision-making under the unanimity practice. The lesson from the Afghanistan affair may have contributed to the willingness of the governments to employ Community action rather than to rely on individual national measures. In that case some governments, to the irritation of others, proved unable (or unwilling) to obtain parliamentary approval for the necessary measures.

(e) Finally, in response to Argentina's "invasion" of the ***Falkland Islands***, "discussions" and "a decision" in EPC culminated in the adoption by the Council of a regulation, also based on article 113, imposing a general embargo on Argentinian imports into the Community. Problems had arisen, however, when it came to extending the embargo beyond the initial period.[304]

On 23 June 1982, in an answer to a question by Mr. Ephremidis criticizing by implication Council action against the Soviet Union, the Council stated:

In establishing the common commercial policy the Council can legitimately take account of a range of factors attributable to the state of relations with one or other country or group of countries. In the present case, the Council considered that the interests of the Community required that imports from the USSR should be reduced. It therefore adopted, on the basis of Article 113 of the Treaty, the commercial policy measures which are the subject of Council Regulations (EEC) No. 596/82 and (EEC) No. 597/82. Article 113 of the Treaty permits the Council to adopt decisions by a qualified majority....

OJ No. C 188, 22 July 1982, p.10. In fact the first mentioned regulation was adopted despite the negative vote of Greece which, however, did not interpose a "vital interest" claim. The Council position in this response can hardly be reconciled with its answer on the embargo against Rhodesia, summarized *supra* in text accompanying note 299.

304 Council Regulation (EEC) No. 877/82 of 16 Apr. 1982, OJ No. L 102, 16 Apr. 1982, p.1, and corresponding Decision of the representatives of the Governments of the Member States of the European Coal and Steel Community meeting within the Council of the same day, *id.* at p.3, were adopted unanimously. In addition to the discussions and decision in the EPC, the preamble of the regulation refers also to a U.N. Security Council resolution on the "invasion" and to consultations under art. 224 as well as to art. 113. Products in transit or to be imported in execution of existing contracts were exempted. The embargo was limited in time but it was extended twice, first by Council Regulation (EEC) No. 1254/82 of 18 May 1982, OJ No. L 136, 18 May 1982, p.1, and Decision of the representatives of the Member States of the European Coal and Steel Community meeting within the Council of the same day, *id.* at p.2; and then, without any time limit, by Council Regulation (EEC) No. 1254/82 of 24 May 1982, OJ No. L 146, 25 May 1982, p.1, and Decision of the representatives of the Member States of the European Coal and Steel Community meeting within the Council of the same date, *id.* at p.2. There was, however, no unanimity in support of the extension. Italy and Ireland declared that for political reasons they would not observe the embargo and would limit themselves to taking measures against trade diversion caused by their non–observance; and Denmark was prepared to cooperate subject to approval (subsequently obtained) by its Parliament. Yet the above measures extending the embargo do not provide any exceptions for the three dissenting Member States. This anomaly obviously raises serious legal questions which have not been officially answered. After Argentinian surrender, the regulations and decisions imposing the embargo were repealed by Council Regulation (EEC) No. 1577/82 of 21 June 1982, OJ No. L 177, 22 June 1982, p.1, and Decision of the representatives of the Member States of the European Coal and Steel Community meeting within the Council of 21 June 1982, *id.* at p.2. *See* Bruha, *Handelsembargo gegen Argentinien durch EWG–Verordnung?*, 98 DVBL 674 (1982). Bruha concludes that the embargo regulations based on art. 113 were illegal: because they were motivated exclusively by foreign–policy and security reasons they could not be viewed as legitimate commerical policy measures. He believes that, despite the initial unanimous support,

iii) The division of functions and the "federalist" tension

It is characteristic of the basic differences between the European and American systems that whereas in the former the imposition of sanctions raised the ubiquitous problem of State power against Community power, in the latter the controversy arose exclusively at the federal level, between the President and Congress, or between the Federal Government and individuals contesting the validity of federal action under federal law and the Constitution.[305]

European scholars and practitioners disagree on a variety of issues concerning sanctions, some real, others imaginary. Subject to one dissenting voice, however, it is widely agreed that, in contrast with its position in GATT, the Community has not "replaced" the Member States in the United Nations and thus is not bound as such by a Security Council resolution.[306] Beyond that, the ambiguity of articles 224 and 225 allows for a wide range of interpretations

the new embargo practice based on art. 113 cannot be viewed as representing "either political or legal consensus." *Id.* at 682. There is, however, substantial earlier authority in support of Community jurisdiction to impose sanctions on the basis of art. 113: Petersmann, *supra* note 301, at 25–26; Schröder, *Wirtschaftssanktionen der Europäischen Gemeinschaften gegenüber Drittstaaten, dargestellt am Beispiel des Iran-Embargos,* 23 GERMAN Y.B. INT'L L. 111 (1980) (Schröder appears to believe that art. 113 may be employed if all Member States agree); also by implication probably Everling, *Das europäische Gemeinschaftsrecht im Spannungsfeld von Politik und Wirtschaft,* in EUROPÄISCHE GERICHTSBARKEIT UND NATIONALE VERFASSUNGSGERICHTSBARKEIT, FESTSCHRIFT FÜR HANS KUTSCHER 155, 171 (G. Grewe, H. Rupp & H. Schneider eds., Baden-Baden, Nomos, 1981). *See also* Meng, *infra* note 308; Kuyper, *Community Sanctions Against Argentina: Lawfulness Under Community and International Law,* in ESSAYS IN EUROPEAN LAW AND INTEGRATION, *supra* note 165, at 141; and *see generally,* Dupuy, *Observations sur la pratique récente des "sanctions" de l'illicite,* 87 REV. GÉN. DR. INT. PUB. 506, 532–33 (1983).

305 In the Rhodesian case the President was able to implement the U.N. Security Council resolution by drawing upon the United Nations Participation Act, an Act of Congress adopted in implementation of the U.N. Charter. However, the Congress revoked the President's authority, thus placing the U.S. in violation of the U.N. Charter, and a court action against this Congressional measure proved unsuccessful. Diggs v. Schultz, 470 F.2d 461 (D.C. Cir. 1972), *cert. denied,* 411 U.S. 931 (1973). The President's authority to apply sanctions against Southern Rhodesia was restored by Congress in Pub. L. No. 95–12, 95th Cong., 91 Stat. 22, 18 Mar. 1977. Reid, *Congressional Power to Abrogate Domestic Effect of U.N. Treaty Commitment,* 13 COLUM. J. TRANSNAT'L L. 155 (1974). *See generally supra* text accompanying note 219. In the Iranian case, companies with claims against the Iranian Government pending before American courts challenged the President's power to apply sanctions in a way that would interfere with the judicial proceedings and contested his power to conclude an agreement with Iran whereby the claims were to be referred to international arbitration. The Supreme Court upheld the President's power. Dames & Moore v. Regan, 453 U.S. 654 (1981).

306 The lone voice is O. JACOT–GUILLARMOD, *supra* note 212, at 191. *See generally* P.J. KUYPER, *supra* note 299, at 192; Meier, *Zur Kompetenz der EG-Mitgliedstaaten zur Durchführung von Sanktionsbeschlüssen des Sicherheitsrats der Vereinten Nationen,* 25 RIW/AWD 247, 250 (1979).

regarding the impact of these articles on Community commercial policy power and generally its role in this context. On the one hand, the bureaucrats see in article 113 a convenient way for bypassing national parliaments and obtaining quick action, but on the other hand, they conjure up a myriad of contingencies which in their conception call for preserving exclusive national powers.[307] However, in the light of the Council action in the Polish and Falkland Islands situations, the Community power to impose economic sanctions appears now established in practice, without necessarily precluding the power of a Member State to protect its essential interests as contemplated in article 224.[308]

IV. Concluding Observations

The contemporary European system for conducting foreign affairs is unprecedented, unparalleled, and hybrid. In this system foreign affairs are conducted neither strictly by states, nor by the central authority alone (as in federal states generally); rather, some affairs are conducted by individual states alone; some by the states in consultation with each other within the European Political Cooperation mechanism; some by the Community as an entity; and some by the Community together with or in parallel to the states. The European system is in flux, with the Community in some contexts replacing the Member States, in others appearing as an additional person in the international arena. Although the scope of Community foreign affairs is growing, foreign policy is still largely determined by the Member States within as well as outside the Community institutions. Because the Council works like a conference of states, Community foreign policy represents the sum of particular national interests of the Member States rather than a common interest.

[307] Per Lachmann of the Danish Foreign Ministry worries about the following questions: If art. 113 is held to apply, would it be possible for Member States individually to discontinue the sanctions? What would happen if new sanctions or amendments were proposed in the U.N. Security Council? Would the Community then be exclusively competent to determine the vote and what about U.K. and French veto rights? *See* Division of Powers, *supra* note 71, at 141. Interestingly, even the members of the legal staff of the Commission disagreed among themselves. *Id.* at 140–42. On the discontinuance of the sanctions against Argentina, *see supra* note 304.

[308] *See* in this sense C.–D. Ehlermann, The Scope of Article 113 of the EEC Treaty (paper presented at the European University Institute in February 1982); and Meng, *Die Kompetenz der EWG zur Verhängung von Wirtschaftssanktionen gegen Drittländer,* 42 ZaöRV 780 (1982).

A. On the Value of the Comparison

1. The Significant Variables to the Comparison

While *prima facie* Europe before the Community might be compared to the thirteen American states before the Union, the contextual reality is wholly different. Moreover, the American states moved to complete union for foreign policy purposes in one step, with individual states withdrawing completely from foreign affairs. Europe has not moved in one step to such a union and, as of today, its gradual movement is not headed towards the type of union in which the states would disappear as international persons. In the 1980's, surely, Europe is in a situation very different from that of the United States, whether in 1787 or since. States of Europe continue to have international personality, and to act on the international scene largely like other states, although in some areas they have given the Community powers to act.

In relation to its constituent states, the foreign affairs systems of the United States is essentially as originally created by the Constitution. Important developments since 1789 were in the allocation of authority within the Federal Government, and not between the Federal Government and the states. In Europe, on the other hand, there is a continuing tension between the Member States and the Community. The precise allocation of foreign affairs power between the Community and the Member States is determined in the context of that tension, and it is articulated through interpretation of the constituent Treaty, with different perspectives by different Member States as well as by the Community institutions, and with the Court of Justice acting as ultimate umpire. Because of the reluctance of the Member State Governments, the Community political institutions have not been prepared to take full advantage of the Community foreign affairs power as defined liberally by the Court.

The continued existence of the states of Europe as major, if not predominant, international actors is perhaps the principal feature that raises serious question about the comparability with the United States system at both the political and constitutional levels. Nevertheless, on the assumption that the Europeans will wish to pursue the integration process, United States example and experience may serve to suggest particular devices by which democratic entities retaining substantial domestic independence can reduce their international sovereignty in pursuit of a more effective common role on the international scene.

2. Ways in Which the American Experience Can Be Used to Provide Guidelines for Community Development

a) As a Source of Ideas for Developing European Legal Doctrines

The experience of the United States, a country with democratic values and institutions kindred to those of Europe, may offer useful principles and techniques, whether by interpretation or formal amendment, as regards, for example:

- "filling in the gaps" in the attributions of foreign affairs powers to central authorities;

- determining limitations on the foreign affairs powers of the central authorities, to be derived from specific prohibitions in the constitutive document, from the basic character of the central institutional system, and above all, from principles of concern for individual human rights;
- rights and remedies for individuals;
- the role of the judiciary;
- the supremacy of central authorities in foreign affairs and procedures for making it effective against the states;
- the use of the pre-emption doctrine to determine whether, in a particular case, central foreign affairs power excludes state power;
- the status of international agreements in "internal" law and remedies for enforcing them in that law (including the concept and import of "directly applicable and effective" treaties);
- claims by central authorities against third states for violation of international law and response to third states' claims of such violations by central authorities;
- assuring compliance by central authorities with international law on treatment of aliens by extending to them the protection of basic human rights available to citizens; and
- assuring compliance by central authorities with international law by extending central power to foreign affairs issues such as the "act of state" and sovereign immunity of foreign states, and generally removing such issues from power of individual states.

Within the sphere of its competence, that is essentially in economic affairs, the Community has already evolved its own variants of a number of these techniques. In some respects, such as the weight accorded to international agreements in its internal legal order, the Community doctrine, if not its practice, represents a clear advance over the American rule. Also, the judiciary in the Community has played a more decisive role in foreign affairs than American courts. While the United States Supreme Court has had only occasionally to confirm the legitimacy of federal action or to strike down interference by individual states, the Court of Justice has been called upon to employ its independent power for the purpose of enforcing Community authority to replace the Member States in the international arena. Yet American practice, extending as it does over more than two centuries, may be helpful, especially because of its longer historical perspective and the amplitude of the material.

b) As a Model for Possible Allocations of Powers Within the Central Institutions

The United States experience may be particularly relevant in suggesting allocations of power within the central institutions, again taking into account the differences in those institutions and in the role of the component states in the two systems. The United States experience is especially suggestive as regards:

- the distribution of authority between President and Congress with respect to the daily conduct of international relations, and representation of the United States in informal international intercourse as well as international bodies and activities;

- extensive delegation of authority by Congress to the President, with devices (*e.g.*, the legislative veto) designed to supervise the uses of delegated authority or to terminate the delegation;
- improving the expertise and facilities of Congressional committees dealing with foreign affairs; and
- accepting a treaty with a third state as a sufficient basis for appropriation by Congress of the funds necessary for implementation of the treaty.

c) As a Cautionary Tale

However, the United States example can also suggest features which Europe should avoid. In fact, the United States, despite the Federal Government's monopoly of foreign affairs powers, often does not "speak with one voice" and experiences chronic deficiencies in evolving sustained foreign policy. This is due in part to the "Presidential system" in which the President is often unable to rely on the required majority support in the Senate; in part to the power competition and faulty coordination among Executive Departments and between them and the White House foreign relations contingent; and also to frequent lapses in communication between the Executive and Congress. Features to be particularly avoided include:

- delay and frustration such as occur in the Senate for treaties laboriously negotiated by the Executive;
- uncertainty as to the scope of the President's sole authority, especially his independent power to enter into executive agreements;
- subjecting international law and treaties to "repeal" by Congressional legislation;
- the "case or controversy" requirement that bars courts from giving opinions for institutional guidance;
- obstacles to access to courts in the form of technical requirements of standing, and the uncertain and controversial doctrine rendering certain "political questions" nonjusticiable; and
- "overjudicialization" and complexity of administrative procedures particularly in international trade matters.

B. Prospects for Europe

The American experience will become more interesting for the Europeans if and when the Community Council begins to act as a genuine Community organ rather than as a diplomatic conference of the Member States. The Council would have to honor the principle of majority voting as required in the Treaty and recognize the political, administrative and managerial functions of the Commission.[309] The Commission in turn would have to assert with greater vigor

[309] However, a modification of Council practice along the above lines will not suffice to alter the fundamentally inadequate process of the bureaucratic decision–making in the Community. Everling, *supra* note 304, at 168.

its role as an important, if not the leading, institution in foreign affairs. Finally, in Europe as in the United States, it is hard to find a policy issue that is not both "domestic" and "international" in its implications. The European Parliament will have to be given a more compelling voice in both domestic and foreign policy, not only to strengthen democracy in the Community but also to assure broad political support for common action.

A cardinal fact of American constitutional history has been the massive accretion of Presidential power in the twentieth century. Because of his control over the foreign affairs establishment and the military, he has become truly the "sole organ" capable of responding effectively to the needs of a centralized foreign policy. At this juncture, there is no evidence that an organ equipped with centralized diplomacy and other requisite instrumentalities will emerge in Europe in the foreseeable future. Although fully centralized foreign affairs power has never been seriously questioned in the United States, the same degree of centralization may not prove necessary or even desirable for Europe. The European Political Cooperation mechanism does not point in the direction of centralization. It remains to be seen how, in the longer run, this mechanism can be brought into an organic relationship with the Community if the essential character and dynamics of the integration process are to be preserved.[310]

[310] The "Solemn Declaration on European Union," adopted on 19 June 1983 by the Heads of State or Government "meeting within the European Council," became available after the completion of this study. It does not purport to bring about any substantive change in the relationship between the Community and the EPC; it calls, however, *inter alia*, for a better coordination of the two processes within the "European Union," full Commission association with the work of EPC and the inclusion of political and economic aspects of security within the EPC scope. For the text of the Declaration with a commentary, *see* Neville-Jones, *The Genscher/Colombo Proposals on European Union*, 20 C.M.L. REV. 657 (1983); *see also* BULL. EC 6-1983, at p.24. *See also* the Draft Treaty Establishing the European Union and the Resolution of the European Parliament concerning the Draft, OJ No. C 77, 19 March 1984, p. 33; BULL. EC 2-1984, at p. 7; BULL. EC 9-1983, at p. 7.

Part II

The Social and Economic Dimension

Migrant Workers and Rights of Mobility in the European Community and the United States: A Study of Law, Community, and Citizenship in the Welfare State

Bryant G. Garth*

> [I]n the words of Mr. Justice Cardozo: "The [U.S.] Constitution was framed ... upon the theory that the peoples of the several States must sink or swim together, and that in the long run prosperity and salvation are in union and not division."
>
> Was this formulation in the minds of the framers of the Treaty of Rome, Article 48 of which says, "[t]he free movement of workers shall be ensured within the Community" and which continues to the effect that such freedom of movement "shall involve the abolition of any discrimination based on nationality between workers of the Member States as regards employment, remuneration and other working conditions"? Probably not, but the concept and spirit informing both statements remains identical.

Lord Mackenzie Stuart, Judge of the Court of Justice of the European Communities**

> [T]here is a kind of basic human equality associated with the concept of full membership of a community – or, as I should say, of citizenship – which is not inconsistent with the inequalities which distinguish the various economic levels in society. In other words, the inequality of the social class system may be acceptable provided the equality of citizenship is recognized.

T. H. Marshall***

* Associate Professor, Indiana University School of Law (Bloomington); B.A. Yale 1972; J.D. Stanford 1975; Ph.D. (European Doctorate) European University Institute, Florence, 1979. I would like to acknowledge the tremendous help of Dr. Jean Amphoux, Legal Service of the Commission of the European Communities, in facilitating the gathering of materials on and my understanding of European Community law. The comments of Professor T. Alexander Aleinikoff have also been quite illuminating on the subject of U.S. immigration law. Many thanks also to Adrian Lesher, a student at the Indiana University School of Law, who contributed to the research, discussed many of the ideas in the paper with me, and provided a number of useful stylistic suggestions.

** Mackenzie Stuart, *Trade Restrictions, Federalism and the Judiciary: Comparative Perspectives: Review of T. Sandalow and E. Stein,* Courts and Free Markets: Perspectives from the United States and Europe, 81 Mich. L. Rev. 1122, 1128 (1983) (footnotes omitted).

*** T. H. Marshall, Class, Citizenship, and Social Development 70 (Westport, Conn., Greenwood Press, 1973).

I. Introduction

The free movement of workers across state (or Member State) boundaries is a defining feature of the European Economic Community and the federal system of the United States.[1] This mobility provides individual economic opportunities, while at the same time promoting economic, social, and political integration. The Project that led to this study focuses on "legal integration," and it is clear that legal rights to mobility occupy a distinctive position in measuring any legal contribution to integration (or community). Anyone familiar with the European Community and the United States, in addition, can see obvious parallels in how mobility is fostered in the two settings. In the United States, despite some challenges by individual states in periods of economic uncertainty, free personal mobility remains a fundamental component of the system,[2] while the European Community has progressed very far in twenty years toward a comparable end – sometimes optimistically termed "European citizenship."[3] Furthermore, in each setting, again consistent with this Project's inquiry into the role of law and legal institutions, we can see that the "community" and "federal" constitutional courts – the European Court of Justice and the U.S. Supreme Court – have played leading roles in breaking down barriers to mobility. Recognizing these rough parallels, one purpose of this essay will be to provide a relatively simple and straightforward comparative study, examining and contrasting the legal structures and evolution of migration policies within the United States and the European Community. In Lord Mackenzie Stuart's words quoted above, the study can explore just how similar the "concept and spirit" of community has become in Europe and the United States.

It is also important, however, that comparison take place at two other levels. First, the comparison of legal approaches to mobility *within* federal entities, while instructive, fails to give the full picture necessary to understand the legal treatment of migrant workers in either the European Community or the United States. Since free movement within relates to opportunities to move from without, the concerns that arise in the discussion of intra-Community mobility

[1] *See especially* the useful contributions by Rosberg, *Free Movement of Persons in the United States*, and Leleux, *The Role of the European Court of Justice in Protecting Individual Rights in the Context of Free Movement of Persons and Services*, in COURTS AND FREE MARKETS: PERSPECTIVES FROM THE UNITED STATES AND EUROPE 275 & 385 (T. Sandalow & E. Stein eds., Oxford, Clarendon Press, 1982).

[2] For a recent example, from 1 April 1980 to 1 July 1982, the population of the Midwest-North Central region of the United States declined by 1.5% while the population of the West increased by 1.5%. Herbers, *Industrial Flight in Minnesota*, New York Times, 12 April 1983, at 33.

[3] As early as 1968, the Vice President of the European Communities called the provisions on worker mobility an "incipient form ... of European citizenship." *See, e.g.*, Plender, *An Incipient Form of European Citizenship*, in EUROPEAN LAW AND THE INDIVIDUAL 39, 40 (F. Jacobs ed., Amsterdam, North-Holland, 1976). The theme has also recently been developed in, *e.g.*, Evans, *European Citizenship*, 32 AM. J. COMP. L. 679 (1984), which appeared while this chapter was in press.

must also be treated with respect to migration from *outside* the United States or European Community. This migration, both legal and illegal, has posed a number of perplexing problems that merit attention here. Legal developments surrounding Turks in the Federal Republic of Germany, Algerians in France, and Haitians and especially Mexicans in the United States, in fact, have recently dominated discussion of the phenomenon of labor migration. Indeed, as the examples of Greece, Portugal, and Spain show, migrant workers from outside the Community may become members of the Community entitled to assert Community rights. We cannot assess the role of migration for work in the European Community without understanding the implications of expansion.

Second, "legal" discussions of major social phenomena cannot proceed merely by reference to trends in laws and court decisions. The law provides an interesting picture, and it is necessary to understand what that picture tells us. But it is equally important to consider political and social dimensions that the legal picture tends to hide. The phenomenon of migrant workers is a remarkable and controversial feature of the last thirty years in Europe and the United States, and a legal study provides a unique vantage point from which to gain more general insights. One task of this essay will thus be to try to relate the law and sociology of worker mobility to broader economic, legal, and political issues of citizenship and community.

The remainder of this study is divided into five parts. Part Two provides introductory background on the history of migration and immigration and the emergence of the migrant status in modern legislation. It examines the various justifications and explanations that have been advanced for labor mobility generally, movement within the European Community and the United States, and restricted movement from outside the United States and the European Community. It is important to understand restrictions on mobility as they relate to the divisions between the developed and less developed world and the rise of the positive state in the twentieth century. The development of the status of migrant worker can be understood as a specific response to the economic organization of the developed welfare states.

Part Three compares the structures and legal evolution of the principle of free movement of workers in the United States and the European Community. This requires an analysis of the constitutional frameworks, institutional settings, and leading cases dealing with mobility across borders within the relevant community. Basic differences between the United States and the European Community exist; most obviously, we find a right to travel for all *individuals* in the United States contrasted with a right of free movement of *workers* in the Community – a right that no doubt owes something to the development of the status of migrant worker. As already noted, however, the Community – aided by liberal decisions of the European Court of Justice – has moved far beyond the strict notion of mobility of individual workers to work. There are rights to migrate to work, to migrate to search for work, to bring families, to prepare for work, to obtain benefits, to reside permanently, to join labor unions, and sometimes even to vote.

Nevertheless, the lengthening catalog of rights in the Community eventually hits a critical difference with the United States. The most important citizenship in the Community remains that of individual countries, while individual state citizenship has practically lost its relevance in the United States. As we shall see, the comparison reveals a significant current difference in the "communities." It is clearly accepted in the legal and constitutional structure of the United States – but not in the European Community – that no state can attempt to solve its economic and social problems by closing its borders or exporting those who become a burden on the state.

The straight comparison of U.S. federalism and European supranationalism must next be expanded. Legal and structural analyses of rights within the relevant community, as noted above, are unduly narrow and can in fact be misleading. Part Four therefore explores the position of migrants, legal and illegal, from outside the European Community or the United States. In Europe, the situation is complicated by the inability of the European Community to coordinate Member State policies with respect to migration from outside, and we must therefore discuss briefly some of the immigration policies in particular countries. The most important concern here, however, is to develop the relationship between the rights or lack of rights of less-privileged migrants and the more privileged individuals moving within the United States or the European Community.

Part Five then adds a further complicating dimension. It seeks to go beyond the picture of formal rights provided to individuals by the law to some assessment of how those rights operate in practice and what social functions they serve. In part, of course, the problems are those of all ethnic, racial, or linguistic minorities,[4] but the status of migrant (and non-citizen) creates special problems. And while little data are available, we can make some preliminary assessments in part on the basis of work that has been done on the enforcement of rights generally. Put simply, we especially need to be alert to the symbolic and social control functions of the law when examining the situation of migrant workers.

The concluding part of this study then summarizes and addresses more specifically three principal themes. It attempts first to evaluate the role of law and legal structures of mobility in integration (and non-integration) in the European Community and the United States. Legal developments, we see, have both created and responded to the problems of migrant workers. And while similar trends can be found within the different structural settings of the European Community and the United States, the Community itself serves basically only to complicate approaches that are still left essentially to the individual Member States. This study therefore should lead to an understanding of the complicated role that legal developments have played for migrant workers in the two federal entities. Too much free movement, we even see, could *hinder* tendencies toward further integration.

[4] Glazer insists this aspect is of paramount importance in N. Glazer, Ethnic Dilemmas 1964–82, ch. 16 (Cambridge, Harv. U.P., 1983).

The second theme centers on the legal status of "migrant worker," which exists with some variations within the Community, within each Member State, and in the United States. The migrant worker is relatively new to the law; it suggests a legal status somewhere between immigrant or citizen, with full rights of participation in the host country, and outsider or alien, with essentially no ability to claim legal rights. This status raises unique and novel questions of law and politics.

Michael Walzer, a distinguished political theorist at Princeton University, provides a moral argument against the status of migrant worker.

> The processes of self-determination through which a territorial state shapes its internal life must be open, and equally open, to all those men and women who live in the territory, work in the local economy, and are subject to local law. Hence, second admissions (naturalization) depend on first admissions (immigration), and are subject only to certain constraints of time and qualification, never to the ultimate constraint of closure. ... Political justice is a bar to permanent alienage – either for particular individuals or for a class of changing individuals. There cannot be a fixed status between citizen and foreigner (though there can be stages in the transition from one of these political identities to the other).[5]

He refuses to recognize the possibility of a status that entitles an individual to work but not to have the opportunity to reap the benefits of full citizenship. His objections, we shall see, are reflected in legal struggles about migrant workers and their rights. Despite the strong attraction in Europe and the United States of the idea of migrant or guestworker – who comes, works when needed, and then leaves – it is very difficult to place that kind of citizenship in the law and have it enforced by public authorities. As a result, we find a rethinking of the migrant worker status and a number of proposals to transform it in law and practice. The European Community has further complicated the problem of rights of migrant workers with its own unique status of "Community worker," and it too must be evaluated practically and in light of Walzer's powerful critique.

The third underlying theme applicable to labor migration both from within and without the relevant community concerns the question of shared responsibility for social and economic problems. Migration typically comes from poor regions to places significantly better off, and it often leads to new social problems of poverty, housing, and discrimination in the place of arrival. A real "community" (not Community) perspective on these problems would treat them in large part as the responsibility of the host country (or a larger federal entity). A less communitarian perspective would be to recognize that certain obligations come with a willingness to admit or tolerate the presence of foreign workers, but to insist also that once the workers no longer have employment, the obligation stops and the guests ought to leave. Part of the inquiry into the status of migrant worker in its various settings, therefore, involves an examination of what social rights are given to migrants who do not or cannot work. The

[5] Walzer, *The Distribution of Membership,* in BOUNDARIES: NATIONAL AUTONOMY AND ITS LIMITS 1, 31 (P. Brown & H. Shue eds., Totowa, N.J., Rowman & Littlefield, 1981).

question naturally concerns the extent to which one country or state can attempt to ameliorate problems such as unemployment or an overburdened welfare state by exporting a certain sector of the victims of those problems. Welfare state governments have had a difficult time resisting the attraction of workers who seemingly will not become burdens on limited state resources, but they have also had difficulty confining workers to that position.

Finally, it is important to specify what this study will not cover. Much of the European Community scholarship on mobility concerns the freedom of establishment and the freedom to provide services within Community Member States.[6] Both these freedoms enable self-employed persons, the liberal professions, and others to migrate to set up a business or provide a service, and the Community has been active in helping to reduce barriers to mobility. Nevertheless, these topics will not be explored here. This study addresses what the editors have termed "European identity" and its U.S. federal counterpart, and these concerns dictate that the Community focus be on European rights to migrate as they have developed from the freedom of worker mobility.

II. The Development of the Migrant Worker as a Legal Status: Safeguard for the Welfare State

The legal status of migrant worker is a recent development, becoming important largely in response to the economic situation that existed after World War II. According to Ansay, "Until the beginning of the twentieth century, one characteristic of migration was its permanency. Migration was for immigration, for the purpose of permanent settlement."[7] As a matter of accepted international law, it was not even clear until the middle of the eighteenth century that States had the right to exclude potential immigrants; and after a period of some restrictions, the situation in Western Europe in the last half of the nineteenth century was generally rather liberal.[8] Castles and Kosack, for example, document considerable immigration to France, Germany, and Great Britain prior to World War I.[9] This is not to say that borders were truly open, or that European countries, with the exception of France, actually sought to increase their populations through immigration, but the relevant distinction in

[6] These subjects, covered by EEC Treaty arts. 52–66, are discussed in the works cited *infra* note 48.

[7] Ansay, *Legal Problems of Migrant Workers,* [1977] III REC. DES COURS ACAD. DR. INT. 3, 7.

[8] *See, e.g.,* R. PLENDER, INTERNATIONAL MIGRATION LAW 46–47 (Alphen a/d Rijn, Sijthoff, 1972).

[9] S. CASTLES & G. KOSACK, IMMIGRANT WORKERS AND CLASS STRUCTURE IN WESTERN EUROPE 16–21 (London, O.U.P., 1973).

law and in policy was that between immigrants and outsiders, with little thought of a special status for migrant workers.[10]

The relatively open immigration policies in the nineteenth century in the United States are of course well-known. Commentators suggest, for example, an average of 600,000 immigrants per year from 1880 to 1914, while the U.S. population more than doubled from 50 to 105 million.[11] The first efforts to restrict immigration to the United States did not begin until late in the nineteenth century, and their aims were mainly to curb immigration of populations thought to be less desirable. The early initiatives culminated in a system adopted in the 1920's based on nationality of origin, but even then, the border between Mexico and the United States remained completely open until 1924. And no numerical quota limited qualified immigrants from Mexico until 1965.[12]

Problems of finding immediate employment for returning soldiers reduced immigration in Europe and the United States in the post-World War I period. More importantly, however, the depression of the 1930's put a stop everywhere to the encouragement of voluntary immigration.[13] In France, for example, "Thousands of foreigners were sent back to their countries of origin by the trainload."[14] Similarly, the very permissive situation for Mexican immigrants in the United States changed quickly with the onset of the depression:

> [X]enophobic notions surfaced almost immediately following the crash and forced the deportation and repatriation of hundreds of thousands of documented and undocumented Mexicans working and living in the United States as well as the removal of United States citizens of Mexican descent.[15]

Economic scarcity led to the favoring of American citizens and white ethnic groups.[16] New immigrants and temporary residents fared poorly, regardless of their legal rights to remain and look for work.

10 That does not mean, of course, that there were no steps along the way between foreigner and citizen. Persons admitted to the territory were, however, not thought of as temporary guests who could never claim citizenship. It appears that there has been less of a tendency recently, therefore, to posit any right to claim citizenship. *See* R. PLENDER, *supra* note 8, at 284–86.

11 *See, e.g.*, Johnson, *The Labor Market Effects of Immigration*, 33 INDUS. & LAB. REL. REV. 331, 341 (1980); Adams, *A Dubious Host*, [1983] WILSON QUARTERLY 101, 106 (No. 1); Seller, *Historical Perspectives on American Immigration Policy: Case Studies and Current Implications*, 45 LAW & CONTEMP. PROBS. 137 (1982). *Cf.* P. EHRLICH, L. BILDERBACK & A. EHRLICH, THE GOLDEN DOOR: INTERNATIONAL MIGRATION, MEXICO, AND THE UNITED STATES (New York, Wideview Books, 1981) [hereinafter THE GOLDEN DOOR].

12 The first law limiting numbers of immigrants was passed in 1921. The similar act of 1924, Pub. L. No. 139, 43 Stat. 153 (1925) remained in effect essentially until 1952. A survey of the later law can be found in G. GOODWIN-GILL, INTERNATIONAL LAW AND THE MOVEMENT OF PERSONS BETWEEN STATES 123–35 (Oxford, Clarendon Press, 1978).

13 *See* Fields, *Closing Immigration Throughout the World*, 26 AJIL 671 (1932).

14 *See* S. CASTLES & G. KOSACK, *supra* note 9, at 23.

15 *See* Lopez, *Undocumented Mexican Migration: In Search of a Just Immigration Law and Policy*, 28 U.C.L.A. L. REV. 615, 663 (1981).

16 *See id.* at 663: "[In] the 1930s, poor white farmers from Oklahoma, Arkansas and Texas ... filled most of the slackened demand for labor in large agricultural enterprises."

The period following World War II produced considerable movement of individuals into Western Europe.[17] As the economies rebounded and expanded greatly in the post-War period, shortages of domestic labor were met in Belgium, France, the Federal Republic of Germany, the Netherlands, and the United Kingdom by active recruiting from countries with lower standards of living and surpluses of labor.[18] The resultant influx into the Federal Republic of Germany is well-known and dramatic. First East Germans, then Italians, and then non-EEC workers came in great numbers. The size of the foreign population was 485,763 in 1951; 3,438,700 in 1972; and 3,981,300 in 1978.[19] By 1978 there were an estimated 12.5 million foreign workers and their dependents within the (then) nine Member States of the European Community.[20] Estimates of the situation vary considerably today, but the numbers have not diminished (although the status of Greeks has changed). One view is that migrant workers and their families in the ten European Community countries make up some 7.3 percent of the population.[21] This unprecedented increase in the number of foreigners, and its impact on foreign and domestic societies, has been noted as one of the critical features of the post-War economy.[22]

It is difficult to trace with precision the evolution of social and legal policies toward these foreign workers.[23] There are national variations that cannot be neglected, and it is not clear in any event that initial policies were carefully thought out and implemented. What does appear to be evident is that, with the limited exception of France, the general assumption was that the foreigners would come, work, and return to their home countries when (and if) work was no longer available, and that the depression policies of illegal deportation

[17] *See generally* A. Bouscaren, International Migrations Since 1945 (New York, Praeger, 1963). Since this is a comparative study of the European Community and the United States, countries such as Switzerland, which have been heavily dependent on migrant labor, will not be examined specifically.

[18] *See, e.g.*, S. Castles & G. Kosack, *supra* note 9, at 28–41; M. Piore, Birds of Passage: Migrant Labor and Industrial Societies (Cambridge, Cambridge U.P., 1979).

[19] *See* Rist, *The European Economic Community (EEC) and Manpower Migrations: Policies and Prospects*, 33 J. Int'l Aff. 201 (1980).

[20] *Id.*

[21] *See, e.g.*, Fouquet, *As Boom Times Fade, Europe Struggles to Absorb 9 Million Immigrants*, Christian Science Monitor, 18 Oct. 1982, at 3. Some recent indications can be found in Comm'n of the EC, Report on Social Developments – Year 1982, at 34, 36, 38, 39, 40, 48 (Brussels, Office for Official Pubs. of EC, 1983) (reporting 878,577 foreigners in Belgium; 49,689 work-permit holders in Denmark; 1,832,166 foreign workers and 4,667,000 foreign residents in the Federal Republic of Germany; 35,000 foreign workers in Greece; and 220,000 foreign workers in the Netherlands). The French press recently reported 4,318,068 foreigners living in France as of 1 Jan. 1982. *4,318,068 étrangers vivent en France*, Le Figaro, 4 July 1983.

[22] *See especially* C. Kindleberger, Europe's Postwar Growth: The Role of Labour Supply (Cambridge, Harv. U.P., 1967).

[23] *See, e.g.*, Ansay, *supra* note 7; Immigrant Workers in Europe: Their Legal Status (E. Thomas ed., Paris, UNESCO, 1982) [hereinafter cited as Immigrant Workers in Europe].

would not have to be duplicated. Migration was not to be seen as a first step toward immigration. After a while even in France the Government "no longer assumed that assimilation of foreign workers was in the long-term interest of France."[24] The German term *Gastarbeiter* or guestworker best captures the general assumption, and the Government in Germany was quite clear in its orientation toward foreigners: "*Deutschland ist kein Einwanderungsland.*"[25]

The laws and regulations within the host countries of the European Community gradually adapted to fit this important new halfway point between immigration and exclusion.[26] Formal legal requirements of work and residence permits were especially well-suited to prevent permanent settlement when work was no longer available. And generally, as the authors of a recent UNESCO study of the legal status of migrants found, "law-makers ... endeavoured to establish a system for regulating movements of persons and to serve economic interests as well as possible."[27] As we shall see, there is some ambiguity about whether this vision of the migrant status – serving national economic interests – lies beneath the system of free movement of workers within the European Community, but it quite clearly came to characterize the increasingly important migration from outside the Community (at least until the severe recent halt on movement into the Community, discussed below).

In the United States, we find a similar movement toward the creation of this intermediate status, applicable especially to Mexican workers during and after World War II.[28] In 1942 the United States agreed by treaty with Mexico to establish the *Bracero* program and provide farm labor for the American war effort.[29] This program, despite considerable criticism from the start, survived until 1964 (and a small scale version still exists) and employed some five million

[24] Martin & Miller, *Guestworkers: Lessons from Europe,* 33 Indus. & Lab. Rel. Rev. 315, 318 (1980). One commentator notes a change beginning in 1969, after which non-European immigrants were referred to as an "unassimilable island." *See* M. Schein, The Third World in France (paper prepared for delivery at the 1983 Convention of the International Studies Association, Mexico City, 5–9 Apr. 1983).

[25] *See, e.g.,* Böhning, *Guestworker Employment in Selected European Countries – Lessons for the United States,* in The Border that Joins: Mexican Migrants and U.S. Responsibility 99, 101 (P. Brown & H. Shue eds., Totowa, N.J., Rowman & Littlefield, 1983) [hereinafter cited as The Border that Joins].

[26] *See generally* Immigrant Workers in Europe, *supra* note 23.

[27] Thomas, *Conclusion,* in *id.* at 240. *See also* Lyon-Caen, *Les travailleurs: étude comparative,* [1975–1] Dr. soc. 1, 3.

[28] *See, e.g.,* Garcia y Griego, *The Importation of Mexican Contract Laborers to the United States, 1942–1964: Antecedents, Operation and Legacy,* in The Border that Joins, *supra* note 25, at 49; Immigrants – and Immigrants: Perspectives on Mexican Labor Migration to the United States (A. Corwin ed., Westport, Conn., Greenwood Press, 1978) [hereinafter cited as Immigrants – and Immigrants]; G. Kiser & M. Kiser, Mexican Workers in the United States: Historical and Political Perspectives (Albuquerque, U. New Mexico P., 1979) [hereinafter cited as Mexican Workers in the United States].

[29] Act of 4 Aug. 1942, 56 Stat. 1759 (1943).

Mexican laborers.[30] Only men were eligible, and they were tied closely to available opportunities in agriculture. If opportunities disappeared, the workers had no choice but to return to Mexico.

The status of migrant, as noted before, is not universally praised or accepted. Recent developments in Western Europe suggest that political forces make the maintenance of this status rather difficult either within a community or in its relations with outside communities. Before exploring the problems that have emerged in the past decade, however, it is important to ask why this novel legal half-way point arose and in whose interests it was created. This legal status must be understood in order to evalute the right of migration in the European Community and its relationship to migration from outside the Community.

The status of migrant worker has a number of advantages from the perspective of employers and governments in welfare states. Indeed, several commentators, among them John Kenneth Galbraith, contend that it in fact serves everyone's interests.[31] For present purposes, however, it will suffice to point out that Galbraith's optimism has not been accepted by all. The evidence is especially thin on the benefits to the countries exporting labor,[32] although that is not within the scope of this essay. There is also skepticism about the migrant's status because of the rather harsh legal approach often taken by a country or community that is hosting foreign workers.[33]

Little analysis or research is necessary to see the economic advantages of the migrant worker from the point of view of the employer and host welfare state governments.[34] First, it is clear in both Europe and the United States that first generation migrant workers often take the least desirable jobs in the economy – positions that would be difficult to fill with nationals. The extent of this "dual market" for labor – one for nationals seeking regular employment in desirable jobs and the other filling marginal positions such as domestic work – is debated among scholars,[35] but certainly it operates for many kinds of undesirable work. A number of the other economic advantages of the status of migrant worker, however, are tied to the idea of "rotation" – where what will be termed here the

[30] A short description can be found in Lopez, *supra* note 15, at 663–72. *See infra* notes 209–11 and accompanying text.

[31] *See* J. GALBRAITH, THE NATURE OF MASS POVERTY (Cambridge, Harv. U.P., 1979). Support for different reasons can be found in M. OLSON, THE RISE AND DECLINE OF NATIONS: ECONOMIC GROWTH, STAGFLATION, AND SOCIAL RIGIDITIES (New Haven, Conn., Yale U.P., 1982).

[32] *See, e.g.*, Macmillan, *The Economic Effects of International Migration: A Survey*, 20 J. C. M. STUD. 245 (1982); Johnson, *supra* note 11.

[33] *See infra* § IV for an assessment of the merits of that skepticism.

[34] Among other commentators underlining the economic basis of this status are Ansay, *supra* note 7; Böhning, *supra* note 25; Martin & Miller, *supra* note 24; J. POWER, MIGRANT WORKERS IN WESTERN EUROPE AND THE UNITED STATES (New York, Pergamon Press, 1979).

[35] *See* M. PIORE, *supra* note 18. *Compare* Fogel, *United States Immigration Policy and Unsanctioned Rights*, 33 INDUS. & LAB. REL. REV. 295 (1980) *with* Piore, *Comment*, 33 INDUS. & LAB. REL. REV. 312 (1980). *See generally* Böhning, *supra* note 25, at 105–16.

"ideal migrant worker" comes, provides labor to promote economic growth, and leaves when the economy takes a downturn.[36]

Migrant workers may require fewer services from the host country than most national workers. For example, if the worker comes alone, without dependents, as was mandated by law under the U.S. Bracero program, then the host country can save in social capital investment in education, housing, medical care and the like. Furthermore, the migrant worker tends to be younger than the typical non-migrant and accordingly should require fewer resources for medical care and social security.[37] Similarly, even if family members come, social absorption costs can be reduced or avoided, since the host country in theory need not worry about integrating workers or their families into the mainstream of the society. Foreign workers and families from different cultural backgrounds and different ethnic groups need not be socialized to the values and culture of the host country.

Finally, the presence of migrant workers can protect domestic workers from the adverse effects of unemployment and a recession. The example of the Federal Republic of Germany is well-known. The recession beginning in 1973 brought a reduction in the foreign worker population by at least one-half million persons.[38] In one sense, this provides a modern example of a "reserve army of the unemployed," but more significant now is the connection to the modern welfare state. Migrant workers are aptly described by the German term *Konjunkturpuffer* – "safety-valve role" – and the equally striking French reference – *un amortisseur de conjoncture*.[39] With the demise of the philosophy of laissez-faire, especially after World War II, governments have been considered responsible for promoting full employment among their nationals. The presence of migrant workers can ease the pressure on governments to act. The essential idea is that there is no social duty owed to guestworkers; they are invited to stay only as long as there happens to be a demand for their services. Similarly, the governmental obligation to provide unemployment benefits to those who lose their jobs may be seen as inapplicable to migrant workers, thus reducing considerably the state's expenditures in a time of recession.

From an employer's perspective, there are also obvious advantages, the first of which is that an employer need not set up business elsewhere to take advantage of the relatively low cost of foreign labor. In addition, foreign workers tend to be more docile, less well-organized than the domestic workforce, and

36 "Rotation" in its purest form means an official policy to "maintain a rapid turnover of foreign workers, in order to prevent their gaining residence rights and settling down." S. Castles & G. Kosack, *supra* note 9, at 38.

37 A review of the literature on this question of the use of resources by migrant workers is found in Macmillan, *supra* note 32.

38 *See, e.g.*, R. Rist, Guestworkers in Germany: The Prospects for Pluralism 62–63 (New York, Praeger, 1978).

39 On the Federal Republic of Germany, *see, e.g.*, Honekopp & Ullman, *The Status of Immigrant Workers in the Federal Republic of Germany*, in Immigrant Workers in Europe, *supra* note 23, at 115, 141. The French term is from Lyon-Caen, *supra* note 27, at 2.

easier to terminate: In both the United States and Europe, it has certainly been to the employer's advantage to encourage the development of migrant labor programs.[40]

It should be noted that labor unions are the most obvious domestic interest group standing to lose from a large influx of foreign labor; but this potential opposition could be overcome fairly easily as long as the economies were expanding and providing enough employment for the domestic labor force. Labor unions in a recession, moreover, have the same general interest as the government in helping to encourage guests to go home. The labor movement has a tradition of international solidarity, but foreign workers and concrete economic interests cut against that tradition.[41]

Migrant workers therefore serve a very "useful" function in modern welfare states – fueling economic growth in times of demand for labor while avoiding the risk of high welfare state costs in time of economic slowdown. This economical status, it is true, tended to break down as a formal category when recession came in the 1970's, and despite economic benefits the Bracero program did not last into the 1970's as a major program in the United States.[42] The now universally accepted conclusion in the European countries is that not enough workers went home.[43] But the migrant status has strong attractions, as we have seen, and pressures to refine it or even to maintain it informally are bound to continue. It is premature, as the conclusion of this study will suggest, to see the status of migrant worker as a "failure."

For the moment, however, it is important only to understand the attractions of the migrant legal status for modern welfare states, and to see the assumptions on which the guestworker idea depends. We can then turn specifically to the peculiar kind of migrant status created within the European Community and how it relates, or fails to relate, to the welfare state safety-valve role that migrant workers seem to have been structured to fulfill. Indeed, the migrant status as just described is the antithesis of an expanded community; it is designed to exploit foreign workers to safeguard the well-being of the domestic economy and citizens. Nevertheless, this essentially anti-community idea apparently has served as the basis of some evolution toward legal integration and the creation of a European welfare state community. The following comparison of the United States and the European Community will serve, among other purposes, to illuminate the accomplishments and limits of that evolution.

[40] *See generally* S. Castles & G. Kosack, *supra* note 9; J. Power, *supra* note 34, at 53.

[41] *See infra* notes 272–78 and accompanying text; J. Berger & J. Mohr, A Seventh Man: Migrant Workers in Western Europe 144–45 (New York, Viking, 1975); S. Castles & G. Kosack, *supra* note 9, at 116–79; Markovits & Kazarinov, *Class Conflict, Capitalism, and Social Democracy: The Case of Migrant Workers in the Federal Republic of Germany,* 10 Comp. Pol. 373, 386–87 (1978).

[42] *See infra* notes 202–08 and accompanying text.

[43] *See infra* notes 159–75 and accompanying text.

III. Migrant Workers and Rights to Mobility in the European Community and the United States: The Idea of a Community Welfare State

The United States and the European Community are sufficiently similar in structure to make it tempting to go too far in finding parallel developments between them. We can point to the U.S. Constitution and the federal system it created, and show how it evolved with the help of the U.S. Supreme Court toward free mobility and what is now termed a fundamental right to travel.[44] We can turn to the European Community, show the somewhat "ambiguous" commitment of the Treaty of Rome at the outset to freedom of movement for workers[45] and non-discrimination on grounds of nationality,[46] and highlight the extraordinary progress that has been made. An ingenious, "teleologically" oriented Court of Justice,[47] supported to a large extent by the Commission of the European Communities, has pushed beyond a privileged version of the unpromising migrant worker status toward something akin to the U.S. right to travel.

A number of carefully written books and articles explain the now accepted liberal interpretation of "worker," the right to enter and seek work, the important rights of families and survivors of a worker, the right to social advantages including social security, rights to join labor unions, and rights even to reside permanently.[48] Work permits have been abolished and Community nationals

[44] Two recent studies especially useful to examine the rights of migration and state citizenship in the United States are Rosberg, *supra* note 1; and Varat, *State "Citizenship" and Interstate Equality*, 48 U. CHI. L. REV. 487 (1981).

[45] EEC Treaty article 48, of course, mentions only freedom of mobility of workers. As Plender points out, the early discussions of the European Community, represented in the *Spaak Report*, "wrote of the need to make rational use of the 'factors of production' in the Member States, and identified those factors as capital and manpower." R. PLENDER, *supra* note 8, at 39. *See generally* D. COLLINS, THE SOCIAL POLICY OF THE EUROPEAN ECONOMIC COMMUNITY (New York, John Wiley & Sons, 1975).

[46] *See generally* B. SUNDBERG-WEITMAN, DISCRIMINATION ON GROUNDS OF NATIONALITY: FREE MOVEMENT OF WORKERS AND FREEDOM OF ESTABLISHMENT UNDER THE EEC TREATY (Amsterdam, North-Holland, 1977).

[47] *See, e.g.*, Leleux, *supra* note 1, at 386.

[48] *See, e.g.*, COMM'N OF THE EC, COMPENDIUM OF COMMUNITY PROVISIONS ON SOCIAL SECURITY (Luxembourg, Office for Official Pubs. of EC, 1980); E. CEREXHE, LE DROIT EUROPÉEN: LA LIBRE CIRCULATION DES PERSONNES ET DES ENTREPRISES (Leuven, Editions Nauwelaerst, 1982); B. GOODWIN-GILL, *supra* note 12, at 168–86; T. HARTLEY, EEC IMMIGRATION LAW (Amsterdam, North-Holland, 1978); P. LELEUX, EXAMEN APPROFONDIS DE QUESTIONS DE DROIT EUROPÉEN (Brussels, Presse Universitaire de Bruxelles, 1979); LA LIBRE CIRCULATION DES TRAVAILLEURS DANS LES PAYS DE LA CEE (M. Maziotti ed., Milan, Giuffrè, 1974); S. NERI, LE CHAMP D'APPLICATION DU DROIT COMMUNAUTAIRE EN MATIÈRE DE LIBRE CIRCULATION DES TRAVAILLEURS (Milan, Franco Angeli, 1982); Evans, *European Citizenship*, 45 MOD. L. REV. 497 (1982); Ress, *Free Movement of Persons, Services and Capital*, in THIRTY YEARS OF COMMUNITY LAW 285 (Luxembourg, Office for Official Pubs. of EC, 1983); Seche, *Free Movement of Workers Under Community Law*, 14 C.M.L. REV. 385 (1977).

have the right to compete on equal terms with others for all private positions *anywhere* within the Community. Obviously these go much beyond any "rotation system" of migrant workers and provide some evidence of a movement toward Community citizenship where all citizens of the Community share basic Community rights.[49] If we spell out and list these rights, and then compare them with what is available for mobility within the United States, we cannot fail to be impressed with the progress that has been made.

Without underestimating that progress, my purpose here will be to understand some aspects of the comparison that have not been developed as well. The right to mobility in the European Community and the United States will be discussed, but the vehicle initially will be a series of leading court cases chosen to suggest not just what rights exist, but also what assumptions, approaches, and limitations there are in the catalog of rights developed in the Community. In part my purpose is to avoid repeating a story that is now very familiar and, especially with regard to social security,[50] full of technical details that would overwhelm a comparative discussion. But it is also important to see beyond the proliferation of rights to the problem of what really is meant by the pivotal ideas of integration and community and how legal structures relate to those ideas.

A. Illustrative Cases

The case of *Roland Rutili v. Minister for the Interior*,[51] decided in 1975, exemplifies the approach to the free movement of workers taken by the European Court of Justice. Rutili, an Italian citizen (solely by virtue of his father's nationality), was a permanent resident in France and a political and trade union activist. He initially faced deportation charges for his activities during and after the May 1968 events, but the Minister for the Interior later limited the order to a ban on residence in the *départements* of the Lorraine. Rutili appealed to the *Tribunal administratif* of Paris to annul the restriction, and the *Tribunal* requested a preliminary ruling by the European Court of Justice under article 177 of the Treaty of Rome. Rutili claimed the order violated article 48 of the Treaty, which guarantees the free movement of workers, and Council directives issued pursuant to that article.

One obvious point apparent from this case is that the formal guarantees of article 48 now go much beyond a narrow Community interest in labor mobility to promote economic efficiency and safeguard welfare states. Rutili's rights, in

[49] *See, e.g.*, Evans, *supra* note 48; EUROPEAN LAW AND THE INDIVIDUAL, *supra* note 3.

[50] *See, e.g.*, J. HOLLOWAY, SOCIAL POLICY HARMONISATION IN THE EUROPEAN COMMUNITY (Westmead, Gower, 1981); P. WATSON, SOCIAL SECURITY LAW OF THE EUROPEAN COMMUNITIES (London, Mansell, 1980); Knorbel, *Social Security Cases in the Court of Justice of the European Communities, 1978–1980* (pts. 1 & 2), 18 C.M.L. REV. 529 (1981), 19 C.M.L. REV. 105 (1982); Wyatt, *The Social Security Rights of Migrant Workers and Their Families,* 14 C.M.L. REV. 411 (1977).

[51] Case 36/75, [1975] ECR 1219.

fact, have little or nothing to do with whether French employers have work for Italians. Rutili is not a "foreign" worker in any practical sense; he was born in France, has a French wife and French children, and he permanently resides there. Nevertheless, as an Italian he can claim and enforce Community rights. The rights are available to any citizen of a Member State.

Citing article 48 and directives issued thereunder, the Court's decision explains that Rutili has a right to reside in France. It does not matter, furthermore, whether Rutili was employed – a worker in fact – at the time of the contested order. He still possessed these rights because he had worked long enough in the past in France. He therefore can now reside on the same terms as French nationals[52] unless his expulsion could be justified by essentially Community-defined grounds of public policy, public security, or public health.[53] These grounds, in addition, would have to relate to Rutili's "individual circumstances," and "personal conduct" – not, for example, because of high unemployment in France or a desire to preserve jobs for French nationals.[54] And while Rutili's personal conduct was at issue, it did not come within the Community exceptions. Indeed, the Court suggested that he could not be penalized for exercising rights to engage in political and trade union activity.

This decision thus reveals considerable movement toward the recognition of what the Commission termed in its submission to the Court a "basic human right to move freely within a State and to choose to reside there."[55] Rutili was free as an Italian to reside in France, work there, and even engage in certain political activity under the same conditions as French nationals, and France could not decide to expel him, even if unemployed, unless it could justify expulsion under specific criteria that must be judged by a Community standard. The limits to the right claimed by Rutili can be explored below, but the first point is to see how far the Court has gone to recognize a Community right to move and reside anywhere in the Community no matter what the needs of employers or the government's general dislike for an individual.

A useful and comparable American case is *Edwards v. California*,[56] decided by the U.S. Supreme Court in 1941. The controversy arose out of the considerable migration to California from other states during the Great Depression of

52 To the same effect is EEC Treaty art. 7 (non-discrimination on grounds of nationality). *See, e.g.*, B. Sundberg-Weitman, *supra* note 46.

53 [1975] ECR 1219, at 1231. A recent judgment discussing *ordre public* in the context of prostitution is Joined Cases 115 & 116/81, Rezguia Adoui v. Belgian State and City of Liège; Dominique Cornuaille v. Belgian State, [1982] ECR 1665. A useful short discussion can be found in D. Lasok, The Law of the Economy in the European Communities 108–12 (London, Butterworths, 1980). *See also, e.g.*, Druesne, *Ordre public et garanties procédurales offerts aux travailleurs migrants*, 16 R.T.D.E. 428 (1980); G. Goodwin-Gill, *supra* note 12, at 299–306.

54 [1975] ECR 1219, at 1241. *See* sources cited *supra* note 53.

55 [1975] ECR 1219, at 1226.

56 314 U.S. 160 (1941).

the 1930's. Invoking a law enacted in 1860 and in fact typical of that period,[57] California officials arrested Edwards for bringing his brother-in-law, an indigent, into California from Texas. When the statute permitting the arrest was challenged, California responded that other states should not be able "to get rid of their poor ... by low relief and insignificant welfare allowances and drive them into California to become our public charges."[58] The Court unanimously rejected that argument. The federal union, it found, places limits on state power:

> And none is more certain than the prohibition against attempts on the part of any single state to isolate itself from difficulties common to all of them by restraining the transportation of persons and property across its borders. ... [T]he peoples of the several States must sink or swim together, and ... in the long run prosperity and salvation are in union and not division.[59]

This notion of a national "community" raises two immediate questions. First, what prompted the Court in the early 1940's to decide to overrule a relatively typical state law that attempted to deter the movement of indigents into the state? And second, what is the source of this "right to travel" nowhere mentioned explicitly in the U.S. Constitution? As in the European Community, the Court took an expansive view of rights to mobility required by the federal union.

No doubt the Supreme Court's opinion derives in part from social trends toward one nation through improvements in transportation and communication and the growth of commerce. But another critical underlying assumption appears to be an assumed *national* responsibility to address the problem of poverty:

> Recent years, and particularly the past decade, have been marked by a growing recognition that in an industrial society the task of providing assistance to the needy has ceased to be local in character. The duty to share the burden, if not wholly to assume it, has been recognized not only by State governments, but by the Federal government as well. The changed attitude is reflected in the Social Security laws under which the Federal and State governments cooperate for the care of the aged, the blind and dependent children.[60]

We see the importance of the idea of social welfare as at least partly a national responsibility, suggesting that there is no real reason states ought to be able to protect themselves from having to support the poor. The states can "sink or swim" together in part because the Federal Government will "share the burden," and from a federal point of view it does not matter whether poverty is in Texas or California.

[57] Interestingly, the Articles of Confederation that preceded the adoption of the U.S. Constitution in the late 18th century stated in Article IV that the privileges and immunities of a state should be available to free inhabitants of each of the states *except for* "paupers, vagabonds and fugitives from justice." *See* Rosberg, *supra* note 1, at 280.

[58] 314 U.S. 160, 168.

[59] *Id.* at 174.

[60] *Id.* at 175.

The source of this right to travel, interestingly enough, was found by the majority opinion to be in Congress' exclusive power "to regulate interstate commerce."[61] States could not enforce barriers to trade that unconstitutionally burden interstate commerce. For the Court's majority, therefore, labor mobility was linked to the American common market, even if it was interpreted rather expansively.

The concurring Justices, however, developed a more compelling justification for the Court's result, based on the "privileges and immunities" clause of the fourteenth amendment to the Constitution, enacted in 1868.[62] According to Justice Jackson, the right to mobility stemmed from the "human rights" of national citizenship:

> This Court should ... hold squarely that it is a privilege of citizenship of the United States, protected from state abridgement, to enter any state of the Union, either for temporary sojourn or for the establishment of permanent residence therein and for gaining resultant citizenship thereof. If national citizenship means less than this, it means nothing.[63]

The idea suggested by Justice Jackson has been elaborated more recently by the Supreme Court, and we shall move next to one of the leading examples; but it is important to emphasize the relationship of the U.S. right to travel to the notion of primary *federal* citizenship and some *federal* responsibility for social welfare in the states. We can return to these characteristics in contrasting the structure of the European Community.

A U.S. Supreme Court case decided in 1969, *Shapiro v. Thompson*,[64] gives a more current perspective on the issues of mobility and community. Again the challenge was to various state laws discouraging the poor from moving to a new state. These statutes limited welfare benefits to persons who had resided for at least one year in the state. The Supreme Court held that these laws infringed a fundamental right to travel,[65] and that asserted justifications of the states – interests in administrative efficiency, in proving residency, in encouraging work, and in deterring migration – were either impermissible or not sufficiently compelling to justify discrimination against the newly arrived. In Justice Brennan's words, "a State may no more try to fence out those indigents who seek higher welfare benefits than it may try to fence out indigents generally."[66]

Those words, we shall see, cannot quite be applied to the European Community, but cases like *Michael S. v. Fonds national de reclassement social des han-*

61 U.S. CONST. art. I, § 8, cl. 3.

62 There is also a privileges and immunities clause applicable to rights of national citizenship in U.S. CONST. art. IV, § 2.

63 314 U.S. 160, 183.

64 394 U.S. 618 (1969).

65 The Court noted that, "We have no occasion to ascribe the source of this right to travel interstate to a particular constitutional provision," referring to the two privileges and immunities clauses and the commerce clause. *Id.* at 630.

66 *Id.* at 631.

dicapés,[67] decided in 1973, point toward some right of mobility even to maximize welfare state benefits unrelated to work. The plaintiff, Michael S., born in 1954, came to Belgium with his Italian parents in 1957. His father worked in Belgium until 1962, stayed, and earned a pension until his death in 1971. Plaintiff in 1970 applied to a certain rehabilitation program for the handicapped, under a law that applied "to persons of foreign nationality ... on condition, *inter alia*, that such persons had established their residence in Belgian territory before the incapacity was first diagnosed."[68] The reason eligibility was limited was obviously to discourage entry of a handicapped individual into Belgium in order to take advantage of liberal benefits.

Nevertheless, interpreting a Council Regulation of 1968,[69] the European Court of Justice found that Michael S. was eligible for the benefits. The Court first looked to article 7 of the Regulation, which defines the relationship of equality between nationals and Community citizens. Article 7(1) mandates equality "in relation to any conditions of work and employment, in particular in matters of remuneration, dismissal, and reinstatement in occupation or re-employment if he becomes unemployed."[70] Article 7(2) then requires that the Community worker enjoy "the same social benefits ... as the workers of that State."[71] These provisions certainly go far to promote mobility of workers but, as the Court points out, Michael S. has not been a worker, and these provisions by their terms do not apply to families of workers.

Article 12 of the Regulation, however, allowed the Court to reach further. This article recognizes that the policy favoring mobility requires that the family be given some rights as well:

[T]he children of a national of a Member State, who is or has been employed in the territory of a Member State, shall be admitted to courses of general education, apprenticeship and vocational training under the same conditions as the nationals of that State, if those children reside in its territory.[72]

Building upon this language and the goal of integration of the family in the environment of the host country, the Court held that "the child can take advantage of the benefits provided by the laws of the host country with a view to the rehabilitation of the handicapped under the same conditions as nationals who are in a similar position."[73] As in *Shapiro*, it is impermissible to discriminate in

[67] Case 76/72, [1973] ECR 457.

[68] *Id.* at 459.

[69] Council Regulation (EEC) No. 1612/68 of 15 Oct. 1968 on freedom of workers within the Community, JO No. L 257, 19 Oct. 1968, p. 2 ([1968] II OJ (Special English ed.) at 475). Copies of the various regulations are available in T. HARTLEY, *supra* note 48, and the Commission has published the official texts as LA LIBRE CIRCULATION DES TRAVAILLEURS À L'INTÉRIEUR DE LA COMMUNAUTÉ (Luxembourg, Office for Official Pubs. of EC, 1975).

[70] [1973] ECR 457, 463.

[71] *Id.* at 463.

[72] *Id.* at 464.

[73] *Id.*

the provision of certain benefits against individuals who have exercised their right to move and then remain, even if the purpose of the move might be in part to take advantage of liberal social welfare benefits.

B. U.S. Federal and European Community Rights

The comparison of the cases thus points to important similarities. In general terms, the idea is that discrimination against those who choose to exercise a fundamental right to move and take up residence is prohibited. We need, however, to go deeper into this right of equal protection before discovering the real similarities and differences.

First, the rights to equal treatment in the United States for state citizens and new arrivals to the state are not quite as clear as *Shapiro v. Thompson* suggests. The Supreme Court has found, for example, that certain durational requirements can be imposed by states even if the result is to discriminate against new residents and inhibit interstate mobility. Such requirements have been upheld respecting in-state tuition rates for universities,[74] divorce,[75] and admission to the bar,[76] although the reason given is a relatively narrow one – to ensure that only bona fide residents claim rights available only to residents. Nevertheless, the Court has continued to strike down laws that seek to prefer established residents over newcomers, most recently, for example, an Alaskan law that provided for state dividends from oil resources on the basis of length of residency in Alska.[77] In rejecting Alaska's efforts to justify the preference, the Court once more insisted that the right to travel "protects new residents of a state from being disadvantaged because of their recent migration."[78]

Second, the rights to mobility within the Community stop short of the U.S. right to travel even if, as the preamble to Regulation 1612/68 states, "The freedom of movement constitutes a fundamental right of workers and their families" in the European Community.[79] Without detailing the various directives,[80] regulations,[81] and court cases, setting out the rights to mobility and to

[74] *See* Starns v. Malkerson, 401 U.S. 985 (1971) (summary affirmance).

[75] Sosna v. Iowa, 419 U.S. 393 (1975).

[76] *See, e.g.*, Rosberg, *supra* note 1, at 341–44. The contrasting situation for lawyers in the EC will not be treated in this study; lawyers are not really part of the group of individuals we think of when we consider the disadvantaged status of migrant workers. *Cf.* Freeman, *A Common Market for Professionals,* 33 C.L.P. 57 (1980); *see also* Friedman & Teubner, *Legal Education and Legal Integration: European Hopes and American Experience, infra* this book, at nn. 65–69 and accompanying text.

[77] Zobel v. Williams, 457 U.S. 55 (1982).

[78] *Id.* at 60 n. 6.

[79] *See supra* note 69.

[80] On the various types of Community legislation *see, e.g.*, T. Hartley, The Foundations of European Community Law 81–100 (Oxford, Clarendon Press, 1981). The impact of regulations is discussed in *id.* at 197–204.

[81] *See id.* The impact of directives is treated in *id.* at 204–16.

benefits, such as social security, it is useful here to explore briefly just what the rights entail today and contrast them with those of the United States. The comparison will return to the ideas found in the cases just discussed.

A national of a Community Member State currently has a right to travel that includes the right to enter the territory of any other Member State "merely on production of a valid identity card or passport."[82] The purpose for entering must be connected to a "worker" status derived from Community law, but the individual's rights do not depend on an offer of employment "actually made" as article 48(3) seems to suggest. The individual may enter for a period of at least three months to look for work.[83] Any unemployment benefits due from the home state must continue to be paid.

In addition, if the potential Community worker secures employment, he or she is automatically entitled to a residence permit valid for at least five years.[84] The permit cannot be withdrawn on the sole basis that the worker has lost the work because of temporary incapacity or involuntary unemployment,[85] and it can be renewed under fairly liberal conditions.[86] Renewal is replaced by a right to reside indefinitely under certain conditions even if work has ceased. This right is available to workers and self-employed personnel who reach the age of retirement, those permanently incapacitated from illness or injury, and frontier workers.

As shown by the *Michael S.* case and other cases perhaps going even farther,[87] these rights to reside extend to the family of a worker, including the spouse, dependent children and other dependent members of the family.[88] They have essentially the same rights as the worker, plus rights to the same education and

[82] *See* D. Lasok, *supra* note 53, at 101.

[83] *See, e.g.*, Evans, *supra* note 48, at 504. The three month provision comes from the "interpretive declaration" adopted by the Council of Ministers. The statement reads:

> les personnes visées à l'article 1 [de la directive 68/360], ressortissants d'un Etat membre et qui se rendent dans un autre Etat membre pour y rechercher un emploi, disposent à cette fin d'un délai minimum de trois mois; si elles n'ont pas trouvé d'emploi à l'expiration de ce délai, il pourrait être mis fin à leur séjour sur le territoire de ce deuxième Etat. Toutefois, si les personnes susvisées, au cours de la période précitée, devaient être prises en charge par l'assistance publique [aide sociale] du deuxième Etat, elles pourraient être invitées à quitter le territoire de ce deuxième Etat.

See Druesne, *Les prolongements de la libre circulation des salariés: droit de séjour et progrès social*, 18 R.T.D.E. 556, 558 (1982).

[84] *See* Council Directive (EEC) No. 68/360 of 15 Oct. 1968 on the abolition of restrictions on movement and residence within the Community for workers of Member States and their families, art. 6, JO No. L 257, 19 Oct. 1968, p. 13 ([1968–II] OJ (Special English ed.) at 485). The right of residence is not, it should be noted, dependent on the permit, but arises from the Treaty and Directive. Case 48/75, *Royer*, [1976] ECR 497.

[85] *See* Directive No. 68/360, *supra* note 84, at art. 7.

[86] *Id.*, arts. 6 & 7.

[87] *Cf.* Case 32/75, Cristini v. Société nationale des chemins de fer français, [1975] ECR 1085 (discounts to large families by the French railroads must be offered to the Italian family of a deceased worker in France). *See* Leleux, *supra* note 1, at 391.

[88] *See, e.g.*, D. Lasok, *supra* note 53, at 105.

other opportunities available to national children. The rights terminate if the connection with a worker is severed, such as through divorce,[89] but as in the case of *Michael S.*, the family may remain under certain circumstances after the death of a working member.

The worker and the family, then, are entitled to share in the welfare state benefits of the host country, including housing,[90] medical care, and, as provided by the extensive jurisprudence of article 51, social security rights at least equal to what the national workers receive.[91] As in *Shapiro v. Thompson*, the newly arrived migrant worker cannot be deprived of social security rights available to nationals of the state, even if the host country would prefer to deter immigration or save money. Obviously this moves to some extent toward the idea of one community – "we sink or swim together" – as described by the U.S. Supreme Court.

This achievement thus goes well beyond the typical category of migrant worker. In Böhning's words,

> This system of freedom of movement for workers represents a truly remarkable advance into one of the most sensitive areas of every modern nation state. Whereas hitherto migration of workers was handled by the authorities of the receiving country, freedom of movement has become a Community affair. The notion of "immigrant" or "temporary migrant" has been replaced by that of *Community worker*. The same commissioner who in 1961 saw free movement in terms of a factor of production, proclaimed in 1968 that it constituted "an incipient form – still embryonic and imperfect – of European citizenship."[92]

The limits of embryonic European citizenship must now be considered. First, mobility has to be connected to the status of worker in the European Community. Rutili had worked in France and *for that reason* could not have his right to free movement curtailed. The father of Michael S. had worked in Belgium, and only that link enabled Michael S. to claim benefits. But "workers" is a flexible category, and the Court of Justice has been notably expansive in interpreting worker under article 48 (and article 51, dealing with social security). In 1982, for example, the Court found that a British woman, Ms Levin, could not be refused a Dutch residence permit simply because her pay would have been less than what the government in the Netherlands consid-

89 This is explained *id.* at 105–06.

90 *See* Regulation 1612/68 arts. 9, 10, *supra* note 69. Art. 10 does provide that for families to come the worker "must have available for his family housing considered as normal for national workers in the region where he is employed." This provision and its background are discussed in W. Böhning, The Migration of Workers in the United Kingdom and the European Community 17 (London, O.U.P., 1972).

91 According to P. Watson, *supra* note 50, at ix, "In it [the case law of the Court of Justice] can be found not only the interpretation and implementation of Community law, but a real expansion of the rights of the migrant as set out in Community legislation." Holloway also points out how the Court has maximized the rights of migrant workers even when it leads to some discrimination *in favor of* their rights. J. Holloway, *supra* note 50, at 186–87. *See also* Ress, *supra* note 48, at 316.

92 W. Böhning, *supra* note 90, at 18–19.

ered necessary for subsistence.[93] Moreover, the Court added, it would not matter if it could be shown that her purpose in coming to the Netherlands was other than to obtain employment. She was protected because she had in fact obtained a "genuine" occupation.[94] Obviously this makes it easier to take advantage of Community rights, even if there still must be some tie to work.[95]

While it is conceivable that a Community family subsequent to the *Michael S.* case could migrate in order to obtain higher social welfare benefits than would otherwise be available, it is clear that the European Community is not a federal welfare state in the image of *Edwards* and *Shapiro*. First, the right to move freely to search for work obviously does not mean a right to move to and collect welfare benefits provided by the new country. Indeed, as emphasized by Sundberg-Weitman, the three month right to search "is not absolute: the host country may expel a person who is in need of social assistance."[96] Similarly, while a person involuntarily unemployed or temporarily disabled can continue under a residence permit, it is not possible to quit work and continue to claim an indefinite right to reside. While the directive is not specific, it appears that a person voluntarily unemployed can in fact lose the residence permit.[97] And while the social security provisions under article 51 go far to maximize benefits to migrant workers, thereby forcing a country to pay generous benefits[98] to persons who are not their citizens nor even entitled to reside there, only social security benefits available as of right fall within this scheme. Other welfare state benefits, such as social and medical assistance in several countries, are outside its scope.[99]

The nature of the economic rights is not the only limitation on mobility. Free movement of workers brings with it no clear political rights, even if *Rutili* did suggest that some rights to engage in political activities may not be suppressed.[100] It is a basic tenet of Western political theory that individuals should have a voice in the political decisions that affect them, and nothing in the Treaty

[93] Case 53/81, Levin v. Staatssecretaris van Justitie, [1982] ECR 1035. *See generally* Druesne, *supra* note 83.

[94] [1982] ECR 1035, at 1044.

[95] *See* the discussion in Evans, *supra* note 48.

[96] B. Sundberg-Weitman, *supra* note 46, at 140–41.

[97] *See* the explanation in D. Lasok, *supra* note 53, at 102–03; E. Cerexhe, *supra* note 48, at 93; Council Directive (EEC) No. 73/148 of 21 May 1973, on the abolition of restrictions on movement and residence within the Community for nationals of Member States with regard to establishment and provision of services, art. 4, OJ No. L 172, 28 June 1973, pp. 14, 15.

[98] *See* D. Lasok, *supra* note 53, at 130. *See* J. Holloway, *supra* note 50; P. Watson, *supra* note 50; *see also infra* notes 126–27 and accompanying text.

[99] *See, e.g.*, D. Lasok, *supra* note 53, at 118. Of course, some social benefits are available to workers and their families in any event under Regulation 1612/68, art. 7, discussed *supra* text accompanying notes 70–71.

[100] Evans, for example, points out that there is no right to migrate to engage in a demonstration. Evans, *supra* note 48, at 510.

of Rome gives workers such rights.[101] It is true that steps have been taken, after some difficulty, to allow Community workers to participate in labor unions,[102] but there remain serious obstacles connected with political aspects of such participation.[103]

Community institutions have since the 1970's made a number of proposals to move closer to European citizenship, including enhanced mobility and some political rights. The proposals would require action to move beyond the Treaty provisions on mobility of workers.[104] Many of the proposals include provisions for participation in local elections, which a few countries allow to all foreign workers,[105] although more recently the emphasis in Community discussions has been on simply extending the scope of free movement beyond the seeking and taking of employment activities. A notable recent effort is a proposed Directive submitted by the Commission to the Council in the summer of 1979.[106] Despite the objections of the Parliament, which wished to go further, the Commission proposal for free movement would have given Community nationals a right to permanent residence *only* if able to support themselves financially.[107] There would be free movement, but the proposal would discourage "population migrations being undertaken with the sole aim of obtaining the most favourable social benefits."[108] Even as proposed, the Council has yet to approve this Directive.

101 Compare cases holding that there are such rights for those who migrate to another state in the United States. *See, e.g.*, Dunn v. Blumstein, 405 U.S. 330 (1972).

102 For the arduous negotiations with respect to union participation, *see* Evans, *Development of European Community Law Regarding Trade Unions and Related Rights of Migrant Workers*, 28 I.C.L.Q. 354 (1979).

103 *Id.* at 365.

104 Extensions of the EEC Treaty can be based on the authority of art. 235, which provides.

> If action by the Community should prove necessary to attain, in the course of the operation of the common market, one of the objectives of the Community and this Treaty has not provided the necessary powers, the Council shall, acting unanimously on a proposal by the Commission and after consulting the Assembly, take the appropriate measures.

See generally, Evans, *supra* note 48, at 509; T. Hartley, *supra* note 80, at 88–96; Ress, *supra* note 48, at 323; J. Weiler, Supranational Law and the Supranational System: Legal Structure and Political Process in the European Community 255–392 (Ph.D. thesis, Florence, European University Institute, 1982).

105 In 1975, the Commission proposed, *inter alia*, that nationals of Member States be granted "special rights," including certain political and civil rights and the right to vote and hold office in at least local elections. Bull. EC 7/8–1975, at p. 12, points 1301, 1302, 1303.

106 *See* the discussion in Evans, *supra* note 48, at 509–13.

107 *Id.* at 511.

108 Comm'n of the EC, Amended Proposal for a Council Directive on a Right of Residence for Nationals of Member States in the Territory of Another Member State, Doc. COM (80) 358 final (27 June 1980), p. 3.

The problems in adopting even this Directive, and in proposals to broaden the rights of Community workers beyond economic rights toward political and social ones, suggest difficulties in the incremental approach toward European citizenship and what might be termed a European welfare state. The Federal Republic of Germany can stop Community nationals from residing there to take advantage of social welfare benefits to the poor, but California cannot stop U.S. nationals from doing the same. The European Community has moved some distance, as discussed above, toward the idea of a Community that sinks or swims together, but proposals to go further have gone nowhere and appear structurally doomed to failure.

C. Citizenship and Residence

The Community position can be better understood and better contrasted with the United States, however, if we examine it from another approach – fully confronting the question of citizenship. As the more perceptive commentators on the Community political structure have pointed out,[109] the question of citizenship has two aspects. First, it is clear that Community law does not prevent Member States from determining who their full citizens are: The Member States still have a "right to treat nationals of other states as aliens,"[110] lacking any claim to full political and economic participation in the society. In Lasok's words, "Indeed equality, it seems, can be achieved only through a common Community citizenship and the harmonization of the relevant legislation."[111] Second, the status of "residence" needs to gain more importance before a more coherent right to travel can be produced:

S'il est évident que les auteurs du traité ne pouvaient garantir d'une manière absolue le bénéfice de la libre circulation des personnes et des services, ils auraient pu *ratione personae* se référer à d'autres critères que celui de la nationalité, en particulier au critère de la résidence dans un Etat membre.[112]

In the United States state citizenship has a very restricted meaning, and federal citizenship is regulated by the Federal Government. In the European Community Member State citizenship is critical and is hardly affected by Community institutions. In certain situations the consequences are nevertheless very similar. Non-U.S. citizens cannot hold a number of state *or* federal political offices.[113] And the Member States have the right to limit their political

[109] *See, e.g.*, Evans, *supra* note 48, at 515; Ress, *supra* note 48, at 322; *infra* notes 110–112.
[110] Leleux, *supra* note 1, at 393.
[111] D. Lasok, *supra* note 53, at 112. This is not to say, of course, that work towards legal harmony and the reduction of barriers to mobility is futile. Progress has certainly been made in reducing barriers, including notably those with respect to the mutual recognition of diplomas and the like. The point here, however, is to underscore the structural obstacles that hinder certain kinds of Community progress.
[112] E. Cerexhe, *supra* note 48, at 33.
[113] A recent example is Cabell v. Chavez-Salido, 102 S. Ct. 735 (1982) (permanent resident aliens in California can be prevented by state law from becoming probation officers). *See generally, Developments in the Law – Immigration Policy and the Rights of Aliens,* 96 Harv. L. Rev. 1286, 1405—15 (1983) [hereinafter *Developments in the Law*].

offices to their own nationals.[114] Neither the U.S. Supreme Court nor the Court of Justice, it might be noted, has done very well in defining just what political offices can be limited solely on the basis of citizenship. These references to U.S. national and Member State citizenship, however, raise few structural problems and are indeed rather obvious. More interesting is how the differences between *European* and U.S. citizenship lead to some peculiar and irreconcilable outcomes.

State citizenship in the United States means nothing more than that an individual has obtained residence in the state and intends to remain indefinitely. It is therefore available easily and as a matter of right. The problem, for example, with one-year welfare residence requirements from this perspective is that they prevent full state citizenship to new arrivals who intend to remain. As a result of this notion, *federal citizens* who are new arrivals – and new state citizens – receive virtually all the state political rights,[115] such as the right to vote and hold office, and all the economic and social rights that those already there have available to them. The very few exceptions, relating mainly to what is a bona fide intent to remain, can be justified consistent with this view of state citizenship.

The situation differs profoundly in the European Community. There is no right to immigrate beyond a right to residence derived from work. That right does not in any way challenge the Member State's control over its citizenship – the only status that brings full rights to reside, vote, hold political office, and the like. Rutili, an Italian permanent resident in France with a French wife and children, had no right under Community law to demand full French citizenship. "Community" citizenship plus an intent to reside indefinitely in France makes no difference. His rights, in fact, were the same as though he had fulfilled the minimum Community requirements to reside permanently in France after working there. (And of course, if he had been a citizen of a non-Member State residing permanently in France, he clearly would have had no legal recourse.)

The inability under Community law to make residency the crucial variable, in addition, limits the flexibility of the Member States.[116] For example, a Member State might prefer to allocate certain social benefits with a preference to those who intend to reside permanently. Benefits such as family allowances, education, and training for the handicapped, all of which must be provided to Community workers on equal terms with nationals, might be provided less generously to persons and families who do not intend to reside permanently or

114 *See, e.g.*, Case 149/79, Commission v. Kingdom of Belgium, [1980] ECR 3881 (interpreting the exception in EEC Treaty art. 48(4), "employment in the public service," and requiring Belgium to reexamine whether certain positions could be deemed to be in the public service).

115 *See, e.g.*, Rosberg, *supra* note 1, at 339–40.

116 For the United States, Varat (*supra* note 44, at 519) points out that there are two different rights at stake. The first is the right to move to take up residence, which then permits some preference for bona fide residents (who become "citizens" by definition); while the second concerns the rights of those who move without any intention to take up residence.

become Member State citizens by other criteria. Individuals in the United States can move and elect to become citizens of a new state, but if they visit, attend school, or even work in a new state without taking up residency, they often *can* be discriminated against in favor of *bona fide* in-state residents who quite properly are entitled to some priority in receiving state benefits.[117]

This contrast with respect to residence points to a particular vulnerability in Community Member States who *must* provide certain benefits to *any* national of another Member State. Any Italian who can find work in Belgium, for example, can take full advantage of family allowances, educational benefits, and programs for the handicapped such as that Belgium was forced to provide to Michael S. Moreover, Italy can confer its own citizenship on any number of individuals, each of whom may decide to find work – even low paying work, it will be recalled[118] – in Belgium or elsewhere within the Community, and neither Belgium nor Community institutions can compel Italy to stop. The European Community structure allows for a large influx outside the control of the host state. Again, by contrast, an Argentine citizen who lives and works in Italy for twenty years, but does not possess Italian citizenship, does not have the right to work elsewhere in the Community.

Here, too, the United States has a different community framework. The Federal Government can to some extent control the potential migration to California simply by restricting immigration into the country. The European Community has no collective means to control who gets to take advantage of Community rights. Similarly, the exclusive federal control over immigration in the United States leads to rights to mobility for *aliens* just about equal to those available to U.S. citizens. Once the Federal Government allows a person to become a U.S. resident, perhaps subject to federal restrictions, then there is no reason in most instances to let states impose further restrictions.

For example, the U.S. Supreme Court in 1971 held that a *state* could not deny welfare to a non-U.S. citizen who had been granted permanent resident status by the Federal Government.[119] And in 1982 the Court required the University of Maryland to grant in-state tuition rates to alien residents in the state.[120] Indeed, it is generally accepted that a state must provide more benefits in the American federal system to an alien residing in the state than to a U.S. citizen residing in another state. The European Community takes the contrary approach. What matters for Community rights, as opposed to the situation for

[117] *See generally,* Varat, *supra* note 44.

[118] *See supra* notes 93–94 and accompanying text. The potential results are underscored by Joined Cases 35 & 36/82, Morson & Jhanjan v. Netherlands, [1982] ECR 3723. The Court of Justice held that Dutch workers living and working in the Netherlands had no right to bring members of their family to that country; yet, if the Dutch workers had been working in another Member State, article 10 of Regulation No. 1612/68 would have permitted them to bring in their non-citizen relatives.

[119] Graham v. Richardson, 403 U.S. 365 (1976). *See generally, Developments in the Law, supra* note 113, at 1400–04.

[120] Toll v. Moreno, 102 S.Ct. 2977 (1982).

U.S. federal rights, is having nationality within one of the Member States, not residence in the place where benefits are claimed.

An unusual but illustrative recent U.S. Supreme Court case concerned the federal rights of illegal aliens residing in Texas.[121] Texas legislation sought to exclude the non-citizen children of illegal aliens from its schools. The Supreme Court majority held that children of illegal aliens were entitled to the equal protection of the laws of the states, and Texas could not justify its discrimination against them on the common sense ground that it would save state money and discourage illegal immigration. Only the Federal Government, the Court held, might have been able to sanction this discrimination, since primary control over the borders and the rights of non-citizens is vested in that government. Texas lacked the power under the circumstances of the case.[122] In more general terms, the case confirms the fact that only the Federal Government can determine what burdens and benefits relate to the status of alien. In contrast, the rights provided to individuals within the European Community are available only to those who Member States make citizens, and the Community institutions cannot participate in those decisions.

D. Dilemmas of the European Community as a Welfare State

We are now in a position to see that the European Community, in contrast to the United States, is not essentially a single welfare state whose inhabitants sink or swim together. It is also true, however, that individual Member States in the European Community cannot "go it alone" to perfect (or at least protect) their welfare states. The Community worker status allows Member States to stand alone to some degree. Only workers and their families have rights, for example, and they cannot migrate simply to exploit favorable welfare benefits in another country. If the workers become unemployed, similarly, and social insurance runs out, they do not necessarily have rights to social assistance. Quite clearly, the idea is to protect against movement unconnected with opportunities available in the labor market. As stated strongly from a Danish antimarket perspective, "We cannot trade the social welfare in our country for an abstract principle such as European unity."[123]

As the preceding discussion shows, however, the European Community has gone some distance beyond that of independent welfare states who can use migrant workers only for the purpose of safeguarding the benefits of citizens. Most obviously, the Member State cannot explicitly favor its own nationals in employment, social security, education, housing, and the like. Second, it is clear that the Community, in part through the active policies of the Court and Commission, has sought to assume some of the social functions of a "supranational

121 Plyler v. Doe, 457 U.S. 202 (1982). *See, e.g., Developments in the Law, supra* note 113, at 1450–52.

122 457 U.S. 202, at 228 n.23.

123 OJ (Annex) Eur. Parl. Deb., Sess. 1979–80, No. 246, 25 Oct. 1979, at 197.

welfare state." This can be seen, for example, through the perspective adopted by the Commission. The Commission thus emphasized a social welfare role in its 1981 report on poverty in the Community: "There is a limit to the extent to which a Member State can make social progress if it acts alone."[124] Furthermore,

> If every Member State moves together in the battle against poverty, progress will be much less hampered by fears about competition. Those States with the least resources can be helped onwards by transfers of resources within the Community.[125]

Such quotations approach the "sink or swim together" perspective of the American federal system, and there is evidence that the kind of redistribution envisioned by that perspective is already to some degree taking place in the European Community.[126] According to figures produced at a meeting of the European Parliament in June 1980, for example, the Federal Republic of Germany "pays out over BF 1.5 thousand million more annually for the 80,000 Italian children who are still resident in Italy than it would on the basis of Italian legislation."[127] Under Community law Italian workers in Germany whose children are not with them obtain the same family allowance that is paid to Germans supporting children in Germany. Finally, it can be noted that the Federal Republic of Germany has virtually no control over this risk, since neither it nor the Community affects decisions about who is made an Italian citizen and thus able to take advantage of Community rights.

The comparison has highlighted the dilemmas of the European Community if we try to see it as one welfare state. The Community has some characteristics consistent with a single welfare state, as mentioned before, and the Commission and the Court have encouraged such developments. Because of those possibilities of income redistribution, in fact, the Community has faced considerable difficulties in extending the full benefits of Community worker mobility to new Members, beginning with Greece, who would likely join Italy as substantial beneficiaries of the Community social policy as it has developed. Before turning to that problem, however, it is necessary to consider some institutional differences that have not yet been mentioned.

The comparisons show clearly, to repeat, that the United States has evolved much farther than the European Community toward a welfare state where each state's economic and social problems cannot be avoided by the other states. What has not been pointed out is that one essential for this evolution is an active central government capable of taking a federal approach to problems such as poverty and unemployment. Part of the reasoning of *Edwards v. California* depended on the fact that the Federal Government had assumed at least some

[124] Comm'n of the EC, Final Report From the Commission to the Council on the First Programme of Field Schemes and Studies to Combat Poverty, December 15, 1981, Doc. COM (81) 769 final (15 Dec. 1981), p. 147.

[125] *Id.* at 148.

[126] *See generally* J. HOLLOWAY, *supra* note 50, at 260–72.

[127] OJ (Annex) Eur. Parl. Deb., Sess. 1980–81, No. 257, 17 June 1980, at 71.

of the responsibility for the problem of poverty.[128] Obviously Community legislative and executive institutions are not capable, whatever the statements or even ideals of the Commission, of assuming a significant responsibility. Thus, the limitations in the concept of European citizenship as it is understood today should not be seen just as unfortunate barriers to progress. They may be essential to protect the welfare state in Community Member States.[129] Put another way, to have real Community citizenship and a concomitant Community welfare state, Community citizens should be citizens of a government capable in fact of approaching Community problems through effective action at the Community level.

The legal structure, it should already be evident, places real obstacles in the way of the development of a European welfare state community that sinks or swims together. A comparative study of the two federal entities could stop with these observations.

The situation is much more interesting and complicated, however, than is at first evident from a study only of rights of mobility within the Nine. The problem of evaluating the role of rights of mobility – the question of "success" or "failure" – can thus await discussion of formal rights of outsiders and some structural impediments to large-scale enforcement of any of these formal Community rights. We can begin to see the complexity by focusing on current Community approaches to the new and potentially new Member States, Greece, Portugal, and Spain, each of which is a less developed welfare state than the Community countries of Northern Europe.

E. Enlarging the Community: The Fear of Free Mobility

In 1978 the Commission pointed out that the central "social" problem of the enlargement of the Community was the question of extending the right of free movement of workers to countries like Greece, Portugal, and Spain, with lower standards of living and less developed welfare states than most, if not all, of the existing Member States.[130] The result of the negotiations with Greece,[131] conducted no doubt with an eye toward establishing a precedent for negotiations with Portugal and Spain, is instructive.

128 *See supra* note 60 and accompanying text. Of course, much discretion remains vested in individual states over the levels of benefits and availability of certain kinds of social welfare. It may even be that the Federal Government is reducing its responsibility to help states overburdened by essentially national economic problems leading to extraordinary state welfare expenditures. While beyond the scope of this essay, it would be interesting to use the example of the European Community to discuss various versions of the "New Federalism" in the United States. For present purposes the point is only that the European Community lacks an institutional basis even to assume responsibility for smoothing out problems caused by enhanced mobility.

129 *See infra* § V.

130 Bull. EC, Supp. 1/78, 2/78, 3/78.

131 Act concerning the conditions of Accession of the Hellenic Republic, and the adjustment to the Treaties, OJ No. L 291, 19 Nov. 1979, p. 17.

The enjoyment of rights of mobility under the Treaty of Rome was postponed seven years – until 1 January 1988 – after Greece's entry into the Community.[132] Greek workers are to be treated equally, except for some limits on family entry and residence, if they are allowed to enter and work, but their migration can be stopped. The only real encouragement of migration comes from a "Declaration" annexed to the Greek Act of Accession stating that if there are needs for manpower from outside a Member State's regular markets, Greek nationals should have priority equal to that of nationals from other Members States.[133] There is no specific provision, however, for the recruitment of this labor through Community means. Similarly, full rights to social security for a worker's family residing in Greece were postponed three years, until 1 January 1984. The exportation of family allowances has thus been delayed, saving some social security payments, particularly by the Federal Republic of Germany.

While it is not clear that the granting of the full rights of the Community worker status would in fact have led to higher unemployment or increased social expenditures in the existing Member States, there is no doubt that the latter were preoccupied with that possibility. Thus Wathelet refers to

> l'attitude de préccaution qui a conduit à l'adoption d'un calendrier de libération progressive quant à l'accès au travail des membres de la famille du travailleur migrant dans l'adhésion de la Grèce et, plus généralement, aux préoccupations manifestées, notamment en Allemagne, à l'égard des conséquences des migrations sur l'infrastructure sociale.[134]

The welfare state now appears very fragile,[135] perhaps even threatened by a relatively limited mobility and redistribution from richer countries of Northern Europe to the less well off Mediterranean South. The Community is being expanded, but rights of mobility have been delayed. And it may also be that the possibilities for a large community in the American "sink or swim together" sense are diminished by the expansion of the Community to include poor countries whose national welfare policies, for example, the Federal Republic of Germany evidently is not enthusiastic about subsidizing. This possibility points again to the contrast between the European and U.S. legal structures of community. We shall turn to some similarities in the next part of this study, however, combining the perspective of intra-Community rights with the situation of migrant workers from outside the Community and outside the United States. Only then can we begin to appreciate the real dilemmas of an effective "Community" social policy and the related Community right to travel.

[132] A useful discussion of the solution for Greece, and its applicability to Portugal and Spain, is Wathelet, *Liberté de circulation et migrations internationales des travailleurs dans la perspective de l'adhésion de l'Espagne à la Communauté européenne,* in L'ESPAGNE ET LES COMMUNAUTÉS EUROPÉENNES 268, 303–04 (Inst. d'études européennes ed., Brussels, Editions de l'Université de Bruxelles, 1979); more up-to-date (but less accessible) is P. Wathelet, La libre circulation des travailleurs dans la perspective de l'adhésion du Portugal à la Communauté Européenne (provisional draft, n.d.).

[133] Act concerning the conditions of accession, *supra* note 131, at 190.

[134] *See* Wathelet, *supra* note 132, at 280.

[135] *See infra* note 200 and accompanying text.

IV. Protecting Community Welfare States: The Tendencies Toward Failure of the "Ideal" System of Migrant Workers

This essay first explored the idea of the migrant worker as a legal status and then compared the rights of personal mobility within the European Community and the United States. Before adding the dimension of rights of mobility from outside the relevant community, however, it is necessary to clarify the models of community, migrant workers, and welfare state employed before.

The model of a federal welfare state community follows the legal development of the United States, especially over the past thirty years. As the leading judicial pronouncements showed, the model is of a federal government responsible for the economic and social conditions throughout. Barriers to mobility are reduced or eliminated, because it is the right of every citizen of the United States – indeed, everyone permitted to reside there permanently – to migrate freely. If the migration places burdens on the state economies or the state capacities to assimilate migration and provide social services, the idea is that Federal Government is responsible to prevent instability and disruption. The larger welfare state community necessarily takes an *overall* perspective on the social conditions of the inhabitants of the United States. The United States represents in this model only one welfare state, because individual states cannot erect barriers that will maximize the welfare of their citizens.

The model of the "ideal" migrant worker for any single welfare state community is the worker who comes to work, fills a position that would not be filled by nationals, utilizes a minimum of social services, and then leaves if the economy contracts and no longer has a surplus of jobs. This migrant worker serves the safety-valve role described before – "un amortisseur de conjoncture"[136] – which means essentially that when the economy cools down, this individual is sacrificed in order to preserve the welfare state for the community of individuals enjoying free rights of mobility – essentially citizens. We can definitely see elements of this model in the use of migrant workers in the European Community and in the United States. Whether or not we believe that it is a desirable economic or social model, moreover, we can understand its attractiveness, at least in its ideal form, to welfare state employers and governments.

The general consensus, however, is that this model has not been successful, and part of the task here is to understand the limitations and failures of legal attempts to maintain this status. This analysis will proceed in three steps. The first will be to examine the problems caused by the legal and political structure of the European Community described earlier, which is complicated by the creation of two different statuses of migrant workers. The second step will be to see the problems of maintaining the ideal status of migrant worker in any welfare state which purports to respect values of equal justice, democracy and human rights. Then we can confront what can be called the dilemmas of migra-

136 *See supra* note 39 and accompanying text.

tion faced by the United States and the double dilemmas faced by the European Community. We will see why both entities are currently rethinking the question of what to do with foreign labor, and why they are not finding the problems easy to resolve.

A. Community Worker v. Non-Community Worker in the European Community

Several commentators have suggested that the existence of migrant workers from outside the Community poses a major problem for mobility within the European Community. Evans, for example, states that the fall in intra-Community migration since the 1960's

> might be attributable to the fact that the above measures [described in Part III] only provided for Community migrants to enjoy equality of treatment with nationals of the host member State. As far as these measures were concerned, immigrants from third countries might still suffer discrimination. This factor may have rendered such immigrants more attractive to prospective employers than Community migrants. Certainly, there are frequent allegations that employers exploit immigrants from third countries by paying them less than their own nationals and subjecting them to inferior working conditions.[137]

It is true, as Evans and others have also pointed out, that a number of other factors can account for the decline in migration from within the Community, including the relative growth of the Italian economy.[138] But we should recognize that the legal situation within the Community provides a peculiar set of incentives to Member State governments and employers.

If they wish to seek the maximum economic advantage available from workers from outside the country, they are better off recruiting workers from non-Member States. Those workers need not be paid the same as nationals doing the same work, cannot make the same claims as a matter of right to equal housing, to equal social benefits, to benefits to families, to full participation in labor unions, and to stay permanently in a given country. The economic advantages of the ideal migrant worker, we shall see, can be difficult to realize in practice, but it appears that an employer pursuing such advantages is unlikely to seek out workers from another Member State. It will be interesting to see what happens in this respect to workers from Greece, Portugal, and Spain both at the time of joining the Community, when those who are employed are supposed to gain some measure of equality, and at the time when nationals of those countries gain their full Community rights. If jobs are not made available to them, then progress toward European integration will be very difficult to make. Two complications especially hinder such progress.

First, in order for an individual to take advantage of the social welfare provisions of Community law, it is necessary to find work sometime in the country to which an individual wishes to migrate. If workers from outside the

[137] Evans, *supra* note 48, at 498. *See also* J. Holloway, *supra* note 50, at 264.
[138] *See, e.g.*, Wathelet, *supra* note 132.

Community are more attractive to employers of other Member States, then the new rights of mobility to relatively privileged European citizens will amount to little or nothing. Migration in the full sense cannot take place without work, and there will be less work available in fact to Member State nationals if workers from outside the Community are more attractive.

Second, and closely related to the first observation, the Community has no mechanism to cut off, regulate, or even coordinate migration from outside the Community in order to protect the Community benefits of those who are citizens of Member States. In the United States, of course, the Federal Government can not only take action to mitigate the impact of migration, it can also take steps to regulate migration in order to maximize the likelihood that economic opportunities will first be available to persons *within* the larger community.

The situation is no doubt very complicated in fact, but it is clear that the structure of the Community creates incentives that make it very difficult to move very far toward a European welfare state, if that is the goal; and the availability of migrant workers from non-Member States creates a further obstacle to true European citizenship and a European welfare state community.

B. The Failure of the Ideal Migrant Worker in Europe and the United States

In order to understand mobility within the United States and the European Community, and the contribution of migrant workers from outside to that general freedom and economic unity, we must consider the other problems that have been found with efforts to take advantage of the ideal migrant worker in Member States or in the United States. Practical difficulties further challenge the capacity of Community legal and political structures, and they also make clear the complications faced by any effort to build a welfare state community – within one Member State, within the United States, or for the European Community – that maximizes the welfare of community members in part by exploiting the safety-valve potential of foreign migrant workers.

The ideal migrant, as described above, protects the welfare state benefits available to the nationals of a country and enjoys relatively few himself. It can be argued that this ideal migrant serves the economies of both home and host countries, but the economic basis of that contention has been difficult to show.[139] Even if such a system were to be found economically efficient, moreover, for a number of reasons it has proven to be extremely difficult to maintain formally to date in Europe or the United States.

The problems with the status of migrant worker can be explored within domestic legal systems, but first some of the international pressures to provide certain rights to migrant workers should be described. They contribute to the

[139] *See* sources cited *supra* note 32.

difficulty of maximizing the economic value of migrant workers in modern welfare states. First, a number of international organizations, especially the International Labor Organization, have been active in asserting minimal rights for migrant workers.[140] Second, while no human rights treaties create "any express obligation [on a country] to allow aliens to enter its territory,"[141] there is a clear trend in international law to recognize a minimal level of human rights for those who are permitted to migrate for work. At least one commentator, Elsa Chaney, insists that customary international law – binding on all countries – already mandates that "all legal immigrant workers [be accorded] no less favorable treatment than that which they [host countries] apply to their nationals, in relation to the work situation."[142] And the trend in international law, at least until very recently, was to increase the number of rights granted to migrant workers.

Probably the best example of this trend, and of specific rights agreed to by treaty, is the European Social Charter, which became effective in 1965 and has now been ratified by all the countries of the European Community.[143] It provides specifically that "nationals of any one of the Contracting Parties have the right to engage in any gainful occupation in the territory of any other Contracting Party, subject to restrictions based on cogent economic or social reasons."[144] What is most significant, however, is the effort to promote the situation of those who take advantage of that ostensible right to migrate to work. While not going as far as the European Community system of mobility and social rights, the Charter urges positive steps to facilitate effective equality, and "to facilitate as far as possible the reunion of the family of a foreign worker permitted to establish himself in the territory."[145] As interpreted by the European Committee of Experts, which interprets the Charter and reports to the Council of Europe, the European Charter is supposed in addition to weaken the distinction between migrant worker and immigrant:

[140] *See generally* U.N. Sub-Commission on the Prevention of Discrimination and Protection of Minorities, *International Provisions Protecting the Human Rights of Non-Citizens* 21–23, U.N. Doc. E.C.N. 4/Sub. 2/392/Rev. 1, UN Sales No. E.80 x IV.2 (1980); P. SIEGHART, INTERNATIONAL HUMAN RIGHTS LAW (London, O.U.P., 1982); Böhning, *International Migration and the International Economic Order,* 33 J. INT'L AFF. 187 (1979); Chaney, *Migrant Workers and National Boundaries: The Basis for Rights and Protections,* in BOUNDARIES: NATIONAL AUTONOMY AND ITS LIMITS, *supra* note 5, at 37; Swart, *The Legal Status of Aliens: Clauses in Council of Europe Instruments Relating to the Rights of Aliens,* 11 NL Y.B. INT'L L. 3 (1980).

[141] *See* P. SIEGHART, *supra* note 137, at 179.

[142] Chaney, *supra* note 140, at 65.

[143] *See generally* D. HARRIS, THE EUROPEAN SOCIAL CHARTER 145-88 (Charlottesville, U. Va. P., 1984); P. SIEGHART, *supra* note 140, at 489; Swart, *supra* note 140. *See also* Kahn-Freund, *The European Social Charter,* in EUROPEAN LAW AND THE INDIVIDUAL, *supra* note 3, at 181.

[144] European Social Charter, part II art. 18.

[145] European Social Charter, part II art. 19.

"Liberal" regulations should normally make it possible for the foreign worker gradually to have access to activities other than those he was authorized to engage in when entering the host country, and to be perfectly free to do so after a certain period of residence or of activity in his occupation. The letter and spirit of the Article means that, in each State Party, the situation of nationals of other State Parties should gradually become as far as possible like that of its own nationals.[146]

Of course, there is considerable flexibility and ambiguity in the terms of the Charter, and there is no mechanism for enforcement by individual workers, nor even by states who are parties to the agreement.[147] But the Social Charter nevertheless reveals the approach to migrant workers that seems to have been emerging in international law. It is clearly inconsistent with any effort to enforce statements such as the one that "*Deutschland ist kein Einwanderungsland.*"[148]

The European Social Charter has been followed by a European Convention on the Legal Status of Migrant Workers, promulgated in late 1977 by the Council of Europe, and this Convention, while not going so far toward social rights and residency as the Social Charter, does insist on equal treatment and the granting of other rights for families of foreign workers.[149]

Finally, institutions of the European Community have also attempted to promote – at least to a limited extent – the rights of migrant workers from outside the Community. In 1974, the Social Action Program adopted by Council Resolution invoked principles favoring equality of treatment and the improvement of conditions of migrant workers, and the Commission has shown a concern for such migrants and their families in several contexts.[150] We shall return to Community involvement with the conditions of migrant workers from outside the Community,[151] but the point here is simply that the approach of Community institutions contributes to the momentum to provide migrant workers with more rights than the narrowly economic perspective might dictate. Internationally proclaimed norms, in sum, have helped to put the "rotation" or ideal migrant system on the defensive.

146 *See* P. SIEGHART, *supra* note 140, at 186.

147 The Charter relies on a Committee of Experts to oversee its enforcement.

148 *See supra* note 25 and accompanying text.

149 The differences are discussed in Swart, *supra* note 140, at 8. Interestingly, ILO Convention No. 43 of June 5, 1975, which attempted to build on the approach of the Social Charter, has been ratified only by Italy among the countries of the European Community. *See* EC Economic and Social Comm., ACP Migrant Workers and their Families in the EEC (Working Doc. CES 352/82 F/AH/CH/JC, drawn up by Mr Soulat, Brussels, 29 Apr. 1982).

The changing attitudes toward expansive rights for migrant workers is explained by the growing conviction that "too many" migrant workers took advantage of costly social rights, and failed to return home in the recession. *See infra* notes 162–93 and accompanying text.

150 *See* the discussion in Duyssens, *Migrant Workers from Third Countries in the European Community*, 14 C.M.L. REV. 501 (1977).

151 *See infra* notes 233–45 and accompanying text.

The situation as it has developed in specific countries can now be examined. As shown particularly by a recent UNESCO study on the legal status of foreign workers in Europe,[152] legal approaches in a number of individual countries have evolved in a similar direction, beginning with the system described before of residence permits linked to work permits. That system, which purports to allow host countries the maximum flexibility in deciding when workers can enter and how long they can stay, is potentially inconsistent with the international norms just discussed.

The legal regime for migrant workers in the Federal Republic of Germany derives from the "fundamental principle ... that no alien has the right to reside in the country without a residence permit."[153] Residence permits are issued for just one year and are then renewed for two year periods. Administrative authorities may issue permits of unlimited or indefinite duration if the foreign worker has resided continuously for at least five years in the Federal Republic of Germany, holds a special work permit (valid for any occupation and any employer), and satisfies certain other critieria;[154] and a permanent residency permit – the first step toward naturalization – may be granted after eight years of continuous legal residence.[155] A work permit is of course required in order to obtain permission to reside, and the criteria for the work permit take into account whether it will threaten "the job security of German workers."[156] The special work permit – not tied to a specific employer – is obtainable only after five years of continuous and legal employment in the Federal Republic.[157] The legal possibilities, it bears emphasizing, are not guaranteed, even after the difficult criteria are met. They are available from administrative authorities, who *may* but will not necessarily sanction steps toward permanence.

Foreign workers also have limited rights to have their families come to the Federal Republic of Germany. Any member of the family who is sixteen years of age or older requires a residence permit, and the permit is available only after work for three years in the Federal Republic and a showing that adequate housing is available. The general rule, in addition, is that spouses cannot work until after a waiting period of four years.[158]

Under this legal system, the Government of the Federal Republic has the legal power, enforced by the broad discretion given to administrative authori-

[152] *See* IMMIGRANT WORKERS IN EUROPE, *supra* note 23; Ansay, *supra* note 7; THE POLITICS OF MIGRATION POLICIES (D. Kubat ed., New York, Center for Migration Stud., 1979); Lyon-Caen, *supra* note 27.

[153] Honekopp & Ullman, *supra* note 39, at 116. *See generally* Mehrlander, *The Federal Republic of Germany*, in THE POLITICS OF MIGRATION, *supra* note 152, at 145–55; G. GOODWIN-GILL, *supra* note 12, at 16–20.

[154] Honekopp & Ullman, *supra* note 39, at 117–18.

[155] *Id.* at 119.

[156] *Id. See also* Ansay, *supra* note 7, at 19.

[157] *See* Honekopp & Ullman, *supra* note 39, at 120.

[158] *Id.* at 124.

ties, to enforce something like the ideal migrant system.[159] During the years of rapid expansion of the German economy prior to the first oil crisis in 1973, however, there was no reason to invoke the full power of the law. The foreign population was in fact allowed to expand fairly rapidly. It doubled from 1961 to 1967 and increased by a factor of 5.5 again until 1973, reaching some four million or 6.4 percent of the population.[160] From November of 1973 to the present, however, there has been a virtual prohibition on the employment of new foreign workers. With the changed economic climate, the failure to renew residence permits no doubt also reduced significantly the size of the foreign worker population. It has thus been estimated that the foreign worker population shrank by one-fifth between 1973 and 1978.[161]

The German migrant worker system, nevertheless, failed to fulfill its safety-valve role in the way it had been expected. For several reasons discussed below, the Federal Republic did not force large numbers of migrant workers to leave. In fact, only 2.4 percent of the 6.3 million requests for new or renewed work permits in 1974-78 were refused, and even some of those denials may subsequently have been successful.[162] While, according to Böhning, nine out of ten Italian migrants returned on the average to Italy, only three out of ten Turkish workers and five out of ten Yugoslav workers have gone home.[163] Moreover, those who stay in the Federal Republic increasingly brought their families to live with them and also have children at a rate much higher than that of families of German nationals.[164]

The result has been no decline in the total foreign population in the Federal Republic of Germany, only a decline in the number of foreign workers. There were some 4.14 million foreigners present in 1979, compared to 3.97 million in 1973.[165] Thirty percent were from Turkey and 15 percent from Yugoslavia. They now tend to look very permanent. In 1980, 40 percent of all foreigners had resided in the Federal Republic for over eight years and 80 percent over five years.[166] Very few of these de facto immigrants have been encouraged or permitted to obtain German citizenship, suggesting that official policy still considers the foreigners to be "guests," but German policy is beginning to recognize that the migrants are not going away. Their social problems, such as inadequate housing, education, and health care, will have to be addressed by

[159] This may be qualified, of course, by treaties with individual countries, but treaties have not tended to be very liberal in granting rights to migrant workers from outside the European Community. *See* the short summary in R. Rist, *supra* note 38, at 61.

[160] Statistics are *id.* at 61–74; Honekopp & Ullman, *supra* note 39, at 120, 122. Mehrlander, *supra* note 153, at 146–53.

[161] Honekopp & Ullman, *supra* note 39, at 128.

[162] *See* Böhning, *supra* note 25, at 102.

[163] *See id.* at 100.

[164] *See, e.g.*, M. Miller, Foreign Workers in Western Europe: An Emerging Political Force 14 (New York, Praeger, 1981); J. Power, *supra* note 34, at 81; G. Goodwin-Gill, *supra* note 12, at 14–16.

[165] *See, e.g.*, Honekopp & Ullman, *supra* note 39, at 129.

[166] *Id.*

the German Government. It appears that the German welfare state will have to extend some benefits to cover those who, it was once thought, would serve only to protect the benefits extended to German nationals.

France, unlike the Federal Republic of Germany, was traditionally a country that encouraged immigration, and in the 1960's it was relatively easy to come to France, work, and even gain French citizenship.[167] The system of residence and work permits permitted administrative control, but entry regulation was relatively lax. The economic situation in the 1970's brought increasingly severe restrictions on the immigration of workers and their families, and very few foreign workers have been permitted to enter after late 1973.[168] Migration (other than seasonal agricultural workers) has been reduced from 226,066 in 1973 to 50,693 in 1979.[169] It appears, indeed, that while some French liberality can still be seen, the official view has been changed from one of treating foreigners as potential French citizens to seeing them as guestworkers who ought to leave when the economy appears to have no place for them. When the French welfare state underwent the strains of recession and the oil crisis, French legal approaches quickly began to treat foreign workers as having fewer rights and legal entitlements than French nationals.

Probably the most notable example of a French effort to enforce the safety-valve function of foreign workers was a policy, created in June 1977, to provide a financial incentive for foreigners to return home.[170] It covered foreign workers who had been gainfully employed in France for at least five years, even if currently unemployed, with a valid residence and work permit. The program offered air fare for the worker and the spouse, a transport allowance for children, and 10,000 French francs deposited in the country of origin. Any worker who accepted this arrangement could not come back to France and work again. Only some 57,000 out of the four million French foreign population, however, took advantage of this offer, and it was stopped in 1981 by President Mitterrand.[171] The situation in France therefore parallels that in the Federal Republic of Germany. Migrants look very much like immigrants, and the question now is what to do with them.

In short, as numerous commentators now point out,[172] the ideal migrant worker proved difficult to create in Western Europe, including the countries of

[167] *See, e.g.*, Böhning, *supra* note 25, at 102; Moulier & Tapinos, *France*, in THE POLITICS OF MIGRATION POLICIES, *supra* note 152, at 127, 130–38.

[168] Thomas, *The Status of Immigrant Workers in France*, in IMMIGRANT WORKERS IN EUROPE, *supra* note 23, at 41, 42–43.

[169] *Id.*

[170] *Id.* at 54. On hostility to migrants by the Government, *see, e.g.*, Apostolo, *Une politique à la mesure de la crise*, [1976–5] DR. SOC. spéc. 34.

[171] *See* Yerkey, *W. Europe Immigrants Live in No Man's Land*, Christian Science Monitor, 30 Mar. 1982, at 1, 6.

[172] Among them are Benoit, *Face à la crise: le verrouillage européen*, [1976–5] DR. SOC. spéc. 6; Böhning, *supra* note 25; M. MILLER, *supra* note 164, at 12–15; J. POWER, *supra* note 34; R. RIST, *supra* note 38. This is of course the often referred to "lesson from Europe" about the migrant worker status. *See* Martin & Miller, *supra* note 21; Mar-

the European Economic Community. Laws existed to terminate rights of residency and in effect force migrants to return to their countries of origin,[173] but they have not been utilized fully. The 1982 UNESCO study thus concluded,

> As for the theory of the turnover of labour, not only has it been abandoned in the countries that had officially adopted it; in addition, it has always proved to be unrealistic in the sense that it would have been necessary to rely on the compulsory repatriation of migrants in order to put it into practice.[174]

And as others have noted,

> The exact chemistry which permitted permanence is hard to disentangle, but the lesson is clear – even explicit temporary status is very difficult to enforce if individuals have strong incentives to stay.[175]

It is admittedly difficult to ascertain the precise reasons for the difficulties in creating the ideal migrant worker. Several general reasons appear salient, however, and they are worth examining briefly. Without engaging in too much speculation, we can consider concerns linked to the accepted values and legitimacy of democratic states; pressure from third states, bolstered by international agreements and claims described earlier based on customary international law; and direct pressures by interest groups supporting migrant workers.

Part of the explanation is captured in the following quotation, attributed to Max Frisch: "We called for workers, and there came human beings."[176] Economies may be organized on the basis of profit-maximization, but there are limits to what can be done to individuals in the name of economic efficiency. Going too far may jeopardize support for the state and the economic system. As legal scholars have emphasized recently, certain principles proclaimed by modern democratic legal and political systems – such as equality of persons and the generality of laws – are important in justifying the political and economic order,[177] and a legalized category of second-class citizenship is *prima facie* inconsistent with those principles.[178] The inconsistency exists, of course, regardless of whether the second-class citizens are formally entitled to the human rights protections of the legal order. To the extent migrant workers become a more or less permanent feature of a particular country, that country will have to justify its treatment of those workers on other than purely

tin, *Mexican Guestworkers: Solution or Mirage?*, Christian Science Monitor, 25 Jan. 1982, at 23; Martin & Houstoun, *European and American Immigration Policies*, 45 Law & Contemp. Probs. 29 (1982).

173 A summary of the changes in the legal status can be found in Thomas, *supra* note 27, at 240–43.

174 *Id.* at 244.

175 Martin & Houstoun, *The Future of International Migration*, 33 J. Int'l Aff. 311, 314 (1979).

176 Cited in German in Markovits & Kazarinov, *supra* note 41, at 373.

177 *See, e.g.*, R. Unger, Law in Modern Society (New York, The Free Press, 1976); Trubek, *Complexity and Contradiction in Legal Order*, 11 Law and Soc'y Rev. 529 (1977).

178 *See* Walzer, *supra* note 5; Loschak, *Observations sur un infradroit*, [1976–5] Dr. soc. spéc. 43.

efficiency grounds. That may lead to the granting of rights beyond what the ideal migrant should receive as merely an economic "factor of production," and it certainly makes it more difficult to take the ultimate step of expelling migrant workers when the economic demand for their labor diminishes.

It is thus difficult to reconcile the economic logic of the safety-valve role of migrant workers with important values that underpin the political system. This is not to say that it can never be done, nor that an abstraction like "the state" calculates what it can get away with without threatening its legitimacy. The point is that political decisions affecting migrant workers, particularly decisions with a high level of visibility, have been difficult to make solely on the basis that self-interested economic policies justify sacrificing the rights of foreigners. Without recognizing this phenomenon, in addition, it is impossible to explain the pronounced inability of the countries studied here, including the United States with the demise of the Bracero program, to maintain the rotation or ideal migrant system.

In France, for example, we can see several instances where the Government has been forced to retreat from potentially very harsh measures. First, the scheme already discussed, which paid foreign workers to return to their country of citizenship, reveals the tendency to avoid coercive measures. The idea was that a "voluntary" repatriation scheme would not be inconsistent with individual rights and human dignity, as contrasted to more coercive measures. Second, some French efforts have been resisted by institutions that are charged with enforcing legal systemic values, such as the *Conseil d'Etat.* When the Government tried in November 1977 to suspend granting any work permits to members of the families of foreign workers, the *Conseil d'Etat* ruled that the Government had exceeded its authority.[179] The basis for the decision, as described by Eric-Jean Thomas, was that "foreigners residing in France had the same right as French citizens to lead a normal life."[180] The Government also was unable to push the restrictive family policy through other means. According to Thomas,

> The case of France is interesting because that country, after deciding to suspend family immigration, had to go back on that decision owing to the large number of hostile reactions which it elicited, at both the national and international levels.[181]

Even without the legal conscience of the *Conseil d'Etat,* moreover, French policies have been circumscribed. As Böhning reported, the Government proposed in mid-1979 "that work and residence permits be withdrawn from foreigners who were unemployed for more than six months; that the qualification period for permanent resident aliens be raised to twenty years; and that the number of foreigners in the country be reduced by 200,000 each year."[182] The

[179] Dec. of 8 Dec. 1978 [1978] Rec. Leb. 493; Thomas, *supra* note 168, at 51.

[180] *Id.* Of course, it may still be possible for the legislature in France to do what is forbidden to the executive.

[181] Thomas, *Summing-Up and Points of Comparison,* in IMMIGRANT WORKERS IN EUROPE, *supra* note 23, at 211, 221.

[182] Böhning, *supra* note 25, at 103.

Government put aside these plans, however, in response to "an immediate outcry in national and international fora."[183]

Finally, it is notable that President Mitterrand during his campaign criticized some of the restrictive policies of his predecessor.[184] Giscard's policies, despite the promises of his 1974 campaign, were described as immoral, smacking of "racism" (and, interestingly enough, also criticized as ineffective).[185] Upon taking power, the Mitterrand Government thus discontinued the scheme for financial encouragement to depart from Fance and implemented several other relatively liberal reforms.[186] Foreign workers still are not doing well in France, as will be pointed out below, but Mitterrand at least initially appeared to bolster their status.

The German evolution has close parallels to the French inability to enforce the rotation system – parallels all the more striking given the longstanding emphasis in the Federal Republic that immigration was not to be a consequence of labor migration. As in France, there has been much discussion of forcing migrant workers to leave when they no longer have work.[187] Böhning points out that successive Federal Governments "tolerated, even fostered, a climate of legal and material insecurity that has made many a guestworker feel unwelcome."[188] Nevertheless, despite trial balloons in the early 1970's, the official policy has been: "The limitation of the duration of stay of foreign employees will not be effected through [police] measures under the law relating to foreigners."[189] Discussion still continues in Germany about schemes such as the French one to encourage voluntary repatriation, but a 1977 Intergovernmental Commission Report rejected "the notion of lump sum payments as an incentive

[183] *Id.*

[184] *See, e.g.*, Miller, *Reluctant Partnership: Foreign Workers in Franco-Algerian Relations, 1962–1979*, 33 J. Int'l Aff. 219, 227 (1979). *See also, e.g.*, Echikson, *France's Lagging Economy Leads to Crackdown on Foreign Workers*, Christian Science Monitor, 16 Feb. 1983, at 3.

[185] *Id.*

[186] The reforms included amnesty for 120,000 undocumented foreigners in France, new and specific requirements for entry into France, and stronger procedural safeguards. Loi 81–973, JORF, 30 Oct. 1982, p. 2970; Décret 82–442, JORF, 29 May 1982, pp. 1711–12. *See, e.g.*, Vincent, *La réforme de l'expulsion des étrangers par la loi du 29 octobre 1981*, [1982] Recueil Dalloz, I, Doctrine 3054; Evans, *Immigration Law Reform in France*, 32 I.C.L.Q. 516 (1982); M. Schein, *supra* note 24, at 17–18.

[187] *See, e.g.*, R. Rist, *supra* note 38, at 57–88.

[188] Böhning, *supra* note 25, at 102.

[189] *Id.* As Markovits and Kazarinov point out,

> The German government faces a conflict of interest with respect to migrant workers. On the one hand, it seeks to promote the short-run profits of German capital, while on the other it faces a dilemma stemming from occasional attempts to improve the social welfare of the foreign workers. A government which prides itself on social democracy and humanitarian values cannot allow approximately 10 percent of its working population to suffer gross social injustices and discrimination.

Markovits & Kazarinov, *supra* note 41, at 379.

to leave the country."[190] Foreign workers can be very unpopular, but democratic governments find themselves limited in the policies they can adopt openly.

The problem of reconciling fundamental values and the economic status of migrant worker thus creates obstacles to the enforcement of that status. That difficulty, it can now be added, is not simply one that perplexes the minds of decision-makers; it also provides a strong political argument for those who take up the cause of migrant workers. They can force the debate and place the Government on the defensive.

The obvious representative of interests of migrant workers is the country of origin, which can structure its arguments in terms bolstered by the emerging norms of international law discussed before. There are numerous examples of bilateral agreements relating to migrant workers, and those also may provide a basis for international pressure and redress. Turkish efforts on behalf of its citizens in the Federal Republic of Germany, although limited, may help focus some concern,[191] and the sometimes stormy relationship between Algeria and France illustrates the same theme. Mark Miller describes this "reluctant partnership" as "another theatre of bilateral conflict," with the Algerian Government arguing for improved conditions and against forced expulsion, which would also have severe economic repercussions in Algeria.[192]

In addition to these international pressures to humanize the migrant worker situation, migrant groups have asserted their own rights, and they have been aided by labor unions on a number of important issues. Admittedly there are limits to the political rights and political activities open to non-citizen workers and their families, but strikes, demonstrations, demands to be heard, and other forms of political pressure do provide some political power. A recent study,

[190] *See* Mehrlander, *supra* note 153, at 154. Very recent reports are of increasing efforts to encourage migrants to leave through subtle administrative means and even through financial help. *See, e.g.,* Newman, *Western Europe Hints that Foreign Workers Should Go Back Home,* Wall Street Journal, 9 May 1983, at 1. According to one news account in the summer of 1983, the Government just finished a project to be enacted in the autumn. The program would apply to workers unemployed between October 1983 and the end of June 1984, would involve a payment of 10,500 marks plus 1,500 per child, and would apply to some 7,000 persons in 1983 and 12,000 in 1984. The Government, it should be noted, is selling the program as a way to "decongest" foreign areas in Germany in order to facilitate the assimilation of those who remain. Clément, *Le repatriement volontaire d'une partie des travailleurs immigrés va être encouragé par des primes,* Le Monde, 24 June 1983, at 6, col. 3. For Italian pessimism that Community workers might also be involved, *see Bonn vuole mandar via anche i lavoratori CEE,* Corriere della Sera, 23 June 1983. An article reviewing these efforts, which appeared while this chapter was in press, is Gupte, *Germany's Guestworkers,* N.Y. TIMES MAGAZINE, 19 Aug. 1984, at 88.

[191] *See, e.g.,* Kubat, *Turkey,* in THE POLITICS OF MIGRATION POLICIES, *supra* note 152, at 247; Thomas, *The Migratory Phenomenon and Returning Migrants in Turkey,* in IMMIGRANT WORKERS IN EUROPE, *supra* note 23, at 179.

[192] *See* Miller, *supra* note 184. *See generally* M. MILLER, *supra* note 164, at 30–82.

undertaken by Mark Miller, thus insists that commentators who claim that foreign workers lack any power are wrong:

> Contrary to the political quiescence thesis, it will be seen that foreign workers possess considerable resources that are of political significance not only to the migrants themselves but also in terms of national and foreign politics in both the emigrant host and sending societies.[193]

He concludes, in fact, that foreign workers have emerged as "one of the most active elements in advanced industrial labor disputes."[194]

The examples cited by Miller, it should be noted, should not be taken to prove that foreign workers are really turning much political policy toward their interests. The workers at best are able to win a few formal concessions, and, as we shall see, the relative weakness of their groups has important implications for the realization of legal rights.[195] The point here, however, is only that the migrant workers have sufficient power to publicize their plight, draw attention to inconsistencies between stated political and legal values and the economic status of migrants, and to help to prevent governments from ignoring those values that the migrant status seems to belie. It is very hard to deport the unemployed and to prevent the reunification of families of foreign workers.

As a result, as noted before, the foreign population has not diminished enough to enable the status of migrant worker to serve fully its safety-valve purpose in Western Europe, leading in turn to at least three consequences that can now be examined. New labor migration from outside the European Community has for the most part been halted. European countries with large foreign populations must confront the prospect of extending the welfare state to them. And illegal immigration has increased considerably.

First, the halt to new labor migration, already described before, obviously relates in part to the decline in economic growth in the 1970's and 1980's. Even if foreign workers primarily take work that would not be filled by nationals,[196] the general reassessment of migrant workers probably would have taken place anyway. Ray Rist thus argues as follows:

> Though the official pronouncements suggested that the economic turn down and the subsequent increases in unemployment were the basis for the various bans, the issue appears to have been more complex and directly related to the perception of increased social costs. The immigrant labor force was becoming more politicized, the antagonisms with the nationals growing more pronounced, and the social welfare costs were rising.[197]

Put simply, the perception was that the safety-valve function failed doubly. Instead of leaving when the economy declined and protecting the welfare state benefits of citizens, migrant workers stayed, became increasingly permanent, and then drained welfare state benefits further. Given the inability to enforce a rotation system, the costs of migrant workers appear to have exceeded their

[193] *See* M. Miller, *supra* note 164, at 22.
[194] *Id.* at 195.
[195] *See infra* § IV.
[196] *See supra* note 35.
[197] Rist, *supra* note 19, at 212.

economic benefits in the host country. Moreover, it is not just that migrant workers can claim certain benefits from the state and increase unemployment; they increasingly present serious social problems akin to those of other minority victims of discrimination.

Now the concern is what to do with this foreign population, which predictably continued to grow through the reunification of families and the birth of new children. In September 1981 two million immigrant children attended the schools of the European Community countries, and in some cities these children amounted to 30 or 40 percent of the population of school children.[198] The International Labor Organization has referred to a "time bomb" and estimated that one-third of the children in Western Europe will be "foreign" by the end of the century, and these very large numbers are forcing European countries to revise their policies toward assimilation and education.[199] The foreigners are unpopular, they are blamed for the current levels of unemployment, and there have been increasing numbers of violent encounters, but the former migrants still are not leaving in large (enough) numbers. Problems of assimilation present a new challenge to the welfare state, and officials have even feared that it "could collapse under the weight of foreign workers."[200]

C. Undocumented or Illegal Migration and the Status of Migrant Worker

The stopping of legal migration has another consequence; it promotes illegal movement, even in a recession, to take advantage of higher wages and standards of living in developed countries. Numerous sources report a dramatic increase in illegal immigration to the European Community in recent years.[201] Some observations can be made here about that movement, but the better example is of course the United States, where the estimated number of "undocumented workers" is staggering.

Illegal immigration into the United States must be understood against the background of experience with the notorious Bracero program, in effect from 1942 to 1964 and involving some five million male Mexican workers entitled to

[198] *See* OJ (Annex) Eur. Parl. Deb., Sess. 1980–81, No. 274–1, 18 Sept. 1981, p. 291 (remarks of Mr O'Kennedy, Member of the Commission); *see also* Eur. Parl. Working Docs., Sess. 1980–81, No. 1–329/81, 30 June 1981, *Report Drawn Up on Behalf of the Committee on Youth, Culture, Education, Information and Sport on the Education of the Children of Migrant Workers* (Rapporteur, Mrs P.J. Viehoff) [hereinafter cited as *Report on the Children of Migrant Workers]*.

[199] *See* Fouquet, *supra* note 21.

[200] *See* Yerkey, *supra* note 171; Fouquet, *supra* note 21 (both articles quoting officials complaining of the threat to the welfare state posed by the migrant workers).

[201] *See, e.g.*, Power, *The Great Debate on Illegal Immigration - Europe and the USA Compared,* 33 J. Int'l Aff. 239, 244–45 (1979) (although there are stiffer sanctions available in Europe); R. Rist, *supra* note 38, at 77–78.

very few rights indeed,[202] and a modified, much smaller migrant worker program in effect today called the H-2 program.[203] The controversial Bracero program came as close as any official policy can to a perfect rotation system, designed for the import and export of inexpensive agricultural labor.[204] Suffering from economic problems sufficiently serious for the Mexican Government to see for itself a safety-valve function in sending workers away,[205] the bilateral arrangements and their enforcement were structured overwhelmingly to favor the interests of U.S. agriculture.

For the growers the program was a dream: a seemingly endless army of cheap, unorganized workers brought to their doorstep by the government. United States employers benefitted from a risk-free pool of menial labor. They paid no social security, fringe benefits, insurance, or hospitalization. And they determined all the working conditions, hours, wages, and living accommodations.[206]

The program had its critics from the start, including labor unions concerned about competition for jobs and downward pressure on wages. The conditions of the workers gradually became known to the general public, and the "appeal to social justice" began.[207] By the 1960's, finally, "the stark poverty of migrant workers was beginning to trouble the national conscience."[208] John F. Kennedy was President, new social reform policies were being followed, and it had become more difficult in the wake of new civil rights developments to defend inequality on the basis that Mexicans were somehow more suited to "stoop labor" or actually liked the conditions under which they worked. The program thus failed to gain extension past 1964.

All that remains of the approach embodied in the *Bracero* program is a much smaller scale "H-2" program,[209] which allows the importation of 10–30,000 temporary foreign workers annually from Mexico, the Caribbean, and Canada, primarily for harvest work.[210] Here, too, neither social security nor unemployment compensation is available to workers, and no contributions need be made by employers. Not surprisingly, the program has been criticized. The important Select Commission on Immigration Policy Final Report, released in 1981 under the title *U.S. Immigration Policy and the National Interest*, recommended

202 *See supra* notes 28–30.
203 The existing "H-2" program, which allowed in some 36,000 migrant workers in 1981, is discussed *infra* notes 209–10 and accompanying text.
204 *See, e.g.*, Garcia y Griego, *supra* note 28, at 53; Hawley, *The Politics of the Mexican Labor Issue*, in Mexican Workers in the United States, *supra* note 28, at 97; Lopez, *supra* note 15, at 663–67.
205 *See* Garcia y Griego, *supra* note 28, at 70, 67.
206 G. Halsell, The Illegals 9 (New York, Stein & Day, 1978).
207 Hawley, *supra* note 204, at 107.
208 *Id.* at 111.
209 8 U.S.C. § 1101 (a)15(H)(ii).
210 Reubens, *Immigration Problems, Limited-Visa Programs, and Other Options*, in The Border that Joins, *supra* note 25, at 187, 206–08; Select Comm'n on Immigration and Refugee Policy, 97th Cong., 1st Sess., U.S. Immigration Policy and the National Interest 227 (Comm. Print, 1981); Lopez, *supra* note 15, at 672.

no extension of the H-2 program or the adoption of any other enforced migrant status, and it also favored some reforms in the H-2 program itself, including the provision of "the same benefits as U.S. workers."[211] Any debate about migrant workers in the United States must focus above all on the phenomenon of illegal immigration. Illegal immigration, we can see, is the real successor to the *Bracero* program.

While there was substantial illegal immigration even during the *Bracero* program, its dimensions have multiplied since 1964 when that program terminated. Illegal aliens – undocumented workers – fill a large variety of unskilled and semi-skilled positions in the U.S. economy,[212] and the number is now estimated conservatively to be somewhere between three and six million.[213] About half the illegal immigrants come from Mexico (a large portion is also students and others who overstay their visas). The Mexican nationals have been the focus of most attention, and they will also be the principal concern here, but it should be remembered that other groups can also be important, such as the large influx of Haitians and Cubans in recent years.[214]

Reasons for this phenomenon are complex, related no doubt to a great extent to the tremendous differential in wages paid in the United States[215] and Mexico and the termination of the *Bracero* guestworker program as one way to get to the United States legally. The border, moreover, is long and difficult to monitor carefully. It is therefore probably impossible to stop completely this migration. It is misleading, however, to see this movement as the result *merely* of the higher standard of living in the United States.[216] The problem is much more complex and involved with the politics of immigration.

First, most migrant labor, legal or illegal, has been recruited directly or indirectly by employers, and the U.S. Government has been willing to tolerate that employment relationship.[217] In the words of Manuel Garcia y Griego:

211 Select Comm'n on Immigration and Refugee Policy, *supra* note 210, at 42–45, 229.

212 *See, e.g.,* D. North & M. Houstoun, The Characteristics and Role of Illegal Aliens in the U.S. Labor Market: An Exploratory Study (Washington, D.C., Linton & Co., 1976); Cornelius, *Illegal Mexican Migration to the United States: Recent Research Findings and Policy Implications,* in Selected Readings on U.S. Immigration Policy and Law 65 (Washington, D.C., U.S. Government Printing Office, 1980). M. Piore, *supra* note 18; Corwin & Fogel, *Shadowy Labor Force: Mexican Workers in the American Economy,* in Immigrants – and Immigrants, *supra* note 28, at 257; Briggs, *Foreign Labor Programs as an Alternative to Illegal Immigration: A Dissenting View,* in The Border that Joins, *supra* note 25, at 223.

213 *See, e.g.,* Briggs, *supra* note 212, at 243; Reubens, *supra* note 210, at 189.

214 *See generally* Segal, *The Half-Open Door,* [1983] Wilson Quarterly 116 (No. 1); Stepick, *Haitian Boat People: A Study in the Conflicting Forces Shaping U.S. Immigration Policy,* 45 Law & Contemp. Probs. 163 (1982).

215 *See, e.g.,* Bustamonte & Martinez, *Undocumented Immigration from Mexico: Beyond Borders But Within Systems,* 33 J. Int'l Aff. 265 (1979).

216 *See generally* Böhning, *supra* note 25, at 105–16; *Developments in the Law, supra* note 113, at 1438–40.

217 *See, e.g.,* Harwood, *Can Immigration Laws Be Enforced?,* 72 The Public Interest 107 (Summer, 1983); Lopez, *supra* note 15, at 668 ff.

Those who argue that the United States bears no responsibility to Mexican migrants who recently have entered illegally ignore the long-standing involvement of U.S. employers in promoting this flow, and the U.S. government in encouraging the violation of its immigration laws in order to accomplish its foreign policy objectives.[218]

We find governmental acquiescence through budget cuts in border patrols, for example, and in the so-called "Texas Provision" of 1952, which specified criminal punishments for "harboring" undocumented aliens but not for employing them.[219] Texas sought this law precisely in order to allow employers to hire undocumented workers with impunity.

It must be recognized, in addition, that undocumented workers in fact provide the economic benefits of the rotation system.[220] Bustamonte and Martinez emphasize, for example, that the label of "undocumented" makes the job seeker a criminal, or outlaw, which

> implies the possibility that human and labor rights may be violated since there is no defense against an employer of Mexican undocumented immigrants. ... This vulnerable condition acquired by the migrant on crossing the international border without papers is favorable to the employers' interests insofar as a worker protected under the law means higher costs for the employer. ... [T]he situation offers the Mexican worker the possibility of getting work in the United States as long as he is willing to accept the condition arising from the label of undocumented.[221]

Furthermore, illegal immigrants can be made to rotate simply by the Government uncovering their illegal status and deporting them. In Power's words, "Illegal immigration ... suits everyone's short-term interests."[222] It is difficult to make human rights claims or argue for minimal conditions or benefits in favor of outlaws. The system leads to a docile workforce that enjoys very few social services (despite paying some taxes), and can be made to leave with little or no outcry about human rights or inequality. The ideal migrant may be an undocumented one, although here too there may be limits to what societies based on law can tolerate.

D. Current Debates and Policies in the U.S. and the European Community

The current debates about rights to mobility, and the political possibilities for action, must therefore take into account the role of illegal migration in the United States. According to available sources, the flow of illegal migrants has also increased substantially in Western Europe since the closing of borders to

218 Garcia y Griego, *supra* note 28, at 79.

219 *Id.* at 63–64. *See also* Lopez, *supra* note 15, at 667–69.

220 *See* Böhning, *supra* note 25, at 113. Böhning points out that, "It is widely accepted that enforcement efforts are inversely related to the state of the labor market and that INS [Immigration and Naturalization Service] officers turn a blind eye to certain situations of illegal employment." *Id.*

221 Bustamonte & Martinez, *supra* note 215, at 274.

222 Power, *supra* note 201, at 244.

new migrant workers from outside the European Community.[223] We now turn to that policy debate in the United States, which will be followed by the still more complex policy problems faced by the European Community and its institutions. These debates begin to illustrate the interaction today between "economically desirable" laws about labor migration and the concerns for human rights and democratic legitimacy just discussed.

For the United States, a perspective that concentrates only on the welfare of its citizens and lawful residents naturally sees a role for migrant workers. The first problem is that such a program is very difficult today to implement, with human rights pressures tending either to stop migration or defeat schemes designed to prevent migrants from becoming immigrants. The second problem is that, while "illegal" worker migration to a certain extent serves the purpose of a true migrant scheme, it is also difficult legitimately to allow such a system to continue once it has gained public notoriety and it becomes clear that, here, too, "undocumented" does not mean that the workers with that status are not human beings.[224] Finally, since the United States Government is responsible for the welfare of its citizens and residents, and for the control of the entry and stay of foreign nationals in the United States, it must heed the demands of individuals and organizations who contend that migrant workers are displacing U.S. workers from their jobs and exacerbating the problem of unemployment. Because of lower pay and the kinds of jobs undocumented workers fill, the United States is not fully enforcing the safety-valve role of foreign labor. The issue is still hotly debated, but many still feel that jobs filled by undocumented workers would otherwise be filled by U.S. citizens or legal residents.[225]

The Carter administration had little luck with reforms proposed in 1977, and undertook to reach a new policy consensus through the appointment of a Select Commission on Immigration and Refugee Policy, which reported to the President and Congress on 1 March 1981.[226] The Commission, as noted before, rejected any new migrant worker program or extension of the H-2 program, and it also made several proposals for the problem of undocumented migrants.[227] It called for "better border and interior controls," "economic deterrents in the workplace," and "once new enforcement measures have been instituted, legalization of certain undocumented/illegal aliens who are already in this country."[228]

[223] *See supra* note 201.

[224] *See, e.g.*, Corwin, *A Human Rights Dilemma: Carter and "Undocumented" Mexicans*, in IMMIGRANTS – AND IMMIGRANTS, *supra* note 28, at 320. For an optimistic vision of U.S. legal developments *see* Schuck, *The Transformation of Immigration Law*, 84 COLUM. L. REV. 1 (1984).

[225] *Compare* M. PIORE, *supra* note 18, *with* Fogel, *supra* note 35; and Briggs, *supra* note 212, *with* Reubens, *supra* note 212.

[226] *See* SELECT COMM'N ON IMMIGRATION AND REFUGEE POLICY, *supra* note 210.

[227] *Id.* at 48.

[228] *Id.* at 45, 35–86.

The Reagan Administration received the report but then appointed its own Task Force on Immigration and Refugee Policy. This Task Force reported in the summer of 1981. In contrast to the report of the Select Commission, this study proposed several options to create a legal migrant program, and the Administration recommended that there be experimentation with a proposal for a two-year "pilot program" for up to 50,000 Mexican workers.[229] The workers would be free to change employers while in the country for nine to twelve months, but would not work on jobs where there was an adequate supply of American workers. And the workers would not be able to bring spouses or families, receive welfare benefits, food stamps, or unemployment compensation.

The reform bill proposed by the Reagan Administration has been one of the most controversial to be introduced in Congress in recent years. It has undergone substantial amendment, which has among other things resulted in the abandonment of the proposed pilot program. The bill which passed the Senate but not the House in 1983 – the Simpson-Mazzoli bill – would: (a) provide for employer sanctions (penalties on employers hiring undocumented workers), now opposed by not only the Chamber of Commerce but also by Hispanic groups who see it as a form of invidious discrimination; (b) increase the border patrol; (c) grant amnesty to numerous undocumented individuals who must wait five years for citizenship and at first are ineligible for federal welfare benefits; and (d) streamline the H-2 program for seasonal agricultural workers, although the effect on numbers in the program is not specified. In addition, the new bill would maintain the number of individuals allowed to immigrate for non-political reasons at 425,000 annually.[230] For the moment, proposed reforms include no new guestworker program, but the debate is continuing and the status of the streamlined H-2 program unclear. The question remains whether there are ways legitimately to gain the benefits of migrant labor without incurring potentially intolerable social costs. Individual European countries have not succeeded in developing an acceptable legal order formally premised on a safety-valve role for foreign workers, and it is not clear if the United States will make its own effort in the future.

229 *See, e.g.,* Abrams, *American Immigration Policy: How Strait the Gate,* 45 LAW & CONTEMP. PROBS. 107, 125–34 (1982); Briggs, *supra* note 212, at 235; Hiller, *Immigration Policies of the Reagan Administration,* 44 U. PITT. L. REV. 495 (1983); Lansing & Alabart, *The Reagan Administration Proposals on Immigration: The Problem of the Undocumented Alien in the United States,* 13 CAL. W. INT'L L.J. 1 (1983); Semler, *Temporary Foreign Labor: The Administration's "Guestworker" Proposal,* 15 CLEARINGHOUSE REV. 642 (1981).

230 The current situation is described in COMM. ON THE JUDICIARY, REPORT TO ACCOMPANY S. 529. IMMIGRATION REFORM AND CONTROL, S. Rep. No. 98–62, 98th Cong., 1st Sess. (1983). After this chapter went to press, there was another inconclusive effort to pass the bill. Interestingly, the decisive issue seems to have been costs. King, *Costs of Immigration Reform, Measured and Unknown, Drowned 1984 Bill,* N.Y. Times, 17 Oct. 1984, at 9.

The situation within the European Community is even more complex. Individual countries, as noted before, have stopped much of the legal migration from outside the Community, and it appears that already there has been a large increase in illegal immigrations despite the availability of sanctions on employers. Estimates begin with the figure of about 600,000 reported by the Commission of the European Communities in 1979.[231] But the problem is not just controlling the situation within individual countries; again it relates to the peculiar legal structure of the European Community.[232] As we shall see, the migrant worker problem for individual countries is necessarily a Community concern.

Most obviously, the efforts to make European jobs available first to Europeans, as U.S. jobs are still available (within the limits of federal control over worker migration from outside) first to U.S. nationals, suffer by the weaknesses of European Community institutions. They can neither control legal nor illegal immigration into Member State countries, nor have any impact on who becomes a national of a Member State and therefore able to invoke Community rights of mobility. In addition, the Community, as noted before, lacks an institutional structure capable of ameliorating the problems of legal and illegal immigrants from outside the Community. These dilemmas, which go beyond those faced by the individual Member States, further hamper European Community efforts to develop coherent policies that treat the problem of migrants from a welfare state community perspective. The relatively few efforts that have been undertaken demonstrate these problems in Community policy-making and structure. Member States have been forced to react to concerns about the human rights of migrant workers, but the European Community, feeling similar pressures to react, is institutionally incapable.

In the late 1960's and early 1970's, according to the Commission's former Director General for Social Affairs, pressures built for the Community "to be seen to be more than a device to enable capitalists to exploit the common market; otherwise it might not be possible to persuade the peoples of the Community to accept the disciplines of the market. The common market had to evolve into a genuine Community. ..."[233] At first the proposed reforms were fairly ambitious, including improvements in working conditions, better employment opportunities, and more worker participation. The change in economic climate after 1973, however, sharpened the focus on the plight of the migrant workers in the Community.[234] Additionally, enthusiasm for Community-wide welfare state policies dampened during the recession, as Member States concentrated on the welfare of their own citizens.

The first explicit Community social attention to problems of migrant workers occurred with the Social Action Program adopted by Council Resolution on January 21, 1974. In 1976 another Resolution of the Council clarified

[231] *See* Power, *supra* note 201, at 244–45.

[232] *See supra* notes 93–122 and accompanying text.

[233] Shank, *The Social Policy of the European Communities*, 14 C.M.L. Rev. 375, 378 (1977).

[234] *Id.* at 379.

and expanded the approach taken before.[235] The aims of these programs were to promote consultation about migration policy from non-Community countries, the control of illegal immigration, and the treatment of non-Community migrants. As stated strongly by the Commission in 1976,

> the Community finds itself with a large unassimilated group of foreign workers who share almost all the obligations of the society in which they live and work but, more often than not, have a less than equal share in its benefits and rights. This situation is in the long term intolerable – degrading for the migrant and dangerous for the Community.[236]

Thus, it was suggested, "one of the basic objectives of an action programme for migrants must be the progressive elimination of all discriminations against them in living and working conditions, once, in the case of third country migrants, they have been legally admitted to employment in the Community."[237] The Commission has continued to take this position, as has the Parliament in recent years, but the Council has not moved to implement concrete measures.[238]

First, a directive concerning the fight against illegal immigration, proposed in 1976 by the Commission and revised in 1978, has been blocked by the Council of Ministers.[239] The aim of harmonizing national legislation to suppress illegal migration and work has not been fostered at the Community level. The fate of a Commission proposal for a Council directive on the education of the children of migrant workers is also instructive. While the Commission and Parliament favored coverage including children of migrant workers from both inside and outside the Community, the Council in July 1977 limited the scope to children of migrant workers of Member States.[240] And a 1979 communication of the Commission concerning consultation about immigration policies for nationals of non-Member States has not been pursued by the Council. It is clear that the Council, representing more directly the views of Member States, has taken a very different perspective than the Commission or Parliament during the past eight or nine years. The differences clearly reflect the strains on any "communitarian" policies during economic recession, but they also underline the lack of an institutional basis to resist Member State efforts to concentrate above all on maintaining their own welfare states for their own nationals.

It is true, as pointed out by the Commission in late 1981, that "[t]he Community needs to be seen to have an active social policy," and that social policy

235 *See generally* Duyssons, *supra* note 150, at 512–19; *supra* notes 105–08 and accompanying text.

236 BULL. EC, SUPP. 3/76, at 21.

237 *Id.*

238 Even the expenditures of the European Social Fund have been limited largely to migrant workers from Member States. *See, e.g.*, Stabenow, *The European Social Fund*, 14 C.M.L. REV. 435 (1977).

239 *See* the discussions in Power, *supra* note 201, at 245; and Duyssens, *supra* note 150, at 517.

240 *Id.* at 518. *See generally* EC Economic and Social Comm., *supra* note 149; *infra* note 299 and accompanying text.

would have to confront the plight of migrants.[241] Describing results of pilot programs on the problem of poverty in the Community, the Commission thus noted: "A common theme throughout the Poverty Programme has been the identification of the disadvantaged position of immigrants and the developing problem of the children of immigrants."[242] Calling for more Community anti-poverty efforts, the Commission emphasized that "[i]f every member State moves together in the battle against poverty, progress will be much less hampered by fears about competition. The State with the least resources can be helped onwards by transfers of resources within the Community."[243]

The Commission takes a position analogous to what a national welfare state government might take, insisting not only that "we ought to sink or swim together," but also that the Community must control who has Community rights to claim against Member States. Furthermore, the Community's legitimacy may depend on its being able to establish itself as a progressive social institution, not just a common market, and a progressive policy should allow it to deal with all foreign workers and their problems, not just the much smaller number of Community workers. Indeed, as the previous quotation suggests, the common market can be seen to hinder "going it alone" to improve social benefits in one Member State country,[244] whether the benefits are directed to Community workers, migrant workers, or legitimate immigrants. Yet Community institutions for controlling migration, both legal and illegal, do not allow the European Community to take these affirmative steps.[245] Ultimately we find the same structural limitations that impede the development of a full right to travel for all Member State citizens. We run again into the difficulty of using mobility policies to effect the redistribution of welfare state benefits within the European Community. With the addition of new Member States from the south, the costs of "community" would be even greater for the better-off states of the north who do not, to repeat the dissenting Danish view quoted earlier with respect to rights of Community workers, wish to give up their advanced welfare states in the name of an abstraction – European unity.

[241] Comm'n of the EC, *supra* note 124, at 148.

[242] *Id.* at 135.

[243] *Id.* at 148.

[244] This theme is discussed usefully in Heller & Pelkmans, *The Federal Economy: Law and Economic Integration and the Positive State – The U.S.A. and Europe Compared in an Economic Perspective, supra* this vol., Bk. 1, at §§ I & II.

[245] According to the Commission's Report on Poverty,

> The principle of free movement of persons is of particular importance at a time when levels of unemployment vary between Member States and within Member States. Any worker who loses a job in one part of the Community has a right to seek it in another. But the full measure of this right depends upon the social protection available to a worker who crosses a national frontier in search of work. What happens to a worker if he exhausts his right to social insurance benefits? In some countries a worker has a legal right to social assistance and in some he has not. This is an impediment to the exercise of free movement of workers.

Comm'n of the EC, *supra* note 124, at 146.

V. The Realization of Rights: The Failure of the System of Making More Rights Available While Preserving the Status of Migrants

The previous section described a tendency, promoted by emerging norms of international law and the values considered essential to democratic societies, to move beyond the ideal migrant status in law toward minimal economic and social rights, incuding the right to stay. The evolution is especially notable in the European Community, where migrant workers from Member States – Community workers – have a legal claim to equal treatment with nationals in most economic and social respects. And the trend generally is toward at least equal pay, living, and working conditions; rights to join labor unions; some protection of social security rights; due process rights to a hearing; and a strong tendency to allow family reunification. There are limits to these rights, and rights to equal treatment may not include such remedial rights as bilingual education for children, mandated, for example, within the European Community for Member State children but not for children of workers from outside the Community.[246] Nevertheless, there has been progress, and several leading commentators suggest that we focus our attention on how to make more progress in legitimating a reformed migrant worker status: "the overriding issue is regularization of the status of migrant workers."[247] Regularization can, it is hoped, "provide needed workers to alleviate labor shortages and mitigate if not eliminate the most negative features of the migrant worker's condition."[248] It would hopefully be the culmination of the movement to extend rights that is apparent in the explicit policies rejecting the harshness of the rotation systems in its ideal legal form.

Some problems with the hope of reform and regularization from the host country's point of view have already been examined. It imposes costs, particularly in times of economic recession, if too many migrants and their families become de facto immigrants. The economic benefits of migrants who return home must thus be balanced against the social costs of managing those who do not. The potential costs can be very great, raising at least the perception that they somehow threaten the welfare state.[249] Migrant or de facto immigrant families tend to be economically disadvantaged, suffer discrimination as members of minority ethnic groups, have language difficulties, and also tend to have rather larger families, which contribute to what has been called the "time bomb" of second generation children.[250]

The focus can now shift from the cost-benefit concerns of the economy and state to the position of the migrant. The migrant status, as we have seen, no

246 *See* the summary of rights in Chaney, *supra* note 140, at 60–61; *supra* note 140.

247 Chaney, *supra* note 140, at 64; The Golden Door, *supra* note 11, at 350; *Developments in the Law, supra* note 113, at 1459–62.

248 Chaney, *supra* note 140, at 64.

249 *See supra* note 200 and accompanying text.

250 *See supra* note 199 and accompanying text.

doubt offers some economic opportunities otherwise unavailable to individuals, but the question is whether the status can be shaped so that those who take advantage of it are not de-humanized and maintained in conditions that are intolerable when measured by human rights standards. Put another way, the question is not simply whether individuals searching for economic opportunities are "willing" to work under conditions that do not fulfill basic criteria of human rights. If it were, we might justify slavery when the product of some sort of "agreement." The question is whether the migrant status, even if regularized consistently with the more progressive treaties and conventions, such as the European Social Charter, comports with values of human dignity that our societies profess. That requires an examination of the prospects for enforcement of rights provided by reform and regularization.

A. Enforcing Migrants' Rights: The General Problem

Since most of the legal "migrant" workers – even if seemingly permanent – are those from countries outside the European Community, such as Turkey, Algeria, and Yugoslavia, the discussion will concentrate on the conditions of these groups. The ideas developed in that context, however, will also be related to the situation of Community workers entitled to the protection of European Community law and illegal or undocumented workers best exemplified by Mexican workers in the United States.

The important questions are: first, whether migrant workers generally have been able to take advantage of the rights that they have obtained to date; second, whether reforms that clarify and to some extent expand the rights of migrants can be realized. Definitive answers to these questions cannot readily be obtained, particularly since empirical data on specific legal rights and living conditions are lacking. But some ideas can be developed on the basis of more general empirical studies, some additional fragmentary information, and some plausible assumptions about the conditions favorable and unfavorable to legal rights enforcement.

The typical problems of migrant workers have been well-documented. In 1973, after surveying the working, housing, vocational training, and educational conditions of migrant workers in Europe (including Switzerland), Castles and Kosack concluded as follows:

> Our study has shown that immigrant workers in all the countries concerned share the same basic position: they have the poorest conditions and lowest status in every social sphere. ... [I]mmigrants are highly concentrated in a limited range of occupations and industries: those offering the lowest pay, the worst working conditions, and the lowest degree of security. ... Immigrants have a similar disadvantageous position outside work.[251]

The 1981 European Commission report on poverty cited some improvement in housing conditions in France and Germany, with better conditions available in

[251] S. Castles & G. Kosack, *supra* note 9, at 474. *See also* Markovits & Kazarinov, *supra* note 41.

the United Kingdom, but the theme of higher unemployment, substandard housing, and grossly inadequate educational policies still emerges very strongly.[252]

One of the reasons for these social conditions, as many commentators have noted, is that rights proclaimed for migrant workers and their families are often not translated into practice. According to Rist,

> The policies governing the lives of the immigrant laborers in the countries of the European North are a patchwork of confusion and contradiction. This is particularly evident when one examines the slippage between pronouncements of concern for the integration and well-being of the workers and the realities that tend to produce opposite outcomes.[253]

Thus Ansay, after discussing the rights to equal treatment based on international agreements and German law, describes the impact of those laws as follows:

> Even if there is an equality on paper, in reality, migrant workers have less chance to benefit from provisions regulating work-place conditions than would appear. There are various legal and non-legal factors which put migrant workers in less favorable conditions.[254]

He points out, for example, that provisions on residence and work permits hinder equality; that social selection criteria in terminating employment operate disproportionately against foreign workers; hiring criteria often favor German applicants over foreigners; and inequalities in pay often exist in practice.[255] In these respects and others, Ansay points out, the situation in the Federal Republic of Germany is typical. Language problems, unavailability of lawyers, and lack of knowledge of rights seriously hinder enforcement. Furthermore, "even if workers know the law and are able to find a competent lawyer, they are often afraid of losing their jobs and are discouraged by the prospect of expulsion."[256]

In part, of course, these problems are ones already faced by citizens who are poor, or members of minority and other disadvantaged groups supposed to be beneficiaries of welfare state rights:

> Immigration law has much in common with other fields of law that are typical products of the modern welfare state in Western Europe. ... [B]eneficiaries are dependent, suffer from social isolation, [and] are confronted with complicated and detailed legislation or the lack of information.[257]

252 *See* Comm'n of the EC, *supra* note 124, at 46, 133.

253 Rist, *supra* note 19, at 211–12. *See also* Duyssens, *supra* note 150, at 511.

254 Ansay, *supra* note 7, at 26.

255 *Id.* at 26–27.

256 *Id. See also* Evain, *Une "reprise en main" ne saurait tenir lieu de politique,* [1976–5] Dr. soc. spéc. 39; Thomas, *supra* note 181, at 233 ("in the event, only a minority of foreigners benefit from their [reform] efforts"); Soubiran, *Les difficultés d'exercice du droit d'accéder à la justice pour les travailleurs étrangers: Pour une étude des facteurs qui encourent à l'ineffectivité du droit,* [1980] Procès 103.

257 Groenendijk, *The Working Group on Legal Aid for Immigrants: A Public Interest Law Organization in the Netherlands,* in Innovations in the Legal Services 165, 175 (E. Blankenburg ed., Cambridge, Mass., Oelgeschlager, Gunn & Hain, 1980).

The problems, however, are complicated technically by the tremendous discretion typically vested in authorities who administer immigration law,[258] and obviously it is more difficult to enforce rights if those who are classified here as migrant workers really do migrate and lose contact with the place where a claim of right must be made.[259] Moreover, as will be explained below, other features of the migrant status make enforcement even more problematic.

Not very much attention has been paid to this problem of enforcement, even with respect to Community workers with rights under European Community law. An interesting conference on the problems of migrants in three countries and how to remedy them, held in 1972 in Amsterdam, resulted in a book entitled *Foreigners in Our Community: A New European Problem to be Solved.*[260] The optimistic mood of that title, however, cannot be found in more recent writings. The approach taken now tends to be more critical, and there are persuasive reasons for pessimism today.

It should first be noted, however, that some measures can be singled out that improve the possibilities for legal redress. Increasingly, for example, consistent with international treaties discussed before, due process rights to a hearing are provided prior to expulsion.[261] European Community law of course provides this right for nationals of Community Member States, and the quality of the hearing must be assessed by Community law.

Similarly, rights of access to court are derived from article 6 of the European Convention on Human Rights, which the European Court of Human Rights has interpreted to mean a right of "effective access" including, where necessary, free legal aid.[262] Other, more recent, conventions are to the same effect, suggesting at least a formal right to invoke the courts and obtain a hearing.[263]

Nevertheless, we cannot expect very much from the provision of lawyers and hearings to go with the expansion of rights available to migrant workers. A situation of unenforced rights, we must recognize, is not merely "a problem to be solved"; it reveals ambiguities and conflicts underlying the policies represented in the rights.[264] It is not sufficient, in other words, to see the proclama-

[258] *See* Ansay, *supra* note 7, at 18–23; Honekopp & Ullman, *supra* note 39, at 135–36; Loschak, *supra* note 178, at 46–49.

[259] These problems for migrant workers in the United States are pointed out, *inter alia*, in II LEGAL SERVICES CORPORATION, SPECIAL LEGAL PROBLEMS AND PROBLEMS OF ACCESS TO LEGAL SERVICES OF PEOPLE WITH LIMITED ENGLISH SPEAKING ABILITIES, MIGRANT AND SEASONAL FARMWORKERS, INDIVIDUALS IN SPARSELY POPULATED AREAS 142–318 (Wash. D.C., Legal Services Corp., 1978).

[260] FOREIGNERS IN OUR COMMUNITY: A NEW EUROPEAN PROBLEM TO BE SOLVED (H. van Houte & W. Melgert eds., Amsterdam, Keesing, 1972).

[261] *See, e.g.*, G. GOODWIN-GILL, *supra* note 10, at 201–81; Swart, *supra* note 140, at 18–20; U.N. Sub-Commission, *supra* note 140, at 35–36.

[262] *See, e.g.*, Airey Case, Judgment of 9 Oct. 1979, Series A: Vol. 32 (Pubs. of Eur. Ct. H.R., 1980); Swart, *supra* note 140, at 46.

[263] *See* sources cited *supra* note 261. G. GOODWIN-GILL, *supra* note 12, at 263–81, suggests however, that the right to a hearing is not completely clear.

[264] *See, e.g.*, Cappelletti & Garth, *Access to Justice as a Focus of Research*, 1 WINDSOR Y.B. OF ACCESS TO JUSTICE *ix* (1981).

tion of rights as leading necessarily or even probably to their enforcement on a large scale, and this is especially true for migrant workers.

The sources of these rights provide a first indication of the likelihood of their enforcement. One source is a developing set of norms in international treaties and customary law. Another source, probably more important, is the necessity of reconciling the ideals of the legal system and democratic governments – equality of treatment and human dignity, for example – with the reality of the conditions of migrant workers as publicized by migrant groups and various other social groups sympathetic to their plight. The rights that are extended to migrant workers can thus be seen as reactive. They are not the product of a widely supported social program, but instead reflect a response to criticism based on liberal values. Of course, all legislation reflects a diversity of goals and motives, and enactment does not necessarily mean that there is a consensus in favor of enforcement, but the symbolic functions of legal rights are especially notable for migrant workers. If the real problem is *criticism* of the conditions of migrant workers, not the conditions themselves, then the legislative attention is above all meant to mute that criticism. It is unlikely to lead to much improvement of the conditions of migrant workers.

The probable situation can be understood better by examining the requirements for the widespread enforcement of rights in basically market economies. Enforcement, it can be demonstrated, is most likely when there is political power that can be mobilized to obtain enforcement in the courts or to compel governmental machinery to act; or, perhaps even better, when the market itself provides incentives that lead organizations with economic and political power to push for enforcement.[265] In other words, some enforcement may come either by political parties or interest groups able to resist complaints of business groups, or by business groups themselves finding that enforcement in fact enhances their profits in a market economy. Neither of these coincidences is likely to occur at all for migrant workers.

Beginning with the most obvious point, the status of migrant worker is economically valuable *because* migrant workers are supposed to take low paying jobs, provide a more docile work force, make few demands on the welfare state, and fulfill a safety-valve role by minimizing unemployment in times of economic downturn: "Industrialists and employers' groups have been (understandably) the strongest advocates of migration."[266] But that advocacy relates to the lack of rights or, at least, the lack of enforcement of rights on a large scale. Even some enforcement, we have seen, leads to cries that the welfare state may collapse,[267] and more widespread enforcement quite obviously does not coincide with the economic motives of business[268] or government.

265 *Cf.* Garth, *Why Consumer Remedies Fail: Review of L. Nader,* No Access to Law, 81 MICH. L. REV. 984 (1983).

266 J. POWER, *supra* note 34, at 53.

267 *See supra* note 200.

268 Sometimes, it should be noted, the interests of larger enterprises favor enforcement to discipline small businesses and maintain a competitive advantage, but there is no evidence that this has happened for migrant workers.

Economic motives point in fact in the opposite direction. Widespread enhancement of opportunities to gain better employment, more social benefits, better housing, and quicker family reunification leads to increased costs and, most probably, fewer returns of migrant workers and their families to their countries of origin.

The question is whether a compensating political power can break the logic of the migrant workers' economic position and promote the realization of rights that have been proclaimed in their favor. To begin again with the obvious, migrant workers simply lack most political rights. With the limited exception of voting in some local elections, for example, foreign workers have no right to vote to elect the individuals who make the crucial decisions affecting their rights in the country where they work. In addition, there may be restrictions on other forms of political activity. Mitterrand finally liberalized possibilities for organized political activity, but there had been very severe limits in France, and Germany is still not very liberal.[269] Such limitations certainly affect the assertion of the rights of foreign workers. The British sociologist, T. H. Marshall, insisted that social welfare rights depended on the earlier development of civil rights, including "the right to follow the occupation of one's choice in the place of one's choice,"[270] and political rights; and one implication of this thesis might be that social rights are difficult to enforce when cut off from the base in other "citizenship rights."

One knowledgeable commentator, as noted before, nevertheless published a book in 1981 in support of the thesis that foreign workers in Western Europe are "an emerging political force."[271] Focusing on recent experiences in France, Germany, and Switzerland, Miller's book points out several ways that foreign workers can assert political power. There is no doubt that his analysis is correct in explaining how rights tend to get proclaimed, but a closer look shows the limits on enforcement that can be expected. Miller's discussion focuses on two styles of participation – one through organization and trade union activity, and the other through direct political action such as strikes, demonstrations, and even violent outbursts.

Miller appropriately looks first to labor unions, where he finds an "increasing rate of foreign worker unionization."[272] By 1980, in the Federal Republic of Germany, 35 percent of foreign workers and 47 percent of Turks were unionized.[273] Labor unions have indeed supported claims to equal rights in a variety of settings. Furthermore, measures that promote industrial democracy, such as co-determination in the Federal Republic of Germany[274] and French

[269] Thomas, *supra* note 181, at 234. *See also infra* note 280.

[270] T. Marshall, Class, Citizenship and Social Development 75 (Westport, Conn., Greenwood Press, 1973).

[271] M. Miller, *supra* note 164.

[272] *Id.* at 155.

[273] *Id.* No data were available for France, but Miller reported that 75% of foreign workers were employed where there was little unionization. *Id.* at 150.

[274] *Id.* at 167.

employee committees,[275] allow foreign workers to participate in business decisions as well as in union affairs.[276] No doubt some gains have been made in recent years.

Nervertheless, there is a fundamental ambiguity in the unions' commitment. As one study noted, "The unions appeal for improved living conditions for migrants. But they have never been able to think or act beyond the proposition that the migrant worker *belongs* to the country he has left and therefore does not belong where he works."[277] An empirical study in France in 1975 thus concluded that legal rights of foreign employees did not accomplish much for them in fact. Thomas summarizes the study as follows:

> (a) in general, immigrant workers ... are paid the lowest wages; (b) they are called to account for breaking factory rules more often than French workers; (c) French workers show their hostility whenever they find themselves in competition with immigrant workers; (d) immigrants are ill at ease in factory unions and are not willing to accept responsibilities.[278]

The dilemma is that foreign workers still are considered foreign – not belonging to the country where they work. Steps to promote full integration are unlikely to be taken, especially since foreign workers are potential competitors with those who are seen more clearly to belong. As will be suggested below, labor unions may be changing in this attitude, but the change relates to the fact that new foreign migrant workers are not being admitted. We are not really seeing internationalism or solidarity with migrant workers, but rather more attention being paid to the group that has de facto become immigrants.[279]

Foreign workers have also benefited from their own organizations and local consultative institutions.[280] While there have been restrictions on foreign associations, most notably in the Federal Republic of Germany but also in France,[281] there is some potential for such self-help organizations to strengthen the position of foreigners.[282] There is also potential for consultative institutions such as immigrants' councils set up to facilitate some political participation, but the councils to date – in part because they have been granted no

275 *See* Thomas, *supra* note 168, at 79–80.

276 *Id.* at 78–79.

277 J. Berger & J. Mohr, *supra* note 41, at 145. Thus a description of the role of organized labor in the Federal Republic of Germany provided,

> Although not fundamentally opposed to immigration, they are anxious to ensure that the unions continue to defend the rights of all workers, both German and foreign. They are in favor of the current policy of reducing the active foreign population.

Honekopp & Ullman, *supra* note 39, at 140. *See also* Lyon-Caen, *supra* note 27, at 5.

278 Thomas, *supra* note 168, at 80. *See also* S. Castles & G. Kosack, *supra* note 9, at 116–79; R. Rist, *supra* note 38, at 120–32.

279 Thomas, *supra* note 181, at 237.

280 *See* M. Miller, *supra* note 164, at 124–27.

281 R. Rist, *supra* note 38, at 146–48; Thomas, *supra* note 181, at 235.

282 *See, e.g.*, Groenendijk, *supra* note 257.

specific power – have not been very successful.[283] And for both kinds of organizations the same dilemma is faced: there is no real possibility for strong organizations that will be able to protect and assert migrant worker rights as long as they are thought to represent migrants.[284]

Without belaboring the obvious, the same point energes with respect to direct political action, which can lead to political concessions.[285] First, the concessions may often be largely symbolic, returning to the problem of enforcement. And second, the limited power to make demands by direct action – for rights or their enforcement – is attenuated further by the migrant status. Disruptive protest need not be accommodated by political compromise, and indeed it can be dealt with by sending away disruptive individuals.[286] Protests and demonstrations have no doubt publicized the plight of migrant workers, contributing to efforts to legitimize their status in Western democracies. But migrants for the most part lack the means to compel effective enforcement.

One other possibility (mentioned before as a source of rights) should be considered – pressure from the home country of the migrant worker.[287] Again there is clearly potential for this kind of strengthening of the power of migrant workers, but home countries tend to be relatively poor with little bargaining power. The record to date is one mainly of pronouncements, agreements, and other policy statements, but it is hard to see the home country getting very far in terms actually of mobilizing rights enforcement.[288] The same is true, at least to date, of institutions like the Council of Europe that are supposed to monitor compliance with human rights treaties.

There are numerous examples of actions with respect to migrant workers that appear more calculated to quiet debate than to improve living and working conditions. Thus French President Giscard d'Estaing, who campaigned in 1974 to better the situation of foreign workers, proclaimed and publicized several reform measures, especially in housing, and then "began an administrative crackdown on foreign workers in a period of growing unemployment."[289] President Mitterrand also made promises, and then publicized several measures including the legalization of over 100,000 foreigners and reforms to prevent summary expulsions, but the situation has not been improving and his attitude seems also to have changed in practice.[290]

[283] This is in effect conceded by M. MILLER, *supra* note 164, at 124–44. *See also, e.g.*, Thomas, *supra* note 181, at 237.

[284] There is also less of an incentive for the Government to try to gain the support of or even prevent disruption by the organization and its membership.

[285] *See, e.g.*, F. PIVEN & R. CLOWARD, POOR PEOPLE'S MOVEMENTS: WHY THEY SUCCEED, HOW THEY FAIL (New York, Pantheon, 1977).

[286] *See, e.g.*, R. RIST, *supra* note 38, at 148.

[287] *See generally* M. MILLER, *supra* note 164, at 30–80.

[288] Algeria's largely unsuccessful efforts are in fact documented by Miller, *supra* note 184. *See also* Echikson, *supra* note 184.

[289] Echikson, *supra* note 184; Apostolo, *supra* note 170.

[290] Echikson, *supra* note 184. *See generally* M. SCHAIN, *supra* note 24 (documenting the lack of power of non-Europeans in France).

Recognition of basic rights and hesitancy to evict or deny family unification help reconcile democratic societies to foreign workers. But there is a clear inconsistency between recognizing and enforcing the rights of migrant workers and the economic status that they represent. As German commentators recently emphasized:

Everything that is being done today to tackle the social problems of foreigners and integrate them into German society has to contend with difficulties created by these inconsistencies. Even though greater attention is being paid to the humanitarian and social demands of the foreign population, the present economic recession is a constant reminder of the fact that the economic and political aspects of the labor market situation still carry more weight in the Federal Republic than all other considerations.[291]

Finally, as the quotation suggests, political pressures come from at least two directions. There is the pressure to reconcile the status of migrant workers with basic human rights and values, but there is also popular nationalistic pressure to make foreign workers the scapegoat for high unemployment. Since foreigners are still deemed to be guests, even though they increasingly have tended to become permanent, political leaders who would otherwise refrain from attacks on particular groups feel free to exploit prejudices against foreigners. Recent statements reported in France, Germany, and the United Kingdom, for example, leave little doubt about the propensity to seek to turn migrant workers who fail as safety-valves against unemployment into scapegoats for unemployment.[292]

B. European Community Rights and Their Enforcement

The situation with respect to rights of citizens of European Community Member States is difficult to ascertain. There are several distinguishing features even beyond the fact that the available rights and remedies are both more clear and more extensive. Most obviously, there are Community institutions like the Commission and Court available to monitor the enforcement of Community rights.[293] In addition, there is a lesser likelihood of ethnic prejudice against Europeans. Unfortunately, we have little information in fact on the level of enforcement of Community rights by workers and their families, and the available evidence suggests that the problems found for non-Community migrants also exist to some extent for Community workers.[294]

291 Honekopp & Ullman, *supra* note 39, at 126. *See also* Duyssens, *supra* note 150, at 507–12.

292 Recent statements are reported in Fouquet, *supra* note 21. *See also* Apostolo, *supra* note 170 (France).

293 The procedures for enforcement are described in T. Hartley, *supra* note 80, at 283–350.

294 A powerful statement of the potential problems is Economides & Weiler, *Accession of the Communities to the European Convention on Human Rights,* 42 Mod. L. Rev. 683 (1979). *See generally* J. Weiler, *supra* note 104, at 409–520. An indication of some of the potential complexities is O'Keeffe, *Practical Difficulties in the Application of Article 48 of the EEC Treaty,* 19 C.M.L. Rev. 35 (1982).

First, Community involvement in bolstering the social position of workers from Member States has been justified to a great extent by the same kind of reasoning that has promoted the proclamation of rights to migrant workers generally. The statement in favor of a stronger social policy, quoted before, was that the European Community "had to be seen to be more than a device to enable capitalists to exploit the common market; otherwise it might not be possible to persuade the peoples of the Community to accept the disciplines of the market."[295] More recently, the Commission emphasized in 1981 that "the Community needs to be seen to have an active social policy."[296] These statements are not hypocritical, but they show that the source of concern for social conditions is primarily one of image. Such a concern, without more, is not deep enough to lead to very much actual change.

Second, if we look for powerful political or economic groups interested in fostering efforts to go beyond image and proclaimed rights, we run into the same problem found for non-Community migrant workers. It may be, as the Court suggested in *Rutili*, that Community workers have political rights of speech and association in Member States, but there decidedly is no right to vote. And, if we look to monitoring and enforcement at the Community level, we find little activity by "underrepresented interests"[297] such as migrant workers. In fact, the Community has little concrete basis anyway to compel enforcement within Member States of the rights of migrant workers. Enforcement is a general problem for Community institutions even when there is a strong consensus and interest in effectiveness.

One example is the directive on the education of the children of foreigners, obviously crucial to families who take advantage of rights of mobility. As noted before, the Commission's proposal to include all children was blocked by the Council.[298] The directive adopted in July 1977 applies only to the children of Member State nationals. Even that directive, however, had not been implemented four years later even on the formal level.[299] Member States did not take the requirement completely seriously, and there was little the Commission and the Parliament could do to speed up the process. National pressures to implement were lacking, and the Community pressures were limited as well. It is difficult, in short, to find a source of political power today to ensure that individuals' Community rights are implemented effectively.

[295] *See supra* note 233 and accompanying text.

[296] *See supra* note 241 and accompanying text.

[297] *See* E. Rehbinder & R. Stewart, Environmental Protection Policy, ch. 6, & p. 269 ff (2 Integration Through Law Series, 1985). *Cf.* Norman, *La participation des organisations de travailleurs au processus de décision dans la Communauté européenne*, 5 Rev. int. eur. 219 (1982).

[298] *See supra* notes 239–40 and accompanying text.

[299] This was reported and lamented by the Parliament in 1981. *See Report on the Education of the Children of Migrant Workers, supra* note 198.

C. Regularizing the Migrant Status and Realizing Rights: Policies in Opposition

The implications of the apparent inability to enforce the rights that purport to bolster the migrant status will be explored in the next section, but a summary of the preceding discussion may first be helpful. From the point of view of the migrants "with rights," we see that the prospects for widespread enforcement are not very great. Part of the difficulty is that evident for all welfare state rights that favor relatively disadvantaged groups, but the situation is much worse for those who are termed migrant workers. The implication is that they are guests whose problems really are not those of the host country but rather those of the country of origin. Concerns about human rights and democratic values make it politically problematic to give migrant workers too few formal rights, and a substantial number of individuals gain from the rights that are declared. But relatively symbolic concerns about abstract values and human rights cannot mask the economic underpinning of the migrant status and provide the power and interest of host countries to go very far in the direction of enforcement. European Community rights have a somewhat greater reach, which makes some practical differences treated in the next section, but we can also expect problems in enforcement here as well. And, needless to say, whatever "rights" illegal foreign workers have can by definition reach few of them. The risk of expulsion is simply too great.

VI. Beyond Successes and Failures: Migrant Workers, Community Workers and Welfare States

Preceding sections of this study appear to point in contradictory directions. We find too many rights and too few both for workers in the European Community and for migrant workers from outside the Community and the United States. We find also too much enforcement, which seems to deter mobility within the European Community and, with respect to migrant workers generally, even to threaten the economic and social foundations of the welfare state. Yet we also see too little enforcement, suggesting that the beneficiaries of the reformed migrant or Community worker status do not realize many of the benefits to which they are entitled. This concluding section will tie these themes together and assess the current reality and prospective developments in rights of mobility and the migrant worker status for the welfare states of the European Community and the United States.

Worker mobility, it will be recalled, fulfills two different roles in a modern welfare state – one essentially communitarian and the other decidedly anti-communitarian. The communitarian vision of mobility is that all citizens (or persons with full legal rights) can move freely within the community and enjoy whatever benefits are available in any given region within the community. No region can attempt to go it alone by excluding or deterring persons from traveling or residing there. There can be persons called migrant workers, but their distinguishing feature would not be that they are entitled to few rights, but rather that they tend to work in positions requiring movement with different seasons. Agricultural workers who never settle in a particular place may indeed live a disadvantaged existence. It is more difficult to prevent discrimination and enforce all kinds of rights when an individual lacks ties and continuity with a particular locale;[300] but only a small fraction of the population of developed countries engages in such activities, and it is at least clear that the national government has a responsibility to ameliorate their plight.

In contrast, the migrant worker status central to post-war Europe and the United States is anti-communitarian; it is built on the principle of exclusion from rights that come with full membership in the community. The purpose is to protect a given community's economic and social benefits by having a group of citizens of another country bear a portion of the risk of economic downturn or welfare overcommitment. The status of migrant worker in this sense has been created in two basic situations. First, it can be embedded in the law, and, second, it can be the result de facto of illegal immigration for the purpose of taking up employment offered in the host country.[301]

The United States, with strong constitutional precedents establishing a right to travel over the past forty years, provides a modern example of a communitarian federal entity. The community for the purposes of mobility is clearly the larger one, and federal citizenship is paramount.[302] Individuals can migrate even if they are indigent and even if they may become an economic and social burden on the state of destination. They also will quickly be able to vote and participate fully in the political life of the new place of residence. The responsibility for dislocation problems is shared by the larger federal government, which views the economy from the perspective of the entire federal system.

Notable examples of the legalized status of migrant worker have included the Federal Republic of Germany and, to a lesser extent, France, but as we have seen, neither really has enforced the right to expel that is implied by the migrant status in its pure sense.[303] In fact the ideal migrant system was not even retained formally in the law through the 1970's. New efforts to find an acceptable version of this migrant status continue. While not found clearly in the Simpson-Mazzoli bill for immigration reform in the United States, a Reagan task force supported experimentation and commentators have promoted some new version of the migrant status. The formal migrant status is not yet dead in Europe or the United States. Similarly, while the United States, with the very large illegal or undocumented working population, especially from Mexico, provides the best recent example of a de facto migrant worker status, it also is found increasingly in the European Community countries.[304]

[300] *See* LEGAL SERVICES CORPORATION, *supra* note 259, at 142–318, for a detailed study of these problems in the United States.

[301] *See supra* notes 23–40, 152–71, 201–22 and accompanying text.

[302] *See supra* notes 56–66, 113–22 and accompanying text.

[303] *See supra* notes 162–65, 170–71 and accompanying text.

[304] *See supra* notes 201–22 and accompanying text.

The European Economic Community cannot be made to fit the communitarian vision of worker mobility. Workers have many rights under Community law as proclaimed by the European Court of Justice. The "Community worker" status goes substantially further than the ideal migrant status would dictate, but even Community workers do not have the kind of personal mobility that lets them choose where to live within the larger community. And, while the catalog of rights has developed very far, proposals to go farther in the past ten years have not been adopted. The European Community seeks to prevent persons from becoming a social and economic burden in the new place of residence. Citizenship, bringing with it full rights to participate in economic and political affairs, is still under the control of individual Member States; and maximum mobility rights, where citizenship is really just an incident of residence, cannot be obtained from the European Community with its current structure.

Furthermore, in contrast to the situation in the United States, there is no central institutional structure that can address – or at least have some overall responsibility for – the problems of enforcing the rights of those who migrate. The European Community can undertake studies, make recommendations, and fund pilot projects, but there is nothing, for example, to compare with the federal anti-discrimination laws and enforcement machinery in the United States, the federal courts, or the federally funded Legal Services Corporation (which still survives despite attacks by the Reagan Administration).[305] Structural constraints make it very difficult or even impossible for the European Community to evolve toward a community in the legal and practical sense described above. The political aim of European citizenship appears very far off.

European mobility within the first nine Member States (and at least Greece from 1988), moreover, is made less likely – less desirable from the point of view of employers and the relatively richer Member States – by the availability of migrant workers from outside the European Community who are not even entitled to claim the rights of Community workers. Whether or not Community workers realize their rights fully, it is at least clear that they do cost more in social security and other benefits than do those from outside the Community. The claim of Michael S., for example, could not have been made by a national of Turkey. Furthermore, from the point of view of the especially disadvantaged (non-Member State) workers, it is even more difficult to enforce what rights they do have. There is not even an institutional basis akin to the Commission and Court of the European Communities, which themselves can hardly claim to be adequate for the rights of *Community workers.*

Nevertheless, even migrant workers from outside tend to be granted minimal rights to certain social benefits, including the potentially costly ones of staying

305 *See* Economides & Weiler, *supra* note 294, at 694. The enforcement role of legal services for the poor is considered in B. GARTH, NEIGHBORHOOD LAW FIRMS FOR THE POOR: A COMPARATIVE STUDY OF RECENT CHANGES IN LEGAL AID AND IN THE LEGAL PROFESSION (Alphen a/d Rijn, Sijthoff, 1980).

and allowing family reunification in the host country. Even if not all can enforce these rights, in any event, enough have done so that the host country claims that the migrant status seems not to be serving the safety-valve function that was originally envisioned by its proponents. It has thus proven so far to be very difficult to operate openly on the assumption that certain individuals are just "workers" who lack an entitlement to basic rights as human beings. The contrast between the ideals of the political system and the values proclaimed by the legal system, on the one hand, and the ideal migrant worker status, on the other, have been too stark to justify legitimately.

The same is becoming true, it appears, for the individuals who migrate illegally to take up employment opportunities. While it is possible for a time to look the other way and maintain that those who are present illegally are outlaws and therefore entitled to no rights, it has become increasingly clear that the host country bears some of the responsibility for the situation, and these migrants too are human beings. Pressures mount to legitimize the situation of these individuals as well, raising the specter of a repeat of the evolution of the more formal migrant status. In the United States, for example, the Supreme Court has found that the children of undocumented aliens are entitled to a free public education. They are in fact persons under the fourteenth amendment to the U.S. Constitution. And the Texas Supreme Court has also recently found that an undocumented farm worker injured through the fault of the employer can bring suit in Texas state courts.[306] He is a person with capacity to sue.

This brief summary points to a general conclusion, that the status of migrant worker – something short of a full right to travel – has not been a successful innovation. It has not worked out well from the individuals' point of view nor according to the perspective of states that intended to protect their citizens from economic problems and maximize the achievements of the welfare state for its citizens. As noted before, it is easy today to find commentators who denounce the migrant status as a failure.[307] And there are others, among them Michael Walzer, quoted earlier in this essay, who denounce the status as inherently immoral.[308] The migrant worker status appears in many ways to be unpromising, even in the enlightened form of Community worker in the European Community.

Before concluding the study, however, it is necessary to look a little more carefully at the ambiguities revealed in the previous sections. Certainly the migrant status, or even the status of Community worker, does not appear to have any real chance of fulfilling what might once have been seen as its potential. But politics and the law operate at subtle levels, and one must be careful before attributing unambiguous "aims" or "purposes" to particular policies. A second look at the European Community, followed by a second look at the status of migrant worker, will show that the often-criticized and "undesirable" status quo still serves important functions in our societies. We will then

306 *See* Puga v. Donna Fruit Company, 634 S.W.2d 677 (Tex. 1982).
307 *See supra* note 172 and accompanying text.
308 *See supra* note 5 and accompanying text.

consider finally what might be done in the future with these intermediate statuses between outsider and citizen, and what that means for welfare states and ideals of community in the European Community and the United States.

A. Rethinking the "Failure" of Community in the EC

The rights of mobility within the European Community, to repeat, contrast notably with the comparable right of travel within the United States, and there does not in fact appear to be increasing use of Community rights of mobility. In one sense, therefore, we can see that the "community" vision of the European Community – European citizenship – has not fulfilled its promise. A conclusion of failure, however, would be oversimplified. It is essential first to consider the benefits of the current system, and they are significant whether approached from the individual, national, or European Community points of view.

First, we can repeat the achievements gained for individuals. Because of the evolution of the European Community, individual citizens of Member States have rights to mobility that they would not otherwise have. If they find opportunities for employment anywhere in the Community, they can choose to take advantage of them, bring their families, and enjoy many social benefits equal to those provided to nationals of the country. Relatively low numbers of persons have been making these moves; the rights fall well short of Community citizenship; and practical enforcement is difficult. But some formal rights have been created, and they enhance considerably the options available to citizens of Member States.

Second, from the perspective of individual Member States, we must recognize that Community citizenship would hardly be an unambiguous good; there is no consensus in the European Community that rights of mobility should be developed fully. The theme of "we sink or swim together" cannot realistically dictate policies in the European Community. Of course, the economies of the Member States have become very closely related from the general policies of the European Community, but the question here is whether Member States would accept a potentially significant redistribution of welfare state benefits to persons whose only qualification is the citizenship of another Member State. It is hard to use the label of failure when no Member State really wants "success."

Despite a lack of consensus in support of redistribution, moreover, the situation has evolved in a subtle way that does lead to some transfer from the better-off Member State to the citizens of the less well-off Member States. As noted before, for example, Italian children, living in Italy, receive more substantial benefits if a parent works in the Federal Republic of Germany than if that parent works in Italy. And Community policies which presumably are in the process of implementation prescribe bilingual education for children of Community workers. It is clear from the opposition to immediate granting of full Community rights of mobility to nationals for new Member States – Greece, Portugal, and Spain – that there is awareness of this redistributive effect and its potential cost. Nevertheless, the status quo is accepted generally by Member

States, and agreement has been reached on the extension of full Community rights, even if belatedly, and that will lead to even more sharing of the welfare state benefits among all nationals of Member States. It can be suggested, therefore, that the intermediate status of Community worker has served European unity by establishing some precedents for and habits of redistribution of welfare state benefits – without at the same time going so far that the wealthier states have challenged the Community's power or legitimacy. Perhaps this situation should be considered a "success," even if limited in comparison to the utopian standard of community in Europe.

Moreover, too much redistribution through rights of mobility could be seen as an *obstacle* to progress in the development of the European Community. Open economic borders, it has been noted, can discourage social policy innovation.[309] To return to the example cited before, the Federal Republic of Germany may be reluctant to raise child allowances or build better public housing. First, such policies may cost more because of the potential extension to Community workers; and, second, policies may attract more Community workers to the extent that decisions to migrate or stay are affected by levels of benefits, and then costs would go up further. To the extent that borders are not now fully open, and rights not fully exploited, there is less of an incentive to minimize social benefits and programs. Further, social democratic and labor political parties in Northern Europe have less reason to oppose Community involvement today if they do not consider Community rights to be obstacles to their domestic social reform policies.

Third, it is important to remember the limitations of Community institutions in developing and implementing social policies. If Community rights lead to problems for the social welfare programs in Member States (and to further problems of discrimination and antipathy toward migrants), that is not just a concern of a Member State trying to protect its own nationals. It is also a problem for the Community. "Progress" in Community rights to mobility, in other words, could lead to problems that individual Member States cannot handle effectively, and then it would be necessary for Community institutions to act. If they cannot act, then the European Community will be seen as an impersonal common market antithetical to concerns of social justice and welfare. As persons involved in Community institutions have noted, the social policy must at least be seen to be commensurate with whatever social dislocations might result from the Community's existence. At this point it is not at all clear that Community institutions could "keep up" in this sense with further extensions in Community mobility. The Community is in part legitimated by the rights that have already been proclaimed, and that helps ensure the Community's survival. But too much enforcement could undermine that legitimacy by creating new problems that neither the Community nor Member States could handle effectively.

309 *See supra* notes 241–45 and accompanying text. An interesting discussion of the interaction between Community law, with its limits, and domestic social legislation is Evans, *Workers and the Common Market: The* Sergius Oebel *Case,* 133 New L. J. 35 (1983).

Proposals have been made to push the rights of mobility closer to the idea of a right to travel as in the United States. Proposals are also made to improve and further develop the Community's social policy. It is important to see how those situations relate, and indeed that they may coexist in a kind of political and legal equilibrium more or less acceptable throughout the Community. This equilibrium could be unstable; alternative futures, discussed below, are certainly imaginable. But the intermediate status of Community worker, with the mix of rights now created and enforced, does help to sustain the Community at its current level of integration.

More development toward integration in terms of personal mobility, however, does not appear to be a question of a little more of this or that. A new equilibrium would need to be found, requiring a new and different common understanding among the Member States. That does not mean that the status quo is a failure, however; it means only that the obstacles toward a communitarian right to travel are very strong and show no signs of collapsing. Those possible European futures can be outlined after the somewhat analogous "successes" of migrant workers more generally are examined.

B. Rethinking the "Failure" of the Status of Migrant Worker

The ideal migrant worker to date has not survived well as a legal status enforced openly by the law, but on the other hand, the rights somewhat grudgingly granted to migrant workers do not appear to have brought them many concrete benefits. Here, too, however, the conclusion of failure may be a bit hasty from several points of view, beginning with the individual one.

First, many individuals from poor countries may "prefer" to migrate with few rights or lax enforcement if the alternative is that the jobs simply are not provided to them. Equality could mean that their services will simply no longer be sought. This libertarian reasoning, admittedly, requires the subordination of human rights to economic practicalities, and it raises important issues of legitimacy that can better be explored below. For present purposes, however, we must at least recognize that individuals are in fact attracted by the possibility of work in wealthier countries, even if few rights are available or enforced.

Assuming that some basic human rights are proclaimed, in any event, it is clear that there are some beneficiaries of the reforms in the "regularized" legal status of migrants. Families have been reunified in the host country and rights of residence invoked; and the result of these claims of right has been to weaken the distinction between migrant and immigrant. Further change beneficial to foreign workers may also result from this change in de facto status. Policies are admittedly still ambiguous; foreigners continue to be treated as outsiders in many ways, but we are seeing the gradual realization that their problems will need to be addressed. A large percentage of the foreigners simply will not go away. The children of foreigners must therefore be educated, or they truly will become a time bomb waiting to disrupt host societies. This is not to suggest that these de facto immigrants as a group are going necessarily to gain substantial political or economic power, but attention to their problems will have to increase, and a number of them will gain from policies aimed at fostering – albeit reluctantly – their social integration.[310]

From the perspective of countries who have utilized migrant workers, in addition, it is also too simplistic to label the policies a failure. Certainly it is true that a number of migrant workers – deemed by the authorities to be too many – did not return to their home countries, and those who did not return may impose a substantial social cost. It is hard to know, however, how seriously to take hyperbolic statements about threats to the welfare state. It also should not be forgotten that foreign workers did in fact make major contributions to postwar economic growth; and many foreigners did return home during the recession. Economic interests, even those implicit in the rotation system, have often been served.

Those who failed to return may become relatively costly to the host state – perhaps even too costly in some sense. Still, they also have served some social functions in the interests of the host state. While they failed to provide the optimally effective safety-valve that once was contemplated for the welfare state, they do provide a convenient scapegoat for high unemployment that can deflect attention from the government and its inability to cope with straitened economic circumstances. It is extraordinary that in numerous countries, including the United States, even illegally present foreigners are blamed for high unemployment notwithstanding evidence that they share little, if any, of the responsibility. Finally, first generation foreign workers tend to hold the lowest paying and least desirable positions in the economy, which keeps them attractive to many employers even when unemployment is high.

There is a kind of equilibrium that must be considered here as well. Considerations of human dignity, human rights, and equality have led to the extension of rights to foreign workers. The costs of full enforcement are considered to be very high; yet the proclamation of rights may be enough to legitimate the disadvantaged situation of foreign workers. Relatively little real pressure for enforcement can be mustered. De facto immigrants, we have noted, gain some rights and are emerging as a social group whose problems must be confronted at some point. But "de facto immigrant" is still a fluid status. Since these "immigrants" remain "foreigners," a reluctant, slow, and frugal effort to improve their living and working conditions can be justified because they still are not considered to *belong*. They may not, therefore, call for the same social investment that might be considered for de jure immigrants who officially and legally do belong. What can be expected is a policy aimed much more at avoiding conflict and social disruption among those who insist on staying rather than a policy to develop the social capital of a social group which is expected more fully to be assimilated.

310 Such policies would be more like those adopted by Sweden, for example. *See* Widgren, *The Status of Immigrant Workers in Sweden*, in IMMIGRANT WORKERS IN EUROPE, *supra* note 23, at 145. For the continuing reluctance, however, *see* recent press reports cited *supra* note 190.

Migrants become immigrants, in sum, but many return home and even de facto "immigrants" possessing important legal rights can still be seen as outsiders, unable to make and enforce substantial demands on the state that hosts them. The legal status of migrant has evolved significantly, and in practice the rotation system has not been sustained by formal legal policies. But, again in practice, even the new "migrant with rights" provides many of the "benefits" of the ideal migrant or rotation system, and the same is also clearly true for the system of "illegal" migrant workers tolerated for their contribution to a host country. Policies that legitimate the system, or succeed in branding migrant workers as outlaws unworthy of legitimation, mask the harsh realities dictated by the economics of migrant labor by providing and granting rights that aid some portion of the migrant workers and their families; but in an important way the economic function, served by the use of a category of workers carefully denied the full rights of citizenship, remains dominant. The reality probably is that migrant workers do help save the welfare state and preserve its social benefits for nationals of the particular country.

C. Community Workers and Migrant Workers in the Future: Tentative Conclusions and Alternative Futures

The rights of European Community workers admittedly do not measure up when compared to the right to travel for nationals within the United States. They could thus be considered a failure. The safety-valve function of migrant workers from outside the European Community and the United States, in addition, failed in the sense that governmental responsibilities had to be recognized to the non-citizens who came to work. But the rough equilibrium of the status quo needs to be explained; adjustments in legal rights and their enforcement inevitably obtain some "success" because they tend to adapt to prevailing social and economic interests in a given state and society. Certainly we should not have expected legal rights to be proclaimed and enforced completely in opposition to dominant societal interests.

That does not mean that the adaptation is stable, or that it will not break down from economic and social factors unrelated to the phenomenon of worker migration. If foreigners are blamed for unemployment, for example, this could conceivably lead to large-scale expulsion regardless of whatever rights are proclaimed. Even the limited benefits provided to foreign workers and their families may be considered too expensive to continue. Alternatively, expanding economies might once again lead to a more open system of allowing labor migration. These and other considerations will help to determine the future of Community workers, migrant workers, and those who are now de facto immigrants. With the wide range of possibilities in mind, however, it is still possible to outline alternative futures and their strengths and weaknesses, beginning with variations on what now has been found to be a very complicated status quo. Two other broad possibilities, closing borders and expanding communities, will subsequently be considered.

The status quo for the European Community is a complicated mixture of substantive Community rights, fewer rights for migrants from outside the Community, and incentives that militate against broad enforcement of either set of rights. The political source of the rights is to a large extent simply a desire to appear to be treating workers as human beings and to make the Community seem to have an effective social policy. The mobility of Community workers can nevertheless be impeded by the availability of other foreign workers who are still cheaper and less likely to take advantage of social welfare rights available in a Member State. We thus find considerable attention to the proclamation and extension of rights, but the reality looks very different. The rights serve important symbolic functions, both for the Community and individual Member States, but the system is structured to minimize the extent to which those rights lead to enforced claims against Member States anxious to safeguard their welfare states or at least not to have to extend social benefits to outsiders. There is always the potential to disrupt this kind of rough equilibrium, since it depends on a contrast between stated values and actual implementation,[311] but it may nevertheless endure indefinitely.

It could also be, however, that the proclamation of rights will help generate more pressure for their enforcement – at least on a broader scale than takes place today. We can imagine reforms that make legal assistance more accessible, for example, or strengthen self-help by groups of foreign workers who organize for their own benefit.[312] This kind of logic can be seen with respect to other rights and the groups supposed to benefit from them. Once rights are proclaimed, the demonstration of a "gap" in enforcement may also generate some political interest in reform. For European Community rights, at least, there are institutions charged to some extent with the task of overseeing their enforcement.

Two factors, however, counsel continued skepticism about this possibility, even in the European Community. First, the history of the enforcement of many new rights typical of the last thirty years is not very promising, and we should expect less power and effort for groups who at best are treated as de facto immigrants. If disadvantaged groups generally fare poorly, then *these* disadvantaged groups should even fare worse.[313] Second, if an "unacceptable" level of persons do vindicate their rights, we can expect a reaction that reduces the likelihood that it will happen in the future. One possibility, of course, which is discussed below, is simply to stop the entry of foreign workers. Another is to use illegal entry and the status of outlaw to minimize the rights that can be claimed. Such policies may not work indefinitely, but they can reduce the pressure for potentially costly rights to be proclaimed and enforced.

[311] *See supra* note 177 and accompanying text.

[312] *See, e.g.*, Groenendijk, *supra* note 257; *supra* note 280.

[313] Obviously there is less need to respond for social control purposes when one alternative is simply expulsion for disruptive behavior. *Cf.* F. Piven & R. Cloward, *supra* note 285.

The "reaction" can also take a different form, corresponding to the general reaction to the perceived costs of the modern welfare state and a demand to regularize the status of migrant workers. Those who recognize the economic virtues of migrant workers but are unhappy with how foreign workers have been treated sometimes call for the regularization of the status of migrant workers.[314] They argue that countries should take seriously the human rights provisions that have increasingly been established for migrant workers. They thus call also for more reform and better monitoring and surveillance. Because of the problems discussed above of welfare state costs, however, and the tendency of migrants to become de facto immigrants, it is doubtful that potential host countries who want the economic benefits of *migrant* workers will choose to go very far with rights for an individual and family to stay, to obtain unemployment compensation, and to get paid social security benefits. That kind of reformist regularization probably will lead in practice back to the status quo of primarily symbolic rights for migrant workers.

Demands for regularization may be turned in a different direction, however, that has not yet been discussed fully. As the initial Reagan Administration proposals suggest, it is possible to retreat from many human rights proclaimed for migrant workers and concentrate on maintaining and improving the economically most attractive status (from the U.S. perspective).[315] The proposals called for experimentation with a guestworker program that would have allowed for no family reunification, no unemployment compensation, and no social security, thus creating explicit inequalities between nationals and foreign workers. The question is whether these inequalities, which appear contrary to emerging international human rights, can be acceptable to a democratic society committed to individual rights. The recent history of migrant workers, with the progressive ameliorization of their status in Europe, suggests that these overt inequalities will be considered unacceptable and illegitimate; but the current critiques of the welfare state as too expensive may support a new form of legitimacy based primarily on economic "reality."

For example, it can be argued that many so-called human rights for migrant workers simply are social rights that are too expensive to justify. Either they would impose too many burdens on the state, which already feels pressures to reduce its social expenditures, or they impose too high costs on employers, who will then not find it to be in their economic interests to hire. Moreover, the argument goes, foreigners do want to work even if benefits are low, and their "choice" can be respected.[316] "Economic logic" today, in contrast to the "so-

[314] *See supra* notes 247–48 and accompanying text.

[315] *See supra* notes 223–30 and accompanying text; Cornelius, *Proposal for a System of Temporary Migration Visas*, in SELECTED READINGS ON U.S. IMMIGRATION POLICY AND LAW, *supra* note 212, at 188. Some hints of the potential retreat in Europe are evident from the fate of treaties after the period of recession. *See supra* note 149.

[316] That argument can be bolstered, at least from the perspective of the United States, by noting empirical studies showing that most Mexican migrants fully intend to return to Mexico and do not stay long in the United States. Even if granted permanent residency

cial logic" in the past couple of decades, may be mustered in support of a legitimated rotation or ideal migrant system. It remains to be seen whether the Reagan Administration will be able to promote this view, or whether norms of human rights and human dignity will pose too great obstacles. It does appear, however, that "regularization" would have to be developed along these lines if the intent really is to create harmony between what rights are available and what is generally enforced. The harmony can come not from a great increase in enforcement but rather from a reduction in rights.

The three variations on the status quo – accepting in some manner the status of migrant worker – return us to the problem posed initially by Walzer, but now we can see the full extent of the dilemma. If we accept the status of migrant workers, or perhaps even the variant of Community worker, we will have a general situation where the human rights guarantees available to the individuals who migrate are unlikely to prevent the emergence of a second class status that falls beneath what most sympathetic observers, such as the International Labor Organization, have found to be essential to make the role of migrant worker consistent with modern notions of human dignity. And there is a movement to resolve that inconsistency by readjusting downward the minimum requirements considered necessary for human dignity. All the trends to upgrade the legal situation of migrant workers could thus culminate ironically in acceptance and enforcement of a legal status that responds almost exclusively to the host country's economic concerns.

It is highly unlikely that the European Community would engage in that kind of explicit retreat for Community mobility. Still, if Member States revive something close to the ideal migrant system or allow considerable illegal immigration causing the same systemic effect, then we cannot expect rights of mobility to be exploited fully within the European Community by the citizens of Member States, even including the many new potential Community workers first from Greece and later from Portugal and Spain. This problem leads to the two remaining choices for the future, exclusion and inclusion. The European Community might lessen the impact of non-Community foreign workers, for example, by making Community rights turn not on work but simply on membership within the European Community. Walzer would have countries

status, most refuse to apply for U.S. citizenship. A system of rotation, therefore, is seen to make more sense for Mexicans than for, say, Turks in Germany, who tend to overstay their welcome. One response to this line of reasoning is simply that if most or nearly all Mexicans plan to and in fact do return to Mexico, there is no necessity to make a legal status to force a return on those few who have invested time in the United States, contributed to economic growth, and developed important ties that make them wish to stay. Moreover, if the idea is to have the status in order to make sure that costly social benefits are not paid to migrants, two questions can be raised. First, does this mean that seniority will not lead to full social benefits – at least formal equality with permanent residents? And second, what would be the implications for the economy and society of two more or less fixed kinds of workers in terms of the compensation and benefits they receive?

choose either exclusion or inclusion (with the possibility of immigration) rather than an intermediate status. These choices are available also to the European Community, its Member States, and to the United States.

A modification of the policy of exclusion is not realistically available to the individual Member States of the European Community with respect to persons who are nationals of other Member States. It would imply the dissolution of the European Community. Individual Member States, however, have essentially stopped the legal (but not illegal) influx of foreign workers from outside the Community. This could mean they are willing to forego the economic benefits of the migrant worker status because of the potential cost, but it is hard to be sure at this point. If European economies revive in the next few years, the demand for foreign labor will increase, and that will be the test of whether a policy of exclusion is adopted toward workers whom governments are unable or unwilling to admit to full citizenship (or at least the realistic possibility of full citizenship). That approach would continue the idea that economic growth should redound first and foremost to citizens, but it would also recognize that temporary foreigners imported on a large scale – guestworkers – should neither contribute to nor benefit from domestic economic policies. This approach is fully consistent with Walzer's view and would lead to immigration *only when the economy is prepared to absorb the immigrants permanently*.

A coordinated Community policy could also develop along similar lines to maximize *Community* mobility. Member States could agree to restrict the entry (legal and illegal) of nationals from outside the Community. Then, if the economies of Member States begin to expand, they will necessarily rely first on the citizens of other Community countries. Obviously this kind of approach would enhance Community mobility, lead to more employment by Community nationals outside their home countries, and accordingly lead to more families taking advantage of the relatively generous rights to social security and education and to reside in a country where a family member has worked. This kind of development, it should be noted, could also be seen as an enhancement of inclusive policies within the European Community, and it will be considered in that light below.

Before looking at policies of inclusion, however, the policies of the United States can be mentioned. There is a substantial body of opinion here, too, that rejects the status of migrant worker – legal or illegal – and instead calls for carefully controlled borders that allow migration only when potentially part of the process of immigration.[317] The Carter Administration proposals essentially followed that approach, trying to gain control over the flow of individuals into the United States and granting some kind of amnesty to those the Federal Government is willing to absorb permanently. The current version of Simpson-Mazzoli is comparable, even if it is unclear whether the H-2 program would be expanded.

[317] *See, e.g.*, SELECT COMM'N ON IMMIGRATION AND REFUGEE POLICY, *supra* note 210; *cf.* Graham, *Illegal Immigration and the New Restrictionism*, CENTER MAGAZINE, May–June 1979, at 54. This is not to imply that the U.S. could ever get complete control over its borders.

These approaches are consistent with international law and practice over a long period of time and accept the traditional assumption that countries owe a duty to provide social benefits only to their own or those that they choose to admit consistent with national political and economic interests. This policy of exclusion also satisfies general human rights concerns, since *those who are admitted* are given the opportunity to have all the rights of nationals. It avoids the dilemma of migrant workers who, it turns out, receive political promises but tend to get little beyond what it is in the economic interest of the host country to provide.

It remains to consider the more communitarian and universal approach – broadening or deepening the relevant community entitled to free mobility in search of economic opportunity or a higher standard of living. The legal picture of the federal system in the United States illustrates that kind of community, as does, of course, the situation *within* any given Member State as far as *its* nationals are concerned. The European Community does not currently have a legal structure that would permit the development of a community in that sense. A number of steps toward that kind of community can be imagined, beginning, as noted before, with the coordination of migration policies for persons from outside the European Community. But each of the "first steps" – mobility divorced from work, the extension of political rights, the development of a meaningful European citizenship, or the strengthening of Community political institutions – is closely related, and progress toward community would require a fundamental change in the structure that makes all those first steps so unlikely.

Completely open mobility within the Community would require Member States with a higher standard of living to give up an important measure of control over their own social welfare policies and their ability to construct and maintain their own, separate welfare states. The risk, even greater with the expansion from nine to ten or twelve Member States, is that a higher standard of living will attract individuals from the poorer south who will then exhaust the resources of the northern welfare states. It is a risk the North once ran and the South – e.g. California and Texas – now run in the U.S. federal system, but it is not a risk that Denmark and the Federal Republic of Germany would care to face fully. They do face it to some extent in the complicated political economy of the European Community today, but they guard against full exposure. Full exposure would require a commitment to the *Community welfare state* – at whatever level it could be maintained – above the interests of individual Member States. It may be that such a commitment will sometime exist. It could also be that the limited redistribution that already takes place will help prepare for that larger commitment. But the undeniable fact, as noted before, is that the current "equilibrium" in the Community does not appear to be shifted substantially in favor of a deeper legal community.[318]

[318] *Cf.* the discussion of the Community's legal and political equilibrium in J. Weiler, *supra* note 104.

The European Community reluctance to take the inclusive or truly communitarian approach to personal mobility points to the difficulty of finding a duty to share the welfare state with relatively disadvantaged peoples of different countries. The better off Community Member States do not want to have a duty to take care of the needy from countries like Greece, Portugal, and Spain, that have a lower standard of living. Even more difficult would be a duty to share with non-Member States or, in the case of the United States, to share with Mexico. The general issue of sharing, indeed, merits some additional attention, since it goes beyond the question of rights of personal mobility. It has been at the core of international relations since at least the 1960's.

Whether a sharing approach will ever become compelling with respect to Mexico, Turkey, Algeria, or even Greece is difficult to determine, but a brief discussion of some developments in international law and relations might help highlight the issues. Some writers in the 1960's argued that "the world community is bound to become a welfare community, just as the nation state became a welfare state."[319] So far that idea has proved to be naive. Similarly, when the majority of the world's nations joined to demand a New International Economic Order, implying some redistribution of the world's wealth,[320] they also were largely resisted by the developed countries.[321] Now world legal attention has been focusing on human rights concerns, but the same issue recurs and underlies the problem of human rights to mobility. There is now renewed attention to a so-called "third generation" of human rights, beyond either the first generation of political and civil rights, or the second of economic, cultural, and social rights, with both generations represented by United Nations human rights covenants.[322] The third generation is supposed to involve obligations to people who are not nationals or residents, such as rights of self-determination, to development, and to share in the "common heritage of mankind"; and a true right to migrate would be placed within this category.[323] This generation of human rights, however, faces the same obstacles as global formulas for redistribution implied in the world welfare state and the New International Economic Order. Indeed, the existing human rights provisions underline the problem of further development in mobility. The Universal Declaration of

[319] Röling, quoted in R. TUCKER, THE INEQUALITY OF NATIONS 57 (New York, Basic Books, 1977).

[320] *See, e.g.*, L. HENKIN, HOW NATIONS BEHAVE: LAW AND FOREIGN POLICY 192–211 (New York, Columbia U.P., 1979); Fatouros, *The International Law of the New International Economic Order: Problems and Challenges for the United States*, 17 WILLAMETTE L.J. 93 (1980).

[321] *See, e.g.*, A. ROBERTSON, HUMAN RIGHTS IN THE WORLD (New York, St. Martin's Press, 1982); L. HENKIN, *supra* note 319, at 228–239.

[322] *See, e.g.*, Sohn, *The New International Law: Protection of the Rights of Individuals Rather than States*, 32 AM. U.L. REV. 1, 48–62 (1982).

[323] A useful discussion of the human rights phenomenon and the mobility of persons is Böhning, *International Migration and the International Economic Order*, 33 J. INT'L AFF. 187 (1979).

Human Rights is typical. While everyone has the right "to leave any country, including his own,"[324] there is no right to compel any country, except his own, to accept him.[325] We should be skeptical that current debates will lead to a *right* of the poor, the unemployed, or even political refugees to choose a country for immigration purposes.

On a more limited scale, nevertheless, perhaps the argument for inclusion could be more successful. There are special relationships that sometimes require countries to do more than narrow national economic and political interests might dictate. The arguments, for example, for Algerian rights with respect to France, and Mexican rights in the United States, can be made fairly simply.[326] And some Algerians and Mexicans may benefit from that argument. Political realities today, especially with economies still very weak, admittedly suggest that it is still naive to expect very much from increased immigration opportunities just because of a special historical relationship that might justify sharing the welfare state with some who otherwise would be excluded.[327] Nevertheless, there may be more potential in this approach than in the efforts to modify the status quo of rights for migrant workers *as migrant workers*. Broadened community responsibility – the strategy of inclusion – at least offers the possibility that the individual will be able to claim benefits as an insider – someone who truly belongs.

The evaluation of the legal status of migrant worker, or its modified version of Community worker, will finally depend on which of the futures emerges. It could be that the migrant worker status will be maintained as a unique modern creation designed primarily to preserve and protect welfare states for their nationals. It could also be that the costs we have seen will lead to the abolishment of the status of migrant worker and the adoption of more restrictive policies of immigration. Neither of those potential developments appears attractive to those who seek to redefine welfare state communities to include persons who traditionally are considered outsiders. But if the status is *transitional*, building special relationships on the way to a deeper commitment to a much greater sharing of the advantages of the welfare state, the justification might be stronger. It is difficult to be optimistic that the system of Community workers is in fact a mere stage in the evolution toward European unity, and even more difficult to believe that new guestworkers from Mexico really presage policies

[324] UNIVERSAL DECLARATION OF HUMAN RIGHTS, art. 13(2).

[325] *See, e.g.*, P. SIEGHART, *supra* note 140, at 179 ("Nowhere in any human rights treaty has any State accepted any express obligation to allow aliens to enter its territory.").

[326] This is the theme, for example, of THE GOLDEN DOOR, *supra* note 11; Lopez, *supra* note 15.

[327] One proposal, interestingly enough, has been for a "North American Economic Union" with Canada, Mexico, and the United States, which raises anew the questions involved with the migrant status in the European Economic Community. THE GOLDEN DOOR, *supra* note 11, at 328–30.

that will lead the United States to share much more generously with its southern neighbor. But from a socially or human-rights oriented perspective, the defense of the status of migrant or even Community worker depends on the possibility of expansion of welfare state communities.[328]

[328] This is not to say that the best or most efficient way to share resources, if that is the goal, is to open the borders to increased immigration. Although beyond the scope of this study, it is obviously useful to a developing country to have aid and investment that create employment *within* the country rather than simply opportunities to move elsewhere. *Cf.* Hofstetter, *Economic Underdevelopment and the Population Explosion: Implications for U.S. Immigration Policy*, 45 LAW & CONTEMP. PROBS. 55, 65–79 (1982).

Legal Integration and the Free Movement of Goods: The American and European Experience

DONALD P. KOMMERS* and MICHEL WAELBROECK**

I. Introduction

A. Purpose and Method

The purpose of this paper is to consider the relevance of the American federal experience to the European Community's effort to create a common trading area free of restrictions on the movement of goods between its Member States. What is being attempted in Europe is nothing less than the creation of a supranational legal order reminiscent of the unified transcontinental legal order that has been achieved in the United States. Given the diverse cultures, legal systems, political traditions, and historical experiences that characterize European nations, the system outlined in the EEC Treaty is really a massively audacious experiment in federalism, one of the closest and most successful analogues of which is the governmental structure of the United States.

The American federal experience seems particularly relevant to the European enterprise in light of the judiciary's contribution to the promotion of legal integration in the United States. The U.S. Supreme Court has played a central role in the integration of an economy once fragmented by the traditions and special interests of the various states. This role has grown out of its interpretation of the commerce clause, which declares very simply, "The Congress shall have the power ... [t]o regulate commerce ... among the several States."[1] Whether in spite of or because of its brevity – and corresponding ambiguity – the commerce clause has been the most fertile source of American constitutional doctrine affecting the relationship between federal and state governments. The purpose of the commerce clause was to bind the nation into a single economic unit,[2] but without depriving the states of those powers to reg-

* Professor of Law, Notre Dame Law School.
** Professor of Law, Université Libre de Bruxelles.

1 U.S. CONST. art. I, § 8, cl. 3.

2 Harlan F. Stone, Chief Justice of the United States Supreme Court from 1941 to 1946, once remarked that "the Commerce Clause and the wise interpretation of it, perhaps more than any other contributing element, have united to bind the several states into a union." *See Fifty Years' Work of the United States Supreme Court*, 14 A.B.A.J. 430 (1928).

ulate and govern areas of life which are reserved to them under the tenth amendment. The Supreme Court's task in interpreting the commerce clause has been the very delicate one of balancing the national interest in a common market with more specialized local needs.

The European Court of Justice has begun to play a corresponding role in the creation of an integrated legal order among the Member States of the European Community. The EEC Treaty obligates Member States to dismantle their trade barriers, although its derogation clauses permit them to enact legislation with restrictive effects on commerce if such legislative measures are in furtherance of certain legitimate policy goals. These derogation clauses are written in broad language, conferring upon the European Court a large leeway for interpretation, challenging its ingenuity to press ahead with legal integration while at the same time respecting certain policy choices of Member States.

Our plan is to consider several substantive policy areas common to the "free market" jurisprudence of the American and European tribunals. The judicial cases examined fall mainly into what is known in the United States as "dormant" commerce clause analysis; that is, they deal with state and Member State legislation designed to protect public health or safety, foster public morality, provide for the general welfare, or to promote certain socio-economic interests. The selection of identical issue areas within these general categories was not altogether possible since the American and European cases are products of vastly different eras and socio-political contexts. We have tried to deal with contemporary issues of concern to both the United States and EEC. Yet our task is not primarily one of illuminating substantive judicial policy; it is rather one of comparing and explaining the uses of judicial power for the purpose of fostering and achieving an integrated economy. More specifically, we propose to examine and evaluate the techniques used by the Supreme Court and Court of Justice in reconciling federal (or Community) values oriented toward an open market with state (or Member State) values based on local interests. Thus, we are less interested in a purely formal analysis of the applicable legal rules affecting the free movement of goods than in the interplay between the various legal, political, and economic factors reflected in the process of constitutional interpretation by the two courts.

B. Judicial Review and Integration Politics

The creation of "a more perfect union" was the overriding objective of the Constitution of the United States.[3] The Constitution converted a confederacy of states – a mere "league of friendship" in the words of the Articles of Confederation – into a federal union marked by independent states and a strong national government. The independence of the states, however, was confined

[3] For an extended discussion of the considerations behind the adoption of the U.S. Constitution, *see* Jacobs & Karst, *The "Federal" Legal Order: The U.S.A. and Europe Compared – A Juridical Perspective, supra* this vol., Bk. 1, at §§ I–II.

to their reserved powers under the tenth amendment, which presumably extended to the internal commerce of each state. But the power to regulate commerce among the states was delegated to the Federal Government. Indeed, a chief justification for the creation of a more perfect union was to tear down existing trade barriers among the states. "Under a vigorous national government," wrote Alexander Hamilton, "the natural strength and resources of the country, directed to a common interest, would baffle all the combinations of European jealousy to restrain our growth."[4] Thus did Hamilton seek to establish an inexorable link between a truly national economy and America's *political* existence as a nation.

Hamilton was equally astute, as was James Madison, in perceiving a connection between a federal judiciary, independent of the states, and a unified national economy. Coincidentally, Hamilton, of all the Founders, advanced the strongest argument in favor of judicial review.[5] The judiciary would most certainly be empowered, in his view, to invalidate state laws incompatible with the Constitution. After all, the Constitution was national law as well as a law of superior obligation and, even though Congress was unlikely in the early years of the new republic to make use of its affirmative power over commerce, a federal judiciary could be expected to reject state laws and especially state judicial decisions incompatible with the principle of national supremacy in the field of commerce. Madison, well aware of the relationship between the absence of a national judiciary and "the prevalency of a local spirit," also underscored the "necessity of a superintending authority over the reciprocal trade of confederated states," a view reinforced in his mind by the commercial experience of other federated systems such as Switzerland, Germany, and the Netherlands.[6]

Nearly two centuries later, with the American experience recorded in history, the Founders of the European Community placed equal emphasis on the importance of judicial power in achieving economic integration. Of course, they could not predict how in fact the Court of Justice would operate, but their expectations were clear. That these expectations were largely fulfilled is one of the wonders of the European Community experience. As Henry G. Schermers has remarked: "It is to the credit of the Court that it always protected the Community interest, even against the wishes of the Member States, and that it did not accept a right of the collective Members – or the majority of them – to give an interpretation of the Community Treaty, but rather adhered to the original intentions."[7] Indeed, in light of the considerable deficiencies in the EC's federal character, judicial power in the Community

[4] THE FEDERALIST No. 11, at 87 (A. Hamilton) (C. Rossiter ed., New York, The American Library, Inc., 1961) [hereinafter all references are to this edition].

[5] *Id.* No. 81.

[6] *Id.* No. 42, at 268 (J. Madison). On the "prevalency of local spirit" *see id.* No. 81, at 486 (A. Hamilton).

[7] Schermers, *The Role of the European Court of Justice in the Free Movement of Goods*, in 1 COURTS AND FREE MARKETS: PERSPECTIVES FROM THE UNITED STATES AND EUROPE 222, 222–23 (T. Sandalow & E. Stein eds., Oxford, Clarendon Press, 1982).

context may in retrospect appear even more significant than it was in the American experience. Still, the example of the United States Supreme Court was available, showing how judicial power can be used to vindicate constitutional principles and legitimize a policy of legal integration.[8]

Free trade and judicial review appear to be natural allies in federal systems of government, just as the reality of judicial review itself tends to be associated with the phenomenon of federalism. Judicial review, as the American and European Founders realized, is potentially a powerful tool in the creation of any integrated economy. It seems uniquely capable of filling in the gaps of a constitution whose ostensible purpose is to break down trade barriers among states. Yet there is nothing magical about judicial review. Its success as a tool of legal integration depends as much on the wisdom and prudence of judges entrusted with the business of constitutional interpretation as on the social, economic, and political context in which it is exercised. Experience seems to show that judicial review works best in advanced pluralistic democracies marked by political moderation or stability and a high measure of individual liberty as well as entrepreneurial freedom,[9] traits common to the United States and Europe.

II. The United States

A. Elements of American Federalism

Created to form "a more perfect union," the Constitution of the United States contains a general enumeration of the powers of the Federal Government, together with a provision that this enumeration is to be construed to include all powers "necessary and proper" for carrying out the enumerated powers.[10] At the same time, according to the tenth amendment, "The powers not delegated to the United States by the Constitution, nor prohibited by it to the States, are reserved to the States respectively, or to the people." Under the American concept of federalism, then, power is divided between a national government of enumerated powers and state governments of "residual powers." This concept

[8] For a detailed analysis of the role of the judicial branch in the integration process, comparing the US and EC experiences, *see* Cappelletti & Golay, *The Judicial Branch in the Federal and Transnational Union: Its Impact on Integration, supra* this vol., Bk. 2.

[9] *See* Kommers, *Judicial Review: Its Influence Abroad*, 428 ANNALS 62–63 (November, 1976).

[10] U.S. CONST. art. I, § 8, cl. 18

"Let the end be legitimate, let it be within the scope of the constitution, and all means which are appropriate, which are plainly adapted to that end, which are not prohibited, but consist with the letter and spirit of the constitution, are constitutional," wrote John Marshall in McCulloch v. Maryland, 17 U.S. (4 Wheat.) 316, 421 (1819). Marshall's historic opinion in this case is significant not only for the doctrine of federal supremacy which it espouses, but also for its conception of the federal union as an inviolable entity established in perpetuity.

of the federal system is rounded out, finally, by article VI, which declares the Constitution and all federal laws (and treaties) made pursuant thereto as the "supreme law of the land."[11]

American federalism, as defined by the Constitution, is easy enough to understand. The reality, however, has been incredibly complex as well as the subject of bitter political conflict. Even in the simple society of nineteenth century America, it became clear that the "more perfect union" was not going to happen by itself. It surely would not be consummated in politics. Force could achieve it, as the Civil War showed, but coercive techniques over the long haul would never legitimate it. The legitimation of American federalism and the national free trade area implied by it could only be achieved by some vehicle of legal integration. The institution in American life most capable of serving as this vehicle was the Supreme Court, in part *owing* to its "insulation" from politics. Its authority to review legislation in the light of the Constitution, especially under the supremacy clause, identified the Court originally as a potentially powerful centralizing agency.

As history has shown, the Court did function early on as a strong centralizing institution in the American system, particularly in the area of trade and commerce. Yet its effectiveness, and the legitimacy of its own decisions, ultimately depended upon its sensitivity to political reality. That reality included powerful local interests and other centrifugal forces, including the nineteenth century notion of dual sovereignty, that tended to undercut the "more perfect union" implicit in the constitutional framework. At the same time, the Court could only retain its institutional integrity and thereby remain in control of legal development by recognizing the independent character of constitutional principles and by keeping its collective eye well fixed on the broad purposes of the American federal system.

The following account of American commerce clause jurisprudence describes the theories and interpretive techniques by which the Supreme Court has sought to maintain the balance between national and state interests in the field of trade and commerce. Our plan is to present a very brief historical overview of this constitutional jurisprudence and then to show how the Supreme Court has applied the commerce clause in selected problem areas related to trade and commerce.

B. Interstate Commerce and State Power: An Historical Overview

During the three decades following *Gibbons v. Ogden,*[12] the seminal case which broadly construed the federal commerce power, two principal theories of the commerce clause contended for supremacy in American constitutional

[11] U.S. CONST. art. VI, cl. 2.

[12] 22. U.S. (9 Wheat.) 1 (1824). "This power [to regulate commerce]," wrote Chief Justice Marshall, "like all others vested in Congress, is complete in itself, may be exercised to its utmost extent, and acknowledges no limitations, other than are prescribed in the

thought. The first theory held that the affirmative grant of the commerce power to Congress precludes by its own force all state regulation or taxation of interstate commerce. The second held that the states are free to regulate and tax as they see fit until Congress steps in with legislation of its own. Both theories were presented to the Supreme Court in *Gibbons.* Both were tempting theories because they contained the seeds of a coherent and predictable jurisprudence. Chief Justice Marshall seemed to lean toward the first; his successor, Chief Justice Roger B. Taney, leaned strongly toward the second. Neither view, however, had been fully accepted by the Court. The exclusive national power theory was undesirable for a compelling practical reason: Congress simply could not legislate on all matters pertaining to interstate commerce. The concurrent state power theory was unacceptable for an equally compelling doctrinal reason: It would have defeated the very purpose of the commerce clause. The history of commerce clause jurisprudence is largely an attempt to stake out a middle ground between these polar positions.

1. The Negative Commerce Clause

The full text of the commerce clause reads: "The Congress shall have the power ... to regulate commerce with foreign Nations, and among the several States, and with the Indian Tribes."[13] Although phrased in terms of an affirmative grant of power to Congress, the clause has been interpreted as a restraint on the states as well, even in the absence of federal legislation. Thus, by its own force, the commerce clause constitutes a limitation on state power over commerce. "The very purpose of the Commerce Clause," the Court has written, "was to create an area of free trade among the several states."[14] In the more pungent language of Justice Cardozo, the commerce clause "was framed upon the theory that the people of the several states must sink or swim together, and that in the long run prosperity and salvation are in union and not in division."[15] More recently, in words that might have been voiced by the Court of Justice in the European context, the Supreme Court declared: "However available [are

constitution." *Id.* at 196. In *Gibbons* a person engaged in the coastal trade pursuant to a federal license challenged New York's grant of a monopoly to operate steamboats within its waters. In Marshall's view, the state law was inconsistent with federal law. Thus, given his definition of the federal commerce power, he easily proceeded to the next step and, on the basis of the supremacy clause, invalidated the New York statute.

Building on Marshall's expansive definition of "commerce" as "commercial intercourse between nations, and part of nations, in all its branches," the Supreme Court today interprets "interstate commerce" to include every species of travel, communication, and movement of any kind across state lines, whether for profit or not, as well as "every species of commercial negotiation which will involve sooner or later an act of transportation of persons or things, or the flow of services or power, across state lines." *See* The Constitution of the United States Annotated 143–44 (Washington, U.S. Gov't. Printing Office, 1973).

[13] U.S. Const. art. I, § 8, cl. 3."

[14] McLeod v. J.E. Dilworth Co., 322 U.S. 327, 330 (1944).

[15] Baldwin v. G.A.F. Seelig, Inc., 294 U.S. 511, 523 (1935).

certain restrictions] in an international system of trade between wholly sovereign states, they may not constitutionally be employed by the States that constitute the common market created by the Framers of the Constitution."[16] The Supreme Court has sounded this theme of economic unity so frequently that it easily ranks as the most familiar refrain in American constitutional law.

As a federal institution armed with the power to review state legislation for conformity with the Constitution, the Supreme Court has borne the principal responsibility for working out the negative implications of the commerce clause. Pointing to the critical importance of this role, Justice Holmes once remarked:

> I do not think the United States would come to an end if we lost our power to declare an Act of Congress void. I do think the Union would be imperiled if we could not make that declaration as to the laws of the several states. For one in my place sees how often a local policy prevails with those who are not trained to national views and how often action is taken that embodies what the Commerce Clause was meant to end.[17]

Indeed, most of the legislation nullified by the Supreme Court in the nineteenth century was in the form of state and local legislation challenged under the commerce clause.[18]

Yet, the national interest in maintaining a common market has not been construed as an absolute prohibition of state legislation impinging upon commerce. Ever since *Gibbons* the Court has acknowledged that under the tenth amendment the states possess residual powers (often termed "police powers") to provide for the safety, health, morals, and general welfare of their inhabitants. American federalism no less than European "federalism" is predicated on the assumption that the constituent units of the federal union are also capable of providing for the common good. Indeed Congress has frequently exercised its incontestable power over interstate commerce for the specific purpose of assisting the states in carrying out their police powers. Moreover, the case law affirming the validity of state legislation affecting or regulating interstate commerce, when passed out of a legitimate concern for the well-being of its people, is substantial.[19]

16 Great Atl. & Pac. Tea Co. v. Cottrell, 424 U.S. 366, 380 (1976).

17 O.W. HOLMES, COLLECTED LEGAL PAPERS 295–96 (New York, Harcourt, Brace & Howe, 1920).

18 Between 1829 and 1932 the Supreme Court upheld state regulation in 355 cases in which state laws or actions were challenged on commerce clause or federal pre-emption grounds. During the same period the Court struck down state regulatory measures as violative of the commerce or supremacy clause in 239 cases. Of these, state regulation was held invalid in 181 cases although there had been no congressional action. Most of the latter involved some variation of *Cooley* rule analysis. A complete list of these cases is included in C. GAVIT, THE COMMERCE CLAUSE OF THE UNITED STATES CONSTITUTION 541–56 (Bloomington, The Principia Press, 1932).

19 The following is an extensive, but by no means exhaustive, list of areas of regulation by states which have been upheld though they in fact affect or regulate interstate commerce:

2. Judicial Techniques: Preserving the Federal Balance

Within the federal framework just described, the Court's task is to formulate theories that strike an adequate balance between the interests of state and nation, a task requiring a high level of practical wisdom from those Justices seeking to work out the negative implications of the commerce clause. The interplay between state regulation and the commerce clause has resulted in several doctrinal formulations over the years for determining whether the states have overstepped their proper bounds. At the basis of each of these formulations is the belief that the values of the commerce clause can be promoted and realized without trenching on the legitimate interests of the states.

The first approach focuses on the *nature* of the power being exercised. This was Marshall's original strategy in *Gibbons v. Ogden.*[20] He denied the right of the states to regulate interstate commerce as such. Unlike the taxing power, the commerce power in his view was indivisible. But he did acknowledge the right of states to enact "inspection laws, quarantine laws, [and] health laws of every description," even though such laws "have a remote and considerable influence on commerce."[21] When the states enact such laws they are not regulating commerce at all but rather exercising their "police powers" under the tenth amendment. But the line between the commerce and police power soon got very murky, as *Willson v. Black-Bird Creek Marsh Co.*[22] readily showed. There Mar-

1. *Advertising:* Head v. New Mexico Bd. of Examiners in Optometry, 374 U.S. 424 (1963); Railway Express Agency, Inc. v. New York, 336 U.S. 106 (1949).

2. *Sale of goods on consignment which move in interstate commerce but are sold exclusively intrastate:* Hartford Accident & Indem. Co. v. Illinois, 298 U.S. 155 (1936); Schafer v. Farmers Grain Co., 268 U.S. 189 (1925).

3. *Food inspection:* Jones v. The Rath Packing Co., 430 U.S. 519 (1977). *See generally,* Annot., 25 L.Ed.2d 846 (1971); Zuber v. Allen, 396 U.S. 168 (1969); Florida Lime & Avocado Growers, Inc. v. Paul, 373 U.S. 132 (1963); Pure Oil Co. v. Minnesota, 248 U.S. 158 (1918); New York *ex rel.* Lieberman v. Van de Carr, 199 U.S. 552 (1905).

4. *Quarantine laws:* Compagnie Française De Navigation à Vapeur v. Louisiana St. Bd. of Health, 186 U.S. 380 (1902); Louisiana v. Texas, 176 U.S. 1 (1900). *But see* City of Philadelphia v. New Jersey, 437 U.S. 617 (1978) (limiting the scope of such laws); Morgan v. Louisiana, 118 U.S. 455 (1886).

5. *State game protection laws:* Baldwin v. Montana Fish and Game Comm'n, 436 U.S. 371 (1978), *but see* Hughes v. Oklahoma, 441 U.S. 322 (1979) (which overruled the long standing precedent of Geer v. Connecticut, 161 U.S. 519 (1896)); Bayside Fish Flour Co. v. Gentry, 297 U.S. 422 (1936); New York *ex rel.* Silz v. Hesterberg, 211 U.S. 31 (1908).

6. *Where the state acts as a buyer of goods in commerce:* Hughes v. Alexandria Scrap Corp., 426 U.S. 794 (1976); Reeves, Inc. v. Stake, 447 U.S. 429 (1980) (both holding that state action which entails the state government's "entry into the market" is distinguishable from state action which interferes "with the normal functioning of the interstate market"). *See infra* text accompanying notes 92–97.

[20] 22 U.S. (9 Wheat.) 1 (1824).

[21] *Id.* at 18.

[22] 27 U.S. (2 Pet.) 245 (1829).

shall sustained the State of Delaware's right to dam a navigable stream, even though the dam obstructed the navigation of a sloop operating under federal law. The case was decided on police power grounds. Yet a touch of interest balancing can be detected in Marshall's discussion of the gravity of the state's concern for the health of its citizens and for improving the value of local property. It was also clear from the nature of the stream dammed that navigation in U.S. waters was not going to be affected substantially. *Willson* made clear that a more convincing doctrinal apparatus would be needed to map a more predictable boundary between federal and state power.

Cooley v. Board of Wardens[23] sought to provide that apparatus and at the same time to forge a compromise between the exclusive national and concurrent state power theories of the commerce clause. Shifting emphasis from the nature of the power exercised to the nature of the subject regulated, *Cooley* established the general rule that states may freely regulate those subjects of commerce which are local and susceptible to diverse treatment but may not legislate with respect to those subjects which in their nature require national uniform legislation. While the application of the *Cooley* rule could usually be justified in terms of the particular result reached by the Court, an adequate standard for determining which subjects of the commerce power are "local" or "national" had not been developed. Declaration often substituted for judicial analysis. In this sense, the *Cooley* rule suffered from the same defect as the police-power regulation of commerce dichotomy. It offered little basis for predicting when or under what circumstances state legislation would be invalidated in the absence of federal legislation.

A third formula that the Court frequently followed in the years after *Cooley* was the "direct-indirect" burdens test. Under this test regulations burdening interstate commerce "directly" were invalid, whereas those burdening it "indirectly" or "incidentally" were valid.[24] In direct-indirect burdens analysis, however, the focus of judicial inquiry was not always clear. Its rhetoric was frequently indistinguishable from police-power analysis. Occasionally, as in the *Minnesota Rate Cases*,[25] it resembled *Cooley*-type reasoning. However, Chief Justice Hughes' detailed empirical examination in the *Rate Cases* of the actual effects of Minnesota's railroad shipping rates foreshadowed Justice Stone's

23 53 U.S. (12 How.) 299 (1851). Specifically, the *Cooley* language reads: "Whatever subjects of this [commerce] power are in their nature national or admit only of one uniform system, or plan of regulation, may justly be said to be of such a nature as to require exclusive legislation by Congress." *Id.* at 319.

24 Examples of this approach are Bayside Fish Flour Co. v. Gentry, 297 U.S. 422 (1936); Hebe Co. v. Shaw, 248 U.S. 297 (1919); Sligh v. Kirkwood, 237 U.S. 52 (1915); Capital City Dairy Co. v. Ohio, 183 U.S. 238 (1902); Smith v. St. Louis Sw. Ry. Co., 181 U.S. 248 (1901); Plumley v. Massachusetts, 155 U.S. 461 (1894). The direct-indirect approach was also used to determine the validity of federal legislation under the commerce clause. The best examples of the application of this test in federal commerce power cases are Carter v. Carter Coal Co., 298 U.S. 238 (1936) and Schechter Poultry Corp. v. United States, 295 U.S. 495 (1935).

25 *See, e.g.*, Simpson v. Shepard, 230 U.S. 352 (1913).

assault on the direct-indirect dichotomy in the late 1920's. Stone wrote that the test was "too mechanical, too uncertain in its application, and too remote from actualities, to be of value."[26] It was a form of judicial nominalism that used "labels to describe a result rather than any trustworthy formula by which it is reached."[27]

The modern period of commerce clause analysis, beginning roughly in the 1930's, finds the Court leaning heavily toward the balancing formula long advocated by Justice Stone. In the newer cases *what* is regulated is less important than *how* it is regulated. The practical operation of a regulatory scheme is more important than whether it affects intrastate or interstate commerce directly or incidentally. Engaging in a process somewhat reminiscent of substantive due process analysis, the Court now begins to consider the reasonableness of state regulations. It should be noted, however, that the balancing approach was not a novel judicial technique. The weighing of state and federal interests was implicit in much of our inherited commerce clause jurisprudence.[28] By the same token, the balancing approach is heavily interlaced today with police-power and "direct-indirect" terminology as well as with *Cooley* rule analysis. These methods of analysis have been used for mutually reinforcing purposes and frequently on behalf of the national interest in maintaining freedom of commerce across state lines.

The significance of these judicial approaches to the commerce clause should become clearer in the subsequent discussion of specific problem areas. Our purpose, once again, is to show how the Supreme Court has used its authority to create an integrated national economy. Constitutional doctrine, the institutional role of the judiciary, and considerations of public policy are important elements of the following treatment. The constitutional cases to be discussed reflect the Supreme Court's past and continuing concern for the implications of the negative commerce power.

C. Public Health and Safety

The right of the states to provide for the health and safety of their people is a principle that has been entrenched in American constitutional law at least since *Gibbons.* Yet state legislation justified on the grounds of public health and safety has not always survived commerce clause analysis.[29] In fact, such legisla-

[26] DiSanto v. Pennsylvania, 273 U.S. 34, 44 (1927) (Stone, J., dissenting).

[27] *Id.*

[28] *See, e.g.,* Willson v. Black-Bird Creek Marsh Co., 27 U.S. (2 Pet.) 245 (1829); and *supra* text accompanying note 22.

[29] Cases striking down such legislation include Kassel v. Consolidated Freightways Corp., 450 U.S. 662 (1981) (regulation of trailer truck lengths); Raymond Motor Transp. Inc. v. Rice, 434 U.S. 429 (1978); Great Atl. & Pac. Tea Co. v. Cottrell, 424 U.S. 366 (1976) (regulations affecting the sale of milk); Bibb v. Navajo Freight Lines, Inc., 359 U.S. 520 (1959) (regulation of mud flaps on tractor-trailer trucks); Dean Milk Co. v. City of Madison, 340 U.S. 349 (1951); and Southern Pac. Co. v. Arizona, 325 U.S. 761 (1945) (regulation of length and make-up of trains passing through the state).

tion has been struck down on several occasions in recent years. Our purpose in this as in the other sections is to examine methods of constitutional interpretation used by the Court in deciding challenges to state health and safety legislation, to show how the Court has applied these methods in specific situations, and to consider the Court's role as an instrument of legal integration.

The interplay between the commerce clause and state health and safety legislation finds its most relevant expression in the line of modern transportation cases ranging from *South Carolina State Highway Dept. v. Barnwell*[30] to *Kassell v. Consolidated Freightways Corporation of Delaware*.[31] These cases are particularly relevant for comparative purposes because arguably legitimate health and safety legislation may have an adverse impact upon instruments of commerce as well as on the free movement of goods. They also serve as a convenient vehicle for our discussion of the Court's role in reconciling conflicts under the dormant commerce clause. The pattern of analysis followed by the Supreme Court in these cases is the subject of fervid dispute among the Justices. The intra-court debate centers on the judicial role itself and the extent to which judicial power should be used to invalidate existing and arguably legitimate state policy.

In *Barnwell*, the Supreme Court sustained a South Carolina law prohibiting the use on its highways of trucks more than 20,000 pounds in gross weight or 90 inches in width. In doing so, the Court overruled a lower court decision which held these limitations invalid as an unreasonable burden on interstate commerce. Its analysis stressed the local character of highway traffic and the traditional interest of the state in providing for the safety of its residents. It was *Cooley* reasoning with police-power overtones. The result in the case seemed foreordained by the Court's finding that the law: (1) regulated a local activity; (2) was enacted as a safety measure; and (3) did not discriminate against interstate commerce. Ironically, Justice Stone, who recommended a balancing of national and state interests in his *DiSanto* dissent,[32] appeared to eschew the balancing approach here, for there was no real effort to weigh the burden of the state's regulation upon interstate commerce against its local interest in safety. In upholding the law on the basis of its mere reasonableness, the Court refused to second-guess the state's policy judgment. Such deference to state legislation was thought to be the proper judicial approach to preserving the value of American federalism, although Congress might have stepped in at any time to reorder the state's priorities with uniform national regulation.

A few years prior to *Barnwell* the Court had even sustained Michigan's denial of a license to an interstate motor carrier requesting permission to use a badly congested highway connecting Cleveland (Ohio) and Flint (Michigan).[33] The state introduced evidence showing that the addition of another carrier to the

30 303 U.S. 177 (1938).
31 450 U.S. 662 (1981).
32 *See* DiSanto v. Pennsylvania, 273 U.S. 34, 44 (1927) (Stone, J., dissenting).
33 Bradley v. Public Utils. Comm'n, 289 U.S. 92 (1933).

highway "would create and maintain an excessive and undue hazard to the safety and security of the traveling public." That was enough for the Court, especially since the carrier was free to seek a license to carry on its interstate trade over other highways. This case is often contrasted to *Buck v. Kuykendall*,[34] where the Court struck down the State of Washington's denial of a certificate of public convenience and necessity to an interstate bus line operating between Washington and Oregon on the ground that passenger traffic was already adequately served. The Court viewed this action as a direct restraint on competition and thus incompatible with one of the basic values of the commerce clause. The Court tended generally, however, to sustain nondiscriminatory health and safety legislation of the *Barnwell* and *Bradley* variety.

In these early cases it seems clear that the court was unwilling to strike down state or local regulation merely because of its impact on interstate commerce. State legislation designed to protect local residents against the hazards of interstate travel would be sustained if not ostensibly enacted to favor the local economy or to discriminate against out-of-state trade. Difficult problems of modern technology were also entangled in these cases, and the Court seemed willing, in the absence of uniform national legislation, to allow local policies involving complex relationships between highway use and construction to stand.

In three leading transportation cases decided between 1945 and 1980 the Court played a more centralizing role in its interpretation of the dormant commerce clause. In *Southern Pacific Co. v. Arizona*[35] – the main bridge to contemporary commerce clause analysis generally – the Supreme Court invalidated Arizona's long-train law which prohibited the operation of trains of more than fourteen passenger or seventy freight cars. In *Bibb v. Navajo Freightlines, Inc.*,[36] the Court nullified Illinois' detailed specifications for rear fender mudguards required on all trucks and trailers. In *Raymond Motor Transportation, Inc. v. Rice*,[37] finally, the Court struck down Wisconsin's prohibition of trucks longer than fifty-five feet which had effectively banned from the state's highways the sixty-five foot long double-trailer units normally used by interstate trucking companies and permitted in most states. In each case public safety and welfare was the ostensible purpose of the statute. In each case the regulation was, for the most part, nondiscriminatory. But in each case the Court nevertheless looked carefully at the nature and extent of the burden on commerce, and in each case found that the national interest in the uninterrupted flow of traffic must prevail.

In assessing the implications of the negative commerce clause the Supreme Court turned increasingly over the years to the weighing of burdens, or

[34] 267 U.S. 307 (1925). This case, incidentally, arose ten years prior to the enactment of the Federal Motor Carrier Act, conferring upon the Interstate Commerce Commission extensive authority over interstate motor carriers.

[35] 325 U.S. 761 (1945).

[36] 359 U.S. 520 (1959).

[37] 434 U.S. 429 (1978).

balancing test. The Court elevated this technique to the level of official doctrine in *Pike v. Bruce Church, Inc.*,[38] where it set forth the general rule for the judicial determination of the validity of state statutes affecting interstate commerce:

> Where the statute regulates evenhandedly to effectuate a legitimate local public interest, and its effects on interstate commerce are only incidental, it will be upheld unless the burden imposed on such commerce is clearly excessive in relation to the putative local benefits. ... If a legitimate local purpose is found, then the question becomes one of degree. And the extent of the burden that will be tolerated will of course depend on the nature of the local interest involved, and on whether it could be promoted as well with a lesser impact on interstate activities.[39]

Under the balancing approach of *Pike* the Court has been extremely reluctant to strike down state health and safety legislation. In eschewing "incidental effects" analysis the Court has generally been unsympathetic to arguments showing the "degree" of impact of such legislation upon commerce. In short, state safety and health legislation is still colored by a strong presumption of constitutional validity and only discrimination of a particularly egregious kind is likely to defeat that presumption.[40]

38 397 U.S. 137 (1970).

39 *Id.* at 142 [citations omitted].

40 This modern deference to state safety regulation was manifested in Ray v. Atlantic Richfield Co., 435 U.S. 151 (1978), where the exercise of state police power was challenged under the supremacy clause. Both the Federal Ports and Waterways Safety Act of 1972 and the State of Washington's Tanker Law sought to regulate the design, size, and movement of oil tankers in Puget Sound, an estuary consisting of 2,500 square miles of inlets, bays, and channels in the northwestern part of Washington. Speaking through Justice Byron R. White, the Supreme Court held that two of the three operative provisions of Washington's Tanker Law had been pre-empted by the federal statute. The Court's ruling on the third operative provision, a tug escort requirement, is a modern echo of the *Cooley* rule: "Similar in its nature to a local pilotage requirement, a requirement that a vessel take on a tug escort when entering a particular body of water is not the type of regulation that demands a uniform national rule." *Id.* at 179. Because local pilotage regulation fits clearly into the category of safety rules traditionally enacted by the states, the commerce clause objection to the tug escort requirement was rejected. Even though the federal statute allocated specific authority to the Secretary of Transportation to promulgate tug escort rules, in the absence of such rules the Court's presumption was also against pre-emption under the supremacy clause, clearly a further presumption of shared federal and state responsibility over the *movement* of vessels in Puget Sound.

With regard to pre-emption, it should be noted here that under the supremacy clause, federal law pre-empts state law when Congress clearly manifests its intention to occupy a given field within its enumerated powers. If this intention is not manifest, the congressional purpose may be evidenced in other ways. The scheme of regulation may be so pervasive as to make reasonable the inference that Congress left no room for the states to supplement it. *See* Pennsylvania Ry. Co. v. Public Serv. Comm'n, 250 U.S. 566 (1919). A conflict may also be found when it is physically impossible to comply with federal and state law at the same time. *See* Florida Lime & Avocado Growers, Inc. v. Paul, 373 U.S. 132 (1963). Or an Act of Congress may touch a field in which the federal

Then what explains the strong interventionist role of the modern Court in the aforementioned transportation cases? One answer is the balancing technique itself, which requires the Court independently to assess "purpose," "local interest," and especially the "burden" on commerce, all key ingredients of *Pike's* analytical framework. Constitutional doctrine does not, of course, evolve in a vacuum. The balancing technique reached maturity within the context of advanced technology, an increasingly complex system of interstate transportation, and the astronomical growth of the trucking industry, together with intense competition among interstate carriers generally. In the absence of federal legislation, these pressures were likely to generate counterpressures in state legislatures calling for the protection of local economic interests, frequently in the guise of safety and health legislation. In this context it made good sense for the Court to substitute a higher level of scrutiny over the relationship between ends and means for the low level of judicial review manifested by *Barnwell's* test of reasonableness. The mere "incantation of a purpose to promote the public health or safety," the Court has said, "does not insulate a state law from commerce clause attack."[41]

On the other hand, balancing is a practical method for reconciling legitimate local interests with free market values. State legislation not clearly discriminatory is presumptively valid. The presumption can be overcome, however, by empirical data showing that the state's interest in health or safety is illusory or excessively burdensome on commerce relative to the proclaimed safety interest. In *Raymond*, for example, the Court was impressed with the uncontradicted evidence marshalled by interstate trucking firms and highway officials that Wisconsin's regulatory scheme in fact contributed very little to highway safety. Under the *Pike* test, therefore, the "putative local benefits," against the backdrop of affidavits showing a heavy burden on interstate trucking firms, in terms of both expense and delay, were heavily outweighed by the burden on interstate commerce.

Suffice to add, however, that while the Justices were unanimous in striking down the statutory scheme in *Raymond*, they were deeply divided over whether the *Pike* test should apply to the Wisconsin circumstances. The plurality opinion was written within the *Pike* framework. But Justice Blackmun's concurring opinion, joined by three Justices,[42] concluded that Wisconsin's regulatory scheme even failed the basic rationality test. Thus balancing was not needed here, for the state's "safety interests have not been shown to exist as a matter of law."[43] But if such safety interests had been shown to exist there is language in the concurring opinion suggesting that the balancing formula of *Pike* would have been applied differently than by the plurality, echoing the

interest is so dominant that the federal system will be assumed to preclude enforcement of state laws on the same subject. *See* Hines v. Davidowitz, 312 U.S. 52 (1941). *See also* Pennsylvania v. Nelson, 350 U.S. 497 (1956) (concerning internal security regulation).

41 Kassel v. Consolidated Freightways Corp., 450 U.S. 662, 670 (1981).

42 Justice Stevens did not participate in the case.

43 434 U.S. 429, 450.

divergences that have fractured the Court in dormant commerce clause cases at least since *Southern Pacific*.[44]

These divergences were clearly and dramatically revealed in *Kassel v. Consolidated Freightways*,[45] a 1981 case that raised serious questions about what information is to be balanced within the analytical framework of *Pike*. *Kassel* was similar to *Raymond* except that here Iowa sought to justify the safety basis for its ban on the use of double-trailer and very long trucks on its highways. But the evidence introduced in the *trial court* seriously damaged Iowa's safety rationale. On the basis of its own examination of the trial record a plurality of four Justices (Powell, joined by Blackmun, White, and Stevens) concluded, after remarking that Iowa's law is now out of step with the laws of all other midwestern and western states, that the "state law cannot be harmonized with the Commerce Clause."[46] Manifesting a clear willingness to make judgments of fact and value in cases such as *Kassel*, the plurality found that the safety feature of the regulation is "marginal" and the interference with commerce "substantial."[47]

Justices Brennan and Marshall, who concurred in the result, faulted the plurality for relying on "the vagaries of litigation rather than on the judgments made by the State lawmakers."[48] The judicial task, in their view, "is to balance the burden imposed on commerce against the local benefits sought to be achieved by the State's *lawmakers*."[49] And if it is determined that the "lawmakers could rationally have believed that the challenged regulation would foster [the] purposes [of safety]," the Court may not then "second-guess the empirical judgments of lawmakers concerning the utility of legislation."[50] Thus, in this view, the discovery that a state law is a rational safety mea-

[44] In *Southern Pacific* Justice Stone, writing for the majority, reviewed extensively, the circumstances and facts of Arizona's long-train regulations, finding them an excessive burden on interstate commerce. Justices Black and Douglas, however, accused the Court of acting like a "super-legislature." The record showed that long trains endanger the lives of railroad employees. Arizona's requirement of short trains was therefore a legitimate safety measure and a state policy judgment that is not "a matter for judicial determination." Judicial interference was not warranted on the grounds that a safety measure burdens interstate commerce. In Douglas' view, shared by Black, judicial intervention was justified "only where the state legislation discriminated against interstate commerce or was out of harmony with laws which Congress had enacted." *See* Southern Pac. Co. v. Arizona, 325 U.S. 761 (1945).

[45] 450 U.S. 662 (1981).

[46] *Id.* at 670.

[47] Consolidated Freightways demonstrated to the Court's satisfaction that Iowa's law substantially burdened commerce. The evidence showed that trucking companies which use 65-foot double-trailer trucks must route them around Iowa or detach the trailers and ship them through the state separately. Either way, the additional cost to the trucking companies was about U.S. $12.6 million per year.

[48] 450 U.S. 662, 678.

[49] *Id.* at 680.

[50] *Id.*

sure ends the judicial inquiry *unless* the Court finds that the statute is discriminatory, in which case it *must* be struck down as incompatible with the commerce clause. The legislative history behind the statute revealed to the satisfaction of these Justices that its real purpose was protectionist in nature and thus unconstitutional "even if the burdens and benefits are related to safety rather than economics."[51]

The three remaining Justices (Rehnquist, Burger, and Stewart) dissented, maintaining that neither of the above approaches was sufficiently sensitive to state safety concerns. Justice Rehnquist proceeds to remind us that the commerce clause is "a grant of authority to Congress, not to the courts."[52] He would not invalidate a state law when balancing yields a result showing that safety benefits are outweighed by burdens on commerce. Rather, the safety benefits must be "demonstrably trivial while the burden on commerce is great."[53] He regards Brennan's approach to discriminatory legislation as excessively harsh and somewhat simplistic since state laws impinging upon commerce are often informed by both safety and protectionist considerations. It is clear, in any case, that the balancing test ensures that the Court will continue to function as a vital decision-maker in the field of interstate commerce.

D. Public Morality

In the principal European case involving a public morality defense of a Member State law impeding the free flow of goods, the Court of Justice sustained England's policy of excluding obscene materials from other countries.[54] There are no modern cases in American constitutional law which have challenged state obscenity legislation directly on commerce clause grounds. The two closest cases in this respect were decided in 1914. Both upheld, over commerce clause objections, state censorship laws requiring all films to be screened upon their distribution for showing in the state. In one case the Court reaffirmed, without much analysis, that the control of public morality is within the police power of the state,[55] while in the other the Court held that since the films at issue had ended their interstate journey and were now "mingled as much as from their nature they can be with other property of the State," they were subject to state

[51] *Id.*
[52] *Id.* at 689.
[53] *Id.* at 692.
[54] Case 34/79, Regina v. Henn and Darby, [1979] ECR 3795 (discussed *infra* text accompanying notes 172–81). *See also* Catchpole & Barav, *The Public Morality Exception and the Free Movement of Goods: Justification of a Dual Standard in National Legislation*, [1980-1] L.I.E.I. 1-21. Only the free movement implications of the public morality exceptions are examined in this paper. For a detailed consideration of the "human rights" aspects of such limitations comparing the US and EC approaches, *see* Frowein, Schulhofer & Shapiro, *The Protection of Fundamental Human Rights as a Vehicle of Integration*, *infra* this book.
[55] Mutual Film Corp. v. Hodges, 236 U.S. 248 (1915).

regulation.[56] Today, of course, the foremost line of attack on state and local obscenity legislation is through the first and fourteenth amendments.

It is interesting to note, however, that in the early 1970's the Supreme Court upheld Congress' use of the commerce power to ban the importation of obscene material from foreign countries as well as across state lines within the United States, even though in a case sustaining this power the material was transported by a private carrier and for the private use of the transporter.[57] Actually, as early as 1913 the Court had approved a congressional measure taking the facility of interstate transportation away from the "debasement of obscene literature."[58]

Congress's power under the commerce clause has been held to include the authority to regulate or totally prohibit certain types of commerce which promote "immorality, dishonesty, or the spread of any evil or harm to the people of other states from the state of origin."[59] What is interesting about federal statutes such as these is that their objectives are unrelated to the purely commercial aspects of commerce. The White Slave Traffic Act (The Mann Act), prohibiting the transportation of women from one state to another for immoral purposes, is an illustration of these statutes. Wholly compatible with state law, and upheld in *Caminetti v. United States*,[60] it is a paradigm example of cooperative federalism. But the power has also been exercised in opposition to local law or custom, a leading example of which is the Civil Rights Act of 1964.[61] Provisions of the act forbidding discrimination in hotels, restaurants, and other places of public accommodation were upheld as a proper exercise of the commerce power in *Heart of Atlanta Hotel v. United States* and *Katzenbach v. McClung*.[62]

56 Mutual Film Corp. v. Industrial Comm'n of Ohio, 236 U.S. 230, 241 (1915).

57 *See* United States v. Orito, 413 U.S. 139 (1973) and United States v. 12 200-ft. Reels, 413 U.S. 123 (1973). *See also* United States v. Thirty-Seven Photographs, 402 U.S. 363 (1971). With regard to the legitimacy of a federal ban on mailing obscene materials, *see* Smith v. United States, 431 U.S. 291 (1977).

58 Hoke v. United States, 227 U.S. 308 (1913).

59 That Congress has such power under the commerce clause was first enunciated in Champion v. Ames, 188 U.S. 321 (1903) and reinforced in United States v. Darby, 312 U.S. 100 (1941).

60 242 U.S. 470 (1917). *See also* Brooks v. United States, 267 U.S. 432 (1925); Williams v. United States, 443 F.2d 1151 (5th Cir., 1971) (the Dyer Act, criminalizing interstate traffic in stolen vehicles, 18 U.S.C. § 2312); United States v. Jackson, 390 U.S. 570 (1968); United States v. Cassidy, 571 F.2d 534 (10th Cir.), *cert. denied*, 436 U.S. 951, *reh'g denied*, 439 U.S. 884 (1978) (upholding all portions of the Lindbergh Law punishing interstate transportation of kidnapped persons, 18 U.S.C. § 1201); Perez v. United States, 402 U.S. 146 (1971) (loan sharking provision of the Consumer Credit Protection Act, 18 U.S.C. § 891 *et seq.)*; United States v. Orito, 413 U.S. 139 (1973) and Smith v. United States, 431 U.S. 291 (1977) (transportation of obscene materials by common carrier in interstate commerce, 18 U.S.C. § 1462, and sending of obscene materials through the mails, 18 U.S.C. § 1461).

61 78 Stat. 241, 243, 42 U.S.C. § 2000 *et seq.*

62 379 U.S. 241 (1964) and 379 U.S. 294 (1964). *See also* Champion v. Ames, 188 U.S. 321 (1903) (Act of 1895 "for the suppression of letters," 28 Stat. 963) and United States v. Darby, 312 U.S. 100 (1941) (the Fair Labor Standards Act banning from interstate

In the absence of congressional legislation, however, what has been the role of the court in dealing with "public morality" legislation in the face of commerce clause objections? Let us continue with the aforementioned examples of obscenity and racial discrimination. Of course, the fact that Congress has added its voice to the chorus of state laws regulating commercial traffic in obscenity would – and should – probably act as a restraint on judicial intervention. A posture of restraint may be justified further by an implicit assumption that states are empowered to protect the social interest in public morality. For one thing, judicial competence in this field is severely limited. Balancing interests in the transportation cases, where proof of safety is readily available, is one thing; balancing in the obscenity field, where the evidentiary basis of state regulation is largely absent, is quite another. Still another important consideration for the Supreme Court is the unity and consistency of its constitutional jurisprudence generally. In this connection, recent first amendment obscenity cases seem relevant. Under the leadership of Chief Justice Burger, the Supreme Court is creating a "new federalism" in this area by rejecting a *national* uniform standard for determining what appeals to a "prurient interest" or is "patently offensive."[63] In *Paris Adult Theatre I v. Slaton,*[64] the Chief Justice, speaking for the majority, acknowledged the state's power under the commerce clause: "Commercial exploitation of depictions, descriptions, or exhibitions of obscene conduct on commercial premises open to the adult public falls within a State's *broad power to regulate commerce* and protect the public environment."[65]

Racial discrimination has also been the subject of the Court's dormant commerce clause jurisprudence. *Morgan v. Virginia*[66] was a challenge to a state statute requiring racial segregation on all motor vehicle carriers, both interstate and intrastate. The law was passed in the exercise of the state's police power to avoid friction between the races. At a more general level the statute also reflected a particular version of social morality. A carrier otherwise integrated under its own rule would thus be required, when entering Virginia, to separate white and black passengers. The statute was attacked as an unconstitutional interference with the federal power over interstate commerce.

The approach of the Court in this case was somewhat different than in the transportation cases discussed earlier, where various modes of judicial activism were employed to keep commerce free from excessive delay or interruptions. The judicial reasoning in *Morgan* is more abstract in quality and seems well suited to the result that the Court sought to achieve. The Court struck down

commerce the products of child labor, 29 U.S.C. §§ 201–219). Perhaps a better example of a congressional act justified on commerce clause gounds but without any clear connection with commerce in the usual sense is Title VII of the Omnibus Crime Control and Safe Streets Act (18 U.S.C. § 1202(a) (13)). *See* Scarborough v. United States, 431 U.S. 563 (1977).

63 *See* Miller v. California, 413 U.S. 15 (1973).

64 413 U.S. 49 (1973).

65 *Id.* at 68–69 (emphasis added).

66 328 U.S. 373 (1946).

the Virginia regulation because "seating arrangements for the different races in interstate motor travel require a simple, uniform rule to promote and protect national travel."[67] By applying the *Cooley* rule in this case the Court was able to concentrate on the general purpose behind the commerce clause. Although Justice Stanley Reed, speaking for the majority, employed the language of "undue burdens," there was in fact no empirical evidence to show the extent of the actual burden on commerce flowing from the requirement of segregation. No such evidence was available, and was unlikely ever to be marshalled. The real key to the Court's reasoning is to be found in the principle of equality in all public conveyances, a principle set forth expressly by the Court seventy years earlier in *Hall v. DeCuir*,[68] which invalidated segregated practices on interstate vessels navigating the Mississippi River. "Such regulations," said the Court in *Morgan*, "hamper freedom of choice in selecting accommodations."[69] To sustain the point, the Court referred to the inevitable disturbances in the comfort of passengers caused by local segregative practices. The "cumulative effects" of such practices, wrote Justice Reed, mindful of the many different state rules on this matter, "make local regulation impracticable."[70] For Justice Frankfurter, too, the "crazy-quilt [pattern] of State laws ... operate[s] to burden commerce unreasonably."[71]

The Court strongly implies that such practices also interfere with the freedom of business enterprises, a concern that was much more explicit in *DeCuir*. If commerce is to flourish, the Court seems to suggest, carriers must be left free to provide for the comfort of their passengers, a matter requiring uniformity of practice along the route of travel. The Court registered no approval or disapproval of local segregation. Its reasoning sought to promote a fundamental value of the commerce clause, namely a uniform and predictable context within which to conduct interstate business. In this sense, the decision in *Morgan* could be welcomed by both business and governments. The economy can be "balkanized" in ways other than by throwing up trade barriers. It can also be obstructed by hostility in human relations generated by conflicting regulations of a purely social nature. *Morgan* thus represented an intelligent and wise furthering of commerce clause values.

Colorado Anti-Discrimination Commission v. Continental Air Lines[72] represented a reverse situation in the racial field. There an interstate airline company claimed that the state, by seeking to enforce a policy of nondiscrimination in hiring practices, imposed an undue burden upon commerce.[73] The Court

[67] *Id.* at 386.
[68] 95 U.S. 485 (1877).
[69] 328 U.S. 373, 383 (1946).
[70] *Id.* at 381–82.
[71] *Id.* at 388 (Frankfurter, J., concurring).
[72] 372 U.S. 714 (1963).
[73] Continental Airlines also claimed that the field of law concerning racial discrimination had been pre-empted by federal laws such as the Railway Labor Act and the Civil Aeronautics Act of 1938. The Court rejected the pre-emption argument.

rejected the Colorado Supreme Court's application of the *Cooley* rule to this case. The Court distinguished between transportation of passengers, the process involved in *Morgan* and *DeCuir*, and hiring employees, which it deemed a much more localized activity and thus within the rightful authority of the state. In actuality, the Court sought to harmonize its interpretation of the commerce clause with the value of nondiscrimination inherent in the due process and equal protection clauses of the fourteenth amendment.

E. Environmental Protection

The United States, like other advanced industrial democracies, has committed itself to a nationwide effort to protect the environment. In doing so Congress has been sensitive to policy considerations of federalism. At the same time, the various states have also been active in enacting environmental protection laws of their own, raising questions of their compatibility with federal law and, owing to their enormous diversity, raising equally serious questions of their validity under the negative commerce clause. Both situations have begun to generate constitutional litigation,[74] supplying the Supreme Court with fresh material for reassessing the nation-state relationship within the American federal system.

Our consideration of standards or techniques used in the constitutional analysis of state laws designed to protect natural resources and the environment requires some discussion of recent cases involving Congress's power over the same field of public policy. An unbroken line of precedents stretching back to 1937 had firmly established the legitimacy of federal legislation regulating any local activity affecting interstate commerce. As a general rule, the judicial discovery of any rational basis whatsoever to support a congressional judgment regulating some intrastate matter affecting commerce was enough to sustain the validity of the legislation.[75]

In 1976, however, in a drastic reversal of its non-interventionist approach to congressional legislation under the commerce clause, the Court invalidated sections of the Fair Labor Standards Act which extended federal minimum

[74] *See* Note, *State Environmental Protection Legislation and the Commerce Clause*, 87 HARV. L. REV. 1762–85 (1974). For a more general and detailed discussion and comparison of environmental protection policy in the US and the EC *see* E. REHBINDER & R. STEWART, ENVIRONMENTAL PROTECTION POLICY (2 Integration Through Law Series, 1985).

[75] *See* Wickard v. Filburn, 317 U.S. 111 (1942), where the Court even upheld the application of a marketing quota to a small farmer whose excess wheat crop was fed to his own poultry and livestock. ("That the appellee's own contribution to the demand for wheat may be trivial by itself is not enough to remove him from the scope of federal regulation where, as here, his contribution, taken together with that of many others similarly situated, is far from trivial." *Id.* at 127–28.) This "cumulative effect" standard has served as a justification for far-reaching congressional regulatory measures in the area of civil rights, criminal behavior, and the local sale of foods, additives, and drugs. *See also* Perez v. United States, 402 U.S.146 (1971).

wages and maximum hours provisions to nearly all state employees.[76] Described by Justice Brennan (dissenting) as a "startling restructuring of our federal system and the role ... creat[ed] therein for the federal judiciary," *National League of Cities v. Usery* held that the tenth amendment limits the reach of the federal commerce power when that power impinges on functions essential to the existence of the states as states. Congress had interfered with the states' ability, said the Court, "to structure integral operations in areas of traditional [state] governmental functions."[77] Here, of course, the function was that of hiring and compensating state employees. The Court's functional analysis, however, contained no clues as to what other kinds of state activities would be regarded as essential to the states' existence and therefore unreachable by federal legislation. Nor was it clear if emphasis in future would be on *traditional* state functions or simply on functions essential to a state's existence.

It is important to understand the political context of *Usery*, which arrived at the Court at a time of general popular discontent with the growth of federal power and bureaucratic controls over the national economy. The 1970's witnessed increasing demands, reflected in both the Nixon and Carter Administrations, for the devolution of authority and for federal deregulation, a "movement" culminating in the "New Federalism" of President Ronald Reagan. *Usery* was one manifestation of the "New Federalism," evidencing "an abiding concern for the maintenance of an effective state role in the federal system and a willingness by the Court's [five person] majority to use its authority to nurture and sustain that role."[78] Subsequent events, however, showed that the impact of *Usery* would be limited. In 1982 the Court sustained the application of a federal statute regulating utilities to state owned gas and electric companies and, in 1983, upheld the application of the federal Age Discrimination in Employment Act to state conservation employees.[79] Thus it caused no great surprise when in 1985 the Court, by a 5:4 majority, overruled *Usery*, largely on the grounds that the "traditional governmental functions" test for state regulatory immunity "is not only unworkable but is inconsistent with established principles of federalism and, indeed with those very federalism principles on which [*Usery*] purported to rest."[80] These outcomes were foreshadowed, in

76 National League of Cities v. Usery, 426 U.S. 833 (1976).

77 *Id.* at 852.

78 Blumstein, *Some Intersections of the Negative Commerce Clause and the New Federalism: The Case of Discriminatory State Income Tax Treatment of Out-of-State Tax-Exempt Bonds*, 31 VAND. L. REV. 473, 488 (1978).

In his majority opinion Justice Rehnquist prefers to examine the *nature* of the state *function* affected by the federal statute. He does not rest his case on the actual effects that the statute had on the state's independence. Blumstein correctly observes: "The opinion by Justice Rehnquist in *Usery* reflects the majority's attempt to breathe new life into commerce clause doctrine of an earlier era in order to restore the Court's role as a check on federal congressional intrusion on certain of the state's undefined essential functions." *Id.*

79 FERC v. Miss., 456 U.S. 742 (1982); EEOC v. Wyo., 103 S. Ct. 1054 (1983).

80 Garcia v. San Antonio Metro. Transit Auth., 105 S. Ct. 1005 (1985) [Eds.].

1981, by *Hodel v. Virginia Surface Mining and Reclamation Association.*[81] There the Supreme Court unanimously sustained the Surface Mining Control and Reclamation Act of 1977, a nationwide program designed to protect society and the environment from the adverse effects of surface coal mining operations. Sensitive to local interests, however, "the Surface Mining Act establish[ed] a program of cooperative federalism that allows the States, within limits established by federal minimum standards, to enact and administer their own regulatory programs, structured to meet their own particular needs."[82] But in the absence of approved state legislation, the full responsibility of enforcement rested on the Federal Government. The majority distinguished *Hodel* from *Usery,* indicating that here the full force of the law fell not on the "States as States" but on the individuals and private businesses whose behaviour Congress had rational basis for believing affected interstate commerce.

Yet, where environmental legislation is concerned, the Court has shown special deference to state legislation, as manifested in *Huron Portland Cement Co. v. City of Detroit.*[83] *Huron* differs from *Hodel* in that state legislation itself is the subject of the constitutional challenge, on both federal pre-emption and negative commerce clause grounds. Portland Cement claimed that Detroit's Smoke Abatement Code had been pre-empted by federal laws governing the inspection and certification of commercial shipping vessels. Barring pre-emption, the company maintained that air pollution was a subject requiring uniform national legislation. The company appeared to be on solid ground: it would have to restructure its boilers to meet Detroit's minimum pollution standards and risk subjection to the cumulative burdens of multiple state requirements. In a terse opinion, however, Justice Stewart rejected the pre-emption argument and was equally swift in his dismissal of the state's negative commerce clause case. He stated:

> The ordinance was enacted for the manifest purpose of promoting the health and welfare of the city's inhabitants. Legislation designed to free from pollution the very air that people breathe clearly falls within the exercise of even the most traditional concept of what is compendiously known as the police power.[84]

The Court's rejection of balancing in *Huron* was surprising in light of the transportation cases carefully setting forth standards for weighing benefits and burdens. But the use of the balancing technique might have dictated the opposite result in *Huron.* On the other hand, the decision was handed down in 1960, around the time that the country was just beginning to become concerned with

[81] 452 U.S. 264 (1981). *See also* Hodel v. Indiana, 101 S. Ct. 2376 (1981) (upholding related constitutional challenges to the Surface Mining Act); United States v. Helsley, 615 F.2d 784 (9th Cir. 1979) (upholding the Airborne Hunting Act); Friends of the Earth, Inc. v. Carey, 552 F.2d 25 (2d Cir.), *cert. denied,* 434 U.S. 902 (1977) (upholding the Clean Air Act); and Sierra Club v. EPA, 540 F.2d 1114 (D.C. Cir. 1976), *cert. denied,* 430 U.S. 959 (1977) (upholding the Clean Water Act).

[82] 101 S. Ct. at 2366.

[83] 362 U.S. 440 (1960).

[84] *Id.* at 442.

its polluted atmosphere. Although air pollution was clearly a national problem, a national solution seemed far off, and the Court under the circumstances might well have believed that state initiatives would best serve the national welfare in the long run. After all, the states had not yet lost their vitality as laboratories of social experimentation.

Yet, nearly twenty years later, in *City of Philadelphia v. New Jersey*,[85] the Supreme Court made clear that it would not tolerate an environmental measure that clearly discriminated against interstate commerce in such a way as to isolate the state from common problems afflicting the nation at large. New Jersey had prohibited the importation of most solid or liquid waste which originated or was collected outside the territorial limits of the state. New Jersey, of course, is a small state with limited landfill sites in which to dispose of waste material. Businesses immediately affected by the statute were the private landfills in New Jersey and several cities in other states that had contracts with these operators for waste disposal.

A threshold question before the Court in this case was whether waste material was to be considered an article of commerce at all in view of the "valueless" character of the product.[86] Here Justice Stewart (author of the *Huron* opinion), speaking for the majority, simply declared that "the banning of 'valueless' out-of-state wastes ... implicates no constitutional protection."[87] In fact, the Court distinguished the circumstances of this case from those cases upholding state quarantine laws banning the importation of noxious articles such as "diseased livestock that required destruction as soon as possible because their very movement risked contagion and other evils."[88] Here the harm appeared to be caused after the disposed waste material is buried in landfill sites. Although Justice Stewart cited cases invoking the balancing standard, he did not employ benefits and burdens analysis. Despite the Court's acknowledgment that environmental protection was part of the legislative purpose, that purpose was not relevant in view of the protectionist character of the means used to accomplish the end. The means used here, said the Court, "reflected ... the evils of economic isolation and protectionism."[89] And thus, concluded the Court, "where simple economic protectionism is effected by state legislation, a virtually *per se* rule of invalidity has been erected,"[90] in which case, it would appear, balancing is no longer necessary. The Court's focus on the threshold question of discrimination anticipated a clear ruling of invalidity in the New Jersey case.

The same "non-balancing" and largely formalistic approach was taken by the Court in *Sporhase v. Nebraska*.[91] In that case, decided in 1982, Colorado residents challenged the validity of a Nebraska statute forbidding withdrawal

85 437 U.S. 617 (1978).

86 *See* Bowman v. Chicago & Nw. Ry. Co., 125 U.S. 465 (1888).

87 437 U.S. 617, 622.

88 *Id.* at 628-29.

89 *Id.* at 623.

90 *Id.* at 624.

91 102 S. Ct. 3456 (1982).

of ground water to a neighboring state which denied such privileges to Nebraska. The ostensible purpose of the statute was to conserve and preserve scarce water resources, a purpose ordinarily warranting a posture of judicial deference to the state's "health and safety" concerns. Nebraska's reciprocity provision with respect to the transportation of water outside the state was regarded, however, as discriminatory legislation. As a result, the statute was reviewed with "strictest scrutiny," and without any balancing whatsoever. This standard was applied after the Court decided, for the first time, that ground water is an "article of commerce" subject to congressional regulation.

Another recent intersection between the negative commerce clause and state environmental protection legislation occurred in *Minnesota v. Clover Leaf Creamery Company*,[92] a case involving a state ban on the retail sale of milk in plastic non-returnable, non-refillable containers. Designed to "promote resource conservation, ease solid waste disposal problems, and conserve energy," the Minnesota statute forbade the bottling of milk in *plastic* non-returnable containers, but permitted "the use of ecologically undesirable paperboard milk cartons." The object was "to stop the introduction of the plastic nonreturnable container before it became entrenched in the market." In a 6-2 decision, the Court upheld the validity of the statute over commerce clause objections. Justice Brennan, writing for the majority, did not find "protectionism" inherent in this statute, even though it would promote the interests of the pulpwood over that of the plastics industry and substantially affect the practices of the dairy industry in and out of the state. First, the statute was not found to discriminate between interstate and intrastate commerce; in-state and out-of-state interests were treated equally. Second, the burden imposed on interstate commerce was found to be "relatively minor" against the backdrop of "the substantial state interest in promoting conservation of energy and other natural resources and easing solid waste disposal."[93]

Given the legitimacy of the legislative purpose behind the statute, in the absence of clear proof of a "clearly excessive" burden on commerce, the Court ruled in favor of the state. Justice Brennan's opinion has the faint ring of "rational basis" analysis despite his ostensible use of the balancing technique. Yet the balancing standard was employed only *after* the Court had characterized the Minnesota regulatory scheme as nondiscriminatory. The Court's deference to the state in this case is of a piece with its decision in *Huron*. First, the statute seemed very clearly directed to a well-recognized environmental problem, namely the conservation of energy and the elimination of litter and refuse from

[92] 449 U.S. 456 (1981).

[93] *Id.* at 473. ("Milk products may continue to move freely across the Minnesota border, and since most dairies packaged their products in more than one type of containers, the inconvenience of having to conform to different packaging requirements in Minnesota and the surrounding States should be slight. Within Minnesota, business will presumably shift from manufacturers of plastic nonreturnable containers to producers of paperboard cartons, refillable bottles, and plastic pouches but there is no reason to suspect that the gainers will be Minnesota firms, or the losers out-of-state firms." *Id.* at 472-73 (footnotes omitted)).

the land. Second, in the light of the statute's nondiscriminatory character, the burden of the legislation is one that probably falls equally on local and other states' interests, thus insuring that a state's own political processes will serve as a check against unduly burdensome regulation. We shall return later to a discussion of the "political checks" doctrine.

F. Social and Economic Policy

Given the structure of the American federal system, how far may the states go to promote various social and economic objectives? May they impose restrictions on the importation and exportation of goods for the purpose of stabilizing their economies? May they preserve their natural resources for the welfare and benefit of their own people? May they justly concern themselves with improving the quality of the goods and services destined for out-of-state consumption? The doctrinal response to these queries is currently in a state of flux.[94] We deal here only with recent illustrative cases. But first it is necessary to consider the landmark case of *H.P. Hood & Sons v. Du Mond*.[95]

1. Hood v. Du Mond : The Judicial Centerpiece

Hood sounds the central theme of the case law involving state legislation restrictive of certain trade practices. Its standard of review has sounded the death knell of state regulatory schemes whose purpose or effect is to restrict the exportation or importation of goods, to shield local business from competition by out-of-state concerns, to favor in-state residents by exacting higher prices from nonresident purchasers, and to place restrictions on the entry of businesses into the state or, alternatively, to pressure out-of-state businesses to locate within the state. The purpose behind such legislation is a critical aspect of judicial analysis, although varying judicial criteria have been used to determine whether the state has exceeded its power under the negative commerce clause.

The *Hood* Court struck down a New York regulatory scheme that on its face seemed sensibly crafted to protect the local milk market against destructive business practices. The case arose out of New York's refusal to grant *Hood*, a milk distributor who sold his products in Massachusetts, a fourth receiving station in New York, on the ground that another plant would disrupt competition in a market already adequately served. Speaking through Justice Jackson, the Court viewed the regulation as a discriminatory trade barrier. In a frequently quoted passage, Justice Jackson described the main purpose of the commerce clause:

[94] Good analytical surveys of the Court's recent commerce clause jurisprudence are: Schwartz, *Commerce, the States, and the Burger Court*, 74 Nw. U.L. Rev. 409-39 (1979); Blumstein, *supra* note 78; and Tushnet, *Rethinking the Dormant Commerce Clause*, 1979 Wis. L. Rev. 125-65 (1979).

[95] 336 U.S. 525 (1949).

Our system, fostered by the Commerce Clause, is that every farmer and every craftsman shall be encouraged to produce by the certainty that he will have free access to every market in the Nation, that no home embargoes will withhold his export, and no foreign state will by customs duties or regulations exclude them. Likewise every consumer may look to the free competition from every producing area in the nation to protect him from exploitation by any. Such was the vision of the Founders: such has been the doctrine of this Court which has given it reality.[96]

That a "state in its dealings with another may not place itself in a position of economic isolation" had already been raised to the level of "ultimate principle" in *Baldwin v. G.A.F. Seelig, Inc.*[97] In Justice Jackson's view, legislation that is protectionist and isolationist in "purpose" or "practical effect" warrants virtually summary rejection by the Court if the national interest in a common market is to be preserved.

The approach of *Hood*, however, is in sharp contrast to the balancing formula used in *Pike* and indeed to the benefits-burdens analysis that the Court had used increasingly in the ten years preceeding *Hood*. There, as just noted, Justice Jackson articulated the ultimate principles governing the judicial construction of the negative commerce clause. But ultimate principles, like general propositions, as Justice Holmes once reminded us, do not resolve concrete cases. The highly conceptualistic approach of Justice Jackson seemed calculated to support his well-known federalist views. But Justice Black, in a strong dissent, did not detect this brand of federalism in the Founders' vision. Moreover, he could discern no "hostile" or discriminatory intent behind New York's legislative scheme. Both Justices agreed that discrimination against interstate commerce was *per se* invalid. But they clearly had different notions of what constitutes discrimination. In subsequent cases, however, particularly those decided since 1975, considerations of federalism have loomed much larger than previously. Still the spirit of *Hood*, revivified in *Allenberg Cotton Co., Inc. v. Pittman*,[98] continues to haunt the corridors of commerce clause analysis, as some of the following cases show.

2. Regulating Competition

Hood declared that New York had unconstitutionally restricted New York products from moving freely in interstate commerce. By favoring local producers and consumers of milk New York had imposed an unjustified economic restraint on interstate commerce. The Court was clearly signaling in *Hood* that it would scrutinize state and local regulatory schemes with a particularly sharp eye when the purpose or result of them is to restrain the importation or exportation of legitimate articles of commerce. Any number of state statutes have been invalidated, long before *Hood*, and afterwards, for imposing such restraints.[99]

[96] *Id.* at 539.
[97] 294 U.S. 511 (1935).
[98] 419 U.S. 20 (1974).
[99] Leading cases are Dean Milk Co. v. City of Madison, 340 U.S. 349 (1951) (invalidating a local ordinance forbidding the sale of pasteurized milk unless processed and bottled at an approved pasteurization plant within a radius of five miles from the center of

Recent cases decided by the Burger Court have continued this strong interventionist approach to state legislation that severely burdens or discriminates against interstate trade. These include *City of Philadelphia v. New Jersey*;[100] *Great Atlantic & Pacific Tea Co. v. Cottrell*,[101] invalidating a Mississippi regulation conditioning the sale of out-of-state milk in Mississippi upon a reciprocity agreement signed by other states; *Pike v. Bruce Church, Inc.*,[102] nullifying Arizona's requirement that locally grown cantaloupes be packaged and labeled inside the state prior to their shipment in interstate commerce; *Hughes v. Oklahoma*,[103] striking down Oklahoma's attempt to prohibit the commercial sale of its natural minnows outside of the state; *Lewis v. BT Investment Managers, Inc.*,[104] invalidating a Florida law prohibiting out-of-state bank holding companies to conduct an investment advisory business within the state; and *Hunt v. Washington State Apple Advertising Commission*,[105] striking down a North Carolina statute requiring all closed cartons of apples shipped into the state for sale to bear only the simple grade or standard adopted by the United States Department of Agriculture and not the quality ranking supplied by another state. It is significant that four of these cases were decided unanimously, while the remaining two were handed down by 7-2 majorities.

a) Countervailing Themes

Yet strong federalistic counterthemes appear in other recent commerce clause cases, raising in the minds of some commentators serious questions about the strength of the *Hood* precedent.[106] Foremost among these cases are *Hughes v. Alexandria Scrap Corporation*,[107] *Reeves, Inc. v. Stake*,[108] *Exxon Corporation v. Governor of Maryland*,[109] and *White v. Massachusetts Council of Construction Employers, Inc.*[110]

In *Exxon*, Maryland flatly prohibited producers and refiners of petroleum products from establishing or operating retail service stations in the state. The statute was enacted in response to the favoritism that huge integrated oil companies showed to their affiliated retail outlets during the fuel shortage of 1973.

Madison); Foster-Fountain Packing Co. v. Haydel, 278 U.S. 1 (1928) (invalidating a Louisiana policy of favoring certain shrimp-related canning industries); and Pennsylvania v. West Virginia, 262 U.S. 553 (1923) (invalidating a West Virginia statute designed to preserve its resources in natural gas by preferring its own inhabitants).

100 437 U.S. 617 (1978). *See supra* text accompanying note 74.

101 424 U.S. 366 (1976).

102 397 U.S. 137 (1970). *See supra* text accompanying note 38.

103 441 U.S. 322 (1979).

104 100 S. Ct. 2009 (1980).

105 432 U.S. 333 (1977).

106 *See, e.g.*, Note, *The Commerce Clause and Economic Self-Protection: Has the Supreme Court Retreated from* Hood?, 14 GA. L. REV. 101 (1973).

107 426 U.S. 794 (1976).

108 447 U.S. 429 (1980).

109 437 U.S. 117 (1978).

110 103 S. Ct. 1042 (1983).

The state's effort to control the retail gasoline market was upheld by a deeply divided Court in the face of the objection that it favored local independent retailers over producers and refiners engaged in the interstate retail enterprise. The objection had merit. But the majority concluded that the state neither discriminated against out-of-state business nor interfered with the interstate flow of oil products. In so concluding, the Court seemed to minimize the practical effects of the state's policy. The finding of nondiscrimination, incidentally, was premised on the fact that no local producers or refineries had been favored by the state, although the statute clearly did favor a certain species of business enterprise.

Alexandria Scrap, Reeves, and *White* also sustained state or local laws challenged on the ground that they favored local citizens and business interests. *Alexandria Scrap* upheld a Maryland program designed to remove abandoned automobiles from the state's roadways and junkyards by offering a bounty to scrap processors who disposed of Maryland-titled automobiles. While both Maryland and non-Maryland processors were eligible, out-of-state processors were subject to more stringent documentation requirements, thereby measurably increasing the financial burden of doing business in Maryland, and making it difficult for them to compete with in-state processors. Because Maryland was participating in the market, rather than *regulating* it, the Court held that the commerce clause was not implicated in the state scheme. Nothing in the commerce clause, held the Court, forbids a state from entering the market as a purchaser of potential articles of interstate commerce and from restricting its trade to its own citizens.

Reeves involved a South Dakota owned and operated cement plant which sold its product in interstate commerce. During a shortage in the supply of cement South Dakota suddenly decided to give priority to in-state customers. Over the dissent of the Justice who wrote the majority opinion in *Alexandria Scrap,* the Court sustained the state's action, again underscoring the "basic distinction between States as market participants and States as market regulators."[111] The two cases – *Alexandria Scrap* and *Reeves* – stand for the proposition that when a state or local government enters the market as a participant it is not subject to the restraints of the commerce clause.

White, on the other hand, seemed to involve a governmental scheme closely related to the regulation struck down in *Hood,* and clearly distinguishable from *Alexandria Scrap* and *Reeves.* Here Boston required that all city construction projects financed by city funds be performed by a work force at least half consisting of *bona fide* residents of Boston, effectively restricting the ability of pri-

[111] 447 U.S. 429, 436. The four dissenting Justices argued that a state cannot be considered just another market participant because, as a state, it makes its market decisions based on factors quite different from those which dominate the decisions of private individuals. In *Alexandria Scrap,* Maryland had simply entered the market essentially to satisfy its own needs. Its bounty became a contributing market force but left the interstate market free. By contrast, in *Reeves,* South Dakota cut off interstate commerce.

vate employers or contractors to hire nonresidents, and thus curtailing nonresidents' access to jobs with private companies. A majority of seven Justices, however, did not regard the case as one *regulating* private economic relationships. Following *Alexandria Scrap* and *Reeves* the Court treated the city as a market participant when using its funds to enter into contracts for building construction. In so holding, the Court did not find it necessary to consider the impact of the city order on out-of-state residents. Burdens analysis, said the Court, commences only after it is established that market *regulation* rather than *participation* is the object of the statute. In the end, *White* illustrated the extent to which a doctrinal outcome is dependent on the Court's characterization of the facts and of the constitutional issue.

b) Taxation of Interstate Commerce

The Court's tolerance of legitimate local concerns with respect to matters affecting interstate commerce and its corresponding intolerance of pro- tectionism is echoed in those cases involving state taxation of interstate commerce. After all there is no question about the regulatory character of tax legislation. Yet the tax cases manifest greater solicitude for the position of the states in the federal union than do the regulatory cases. Constitutional doctrine had long held that the states could not impose any form of direct taxation on interstate commerce. But traditional doctrine has been substantially eroded as the Court has formulated new criteria for determining the validity of state attempts to tax commercial activities within the state which are part of interstate commerce. Recently, in *Complete Auto Transit, Inc. v. Brady,*[112] the Court held that even a tax on the "privilege of doing business"[113] in a state will not be considered an impermissible burden on interstate commerce as long as the activity (1) has a substantial nexus with the taxing state, (2) is fairly apportioned, (3) does not discriminate against interstate commerce, and (4) is fairly related to the services supplied by the states. In short, as the Court noted in an earlier opinion, "It was not the purpose of the Commerce Clause to relieve those engaged in interstate commerce from their just share of tax burdens even though it increases the cost of doing business."[114]

Commonwealth Edison Co. v. Montana,[115] decided in 1981, not only shows the readiness with which the Supreme Court is prepared to discard old doctrines but also underscores the widening freedom of the states to tax goods and resources destined for interstate shipment. Here, as in *Brady,* the Court rejects

112 430 U.S. 274 (1977).

113 The Court had previously held that a tax so labeled was an impermissible burden on interstate commerce. Spector Motor Serv., Inc. v. O'Conner, 340 U.S. 602 (1951). *See also,* Railway Express Agency v. Virginia, 358 U.S. 434 (1959) (*Railway Express* II). The Court had signaled its rejection of the *Spector* rule in Northwestern States Portland Cement Co. v. Minnesota, 358 U.S. 450 (1959); Colonial Pipeline Co. v. Traigle, 421 U.S. 100 (1975); and Railway Express Agency v. Virginia, 347 U.S. 359 (1954) (*Railway Express* I).

114 Western Live Stock v. Bureau of Revenue, 303 U.S. 250, 254, (1938).

115 453 U.S. 609 (1981).

older criteria such as the "direct-indirect effects" standard, and expressly disapproves of the mechanical approach of *Heisler v. Thomas Colliery Co.*[116] which held that a tax is not subject to the strictures of the commerce clause if levied on goods prior to their entry into interstate commerce. What is important now is the practical consequences of a tax measured by *Brady's* four-part test. Under this test, a deeply divided court found in favor of a Montana severance tax of up to 30 percent of the contract sales price on the mining of coal, even though Montana owns 25 percent of all known coal reserves in the United States and ships 90 percent of its coal to other states. Over the objection that this high tax rate impermissibly burdened and discriminated against interstate commerce because the tax burden is borne primarily by out-of-state consumers, the Court held that the state tax was a legitimate revenue measure properly apportioned to the general activities of the state government. The tax did not discriminate, said the Court, since it fell equally on in-state and out-of-state purchasers. In effect, those who challenged the tax argued that residents of one state are entitled to buy the richly endowed resources of another state at reasonable prices. The Court was not convinced that "the commerce clause, of its own force, gives the residents of one state the right to control in this fashion the terms of resource development and depletion in a sister state." In any case, the Court concluded, the judiciary was not institutionally equipped to determine the appropriate amount or level of taxation. That Congress had not yet seen fit to enter the field with legislation of its own merely confirmed, at least in the mind of Justice White, the propriety of judicial restraint in this case.

But the Court shows no such restraint when the effect of a state tax is to halt interstate commerce altogether. Thus, in *Boston Stock Exchange v. State Tax Commission*[117] a unanimous Court struck down New York's stock transfer tax, the effect of which was to favor the New York Stock Exchange since the tax gave an advantage to sales made within New York. The tax was found to be discriminatory because it operated as an incentive for out-of-state residents to negotiate stock transfers in New York and, alternatively, encouraged New York residents to keep their business in the state, a practice that violated the free trade purpose of the commerce clause.

3. Quality Control Legislation and Conservation of Wild Life

Hunt v. Washington State Apple Advertising Commission[118] and *Hughes v. Oklahoma*[119] will serve, finally, as appropriate vehicles for summarizing the Court's basic approach to legislation intended to enhance the quality of a product and to preserve certain natural resources. Both statutory objectives are likely to implicate the commerce clause. Washington State, a leader in the apple growing industry, sought to protect the reputation of Washington apples by

[116] 260 U.S. 245 (1922).
[117] 429 U.S. 318 (1977).
[118] 432 U.S. 333 (1977).
[119] 441 U.S. 322 (1978).

establishing a stringent, mandatory inspection program which requires all apples shipped in interstate commerce to be tested under strict quality standards and graded accordingly. Washington challenged the validity of North Carolina's rule, unique in the fifty states, requiring all closed containers of apples shipped into or sold in the state to display the single uniform standard established by the U.S. Agriculture Department or none at all. The case was a classic confrontation between one state's desire to maintain the quality of its goods and another state's desire to protect its residents from fraud and deception in the marketing of apples. The question raised was whether one state can insist on the application of its quality control standards when those standards are superior to those employed by other states.

The Supreme Court unanimously invalidated the North Carolina statute. Although neutral on its face, the impact or practical effect of the law was considered to be discriminatory. The statute was found to be flawed in three respects: (1) it multiplied the costs of Washington apple dealers doing business in North Carolina; (2) it deprived Washington's apple industry of the economic advantages it had earned throughout the nation, owing to its inspection and grading system; and (3) it had a "leveling effect" which protected the North Carolina apple industry from competing with out-of-state products. In short, the North Carolina statute not only hindered competition in the sale of apples, but also, by depriving purchasers of valuable information concerning the quality of the closed apple containers, tended to defeat the state's declared intention of eliminating the problems of deception and confusion among consumers.

The significance of *Hughes* is that it brought state regulation of wildlife within the mainstream of modern commerce clause analysis. Under the theory of *Geer v. Connecticut*,[120] which *Hughes* overruled, a state "owned" the wildlife within its borders and could thus restrict its use to the social and economic benefits of its own citizens. *Geer* stood out as an anomaly in commerce clause jurisprudence, for the Court had long rejected the "legal fiction of state ownership" with respect to other kinds of natural resources. Oklahoma, as part of its resource conservation code, banned the shipment for sale outside of the state of minnows which were seined within the state's own waters. (The ban did not apply to hatchery-bred minnows.) The fish could, however, be procured and sold within the state in any quantity.

The statute was invalidated over the strong dissent of Justices Rehnquist and Burger. The Court found the statute discriminatory on its face, but administered the death blow under the analytical framework of *Pike*. While recognizing that the protection of wild animals is a legitimate local purpose similar to the state's interest in protecting the health and safety of its citizens, the majority did not find that Oklahoma's law served that purpose. Less restrictive means to achieve the end were available to the state. Blocking the flow of interstate trade at the state's border was a burden on commerce that could not be offset by the actual benefits gained. Interestingly, the Court's balancing rhetoric intermin-

[120] 161 U.S. 519 (1896).

gles with the language of *Hood:* the Justices issued somber warnings against the "balkanization" of the economy and underscored once again the basic principle that "our economic unit is the Nation."

G. Concluding Remarks

The results of the cases discussed in this section on the American commerce clause cannot easily be explained by the doctrinal techniques used by the Court in arriving at its conclusions. The balancing technique, which appears to prevail in those cases not involving discrimination against interstate commerce, contains few ingredients capable of predicting judicial outcomes. On the other hand, it is not always a simple matter even to discern whether a state statute impinging on commerce is discriminatory. Such discrimination may depend as much on how the Court characterizes the legislation in question as on the facts themselves. Still, the outcome of most cases discussed in this section seems intuitively correct, largely because they reflect satisfactory compromises between state and federal interests.

Yet, more or less consistent patterns do emerge from this survey, especially if we look at the cases, as Vincent Blasi has done,[121] in terms of the effect of the state law under challenge rather than in terms of the policy area represented by the law. For example, the Court has usually invalidated state laws restricting the exploitation of its natural or created resources to its own citizens.[122] One significant exception to this general rule is the situation in which the state acts as market participant rather than as regulator. By the same token, as manifested by *Hunt v. Washington Apple Advertising Commission*, the Court has tended to strike down state laws that control the manner in which out-of-state goods are marketed within the state.[123] Also struck down, and largely as a matter of course, are state laws barring interstate dealers from selling to local customers.[124] On the other hand, the Court almost invariably upholds state regulations restricting the entry of goods for health and safety reasons.[125] As the cases analyzed in this section show, the Court has also been sympathetic to state laws designed to ensure the quality of local products, although it "has charted a mixed and uncertain course regarding laws that regulate business transactions in order to protect producers from being deceived or exploited by interstate dealers."[126] Finally, if the state is acting as a market participant, it may seek to alleviate unemployment by requiring interstate companies to hire a certain

[121] Blasi, *Constitutional Limitations on the Power of States to Regulate the Movement of Goods in Interstate Commerce*, in 1 Courts and Free Markets, *supra* note 7, at 174–221.
[122] *Id.* at 192-97.
[123] *Id.* at 199–207.
[124] *Id.* at 207–11.
[125] *Id.* at 211–18.
[126] *Id.* at 197.

percentage of local residents.[127] Under the Court's decisions states are also permitted to stabilize their economies by imposing price controls on products bought and sold within state borders.[128]

III. The European Economic Community

A. Introduction

The complicated web of dormant commerce clause jurisprudence in the United States has been spun from the implications of the brief constitutional command conferring upon Congress the power to regulate commerce among the states. The EEC Treaty, by contrast, contains numerous provisions specifically aimed at prohibiting impediments to intra-Community trade, but which exist in the context of a more temporally limited jurisprudential tradition. Still, the issues that arise in the course of interpreting the provisions of the Treaty are equally complex, and thus the solutions crafted in the Community legal system to these problems of competing government authority may be, for Americans, much more than a comparative legal curiosity.

We turn our attention in this section first to those provisions of the EEC Treaty which establish the principle of the free movement of goods – in general, to those articles which prohibit direct or indirect restrictions on imports and exports. We then turn our attention more carefully to the interpretation by the Court of Justice of the recognized exceptions to the principle of free movement of goods – in particular, to those based on reasons of public health, safety or morality, and on the legitimate protection of consumers and of other accepted national social and economic interests.

B. The Free Movement of Goods Guaranteed in the Treaty

1. Import Restrictions

The most general provision relating to import restrictions is article 30, which prohibits all measures having an effect equivalent to quantitative restrictions on imports. This notion has been interpreted by the Commission as governing all "measures, other than those applicable equally to domestic and imported products, which hinder imports which could otherwise take place, including measures which make importation more difficult or costly than the disposal of domestic production.[129] According to the Court, the notion includes all mea-

127 White v. Massachusetts Council of Constr. Employers, Inc., 103 S. Ct. 1042 (1983).
128 Blasi, *supra* note 121 at 188–91.
129 Commission Directive No. 70/50 of 22 Dec. 1969, JO No. L 13, 19 Jan. 1970, p. 29 ([1970-I] OJ (spec. Eng. ed.) at p. 17).

sures capable of hindering intra-Community trade, whether directly or indirectly, actually or potentially.[130]

It results from both these definitions that it is not necessary to establish that a measure has in fact produced a restrictive effect; the mere potentiality of such effects is sufficient to make article 30 applicable.[131] It is further not required that the measure discriminate against *all* imported goods or in favor of *all* domestic products; the restriction imposed by France on the advertising of grain alcohols (such as whisky and gin) was held to constitute a measure of equivalent effect inasmuch as it did not apply to alcohol made from cane sugar or from wine and fruits (of which France is a major producer), even though certain domestic products, such as "pastis," were also subject to the ban.[132] Similarly, a measure which discriminates only against products imported via certain channels (*e.g.* parallel imports) is prohibited by article 30 even though products imported via other channels (*e.g.* imports via the appointed exclusive distributor) are treated like domestic products.[133] Finally, the fact that the authorities of the importing country are empowered to grant derogations from the restrictive measure and that they frequently exercise that power does not prevent the measure from being equivalent to a quantitative restriction.[134]

Although the Commission initially considered that measures which are equally applicable to domestic and imported products (such as measures regulating the shape, size, weight, composition, presentation, identification or packaging of products) are prohibited only where their restrictive effect on the free movement of goods "exceeds the effect intrinsic to trade rules,"[135] the broad definition used by the Court does not make any distinction between "discriminatory" measures and measures which are "equally applicable." If a given measure, whatever its nature, makes the import of goods from other Member States more difficult or costly than the disposal of domestic production, it falls under the Court's definition. Nevertheless, as we shall see, the Court accepts that equally applicable measures may lawfully produce certain restrictive effects if they are justified by an overriding consideration of general interest.

Article 36 provides a certain number of exceptions to the prohibitions of article 30. It allows Member States to prohibit or restrict imports if this is "justified on grounds of public morality, public policy or public security; the protection of health and life of humans, animals or plants; the protection of national treasures possessing artistic, historic or archaeological value; or the protection

[130] This definition was used for the first time in Case 8/74, Procureur du Roi v. Dassonville, [1974] ECR 837, 852. It has been repeated in a steady line of decisions since then.

[131] This has been confirmed by the Court in Case 12/74, Commission v. Federal Republic of Germany, [1975] ECR 181 (the "Sekt and Weinbrand" case).

[132] Case 152/78, Commission v. French Republic, [1980] ECR 2299.

[133] Case 104/75, De Peijper, [1976] ECR 613.

[134] Case 82/77, Openbaar Ministerie of the Kingdom of the Netherlands v. Van Tiggele, [1978] ECR 25.

[135] Commission Directive No. 70/50, *supra* note 129, art. 3.

of industrial and commercial property." The scope of this exception is limited by the requirement that the prohibition or restriction may not "constitute a means of arbitrary discrimination or a disguised restriction on trade between Member States."

2. Export Restrictions

Article 34 provides that "quantitative restrictions on exports, and all measures having equivalent effect, shall be prohibited between Member States."

Initially, it appeared that the Court was prepared to consider that any measure restricting production of a given product was prohibited by this provision.[136] However, later decisions indicate that article 34 applies only if the object or the effect of the Member State measure is specifically to restrict exports by a Member State treating differently its domestic trade from its export trade.[137] The difference in result is probably explicable by the fact that the earlier case of *Van Haaster* was not concerned with the interpretation of article 30 as such, but with an identically-worded provision contained in a regulation setting up a common organization of the market in the agricultural sector. While the Court's conclusion in that case is based on the interpretation of the phrase "measure of effect equivalent to an export prohibition," its reasoning indicates that it considered that the agricultural regulation at issue had pre-empted the field, thus making all possibility of intervention by the Member States in the production and marketing of the products unlawful.[138]

The different treatment of the phrase "equally applicable measures" under articles 30 and 34 has been regretted by Advocate General Capotorti.[139] It would seem, however, that measures which apply equally without distinguishing between products sold on the domestic market and export products are less likely to have protective effects than measures which apply equally to imported and to domestic products. Whereas the impediment to imports resulting from diverging Member State requirements is, by its very nature, susceptible of protecting national production, the impediment to export is, at most, capable of putting exported products in a disadvantageous competitive position on the markets of other Member States. It is not surprising that the Court should not be so concerned by such a result. Moreover, the application of article 34 to national measures limiting production would give that provision an excessively wide coverage. If this were the interpretation of the

136 Case 190/73, Officier van Justitie v. Van Haaster, [1974] ECR 1123.

137 Case 15/79, P. B. Groenveld B. V. v. Produktschap voor Vee en Vlees, [1979] ECR 3409; Case 155/80, Summary Proceedings against Oebel, [1981] ECR 1993.

138 Koppensteiner, *Vertikale Preisbindung durch Gesetz als Maßnahme gleicher Wirkung wie eine mengenmäßige Einfuhrbeschränkung*, 23 RIW/AWD 581, 589 (1977); Baumann, *Common Organizations of the Market and National Law*, 14 C.M.L. Rev. 303, 322 (1977).

139 *See* the Opinion of Advocate General Capotorti in Case 155/80, *Oebel*, [1981] ECR 1993, 2012.

provision, then legislation imposing a requirement of obtaining planning permission before constructing a factory could arguably fall under article 34, as could legislation relating to health and safety at work.[140]

The exceptions of article 36 apply to restrictions on export as well as to restrictions on import.

3. Import Taxes and Discriminatory Internal Taxes

Article 9 prohibits, *inter alia*, all customs duties on imports and charges having equivalent effect. Initially, the Court considered that a charge had an effect "equivalent" to an import duty only if it had a protective effect.[141] However, in a judgment of 1969, the Court considered a Belgian tax on the import of raw diamonds to be a charge of equivalent effect. It was clear that this tax did not have any protective effect, since raw diamonds are not produced in Belgium. Nevertheless, the Court considered that since the tax was levied by reason of the fact that the goods crossed the border, it had to be regarded as equivalent to a customs duty.[142] The Court also stated in the same case that the fact that the amount of the tax was extremely small (0.33%) did not exempt it from the prohibition.

The Court considers that when a tax is levied both on domestic products and on imports, it does not fall under article 9 but constitutes an internal tax covered by article 95. That provision prohibits Member States from imposing any internal tax of any kind on the products of other Member States in excess of that imposed on similar domestic products.

The distinction between the respective fields of application of article 9 and of article 95 has given rise to problems where a tax, although part of a system of internal taxation, is levied on imported products of which no domestic production exists (e.g. Italian lemons imported into Germany). The Court has held that the fact that no domestic production exists is irrelevant, the decisive factor being that the tax is part of a general system of taxation applicable to all products.[143] Difficulties can also arise where the tax imposed on the imported product is not levied at the same marketing stage or according to the same modalities as the tax on the domestic product. The Court held that it was no defense to the illegality of a French tax on imported lard that animals slaughtered in France would already have been subject to a similar charge at an earlier stage of

[140] *See* Oliver, *Measures of Equivalent Effect: a Reappraisal*, 19 C.M.L. Rev. 217, 239 (1982); VerLoren van Themaat, *De Artikelen 30–36 van het EEG-Verdrag*, R.M. Themis 378 (1980); Barents, *New Developments in Measures Having Equivalent Effect*, 18 C.M.L. Rev. 271, 302–03 (1981).

[141] Joined Cases 2 & 3/62, Commission v. Grand Duchy of Luxembourg and Kingdom of Belgium, [1962] ECR 425.

[142] Joined Cases 2 & 3/69, Sociaal Fonds voor de Diamantarbeiders v. SA Brachfeld and Sons and Chougol Diamond Co., [1969] ECR 211.

[143] Case 90/79, Commission v. French Republic, [1981] ECR 283 (tax on the use of reprographic instruments).

processing.[144] The Court has also held that when a tax, although apparently imposed evenhandedly on imports and on domestic products, was refunded to domestic producers in the form of a subsidy, it amounted in reality to a charge of equivalent effect prohibited by article 9, since in the final analysis the financial burden was borne only by the importers.[145]

The operation of article 95 does not require that the discriminatory tax place *all* imported products in a less favorable position than competing domestic products. Thus, the Court condemned the Danish system according preferential tax treatment to *akvavit*, most of which is domestically produced, even though the effect of the tax was to protect *akvavit* against all other alcoholic beverages, whether domestically produced or imported, and although there were some imports into Denmark of *akvavit* made in other EEC countries.[146] In judgments rendered on the same day, the Court condemned equally, as incompatible with article 95, the French tax system benefitting cognac and *armagnac* and the Italian tax system benefitting brandy and *grappa*, even though, here too, the discrimination did not affect all alcoholic beverages imported from other Member States and even though it affected adversely some alcoholic beverages which were produced in the countries imposing the tax.[147] The same principle was applied in the *Kortmann* case, where the Court held that an internal tax was contrary to article 95 if it discriminated against parallel imports, even though the tax burden imposed on products imported by the appointed distributor was not greater than the burden imposed on the domestic products.[148]

4. Export Taxes

Article 16 provides for the abolition between Member States of all customs duties on exports and charges having equivalent effect. Although there is no express prohibition against the imposition of discriminatory internal taxes on exports between Member States, the Court has held that the basic prohibition against discrimination contained in article 95 applies also to taxes imposed by reason of the export of a given product.[149]

Although normally internal taxes levied on a product or its constituent elements are refunded in case of export, the Treaty imposes no obligation on Member States to effect such a refund. The only obligation which the Treaty

144 Case 132/78, Denkavit Loire S.à.r.l. v. French State, [1979] ECR 1923; the Court had already adopted a similar approach in Case 87/75, Bresciani v. Amministrazione Italiana delle Finanze, [1976] ECR 129, and Case 35/76, Simmenthal SpA v. Italian Minister for Finance, [1976] ECR 1871.

145 Case 77/72, Capolongo v. Azienda Agricola Maya, [1973] ECR 611.

146 Case 171/78, Commission v. Kingdom of Denmark, [1980] ECR 447.

147 Thus, anisated spirits were included by the French legislation in the same category as, *e.g.*, whiskey and gin. *See* Case 168/78, Commission v. French Republic, [1980] ECR 347; Case 169/78, Commission v. Italian Republic, [1980] ECR 385.

148 Case 32/80, Officier van Justitie v. Kortmann, [1981] ECR 251.

149 Case 142/77, Statens Kontrol med Ædle Metaller v. Larsen, [1978] ECR 1543.

provides is the prohibition of any refund of internal taxes in excess of the internal taxation actually imposed, directly or indirectly, on the exported product.[150] Member States are free, therefore, to effect only a partial repayment[151] or not to make any repayment at all.[152] The fact that double taxation may result if a tax is imposed on the same product in the importing country does not constitute a violation of article 95.

5. Other State Interventions Affecting Imports and Exports

The Treaty contains several provisions which are designed to cope with other types of Member State interventions capable of restricting imports or exports. Thus, articles 92 to 94 provide for supervision by the Commission of Member State aids which distort or threaten to distort competition and affect trade between Member States. However, since there is no directly enforceable prohibition on Member State aids,[153] these provisions offer individuals a less effective remedy than those which have been described above.

Article 37, which provides for the "adjustment" of Member State monopolies of a commercial character with a view to ensuring that no discrimination exists regarding the conditions under which goods are procured and marketed between nationals of Member States, is of more interest, especially since it has been interpreted by the Court as calling for the abolition, with direct effect in domestic law, of the exclusive rights of import and export previously enjoyed by those monopolies.[154] If one compares this provision, and the interpretation given to it by the Court of Justice, with the U.S. cases of *Hughes v. Alexandria Scrap Corporation* and *Reeves, Inc. v. Stake,*[155] one may wonder whether the EEC law concerning state involvement in business is not more advanced than the U.S. law on the subject.

C. The Protection of Legitimate National Interests

Having examined the Treaty provisions dealing with restrictive State interventions in the import and export field, we shall now examine in more detail the extent to which the interpretation given to these measures by the Court of Justice allows due consideration of legitimate national interests, such as the need to ensure the preservation of public health and safety, public morality, consumer protection, and certain social and economic interests, such as quality promotion, the protection of certain social classes or forms of business, and energy conservation. The fact that some of these interests are specifically mentioned in article 36 does not indicate how a given measure should be examined

150 EEC Treaty art. 96.
151 Case 27/74, Demag AG v. Finanzamt Duisburg-Süd, [1974] ECR 1037.
152 Case 142/77, Statens Kontrol med Ædle Metaller v. Larsen, [1978] ECR 1543.
153 *See* Case 77/72, *Capolongo,* [1973] ECR 611.
154 Case 59/75, Pubblico Ministero v. Manghera, [1976] ECR 91.
155 *See supra* § II.F.2.a.

to determine whether it is "justified" by one of the listed exceptions. Moreover, article 36 allows for exceptions to be made only to the prohibition of article 30; it cannot be used to justify discriminatory or protective taxes covered by articles 9, 16 or 95, or other obstacles to trade.[156]

1. Public Health and Safety

Public health and public safety are both expressly mentioned in article 36 among the reasons by which import and export restrictions may be justified. Most of the cases decided to date have concerned restrictions allegedly justified by considerations of public health. It can be assumed, however, that the Court would apply the same tests to restrictions based on considerations of public safety.

When it is faced with a claim by a Member State that a restrictive measure is justified by reasons of public health, the first thing the Court does is to verify whether in the absence of the measure there would exist a real risk to public health. Where that is not the case, the Court takes it upon itself to reject the claim. Thus, in the celebrated *Cassis de Dijon* case,[157] the Court did not accept the German Government's argument that the imposition of a standard for minimum alcohol content of liqueurs was justified by the need to combat alcoholism. Similarly, in the *Gilli* case,[158] it found that the prohibition enacted by Italy on the sale of vinegar other than wine vinegar was not justified since other kinds of vinegar were not damaging to human health. And in the German *Meat Preparations* case,[159] the Court decided that a German legal provision prohibiting the sale of meat products prepared from meat which had not been obtained in the country of processing was not necessary to protect public health.

Normally, it is up to the Member State to establish that the protective measure it adopted is justified under article 36.[160] However, to do so it is sufficient if the Member State shows the existence of a risk; it does not have to establish that, in the absence of the measure, public health would inevitably be endangered. Member States have a certain discretion in deciding at what level they wish to place the protection which they want to give to public health.[161] The recent *Nisin* case offers an interesting example of this approach.[162] Nisin is an antibiotic which occurs naturally in small quantities in cheese. The exact extent

156 Case 32/80, Officier van Justitie v. Kortmann, [1981] ECR 251, 267 at recital 11.

157 Case 120/78, Rewe-Zentral AG v. Bundesmonopolverwaltung für Branntwein, [1979] ECR 649.

158 Case 788/79, Gilli and Andres, [1980] ECR 2071.

159 Case 153/78, Commission v. Federal Republic of Germany, [1979] ECR 2555.

160 Case 251/78, Firma Denkavit Futtermittel GmbH v. Minister für Ernährung, Landwirtschaft und Forsten des Landes Nordrhein-Westfalen, [1979] ECR 3369, 3392 at recital 24.

161 Case 104/75, De Peijper, [1976] ECR 613, 635 at recital 15.

162 Case 53/80, Officier van Justitie v. Koninklijke Kaasfabriek Eyssen BV, [1981] ECR 409.

of the health risk created by excessive consumption of nisin is not yet completely known. The laws of the Member States relating to the addition of nisin to cheese fall into three groups. In France and in the United Kingdom its use is permitted without limits, subject, in the case of the United Kingdom, to an obligation to specify on the label that the cheese "contains permitted preservatives." In Belgium, Denmark, Ireland and Italy, the use of nisin is permitted up to specified limits, which vary. In Germany, Luxembourg and the Netherlands, the addition of nisin is forbidden except in products destined for export. An expert consultative body in the Netherlands had recommended the relaxation of the Dutch law prohibiting the addition of nisin to cheese so as to permit the addition of nisin up to a specified limit.

In its judgment, the Court rejected the Commission's argument that it was up to the Dutch Government to establish that an outright prohibition on the addition of nisin was necessary for the protection of public health. The Court considered that in view of the lack of certainty as to the extent of the risk which the absorption of nisin could create, especially in view of the different eating habits in the various Member States, the prohibitory provision of the Dutch law could be considered as justified on grounds of public health.

In determining whether a measure is "necessary" to ensure the protection of public health, the Court takes into account the extent of the burden which the measure imposes on trade between Member States. Thus, in the German *Meat Preparations* case, the Court insisted that the effect of the measure was to discriminate against processors of meat who imported their raw material from another Member State as against those who obtained their supplies of meat within their own country. Although the measure did not prevent the import of products from another Member State (as long as they were made from meat coming from that Member State), the Court insisted on the fact that the hindrance to intra-Community trade resulting from the measure was out of proportion with regard to the objective pursued.

The Court also examines whether a measure, although necessary, can be replaced by a less restrictive alternative. Thus, in the *De Peijper* case,[163] a Dutch legal provision required parallel importers of pharmaceutical products to submit to the national health authorities certain documents which could be obtained only from the manufacturer of the products or his appointed distributor. The effect of this provision was to make all parallel imports of pharmaceutical products dependent on the good will of the manufacturer or of the official distributor. The Court considered that such a regulation could not benefit from the exception provided in article 36 since public health could be protected as effectively by less restrictive measures, such as collaboration between the Dutch authorities and those of the Member State in which the pharmaceutical products in question were produced. The decision is interesting, insofar as it implies that under certain circumstances the national authorities have a positive duty to collaborate between themselves in order to

[163] Case 104/75, De Peijper, [1976] ECR 613.

minimize the burden to interstate trade which results from administrative controls necessary to protect public health.

In addition to verifying that there exists a real health risk, that the protective measure does not impose an excessive burden on interstate trade, and that the measure cannot be replaced by a less restrictive alternative, the Court also examines whether it does not constitute a "disguised restriction" or an "arbitrary discrimination" within the meaning of the last sentence of article 36. The fact that the measure applies only to imports creates a strong presumption that it is arbitrary. However, this presumption can be rebutted if it is shown that adequate safeguards are enforced on the Member State level to prevent a similar health risk from arising. Thus, in the *Rewe-Zentralfinanz* case of 8 July 1975, the Court considered that phytosanitary import inspections could lawfully be carried out by Germany to prevent imports of diseased apples if effective measures were also taken internally to prevent the marketing of contaminated domestic products and if there was reason to believe that a risk of propagation of the disease would exist if no inspection was held on importation.[164] Similarly, in the *Nisin* case, the fact that the Dutch prohibition did not apply to cheese exported to other Member States was not considered to be an indication that the prohibition on use of nisin in cheese marketed in the Netherlands was an arbitrary discrimination or a disguised restriction on trade between Member States, since the dangers of nisin for human health were not assessed in the same manner in all Member States.[165]

In the case concerning the regulation of the advertising of alcoholic beverages in France, the Court accepted that, in principle, restrictions on the advertising of alcoholic beverages can be justified under article 36 as necessary to combat alcoholism. However, when the restriction does not apply evenhandedly but allows for important exceptions in favor of certain beverages made in the Member State imposing the restrictions, it constitutes an arbitrary discrimination in trade between Member States, thereby precluding the possibility of invoking article 36.[166]

The obstacles to free trade resulting from exceptions justified under article 36 are not necessarily permanent. The Treaty provides in article 100 for the adoption of Council directives to harmonize Member State provisions which directly affect the establishment or functioning of the Common Market. Numerous directives have been adopted under that provision to harmonize Member State legislation concerning food additives, veterinary and sanitary inspections, the marketing of pharmaceutical products, etc. The Court has repeatedly stated that the purpose of article 36 was not "to preserve certain matters to the exclusive jurisdiction of Member States but to permit national laws to derogate from the principle of free movement of goods to the extent to which such derogation is and continues to be justified for the attainment of the

164 Case 4/75, Rewe-Zentralfinanz eGmbH v. Landwirtschaftskammer, [1975] ECR 843.
165 Case 53/80, *Koninklijke Kaasfabriek Eyssen,* [1981] ECR 409.
166 Case 152/78, Commission v. French Republic, [1980] ECR 2299.

objectives referred to in that Article."[167] When directives have been adopted under article 30, recourse to article 36 therefore ceases to be justified.

The result is that, as the activities of the Community in the field of harmonization progress, this will result in a progressive narrowing of the scope of application of article 36. However, to the extent a directive only provides for a minimum harmonization or deliberately leaves certain aspects open, the Member States retain their power to invoke article 36 to justify measures restricting imports.[168]

Although, in the absence of a Community directive, sanitary inspections of imported products can be justified under article 36, Member States are not allowed to levy duties on the occasion of such inspections. Such duties must be considered as charges having an effect equivalent to customs duties, at least where no comparable duty is imposed on the marketing of the same domestic products.[169] If a duty is charged according to the same or comparable criteria on domestic products, the duty will be considered as an internal tax subject to article 95 and not as a charge of equivalent effect to a customs duty.[170] The Court decided in the *Bauhuis* case that where sanitary controls had been harmonized throughout the Community by providing that the inspection should be effected in the country of export, it was permissible for that country to charge a reasonable amount as compensation for the inspection. Although article 16 prohibits taxes that have an equivalent effect to an export duty, the Court considered that, since such inspection was not a measure "unilaterally imposed by each Member State" but was effected in accordance with the provisions of the Community directive, the taxes charged on the occasion of these inspections did not constitute charges of equivalent effect if their amount did not exceed the real costs of the inspection.[171]

2. Public Morality

In the only case rendered to date in which the Court had to deal with national restrictions based on grounds of morality, the Court adopted a cautious approach. To a large extent, this is understandable since the requirements of public morality do not readily lend themselves to objective ascertainment. As Advocate General Warner pointed out.

> [A]lthough no doubt the opinions of experts may differ on what may justifiably be prescribed for the protection of indications of origin, of consumers generally, and of the health and life of humans, animals or plants, those are matters which, at the end of the

[167] Case 5/77, Tedeschi v. Denkavit Commerciale s.r.l., [1977] ECR 1555; Case 35/76, Simmenthal SpA v. Italian Minister for Finance, [1976] ECR 1871.

[168] Barents, *supra* note 140, at 279-80; Masclet, *Les articles 30, 36 et 100 du Traité CEE à la lumière de l'arrêt* Cassis de Dijon, 16 R.T.D.E. 611, 617-19 (1980).

[169] Case 29/72, S.p.A. Marimex v. Italian Finance Administration, [1972] ECR 1309; Case 39/73, Rewe-Zentralfinanz eGmbH v. Direktor der Landwirtschaftskammer Westfalen-Lippe, [1973] ECR 1039.

[170] Case 32/80, Officier van Justitie v. Kortmann, [1981] ECR 251.

[171] Case 46/76, W.J.G. Bauhuis v. The Netherlands State, [1977] ECR 5.

> day, are susceptible of objective assessment. They are, moreover, matters on which it is, by and large, possible to prescribe a solution applicable uniformly in all Member States. ... A different approach is, however ... inevitable, when the question under consideration is that of the circumstances in which a Member State may be justified in imposing prohibitions or restrictions on imports "on grounds of public morality". The concept of "public morality" is not one that can be made the subject of objective assessment, or of a Community-wide definition. It is a matter of individual opinion, rather than of expert opinion.[172]

The European Court of Human Rights adopted a similarly cautious attitude when it was confronted with a similar problem in the *Handyside Case.*[173]

In the *Henn and Darby* case, the Court had to decide whether the application of the United Kingdom legislation on pornography to imports of publications of Danish origin was justified under article 36. It appears that the UK legislation applied a dual standard. It allows prevention of imports of "indecent or obscene" material whereas domestic products can be sold throughout most of the United Kingdom (except the Isle of Man and Scotland) even if they are "indecent," as long as they are not "obscene." Moreover, the sale of "obscene" material of UK origin can be justified on the grounds that it is in the interests of science, literature, art or learning or other objects of general concern, whereas import of "obscene" articles can never be justified on those grounds. In spite of this duality of standards, the Court did not consider that the prohibition constituted an arbitrary discrimination or a disguised restriction on trade between Member States. It started out by stating, in a general manner, that "in principle, it is for each Member State to determine in accordance with its own scale of values and in the form selected by it the requirements of public morality in its territory."[174] Referring to the legislation in force in the United Kingdom, the Court declared that "it cannot be disputed that the statutory provisions applied by the United Kingdom in regard to the importation of articles having an indecent or obscene character come within the powers reserved to the Member States by the first sentence of Article 36."[175] As regards the claim that the laws applicable in different parts of the United Kingdom applied different tests, the Court said that

> each Member State is entitled to impose prohibitions on imports justified on grounds of public morality for the whole of its territory ... whatever the structure of its constitution may be and however the powers of legislating in regard to the subject in question may be distributed. The fact that certain differences exist between the laws in force in the different constituent parts of a Member State does not thereby prevent that State from applying a unitary concept in regard to prohibitions on imports imposed, on grounds of public morality, on trade with other Member States.[176]

172 Case 34/79, Regina v. Henn and Darby, [1979] ECR 3795, 3818 at 3821.

173 Handyside Case, Judgment of 7 Dec. 1976, Series A: Vol. 24, p. 22 (Pubs. of Eur. Ct. H.R., 1976). For further discussion of this case *see* Frowein, Schulhofer & Shapiro, *supra* note 54, esp. at § IV.D.

174 Case 34/79, *Henn and Darby,* [1979] ECR 3795, 3813.

175 *Id.*

176 *Id.*

The Court concluded by holding that article 36 properly construed

> means that a Member State may, in principle, lawfully impose prohibitions on the importation from any other Member State of articles which are of an indecent or obscene character as understood by its domestic laws and that such prohibitions may lawfully be applied to the whole of its national territory even if, in regard to the field in question, variations exist between the laws in force in the different constituent parts of the Member State concerned.[177]

The decision is remarkable in many respects. Firstly, it is striking that the Court seems to recognize in its judgment an unbridled freedom of action on the part of the Member States as regards the protection of public morality in their territory. The Court did not follow Advocate General Warner, who had cautioned that "no Member State has an unfettered discretion to impose prohibitions or restrictions on the importation of goods from other Member States on grounds of public morality." In cases involving the right of Member States to derogate from the principle of free movement of persons for reasons of public policy,[178] the Court had stressed that while "the particular circumstances justifying recourse to the concept of public policy may vary from one country to another and from one period to another" the area of discretion which the competent Member State authorities enjoy in this respect is subject to the limits imposed by the Treaty.[179] It seems to follow that, as regards restrictions on imports of goods – as contrasted with restrictions on access of aliens – each Member State has an unlimited discretion to employ the concept of public morality "as understood by its domestic law."

But within the bounds of this discretion, it is arguable that if competing standards of public morality are enforced within a single Member State, the most lenient and not the most stringent one should be applied to goods imported from another Member State. What is allowed within the boundaries of a Member State should be permissible in relation to intra-Community trade.[180]

It is surprising that the Court did not find that the dual standard applied to domestic goods and to imported goods in this case constituted a means of arbitrary discrimination or a disguised restriction on trade contrary to article 36. The Court stated that the laws in force in the United Kingdom, "taken as a whole, have as their purpose the prohibition, or at least the restraining, of the manufacture and marketing of publications or articles of an indecent or obscene character. In these circumstances it is permissible to conclude, on a comprehensive view, that there is no lawful trade in such goods in the United Kingdom." As noted by Catchpole and Barav, this statement seems only partly accurate. Indeed, there is practically no restriction in the United Kingdom on trade in indecent materials. Moreover, there is a lawful trade in obscene materials

[177] *Id.* at 3813-14.

[178] *See* EEC Treaty art. 48, para. 3; art. 56, para. 1.

[179] Case 41/74, Van Duyn v. Home Office, [1974] ECR 1337; Case 36/75, Rutili v. Minister for the Interior, [1975] ECR 1219.

[180] Catchpole & Barav, *supra* note 54, at 16.

provided they possess a scientific, literary or educational value. However, no such articles can be imported into the United Kingdom. Thus, the fact that the "purpose" of the United Kingdom legislation was not to discriminate against pornographic materials produced in other Member States does not exclude arbitrary discrimination within the meaning of article 36.[181]

The singularly permissive attitude adopted by the Court vis-à-vis the United Kingdom legislation on pornography can probably be explained not only by the natural reluctance of international courts to interfere with national conceptions in these areas but also by the facts of the case, which involved imports of undeniably obscene materials.

3. Consumer Protection

All Member States have in force divergent requirements designed to protect consumers and providing detailed rules relating to the composition, quality, packaging, wrapping and labeling of goods.[182] Such requirements can have more or less overt protective effects.

The Commission and the Court have consistently held that measures which lower the value of imported products (such as the obligation to affix the term "foreign" to the product) or which enhance the value of domestic products (by confining to such products certain designations or names) constitute measures equivalent in effect to a discriminatory restriction on trade. Thus in Directive 70/50, in article 2(3) the Commission expressly mentions as contrary to article 30 measures which "lower the value of an imported product, in particular by causing a reduction in its intrinsic value" (paragraph (f)), or which "confine names which are not indicative of origin or source to domestic products only" (paragraph (s)). In the *Sekt and Weinbrand* case,[183] Germany had reserved the designation "Sekt" and "Weinbrand" for products made in Germany. The Court noted that these designations did not relate to products having certain qualities and characteristics by reason of the geographic location from which they came, so that they did not constitute appellations of origin. They could not, therefore, be justified on grounds of protection of industrial and commercial property. Moreover, the need to reserve such designations to German-made products did not appear to be justified by the need to protect the fairness of commercial transactions. Similarly, in the *Irish Souvenirs* case the Court held that the obligation imposed under Irish law on foreign producers of articles featuring typically Irish motifs (such as an Irish hero, event or landscape, a greyhound, a round tower, or a shamrock) to indicate that these products were of foreign origin constituted a discriminatory requirement contrary to article 30. The Irish Government claimed that the measure was justified by the need to protect consumers. However, the Court pointed out that article 36 does not

[181] *Id.* at 18–19.

[182] For a more detailed discussion of consumer protection comparing the EC and US *see* T. Bourgoignie & D. Trubek (with L. Trubek & D. Stingl), Consumer Protection Policy (3 Integration Through Law Series, forthcoming).

[183] Case 12/74, Commission v. Federal Republic of Germany, [1975] ECR 181.

include consumer protection among the reasons justifying a derogation from the principle of free movement of goods. It added that, in any case, the measure was not required to prevent deception of consumers since the nature of the products was not such as to require that they be manufactured in Ireland. The interests of consumers were sufficiently protected by the possibility which domestic producers had of affixing their own mark of origin on their products, without its being necessary to oblige foreign producers to do the same.[184]

The above cases concerned measures which applied *only* to imported products, and which were therefore of a clearly discriminatory character. Where a measure intended to protect consumers applies equally to domestic and to imported products, its evaluation under articles 30–36 gives rise to more delicate problems. In Directive 70/50, the Commission made a clear distinction between discriminatory measures and measures which apply equally to domestic and imported products. It felt that the effects of the latter on the free movement of goods "are not as a general rule equivalent to those of quantitative restrictions, since such effects are normally inherent in the disparities between rules applied by Member States in this respect." It is only where such measures "have a restrictive effect on the free movement of goods over and above that which is intrinsic to such rules," that they may constitute measures of equivalent effect.[185]

The result of the Commission's approach was that measures governing the marketing of products which dealt, in particular, with the shape, size, weight, composition, presentation, identification or packaging of such products could be prohibited only "where the restrictive effect of such measures on the free movement of goods exceeds the effects intrinsic to trade rules."[186] By laying the burden of proving the "excessive" character of the measure on the Community, this approach was clearly inadequate to cope with the problem. During the last twenty years, consumer pressures in favor of increased regulation of the marketing of products have often received warm support from local industry, which views them as a welcome means to protect itself against foreign competition, and from the national bureaucracy, which sees in them a means of advancing its influence. This has given rise to the adoption in Member States of a great number of divergent and more or less arbitrary rules and standards governing the marketing of given products.

The Commission's approach was severely criticized as inadequate by some authors.[187] These authors stressed that the restrictions on trade resulting from

[184] Case 113/80, Commission v. Ireland, [1981] ECR 1625.

[185] Commission Directive No. 70/50, *supra* note 129, eighth & ninth "whereas."

[186] *Id.*, art. 3.

[187] VerLoren van Themaat, *Bevat artikel 30 van het EEG-Verdrag slechts een non-discriminatie-beginsel t.a.v. invoerbeperkingen?*, [1967] SEW 632; Waelbroeck, *La libre circulation des marchandises*, in 1 LE DROIT DE LA COMMUNAUTÉ ECONOMIQUE EUROPÉENNE 37 (J. Mégret, J.-V. Louis, D. Vignes, M. Waelbroeck eds., 2d ed., Brussels, Editions de l'Université Libre de Bruxelles, 1973); M. WAELBROECK, LES RÉGLEMENTATIONS NATIONALES DE PRIX ET LE DROIT COMMUNAUTAIRE 24–40 (Brussels, Editions de l'Université Libre de Bruxelles, 1975).

"equally applicable measures" could be just as serious as those resulting from formally discriminatory ones; in fact, in many cases, the only difference between an "equally applicable" and a "formally discriminatory" measure is a question of drafting. Realistically, all measures which have the effect of making importation more difficult or costly than the disposal of domestic production should be regarded as having an effect equivalent to a quantitative restriction and should be justifiable only on the basis of the grounds mentioned in article 36.

In the celebrated *Cassis de Dijon* case,[188] the Court dissociated itself from the views expounded by the Commission in Directive 70/50. The case involved a German regulatory provision imposing a minimum alcoholic strength of 25 percent for all liqueurs sold in Germany. An importer of French "Crème de Cassis," a well-known French liqueur having an alcoholic strength of only 15–20 percent, was prosecuted for not having complied with that provision. The case was referred to the European Court by the German court under article 177 of the Treaty.

The importance of the judgment results from the fact that the purpose of the measures in issue was not to protect domestic producers, but to protect consumers by increasing the transparency of the market. Nevertheless, its effect was to keep products off the German market which could have competed with German-made liqueurs and which were freely available and lawfully marketed in other Member States.

The approach of the Court is approximately halfway between the approach of Directive 70/50 and that of the authors who had criticized the Directive. The Court did not say that "equally applicable measures" are prohibited only when it is shown that their restrictive effects exceed the effects intrinsic to trade rules. However, nor did the Court say that all measures, whether equally applicable or not, which produce a restrictive effect on imports are prohibited except when they can be justified under article 36. Indeed, the Court seems to have recognized that the restrictive effects resulting from equally applicable measures governing the marketing of products could be justified by considerations not falling within the scope of article 36 *stricto sensu;* it stated that such restrictive effects must be accepted to the extent that the measures in question are justified by overriding considerations of general interest, such as the need to ensure the efficiency of tax controls, the protection of public health, the fairness of commercial transactions and the protection of consumers. However – by contrast with the Commission's approach in Directive 70/50 – the burden is on the Member State to establish that its measures are so justified.

The Court's solution, although satisfactory in practice, raises a number of questions as to its legal foundation. Indeed, the link between the "overriding requirements" of Member States, the legitimacy of which the Court recognizes, and the considerations mentioned in article 36 is not clear. On the one hand, it would seem possible to argue that the "efficiency of tax controls" is a

188 Case 120/78, Rewe-Zentral AG v. Bundesmonopolverwaltung für Branntwein, [1979] ECR 649.

consideration of "public policy" within the meaning of article 36.[189] The fairness of commercial transactions and the protection of consumers can similarly be regarded as considerations of public policy within the meaning of article 36.[190] Alternatively, the fairness of commercial transactions could be considered as part of the notion of "commercial property" which is also mentioned in article 36. However, such an interpretation would be in conflict with the *Irish Souvenirs* case.[191] In that case, the Court made it clear that article 36 must be interpreted restrictively and that it does not authorize restrictions based on the need to protect consumers or fair competition.

Thus, it appears that the *Cassis de Dijon* judgment recognizes that Member States may, when adopting measures which apply equally to domestic and imported products, restrict imports on grounds other than those specifically recognized by article 36. Although the practical result appears satisfactory, the lack of any legal basis in the Treaty for such a distinction raises serious doubts as to its long-term acceptability. Instead of creating an entirely new set of justifications for "equally applicable" measures, we believe the Court would have been better advised if it had based these derogations on a somewhat less restrictive interpretation of article 36.

The *Cassis de Dijon* judgment has had an important influence on the Commission's approach to the task of harmonization of legislation. By giving a broad interpretation to article 30, it has correspondingly reduced the need for harmonization directives. The Commission has stated in a notice published in the *Official Journal of the European Communities* that it interpreted the *Cassis de Dijon* judgment as establishing the principle that any product which is legally manufactured and marketed in a Member State must be admitted to the territories of all other Member States.[192] Although it can be doubted whether the judgment really stands for such a broad principle,[193] it cannot be denied that it will allow the removal of a number of serious barriers to trade without need for the cumbersome and time-consuming integration process set in motion by harmonization directives.

Thus, the *Cassis de Dijon* rule has resulted in the condemnation, as prohibited measures of equivalent effect, of the following national provisions:

- the Italian prohibition on the sale of vinegar excepting vinegar made from wine;[194]

[189] In Case 7/78, Regina v. Thompson *et al.*, [1978] ECR 2247, the Court held that a ban on export of national coins with a view to preventing their being melted down or destroyed in another Member State is justified on grounds of public policy, because it stems from the need to protect the right to mint coinage which is traditionally regarded as involving the fundamental interests of the State.

[190] Opinion of Advocate General Capotorti in Case 120/78, *Cassis de Dijon*, [1979] ECR 649, 672. The question was expressly left undecided by the Court in Case 12/74, Commission v. Germany, [1975] ECR 181, 200 (the "Sekt and Weinbrand" case).

[191] Case 113/80, Commission v. Ireland, [1981] ECR 1625.

[192] OJ No. C 256, 3 Oct. 1980, p.2.

[193] *See* Barents, *supra* note 140, at 292-96; Oliver, *supra* note 140, at 234-36.

[194] Case 788/79, Gilli and Andres, [1980] ECR 2071.

- the obligation imposed by Dutch law to use the word "likeur" on the label of all products having a stated composition and containing ethyl alcohol, sugar, aromatic substances and/or fruit juices;[195]
- the requirement imposed in the Netherlands that the quantity of dry matter contained in bread should fall within certain specified limits;[196]
- the prohibition imposed by Belgian law on the sale of margarine other than in cube-shaped wrappings.[197]

The interesting thing to note here is that many of the requirements which were thus struck down had no overt or even hidden protectionistic purpose but constituted bona fide measures designed to inform consumers and prevent deception. Nevertheless, the Court ruled that the seriousness of the obstacles which they raised to trade between Member States was such that the measures could not be regarded as justified, especially since consumers could have been adequately protected by measures having less far-reaching consequences.

4. Social and Economic Interests

The Court has always been aware that, in the guise of protecting certain legitimate social and economic interests, Member States might adopt measures having a restrictive impact on intra-Community trade.

a) Price Controls

Legislation allowing national governments to prescribe maximum (and sometimes minimum) prices are common in a number of European countries. Such measures, in order to attain their full effect, must generally be applied equally to domestic and to imported goods. Although their main purpose is generally not protective, in certain cases they can have such an effect. Whenever such an effect has seemed likely, the Court has not hesitated to strike down such measures as incompatible with article 30.

Thus, the Court held that

> [w]hilst rules imposing a price freeze which are applicable equally to national products and to imported products do not amount in themselves to a measure having an effect equivalent to a quantitative restriction, they may in fact produce such an effect when prices are at such a level that the marketing of imported products becomes either impossible or more difficult than the marketing of national products. That is especially the case where national rules, while preventing the increased prices of imported products from being passed on in sales prices, freeze prices at a level so low that – taking into account the general situation of imported products in relation to that of national products – traders wishing to import the products in question into the Member State concerned can do so only at a loss, or, having regard to the level at which prices for national products are frozen, are impelled to give preference to the latter products.[198]

195 Case 27/80, Fietje, [1980] ECR 3839.

196 Case 130/80, Fabriek voor Hoogwaardige Voedingsprodukten Kelderman BV, [1981] ECR 527.

197 Case 261/81, Walter Rau Lebensmittelwerke v. De Smedt PvbA, [1982] ECR 3961.

198 Joined Cases 16 to 20/79, Openbaar Ministerie v. Danis and Others, [1979] ECR 3327. In 1976, the Court had already held, for similar reasons, that the fixing of

The fixing of minimum prices applicable equally to domestic products and to imported products may also constitute a measure of equivalent effect insofar as it prevents producers from other Member States from taking advantage of lower production costs by reflecting them in a lower sales price.[199]

Thus, it can be seen that, although the Treaty does not provide for the adoption of a Community economic policy, but for a simple coordination of the economic policies of the Member States,[200] the Treaty rules on free movement of goods severely limit the freedom of Member States in the exercise of some of their control of domestic economic policy. Although price controls are not per se prohibited, their effectiveness is severely reduced to the extent Member States are no longer free, in certain circumstances, to apply them to imported products.

b) Quality Promotion

The Court has recognized that the promotion of the quality of products is a desirable policy objective to be pursued by Member States.[201] However, such an objective can only be pursued by means compatible with the Treaty. Thus, the Court has held that Member States are not allowed to charge a tax designed to compensate them for checking the quality of exported goods and affixing a quality label to them, if the exporter is not free to export without submitting to the control.[202] Such a tax, in the view of the Court, constitutes a charge equivalent to an export duty. The Court has also held that a prohibition on the export of goods which do not meet certain minimum quality standards constitutes a measure having an effect equivalent to a quantitative restriction on export if the same prohibition does not apply to goods sold on the domestic market.[203] In a case involving a prohibition applying equally to exported goods and to goods sold domestically, the Court refused to consider that an export restriction was involved, even though the practical effect of the measure restricted exports more than it restricted domestic sales.[204] Thus, it seems pretty clear that Member States may impose minimum standards for the production of certain goods, as long as they do so without formally discriminating against exports, and even though the result may be to reduce the quantities exported.

c) Protection of Certain Social Groups or Forms of Business

The Court has been reluctant to interfere with national policies designed to protect certain social groups or to encourage certain types of businesses. Thus,

maximum prices could constitute a measure of equivalent effect: in Case 65/75, Tasca, [1976] ECR 291; and in Joined Cases 88 to 90/75, Società SADAM v. Comitato Interministeriale dei Prezzi, [1976] ECR 323.

199 Case 82/77, *Van Tiggele,* [1978] ECR 25.

200 *See* EEC Treaty arts. 103 ff.

201 Case 53/76, Procureur de la République v. Bouhelier and Others, [1977] ECR 197.

202 Case 63/74, W. Cadsky S.p.A. v. Istituto Nazionale per il Commercio Estero, [1975] ECR 281.

203 Case 53/76, *Bouhelier,* [1977] ECR 197.

204 Case 15/79, *Groenveld,* [1979] ECR 3409.

in the *Oebel* case,[205] the Court upheld a German law prohibiting night work in bakeries. The Court expressly recognized that such a prohibition constitutes a legitimate economic and social policy choice which is in conformity with the objectives pursued by the Treaty. It noted that several states inside and outside of the Community had subjected night work in that sector to similar regulations and that a convention had been signed in 1925 within the framework of the International Labor Organization on that subject. Since the prohibition applied both to products sold in Germany and to exported products, it did not constitute a measure of equivalent effect on export prohibited by article 34.[206] The prohibition on night work obviously did not in itself constitute a restriction on import. However, it was reinforced by a prohibition on the transportation and delivery of bakery products to consumers or retail outlets before 5:45 a.m. The accused party claimed that this prohibition prevented trade between Germany and the other Member States. Indeed, in view of the need to deliver the products in time to the consumer, it effectively limited the distance over which they could be transported.

The Court found that, since the prohibition applied only to deliveries to retailers and consumers, products could still be transported and delivered freely at all times to warehouses and intermediaries, and therefore intra-Community exchanges were not hindered to any greater extent than purely domestic exchanges. Trade within the Community remained possible at all times "subject to the single exception that delivery to consumers and retailers is restricted to the same extent for all producers, wherever they are established."[207]

Member States frequently grant tax benefits in order to further certain economic and social objectives. When such benefits take the form of reduced taxation on certain products, the Court has always insisted that such benefits should be accorded to *all* products, whether domestic or imported. Thus, in *Bobie*[208] the Court made clear that at its present stage of development – and in the absence of any unification or harmonization of relevant national provisions – Community law does not prohibit Member States from granting tax advantages, in the form of exemptions from or reductions in duties, to certain types of products or to certain classes of producers for legitimate economic or social purposes, as long as the same advantages are granted to similar products imported from other Member States.[209] However, it is necessary that the conditions governing the tax benefits granted by the Member State be capable of

205 Case 155/80, *Oebel*, [1981] ECR 1993.

206 The Court expressly cited its *Groenveld* judgment in support of this finding. *See Oebel*, [1981] ECR at 2009.

207 *Id.* at 2010.

208 Case 127/75, Bobie Getränkevertrieb GmbH v. Hauptzollamt Aachen-Nord, [1976] ECR 1079.

209 *See also* Case 148/77, H. Hansen jun. and O.C. Balle GmbH & Co. v. Hauptzollamt Flensburg, [1978] ECR 1787.

being met by producers from other Member States.[210] Thus, a Member State would infringe article 95 if it provided that a given tax benefit would be granted only to products whose manufacture can be controlled on the territory of the Member State granting the benefit, since such a condition could not be fulfilled by products coming from other Member States.[211]

The question whether an apparently non-discriminatory tax advantage involves, in reality, a disguised discrimination in favor of domestic products is a difficult one to resolve in practice. Thus, we have seen that the Court considered in the *Spirits* cases that the preferential tax treatment reserved by certain Member States to products *most* (but not all) of which are domestically produced could involve a breach of article 95.[212] The Court said that, in this case, the differential tax rate had a protectionistic effect. It is not clear, however, that the purpose of the tax differentiation was to protect domestic products: indeed, anisette drinks – of which France is a major producer and which are not imported to a substantial extent – were taxed at the higher rate. However, in the *Chemial* and *Vinal* cases, the Court upheld Italian legislation which provided for a heavier tax on sales of ethyl alcohol made from ethylene (synthetic alcohol) than on ethyl alcohol obtained from the distillation of agricultural products (agricultural alcohol), notwithstanding the fact that there is no Italian production of synthetic alcohol whereas Italy is a major producer of the agricultural products used for distillation purposes.[213] The Court contented itself with noting that the tax differential was justified by legitimate economic considerations, *i.e.* conservation of energy resources and finding outlets for excess agricultural production. Moreover, as noted by Advocate General Reischl, Italy is a substantial producer of ethylene and has the necessary industrial infrastructure for transforming ethylene into ethyl alcohol. On the other hand, the agricultural products used in the production of agricultural alcohol are produced not only in Italy but in the other EC countries as well. The differentiated tax system was not, therefore, directed against producers from other Member States any more than against Italian producers.

Thus, it appears that if a differentiated tax system benefits products which are "typically domestic" and discriminates against products which are "typical" of other Member States, it will normally be found to infringe article 95. On the contrary, if the fact that the differentiated tax system affects imported products to a greater extent than domestic products is not due to the particular characteristics of the products but to the existence of the differentiated tax structure

[210] Case 26/80, Schneider-Import GmbH & Co. KG v. Hauptzollamt Mainz, [1980] ECR 3469.

[211] Joined Cases 142 & 143/80, Amministrazione delle Finanze dello Stato v. Essevi SpA and Salengo, [1981] ECR 1413.

[212] Case 168/78, Commission v. French Republic, [1980] ECR 347; 169/78, Commission v. Italian Republic, [1980] ECR 385; and 171/78, Commission v. Kingdom of Denmark, [1980] ECR 447.

[213] Case 140/79, Chemial Farmaceutici SpA v. DAF SpA, [1981] ECR 1; Case 46/80, Vinal SpA v. Orbat SpA, [1981] ECR 77.

itself – and if that structure is justified by legitimate economic or social considerations – then it will be allowed to stand.

The difficulty with the Court's case law in this area is that it involves a judgment as to the protectionist character of differential tax rates which, in turn, implies a review of the reasonableness of the objective pursued by a Member State in adopting the tax differential at issue. In the *Cogis* case,[214] the Italian Government sought to rely on the *Chemial* and *Vinal* cases in order to justify taxing grain alcohol more heavily than wine alcohol. It stressed the fact that there was no natural obstacle to the production of grain alcohol in Italy. Thus, according to the Italian Government, the fact that production of grain alcohol was insignificant was due to a legitimate policy decision to impose a tax on it at a higher rate in order to encourage wine distillation, in conformity with the Community's policy of reducing wine surpluses.

The Court did not accept this line of reasoning. Adhering to its decision in the *Spirits* cases, it noted that the Italian tax system benefitted "the most typical domestic products," whereas grain alcohol, which is almost entirely imported from other Member States, was subjected to a heavier charge. The fact that there also exists a certain domestic production of grain alcohol did not change the result, since it was not disputed that such production involved only minimal quantities. The result of the differential tax rate was therefore to reduce potential consumption of imported products.

The Court carefully avoided referring to the *Chemial* and *Vinal* cases, so that it is difficult to know on what ground it was able to distinguish them. It seems that a possible distinction is that the economic policy arguments advanced in favor of the preferential treatment of wine-based spirits over grain-based spirits appeared less convincing than the reasons justifying the preferential treatment of agricultural ethyl alcohol over synthetic alcohol.

The *Chemial* and *Vinal* test therefore requires an examination of the reasonableness of the national economic policy objective pursued by differential tax rates – an examination which may involve the Court in delicate and controversial judgments having strong political overtones.

IV. Comparative Evaluation

This paper has examined the constitutional jurisprudence of the United States Supreme Court and the European Court of Justice as it relates to the free movement of goods and services across state or national lines. A major purpose of the study has been to assess the judicial role in the promotion of economic integration in Europe and the United States. We were particularly interested in describing the judicial techniques used to resolve conflicts between central and local units of government within the American federal system and the European

214 Case 216/81, Compagnia Generale Interscambi SpA (COGIS) v. Amministrazione delle Finanze dello Stato, [1982] ECR 2701.

Community and in appraising their effectiveness. Although the jurisprudence of the Court of Justice appears to have developed in the absence of any conscious reference to the Supreme Court's commerce clause jurisprudence it converges with American doctrine in several interesting respects. But in other respects the lines of doctrinal development clearly diverge. Our task in these concluding pages is to identify the similarities and differences in the approach of the courts in promoting legal integration in their respective jurisdictions and to consider the relevance of the American jurisprudence to the work of the European Court of Justice.

A. Techniques of Legal Integration: A Comparison

In federal systems of government, constitutional law, judicially defined, is an important tool in bringing about legal integration. We have seen that the highest courts of both the European Community and the United States have played critical roles in establishing the legal framework for the development of a common market. Despite the differences in the language of the commerce clause and that of articles 30 to 36 of the EEC Treaty the jurisprudence of the two courts has unfolded in strikingly similar ways. The prevailing mode of analysis employed by both courts is that of balancing "local" and "national" interests. The Court of Justice uses a balancing test very similar to the analytical framework adopted by the Supreme Court in *Pike v. Bruce Church, Inc.*[215] The balancing technique is clearly designed to promote legal integration without sacrificing vital local interests. Yet variations are to be found in the manner in which the balancing test is applied, as both Courts recognize variations often attributable to differences in the language and purpose of the two Constitutions. These variations are also owing to the type of regulation imposed, the nature of the local interest involved, or the relative impact of the legislation on the integrated economy.

1. Health and Safety Legislation

Balancing has been applied most commonly by the two tribunals in the field of health and safety legislation. The techniques used within the balancing framework are almost identical. These include "legitimate purpose," "burdens," and "less restrictive alternative" analysis. *Legitimate purpose analysis* seeks to insure that local regulations affecting commerce or the free flow of goods falls clearly within the police power (with respect to the United States) or within the exception of article 36 (with respect to the EEC). *Burdens analysis* seeks to determine whether the regulation's impact on commerce is excessive in relation to the benefits derived from the regulatory scheme. *Less restrictive alternative analysis* is an examination of whether an otherwise legitimate purpose that excessively burdens commerce could be achieved by means that would have a lesser impact on the free movement of goods. By seeking to measure the

[215] 397 U.S. 137 (1970).

validity of legislation by its consequences, the balancing formula eschews formalistic reasoning. The strength of the balancing technique is its pragmatism. It is a convenient method of reconciling local and national interests. The weakness of the technique, however, is its inability to predict the result in a given case. Whether judges place their thumb on the state or federal side of the scale often depends on their subjective judgments of fact and degree. Yet balancing can be avoided, and often is, by an initial characterization of a regulatory statute as discriminatory in effect or on its face. Here an almost per se rule of invalidity results unless the state or local community can sustain a difficult judicially imposed burden of proof.

It seems clear that the balancing formula is applied differently by the two courts. The Court of Justice seems to place a much heavier thumb on the Community side of the scale than the Supreme Court places on the federal side. This is manifest with regard to health and safety legislation. Even if the legitimate purpose test is satisfied the Court of Justice requires the Member State to show that there would be a *risk* to health or safety in the absence of the regulation, whereas the Supreme Court, assuming evenhanded legislation, places the initial burden of proof upon those economic interests challenging the regulatory scheme. The activism of the European Court could probably not be duplicated, for a number of political reasons, by the Supreme Court. Yet even the Supreme Court has employed the balancing test largely to vindicate national rather than local interests.

Within the American context, *Cooley* rule analysis continues to play a role in reconciling federal and state interests. Occasionally, such analysis is engrafted onto the rhetoric of the balancing test and is used to assess the extent of the burden on commerce. As noted earlier in the paper, the *Cooley* rule postulates that certain subjects of commerce are local in nature and hence do not require national uniform legislation. The Court of Justice has not sought to classify the subjects of commerce on the basis of their local or Community character. Again, this variation on the balancing test suggests that the Court of Justice is less sensitive to federalistic concerns than the Supreme Court. The overarching purpose of the Court of Justice has been to vindicate the Community's interest in the free movement of goods across Member State borders.

2. Tax Legislation

It is of interest to note, however, that the balancing test is used mainly in the field of regulatory legislation. Both courts find it less adequate as a tool for safeguarding common markets against tax legislation. In the tax field both courts apply a standard of review even more exacting than balancing. Discriminatory tax legislation rarely survives constitutional analysis in the Supreme Court. It has never survived analysis in the Court of Justice. The touchstone of nondiscrimination for both systems is the equal treatment of domestic and "foreign" products within the local tax structure. But once this observation has been made we find the paths of the two courts diverging once again, with the Court of Justice evincing a much more federal-oriented perspective than the Supreme Court. Even nondiscriminatory tax legislation having no protective effect is reviewed with heightened judicial scrutiny by the Court of Justice if the tax has the appearance of a duty on interstate trade as such. As *Brachfeld and Chougol*[216] shows, judicial scrutiny of even an infinitesimal tax on interstate trade will be fatal if the tax does not fall evenhandedly on domestic and foreign goods or businesses. The mere fact that a tax has a discriminatory *structure* – *i.e.* that it applies to imported goods only – will bring about its incompatibility with the Treaty, even though the goods to which it applies are not produced inside the Community and thus could not be said to benefit from a protective effect outlawed by the Treaty. Indeed, both courts have accepted the principle of evenhanded taxation as the *sine qua non* of any viable legal framework designed to establish a common market. On the other hand, the Supreme Court has replaced older formalistic doctrines with a more practical test grounded in the notion of fairness.

The European Court, by contrast, is not prepared to concede that businesses active in interstate commerce should be prepared to pay their share of the costs of doing business in "interstate commerce," in the form of a tax levied by the importing country. It has, however, been willing to concede that when interstate commerce is governed by Community rules, as in the field of veterinary and sanitary inspections of certain agricultural products, the *exporting* Member State may be entitled to collect a tax to cover the costs of the sanitary inspections necessary to entitle the exported products to circulate freely. Thus, in many respects, the European Court adopts a stricter attitude than the Supreme Court. This phenomenon may be explained by the fact that the European Community is, at least at this time, still much less integrated than the United States. The risk that the European Community may be dislodged from its regulatory jurisdiction is still very real, and can only be avoided by the adoption of rather strict and formal rules which do not leave much room for discretion on the part of the Member States.

3. Public Morality Legislation

The balancing approach has also been abandoned by the two courts with respect to public morality legislation. The extremely deferential approach of the European Court in *Henn and Darby*[217] is in sharp contrast to its activism in other areas of local legislation. The posture of the Court in this case has been considered by some as amounting to an abdication of its responsibility to enforce the Treaty. On the other hand, it represents a prudential recognition of the existence of widely varying national standards on a sensitive moral issue. Criticism of the decision has focused less on the Court's deference to public morality legislation than on its tolerance of a double standard as applied to domestic and imported articles. The Supreme Court's treatment of obscenity legislation, on the other hand, occurs mainly within the framework of the first and fourteenth amendments. Under Chief Justice Earl Warren, of course, the

[216] Joined Cases 2 & 3/69, [1969] ECR 211.
[217] Case 34/79, [1979] ECR 3795.

Supreme Court imposed a rather exacting national uniform standard for defining obscenity.[218] But a more conservative tribunal under Chief Justice Warren Burger has reaffirmed the right of local communities to regulate obscenity within the framework of a less exacting federal standard.[219] It is of interest to note here that where commerce as such is concerned the United States has resorted to another technique to control traffic in obscenity, namely federal legislation which strips obscene articles of their interstate character – an affirmative exercise of congressional power that the Supreme Court has approved. *Henn and Darby* comes very close, doctrinally, to the same result for the same reasons, a logic which, if extended to other areas, could halt the forward thrust of legal integration.

4. Environmental and Consumer Protection Legislation

In the environmental and consumer protection field, as well as in the general area of economic policy, the two courts have demonstrated considerable flexibility and creativity in promoting both legal integration and the legitimate interests of federalism. The Supreme Court, even under Chief Justice Burger, remains vigorously interventionist in each of these areas when the effect of local legislation is to restrict competition, to bar the shipment of goods across state lines, or to "balkanize" the economy in any serious fashion. The principle of a unified economy implicit in the cases studied has secured the approval of nearly all of the Justices. But there is a reverse side to this picture which has occasioned far less agreement in the Court. *Hughes v. Alexandria Scrap,*[220] *Reeves v. Stake,*[221] and *White v. Massachusetts Council of Construction Employers* imposed severe restraints on trade just as *Exxon Corporation v. Maryland*[222] effectively favored local independent retail establishments over large interstate refineries operating retail establishments. The Court's finding of non-discrimination in the latter case, and its distinction between the state as regulator and as market participant in the former, is a retreat into formalistic reasoning that ascribes higher importance to logical relationships than to the economic consequences of state activity. On the other hand, the result in these three cases – particularly in *Alexandria Scrap, Exxon,* and *White* – can be justified by persuasive reasons of public policy.

By contrast, article 37 of the EEC Treaty provides the Commission and the Court with means to ensure compliance with the Treaty by the Member States when they act as entrepreneurs. In this respect, the system of the Treaty can be said to be more realistic than that conceived of by the Supreme Court. In view of the importance of the intervention of governments as direct participants in the economy of the Member States, the absence of a provision such as article 37 would have been a very serious lacuna.

218 Roth v. United States, 354 U.S. 476 (1957).
219 Miller v. California, 413 U.S. 15 (1973).
220 426 U.S. 794 (1976).
221 447 U.S. 429 (1980).
222 437 U.S. 117 (1978).

On the other hand, the Supreme Court has displayed particular sensitivity to local interests with regard to state legislation designed to protect the environment, to control the quality of its homegrown or manufactured goods, or to conserve energy. Such legislation clearly falls within the police power of the states. Even though the problems in these policy areas are often national in scope *and* the subject of parallel federal legislation, the Supreme Court has adopted techniques of interpretation clearly designed to further the legitimate interests of federalism. Although *Hodel v. Virginia Surface Mining*[223] represented a unanimous reaffirmation of federal power in the environmental field, the federal statute challenged in this case nevertheless provided and encouraged the enactment of parallel state legislation. The cooperative federalism undergirding national policy here was no small factor in prompting the Court toward a benign view of the state law sustained in *Minnesota v. Clover Leaf Creamery Co.*,[224] where deferential rational basis reasoning again rears its head. Generally, the doctrine of pre-emption tends to be narrowly construed and appropriately so, in areas of policy where high levels of consumer and environmental protection are politically desirable.

The European Court of Justice has been equally opposed to any "balkanization" of the European economy. It has been able to achieve a high level of integration in Europe by its broad construction of the "equivalent effect" clauses of articles 30 and 34. By reading into these clauses a ban on all measures capable of hindering intra-Community trade – directly or indirectly, actually or potentially – the Court has laid a rather solid foundation for the uninterrupted flow of goods within the common market. The Court has even struck down nondiscriminatory price controls having a protective effect on local products. At the same time, the Court has narrowly construed the derogation clauses of article 36, often over the vigorous protests of Member States. It has even pointed out that article 36 does not include "consumer protection" among the reasons for derogating from the "free movement of goods" principle. By contrast, the Supreme Court has broadly interpreted the police power, a term of convenience, as noted earlier, to describe the general authority of a state to provide for the general welfare. Finally, the Court of Justice has expansively interpreted the "doctrine of pre-emption," suggesting that when directives have been adopted under article 30, recourse by a Member State to article 36 is no longer justified. Clearly, the potential here for uniformity is enormous.

But whether such uniformity is politically feasible – or in the long run, possible – is another question. The Court of Justice has recognized that consumer protection and quality control legislation, as well as legislation designed to protect and foster certain kinds of businesses, may be justified if the means used to achieve these objectives are compatible with the Treaty. In fact, the Court has gone beyond the specific language of article 36 to assert that evenhanded measures governing the marketing, sale, and presentation of goods may be justified by "overriding considerations of general interest,"

[223] 452 U.S. 264 (1981).
[224] 449 U.S. 456 (1981).

although the Member State has the burden of showing that such considerations exist. This rule, of course, did not help Ireland when it attempted to require the identification of the geographic origin of certain souvenirs, or Germany when it attempted to impose a minimum alcohol content regulation for liqueurs;[225] indeed, it has sometimes been argued that these two decisions may lead to the enactment of lower Community standards for consumer protection so that they might be more readily accepted on a Community-wide basis. However, the cases offer a substantial number of other examples of national provisions which have been upheld in spite of their potentially restrictive effect because they were considered necessary for the protection of public health, security, morality, consumer protection, or the fairness of commercial transactions. Moreover, the applicability of article 30 does not preclude the adoption of harmonization directives setting Community-wide standards at a level higher than the lowest level prevailing in the Member States. Finally, the Court of Justice considers that, by virtue of the sovereignty which they retain in tax matters, Member States may grant tax exemptions and reductions for legitimate economic and social policy considerations. Thus, the Court of Justice has upheld Italy's heavier tax on synthetic alcohol producers than on the agricultural alcohol industry, a decision somewhat comparable to the result in *Minnesota v. Clover Leaf Creamery Co.*[226] It should be noted, however, that Italy's tax and Minnesota's regulation were sustained only after a showing of evenhanded treatment with respect to both domestic and foreign enterprises. Still the cases illustrate the willingness of both courts to allow local units of government to fill in the gaps of federal and Community law.

B. The Judicial Role and the Relevance of the American Experience

The main conclusion that emerges from this study is that the Court of Justice, in the space of less than two decades, has molded a jurisprudence at least as centralized as that of the Supreme Court. In fact, as we have seen, the Supreme Court has upheld local legislation under the dormant commerce clause that the European Court would probably invalidate under the more restrictive language of the EEC Treaty. The difference in the approach of the two courts owes as much to the constitutional framework within which they function as to techniques of judicial review. The American system is genuinely federal, and even at its birth the "more perfect union" created by the Constitution was far more integrated politically and economically than the European Community. At the same time, as a practical matter, Americans have historically recognized the need to balance the value of integration served by the commerce clause and other equally valid values of decentralization served by the tenth amendment. The EEC Treaty, on the other hand, did not create a general system of government but rather an economic union whose highest value is the principle of free

225 *See supra* text accompanying notes 157 and 183.
226 449 U.S. 833 (1981).

trade. There is always the danger that, because of the less integrated nature of the Community, the achievements realized during the past years will be swept away by the tide of resurgent protectionism. Therefore, it is necessary for the European Court to take a somewhat rigid stance as regards the respective powers of the Community institutions and of the Member States, while the U.S. Supreme Court can afford to be more tolerant of state powers and of state legislation which has potentially restrictive effects when such legislation is justified by a *prima facie* valid motive.

Still, the diverse constitutional structures of the two systems are not the only factors influencing the integrative process, as indeed constitutional texts and modes of constitutional interpretation also play an important role in the judicial creation of a regime of economic integration. The EEC Treaty, which embodies a code of rather specific provisions aimed at the removal of all restrictions on the free movement of goods is a solid foundation on which to build a convincing jurisprudence of free trade. On the other hand, the general language of the commerce clause leaves plenty of room for judicial experimentation with techniques for reconciling state and federal interests. It is also noteworthy that the Court of Justice mainly follows the teleological or functional approach to constitutional interpretation, which strongly emphasizes the evolutionary character of the EEC Treaty. Its main point of reference is the objective goals and purposes of the Treaty, a methodology that allows the Court maximum flexibility in adjusting its decisions to existing practices and circumstances. By contrast, the U.S. Supreme Court has historically relied more heavily upon textual analysis and the subjective intent of the Founding Fathers, the result being a commerce clause jurisprudence highly sensitive to state and local interests. In this connection, finally, it is relevant to point out that whereas American commerce clause doctrine evolved over a long period of time within the context of developing economies the free trade doctrine of the Court of Justice has sprung rather suddenly out of the relatively developed economic context of contemporary Europe.

It can probably be assumed that the judges of the Court of Justice – or at least some of them – were well aware of the meandering course of American commerce clause jurisprudence, with its frequent swings between the poles of centralization and decentralization. Thanks to the United States experience, the European judges were able to take shortcuts. This explains how merely a few years after the first case involving interpretation of article 30 was submitted to them, they were able to adopt a balancing test very similar to the one used by the Supreme Court in *Pike v. Bruce Church*, and thus managed to avoid the vagaries of the "police powers," "direct-indirect" and "*Cooley* rule" tests which plagued U.S. Justices over the years. In this latter respect the integrative drive of the European Court has also benefitted from the European practice of handing down single, institutional opinions. The simple institutional opinion is of course an established practice in Civil Law systems. National courts within the Community entrusted with the enforcement of Court of Justice rulings would probably be put off, if not thoroughly confused, by the diversity of opinion often found in American case law. Imagine Member State courts trying to deal with the approaches to balancing analysis currently dividing the Justices on the U.S. Supreme Court; such divisive behavior in the European Court would probably diminish its authority in the eyes of Member State courts, and detract from its role as an instrument of legal integration.

This is not to suggest, however, that the European Court is any less flexible than the Supreme Court. While constitutional texts are important in understanding decisional outcomes those texts are also subject to interpretation, regardless of their specificity or generality. Thus there would seem to have been nothing inevitable about the path of doctrinal development blazed by the Supreme Court or the Court of Justice. The creativity of the Court of Justice, for example, has been manifested by the introduction of doctrinal formulations such as "overriding considerations of general interest," although this notion would seem inferable from the concept of "public policy" jurisprudence yet to be developed by the Court of Justice. Indeed, the play in the joints of all the derogation clauses is immense. The Court's narrow construction of these clauses is currently a testimony to its determination to underscore the importance of transnational values at a critical time in the development of the Community concept.

And yet interpretations of treaty provisions, however uniform, are only as good as the reasons supporting those interpretations. Some European decisions seem no less conclusory than earlier American decisions applying the "direct-indirect" formula or current decisions applying the balancing test. It is not immediately evident to us why, for example, the result of the *Irish Souvenirs*[227] case is necessarily correct in terms of public policy. Surely it is not the purpose of EEC law to achieve legal integration merely for the sake of legal integration. Transnational policy may not always be the best policy. Local policy may be more enlightened or progressive, or even more efficient. In any case, if judicial authority is to be accepted it must be *convincing*. Persuasive argumentation disclosing the sources of judicial authority, identifying and explaining the purposes for which it is exercised, and exhibiting an appreciation for the limits of judicial power seem necessary for the construction of a lasting and durable jurisprudence.

It is difficult to measure precisely the impact which the activism of the European Court has had in the practical world. Compliance with the Court's judgments has, in a number of cases, been slow. Sometimes, the measures which the Court had held to be incompatible with the Treaty were replaced by other measures, whose illegality had not yet been established, thus forcing the Commission to take renewed action against the defaulting Member States. Although the doctrines of Community supremacy and direct effect go a long way toward making Community law a reality which can be invoked by private citizens in their day-to-day dealings with each other and with Governments, there are a number of cases in which, either because of ignorance, intimidation or the expenses involved, parties renounce invoking their Community rights and prefer to settle on the basis of possibly infringing Member State statutes.

[227] Case 113/80, Commission v. Ireland, [1981] ECR 1625.

In some areas, it cannot be denied that the Court's case law has produced tangible results. This is particularly so in the field of taxes having equivalent effect. Most of these taxes have today been abrogated and those which are still in existence are being litigated either before the domestic courts or before the Court of Justice. The obstacles to trade resulting from divergent national rules concerning the composition, packaging, and labeling of goods are more and more frequently being questioned on the basis of the *Cassis de Dijon* rule and this no doubt constitutes a field in which immense practical changes are proceeding at present.

In other areas the effect of the Court's decisions is less apparent. Member States continue to enforce price control regulations and it does not seem that the effectiveness of these regulations has been substantially affected by the possible application of article 30. True, on isolated occasions, traders prosecuted for infringement of the national regulations have raised the article 30 defense; however, on a macro-economic scale, it does not seem that these cases have seriously affected the course of policies pursued by the Member States. But it is probably in the area of national health and security standards that the results of the Court's case law have been the least visible. Because of the difficulty of showing that such standards are not justified by the existence of a genuine risk, or that they are excessive or can be replaced by less restrictive alternatives, there are relatively few cases in which such standards have been successfully challenged. Also, traders intending to challenge such standards on the ground that they are not justified on the basis of Community law may find themselves exposed to diverse kinds of more or less subtle pressures from the governmental authorities, trade associations or other traders. This is probably the area in which the most work remains to be done if a real Common Market is to be realized. It is also an area in which success will be the most difficult to achieve.

Our final remarks are directed to the general role of courts within federal systems. In the United States, commerce clause jurisprudence has been a particularly cogent vehicle for interpreting the federal nature of the American political system. That jurisprudence has involved two separate but related concerns: (1) the allocation of regulatory power between federal and state governments; and (2) the preservation of the political identity of both federal and state governments within the federal union. With respect to both concerns the Supreme Court has manifested renewed sensitivity toward the role of the state in the federal system, perhaps representing one of those periodic swings of the judicial pendulum referred to earlier. The revival of the tenth amendment in cases such as *National League of Cities v. Usery*[228] and the result in cases such as *Commonwealth Edison Co. v. Montana*[229] are expressions of a "new federalism."

In the complex area of dormant commerce clause jurisprudence the Supreme Court is clearly seeking to identify its judical role in the reconciliation of local

[228] 426 U.S. 833 (1976).
[229] 453 U.S. 609 (1981).

and national interests. In light of Congress' clear authority to pre-empt or reorder state policies affecting commerce some constitutional scholars have advised that the Court stay its hand in dormant commerce clause cases. Up to now the Court has rejected this advice and properly so. As we have noted, it continues to deal harshly with purposeful discrimination. A more serious problem of judicial review arises when discriminatory and nondiscriminatory motives combine to result in the enactment of a scheme to regulate aspects of commerce or when the *impact* of an otherwise facially valid statute is discriminatory. In these situations, the Court has often examined the legislative process to determine whether "out-of-state" interests were adequately represented in the legislature responsible for enacting the "burdensome" legislation. If those interests were adequately represented, *in the absence of corrective federal legislation,* then the Court ought to stay its hand out of proper respect for a constitutional framework limited by separation of powers and federalism. The rational basis reasoning supported by Justice Rehnquist (and before him by Justice Black) seems an inadequate protection of the federal interest in a common market. The political theory just noted – originally associated with the views of Justice Stone – allows the Court to substitute its judgment for that of the legislature if out-of-state interests are not adequately represented. In this way the Court is able to protect the respective interests of both state and federal governments. In this way, too, the Court does not foreclose the future. It allows the dialogue between levels of government to continue, setting the foundation for the further development of cooperative federalism.

The activism of the European Court, on the other hand, may possibly be justified by the absence of fully developed EEC executive and legislative organs. Yet the lack of a fully developed democratic system of political decision-making in the EEC would not justify the Court acting like a legislature or an executive. Still the Court might borrow from the American experience by paying closer attention to the nature of the political process that yields a challenged regulatory scheme within a Member State. By doing so, the Court could help to legitimate the decision-making process in the Member States as well as to enclose its own process of decision-making within a coherent frame.

Part III

The Moral and Cultural Dimension

The Protection of Fundamental Human Rights as a Vehicle of Integration

JOCHEN ABR. FROWEIN* STEPHEN SCHULHOFER**
and
MARTIN SHAPIRO***

I. Introduction

A. Integration and Common Values

When independent political entities, or states, undertake to create some sort of closer union – be it a confederation, federation, or supranational community – a process of integration is set in motion. This process will vary in duration depending on its ultimate goal, which may itself change during the process.

Experience seems to show that the question of common values protected by the legal system cannot be avoided if the process of integration is to continue towards the creation of a union to which all citizens feel a common allegiance. In the United States, we recall, a civil war was fought over what was basically a human rights issue: the question whether there could be different positions on slavery in the various states of the union. In Europe, of course, no civil war as such has been fought over purely human rights questions, but the violations of fundamental human rights in the last two World Wars did help lead Europeans to realize the need to commit themselves to a declaration of fundamental values which all European nations should aspire to protect.

Fundamental human rights can express a common set of minimum standards below which human rights conditions must not fall anywhere in the developing union of states. This presupposes, of course, the condition that these rights bind all public authorities in the union, for only then will fundamental rights have a clear unifying and integrating impact. It is one of the dominant themes of this chapter, however, that the application of uniform standards protecting fundamental rights to *all* public authorities (local, state and federal) may be a goal attained only after a long and difficult process of legal and historical develop-

* Professor of Law, University of Heidelberg; Co-Director, Max-Planck Institute, Heidelberg; Second Vice-President, European Commission of Human Rights, Strasbourg.

** Professor of Law, University of Pennsylvania.

*** Professor of Law, University of California at Berkeley (Boalt Hall School of Law).

ment. In the United States, we will see, the Supreme Court did not issue any important opinion in the area of freedom of speech until 1919; it did not even hint that the free speech standards it was elaborating for the Federal Government might be binding on the states until 1925; and it did not really begin to apply such standards to the states until 1931, sixty-three years after the adoption of the fourteenth amendment.[1] Similarly, in the field of criminal procedure, the Supreme Court reviewed only a handful of important state cases prior to World War I, and began to develop a significant jurisprudence only after 1936.[2]

It is another of the themes of this chapter that throughout the course of the integrative process, the level of applicable minimum human rights standards may vary considerably, from time to time, from place to place, and from one class of rights to another. In our primary example, the United States, the national minimum standard for freedom of speech on political matters in public places is high, although some states place their own standards even higher. Where arguably obscene speech is involved, however, the national minimum standard has waivered.[3] Before 1957 there was no such standard. In that year a low minimum standard was introduced. By 1964 the standard had crept up to so high a level that little or no discretion was left to the individual states, which were left free to bar only the most blatantly pornographic materials. Then in 1973 the federal standard was lowered somewhat to allow states to prosecute a slightly broader category of obscene material if they wished to. It is interesting to note in this regard that a number of different minimum standards may even exist simultaneously in the same area of law. Thus the U.S. federal minimum speech protection standard in the area of libel is high where speech about a public official is involved, but lower where speech concerns a private citizen.[4]

In Europe, similar fluctuations in attitudes toward human rights protection can be detected. Germany, one of the earliest European experiments in unification, provides us with comparable examples. The first attempt to introduce a federal Bill of Rights in Germany was in 1848, when the draft Constitution adopted by the *Paulskirche Parliament* following the 1848 Revolution included a catalogue of fundamental rights, made with the clear intention of unifying particular human rights conditions in the different German states. But the failure of the Revolution also meant the end of the 1848 Constitution and of its famous Bill of Rights. The two succeeding federal constitutions – the Constitution of the North German Confederation of 1867 and of the *Reich* of 1871 – contained no Bill of Rights, despite the strong demands of some liberal deputies from those states which offered the least protection of rights under their state constitutions – such as the two Mecklenburgs – that such federal guarantees be introduced. The main justification for such non-inclusion was clearly

[1] *See infra* § II.B.
[2] *See infra* §§ III.A.1–2.
[3] *See infra* § II.C.8.
[4] *See infra* § II.C.9.

the desire to protect the individual states of the union against the far-reaching changes in their internal systems which would have been brought about by a federal Bill of Rights, for although most states had their own constitutional Bill of Rights, by the mid-nineteenth century the level of protection and the legal remedies available varied greatly from state to state. Despite the lack of a federal constitutional Bill of Rights, however, several important federal statutes adopted between 1867 and 1874 – concerning the free movement of persons, access to industrial activities, and the freedoms of religion and of the press – soon created a subconstitutional system of federal guarantees for fundamental freedoms. It is worth mentioning that the extension of protections to the freedom of movement, as well as to the right to settle and undertake industrial activities under the same conditions in all the states of the federation, was a step very similar to the one taken by the Member States of the EEC when they adopted the Rome Treaty. From 1919 to 1933, and particularly after 1949, the protection of fundamental rights in the German federal system was assured through a Federal Constitutional Bill of Rights binding federal as well as state organs.[5]

In the European Communities, the protection of fundamental human rights does not form part of the written treaty law. It follows that integration through the guarantee of fundamental human rights was not envisaged by the drafters of the EC Treaties. Rather, they hoped that the protection of specific economic freedoms such as the free movement of workers or goods and the freedom of settlement would be a sufficient force for integration. However, the European Convention on Human Rights, a "Bill of Rights" for twenty-one European states within the Council of Europe – including all the EC members – may have an integrative value not to be overlooked in the future context of the EC system. Moreover, the case law of the European Court of Justice at Luxembourg shows that this court will also protect fundamental human rights, as well as general principles of law forming part of the legal tradition of the Member States, and may thus influence the process of integration even though this protection of human rights is formally limited to questions involving acts of the Communities.

Finally, as a cautionary note, it should be recognized that fundamental human rights may be protected in a manner which produces clearly disintegrative effects. With respect to the EC, this would be the case were a Member State's Bill of Rights to be applied to strike down Community legislation or other acts. The Federal Constitutional Court in Germany as well as the Italian Constitutional Court – the latter in a much more cautious manner – have held that such a possibility exists, at least in principle.[6] No case has come before these Courts in which they have found Community legislation to be in violation of the national Bill of Rights; but should that possibility materialize, the result would be disintegrative with respect to the specific subject matter, since Com-

[5] For a detailed discussion of the German developments, *see* Frowein, *Integration and the Federal Experience in Germany and Switzerland, supra* this vol., Bk. 1, esp. at § II.B.4.

[6] *See* Cappelletti & Golay, *The Judicial Branch in the Federal and Transnational Union: Its Impact on Integration, supra* this vol., Bk. 2, at § V.D.1.

munity acts would become inapplicable in some parts of the Community while remaining applicable in others, in clear violation of article 189 of the EEC Treaty.

Modern American experience is not directly relevant on this point because the U.S. Constitution itself provides that it is supreme over state laws and constitutions (article VI). Thus, although a state constitution may guarantee a higher level of rights protection to its citizens than is afforded by the U.S. Constitution, such state protections would never be permitted to defeat the implementation of a federal law. While before the Civil War some American states did argue that state constitutional guarantees might "nullify" or "interpose" themselves against the enforcement of federal law within their domains, that question was settled against the states by the Civil War. The European Convention on Human Rights – as a treaty and not a constitution – clearly does not enjoy such a supreme status vis-à-vis national law and thus must make its influence felt by other means.

B. The Legal Sources and Their Application in Comparison

1. Differences in the Nature and the Applicability of the Legal Sources

In the United States the standards developed in the jurisprudence of the U.S. Supreme Court which bind the states form part of federal constitutional law. Although the first ten amendments to the U.S. Constitution – the Bill of Rights – were held not to apply to the states in the early jurisprudence of the Court, subsequent interpretation of the due process and equal protection provisions of the fourteenth amendment has reversed this holding. Today, the vast majority of guarantees contained in the Bill of Rights bind federal and state organs alike. Uncertainty existed frequently in the past, and may sometimes still exist today, as to the exact reach of this incorporation of elements of the Bill of Rights into the provisions of the Constitution which bind the states. But in theory, the same minimum level of protection is in force throughout the states.

The European Convention on Human Rights is a treaty concluded under public international law. It is clear that its provisions are binding on all the States which have ratified it. Less clear is its binding force on the European Communities, although the Court in Luxembourg has referred to the European Convention on Human Rights when reviewing acts of the Communities.[7]

There is, however, one very important distinction with regard to the applicability of the Convention in the different Member States of the EC. The Convention forms part of municipal law in France, Italy, Germany and in the Benelux countries. Even though in most of these countries its rank is equal, not superior, to a parliamentary statute, courts will not easily apply a law which is in violation of the Convention. They will rather observe a traditional rule of statutory interpretation and interpret legislation in conformity with treaties in

[7] *See id.* at n. 303. *See also infra* notes 211–13 and accompanying text.

force, if at all possible. On the other hand, in Britain, Ireland and Denmark the Convention is not internal law, and will not be applied by the courts as such. British courts have taken notice of the Convention, in attempting to see whether they might interpret British law in light of it. But it is doubtful how far this has become a general practice. In this area, American experience provides no guidance because the Constitution is without question directly applicable in state courts, and is clearly superior to state law.

The European Convention on Human Rights does not contain any rules governing its applicability in the municipal legal order. The European Court of Human Rights has held that article 1 of the Convention was intended to make clear that the rights and freedoms guaranteed in the Convention will be directly secured to anyone within the jurisdiction of the Contracting States. That intention, according to the Court, finds a particularly faithful reflection in those instances where the Convention has been incorporated into domestic law. This jurisprudence seems to confirm the view that there is no obligation under the Convention to apply it as such in the municipal legal order of the Contracting States.

It is a consequence of this weakness of the Convention, as compared with EC law, for instance, that its impact as a tool for integration is severely hampered. Only in those states where the Convention is internally applicable may the municipal courts come to a decision based on transnational standards. In those countries where the Convention is not internally applicable, it is only through lengthy and difficult procedures before the supervisory organs set up by the Convention – the European Commission and Court of Human Rights – that the goal of integration can be finally reached.

The United States experience in this area might appear to be totally irrelevant, given the internal applicability of the U.S. Constitution. At the level of actual practice, however, the U.S. has encountered comparable problems, particularly in the field of criminal justice. American state trial court judges are not part of a federal or even state career service. They are not uniformly trained. They identify themselves strongly with the local communities from which they are chosen (often by popular election) and in which they serve. It has not been uncommon for state criminal court judges to be either ignorant of or resistant to rulings of the U.S. Supreme Court. Integration has been a hard-fought and only partially won battle in American criminal justice even where the Supreme Court has sought to impose federal standards.

The fundamental rights jurisprudence of the European Court of Justice at Luxembourg can be expected to have no direct impact on European integration, as these human rights restrictions apply only to the organs of the European Communities, and not to individual Member States. It will only be when the courts of the Member States look to the Community Court's rulings in these matters that some harmonization of standards will be reached through this jurisprudence. Such a development would not seem to be unlikely. Since the Luxembourg Court often develops its standards by comparing Member State rules, Member State courts may in turn be influenced in their jurisprudence on Community matters by this common standard.

2. The Interpretation of the Rights Guaranteed

The Bill of Rights in the U.S. Constitution has been in a continual state of development for almost two hundred years. Leaving aside all disputes about judicial activism or judicial restraint, it cannot be doubted that this development is one of the clearest examples of judicial law-making. This development was made possible especially thanks to the high authority of the U.S. Supreme Court, established in the very early years of the Republic. This meant that important reforms could be brought about by decisions of the Court. This is true for the whole matter of racial integration, for electoral reforms after 1962, and for the development of the law on abortion, or more generally, on the right to privacy.

It is clear that an international court such as the European Court of Human Rights can hardly claim an authority comparable to that of the U.S. Supreme Court. The history of the European Court of Human Rights covers only a very short period. Established in 1959, the Court had only very few cases referred to it until 1974. During the past several years the jurisprudence has grown considerably, but not in a manner comparable to that of national courts or to that of the Court of the European Communities in Luxembourg. Nevertheless, the European Court of Human Rights has clearly adopted a dynamic approach to the interpretation of the Convention. In several judgments the Court has stressed the need to take into account the development of new principles in the law of the Contracting States.

A good example is the decision in the *Tyrer Case*, concerning judicial corporal punishment on the Isle of Man. The Court expressly recalled that the Convention is "a living instrument which, as the Commission rightly stressed, must be interpreted in the light of present-day conditions."[8] The Court then referred to the development of commonly accepted standards for corporal punishment in the penal policy of the member countries of the Council of Europe. The Court concluded after a careful examination of the manner in which corporal punishment was executed on the Isle of Man that this punishment was degrading in the sense of article 3, and that therefore it violated the European Convention on Human rights.

Again in the *Marckx Case* the Court used the example of legal developments in many European states moving towards full recognition of the principle *"mater semper certa est"* for the interpretation of the Convention. It stressed that the domestic law of the great majority of member countries of the Council of Europe "has evolved and is continuing to evolve, in company with the relevant international instruments towards full recognition of the maxim."[9]

In these cases the harmonizing effect of a dynamic interpretation of the Convention becomes obvious. National rules which have fallen far below the general average standard due to general evolutionary tendencies in other states may eventually come into conflict with the Convention.

[8] Tyrer Case, Judgment of 25 Apr. 1978, Series A: Vol. 26, p. 15, para. 31 (Pubs. of Eur. Ct. H.R., 1978).

[9] Marckx Case, Judgment of 13 June 1979, Series A: Vol. 31, p. 19, para. 41 (Pubs. of Eur. Ct. H.R., 1979).

The analogous American experience in criminal justice is rich, but quite inconsistent in announcing the evolution of new national rights. On a number of occasions the U.S. Supreme Court has professed to follow evolving practices of a majority of American states, or what it has perceived to be a growing movement among the states. In other instances, however, the Court has not hesitated to proclaim new constitutional rights that, in effect, invalidated the laws of thirty or forty states in a single decision.

3. The Relationship to Other Guarantees in the Member State

Of importance for the influence of a transnational Bill of Rights in the process of integration will be its relationship to Bills of Rights in the different member states. In the Federal Republic of Germany, the provisions protecting fundamental rights in the *Land* Constitutions seem to have lost most of their importance, due to the broad and dynamic interpretation of the Federal Constitution in the same area. Not all Constitutions of the German *Länder* include guarantees of fundamental rights. Some, such as Nordrhein-Westfalen or Baden-Württemberg have incorporated the Federal Bill of Rights. Those German *Länder* which have adopted a detailed Bill of Rights in their constitutions, such as Bavaria, nevertheless feel the clearly unifying, and sometimes even supplanting, influence of the Federal Constitutional Court's jurisprudence on the Federal Bill of Rights.

This relationship is more or less the reverse if we look at the European Convention on Human Rights. Here, the transnational protection of fundamental rights has so far been clearly limited to a subsidiary role. Most of the countries which ratified the Convention have their own domestic Bills of Rights. The jurisprudence of the municipal courts will mainly look to this guarantee of fundamental rights even where the Convention is internally applicable. In many instances the national protection of fundamental rights will be stricter and include more rights than the Convention. In the case of Britain, which does not have a written constitution with a Bill of Rights, fundamental rights are still protected, to a large extent, through domestic law and by the courts independently of the Convention.

There is, however, a growing interest in the legal circles of those countries where the protection of fundamental rights is deficient in the future potential of the Convention. This is especially so with respect to review of acts of the legislature. In most countries which have a written Bill of Rights, courts may still not rule on the validity of statutes on the basis of their conformity with fundamental rights guarantees. Of the EC countries, only the Federal Republic of Germany, Ireland, and Italy have had for a number of years a clearly established system of judicial review of legislation. Likewise, of the other countries adhering to the Convention only Austria and, for cantonal legislation, Switzerland, have had such a system for any significant length of time. This means that in many of the member countries challenges to legislation on the basis of alleged violations of fundamental rights guarantees will only be possible through the Convention system. The *Marckx Case*, which questioned the validity of Belgian legislation regarding illegitimate children, is a good example of this type of review. It seems clear that British lawyers may make use of the procedures before Commission and Court in even a much wider area for the protection of fundamental rights, because in Britain there is no general possibility of attacking administrative acts on the basis of alleged violations of a Bill of Rights. This is one explanation for the growing number of important and difficult applications coming to the Commission from Britain.

The American experience here is rich, and indicates that developments need not be uniform or unidirectional. Historically, some states were far ahead of the central government in developing protections for the rights of accused persons. The Supreme Court gradually developed higher and higher standards for the central government's criminal justice system. As a result, an ever-widening gap opened between what was required of federal officials and the standards then applied in most states. During the 1950's and 1960's the Supreme Court, led by Chief Justice Warren, closed this gap by imposing more federal standards on the states. In this process, state constitutional provisions began to appear more and more redundant.

For a number of reasons American lawyers tend to be far more conversant in federal than in state constitutional law. Nevertheless, recent developments make it clear that state constitutions may remain important. In a number of substantive areas, including criminal procedure, freedom of speech, racial discrimination and equality in school financing, some state supreme courts have guaranteed a far higher standard of rights than the U.S. Supreme Court. As civil rights activists have come to perceive the Burger Court as being far less sympathetic to their cause than the Warren Court, there has been a renewed interest in state courts and state constitutions. Both the American and the British experience show that lawyers will seek out favorable forums. It is not necessarily true, however, that the most favorable forum is the one the farthest away.

C. The Methods of Application of Transnational and Trans-State Standards

1. Rules and Restrictions

Superficial examination of the basic texts of the U.S. Constitution and the European Convention on Human Rights leaves the impression of a startling contrast. In the Constitution, rights typically are stated briefly and absolutely. In the Convention, the typical structure is one in which the right is first stated broadly and then qualified by specific restrictive clauses. When one considers additionally the glosses placed on the Constitution by the Supreme Court, however, the similarity between U.S. and European law becomes evident: the written provisions of the Constitution state general rights just as the first clauses of many Convention articles do, and Supreme Court decisions place restrictions on these rights, as do the second clauses of many of the Convention articles. Against the background of this structure of general rights and qualifying restrictions, a central decisional formula of the U.S. Supreme Court becomes the balancing doctrine. The Court repeatedly states that most constitutional rights are not absolute. The right or interest protected by a statute usually can be balanced against the constitutional right infringed upon by that statute. The Court will do the balancing itself with sometimes greater and sometimes less deference to the statute-makers. If one were to enumerate the restrictions on the first amendment created by the Court using the balancing doctrine and similar devices, one would come startlingly close to the list of restrictions on free speech stated in article 10, section 2 of the Convention.[10] Of course, certain rights of the accused, such as the right against self-incrimination, are nearly absolute in the United States, and the Supreme Court does not invoke a balancing doctrine when elaborating them. Another of the key rights, however – that against search and seizure – is stated in the Constitution only in a qualified way, and is subject to explicit balancing considerations by the Supreme Court when it determines whether searches are "unreasonable."[11]

To state that the Supreme Court creates restrictions on constitutional rights through a balancing doctrine is also to say that the Court defines and limits those restriction in its case law. The Convention also limits its own restrictions. The adjudicative system used, rather similar to that employed in interpreting some of the more modern national constitutions such as the German Basic Law, limits these restrictions in several ways. They must, first, be prescribed by law. This will mean that in most cases the restriction must have been adopted by a legislature, whose democratic legitimacy is required by article 3 of the First Protocol of the Convention.[12] As Commission and Court have held, however, Common Law restrictions – such as those developed in the United Kingdom concerning contempt of court – are not excluded from this consideration. Second, the restrictions must have a specific aim, expressly mentioned in the restrictive clause. There we find, for instance, the protection of public order, of territorial integrity, or the rights and freedoms of others as possible justifications for restrictive legislation. Commission and Court will have to decide whether a given statute falls within one of the categories mentioned here. Since, admittedly, these aims are stated in a rather broad manner, with many alternatives, most restrictions potentially will be covered by one of the interests enumerated. Third, the Convention requires that the restriction be "necessary in a democratic society" for the protection of the interests mentioned. It is here, of course, that the most difficult questions arise. How far can Commission and Court review the necessity of a restriction in this sense? The problem

10 *See infra* note 263 and accompanying text.

11 The fourth amendment to the U.S. Constitution reads:

> The right of the people to be secure in their persons, houses, papers, and effects, against unreasonable searches and seizures, shall not be violated, and no warrants shall issue, but upon probable cause, supported by oath or affirmation, and particularly describing the place to be searched, and the persons or things to be seized.

12 ECHR, 1st Protocol, art. 3 provides:

> The High Contracting Parties undertake to hold free elections at reasonable intervals by secret ballot, under conditions which will ensure the free expression of the opinion of the people in the choice of the legislature.

is treated mostly by permitting the state a "margin of appreciation" for its actions, in the particular internal context.

2. The "Margin of Appreciation" and Strict Scrutiny

The first decision on whether a restriction of a human right is "necessary" in the sense of the European Convention on Human Rights must be made by the national parliament. It is clear from the whole system of the Convention that use of the term "necessary" does not imply that restrictions of the same sort must exist in all countries of the Convention to justify the restriction in question. Of course, the interests which may be protected according to the Convention must be considered in their specific national context. What is required to protect national security may be different in a country where a civil war rages in some regions, compared with a country on a small island without external or internal threats.

While the problem of "margin of appreciation" is usually treated as one of potential conflict between national and transnational *levels of government*, it is also one of potential conflict between differing *governing institutions*, the legislatures and courts. In the United States, the question is usually put in terms of a conflict between philosophies of "judicial activism" and "judicial self-restraint," or of "judicial deference" to the "political branches." There, too, questions of the appropriate *levels* and *institutions* of government for the protection of rights are mixed, but the emphasis falls far more heavily on the role of institutions than on conflicts between levels of government. Sometimes the Supreme Court will defer to a state legislature on the grounds that the state government is in a better position to assess local conditions than the Court sitting in Washington. More frequently, though, if the Court does choose to defer to a legislature, it will do so on the grounds that a democratically elected legislature is entitled to strike its own balance between conflicting rights and interests, without interference from an unelected, and thus less democratic, court. This rationale for granting a margin of appreciation is, of course, equally applicable to the state legislatures and the U.S. Congress. It rests not on the relative abilities of state and trans-state governments, but on the relative democratic legitimacy of legislatures and courts. Questions of relative ability also arise between U.S. courts and the Executive Branch. The U.S. Supreme Court has deferred to the U.S. President in a number of instances in which Executive national security policies have infringed upon individual rights. Obviously no question of supremacy arises here. The issue has been the extent to which judges who have no expertise in security matters may question the decision of executives who do. As the transnational European courts become more and more active, these facets of the American experience, as well as the federal aspect, may become increasingly relevant to Europeans.

In the meantime, certain European developments concerning questions of supremacy are instructive. In the *Handyside Case*,[13] the European Court of

[13] Judgment of 7 Dec. 1976, Series A: Vol. 24 (Pubs. of Eur. Ct. H.R., 1976).

Human Rights had to examine British measures taken against the so-called "Little Red School-Book," for their conformity with article 10, section 2 of the Convention.[14] The book – a general "consciousness-raising" guide for school-aged children, dealing with a wide range of issues such as abortion, sex practices and obedience to parents – had been widely distributed on the Continent. In its decision, the Court recognized that the different views prevailing in different Convention states about the protection of morals in a democratic society may lead to a justified restriction in one country, while there may be none in others. It also recognized that the concept of morals may differ from one country to the next. The U.S. Supreme Court has also specifically recognized that local "community standards" have a bearing upon the outcome of obscenity prosecutions.[15]

Certain European cases do, however, raise questions of institutional competence and thus draw our attention to the second aspect of the American experience with the margin of appreciation. In the *Klass Case*,[16] concerning German legislation on secret surveillance, the Court held that the domestic legislature enjoys a certain discretion in the setting of conditions under which a system of surveillance may be operated. While that decision did stress the special significance of the knowledge of local authorities about local conditions, it also raised the question of institutional expertise. Are judges qualified to make judgments about precisely what tactics are needed to combat effectively subversion or foreign infiltration? If they are not qualified to do so, must they leave questions involving fundamental rights to the mercy of the security authorities? These questions are central to such landmark U.S. cases as the *Japanese Exclusion Cases*[17] of World War II, where the Supreme Court deferred heavily to the judgment of military officials and the Executive Branch. More recently, and in a context more closely analogous to that of the *Klass Case*, the American courts have tended to insist on the importance of judicial control. American law generally prohibits secret electronic surveillance in the absence of prior judicial authorization, given only on the basis of probable cause to believe that a crime is about to be or has been committed. In 1972 the Supreme Court rejected an Executive Branch argument to the effect that this requirement of prior judicial authorization should be inapplicable when the President or Attorney General determines that domestic individuals or organizations threaten "the overthrow of the Government by force or other unlawful means, or ... any other clear and present danger to the structure or existence of the Government."[18] Rather, the Court insisted that even when surveillance is prompted by such a serious threat, prior judicial authorization remains necessary. The Court stated explicitly:

[14] *See supra* note 11.

[15] *See infra* § II.C.8.

[16] Judgment of 6 Sept. 1978, Series A: Vol. 28 (Pubs. of Eur. Ct. H.R., 1979).

[17] Hirabayashi v. United States, 320 U.S. 81 (1943); Korematsu v. United States, 323 U.S. 214 (1944); *Ex parte* Endo, 323 U.S. 283 (1944).

[18] United States v. United States District Court, 407 U.S. 297, 302 (1972), *citing* 18 U.S.C. § 2511(3).

> We cannot accept the Government's argument that internal security matters are too subtle and complex for judicial evaluation. ... If the threat is too subtle or complex for our senior law enforcement officers to convey its significance to a court, one may question whether there is probable cause for surveillance.[19]

The U.S. Supreme Court has not yet considered whether some exemption from these principles may be recognized for situations involving foreign intelligence surveillance, but the lower federal court jurisprudence and Congressional legislation responding to it now establish that even in this sensitive area the primacy of judicial control will be preserved, and the regime of exemptions envisaged in the statutory scheme is quite narrow in scope.

In the *Sunday Times Case*[20] the European Court held that the scope of the domestic power of appreciation is not the same for each of the qualifications listed in article 10, section 2. Unlike the conception of morals, the "more objective notion of the 'authority' of the judiciary" is open to more extensive European supervision, which corresponds to a less discretionary power of appreciation. This opinion, however, was not shared by the strong minority, which wrote a forceful dissent in this case. There is, however, common ground between majority and minority as to the competence of the Court to review the proportionality of a given restriction as one element in considering its necessity in a democratic society.

The majority of the Court was of the opinion that the balancing of interests between freedom of the press on one hand and the authority of the judiciary on the other could be achieved independently by the European Court of Human Rights. The strong minority limited its review to the question of whether the national authorities "have acted in good faith, with due care and in a reasonable manner when evaluating those facts and circumstances, as well as the danger that might thereby be occasioned for the interests listed in Art. 10 § 2."[21]

In a later section of this chapter we shall use the *Sunday Times Case* as a vehicle for examining the striking parallelism between developments in legal doctrines and judicial reasoning in the United States and the countries of the European Convention. In *Sunday Times* we encounter concepts such as "strict scrutiny," "compelling state interest," "preferred position," "the presumption of constitutionality," and "principled" versus "ad hoc" "balancing of interests," that have been central to American free speech jurisprudence for many years.[22]

3. Positive Rights and Their Harmonizing Effects

The harmonizing effect of a Bill of Rights will certainly be greater if it contains not only negative rights protecting the individual against state interference, but positive obligations for the state as well. An example of such a right is the one

[19] *Id.* at 320.
[20] Judgment of 26 Apr. 1979, Series A: Vol. 30 (Pubs. of Eur. Ct. H.R., 1979).
[21] *Id.* at p. 50 (joint dissenting opinion).
[22] *See infra* § IV.D.

included in article 6, section 3 (e) of the European Convention on Human Rights, whereby the state is under the obligation to provide for the free assistance of an interpreter if the accused does not understand or speak the language used in court. The European Court of Human Rights held that Germany had violated this provision since German law provided that the costs of an interpreter were to be borne by the accused if he were convicted.[23] The result of this decision may be the harmonization of the legislation on this problem, since other Convention countries currently use the same system formerly used by Germany. But the European Court of Human Rights has gone even further. It has stated that positive obligations may also follow by implication from Convention articles which have a negative or neutral wording. Thus, the Court has held in the *Marckx Case*[24] that respect for family life implies the obligation to protect the family by legislation. In the *Airey Case*[25] the Court found that the access to courts guaranteed under article 6 must be "effective." Therefore, high costs for legal proceedings, in combination with a lack of legal aid, may amount to a violation of the Convention. Again in the *Artico Case*[26] it was held that where the accused has no financial means with which to obtain his own counsel, it is not sufficient to appoint a defense lawyer who merely sees that all procedural requirements of the trial are fulfilled. Rather, the state has a duty to ensure that all the responsibilities of a defense attorney are being adequately met. The Court again stressed the positive obligation created by the Convention in this case.

Positive obligations of a similar nature have been inferred from the basic guarantees specified in the U.S. Bill of Rights. The sixth amendment right to the assistance of counsel has been interpreted as requiring the states to appoint counsel for indigents facing any criminal charge resulting in imprisonment.[27] Because the vast majority of American criminal defendants are poor, most jurisdictions across the country have been forced to establish elaborate mechanisms to provide representation. Some jurisdictions rely on systems for appointing, on a case-by-case basis, attorneys who also maintain an independent practice; compensation schemes for such attorneys vary widely. Other jurisdictions rely on an organized Defender Agency, in which the attorneys handle indigent criminal defense on a full-time basis. Although an important body of scholarly literature suggests significant variances in the quality of defense representation resulting from these different systems, the Supreme Court has not dictated the adoption of any particular approach. Nonetheless, practical considerations and economic constraints have in recent years produced some trends toward uniformity of techniques, at least in the larger cities. Moreover, decisions by the Supreme Court and lower courts have elaborated the contours of the

23 Case of Luedicke, Belkacem and Koç, Judgment of 28 Nov. 1978, Series A: Vol. 29 (Pubs. of Eur. Ct. H.R., 1979).

24 *Supra* note 9.

25 Judgment of 6 Feb. 1981, Series A: Vol. 41 (Pubs. of Eur. Ct. H.R., 1981).

26 Judgment of 13 May 1980, Series A: Vol. 37 (Pubs. of Eur. Ct. H.R., 1980).

27 *See infra* § III.B.2.

principle of adequate representation in some detail, so that there is considerable uniformity in the minimum level of obligation to be satisfied, even if the mechanisms chosen to satisfy the obligation vary from one another. For example, the states must insure that the appointed counsel is professionally competent, that he is appointed under conditions conducive to effective representation (*e.g.* adequate preparation time) and that he in fact performs in a professionally acceptable fashion (*e.g.* appropriately investigating facts and law).[28] In addition, states must enable the defense counsel to obtain the help of other professionals (psychiatrists, ballistics experts, etc.) at state expense when necessary for an adequate defense.[29]

In the area of prison conditions, American courts have likewise deduced from a negative obligation – in this instance, the obligation not to impose "cruel and unusual punishments" – what amounts to a positive obligation – to afford certain minimal levels of safety, living space and medical attention in prison.[30] Some of the judicial decrees in this area impose quite detailed obligations upon prison authorities and in some instances the resulting fiscal consequences for the states have been considerable. Although judicial initiatives of this kind remain controversial, and in a few cases have been restrained by the U.S. Supreme Court, it can scarcely be questioned that some positive obligations necessarily attach when the state exercises its power to imprison; decisions by the federal courts over the past decade have undoubtedly contributed to more uniform appreciation of these obligations among the states.[31]

The American experience in connection with both defense representation and prison conditions suggests both the importance and the limitations of judicial efforts to formulate positive obligations by which the enjoyment of fundamental rights may be protected more effectively. In general, protection of such rights is the responsibility of the legislature, which must decide for which purpose public funds should be spent as a matter of priority.

D. Fundamental Human Rights as a Vehicle for Integration – A Provisional Evaluation

Historical examples of developments in the United States, and also in Germany show that the guarantee of fundamental rights in the constitution or in federal statutes can be of considerable importance for integration. Integration here means, most centrally, the development of equal, or at least equal minimum, standards of protection for human rights in the different constituent parts of the federation or union.

[28] *See* McMann v. Richardson, 397 U.S. 759 (1970); Moore v. United States, 432 F.2d 730 (3d Cir. 1970).

[29] *See* Mason v. Arizona, 504 F.2d 1345 (9th Cir. 1974); Lee v. Habib, 424 F.2d 891 (D.C. Cir. 1970).

[30] *See* Estelle v. Gamble, 429 U.S. 102 (1976).

[31] *See generally* Note, *Review of Prisoners' Rights Under the First, Fifth, and Eighth Amendments,* 18 Duq. L. Rev. 683 (1980).

For European integration it seems difficult to evaluate, at this stage, the possible integrative impact of rules and decisions on questions of transnational human rights. So far, the jurisprudence of the European Commission and Court of Human Rights has tended to be of rather marginal importance for the unification of standards. It seems, however, that this may be about to change. The growing number of cases brought before the European Court of Human Rights suggests that more important and more difficult issues are reaching the Convention organs.

Of course, the role of the European Convention on Human Rights is so far clearly a subsidiary one for the great majority of member countries. The country with the largest population, the Federal Republic of Germany, has a particularly elaborate system of internal protection of fundamental rights. The Federal Constitutional Court can review all public acts on the basis of a constitutional complaint brought by an individual citizen. Even statutes adopted by the Federal or *Land* Parliaments can be attacked by such a complaint if they interfere directly with individual rights. This may explain the fact that only a very few important applications have reached the Convention system from Germany. France recognized the right of individual application under article 25 only very recently, and so up to a short time ago had no applications whatsoever. In Italy, the Convention is apparently not very well known in legal circles, although several important applications are now pending before the Commission or the Court. Only in the United Kingdom can we recognize a definite strategy, selected by experienced lawyers, to bring important test cases before the Convention organs. This was true for the *Handyside Case*, concerning the problem of obscenity as a limitation on the freedom of expression. It was the same for the *Sunday Times Case*, where contempt of court and freedom of the press had to be balanced. But it is also true for the whole series of prisoners' correspondence cases recently decided by the Court,[32] as well as for the *Case of Young, James, and Webster*, in which the applicants attacked certain aspects of the closed-shop system.[33] It seems easily understandable that, in a country where remedies against decisions by public authorities are still less extensive than in most others, the Convention system should be of particular interest. As for the potentially harmonizing influence of this procedure, it may be mentioned that in several important British cases the lawyers quoted decisions of the German Federal Constitutional Court and of the U.S. Supreme Court, based on provisions of the respective Bills of Rights which are essentially equivalent to guarantees applicable under the Convention.

The possibility that the jurisprudence of the European Convention on Human Rights will have a harmonizing effect presupposes that all states will follow its jurisprudence and respect the results. It seems doubtful whether this is the case at present. So far, it would seem that only the state primarily concerned in the case will draw conclusions from the judgment. For instance, one

[32] *See* Case of Silver, *et al.*, Judgment of 25 Mar. 1983, Series A: Vol. 61 (Pubs. of Eur. Ct. H.R., 1983).

[33] Judgment of 13 Aug. 1981, Series A: Vol. 44 (Pubs. of Eur. Ct. H.R., 1981).

has not heard of any changes in the legal systems of those states which charge the convicted defendant for interpreters' fees after the judgment of the Court in the *Luedicke Case*,[34] except in the Federal Republic of Germany, where the decision resulted in an immediate change of procedures and in an amendment of the relevant legislation.

In focusing on integration, we must be careful not to assume that the United States now has a completely integrated system of legal rights, nor that the movement toward the level of integration that currently exists there was steady and inevitable. Historically, for instance, there were greatly varying levels of protection of rights of accused persons in the various states. At crucial times in the development of national (trans-state) standards, the inspiration for many of the leading U.S. Supreme Court cases were opinions from the most advanced states, such as California. Other leading cases came from Southern states that by contrast devoted few resources to protecting the accused. As in Europe, the flow of cases "upward" seems to depend both on differing state legal institutions and on differing levels of activity among state lawyers. And as in Europe, some state high courts are themselves so alert to claims of individual rights that state levels of constitutional protection exceed federal minimum standards.

The U.S. Supreme Court enjoys three major advantages over the European Court of Human Rights in achieving legal integration. The first of these advantages will persist indefinitely. In the United States there is an independent federal criminal law, criminal courts, and police system running parallel to that of the states. The U.S. Supreme Court has historically established high criminal justice standards for the Justice Department, the F.B.I. and the federal district courts long before it has applied comparable standards to the states. Thus, it can experiment with such standards and familiarize the bar and the public with them before imposing them on the states. The Supreme Court's possession of a "captive" system over which it exercises direct authority and which it can use to demonstrate new standards has been an important tool for integration. Paradoxically, there is some evidence that the Supreme Court's recent activism in extending Bill of Rights guarantees to the states has prompted the Court to be more cautious and conservative in recognizing new principles even for limited application within the federal criminal courts, but it is perhaps too early to tell how much this new attitude should be attributed solely to the broadened reach of the Bill of Rights.

A second advantage enjoyed by the U.S. Supreme Court, also likely to be a permanent one, is the existence of lower federal courts whose general jurisdiction extends to claims relating to alleged state infringement of fundamental rights. The U.S. Supreme Court could scarcely begin to review all the important state court decisions rendered each year in matters affecting federally guaranteed civil liberties. As a practical matter, the Supreme Court would have little hope of enforcing uniform standards effectively without the support of the independent system of federal trial and appellate courts throughout the country, now staffed by roughly five hundred federal judges. Persons facing poten-

[34] Case of Luedicke, Belkacem and Koç, *supra* note 23.

tial deprivation of rights to free speech, personal privacy and so on typically can initiate a suit against state authorities (for injunction, declaratory relief or damages) in a federal trial court and thus can be assured of a hearing before a judge oriented to the federal system of guarantees and directly responsible to federal appellate judges. Similarly, defendants convicted in state criminal cases need not rely on the very slim chance that the U.S. Supreme Court will be able to grant review; generally such defendants can obtain a new hearing on their federal constitutional claims before a federal trial judge by invoking the writ of habeas corpus.

As a result, the United States obviously enjoys a considerable advantage as far as the potential for integration is concerned. Major Supreme Court decisions, such as those on the death penalty, often result in almost immediate revisions of the laws or administrative practices of most of the states. Yet the uniformity of response must not be exaggerated. Even legally trained local and state administrators often are unaware of, misunderstand, or deliberately ignore U.S. Supreme Court declarations of law. State statutes in violation of Supreme Court constitutional decisions may remain in force until some individual party challenges them. Indeed, the problem of local compliance with Supreme Court mandates is the subject of a large and complex body of American legal scholarship.

In view of such difficulties, the general jurisdiction of the federal trial courts has been of inestimable importance for achieving compliance with principles articulated by the U.S. Supreme Court. One must wonder about European prospects for realizing legal integration in the human rights sphere in the absence of some comparable mechanism. It may be that the European national judiciaries, being more systematically trained and less politically oriented than their counterparts in the American states, will respond more readily to guidance emanating from the European Court. Nonetheless, over the long run, attention to an enforcement procedure such as that envisaged by article 57 of the Convention[35] and elaboration of techniques for making it effective in the European context may prove crucial for furthering the extent of genuine legal integration.

The last advantage enjoyed by the U.S. Supreme Court is one that the European Court of Human Rights may come to enjoy. While it is true that for most purposes the American Bar is organized state by state, there exists a quasi-national constitutional Bar. Even in state Supreme Courts advocates are more likely to make civil liberties arguments based on the U.S. rather than on state constitutions. The reasons for this fixation on the U.S. Constitution at the expense of the state constitutions are complex, ranging from the existence of large Washington law firms with concentrated expertise in federal

[35] ECHR art. 57 provides:

> On receipt of a request from the Secretary-General of the Council of Europe any High Contracting Party shall furnish an explanation of the manner in which its internal law ensures the effective implementation of any of the provisions of this Convention.

constitutional litigation, to the central place given to the U.S. Constitution in even the most locally-oriented law school curriculums.[36] It may be that American experience in this regard can be informative to Europeans seeking to create a more central place for the Convention on Human Rights in European legal consciousness.

Up to the present time, the harmonizing influence of the Convention system can probably best be shown in the notions of fair trial, of "equality of arms" in criminal procedures, or of the reasonable time for detention before trial. Here, the early jurisprudence of the Commission and the Court have brought about actual changes in the law, and to some extent in the practices of several member countries of the Convention.

At the present time it seems premature to speculate about which method of interpretation and application of the European Convention on Human Rights would be more appropriate for the goal of legal integration. In the near future, it seems that all one can aim for is a growing awareness that common standards for the protection of fundamental rights have a clear bearing on integration.

[36] *See generally* Friedman & Teubner, *Legal Education and Legal Integration: European Hopes and American Experience*, *infra* this book, at § III.

II. Freedom of Expression – Transnational and State Interactions in the American Experience

(*by* Martin Shapiro)

A. The American Experience - An Introduction

We must bear in mind that our comparison of European and American experience is not primarily at the level of the legal doctrines themselves but focuses on the role of law and courts in the achievement of some level of legal integration or harmonization. From this perspective our approach to the American materials on freedom of speech must be historical. The history of the first amendment to the U.S. Constitution – the major source of free speech protections in U.S. law – shows a movement from an initial stage at which the states were the sole actors in free speech jurisprudence through a middle stage in which state and national governments were roughly coequal, to a stage of national primacy accompanied by continued state activity. It is this historical evolution that may be of particular interest to Europeans.

One of the central features of U.S. free speech history is the relative dearth of freedom of speech cases in both state and federal courts. A substantial jurisprudence of freedom of speech is absent from the founding of the Republic until World War I, a period of about 125 years. Adopted in 1791, the first amendment was virtually an integral part of the initial Constitution. In the simplest of terms it read, "Congress shall make no law ... abridging the freedom of speech, or of the press. ..."

At that time most of the original states already had free speech guarantees in their own state constitutions. As new states were formed and entered the union, their constitutions, too, typically contained speech protections. In a number of instances these protections subsequently were strengthened by further amendments. At the formal constitutional level, the U.S. enjoyed a parallel structure of state and federal guarantees.

1. Early Federal Jurisprudence

In the federal jurisdiction there simply were no significant freedom of speech cases until 1917. The Sedition Act of 1798 contained severe infringements upon freedom of speech and was administered to suppress the partisan critics of the Federalist political party that controlled Congress, the Presidency and the Supreme Court. It remains probably the most serious incident of government repression of speech in American history. It is unclear, however, whether the statute was as clearly in violation of the first amendment in the eyes of eighteenth century Americans as it is in those of twentieth century Americans. The controversy that it aroused was so highly partisan, pitting spokesmen for the Federalist Party against those of the Anti-Federalist Party of Jefferson, that no clear doctrines emerged from the public controversy. Perhaps because the federal courts were totally dominated by judges appointed by the Federalist Party, the Anti-Federalist newspaper editors prosecuted under the statute received no comfort there. The constitutionality of the Sedition Act was never tested in the Supreme Court. The Act itself was repealed when the Anti-Federalist Party took control of the Federal Government after the election of 1800. Years later, Congress awarded monetary indemnification to those who had been convicted. The Sedition Act episode left a major question but no jurisprudential development.[37]

It is sometimes argued that the reason that no first amendment cases were decided in the federal courts between 1800 and 1917 is that the Federal Government made no attempt to suppress speech between the era of the soon-repealed Sedition Act and that of the Espionage Act of 1917. This argument is not entirely correct. There were suppression incidents in connection with the Civil War. And a number of post-Civil War postal and customs statutes contained provisions directed against fraudulent and obscene publications. Nevertheless, the Civil War produced no lasting statutory authority to suppress speech, and, until recently, fraud and obscenity were so clearly outside the ambit of constitutionally-protected speech that the postal and customs statutes did not appear to raise any constitutional problems. Some would argue that until the ideological cleavages brought on by World War I, Americans were so devoted to freedom of speech that no judicial intervention on its behalf was necessary because no infringements occurred. Others would explain that absence of litigation at the federal level by supposing that the conformist pressures of American democracy were so great that private and local hostility to dissident speech repressed it effectively and informally without the need of formal, legal repressions by the Federal Government. For whatever reason, the Supreme Court did not render a significant first amendment opinion until 1919.[38]

2. Early State Jurisprudence

At the state level, there is only scattered judicial activity until the turn of the century. From the 1890's until World War I, there is a gradual accumulation of state cases and of surrounding commentary on free speech. The relative importance of this activity is now the subject of debate among historians. American constitutional historians had conventionally remarked that issues of freedom of speech were simply not on the intellectual, legal and political agenda until World War I.[39] This view is now being challenged by a number of young scholars who can point to a small body of pre-World War I legal literature on freedom of speech, several hundred state court opinions, one organized free

[37] *See* L. Levy, Legacy of Suppression, Freedom of Speech and Press in Early American History (Cambridge, Harv. U.P., 1960); J.C. Miller, Crisis in Freedom: The Alien and Sedition Acts (Boston, Little Brown, 1951).

[38] Schenck v. United States, 249 U.S. 47 (1919).

[39] P. Murphy, The Meaning of Freedom of Speech (Westport, Greenwood, 1972).

speech protection group and a number of social action groups that pressed speech claims in order to fend off attempts to repress their activities.[40]

The pre-World War I state cases for the most part involve seven basic situations. The first is libel. There are a great many cases, of course, but most of them cannot properly be said to involve first amendment issues at all. It was not until the 1970's that libelous statements aimed at private persons were perceived as raising any constitutional issues.[41] Some states, however, did hold that the good faith publication of news about public officials was an exercise of constitutionally-protected free speech and thus was privileged. The second category of cases are those involving "scandal sheets," that is, newspapers and magazines that massed news and gossip about crime and sexual misconduct. Although many of their reports were directed against local officials and other politicians, and the scandal sheets sometimes raised claims of freedom of the press, state courts held that such speech might be proscribed as a danger to public morals. Third, there were a substantial number of obscenity cases. Here the freedom of speech issue was almost never raised. Nearly every state had both a constitutional free speech provision and an obscenity statute. Hardly anyone supposed that the two could be in conflict. Fourth, there were a substantial number of labor union picketing cases. In some states a distinction was drawn between peaceful picketing, which was held to be protected by state constitutional free speech provisions, and union activity involving threats, intimidation or violence, which was not. Other state courts held all picketing to be inherently intimidating and therefore lacking in constitutional protection. Even where picketing was granted a degree of protection, courts generally held that union speech rights might not lawfully be exercised to interfere with the property rights of owners or the right of workers to contract freely for their labor.

In these four areas, then, free speech was either never or rarely a salient issue to pre-World War I state judges. In the other three, free speech was more centrally implicated. One of these involved parades and demonstrations by groups like the Salvation Army. On the whole local communities did not object to the substantive messages of Christianity and temperance that such groups deliv-

[40] The greatest 19th century constitutional commentator, Thomas Cooley, had devoted a considerable discussion to the first amendment. So had several other treatise writers. Theodore Schroeder had produced a large body of freedom of speech writings. If one includes obscenity and labor cases, the state court production of cases is detectable, but European readers should remember that a few dozen or even a few hundred cases spread over twenty or thirty years is an almost insignificant drop in the ocean of opinions that American courts issue. The Free Speech League of New York was a very vocal forerunner of such groups as the American Civil Liberties Union, and a number of labor unions and the I.W.W. (a labor movement of revolutionary, anarcho-syndicalist coloration) often raised freedom of speech issues in the course of unionization battles. *See* Anderson, *The Formative Period of First Amendment Theory, 1870–1915*, 24 AM.J. OF LEGAL HIST. 56–75 (1980); Rabban, *The First Amendment in Its Forgotten Years*, 90 YALE L.J. 514 (1980).

[41] *See* Gertz v. Robert Welch, Inc., 418 U.S. 323 (1974).

ered, but they did object to the noise and disruption caused by all the drumbeating and marching. In general courts struck down blanket prohibitions on parades. Some state courts upheld ordinances requiring that licenses for parades and speeches in public places be obtained from local authorities. Others struck down such ordinances particularly if they appeared to be used to discriminate against some speakers in favor of others. A second area that obviously did involve freedom of speech was that of demonstrations and speeches by leftists waving the red flag and/or preaching anarchism and socialism. Here courts uniformly upheld prosecutions for failure to obtain a license or disturbing the peace, usually on the ground that such speech necessarily endangered the public peace. Lastly, there were a scattering of contempt of court prosecutions directed at newspapers that had published news and comments about trials. Some courts upheld all such contempt convictions and others limited the contempt power to comments published before the verdict.

Even when we examine these three areas where free speech claims were openly made and addressed by the courts, the jurisprudence is thin. Some generalizations are possible remembering that they are constructed from very few cases scattered over many years and many states. They are, however, generalizations of the sort that academic lawyers construct rather than the living law of the various states. In general, state courts agreed that a prior restraint of the publication of printed materials was constitutionally forbidden even in areas like libel and obscenity. They also generally held that the public enjoyed property rights in public streets and parks. Like those of other property owners, these rights could not be overridden by the free speech rights of non-owners. Streets and parks were held to be primarily devoted to traffic and recreational uses. Therefore, public authorities might either bar speakers from parks and streets entirely or employ licensing requirements that imposed reasonable limitations on the time, place and manner of speech so as to preserve the primary traffic and recreational uses of their property. In short, the contrary of what later became known as the public forum doctrine[42] was the agreed law although courts would strike down unreasonable regulations, particularly those that were unreasonable in the sense of discriminating in favor of some speakers and against others.

Most importantly, the state courts agreed that speech regulation was an exercise of the state "police power," which in American constitutional law means a general reservoir of powers inhering in the state to protect the "health, safety, morals and welfare" of the people. State courts did not view freedom of speech as an absolute bar to the exercise of the police power or even as enjoying a preferred position. Rather they held that in exercising the police power, the state might balance freedom of speech against the needs of public order and morality in constructing reasonable regulations of speech. State courts were aided in the construction of this balancing standard because, unlike the federal

[42] *See* Kalven, *The Concept of the Public Forum:* Cox v. Louisiana, 1965 SUP. CT. REV. 1. *See infra* text accompanying notes 86–88.

constitution, most state constitutions not only guaranteed the right of free speech but also spoke of responsibilities not to abuse the right.[43]

It should be added to this account of pre-World War I state activities that, following the assassination of President McKinley by an anarchist, New York State passed a criminal anarchy statute prohibiting the advocacy of overthrow of the government by force.[44] There were, however, almost no pre-War prosecutions under this or other statutes.

Thus in the pre-War period while some state constitutional law of freedom of speech was gradually emerging, free speech was not a widely litigated issue. When the United States Supreme Court chose to enter the area, it would not find itself confronted with well articulated bodies of state law or state judges anxious to preserve their state legal traditions.

3. The World War I Outburst

If there is some disagreement among historians about how much freedom of speech jurisprudence had developed before World War I, they are in agreement that a great outburst did occur at that time both at state and national levels.[45] From 1914 to 1917 there was extremely strong opposition to American entry into the war. This opposition did not, however, generate much speech litigation, and abruptly stopped with America's entry into the war. It was not the war itself, but the Russian Revolution, that initiated the modern concern for freedom of speech. When the revolutionary government withdrew from hostilities and the allies responded by sending an expeditionary force to Russia, socialist organizations in the United States responded with a campaign of anti-war propaganda. American anti-communists found this campaign a heaven-sent opportunity to suppress the socialist ideas they hated under the guise of a patriotic drive against those seeking to undermine the American war effort. The drive began during the war but continued in the Red Scare of the immediate post-war period. Both state and federal authorities raided socialist organizations, arrested their members and shut down their publications.[46] The states frequently invoked their old or newly-enacted sedition and criminal syndicalism acts, and the Federal Government employed the Espionage Act of 1917[47] as amended by the Sedition Act of 1918,[48] which proscribed advocacy of resistance to the war effort. As a result, freedom of speech challenges to the constitutionality of these statutes began to pour into state and federal courts.[49]

43 I am indebted for this very important point to Berta Schweinberger, a Ph.D. candidate in the Jurisprudence and Social Policy Program of the Law School of the University of California, Berkeley.

44 1902 N.Y. Laws ch. 371; N.Y. PENAL LAW §§ 160, 161 (1902).

45 *See* P. MURPHY, WORLD WAR I AND THE ORIGINS OF CIVIL LIBERTIES IN THE UNITED STATES (New York, Norton, 1979).

46 H. SCHEIBER, THE WILSON ADMINISTRATION AND CIVIL LIBERTIES (Ithaca, N.Y., Cornell U.P., 1960).

47 40 Stat. 217, 219 (1917).

48 40 Stat. 553 (1918).

49 Z. CHAFEE, FREE SPEECH IN THE UNITED STATES (Cambridge, Harv. U.P., 1942).

The immediate causes of the Red Scare are clear enough. All peoples and governments are more prone to the suppression of speech in war than in peacetime. And, while leftist groups had been active in the U.S. for some time, the success of the Russian revolutionaries suddenly made revolutionary rhetoric appear really dangerous. The deeper causes of both the wave of repression and the rapid emergence of a legal theory of freedom of speech are less clear. American historians have recently been exploring the darker side of the Progressive Movement, which was basically a reform movement aimed at rendering American government both more democratic and more efficient by reducing the power of the old local political elites who ruled the Democratic and Republican Parties. Progressivism, however, also contained an important strand of "nativism," that is of a fear that traditional American values associated with rural life and with the older waves of English and German speaking immigrants would be swept away by the new waves of Italian, Slavic and Jewish immigrants clustered in the cities. Woodrow Wilson was a Progressive President, while the Reds were predominantly Eastern European and urban and often Jewish.[50]

A somewhat parallel explanation argues that Americans had enjoyed a considerable consensus of values after the Civil War, indeed a consensus so strong that it led to the suppression of dissident speech by private pressures to conform, without the need of government intervention. Without government intervention legal questions of free speech could not usually arise. In the few instances in which they did, people united and secure in their political ideology would find it obvious that radical speech was not an exercise of freedom of speech but an abuse of that freedom that ought to be suppressed in the name of public order. After the turn of the century, so it is argued, this consensus broke down. As a result more radical speech took place, appearing more dangerous to those who still espoused the old values, and it could no longer be suppressed by a united front of private opposition. Thus government power was more often invoked. Once the traditional boundaries between "true" speech and "irresponsible" speech had broken down, more people saw the government intervention as a possible violation of constitutional guarantees.[51]

More precisely, it has been argued that in the 1910's and 1920's organized groups came into existence whose aim was to radically challenge traditional American ideology and radically restructure American society. These groups began to formulate freedom of speech claims to protect themselves from government repression. The sudden emergence of freedom of speech jurisprudence in the 1920's is, in this view, not the result of the progress of constitutional thought or the emergence of judicial leaders like Holmes and Brandeis. Rather it is the product of group politics carried into the courts. It occurs when minority but organized political movements seek to invent and invoke constitutional symbols to protect themselves against majority repres-

[50] H. Scheiber, *supra* note 46.

[51] *See* P. Murphy, *supra* note 45; Abrams, *Free and Equal as Compared to What?*, in Reviews in American History 97 (March 1981).

sion and seek to use the courts to protect themselves against majority controlled legislatures and executives.[52] Indeed, most of the great cases of the 1920's that formulated the initial federal freedom of speech doctrines were brought to the Supreme Court by the American Civil Liberties Union (A.C.L.U.) or the International Labor Defense (I.L.D.). The former had sprung from the pacifist movement of World War I and while it purported to be nonpartisan was consistently enlisted in defense of leftist groups and those opposing racial discrimination. The latter was the litigation arm of the Communist Party.[53]

We have paid so much attention to these background factors because they are important in assessing the relevance of American constitutional experience for the European Community. American freedom of speech developments did not occur purely as an autonomous jurisprudential process entirely dependent on the advanced thinking of a few judges. The sudden flowering of a federal constitutional jurisprudence of free speech depended in part on the cataclysmic world events of 1917 and fundamental changes in the basic American political climate. More precisely and immediately it depended far less on judges than on organized private groups and the lawyers they employed to bring litigation and formulate legal arguments that could successfully defend the speakers they favored. By the same token, the movement that has led to the adoption of a European Convention on Human Rights may be seen not as part of an abstract intellectual or jurisprudential trend, but as a reaction to political upheavals in Europe and, in particular, to the wholesale abrogation of fundamental rights by the Fascist and Nazi regimes. In this respect, the American historical background emerges not in contrast to, but rather in closer harmony with the European experience.

B. Incorporation of the First Amendment

1. Historical Background to Incorporation

So far we have noted that freedom of speech issues rarely arose in either state or federal courts before 1917. Moreover, there are almost no instances in which the Supreme Court of the United States heard freedom of speech cases that had initially arisen in state courts under its power to review state court decisions involving federal constitutional questions. In *Barron v. Mayor of Baltimore*,[54] the U.S. Supreme Court had held that the Bill of Rights limited only the Federal Government and was not applicable to the states. The Civil War Amendments did apply to the states. The fourteenth amendment provided that no state should deny to its citizens "privileges and immunities," or the "equal protection" or "due process" of law. With these clauses begins the constitu-

52 P. MURPHY, *supra* note 45.

53 R. CORTNER, SUPREME COURT AND THE SECOND BILL OF RIGHTS chs. 3–4 (Madison, U. Wis. P., 1981).

54 32 U.S. (7 Pet.) 243 (1833).

tional development usually labelled "incorporation" of the Bill of Rights into the due process clause of the fourteenth amendment. The full story of incorporation is most relevant to the nationalizing of the rights of accused persons and will be told in another part of this chapter. The freedom of speech rights guaranteed by the first amendment were those first incorporated so we must present here a brief account of the early stages of incorporation.[55] The immediate purpose of the Civil War Amendments threatened to upset the whole balance of federalism by making the Federal Government, and more specifically the federal courts, the guarantors of a wide range of individual rights against invasion by state officials. In a series of cases from 1873 to about 1910, the Supreme Court at first sought to preserve the old federal balance by reading the Civil War Amendments very narrowly, and then to countenance Federal Government intervention only in the protection of private property rights rather than the wider array of rights protected by the first ten amendments. The Court explicitly rejected the theory that the Bill of Rights had been made applicable to the states by the fourteenth amendment. As a result, even in those instances where freedom of speech claims were raised in state courts, they were not reviewable by the United States Supreme Court. Instead they were treated as claims arising under state constitutional provisions on speech. State supreme courts were the final authorities on state constitutional questions. Until World War I the U.S. Supreme Court had addressed the constitutionality of state government suppression of speech in less than half a dozen cases, none of them conclusive.

Thus when World War I brought an upsurge of conflict over freedom of speech neither state nor federal courts had developed a substantial body of free speech jurisprudence nor had the federal courts asserted any supervisory power over exercises of state police power that might infringe upon speech. Moreover, when the upsurge came, there was a very close parallelism of interests between state and federal jurisdictions. It will be recalled that the Espionage Act of 1917 was the occasion of the burst of free speech cases in federal courts. Provisions of that act making criminal both conspiracy to overthrow the government and advocacy of the same were closely paralleled by state criminal syndicalism and sedition statutes. Prosecutions under such statutes were the cause of an upsurge of speech cases in state courts. So the statutory materials were almost identical in state and federal litigation. Furthermore the speakers being prosecuted were the same. Both state and federal governments mounted prosecutions against revolutionary socialists. When the states did so, it was not really because they feared that the socialists might bring about the overthrow of the state of New York or California. The situation was not at all comparable to one in which the British Government seeks to deal with revolutionaries in Northern Ireland or the Belgian Government with linguistic strife – that is, where a member of the Council of Europe seeks to deal with a threat to its own internal order but one that is no direct threat to other members. In the United States in this period,

[55] For an excellent account of the entire incorporation movement *see* R. CORTNER, *supra* note 53.

both state and federal authorities were seeking to deal with revolutionary parties that sought the overthrow of the national government and only incidentally sought overthrow of the states. With both governments confronting the same speakers under comparable statutes and without differing pre-existing bodies of case law, there was no reason to assume that an abrupt confrontation over free speech would occur between state governments and federal courts. And indeed, none did.

What did occur, however, is that the A.C.L.U. and the I.L.D. became actively involved in both state and federal cases. It was natural of course for lawyers who had lost at trial and on appeal in the state courts to seek some mode of getting to the U.S. Supreme Court because it was the only place left to go. Perhaps even more important, once national free speech groups became active, their ideal target naturally became the U.S. Supreme Court. If that court would render a definitive pro-freedom of speech opinion binding on both federal and state governments, then the groups would be saved the time and expense of fighting out free speech issues in one state after another. Indeed much of the pressure for nationalizing rights in the United States comes from pressure groups which would prefer to fight one battle in the U.S. Supreme Court rather than battles in each of the fifty states plus an additional battle in the federal courts. One lawyer fighting for one client may just as soon win in a state court or persuade a state governor to issue a pardon. A national, organized group devoted to free speech in general, rather than to one particular client, would prefer to win in the U.S. Supreme Court. Indeed in the case that finally nationalized free speech rights, *Gitlow v. New York*,[56] the groups involved actually persuaded the client and the Governor of New York to hold off on a pardon until the case could be appealed from the New York Court of Appeals to the U.S. Supreme Court.[57]

So beginning in 1917 the argument was increasingly presented that the freedom of speech guaranteed by the first amendment against Federal Government encroachment was one of the "fundamental liberties" that the due process clause of the fourteenth amendment protected from state government encroachment. In *Twining v. New Jersey* (1908),[58] counsel had argued that the fourteenth amendment prohibited the states from depriving a person of liberty without due process of law and that the right against self-incrimination guaranteed by the fifth amendment was such a liberty. The right, therefore, was protected by the due process clause against state encroachment. The Supreme Court held that the right against self-incrimination was not such a liberty. But if the word liberty in the fourteenth amendment did not encompass self-incrimination, what did it encompass? The Court could not very well say that it had no meaning. The Court said liberty meant "a fundamental principle of liberty and justice which inheres in the very idea of free government and is the inalienable right of a citizen of such a government."[59]

56 268 U.S. 652 (1925).
57 R. CORTNER, *supra* note 53, at 55.
58 211 U.S. 78 (1908).
59 *Id.* at 106 (1908).

After 1917 counsel for pro-speech groups began to insist that freedom of speech was among the "fundamental principles of liberty which inhere in the very idea of free government."[60] It would have been extremely difficult for the Court to deny their claim. Although there was little American jurisprudence of free speech, American political ideology certainly treated freedom of speech as fundamental to democracy. Of course if freedom of speech came under fourteenth amendment protection, speakers convicted in state courts could seek review by the U.S. Supreme Court.

In the period just after World War I, seven of the nine Justices of the U.S. Supreme Court were extremely conservative. The Court completed its first case concerning prosecution of a leftist speaker under the Espionage Act at about the same time the state courts were engaged in the same questions. *Schenck v. United States* (1919)[61] is best remembered for the opinion by Justice Holmes announcing the "clear and present danger" rule,[62] a rule subsequently used to protect speakers. It is less well remembered that in that case Holmes spoke for a unanimous Court in upholding the conviction of an official in a political party that had published pamphlets urging draft resistance.

A few months later in *Abrams v. United States*,[63] Holmes and Brandeis did use the danger test to challenge the constitutionality of an Espionage Act conviction, but they did so in dissent while their seven conservative colleagues upheld the conviction.

Thus the stage was set for *Gitlow v. New York* (1925)[64] which had momentous consequences for nationalizing the first amendment. While the Court had upheld state limitations on speech in three earlier cases (*Patterson, Fox, Gilbert*[65]) and as late as 1922 had declared that the fourteenth amendment contained no free speech guarantees (*Prudential Insurance*[66]) counsel for leftist speakers convicted in state courts continuously pressed for Supreme Court review. They argued that freedom of speech was among the fundamental liber-

60 R. Cortner, *supra* note 53, at 57.

61 249 U.S. 47 (1919).

62 In explaining the justification for the limitation imposed on free speech in this case, Holmes wrote:

> We admit that in many places and in ordinary times the defendants in saying all that was said in the circular would have been within their constitutional rights. But the character of every act depends upon the circumstances in which it is done. The most stringent protection of free speech would not protect a man in falsely shouting fire in a theater and causing a panic. ... [The] question in every case is whether the words used are used in such circumstances and are of such a nature as to create a clear and present danger that will bring about the substantive evils that Congress has a right to prevent.

Id.

63 250 U.S. 616 (1919).

64 268 U.S. 652 (1925).

65 Patterson v. Colorado, 205 U.S. 454 (1907); Fox v. Washington, 236 U.S. 273 (1915); Gilbert v. Minnesota, 254 U.S. 325 (1920).

66 Prudential Ins. Co. v. Cheek, 259 U.S. 530 (1922).

ties protected by the due process clause. It is clear from the correspondence of the pro-speech groups that they were so anxious to get a Supreme Court pronouncement that they virtually avoided thinking about the kind of pronouncement they were likely to get given the Court's performance in *Schenck* and *Abrams*.[67] With the benefit of hindsight we can see that they were correct, that it was more important to get the Supreme Court to impose the first amendment on the states than to get a favorable decision for speakers out of the Justices when they first made the imposition. In *Gitlow v. New York* and its companion case, both of the counsel for the speakers argued that freedom of speech was a fundamental liberty protected by the due process clause, one of the government counsel conceded the point and the other offered only pro forma opposition to it.[68] In its opinion the Court said

> For present purposes we may and do assume that freedom of speech and the press – which are protected by the First Amendment from abridgement by Congress – are among the fundamental personal rights and "liberties" protected by the due process clause of the Fourteenth Amendment from impairment by the states.[69]

Although the language was equivocal, *Gitlow* did in effect impose the first amendment or something very like it on the states. The first step toward enforcing the Bill of Rights on the states had been taken. It had been taken, however, without the issues having been fully argued by opposing counsel, and without any argument, explanation or rationale by the Justices. Indeed the Court has never offered a full explanation for its incorporation of the first amendment into the fourteenth. In subsequent cases typically it has cited without elaboration the "assumption" language of *Gitlow*.

It must be added that while the majority in *Gitlow* assumes the incorporation, it announces a freedom of speech doctrine wholly unfavorable to speakers and upholds the constitutionality of a state criminal syndicalism statute that punishes the mere abstract advocacy of communist revolution. Holmes and Brandeis invoked the clear and present danger test in dissent. The majority, however, offered two doctrines in opposition to the danger test. First it argued that where a legislature had passed a statute proscribing certain speech because it constituted a danger to government, the courts ought to defer to the legislature's judgment. Second, the majority argued for what became known as the "bad tendency" test. Under the bad tendency test if speech had the tendency to promote revolution, not clearly and presently, but at any future time, the government might suppress it. The Court argued that to insist that the government wait until a present danger of violent outbreaks existed would be to insist that government wait until it was too late to defend itself against the revolutionaries.

So while *Gitlow* imposed national freedom of speech guarantees on the states, it defined freedom of speech very weakly in relation to both state and national government repression of leftist speakers. The first amendment was

67 *See* R. Cortner, *supra* note 53, at 55, 63.
68 R. Cortner, *supra* note 53, at 56–58.
69 268 U.S. 652, 665 (1925).

nationalized, but in the *Schenck-Abrams-Gitlow* version there was not much to it.

Two years after *Gitlow* the Court did finally intervene to free a speaker convicted in state courts, but it did so in language that did not invoke the *Gitlow* assumption or indeed mention the first amendment or freedom of speech at all.[70] In *Whitney v. California* (1927)[71] we encounter a repeat of *Gitlow.* The Court again assumes that freedom of speech is protected by the fourteenth amendment, but upholds a state conviction by invoking the bad tendency test, while Holmes and Brandeis invoke the danger rule.

It was not until a flurry of cases in the early 1930's that it became absolutely clear that the Court had nationalized the first amendment.[72] Those cases simply declare, citing *Gitlow* and without explanation, that the due process clause encompasses free speech guarantees. They also free the speakers. For the first time we get the imposition by the Supreme Court of the first amendment's free speech guarantees on the states in order to protect speakers from state punishment. It should be noted that the same kinds of free speech special interest groups that had earlier pressed for incorporation sponsored these cases as well.[73] So they finally won the victory that had partially eluded them in *Gitlow.*

The most important of these cases in anchoring the incorporation doctrine was *Near v. Minnesota.*[74] This case involved a scandal sheet of the sort that had been involved in some of the pre-War state cases. The Supreme Court struck down the state statute banning such scandal sheets as a prior restraint on the freedom of speech and press.[75] Thus *Gitlow* announces the imposition of federal free speech guarantees on the states in a context of approving both state and federal anti-Red prosecutions under comparable state and federal statutes. And *Near* confirms that position in a context of announcing a federal doctrine opposed to prior restraints on publications parallel to the existing no-prior-restraint doctrines of the states. Indeed it will be recalled that the rule against prior restraints on publications is about the only free speech doctrine that emerges with any firmness from the traditional body of pre-War state jurisprudence.

2. The Causes and Technique of Incorporation

In reviewing the American experience of nationalizing freedom of speech guarantees a number of tentative conclusions arise. First, those who sought nationalization did not face a situation of widely varying and well entrenched

70 Fiske v. Kansas, 274 U.S. 380 (1927).

71 274 U.S. 357 (1927).

72 Stromberg v. California, 283 U.S. 359 (1931); Near v. Minnesota, 283 U.S. 697 (1931); DeJonge v. Oregon, 299 U.S. 353 (1937).

73 The American Newspaper Publishers' Association and the I.L.D.

74 283 U.S. 697 (1931).

75 Indeed in one of the very few pre-War U.S. Supreme Court decisions, Patterson v. Colorado, 205 U.S. 454 (1907) the Court had supported the widely-held state view that prior restraints on speech were certainly contrary to both state and federal constitutional speech provisions.

state bodies of free speech law. Nor did they face a situation in which established federal free speech jurisprudence varied widely from that of the states. Even though they were working over a hundred years after initial and varying free speech provisions had appeared in federal and state constitutions, they wrote upon a clean slate. Neither the Federal Government nor the states had much free speech law at the time of World War I. Second, the nationalization or incorporation occurred at a time when federal and state governments were seeking to suppress the same kinds of speakers using very similar statutes. It came in the context of approving both federal and state suppressions. Third, when the incorporation came, it came almost absentmindedly and was accomplished without debate on or off the Court and with no substantial reaction from state or federal authorities. And fourth, its consolidation came in the context of announcing a federal freedom of speech doctrine that echoed the existing state doctrine against prior restraint. In short, nationalization occurred without a substantive confrontation between state and federal constitutional doctrines. American courts did not do anything much about free speech from 1789 until 1917. When they did, they nationalized free speech guarantees in little over a dozen years without much opposition and indeed without much thought.

A number of factors can be identified as contributing to this historical pattern. Although the immediate post-Civil War Supreme Court had been anxious to nullify the impact of the fourteenth amendment upon federalism, by about 1890 the Court was seeking to use the due process clause of the fourteenth amendment to protect private property against state regulation. It will be recalled that the due process clause applies to "life, liberty or property." As the U.S. Supreme Court built up its own power to intervene under the due process clause in state "property" regulation, it could not totally avoid the claim that if it were required by the amendment to intervene in property matters, it must be required to intervene in liberty matters as well. Thus we get the opinion in *Twining* with its talk of "fundamental liberties." The fundamental liberties language of *Twining* slumbered as far as free speech was concerned because free speech itself was slumbering as a constitutional issue. When World War I and the Russian Revolution awoke the free speech issue, it became impossible to argue that freedom of speech was not a fundamental liberty enjoyed by citizens living under a free government.[76]

Often what at first glance seems to be an enormous judicial initiative by the Supreme Court turns out to be simply a judicial enunciation of an idea "whose time has come," that is an idea that has come to enjoy such high levels of latent popular support that once announced it gains immediate public acceptance. We do not know why or how it happened, but by 1925 it had become so obviously true that freedom of speech was a fundamental liberty of a free people that no one proposed to dispute it. The combination of this widely accepted idea with the Supreme Court's long established position that it was entitled, indeed

[76] Justice Brandeis made this point in dissent in Gilbert v. Minnesota, 254 U.S. 325, 343 (1920).

required, to impose fourteenth amendment due process requirements on the states, made incorporation of free speech undebatable. In other words, the sudden assertion by the Supreme Court of a power to impose national standards of speech rights on the states appeared at the time as a minor, logical, derivation from the Court's slowly built-up power to impose national standards of property rights on the states.

So far we have identified two basic elements in incorporation. The first is an idea whose time has come – the idea that speech was a fundamental right. The second was a well-established political or institutional power, the power of the Supreme Court to impose due process requirements on the states – a role developed for property rights but transferable to free speech rights. A third factor, and one very frequently at play in American constitutional law, is the activity of privately organized and financed groups. It was not the "accident" of individual litigation or any inevitable throwing up of major undecided issues of law by the appellate process that brought the Supreme Court to the decision of the free speech incorporation question. Perhaps the first two factors we have identified would have made the Court's answer to the incorporation question inevitable, but it was the conscious and persistent efforts of a number of free speech interest groups over a period of a dozen years that brought the question to the Court to be answered.

We must conclude then that the creation of trans-state constitutional standards in the area of freedom of speech occurred because of a combination of popular acceptance of freedom of speech as a fundamental value, a previously established judicial review role for the Supreme Court in the enforcement of the due process clause on the states, and the conscious activity of interest groups prepared to fashion litigation that would bring the first two factors together.

3. Challenges to Incorporation

Since *Gitlow* and *Near* established the incorporation of the first amendment into the fourteenth, that incorporation has only been challenged twice. When Justices more favorable to the New Deal of Franklin Roosevelt took control of the Supreme Court in 1937, they established a new standard of judicial review. In effect they held that where Congress or the state legislatures passed legislation regulating business and property interests, the Court would presume the constitutionality of such measures, deferring to whatever balance the legislators had struck between the public welfare and property rights. Remember that the Court had initially moved to enforce freedom of speech rights against the states because speech was a "liberty" protected by the due process clause just as business interests were "property" protected by that same clause. Would it now follow that if the post-1937 Supreme Court would no longer enforce due process property rights against the states, it should not enforce due process liberty rights either? The Court responded to this question with the "preferred position doctrine."[77] That doctrine held that free speech and certain other per-

[77] United States v. Carolene Prods. Co., 304 U.S. 144, n.4 (1938).

sonal liberty interests were preferred over property rights by the Constitution. Therefore, the Supreme Court would not defer to the legislatures in these areas. Instead, it would engage in active judicial review to protect these rights against government infringements. The preferred position doctrine had less to do with logic and more to do with partisan Democratic and Republican politics than most constitutional commentators care to admit.[78] Nevertheless, in various guises, such as the "compelling state interest,"[79] the "fundamental rights,"[80] the "strict scrutiny,"[81] the "peculiar judicial competence"[82] and the "representation reinforcing"[83] doctrines, the preferred position doctrine has survived to the current day. The Court continues to insist that it will enforce national freedom of speech standards on the states.

The second challenge arose in the libel and obscenity areas. It will be recalled that technically one might argue that the first amendment command, "Congress shall make no law," had not been incorporated literally into the due process clause. Instead, the argument runs, the due process clause protects "fundamental rights," and a freedom of speech fundamental right – comparable to, but not exactly the same as that of the first amendment – is protected by the fourteenth. The freedom under the fourteenth amendment may not be as great as that under the first because the first contains an absolute prohibition on government activity while the fourteenth speaks only of no deprivation without due process of law. Moreover, at the time the first amendment was adopted, the states already had obscenity law, and it seems clear that the framers of the first amendment had no intention of displacing such laws. So a number of Justices have argued from time to time that the Court ought not to impose as strict freedom of speech requirements on state libel or obscenity measures as it does on federal ones.[84] As we shall see later, Supreme Court obscenity decisions have come to pay considerable respect to local sentiments, but they have chosen a different route for doing so. While the Court has never explicitly stated that the first amendment as such is directly binding on the states, and technically still always speaks in terms of the liberty and due process of the fourteenth, in effect it applies the same freedom of speech standards to state as to federal action in all areas of speech including obscenity.

78 *See* Shapiro, *The Constitution and Economic Rights,* in ESSAYS ON THE CONSTITUTION OF THE UNITED STATES (M. Judd Harmon ed., Port Washington, Kennikat Press, 1978).

79 Gibson v. Florida Legislative Investigation Comm'n, 372 U.S. 539 (1963).

80 *See* Gunther, *Foreword: In Search of Evolving Doctrine on a Changing Court: A Model for a Newer Equal Protection,* 86 HARV. L. REV. 1 (1972).

81 *Id.*

82 *See* J. CHOPER, JUDICIAL REVIEW AND THE NATIONAL POLITICAL PROCESS (Chicago, U. Chi. P., 1980).

83 *See* J. ELY, DEMOCRACY AND DISTRUST: A THEORY OF JUDICIAL REVIEW (Cambridge, Harv. U. P., 1980).

84 *See, e.g.,* Jackson, J., dissenting in Beauharnais v. Illinois, 343 U.S. 250, 287 (1952) and Harlan, J., concurring in Alberts v. California, 354 U.S. 476, 496 (1957).

C. First Amendment Doctrines and State Discretion

While it is clear that since the early 1930's the Supreme Court has nationalized freedom of speech standards, applying the same doctrines derived from the first amendment to both state and federal governments, it remains to examine the doctrines themselves to see what range of discretion they allow to state and local authorities. In this discussion no attempt will be made to present a systematic survey of first amendment doctrine. Rather we will concentrate on those aspects of the doctrine that have particularly strong implications for either the imposition of strict uniform national standards on the states or the recognition of particularly high levels of state and local discretion.

1. Prior Restraint and Reasonable Time, Place and Manner

As a result of incorporation in the 1930's the Supreme Court began to receive a wide range of state appeals, some involving printed left-wing revolutionary materials, but most involving a wide range of speech problems that had begun to appear in state jurisprudence before World War I – abusive language, speech on the streets and in parks, demonstrations and parades, contempt of court, labor picketing, and licensing requirements for speakers. The anti-prior restraint standard announced in *Near* was a rather strict and uniform national standard, but the same anti-prior restraint rule had dominated most state jurisprudence. So this doctrine did not appear to impose the national will on recalcitrant states. The new Supreme Court jurisprudence also echoed earlier state developments in another area. In dealing with parade and licensing cases, the Court soon evolved a "reasonable time, place and manner" doctrine.[85] Local governments might reasonably regulate speakers' use of streets and parks so long as the regulations did not serve as a disguise for discrimination among speakers based on the content of their speech. (In the United States, local governments are the legal creatures of the states.) "Reasonable time, place and manner" not only echoed earlier state law, but also granted considerable authority to local governments to tailor their regulations to local needs. On the other hand, it did make a national court, sitting far away in the national capital, the ultimate judge of the reasonableness of local regulations.

2. Public Forum

In a related area the Court gradually adopted a doctrine quite contrary to earlier state jurisprudence and one that narrowly limited local government powers. In the late 1930's, the Court began to hold that state governments did not "own" their streets and parks in the same sense that private persons owned private property. Instead streets and parks were "public forums" that must be open to speakers.[86] State and local governments might not ban all speech. Nor

[85] *See* Note, ***The Public Forum: Minimum Access, Equal Access, and the First Amendment,*** 28 STAN. L. REV. 117 (1975).
[86] *See* Kalven, *supra* note 42.

might they balance speech rights against public order, traffic flow or peace and quiet as they typically had been allowed to do under state jurisprudence. Subject only to reasonable time and manner regulation, the states must allow speech in public places even at the risk of traffic disruption and noise. Indeed, they must protect the speaker from the threat of public disorder rather than suppressing the speech. The public forum doctrine became extremely important during the period of civil rights demonstrations in the 1950's and 1960's.[87] It is now being exploited by the American Nazi Party and the Ku Klux Klan. It constitutes the single greatest point of friction between the central courts and local governments. It is a relatively rigid and uniform national standard that severely restricts the authority of local governments to deal with what may appear to them to be major crises.[88] It imposes on those governments a duty not only to tolerate, but to protect speakers. It often necessitates the use of local police to protect speakers. It also often necessitates the use of local police against local citizens and in defense of "outside agitators." Yet the doctrine is the principal bulwark of oral free speech in the U.S.

3. Least Means, Narrowly Drawn, Overbreadth, Facially Invalid, Vagueness and Chilling Effect

Another group of doctrines is less dramatically intrusive on state affairs but ultimately is of equally great significance. The Court often uses the language of "least means," "narrowly drawn," "overbreadth," "facially invalid," "vagueness" and "chilling effect" when referring to statutes restrictive of free speech. The nuances and interrelations of these doctrines are too complex to describe here.[89] Either singly or in combination, however, and pushed to their ultimate logic, they constitute a bold assertion of Supreme Court authority over the state legislative process. Where a state or local government seeks to infringe upon a speech interest in order to serve some other legitimate interest or purpose of government, the Supreme Court will imagine for itself what statute would serve that other interest with the least possible damage to the speech interest. As used by the Court, the concepts are thus similar to the general notion of "proportionality" in Continental law – that the restrictiveness of a legal norm must be in proportion to its legitimate regulatory purpose – a notion which, not surprisingly, is invoked by the European Court of Human Rights in the context of discussing the scope of legitimate state restrictions on speech in the *Sunday Times Case*.[90]

With these American analogues to the European proportionality concept, the U.S. Supreme Court defines what would be an acceptable state statute restricting speech. Such a statute would be narrowly drawn to do as little

87 H. Kalven, The Negro and the First Amendment (Columbus, Ohio St. U. P., 1965).

88 *See* Barnum, *Freedom of Assembly and the Hostile Audience in Anglo-American Law,* 29 Am. J. Comp. L. 59 (1981).

89 *See* L. Tribe, American Constitutional Law 682–88, 710–23, 734–36 (Mineola, N.Y., Foundation Press, 1978).

90 *See infra* § IV.D.2.

damage to speech as possible. It would choose the means to its end least damaging to speech. Its restrictions on speech would be cast in statutory language as precise as possible. Vaguely worded restrictions might "sweep too broadly," restricting some speech that did not need to be restricted in order to achieve the state's goal. Moreover, vague or overbroad restrictions might have a chilling effect on innocent speakers, that is to say they might frighten some speakers into silence because of the risk of prosecution they pose even though the state in fact does not prosecute such speakers. For instance a statute proscribing the use of "insulting and offensive language" about the police might deter speakers wishing to voice vigorous complaints about the police even though in fact only those who called the police "pigs" were actually prosecuted. If the justices can imagine a statute that could achieve the state's legitimate goal with less damage to speech than the actual statute under constitutional challenge, they may declare the actual statute unconstitutional. The Warren Court tended to use these doctrines rather aggressively to substitute its own legislative judgment for that of the states. Several of the Nixon appointees have protested about the excessive use of the doctrines, and the Burger Court has declared that it will use them more cautiously.[91]

4. Clear and Present Danger

So far the doctrines we have talked about have been rather specialized ones. The general free speech doctrines employed by the Supreme Court have been first the clear and present danger test and then the balancing test.[92] The danger test is as old as the Court's interest in free speech, dating from the *Schenck* case of 1919. Its history is full of uncertainty and controversy that need not concern us here. It was the Court's general test only in the 1940's and early 1950's. It announced the general rule that speech should be unrestricted coupled with an exception. Speech might be regulated if it constituted a clear and present danger of a substantive evil that the government had a right to prevent. The danger rule did offer a certain margin of discretion to local governments. They could intervene against speakers whose words constituted such activities as incitement to riot or intimidation of courts. Even more leeway was given by the Court's recognition of labor union picketing as "speech plus" and so subject to more regulation than "pure speech," but most of this regulatory authority passed to the National Labor Relations Board rather than to state governments.[93] Of course the Supreme Court exercised the ultimate judgment as to whether a particular speech had in fact created a clear and present danger. And it was not at all embarrassed to substitute its own factual judgment for that of the state courts which had initially heard the matter.

[91] Broadrick v. Oklahoma, 413 U.S. 601 (1973).

[92] *See* M. Shapiro, Freedom of Speech: The Supreme Court and Judicial Review 46–107 (Englewood Cliffs, N.J., Prentice-Hall, 1966).

[93] *See* M. Shapiro, Law and Politics in the Supreme Court 77–83 (New York, Free Press, 1964).

The danger test survives today in altered and strengthened form in *Brandenburg v. Ohio.* "[T]he constitutional guarantees of free speech ... do not permit a state to ... proscribe advocacy of the use of force or of law violation except where such advocacy is directed to inciting or producing imminent lawless action and is likely to incite or produce such action."[94] In this form it still grants the states some discretion to make exceptions to the general rule forbidding infringement on speech and still leaves the Court as the final judge of whether the facts of a particular instance justify the particular exception made.

5. Balancing

Since the mid-1950's the general freedom of speech test has been the "balancing of interests" test. Government infringements on speech are justified if the interests protected by the statute in question outweigh the speech interests infringed. The balancing test is particularly important in the development of comparisons between U.S. and European speech law. The words of the first amendment are a flat negative – "Congress shall make *no* law" (emphasis added). The first amendment, unlike article 10 of the European Convention on Human Rights, contains no second clause providing for exceptions.[95] Yet if one looks at the case law rather than the text of the amendment alone, American constitutional law is structured in a way parallel to the structure of the Convention. As we shall note shortly, the Court has written in obscenity and libel exceptions. Its clear-and-present-danger, ***Brandenburg*** and "fighting words"[96] doctrines have created an "incitement to violence" exception. And the Court's balancing test is an open-ended authorization to itself to write in whatever other exceptions seem advisable to it from time to time. Using that test it has written exceptions based on national security,[97] integrity of the electoral process,[98] integrity of the judicial process,[99] privacy[100] and other reasons.[101]

[94] Brandenburg v. Ohio, 395 U.S. 444, 447 (1969).

[95] *See supra* § I.C.1.

[96] *See* Chaplinsky v. New Hampshire, 315 U.S. 568 (1942) and Cohen v. California, 403 U.S. 15 (1971).

[97] *See* the various opinions in New York Times Corp. v. United States, 403 U.S. 713 (1971); Dennis v. United States, 341 U.S. 494 (1951); Barenblatt v. United States, 360 U.S. 109 (1959).

[98] Buckley v. Valeo, 424 U.S. 1 (1976).

[99] *See* Nebraska Press Ass'n v. Stuart, 427 U.S. 539 (1976); Richmond Newspapers, Inc. v. Virginia, 448 U.S. 555 (1980); Wood v. Georgia, 370 U.S. 375 (1962). The exception for integrity of the judicial process must be derived largely by negative inference. In most of the relevant cases the Court has upheld the speech right against claims that it was outweighed by fair trial rights, but in each instance the Court has said that it could imagine instances in which the exercise of speech rights would so interfere with the judicial process that the speech might justifiably be curtailed. *See especially* Cox v. Louisiana, 379 U.S. 536 (1965).

[100] Cox Broadcasting Corp. v. Cohn, 420 U.S. 469 (1975); Time Inc. v. Hill, 385 U.S. 374 (1967). Again the exception must be constructed by negative implications. In these

Stated baldly, the balancing test not only is a declaration of absolute judicial discretion but constitutes a considerable downgrading of freedom of speech from its "preferred position." Speech interests are simply to be weighed against other interests. The Court's jurisprudence, however, tends to load the balance in favor of speech. The clearest example is prior restraint. Since its very first prior restraint opinion in *Near*, the Court has repeatedly declared that the constitutional prohibition on prior restraints is not absolute, that there might be instances in which the public interest in a prior restraint overbalances the prohibition. Yet the Court holds in *New York Times v. United States* (1971)[102] that: "Any system of prior restraints of expression comes to this Court bearing a heavy presumption against its constitutional validity."

Gibson v. Florida Investigating Committee (1963)[103] is the case in which the Court first explicitly invoked the balancing standard in reviewing actions by a state government infringing upon free speech. There the Court spoke of the state's need to demonstrate a "compelling" interest to justify infringement on speech. It has continued to use the compelling state interest formula.

In the rather special area of Communist subversion the Court has used the balancing formula as the general justification for upholding various federal statutes. Some of these statutes have required registration of parties that advocate overthrow of the government by force and violence. Others make such advocacy or membership in such an organization a crime. Having upheld the statutes, however, the Court has gone on to distinguish between mere abstract advocacy, which constitutionally may not be punished, and incitement which may be. It also distinguishes between mere membership, which may not be punished, and active membership with the knowledge that the organization seeks to bring about revolution and with the specific intent to aid the organization in bringing about that revolution. Such membership may be punished.[104] In addition in *Pennsylvania v. Nelson* (1956)[105] the Court held that the national government had pre-empted the field of protection of national security so that states might not enact their own national security statutes. However, the states may adopt measures designed to protect state services from abuse or disruption by forbidding or regulating state employment of subversives.

Clearly America's second Red Scare, the McCarthy period of the 1950's, pushed the Court into retreat on freedom of speech questions. The balancing doctrine was the vehicle for the retreat. Nevertheless, using devices such as compelling state interest, the distinction between incitement and advocacy, and

cases the Court found the speech claim outweighed the particular privacy claim, but hinted that the balance might sometimes swing the other way.

101 *E.g.*, the neutrality of the civil service; *see* U.S. Civil Service Comm'n v. National Ass'n of Letter Carriers, 413 U.S. 548 (1973).

102 403 U.S. 713 (1971).

103 372 U.S. 539 (1963).

104 *See* Yates v. United States, 354 U.S. 298 (1957); Scales v. United States, 367 U.S. 203 (1961).

105 350 U.S. 497 (1956).

the requirement of proof of specific intent to bring about the overthrow of the government, the Court of the 1960's and 1970's managed to strike down or render innocuous most of the kinds of state anti-Communist laws it had earlier upheld.[106] It has also made it more difficult to mount successful prosecutions under the federal laws, some of which have been repealed subsequently by Congress.

With all these caveats, it must be concluded that the balancing doctrine at best is ambiguous as to the scope of state speech regulation. On the one hand it allows state legislation when the state can show a compelling state interest, although even when it can show a compelling interest the state must still write a statute that meets the least-means/vagueness/chilling-effect standard. On the other hand, it makes the national Supreme Court the final "balancer" to decide what interests are sufficiently compelling to outweigh the interest in free speech. In dealing with the Federal Government, the Court has recently shown that it is quite willing to balance its way through a very complex legislative scheme, striking down some provisions and upholding others.[107] While a few of today's Justices speak of the special deference owed to the states, it seems probable that the Court will be just as active in reviewing the balances struck by state legislatures between speech and other interests.

6. Ad Hoc versus Principled Balancing

One aspect of balancing doctrine of especial interest, particularly in light of the *Sunday Times Case*, is the long American debate about "ad hoc" or "case-by-case" versus "principled" balancing. In the 1940's and 1950's many commentators decried "rigid" constitutional rules like the clear and present danger test. They argued that because no constitutional right is absolute, every constitutional case ultimately resolves itself into a balancing of interests. As practiced by the Supreme Court this balancing was typically, but not always, done on a case-by-case basis. That is, the particular damage done to the speech interests of a particular set of speakers by a particular statute or other government action was balanced against the particular benefits achieved by that statute or other action. Some of the opponents of ad hoc balancing argued that balancing might be inevitable, but that such balancing should yield general rules or principles stating general standards of protection for speech.[108] The *Sunday Times Case*[109] is a good example of the difference in the two approaches. The House of Lords said that it had taken a fresh look at the conflict between free speech and fair trial interests, had struck a balance between them, and had concluded that on balance the best resolution of the conflict was a general, all-inclusive rule against pre-trial publicity. The European Court of

106 *See* Keyishian v. Board of Regents, 385 U.S. 589 (1967).

107 *See* Buckley v. Valeo, 424 U.S. 1 (1976).

108 *Cf.* Frantz, *The First Amendment in the Balance,* 71 YALE L. J. 1424 (1962) *with* Mendelson, *On the Meaning of the First Amendment: Absolutes in the Balance,* 50 CALIF. L. REV. 821 (1962).

109 Judgment of 26 Apr. 1979, Series A: Vol. 30 (Pubs. of Eur. Ct. H.R., 1979).

Human Rights then ruled that the House of Lords had been in error in formulating such a general rule. The European Court itself engaged in ad hoc balancing leading to the conclusion that in this particular case the kind of publication done by the *Sunday Times* was not sufficiently damaging to the fair trial rights of the particular litigants to justify the particular infringement on freedom of the press.

Ad hoc balancing is a flexible formula that allows courts to yield as much or as little as they like to the balances struck by legislators, administrators or other courts. Thus it would allow a trans-state or trans-national court to defer to the decisions of state or national units. In the United States the Supreme Court's ad hoc balancing has left everyone in a considerable state of uncertainty as to the constitutional protection of freedom of speech. The doctrine allows a feasible constitutional defense of nearly any proposal for limiting speech. After all, no matter how badly speech is infringed, some countervailing interest served by the proposal may be deemed sufficiently weighty to justify the infringement. It is extremely difficult to assess the impact on American federalism of ad hoc balancing. On the one hand, it invites state and local governments to invade speech to the extent that they feel they have compelling state interests in doing so. On the other, it warns them that to do so successfully they must anticipate what particular balance the national Supreme Court will strike. Thus at any given moment the degree of national control depends on the extent to which the Supreme Court gives different weights to various interests than do the states. We cannot, however, derive objective evidence about such differences of weighting from the incidence of Supreme Court reversals of state balances. For in many instances the states may have foregone the particular balance they wanted because they anticipated that the Court's balance would be different. Thus many real state-federal conflicts may be obscured by this operation of the "rule of anticipated reaction" familiar to all students of politics.

7. Content Based Regulation

Perhaps the most rigid national first amendment rule constraining the states is one that seldom serves as the decisive ground of decision, but is nonetheless the very core of American freedom of speech law. No doubt it is so rarely the basis of decision precisely because it is so widely accepted that it is not a feasible option for legislators to violate it. The rule is that regulations of speech may not be based on the content of the speech. No government may ban the exposition of certain ideas or restrict those who espouse certain ideas in favor of those who espouse others. One criticism of both the clear and present danger standard and the balancing formula is that they have allowed covert content based regulation. Certainly American history shows a pattern of repression of socialist and communist speech motivated by hostility to its revolutionary content. Nevertheless, the constitutional bar to content-based regulation is sufficiently strong that states will rarely pass legislation that overtly seeks to ban certain ideas from the intellectual market place. The aversion to content-based regulation is so general, however, that it is inherent in the state as well as the federal constitutions. So, here again, it is difficult to say how much more the states are constrained by the federal rule than they are by their own constitutions.

8. Obscenity

The anti-content regulation core of the first amendment has had important consequences for two areas of law of special concern to the states, obscenity and libel. Obscenity and libel regulation are, of course, content-based regulation. Thus they would seem to be forbidden by the first amendment. Yet the states have always had obscenity and libel laws. Until *Gitlow* and *Near* no problem arose because the states were not bound by the first amendment. Subsequently the Court introduced the doctrine that certain kinds of speech, including obscenity, libel and "fighting words," were excluded from first amendment protection.[110] Indeed the Federal Government itself had enacted obscenity provisions for its mailing and customs statutes long before the announcement of the exclusion doctrine. Although, as we shall see in a moment, much of the substance of the exclusion doctrine has been whittled away, the Court clings to its form because it continues to provide a rationale for content-based regulation of these kinds of speech.

From the 1950's onward the Supreme Court has been engaged in extending greater freedom of speech protection to the "excluded" areas even while continuing to insist they are excluded. In the obscenity area the Court's approach has been to argue that true obscenity is not protected but that the rules for determining whether particular speech is obscene must be such that no non-obscene material is labelled obscene. For if the rules for sorting the obscene from the non-obscene are not carefully constructed, some speech that is protected by the first amendment might wrongfully be labelled obscene and then unconstitutionally punished. In *Roth v. United States* (1957),[111] the Court announced the sorting rule for obscenity: "whether to the average person, applying contemporary community standards, the dominant theme of the material taken as a whole appeals to prurient interest." This standard was announced as the test for both federal and state prosecutions although, as we noted earlier, Justice Harlan suggested that the states ought not to be held to so strict a standard. The subsequent development of the *Roth* standard has been extremely complex and confused and will not be traced here except to note that currently it is modified by the doctrine that obscene material is that which goes substantially beyond the limits of candor current in the community and is without substantial literary, artistic or scientific merit.[112]

From the beginning the Justices recognized that in a nation as diverse as the United States different local communities would have widely varying standards

110 *See* M. Shapiro & R. Tresolini, American Constitutional Law 343–346 (5th ed., New York, Macmillan Co., 1979).

111 354 U.S. 476 (1957).

112 Miller v. California, 413 U.S. 15 (1973).

of obscenity. If the standards were treated as local community standards, then there would be one first amendment rule but its application and results would differ widely from community to community in line with variations in local community mores. Ultimately of course every local decision would be reviewable by one national Supreme Court to assure that basic obedience to the first amendment would be maintained. This would appear to be an ideal federal solution imposing a basic national uniformity but allowing sufficient local flexibility to meet local variations.

Three objections were raised to the local community standards approach. The first of these arose out of the Court's announcement of a single test for both federal and state obscenity prosecutions. If the word local were inserted before the word community in the *Roth* test, local flexibility would be served. Such an insertion would, however, allow federal prosecutors enforcing the mailing statute to track a given sexually oriented publication until the mail truck passed through the most Puritanical local community in the United States, seize it there, and prosecute it there with the benefit of local opinion highly favorable to the prosecutor. Aside from the fundamental unfairness of such a tactic, the result would be that what the whole of the American public were allowed to receive in the mail would be determined by what the most straight-laced American community was willing to read.

Quite apart from this problem, publishers argued that the same result would follow from local standards applied by state and local prosecutors. The economics of publishing are such that a work that cannot enjoy an unfettered national market is not attractive to publishers. If publishers anticipated that a work submitted to them would be subject to obscenity prosecutions in a few dozen or a few hundred American towns, they would not publish it. Thus under a local community standards test, market forces would insure that the tastes of the strictest communities would be imposed on everyone.

Finally, a test that combined local community standards with ultimate review by the Supreme Court would either degenerate into total local control or absorb excessive amounts of the Supreme Court's time. For the only way to assure basic national uniformity under such a vague and varying test would be for the Court to take a great many appeals from state obscenity convictions, view the materials itself and generate a large body of decisions on particular materials that could then guide local prosecutors.

All of these problems could be cured by opting for a single national community standard rather than local ones. The objection to a national standard was not only that it would rob local communities of the power to guard their particular sensibilities, but that in reality there was no national community of taste or sexual sophistication. So to opt for a national standard would simply be to substitute the particular standards of the Justices for those of real communities. The Justices would inevitably read their own tastes into those of a purely fictional national community.

The battle over local versus national community standards continued for many years. At least for state prosecutions, the Court has now opted for local community standards and for considerable deference to juries as the best judges of local standards.[113] The Court now hears few obscenity cases, confining itself largely to those in which local authorities have used obscenity prosecutions as a guise for attacking publications to whose ideas they object and to instances in which convictions are obtained against materials that most Americans would find clearly non-obscene.[114] Local juries in most of the United States have proven surprisingly broad-minded and in most major American cities convictions are extremely difficult to obtain even against clearly pornographic materials. Prosecutions against the printed word are extremely rare; film prosecutions and those against picture magazines are more frequent. The granting of substantial local autonomy does not seem to have significantly constricted the national speech market or flooded the Supreme Court with obscenity cases. Perhaps this is not so much because of the particular legal solution adopted as because the Court's obscenity decisions came during a period of rapid and massive changes in sexual mores. Yet it is hard to tell the chicken from the egg in this area. The Court's own decisions were themselves important factors in opening up wider channels of sexual expression and the increase in sexual expression was itself one of the factors leading to wider public acceptance of that expression.

9. Libel

Somewhat parallel developments occurred in libel law. The Court had included libel in its list of excluded areas until it announced in *New York Times v. Sullivan* (1964)[115] that where a public official was the subject of the speech, some accommodation had to be reached between libel protection for the individual and the traditional first amendment right to criticize government. It has been disputed whether the English common law of seditious libel was carried over into the law of the former American colonies. It will be recalled that the constitutionality of the Sedition Act of 1798 had not been tested. In *New York Times* the Court announced that the first amendment precluded the crime of seditious libel. The rule of *New York Times* is that one may not be held legally responsible for the libel of a public official unless the otherwise libelous statement was uttered with the actual knowledge that it was untrue or with reckless disregard of whether it was or was not true. From a first amendment standpoint such a standard is extremely deficient. It is clear that one could not be punished constitutionally for making even knowingly false or reckless statements about government in general rather than about particular officials. Such punishment would be content-based and thus forbidden by the first amendment. It is the exclusion doctrine that allows the Court to propose a standard for libelous speech directed at individual government officials far less protective of freedom of speech than the normal first amendment standard. On the other hand, public officials enjoy far less protection from libelous speech under the *New York Times* rule than they would under most state libel laws.

113 *Id.*
114 *E.g.*, Jenkins v. Georgia, 418 U.S. 153 (1974).
115 376 U.S. 254 (1964).

Thus *New York Times* represents a major imposition of a uniform national rule in an area of law that had traditionally been within the discretion of the states. The basic concept behind the *Times* rule, however, if not its application to public officials, was one with which the states were already familiar. Many states invoked an "actual malice" test for certain purposes, such as for the awarding of punitive damages. The *New York Times* rule is a restatement of the malice test employed by several states. While the nationalizing of the law substantially invaded previous state law, its malice standard did not provide severe conceptual problems for state courts.

The state courts and the Supreme Court itself have faced severe conceptual problems in deciding who is and is not a public official. The Supreme Court soon moved from public official to "public figure" thus including many persons who do not hold positions in government. It has been struggling in recent years to define the limits of the "public figure" exception and its current jurisprudence is quite unclear about the distinction between public figure and private person.[116] Its uncertainty has had an unsettling effect on state jurisprudence as well.

In short, the *New York Times* rule compromises with older state libel law by being applicable only to public figures, by not extending full first amendment protection even to those who libel public figures and by adopting a libel standard that many states themselves had used for some purposes. Nevertheless, it constitutes a major announcement of a national freedom of speech standard that has sharply altered state law and unsettled state jurisprudence.

In 1974 the Court went even a step further in subjecting state libel laws to a uniform national rule more protective of speech than the state laws had been. In *Gertz v. Robert Welch, Inc.* (1974)[117] the Court held that even where libel of a private person were involved the states might not award punitive or presumed damages nor impose liability without fault. Thus the Court is being drawn deeper into state libel proceedings and appears to be leaving to state autonomy only the core of cases in which real damages are asked by a private person for a knowingly or negligently false statement.

A brief statement about "group libel" seems useful in light of the British Race Relations Act and Continental statutes that proscribe the defamation of racial, religious and national groups. At a time when it considered libel wholly excluded from first amendment protection, the Supreme Court upheld a state "group libel" statute forbidding defamatory statements about racial and other groups.[118] The authority of this decision is now seriously in doubt given the erosion of the libel exclusion and the extent to which statements about race have become an integral part of the public discourse that the Court in *New York Times* says the first amendment is designed to protect.

[116] *See* Time Inc. v. Firestone, 424 U.S. 448 (1976).
[117] 418 U.S. 323 (1974).
[118] Beauharnais v. Illinois, 343 U.S. 250 (1952).

10. State Initiatives

Having traced the major areas in which the Court has imposed uniform national rules on the states, it should also be noted that those rules must be read as floor or minimum standards. The Supreme Court has recently made it clear[119] that state courts, relying on their own state constitutional speech guarantees, may extend protection to speech beyond the protection demanded by the U.S. Constitution. In this instance, the U.S. Supreme Court had flirted with extending the public forum doctrine to the streets, sidewalks, and plazas of privately owned shopping complexes. The Court had eventually retreated from this extension. Relying on its own state constitution, the California Supreme Court then announced a comparable shopping-center public-forum doctrine. The U.S. Supreme Court upheld the California Court.

Obviously, the extent to which state supreme courts develop freedom of speech protections above and beyond those required by the U.S. Supreme Court is of great significance in determining the relevance of American experience to European developments. A number of state supreme court justices have been eloquent on the subject. They have particularly complained of the failure of counsel to present independent state grounds in arguing freedom of speech cases. Unfortunately, state constitutional law is a vast underdeveloped area of American legal scholarship. We simply do not know at the moment what the fifty states do about freedom of speech beyond adjusting themselves to federal constitutional rules.

D. Summary of American Developments

In summary, we might say that the ease and absence of controversy with which nationalization of the first amendment was accomplished resulted from a peculiar combination of circumstances. By the period of *Gitlow-Near*, the legitimacy of judicial review had been long established, as had the Supreme Court's practice of reviewing exercises of the state police power. On the other hand, by this period neither the state nor the national courts had developed a substantial free speech jurisprudence. So in the exercise of its well-grounded power of judicial review the Supreme Court did not have to overcome an entrenched body of law and policy to which the states were wedded, nor did it have to harmonize two bodies of differently structured law. The Court wrote upon a relatively clean slate and during a time when both state and federal authorities were primarily concerned with the same problem – the leftist revolutionary speaker who posed the same threat to both of them, and to whom both had responded with the same kinds of statutes.

The process of "incorporation" was greatly facilitated by the pre-existing agreement that the fourteenth amendment protected "fundamental rights" and by the growing recognition that in a climate of ideological diversity free speech for all factions was the best way to make democracy work. The immediate cause

[119] Prune Yard Shopping Center v. Robbins, 447 U.S. 74 (1980).

of incorporation, however, was the work of a number of highly specialized groups allegedly pursuing freedom of speech for its own sake but actually pursuing it in defense of the left.

The two processes of nationalizing freedom of speech rules and developing such rules then proceeded simultaneously in case-by-case pronouncements by the Supreme Court so that state governments typically were not confronted with the need to suddenly adjust their law to an already existing body of federal rules. Instead the states responded to case-by-case development and change in first amendment doctrine just as did private groups and individuals, that is, by piecemeal litigation in the Supreme Court. The Supreme Court developed many doctrines some more and some less favorable to state autonomy. Of these the public forum doctrine and the least-means/vagueness/chilling-effect complex have imposed the most confining national rules on the states. The reasonable time, place and manner, and clear and present danger tests have allowed the states considerable discretion to meet particular local circumstances but under ultimate national supervision by the Supreme Court. The ad hoc balancing test would seem to allow very broad discretion to the states in passing statutes that incidentally infringed upon speech in pursuit of legitimate state goals, but in the compelling state interest version used by the Supreme Court it has promised more freedom to the states than it has actually given.

In the two areas where the national Supreme Court did confront well established bodies of state statutory and case law – obscenity and libel – it did move toward nationalization much more slowly. It was over thirty years after *Gitlow* that it partially nationalized obscenity standards, forty-five years before it entered the libel field and almost fifty years before it touched the basic body of state law dealing with libel of a private person. In both these areas the Court left more state authority intact than it had in speech generally by employing the exclusion doctrine and such other doctrines as local community standards, the public figure versus private person distinction and the malice test. Finally, it has always been clear that the states might employ independent state constitutional grounds to provide a higher level of protection for freedom of speech than is provided by the national standards.

On the whole freedom of speech has not constituted a major area of conflict between federal and state courts or, more broadly, between federal and state governments. In part this is because the general level of commitment to freedom of speech is roughly the same throughout the country and is part of a national political culture. In part it is because the two great waves of anti-free speech sentiment, that of World War I and that of the 1950's, were nationwide reactions to what was perceived as a foreign threat which was of equal danger to the Federal Government and the governments of all the states.

The freedom of speech problems that arose out of the Southern civil rights movement might have been perceived as pitting national free speech standards against those of one regional group of states. And clearly the public forum doctrine did aid the demonstrators. On the whole, however, the speech claims were so submerged in the racial problem that they were rarely seen as an independent issue. The conflict was perceived as one between national and state race policies, and not speech policies. It should be noted, however, that one of the two major incursions of the Supreme Court into areas of pre-established state speech law arose out of this nation versus region conflict. *New York Times v. Sullivan* occurred because a Southern jury sought to punish a Northern newspaper for its national civil rights stance and its interference in Southern affairs.

With this one exception national and state sentiment on freedom of speech have moved along sufficiently parallel tracks that the nationalization of freedom of speech has been far less of a problem than the problem of precisely what freedom of speech standards should apply at both national and state levels.

III. Towards Transnational Standards of Criminal Justice: The American Experience in Criminal Procedure

(*by* Stephen Schulhofer)

A. Introduction

The relevance of criminal procedure to the study of legal integration cannot altogether be taken for granted. A diversity in laws affecting commerce, corporate finance and even air pollution poses obvious difficulties for federal nations and for the interdependent countries of the international community. The human rights field is more intensely political and at the same time less likely to pose immediate obstacles simply because of a lack of uniformity. Even in this sphere, of course, there are some individual rights that call for uniformity at least at some minimum level of protection. The right to freedom of movement is an obvious example. The preceding section shows how the American experience with freedom of speech has been greatly influenced by direct pressures for uniformity; local diversity in the standards for free speech is difficult to tolerate when it affects debate on issues of national concern, and the economics of publishing make uniform standards at least as important to the press as they are to other industries serving a national market.[120]

Criminal procedure presents an entirely different situation. Diversity in court processes and in the rights of the accused poses no obvious threat to the smooth flow of commerce or to other requirements of economic efficiency. Freedom of movement conceivably could be affected by perceptions about a given nation's procedures for dealing with persons should they become involved with the criminal courts, but it may be doubted whether any such effect has ever been substantial. Perhaps in no legal domain other than land law does uniformity as such have so low a priority as it does in criminal procedure.

The importance of integration in the field of criminal procedure must be sought at a different and more elusive level. Precisely because of their intensely political nature, fundamental human rights cannot be ignored in efforts to build a community linked by ties that transcend economic expediency. The working out of common values and uniform minimum standards of protection in this sphere can be an important (and perhaps a necessary) element in the effort to forge enduring links among nations of diverse cultures and traditions. And attempts to pursue uniformity in such a highly politicized realm can shed light on problems to be expected (and remedies to be deployed) in other sensitive domains. It is from these perspectives that the American experience in criminal procedure may prove suggestive for Europeans.

[120] *See supra* § II.C.8.

B. Substantive Standards for Protecting Rights of the Accused

1. Historical Background

As we have noted previously,[121] early in the nineteenth century, the U.S. Supreme Court held that the provisions of the Bill of Rights were binding only on the Federal Government and imposed no restrictions upon the states.[122] Thus, although most of those amendments were cast in general terms (*e.g.*, amend. VI: "[i]n all criminal prosecutions, the accused shall enjoy the right ... to have the assistance of counsel for his defense"), no provisions of federal law were thought to preclude a state from denying the right to counsel (to indigents or to everyone), from compelling self-incrimination or even from imposing "cruel and unusual punishments." State constitutions often imposed comparable restrictions, but the interpretation of those restrictions was a matter for the state courts. Once a state supreme court had found no violation of state law in connection with a state criminal prosecution, the defendant generally could have no federal constitutional claim to present to the U.S. Supreme Court.

The precise extent of diversity in rights of the accused prior to the Civil War is a subject of some disagreement among scholars of the period, but there can be little question that, overall, there were important divergences among the states. It suffices to consider only one very basic matter, the right to counsel. All of the states except Virginia had specific constitutional provisions protecting this right, and the Virginia courts had construed the state's "due process" clause as implying a right to counsel. Yet, as of 1800, only New Jersey and Connecticut afforded counsel to indigents in all serious criminal cases. In the other states the right to counsel meant only the right to have a retained counsel appear, and usually also the right of indigents to appointed counsel in capital cases.[123] Between 1800 and 1860, ten more states enacted some form of right to counsel for indigents, but the majority did not afford such protection.[124]

On other issues early American law, as actually applied, presents a complex and often obscure picture; but in light of the variety of customs and conditions in states admitted to the Union in the nineteenth century – including several closely linked to French or Spanish legal tradition – the potential diversity is easy to imagine. In any event, the lack of uniformity with respect to such relatively technical issues was wholly overshadowed by the Southern states' acceptance of slavery, which involved the explicit denial of a whole range of fundamental human rights, including even differential treatment of slaves in the criminal process.[125] The deep disagreement over slavery nearly split the Union, and constitutional amendments enacted in the wake of the Civil War made clear

[121] *See supra* § II.B.

[122] Barron v. Mayor of Baltimore, 32 U.S. (7 Pet.) 243 (1833).

[123] W. Beaney, The Right to Counsel in American Courts 21 (Ann Arbor, U. Mich. P., 1955).

[124] *Id.* at 80–83.

[125] *See* A.L. Higginbotham, In the Matter of Color (New York, O.U.P., 1978).

that fundamental human rights would occupy a very different place in the revised federal structure.

The opening words of the fourteenth amendment, enacted in 1868, state: "All persons born or naturalized in the United States, and subject to the jurisdiction thereof, are citizens of the United States. ..." The precise implications of this sentence remain controversial in some of its potential applications, but its wording, together with its position at the outset of the amendment, make clear the importance attached to establishing a national political allegiance and identification, along with concomitant rights to basic personal freedoms. The amendment goes on to provide that no state may "deprive any person of life, liberty, or property, without due process of law." As a result, state criminal procedure for the first time became subject to scrutiny under a federal standard. It remained, however, to determine the content of the "due process" limitation that the states were obliged to respect.

Three schools of interpretation emerged. The first read "due process" to require *fundamental fairness.* Sometimes this meant that a procedural rule found in the Bill of Rights was also held binding upon the states, because it was seen as "fundamental" or "of the very essence of a scheme of ordered liberty."[126] Typically, however, the fundamental fairness approach did not lead the Supreme Court to impose specific rules upon the states. Rather, the Court focussed on the question whether the proceedings in the particular case had been unfair under the "totality" of the circumstances. In *Betts v. Brady,* for example, the Court said: "Due process of law ... formulates a concept less rigid and more fluid than those envisaged in other specific and particular provisions of the Bill of Rights. Its application is less a matter of rule. Asserted denial is to be tested by an appraisal of the totality of facts in a given case."[127] This fundamental fairness approach dominated Supreme Court interpretation of the due process clause for nearly 100 years after the adoption of the fourteenth amendment.

The second school of interpretation, usually referred to as that of *total incorporation,* read "due process" to include all of the rights protected by the first eight amendments. This approach, which received its fullest development in Justice Black's dissenting opinion in *Adamson v. California,*[128] was based primarily on evidence from the legislative history of the fourteenth amendment, indicating that at least some of the amendment's sponsors intended the term "due process" to include or "incorporate" the Bill of Rights. The total incorporation theory undoubtedly also attracted support because it was perceived as less subjective than the fundamental fairness approach, because it provided clearer guidance about the content of the due process requirement, and because it promised broader and more effective protection for the accused. Nevertheless, the historical premises of the total incorporation approach were

[126] Palko v. Connecticut, 302 U.S. 319, 325 (1937). *See also* Twining v. New Jersey, 211 U.S. 78, 99 (1908).
[127] 316 U.S. 455, 462 (1942). *See also* Powell v. Alabama, 287 U.S. 45, 71 (1932).
[128] 332 U.S. 46 (1947).

sharply questioned,[129] and some of its practical consequences were most unwelcome. (Under the seventh amendment, for example, the states would have been required to provide a right to jury trial in all *civil* suits at common law, whenever the amount in controversy exceeded $20.) The total incorporation approach won the votes of four Justices in *Adamson*, but it never commanded a majority of the Supreme Court.

The third school of interpretation, known as *selective incorporation*, became ascendant in the early 1960's, primarily as part of an effort to avoid the excessive subjectivity and uncertainty of the fundamental fairness approach, while also avoiding the excessive rigidity of total incorporation. Under the selective incorporation approach, the Supreme Court examines a particular clause of the Bill of Rights (the right to counsel, the double jeopardy clause, etc.) in order to determine whether the rights protected by that clause are fundamental. If so, then that particular clause is "selectively incorporated" into the due process clause and becomes binding on the states. The selectivity and discretion afforded by this approach permit the Supreme Court to avoid applying certain Bill of Rights provisions to the states; the fifth amendment requirement of a grand jury indictment, for example, probably will never be held binding upon the states. Once a clause is incorporated, however, further selectivity is (at least in theory) precluded; the scope and content of the clause as it applies to the states is identical to its scope and content with respect to the Federal Government.[130]

2. Experience Under the "Fundamental Fairness" Standard

As just mentioned, the "fundamental fairness" interpretation of the due process clause prompted the Supreme Court to eschew efforts to identify concrete, generally applicable requirements. Rather, the Court attempted to ascertain whether a given conviction was unfair under the "totality of the circumstances." We have already examined the use of such an ad hoc balancing approach in free speech cases,[131] and its characteristics in criminal cases were similar. The Court did not necessarily defer to local authorities or allow them a "margin of appreciation"; indeed the "fundamental fairness" concept, which required the Supreme Court to reach its own, essentially subjective judgment under an open-ended standard, did not value the state court's position as such. However, if there was little or no "margin of appreciation" in theory, the states had considerable "room to maneuver" in practice. The "totality of the circumstances" analysis made it difficult to argue that any particular rule or procedure had been held unlawful. Even after an unfavorable Supreme Court judgment in a particular case, a state could always argue that the circumstances in the next case were sufficiently different to warrant a different result.

[129] *See, e.g.,* Fairman, *Does the Fourteenth Amendment Incorporate the Bill of Rights?,* 2 Stan. L. Rev. 5 (1949).

[130] *See, e.g.,* Malloy v. Hogan, 378 U.S. 1, 10–11 (1964); Benton v. Maryland, 395 U.S. 784, 795 (1969).

[131] *See supra* § II.

Moreover, because American double jeopardy concepts do not normally prohibit retrial after reversal of a conviction, a state had relatively little to lose by taking the most narrow possible view of unfavorable Supreme Court precedent.

The consequences of this ad hoc approach, both for uniformity and for absolute levels of protection, are instructive. For reasons not fully understood, there was only a scattering of Supreme Court decisions under the "fundamental fairness" standard for the first sixty years following adoption of the fourteenth amendment.[132] Beginning in the 1930's, however, the Supreme Court became more active in the review of state criminal convictions. In *Powell v. Alabama*,[133] the Court found a violation of due process in a state's failure to make timely appointment of counsel for an indigent, uneducated Black facing capital charges, but subsequently the Court made clear that the due process question would turn on the "totality of the circumstances" in each case.[134] As a result, even by 1960, nearly a century after adoption of the fourteenth amendment, there was still no uniformity of practice in the United States concerning appointment of counsel for the indigent. At that time five Southern states still refused automatic counsel for indigent felony defendants, many more states refused counsel for indigents facing serious misdemeanor charges, and in nearly all states whatever right to counsel existed found its source in state statutory law subject to varying interpretations and provisos.[135]

In those right to counsel cases reviewed by the Supreme Court, the circumstances that would require appointment of counsel were steadily expanded. Indeed in every such case reaching the Court after 1950, the denial of counsel was held fundamentally unfair, and by 1960 the Court had in effect reached the position that the pendency of any major criminal charge was in itself sufficiently serious to outweigh other circumstances and thus to require counsel. Nevertheless, reaching this position "in effect" proved to be quite different from reaching this position in a clear, unequivocal holding. When Justice Harlan, a strong supporter of the "totality" approach, finally agreed to abandon that approach in the counsel context, he wrote (with tactful understatement): "This evolution [in the circumstances requiring counsel] appears not to have been fully recognized by many state courts, in this instance charged with the front-line responsibility for the enforcement of constitutional rights."[136] Whether prompted by lack of perceptiveness or by downright hostility, the attitude of the state courts forced the Supreme Court to promulgate a clear, easily enforceable rule mandating counsel in all felony cases. The Court did this by

[132] *E.g.*, Moore v. Dempsey, 261 U.S. 86 (1923). Mention should also be made of decisions granting relief under the fourteenth amendment's equal protection clause, in cases involving racial discrimination in the selection of the jury. *E.g.*, Strauder v. West Virginia, 100 U.S. 303 (1880).

[133] 287 U.S. 45 (1932).

[134] Betts v. Brady, 316 U.S. 455 (1942).

[135] *See* W. BEANEY, *supra* note 123, at 81–83.

[136] Gideon v. Wainwright, 372 U.S. 335, 351 (1963) (concurring opinion).

abandoning the fundamental fairness test and holding that the sixth amendment right to counsel was selectively incorporated into the due process clause and therefore enforceable against the states.[137] It should be noted, however, that the significance of this step, and the motivation for it, lay not in the incorporation technique itself, but in the relative specificity of the right incorporated, because the sixth amendment language could, just like that of the due process clause, have been read to leave appointment of counsel for indigents to the circumstances of the case.

Supreme Court efforts to control illegal police searches taught similar lessons. The Court had intimated in 1886[138] and held in 1914[139] that evidence obtained in violation of fourth amendment search and seizure requirements was not admissible in *federal* criminal trials. Nevertheless, the fourteenth amendment was viewed as barring such evidence in *state* trials only if the police conduct was so egregious as to "shock the conscience."[140] Even after the Court made explicit in 1949 that state police were bound in principle to comply with fourth amendment standards,[141] it continued to leave the question of the admissibility of illegally obtained evidence to the discretion of the state courts.

This approach resulted in considerable variation in state remedies for victims of illegal search and seizure. As of 1886, at the time of the Supreme Court's *Boyd* decision, no state court had required the exclusion of illegally seized evidence, and leading American evidence commentators insisted that *Boyd* had disturbed ancient Anglo-American tradition favoring the admissibility of such evidence.[142] More recent scholarship suggests, however, that there was no clear authority either for or against the exclusionary rule up to the mid-nineteenth century and that the *Boyd* court was writing on a more or less clean slate.[143] By 1914, when the Supreme Court in *Weeks v. United States*[144] firmly promulgated the exclusionary rule for federal prosecutions, at least one other state (Iowa) appeared to be moving toward that position,[145] and by 1933, roughly twenty years after *Weeks*, at least nineteen states had adopted an exclusionary rule, either by statute or by judicial decision.[146] By this time, however, nearly all the states had taken a definite position on the issue. New York, in a particularly influential opinion, rejected the exclusionary rule in 1926,[147] and

137 Gideon v. Wainwright, 372 U.S. 335 (1963).
138 Boyd v. United States, 116 U.S. 616 (1886).
139 Weeks v. United States, 232 U.S. 383 (1914).
140 Rochin v. California, 342 U.S. 165 (1952).
141 Wolf v. Colorado, 338 U.S. 25 (1949).
142 *See* 4 J. Wigmore, A Treatise on the Law of Evidence § 2183, at 2955 (Boston, Little, Brown, 1905).
143 Wilkes, *A Critique of Two Arguments Against the Exclusionary Rule: The Historical Error and the Comparative Myth*, 32 Wash. & Lee L. Rev. 881 (1975).
144 232 U.S. 383 (1914).
145 State v. Sheridan, 121 Iowa 164 (1903).
146 *See* Elkins v. United States, 364 U.S. 206, 224 (1960); Wolf v. Colorado, 338 U.S. 25, 38 (1949) (Black, J., dissenting).
147 People v. Defore, 242 N.Y. 13, 150 N.E. 585 (1926).

many states followed suit. As of 1949, thirty states opposed the exclusionary rule and only seventeen accepted it; the Supreme Court emphasized this "contrariety of views" when holding in that year that "fundamental fairness" did not make the exclusionary rule constitutionally obligatory.[148]

It should be noted that this diversity of approaches was not in itself regarded as an indication of weakness or incomplete evolution of the American federal system. Rather, it was thought, as Justice Brandeis had written many years earlier, that "[i]t is one of the happy incidents of the federal system that [a state may] serve as a laboratory, and try novel social and economic experiments."[149] Variation in state attitudes toward the exclusionary rule was seen as part of a quest for appropriate remedies for constitutional violations, in which diversity of approach could prove beneficial.

As of 1949, the Supreme Court's search and seizure jurisprudence afforded the states two distinct areas of flexibility. First, the states were free to design their own system of remedies for illegal police behavior. Second, for the one situation in which exclusion of evidence was mandated – outrageous police conduct that "shocks the conscience" – the states could not in theory claim any "margin of appreciation," but the vagueness of this standard, together with the impracticality of Supreme Court review of a statistically significant number of cases, left state court decisions largely free of effective control. The Supreme Court's inability to exert practically significant influence over the states under these standards led not only to lack of uniformity but also to persistent invasions of fundamental rights, without any meaningful remedy. Even in cases accepted for Supreme Court review, the Court often found itself unable to do more than express dismay over clearly illegal searches, while upholding the underlying conviction.[150] Finally in 1961 the Court held in *Mapp v. Ohio*[151] that the fourth amendment exclusionary rule was incorporated into the fourteenth amendment and thus binding on the states. As in the counsel cases, the Court was impelled to impose upon the states a clear, easily enforceable rule, not primarily to guarantee uniformity for its own sake but to provide a practically administrable technique for insuring adequate respect for fundamental rights.

The exclusionary rule remains controversial to some degree, but the highly politicized current debate should not mislead European observers studying the lessons of the 1940's and 1950's. In the American judicial system, at least, adequate respect for fundamental rights could not be achieved under a standard that left broad flexibility to local authorities, who are typically far more sensitive to law enforcement needs than to long-run implications for civil liberties. Even today, the leading critics of the exclusionary rule remain cognizant of this point. Chief Justice Burger, after pointedly detailing the serious problems created by the exclusionary rule, made clear in the *Bivens* case[152] that he

148 Wolf v. Colorado, 338 U.S. 25 (1949).

149 New State Ice Co. v. Liebmann, 285 U.S. 262, 311 (1932) (dissenting opinion).

150 *See, e.g.*, Irvine v. California, 347 U.S. 128 (1954).

151 367 U.S. 643 (1961).

152 Bivens v. Six Unknown Named Agents, 403 U.S. 388, 411 (1971) (dissenting opinion).

opposed abandoning the exclusionary rule until some effective substitute remedy was developed, and he offered detailed suggestions for legislation that might accomplish this goal. Similarly, the recent report of the Attorney General's Task Force on Violent Crime proposed a modification of the exclusionary rule to permit the admission of evidence when illegality results only from a good faith, technical violation by the police officer. This proposal, while potentially significant, nonetheless reaffirms the basic need for the exclusionary rule in the American system.[153]

The problem of police interrogation is worth separate mention because, although it illustrates some of these same themes, the pressures for clear, easily enforceable standards in this instance drove the Court to override legal standards which were rather uniform among the states and which had not previously been considered inadequate even for federal prosecutions. In a series of cases beginning in 1936,[154] the Court held that the admission of an "involuntary" confession in a state criminal trial violated the fourteenth amendment. As with the "fundamental fairness" standard applied in such areas as the right to counsel, the "voluntariness" test required an open-ended assessment of the "totality of the circumstances." Once again, several decades of experience with the test made clear that lower courts could not or would not perform the elusive balancing analysis with an appropriate sensitivity for the constitutional rights at stake. That experience likewise made clear that the Supreme Court's appellate powers were wholly inadequate to insure respect for those rights when its ad hoc balancing approach might serve to correct injustice in only a handful of confessions cases each year.[155] Finally, in 1966 the Supreme Court announced in its *Miranda* decision[156] a series of rather sharply defined rules and explicitly acknowledged that they were prophylactic devices designed to insure respect for the suspect's rights by police interrogators in the first instance and by lower courts later called to rule on the constitutionality of their techniques. The Court not only mandated a series of warnings to be given to the suspect but also announced that once a suspect indicates a desire to remain silent, all questioning must cease. The latter safeguard in effect created a fundamental substantive right previously unknown to federal and state law, because both the fourteenth amendment voluntariness requirement and the fifth amendment privilege against compulsory self-incrimination had permitted continued questioning so long as answers were not "compelled." The difficulty of giving specific content to the concepts of voluntariness and compulsion, together with the need for a readily administrable standard of appellate review, led the Court to a significant redefinition of the substantive rights of the accused in the context of police interrogation.

153 Attorney General's Task Force on Violent Crime – Final Report, para. 40, 29 CRIM. L. REP. 3131 (Washington, Bureau of National Affairs, 19 Aug. 1981).

154 Brown v. Mississippi, 297 U.S. 278 (1936).

155 *See* Schulhofer, *Confessions and the Court*, 79 MICH. L. REV. 865, 867–72 (1981).

156 Miranda v. Arizona, 384 U.S. 436 (1966).

3. Experience Under the "Selective Incorporation" Approach

By the late 1960's, the Court had "incorporated" into the fourteenth amendment, and thus applied against the states, nearly all the significant guarantees of the Bill of Rights. In addition to the provisions respecting searches and seizures, confessions and right to counsel, the Court had incorporated the fifth amendment protection against double jeopardy,[157] the sixth amendment rights to a jury,[158] a speedy trial,[159] to the confrontation of witnesses[160] and compulsory process,[161] and the eighth amendment guarantee against cruel and unusual punishments.[162] These steps did not, however, solve all the Court's problems. It remained necessary to give content to the rights that had been incorporated. In many instances this task was facilitated by a relatively well-developed body of precedent detailing the scope of the Bill of Rights guarantee in federal prosecutions. This was the case, for example, under the double jeopardy clause, where an ample, though somewhat contradictory, case law had developed. In other areas, however, nearly 200 years of adjudication had produced remarkably few decisions. In part this was due to the very specialized focus and relatively limited volume of prosecutions under federal criminal law. The situation also stemmed in part from federal statutes and court rules extending many rather broad safeguards independently of the Constitution; until the 1960's the Court had no occasion to consider the constitutional implications of different procedural arrangements.

The Court's efforts to apply the sixth amendment jury trial provision can serve to illustrate the consequences of this situation. In 1968, in *Duncan v. Louisiana*,[163] the Court incorporated this provision into the fourteenth amendment and made clear that its scope in state cases would be identical to what it had been in federal prosecutions. But the Court had never had occasion to identify with precision the kinds of petty offenses too insignificant to qualify as "criminal" prosecutions to which the sixth amendment jury trial right applied. Moreover, the Court had never even defined the meaning of the word "jury." Although many decisions took for granted that this meant a body of twelve, the point had never been tested because the Federal Rules of Criminal Procedure independently required a twelve-person panel.

In 1970 the Court held in *Baldwin v. New York*[164] that the jury trial guarantee extended to any offense punishable by at least six months' imprisonment. The effect was to invalidate a New York practice permitting trial without jury for any misdemeanor punishable by no more than a year in prison. The difficulties

[157] Benton v. Maryland, 395 U.S. 784 (1969).
[158] Duncan v. Louisiana, 391 U.S. 145 (1968).
[159] Klopfer v. North Carolina, 386 U.S. 213 (1967).
[160] Pointer v. Texas, 380 U.S. 400 (1965).
[161] Washington v. Texas, 388 U.S. 14 (1967).
[162] Robinson v. California, 370 U.S. 660 (1962).
[163] 391 U.S. 145 (1968).
[164] 399 U.S. 117 (1970).

posed by selective incorporation, with its need for a single rule applicable across the nation, were stressed by Justice Harlan in his dissent from this result:

[The Court] ignores both the basic fairness of the New York procedure and the peculiar local considerations that have led the New York Legislature to conclude that trial by jury is more apt to retard than further justice for criminal defendants in New York City. ... "Incorporation" in *Duncan* closed the door on debate, irrespective of local circumstances, such as the backlogs in urban courts like those of New York City. ... Flexibility for experimentation in the administration of justice should be returned to the States. ...[165]

The Court's reasons for rejecting such arguments were perhaps best summarized by Justice Goldberg, responding to similar arguments by Justice Harlan in an earlier case:[166]

[Justice Harlan's] view would have the Fourteenth Amendment apply to the States "only a 'watered-down, subjective version of the individual guarantees of the Bill of Rights.' " ... I do not believe that [state latitude] includes the power to experiment with the fundamental liberties of citizens safeguarded by the Bill of Rights. My Brother Harlan's view would also require this Court to make the extremely subjective and excessively discretionary determination as to whether a practice, forbidden the Federal Government by a fundamental constitutional guarantee, is, as viewed in the factual circumstances surrounding each individual case, sufficiently repugnant to the notion of due process as to be forbidden the States.

Finally, I do not see that my Brother Harlan's view would further any legitimate interests of federalism. It would require this Court to intervene in the state judicial process with considerable lack of predictability and with a consequent likelihood of considerable friction. ... [And,] to deny to the States the power to impair a fundamental constitutional right is not to increase federal power, but, rather, to limit the power of both federal and state governments in favor of safeguarding the fundamental rights and liberties of the individual. In my view this promotes rather than undermines the basic policy of avoiding excess concentration of power in government, federal or state, which underlies our concepts of federalism.

Experience suggests, however, that the incorporation approach has not always served to maximize protection for individual rights. In the same year as the *Baldwin* case, the Court held in *Williams v. Florida*[167] that the common law tradition of a twelve-person jury was a historical accident and that a panel of six jurors satisfied the sixth amendment. In this instance it seems clear that the Court was influenced by the severe inconvenience of requiring twelve-person juries in the context of overburdened state systems, but since the decision interpreted the scope of the sixth amendment, its effect was to permit smaller juries in federal prosecutions as well. Many have doubted whether the Court would have so readily set aside the historical tradition if its holding had applied to federal prosecutions only.[168]

Although *Williams* indicates the ways that a policy favoring clear, across-the-board rules can generate pressure for lowering the absolute level of protec-

165 *Id.* at 134, 138 (dissenting opinion).

166 Pointer v. Texas, 380 U.S. 400, 413–14 (1965) (concurring opinion).

167 399 U.S. 78 (1970).

168 *See id.* at 129 (Harlan, J., concurring).

tion, the danger must not be exaggerated. Most observers would probably agree that in following that policy, the Supreme Court has, on balance, greatly enhanced the protection afforded to fundamental rights in the U.S. In this connection, however, it is of interest that the current majority of the Supreme Court, even while inclined to narrow the rights of the accused in many areas, has not seen fit to return to the philosophy advanced by Justice Harlan. Although at least one member of the Court does continue to adhere to the "fundamental fairness" approach in fourteenth amendment cases,[169] the majority remains committed to the view that once a Bill of Rights provision has been "incorporated," "due process" requires the states to comply with the same detailed safeguards that this provision imposes on the Federal Government.[170]

Of course, it remains possible, within the methodology of selective incorporation, for the Court to decide that a given Bill of Rights provision should be applied flexibly in light of the "totality of the circumstances." In a few discrete areas, the Court has, in fact, rejected relatively bright guidelines in favor of a more open-ended balancing of criteria.[171] In these instances, however, the Court soon ceases frequent intervention in the area, since its ad hoc decisions have such limited reach. The effect is perhaps most notable in speedy trial cases, where the Court has read the sixth amendment guarantee to require a balancing of the circumstances present in each case.[172] As a result, the Supreme Court now renders very few opinions on a subject which, under a similarly open-ended standard, appears to occupy a comparatively significant place in the jurisprudence of the European Court of Human Rights.[173]

In sum, it seems likely that the exigencies of reaching and controlling a far-flung, multi-tiered judiciary whose members are products of highly diverse backgrounds, training and degrees of political accountability, have compelled the Supreme Court, whether liberal or conservative in orientation, generally to favor rather clear, easily administrable standards. This does not necessarily mean, of course, that a Court less solicitous of individual liberty can *force* reductions to a sharply defined and rather low level of protection. We are always speaking only of the criteria used for defining the ***minimum*** level of protection. State courts remain free to provide more extensive protection by interpretations of state law, including bill of rights guarantees in state constitutions. Indeed, state initiatives of this kind have become more common in recent years and are now the subject of a very substantial body of commentary.[174] What one

169 *See* Johnson v. Louisiana, 406 U.S. 356, 366 (1972) (Powell, J., concurring).

170 *See, e.g.*, Crist v. Brest, 437 U.S. 28 (1978); Apodaca v. Oregon, 406 U.S. 404 (1972).

171 *E.g.* Barker v. Wingo, 407 U.S. 514 (1972) (speedy trial). *See also* Manson v. Brathwaite, 432 U.S. 98 (1977).

172 Barker v. Wingo, 407 U.S. 514 (1972).

173 *See infra* §§ IV.C.3 & 5.

174 *E.g.*, Brennan, *State Constitutions and the Protection of Individual Rights*, 90 Harv. L. Rev. 489 (1977); Wilkes, *The New Federalism in Criminal Procedure*, 62 Ky. L. J. 421 (1974); Howard, *State Courts and Constitutional Rights in the Day of the Burger Court*, 62 Va. L. Rev. 873 (1976); Project Report, *Toward an Activist Role for State Bills of Rights*, 8 Harv. C. R. – C. L. L. Rev. 271 (1973).

can see operating at the national level, where the *minimum* level of protection must be defined, is a tension between the needs for flexibility and uniformity. Flexible criteria allow for local differences and also permit desirable variations that mark a healthy system that is federal rather than monolithic. But uniform, sharply defined criteria serve to prevent experimental tinkering with rights perceived as fundamental, and in any event serve the administrative imperatives of a Court that, despite its vast power, cannot easily affect the day-to-day behavior of judges and other public officials who are thousands of miles distant geographically and psychologically.

C. Procedure for Asserting a Federal Bill of Rights Claim

1. The History of Federal Habeas Corpus

Prior to the Civil War, state criminal cases could be reviewed by the Supreme Court, after conviction and after any appeals in the state system, but only to the extent that the accused could claim some infringement of federal law. There were, of course, essentially no federal procedural claims available at this time, but there were important federal substantive rights. Thus, one convicted under a law that interfered with interstate commerce could obtain relief in the Supreme Court. Relief by direct Supreme Court review was in fact the only avenue of redress available during this period. The first Congress in 1789 had given both the Supreme Court and lower federal courts the power to remedy illegal detention by granting release on habeas corpus, but in the case of jailed prisoners this power extended only to those held under federal authority.[175] There was no power to issue habeas corpus on behalf of a prisoner held under state law.[176]

At the same time that the fourteenth amendment granted state defendants the first significant procedural rights, Congress amended the habeas corpus statute so that beginning in 1867 federal judges acquired the power "to grant writs of habeas corpus in all cases where any person may be restrained of his or her liberty in violation of the constitution, or of any treaty or law of the United States."[177] Thus, relief by habeas corpus became available for prisoners held by state authority in alleged violation of federal law.

Habeas corpus acquired fame beyond the Anglo-American world primarily because of its role as a device to test the legality of detention outside the normal judicial process and as a device to insure a prompt hearing for arrested persons at the outset of allegedly unfounded criminal proceedings. These are no longer significant functions of the writ in American practice. Although there remains an extensive list of purposes for which the writ may in principle be used, for American lawyers habeas corpus is first and foremost a *post-conviction* remedy,

175 Judiciary Act § 14, 1 Stat. 81–82 (1789).

176 *Ex parte* Dorr, 44 U.S. (3 How.) 103 (1845). There was a handful of very narrow statutory exceptions to this principle.

177 Act of 5 Feb. 1867, 14 Stat. 385.

that is a device for asserting certain kinds of fundamental claims in a new proceeding (technically, in fact, a civil lawsuit) commenced in a trial-level court after completion of the criminal trial and after pursuit of all normal avenues of direct appeal. In all the states such a remedy, by habeas corpus or some analogous writ, is available in the *state* courts after state conviction, and a prisoner normally must seek such post-conviction relief from a state court (the "exhaustion" requirement) before applying for a *federal* writ of habeas corpus. Today it is not uncommon for a state prisoner, after unsuccessfully claiming violation of his federal rights at trial (in connection with a confession, for example), to present his claim to the state appellate courts, to renew that claim in state post-conviction proceedings (involving both trial and appeal) and then to present the same claim to a federal trial judge, who may reconsider the legal analysis and may even hold an evidentiary hearing to explore more fully the essential facts.

How habeas corpus came to play this role is a question that still evokes intense controversy among American legal scholars. The complex history can be summarized only with some oversimplification.[178] It may be said, however, that the 1867 Act by no means envisaged that every federal claim litigated in a state trial could be relitigated on federal habeas corpus. On the contrary, one convicted by normal judicial process was ipso facto detained in conformity with the Constitution, even if the court had, after a fair hearing, reached an erroneous decision on the merits of some federal issue. The federal courts began to grant relief on habeas, however, when the nature of the federal claim cast doubt on the very jurisdiction of the state court or on the state's ability to afford a fair hearing on the claim. The jurisdiction requirement was steadily expanded, and in 1938 the Supreme Court treated as "jurisdictional" a relatively routine claim – that a defendant's waiver of the right to counsel had been improper.[179] Finally, by 1953 the Court had held that relief on habeas was available following a state's erroneous denial of any federal constitutional claim.[180]

Historical and precedential arguments of some complexity were invoked to support this evolution, but most would agree that two related concerns were decisive. First, onerous or technical state procedures often prevented defendants from raising their constitutional claims effectively in the course of the state criminal trial. This is one facet of the all-important problem of "access to justice." Second, even when claims could be raised, they came before state trial judges who were perceived by the Supreme Court as insufficiently sensitive to federal constitutional rights. These two conditions undermined the federal guarantees in practice because the Supreme Court itself could never hope to

[178] For detailed accounts *see* Fay v. Noia, 372 U.S. 391 (1963); *id.* at 448 (Harlan, J., dissenting); P. Bator, P. Mishkin, D. Shapiro & H. Wechsler, Hart and Wechsler's The Federal Courts and the Federal System 1465–81 (2d ed., Mineola, N.Y., Foundation Press, 1973) [hereinafter cited as Hart & Wechsler].

[179] Johnson v. Zerbst, 304 U.S. 458 (1938).

[180] Brown v. Allen, 344 U.S. 443 (1953).

review all the state court decisions presenting difficult or important federal questions. Moreover, even in cases accepted for review, the outcome would necessarily depend on findings of fact made by the state trial judges, and the Supreme Court could not effectively develop a new factual record when the state court findings seemed incomplete or suspiciously biased. The Court's experience with the process of direct review over the years provided it with a continuing source of evidence of the inadequacy of this process for the effective protection of constitutional rights.

2. Special Problems of Habeas Corpus Procedure

The resulting system of adjudication must seem almost incredibly cumbersome to a foreign observer, and of course it has its critics within the U.S. as well. The controversy has centered on two matters that deserve separate discussion and analysis. The first concerns the availability of habeas relief for federal claims not presented in compliance with state procedure. This "access-to-justice" problem is referred to in the American context as a problem of "waiver." The second area of controversy concerns the availability of a second hearing in a federal, trial-level forum, after a claim *has* been properly presented in state court but rejected on the merits.

a) Waiver

Doctrinal requirements with respect to waiver are intricate and elusive, verging on the incomprehensible even for lawyers immersed in the American system. Yet these requirements play so vital a role in the overall scheme for the protection of civil liberties that an effort must be made to trace their contours.

All procedural systems specify some requirements for the proper presentation of a legal claim. If, for example, a defendant claims that a confession should be inadmissible because coerced, he may be required to raise that objection before trial or at least at the trial itself. Only rarely will a jurisdiction permit the claim to be raised for the first time after trial, at least in the absence of newly discovered and previously unavailable evidence. Similarly, jurisdictions typically require that appeal from a trial court judgment be lodged within a specified time, except in special circumstances that may be defined quite differently from one jurisdiction to another.

In the American system (and perhaps in any federal system) these commonplace requirements take on special significance because of the limited jurisdiction of the Federal Supreme Court. Suppose that a defendant claims that a confession used at his trial had been obtained in violation of his constitutional rights. The state court has affirmed his conviction on the ground that the objection was raised too late, or possibly has dismissed his appeal altogether on the ground that it was not filed in time. Can the federal Supreme Court hear and decide the question whether this person's constitutional rights were violated? In American law the answer is "no." So long as the state court's judgment rests on "adequate and independent state grounds" (*i.e.* the failure to perfect a proper appeal) the federal issue can no longer be considered relevant to the disposition of the case. Whether or not there was error at trial, a judgment not properly appealed will remain undisturbed.

There is a problem, of course, in determining whether the state procedural requirement is really "adequate." This question involves a tension between the need for reasonable opportunities to present federal claims and the need for reasonable state autonomy in designing orderly, fair procedures. Cappelletti and Golay explore the dimensions of this problem, which arises in both civil and criminal contexts in the United States.[181] For present purposes it is best to focus first on the relatively simple kinds of requirements that are widely followed and generally regarded as fair – for example, that objections to improper testimony be made when it is offered or that appeal be filed within a reasonable time. The "adequacy" of such requirements is normally clear, and therefore a failure to comply with them will prevent consideration of any underlying claims of unconstitutionality on direct appeal of the conviction to the U.S. Supreme Court.

Should the same principle apply in habeas litigation? That is, if the defendant has failed to comply with state requirements for challenging use of his confession, can he nevertheless raise his claim in a federal trial court on petition for habeas corpus? Prior to 1963 the answer was again a clear "no." Indeed, it may be hard to imagine how the answer could possibly be otherwise. Since the conviction can stand whether or not there was constitutional error at trial and since the Supreme Court itself has no power whatever to review the case on direct appeal, it may appear illogical, to say the least, to permit a federal trial court to hear the federal claim and order the prisoner's release upon finding the claim valid on the merits. Nonetheless, this is precisely the power that was granted to federal courts hearing habeas corpus claims in the Supreme Court's landmark 1963 decision in *Fay v. Noia.*[182] Though the Court reaffirmed that an "adequate and independent state ground" would foreclose Supreme Court review on direct appeal, it also held that such a ground would *not* foreclose presentation of the claim on habeas unless the defendant had "deliberately bypassed" the state requirement. This strict deliberate-bypass test would normally require proving a conscious choice by the defendant to withhold or abandon his claim, perhaps out of a perception, for example, that introduction of a confession would ultimately work to his tactical advantage. But if the objection was not properly raised because of oversight, neglect or unawareness of the nature of the claim, relief that was foreclosed on direct appeal would remain available on habeas.

The foundations of the *Fay* decision do not readily lend themselves to brief exposition, and much of the Court's historical and conceptual analysis is best omitted for present purposes. The core of the matter may perhaps be traced to a pervasive assumption in American law that constitutional rights should not be lost by inadvertence or accident; a waiver should be valid only if it is "knowing

[181] *See* Cappelletti & Golay, *The Judicial Branch in the Federal and Transnational Union: Its Impact on Integration, supra* this vol., Bk. 2, at § IV.B.3.

[182] 372 U.S. 391 (1963).

and intelligent." If the defendant's right to remain silent can be waived only by a deliberate, well-informed choice, why should his chance to claim violation of that right be forfeited by anything less than the same deliberate, well-informed choice? From this perspective, the *Fay* decision is not really illogical but rather serves to eliminate an illogical anomaly in prior law, under which constitutional rights in theory could not be lost by accident but remedies for defense of them (including redress for the denial of constitutional rights) *could* be so lost.

The need for *Fay* had become acute, moreover, because procedural requirements varied widely from state to state and the fairness or "adequacy" of many of them was not so obvious. For example, after the criminal conviction at issue in *Daniels v. Allen*,[183] a sixty-day time period had been allowed for appeal and this period expired on a Sunday. The appeal papers would have been timely if postmarked on Sunday, but out of caution, defendant's counsel chose to hand-deliver the papers to the court clerk the following Monday to insure the earliest possible receipt. Unfortunately, this was the sixty-first day, and the state courts held the appeal untimely. A divided Supreme Court, deferring to state autonomy in this procedural matter, upheld the "adequacy" of this state ground, which shut the door on a serious coerced confession claim of a prisoner under sentence of death.

Another important aspect of the "adequacy" problem can arise when an entirely reasonable requirement is violated by a lawyer or litigant who is inexperienced, overworked or constrained by an unusual tactical dilemma. In this situation the state procedures as such do not pose an arbitrary barrier to access, but overall context and institutional environment may create such a barrier. In other words, the state rules may be considered *formally adequate* but *contextually inadequate* to insure proper access to justice.

The Supreme Court might have chosen to address both of these problems – that of rules that are arguably unfair even in form (as in the *Daniels* case) and that of rules that are arguably unfair in context, by adopting much stricter standards of "adequacy" in reviewing convictions on direct appeal. To take such a course, however, would have meant relatively serious intrusions upon state autonomy in designing orderly procedures for litigation within the state's own court system. Perhaps for this reason, as Cappelletti and Golay develop more fully,[184] the Court has not been very active in scrutinizing the adequacy of state procedural grounds.[185]

The solution adopted by the Court in *Fay v. Noia* appears, in this light, as a difficult but ingenious compromise. State autonomy in designing procedural rules is in a sense preserved, but federal courts can hear constitutional claims despite non-compliance with state requirements. It is true that where a violation is found, a state will be forced to provide a new trial; in this sense adherence to

183 344 U.S. 482 (1953).

184 Cappelletti & Golay, *supra* note 181, at § IV.B.3.

185 In Henry v. Mississippi, 379 U.S. 443 (1965), the Court hinted at the prospect of serious control over state procedural barriers in the context of direct review of criminal convictions, but this hint has never been pursued.

orderly state procedures is not fully enforced. On the other hand, *Fay* requires new state proceedings only in cases of actual violation. The burdensome task of sorting through the hundreds of cases of *alleged* constitutional violations is borne by federal tribunals. In this sense state procedural requirements are still respected because the states do not have to undertake the difficult sorting process with a hearing in their own courts, when state rules for orderly presentation of claims have not been followed.

The *Fay* rule has proved valuable not only as a device for protecting constitutional rights but also, interestingly, as a tool for integration. Some commentators suggested that the broad availability of the federal habeas remedy might remove the incentive for states to improve the fairness and workability of their own procedures, because defendants would be able to obtain relief in any event from the federal courts.[186] A review of the decisions indicates, however, that this probably has not occurred. On the contrary, it appears that after *Fay*, states began to modify their more technical procedural rules and to hold that formal procedural defaults should be disregarded in the absence of a deliberate bypass.[187] Thus, the *Fay* decision managed, without intruding directly upon state procedural autonomy, to set up a dynamic that has led to a considerable harmonization in state rules of procedure and state standards for permitting relief from a defendant's procedural default.

Experience with the *Fay* rule has led some American lawyers and judges to conclude that in practice it too often undermines valid state rules and improperly impairs the finality of state criminal convictions. Reflecting this concern, the Supreme Court in *Wainwright v. Sykes*[188] decided to abandon the deliberate bypass test, at least in certain contexts, and to substitute a new formula under which a defendant can obtain a federal habeas hearing, after violation of state procedural rules, only if he can show *cause* for the default and *actual prejudice*.[189] Although many attorneys believe that the shift from the *Fay* to the *Wainwright* standard will prove extremely important in actual litigation, the difference between the two formulations is, from a comparative perspective, relatively subtle. The essential point, it seems, is that in the American federal system "adequate" state procedural rules are respected, but such rules nevertheless do not always foreclose independent federal examination of constitutional claims. The contemporary Supreme Court, even with its quite "conservative" orientation, continues to recognize that divergent state procedural

186 *See* HART & WECHSLER, *supra* note 178, at 1493.

187 *See, e.g.*, State v. Carufel, 263 A.2d 686 (R.I. 1970); State v. Knoblock, 44 Wis.2d 130, 170 N.W.2d 781 (1969); State v. Leavitt, 237 A.2d 309 (R.I. 1968). Similar findings were made in an empirical study of post-conviction litigation. *See* Shapiro, *Federal Habeas Corpus: A Study in Massachusetts*, 87 HARV. L. REV. 321, 348 (1973).

188 433 U.S. 72 (1977).

189 In its most recent effort to interpret the "cause" standard the Supreme Court appears to be moving toward a strict standard that will give relatively little weight to problems of what I have called "contextual inadequacy." *See* Engle v. Isaac, 456 U.S. 107 (1982).

requirements can, because of either formal or contextual inadequacy, jeopardize the enjoyment of federal constitutional rights in practice, and accordingly that access to a federal forum must on occasion be afforded despite a failure to comply with valid state rules. The new standard, like the one it replaces, will serve not only as a means for protecting federal rights but also, it may be added, as a tool for harmonization of divergent access rules among the state systems themselves.

b) Relitigation on the Merits

When a federal constitutional question has been fully litigated in state courts, the need for a second hearing in a federal, trial-level forum still commands a considerable degree of acceptance. In 1976, however, the Supreme Court, in *Stone v. Powell*,[190] held that fourth amendment search and seizure claims may no longer be relitigated in federal habeas corpus after an opportunity for full and fair hearing in the state courts. In imposing this restriction on habeas relief, the Justices emphasized two factors. First, fourth amendment remedies are especially costly because they lead to exclusion of highly credible, probative evidence. Second, the Justices stressed their perception that "[d]espite differences in institutional environment and the unsympathetic attitude to federal constitutional claims of some state judges in years past, we are unwilling to assume that there now exists a general lack of appropriate sensitivity to constitutional rights in the trial and appellate courts of the several States."[191]

Although it is hazardous to predict the extent to which such restrictions on habeas relief will be extended beyond the special context of search and seizure claims, to date all indications suggest that the Court will continue to preserve the principal possibilites for relitigation of federal claims on habeas.[192] Similarly, the Attorney General's Task Force on Violent Crime has proposed: (a) restricting the occasions that warrant a new evidentiary hearing to develop facts; and (b) requiring that petitions be filed within three years of the state court judgment.[193] Although American civil libertarians will regard such measures as significant limitations, a European observer can appreciate that the basic concept of federal habeas review continues to enjoy acceptance across a broad spectrum of American professional and political opinion.

D. Conclusions

1. The Comparative Problem: Similarities and Differences in Context

The next section of this chapter explores the role of fundamental rights as a vehicle of legal integration in Europe, and that paper is followed by an overall conclusion that brings into focus the principal similarities and differences

190 428 U.S. 465 (1976).

191 *Id.* at 493–94 n.155.

192 *See, e.g.*, Estelle v. Smith, 451 U.S. 454 (1981); Rose v. Mitchell, 443 U.S. 545 (1979); Schulhofer, *supra* note 155, at 888–91.

193 Attorney General's Task Force, *supra* note 153, at para. 42.

between European and American experience. Before moving on to the larger comparative problem, involving distinct cultures and legal systems, we do well to stress that even within the American context, experience concerning the protection of fundamental rights is not all of a piece. In criminal procedure the U.S. Supreme Court faced the problems of federalism under conditions quite different from those prevailing in free speech cases. In the latter area, as we have seen:[194]

(i) there was (except in libel and obscenity matters) no well-articulated body of doctrine before the Supreme Court entered the field;

(ii) an increasingly well-informed bar and institutional litigants with long-range objectives played a major role in developing test cases and in shaping the Court's agenda;

(iii) there was a close parallelism between the interests of federal and state governments;

(iv) the Court's priorities and its techniques for protecting them reflected a relatively long-standing social consensus and thus enjoyed rather strong popular support.

The contrast to circumstances under which the Court had to function in criminal procedure cases is striking:

(i) State courts had considerable experience, and in some instances a detailed case law, even prior to 1868. By the time the Supreme Court became most active, in the 1960's, state law directly contrary to the Court's preferences was clear and well-entrenched in many states; indeed in some instances institutional arrangements in police and court administration reflected considerable, deep-rooted reliance on such well-developed state law. While some of the Court's initiatives upset prior practice only in a few, seemingly aberrant states (this was true in jury trial and in the initial right-to-counsel cases), the exclusionary rule decision ran counter to the law of roughly half the states, and the Court's interrogation rules changed long-standing practice in every American jurisdiction.

(ii) In death penalty cases institutional litigants developed a well-coordinated strategy and significantly shaped the Court's agenda.[195] In other areas initiatives originating in the bar have had little or no impact. The Court's landmark right-to-counsel ruling came in a case filed by an indigent Florida prisoner and selected by the Justices for review from among thousands of similar, informal petitions filed each year.[196] The exclusionary rule decision came quite unexpectedly in a case pressed by the American Civil Liberties Union in an effort to have the Court clarify the free speech principles applicable to obscenity.[197]

(iii) Federal law enforcement is an effort of relatively small scope and highly specialized focus. Court efforts to protect individual liberties therefore

[194] *See supra* §§ II.A,D.

[195] *See* M. MELTSNER, CRUEL AND UNUSUAL: THE SUPREME COURT AND CAPITAL PUNISHMENT (New York, Random House, 1973).

[196] *See* A. LEWIS, GIDEON'S TRUMPET (New York, Random House, 1964).

[197] *See* Mapp v. Ohio, 367 U.S. 643, 672–75 (1961) (Harlan, J., dissenting).

impinged much more severely upon state interests than they did upon the interests of the Federal Government.

(iv) Decisions in support of the rights of the accused were perceived as affecting in a serious way the personal safety and security of "law-abiding" citizens. The Court's initiatives were far from popular.

That the Court pressed to introduce extensive reform under such conditions is itself a striking phenomenon. Its ability to do so no doubt reflects its extraordinary prestige. Yet even with a position unique among courts of the world, the U.S. Supreme Court has not entirely escaped the consequences of political reaction, and it is still too early to say definitively what lessons should be drawn from the Court's activism in the 1960's. One can see, however, that progress in the field of criminal procedure required the Court itself to take considerable initiative, both in its selection of cases and in the active shaping of doctrine to meet needs that its own experience in adjudication had impressed upon it. "Activism" in this sense – the Court's willingness to lead in identifying a problem, to set its own priorities and in some measure to develop its own solutions – persists today in a Court that, in terms of values and results, differs considerably from its immediate predecessor.

This point may be especially relevant for Europeans studying current American practice with respect to habeas corpus. As suggested by the Supreme Court in *Stone v. Powell*, some narrowing of the habeas remedy now seems justifiable to many Americans, in light of perceptions that insensitivity to federal rights may be less common in state courts today. Yet we cannot assume that this evolution in the attitudes of state judges is wholly unrelated to the active intervention of federal courts reexamining state decisions under the broad habeas jurisdiction of preceding years. Of course, a great variety of legal, social and political circumstances, many of them without parallels in the European context, play a role in explaining the long history of inadequate respect for federal rights in state courts, not only in the Reconstruction South but throughout the nation and well into quite recent times. Indeed it seems rather unlikely that the effort to bring European judges to a full appreciation of the European Convention on Human Rights will require anything close to the extensive measures deployed for a comparable purpose in the U.S. Nevertheless, even in states where judges have been relatively well-trained and free of obvious political bias, the federal habeas corpus mechanism seems to have played a significant role in educating the trial bench in its responsibilities and in promoting awareness of the full implications of federal doctrine. American experience thus draws attention to the importance of a practically effective enforcement system which renders federal relief more than a statistically remote contingency, and which thus translates the abstract guarantees of a federal bill of rights into an everyday reality for trial-level judges who are necessarily preoccupied with more immediate concerns.

2. Policy Implications

Pervasive differences in history, culture and institutional organization between Europe and America plainly preclude a direct copying of American techniques of integration even when they can be judged attractive or successful. The most useful comparative lessons appear to lie in the realm of locating problems to be anticipated and identifying converging or diverging trends in shaping responses to these problems. These matters are explored in the common conclusion to this chapter. Nevertheless, even at the particular and thus highly problematical level of specific technique, American experience may contain lessons relevant for Europeans.

Throughout the present paper we saw how the U.S. Supreme Court was preoccupied during much of its recent history with problems essentially administrative in nature – that is, those related to insuring that its decrees are respected in practice as well as in theory. These administrative concerns caused the Court to become immersed in the details of shaping particular remedies for the vindication of constitutional rights (the exclusionary rule, post-conviction habeas corpus). More strikingly, administrative concerns ultimately proved decisive even at the level of interpreting substantive rights, prompting the Court to replace such open-ended standards as "fundamental fairness" and "voluntariness" with relatively specific, automatic tests leaving much less room for judges to evaluate many factors under the totality of the circumstances.

Sharp differences between the European and American judiciaries, in training, in institutional environment, and also in professional and political accountability, suggest that questions of compliance and practical effectiveness in Europe are unlikely to take precisely the shape that they have taken in the U.S. In more general terms, however, it seems inevitable that in Europe, as in the U.S., intervention by the highest federal tribunal will be at best a remote, statistically infrequent contingency from the perspective of the government officials and trial-level judges who determine the actual meaning of civil liberties in practice. Indeed, in one sense the administrative problem may be even more acute in Europe, because as Professor Frowein points out, both the Commission and the Court in Strasbourg are part-time bodies.[198] Administrative concerns therefore may in time play a role in shaping the standards that the European Court will choose to follow in giving content to fundamental rights. If not, the European Court may, at the very least, have to take into account, overtly or tacitly, the administrative implications of the modes of interpretation it pursues. Similarly, administrative concerns may come to influence European thinking about the role of remedies in the overall scheme under the European Human Rights Convention. Already, the concept of post-conviction relief is not entirely unknown in Europe; witness the German procedure for extraordinary appeal to reopen factual questions,[199] and for petition to the Federal Constitutional Court, in cases of constitutional violation by an act of the judiciary.[200] At the level of the Convention system, Professor Frowein describes below the procedure for individual petition under article 25,[201] a proce-

[198] *See infra* § IV.B.
[199] StPO §§ 359 ff.
[200] GG art. 93, § 1, para. 4(a).
[201] *See infra* § IV.B.

dure that amounts in effect to something resembling, at least in its potential, the American writ of habeas corpus, including even a procedure for independent fact-finding by the Commission in Strasbourg. Problems concerning failure to comply with national procedural prerequisites and concerning relitigation of issues settled at the national level surely will be present in this context, if only implicitly. Europeans will not wish to copy the specifics of American solutions to these problems, but they may find the evolution of American doctrine and technique suggestive with respect to two basic goals that both communities share – insuring that fundamental rights are respected in practice as well as in theory, and harmonizing (within a framework of local autonomy) the all-important procedural rules that determine access to justice when questions of fundamental rights are at stake.

IV. Fundamental Human Rights as a Vehicle of Legal Integration in Europe

(*by* Jochen Abr. Frowein)

A. The Transnational Protection of Fundamental Rights in Europe

1. The European Convention on Human Rights: Its Dynamic Character

The preamble to the European Convention for the Protection of Human Rights and Fundamental Freedoms, signed in Rome on 4 November 1950, recognizes that the aim of the Council of Europe is "the achievement of greater unity between its Members and that one of the methods by which that aim is to be pursued is the maintenance and further realisation of Human Rights and Fundamental Freedoms." The goal of integration by means of the common protection and further realization – which must be understood as a process of development – of fundamental human rights is clearly encompassed by these words. As we have already stated in the Introduction, it is clear that the Convention organs do take into account general developments in the various member countries which go in the direction of a "further realisation of Human Rights and Fundamental Freedoms."[202] When the question arose whether judicial corporal punishment was to be seen as "degrading punishment" in the sense of article 3 of the Convention,[203] both the Commission and the Court referred to recent developments in the penal systems of member countries. The Commission quoted two British reports on corporal punishment,[204] while the Court found that it could not help "but be influenced by the developments and commonly accepted standards in the penal policy of the member States of the Council of Europe in this field."[205] Similarly in the *Marckx Case* the Court used the comparable formula that it "cannot but be struck by the fact that the domestic law of the great majority of the member States of the Council of Europe has evolved and is continuing to evolve, in company with the relevant international instruments, towards full juridical recognition of the maxim 'mater semper certa est'."[206]

In the last sentence of the dissenting opinion by Sir Gerald Fitzmaurice in the *Tyrer Case* the majority of the Court is criticized, even if indirectly, for using article 3 "as a vehicle of indirect penal reform, for which it was not

202 *See* Introduction, *supra* at § I.B.2.
203 *See infra* note 301 and accompanying text.
204 Tyrer v. U.K., App. No. 5856/72, Rep. of 14 Dec. 1976, p. 14 ff (Eur. Comm'n H.R., Strasbourg, 1976).
205 Tyrer Case, Judgment of 25 Apr. 1978, Series A: Vol. 26, p. 15 ff (Pubs. of Eur. Ct. H.R., 1978).
206 Marckx Case, Judgment of 13 June 1979, Series A: Vol. 31, p. 19 (Pubs. of Eur. Ct. H.R., 1979).

intended."[207] Here, one is clearly confronted with a fundamentally different approach to the Convention. Either one accepts that general standards for concepts such as "degrading punishment" may indeed evolve – in which case they must inevitably lead to penal reform when sanctions come into conflict with this notion – or article 3 is to be understood as referring only to a past standard prevailing in 1949 or 1950, which will now be very difficult to establish in a given case. Such an approach would preclude, of course, the achievement of greater unity among the members of the Council of Europe through further development of concepts of fundamental rights by the organs of the Convention.

It will be shown in greater detail below how some consequences for legal integration in Europe have already been brought about by the jurisprudence of the European Commission and the European Court of Human Rights.[208]

2. The Issue of Fundamental Rights in the European Communities

It is the goal of the European Communities to establish specific economic freedoms for the territory of the Member States. The free movement of goods and the freedom to exercise all kinds of professional activities are to be guaranteed throughout the Community. Sometimes these economic freedoms are compared to fundamental rights.[209] The specific methods of legal integration through the establishment of these economic liberties are dealt with in separate chapters of this Project. In the present context, the issue of fundamental rights in the European Community is a more limited one; here, it relates specifically to the application of standards of fundamental rights against acts of the Community. The European Court of Justice has recognized in several decisions that fundamental rights recognized and protected by the Constitutions of the Member States form an integral part of Community law.[210] By this jurisprudence it became clear that the organs of the Community are bound by an unwritten catalogue of fundamental rights. The Court has also stated, moreover, that the European Convention on Human Rights must be taken into account as expressing the common standard of fundamental rights in the Member States of the Community.[211] In its decision in *Hauer v. Rheinland-Pfalz*,[212] for example, the Court discussed in some detail whether the measure concerned – an EEC regulation prohibiting the expansion of existing vineyards – was consistent with article 1 of the First Protocol to the European Convention on Human Rights.[213]

[207] Tyrer Case, *supra* note 205, at p. 32.

[208] *See infra* §§ IV.C,D,E,F.

[209] *See, e.g.*, 3 A. Bleckmann, Europarecht: Das Recht der Europäischen Wirtschaftsgemeinschaft 136 ff (Cologne, Carl Heymanns, 1980).

[210] One of the most important decisions is Case 44/79, Hauer v. Rheinland-Pfalz, [1979] ECR 3727. *See infra* § IV.G.

[211] *See* Case 4/73, Nold v. Commission, [1974] ECR 491; and Case 44/79, *Hauer*, [1979] ECR 3727.

[212] *See* Case 44/79, [1979] ECR 3727, 3745 ff.

[213] *See infra* note 328 and accompanying text.

One may ask, nevertheless, whether this development in Community law has any bearing on the question of legal integration in Europe. It seems that, for at least two reasons the jurisprudence of the European Court of Justice on these matters should not be ignored. On the one hand, the Community legal order as an *autonomous* order is influenced by common standards of fundamental rights, as are the municipal legal orders of its Member States. On the other hand, it is possible to foresee a dialectic development by which the legal order of a Member State will be influenced by the jurisprudence of the Court of the Communities. Since Community law is directly applicable in the domestic sphere it is rather unlikely that national courts will fall behind established Community standards when applying domestic fundamental rights, even in matters which have nothing to do with Community law. To this extent, there may be indirect integration through the jurisprudence of the European Court of Justice concerning fundamental rights and freedoms.

B. The Effect of Transnational Protection of Fundamental Rights by the Organs of the European Convention on Human Rights – The System of Remedies

It is an important feature of the European Convention on Human Rights, as compared with many other international agreements for the protection of human rights, that it not only provides for the creation of two specific organs, the European Commission and the European Court of Human Rights, but that these organs have themselves created an extensive jurisprudence interpreting the Convention.[214] Applications to the European Commission of Human Rights may come from member countries under article 24,[215] but they may also originate – and in practice, do originate most frequently – from individuals, provided the state concerned has recognized the competence of the Commission to receive such petitions under article 25.[216] Most of the states which have

[214] *See* Frowein, *The European and the American Convention on Human Rights – A Comparison*, 1 H.R.L.J. 44 (1980).

[215] "Any High Contracting Party may refer to the Commission, through the Secretary-General of the Council of Europe, any alleged breach of the provisions of the Convention by another High Contracting Party." ECHR art. 24.

[216] (1) The Commission may receive petitions addressed to the Secretary-General of the Council of Europe from any person, non-governmental organisation or group of individuals claiming to be the victim of a violation by one of the High Contracting Parties of the rights set forth in this Convention, provided that the High Contracting Party against which the complaint has been lodged has declared that it recognises the competence of the Commission to receive such petitions. Those of the High Contracting Parties who have made such a declaration undertake not to hinder in any way the effective exercise of this right.
(2) Such declarations may be made for a specific period.
(3) The declarations shall be deposited with the Secretary-General of the Council of Europe who shall transmit copies thereof to the High Contracting Parties and publish them.

ratified the Convention have also recognized the right of individual application; declarations recognizing such a right are in force for Austria, Belgium, Denmark, the Federal Republic of Germany, France, Ireland, Iceland, Italy, Liechtenstein, Luxembourg, the Netherlands, Norway, Portugal, Spain, Sweden, Switzerland and the United Kingdom. Only Greece, Malta, Turkey and Cyprus remain not subject to the jurisdiction of the Commission on applications by individuals.[217] This shows that, for most of the states in Western Europe, the individual has access to an international organ protecting his or her fundamental rights and freedoms.

The control exercised by the Convention organs is intended to be only subsidiary, and therefore the exhaustion of domestic remedies "according to the generally recognized rules of international law" is made a prerequisite for an application by article 26.[218] It is the task of the Commission to decide whether this rule has been complied with, and to determine whether the application is incompatible with the Convention, is manifestly ill-founded, or constitutes an abuse of the right of petition. If this is not the case and the formal requirements are fulfilled – if the petition has been made within six months after a final national decision, is not anonymous, and is not substantially the same as an earlier petition or has not been subjected to another procedure of international investigation or settlement – then the Commission may declare the application admissible.

Through the end of 1982,[219] 297 individual and 9 state applications had been declared admissible. While all state applications – for which only the procedural rules concerning the exhaustion of local remedies and the six-month time limit apply – have been declared admissible, only a small percentage of individual applications reaches the merits stage. The total number of individual applications filed with the Commission up to the end of 1982 was 10,210.

This shows that the chance of an individual application being declared admissible has been far below 5 percent. However, it is also clear that a considerable change in the attitude of the Commission has taken place in recent years. While only 49 individual applications were declared admissible during the first twelve years of the Convention, up to 1967, 166 were declared admissible in the next twelve years. In 1982 alone, 42 applications were declared admissible, which is the highest amount ever.

(4) The Commission shall only exercise the powers provided for in this Article when at least six High Contracting Parties are bound by declarations made in accordance with the preceding paragraphs.

ECHR art. 25.

217 Lists of declarations appear in 1980 Y.B. Eur. Conv. H.R. 26

218 "The Commission may only deal with the matter after all domestic remedies have been exhausted, according to the generally recognised rules of international law, and within a period of six months from the date on which the final decision was taken." ECHR art. 26.

219 Statistics from Eur. Comm'n H.R., Stock-Taking on the European Convention of Human Rights 224 (Strasbourg, Council of Europe, 1982), and Andrews, *Council of Europe - Current Survey,* 9 Eur. L. Rev. 72 (1984).

It is certainly not surprising that an international machinery of remedies for the protection of human rights would take some time to become known and to establish itself. In the early years, when it was uncertain whether many states would accept the right of individual application, the Commission was rather reluctant to declare cases admissible. The Federal Republic of Germany was the only large country to accept the right of individual application early on, in 1955. The United Kingdom followed only in 1966, Italy in 1973 and France in 1981. Declarations recognizing the right of individual petition are normally valid for periods of three to five years; only Iceland, Ireland and Sweden have accepted the right to individual application for an indefinite period. But significantly, no state up to now has failed to renew an article 25 declaration when it lapsed.[220]

These developments may show that some initial reluctance on the part of the Commission to declare applications admissible was quite understandable. The experience of lawyers with the system established by the Convention grows only slowly, and this is certainly an additional reason why for many years only few really important applications were filed. In states with a rather elaborate system of internal remedies, such as the Federal Republic of Germany, most important issues concerning fundamental rights and freedoms are taken care of by the internal machinery. This is true especially where there exists a remedy of constitutional complaint, or of appeal to a Constitutional Court. In recent years the most difficult applications to the Commission have come from countries where the system of internal remedies does not allow for specific complaints concerning the violation of fundamental rights, especially from Britain. The *Sunday Times Case*,[221] raising important issues of freedom of the press, and the *Case of Young, James, and Webster*,[222] challenging aspects of the closed shop – both against the United Kingdom – are two examples of this phenomenon. It is notable that applications originating from the United Kingdom are frequently prepared by very highly qualified lawyers. Apparently the British Bar has become aware of the potential contained in a Bill of Rights which does not otherwise exist in British law.

As soon as an application has been declared admissible, the Commission investigates the case and puts itself at the disposal of the parties with a view to securing a friendly settlement, as provided for in article 28.[223] A friendly settle-

[220] The United Kingdom has, however, not renewed the declaration for the Isle of Man after the judgment in the *Tyrer Case*.

[221] Judgment of 26 Apr. 1979, Series A: Vol. 30 (Pubs. of Eur. Ct. H.R., 1979).

[222] Judgment of 13 Aug. 1981, Series A: Vol. 44 (Pubs. of Eur. Ct. H.R., 1981).

[223] Art. 28 provides that in the event of the Commission accepting a petition referred to it:

(a) it shall, with a view to ascertaining the facts, undertake together with the representatives of the parties an examination of the petition and, if need be, an investigation, for the effective conduct of which the States concerned shall furnish all necessary facilities, after an exchange of views with the Commission;

(b) it shall place itself at the disposal of the parties concerned with a view to securing a friendly settlement of the matter on the basis of respect for Human Rights as defined in this Convention.

ment has been reached in a number of cases, altogether 22 up to 1982. If this proves to be impossible the Commission adopts a report, in the form of a non-binding judgment. The report goes to the Committee of Ministers, but the Commission can then refer the case to the Court, provided the state concerned has accepted the Court's jurisdiction. The jurisdiction of the Court has been accepted by all the states which have accepted the right of individual application, and in addition by Greece and Cyprus.[224]

Again, a noticeable change in Commission practice has taken place in this area in recent years. While only 11 cases had been referred to the Court up to 1973, since then the Commission has brought more than 40 applications before the Court. The Court has pronounced between 5 and 10 judgments every year in recent times. This is, of course, hardly comparable to the caseload of a national Supreme Court or to that of the Court of Justice of the European Communities. But considering that the Commission and the Court in Strasbourg are only part-time bodies, the output of the last few years is not at all negligible. And it should be stressed that the Commission's Secretariat, and the Office of Registrar of the Court fulfill the very important task of disseminating information about new developments by continually publishing and circulating decisions and reports.

The procedures employed before the Commission and the Court are different in several respects. The individual applicant is a real party only before the Commission, which sits *in camera*. The applicant is not a party before the Court; only the Commission and the respondent party, the State, have standing in this forum. This is a considerable deficiency of the system agreed to in 1949–1950. Fortunately, in practice the applicant is represented by his lawyer, who may adress the Court under Rule 30 of the Rules of Court 1982. Thereby, in fact, the Court will hear extensive written and oral arguments on behalf of the applicant. This system, although not provided for by the text of the Convention, is a most effective innovation for the protection of the rights of the individual applicant. In fact, even before 1982 the Court already frequently quoted the submissions of the applicant's counsel made while addressing the bench as a member of the Commission's delegation.[225]

Although the system of remedies set up by the Convention is rather complex, experience has shown that it can, nevertheless, function effectively for the development of common European standards for the protection of fundamental rights. While in most substantive areas the jurisprudence generated by the European Court and Commission of Human Rights cannot even approach the degree of legal sophistication and detail – and consequent value as a tool of integration – represented by almost two hundred years of rulings on similar human rights issues by the U.S. Supreme Court, in certain areas the European Court of Human Rights has succeeded in creating definite Euro-

[224] *See supra* note 217, at 603.

[225] *See, e.g.*, Airey Case, Judgment of 6 Feb. 1981, Series A: Vol. 41, p. 9 (Pubs. of Eur. Ct. H.R., 1981); Deweer Case, Judgment of 27 Feb. 1980, Series A: Vol. 35, p. 14 (Pubs. of Eur. Ct. H.R., 1980).

pean human rights standards of its own, and more importantly, in setting up a perceptible legal framework that makes future legal developments inevitable. We shall now examine the developments in some of these human rights areas, focusing especially on two for which we have a record of extensive American experience – the areas of rights of the accused in criminal procedure, and freedom of expression. We shall then move on to some other developments of Convention law for which we have not offered parallel U.S. examples, but which are, particularly in the light of the still limited corpus of European jurisprudence, central to our appreciation of the influence of the European Convention on legal integration in Europe.

C. Towards Transnational Standards of Criminal Justice: The Limited European Experience

1. Introduction

The European Convention on Human Rights was not drafted with the goal of changing the vastly different systems of criminal justice that exist in the now twenty-one member countries of the Convention. While the adversary procedural system of the Common Law tradition is practiced in Great Britain and Ireland, as well as in Malta and Cyprus, different versions of what is called the inquisitorial system are in force in the other Convention countries. But despite this key difference, it is now already quite noticeable that some harmonizing influence is being exercised in this area through the jurisprudence of the Convention organs. National high courts look more frequently to the Convention and to the interpretative jurisprudence of the Commission and Court when rulings on human rights issues relate to the criminal process. Furthermore, Parliaments of several member countries have amended their codes of criminal procedure to bring them in line with decisions of the Commission and the Court.

2. The Deprivation of Liberty on the Basis of Reasonable Suspicion

a) The Convention Basis

Article 5, paragraph 1 (c) of the Convention justifies detention on remand in rather broad terms; article 5, paragraph 3 then points to the special responsibility of the prosecuting authorities for those who are held in such detention.[226]

[226] (1) Everyone has the right to liberty and security of person. No one shall be deprived of his liberty save in the following cases and in accordance with a procedure prescribed by law:
(a) the lawful detention of a person after conviction by a competent court;
(b) the lawful arrest or detention of a person for non-compliance with the lawful order of a court or in order to secure the fulfillment of any obligation prescribed by law;
(c) the lawful arrest or detention of a person effected for the purpose of bringing him before the competent legal authority on reasonable suspicion of having

The provision does not give a general right to bail, but implies that detention on remand may not be prolonged when it is not necessary to insure the presence of the accused at the trial or necessary for the investigation of the crime. The European Commission on Human Rights was careful to emphasize this point in its early decisions and to reject the view, put forward by some Convention countries, that the practice of crediting time served in detention before trial against the eventual sentence made the prolongation of pre-trial detention less severe.[227] The fact that only *reasonable* suspicion is sufficient to justify detention under article 5, paragraph 1 (c) is important, and makes it necessary to monitor the reasonableness of this suspicion during the investigation. Those held in detention on the basis of a suspicion which later proves to be unfounded have no basis for a claim under article 5, paragraph 5, as long as the detention was reasonable in line with article 5, paragraph 1 (c). Under many national laws a person in this situation may, however, have a claim.[228] It seems that, today, standards for arrest and detention are still quite different throughout Europe.[229] Whether the Convention organs will attempt to exercise some harmonizing influence here in the future is very difficult to foresee.

committed an offence or when it is reasonably considered necessary to prevent his committing an offence or fleeing after having done so;
(d) the detention of a minor by lawful order for the purpose of educational supervision or his lawful detention for the purpose of bringing him before the competent legal authority;
(e) the lawful detention of persons for the prevention of the spreading of infectious diseases, of persons of unsound mind, alcoholic or drug addicts or vagrants;
(f) the lawful arrest or detention of a person to prevent his effecting an unauthorised entry into the country or of a person against whom action is being taken with a view to deportation or extradition.

(2) Everyone who is arrested shall be informed promptly, in a language which he understands, of the reasons for his arrest and of any charge against him.

(3) Everyone arrested or detained in accordance with the provisions of paragraph 1 (c) of this Article shall be brought promptly before a judge or other officer authorised by law to exercise judicial power and shall be entitled to trial within a reasonable time or to release pending trial. Release may be conditioned by guarantees to appear for trial.

(4) Everyone who is deprived of his liberty by arrest or detention shall be entitled to take proceedings by which the lawfulness of his detention shall be decided speedily by a court and his release ordered if the detention is not lawful.

(5) Everyone who has been the victim of arrest or detention in contravention of the provisions of this Article shall have an enforceable right to compensation.

ECHR art. 5.

227 Wemhoff Case, Judgment of 27 June 1968, Series A: Vol. 7, p. 21 ff (Pubs. of Eur. Ct. H.R., 1968).

228 This is, for instance, the case under German law.

229 *See* Trechsel, *The Right to Liberty and Security of the Person*, 1 H.R.L.J. 88, 90 (1980).

b) Towards a Common Notion of Liberty

Three important judgments of the European Court of Human Rights have clarified the notions of liberty and detention as used by the Convention. In the *Guzzardi Case* the Italian Government had argued that a person compelled to take up residence on a small portion of an island comprising 2.5 sq. km., and guarded by *Carabinieri*, was not deprived of liberty. The Court held to the contrary, as had the Commission, making it clear that administrative measures could not in fact lead to a result indistinguishable from a state of detention without falling under the control of the specific guarantees of the Convention.[230] In the *Engel Case* the notion of deprivation of liberty had to be defined in a military context, and here the Court placed the main emphasis on the notion of incarceration.[231] In the *Van Droogenbroeck Case*, someone who under Belgian law was placed "at the disposal of the Government" as the consequence of a criminal conviction, but in fact was at liberty, was permitted to complain about the possibility of being put back later into a special institution. This means that the guarantees of personal liberty may not be circumvented by a system of conditional liberty.[232]

c) The Necessity of Court Review (Habeas Corpus)

Persons detained on the basis of reasonable suspicion must be brought "promptly" before a judge or other officer in the sense of article 5, paragraph 3, who must decide on the legality of the detention. It is most preferable that this officer be a real judge acting in complete independence and deciding on the substantive grounds of detention. In the *Schiesser Case* the Court held, as had the Commission, that a District Attorney in Zürich qualified as an officer in the sense of article 5, paragraph 3, although he also acts as the investigating and prosecuting authority.[233] The Court stressed the necessity that he act independently when deciding on the question of detention, and that in the specific case he not act later as prosecutor.

Since the decision to detain falling under article 5, paragraph 3 (which must be taken within three to four days of arrest) is not necessarily a decision made by a judge, Court control of the "lawfulness" of the detention in the sense of article 5, paragraph 4 is of crucial importance. It is clear that the writ of habeas corpus lies in the background of this Convention guarantee. Interestingly enough, the availability of habeas corpus has become one of the main issues creating difficulties in interpreting the provision. The control of the lawfulness

[230] Guzzardi Case, Judgment of 6 Nov. 1980, Series A: Vol. 39, p. 32 ff (Pubs. of Eur. Ct. H.R., 1980).

[231] Engel Case, Judgment of 8 June and 23 Nov. 1976, Series A: Vol. 22, p. 25 ff (Pubs. of Eur. Ct. H.R., 1977).

[232] Van Droogenbroeck Case, Judgment of 24 June 1982, Series A: Vol. 50 (Pubs. of Eur. Ct. H.R., 1982).

[233] Schiesser Case, Judgment of 4 Dec. 1979, Series A: Vol. 34, p. 11 (Pubs. of Eur. Ct. H.R., 1979). *See also now* McGoff Case, Judgment of 26 Oct. 1984, Series A: Vol. 83 (Pubs. Eur. Ct. H.R., 1984).

of detention under article 5, paragraph 4 can be merely a control of procedural forms, or it can include an investigation of substantive grounds for the detention. The Commission and the Court have held that procedures under article 5, paragraph 4 must include a hearing of the position of the detained person, either in person or through some form of representation.[234] In the *Winterwerp Case*, concerning the Dutch system for the internment of mentally ill persons, the Court left open, however, the question whether control by a court under article 5, paragraph 4 covers only the formal propriety of the procedure followed, or also the substantive justification for the deprivation of liberty.[235] The Commission, the Government of the Netherlands, and the applicant were all agreed that the control must cover both. The U.K. Government had taken the opposite view in a memorandum filed with the Commission which was referred to the Court. This problem was the main issue in the case *X v. The United Kingdom*, again dealing with detention for unsoundness of mind.[236] The Court reasoned as follows:

> On the other hand, in the Court's opinion, a judicial review as limited as that available in the habeas corpus procedure in the present case is not sufficient for a continuing confinement such as the one undergone by X. Article 5 § 4, the Government are quite correct to affirm, does not embody a right to judicial control of such scope as to empower the court, on all aspects of the case, to substitute its own discretion for that of the decision-making authority. The review should, however, be wide enough to bear on those conditions which, according to the Convention, are essential for the "lawful" detention of a person on the ground of unsoundness of mind, especially as the reasons capable of initially justifying such a detention may cease to exist. This means that in the instant case Article 5 § 4 required an appropriate procedure allowing a court to examine whether the patient's disorder still persisted and whether the Home Secretary was entitled to think that a continuation of the compulsory confinement was necessary in the interests of public safety.

It would seem then that the guarantee of article 5, paragraph 4 can be a meaningful one only if it goes to the substantive grounds for the detention. One may only wonder whether some sort of harmonizing effect will flow from this development, especially for the mother country of habeas corpus.

3. The Length of Pre-Trial Detention (Detention on Remand)

Most important as an example of legal integration through the application of the European Convention on Human Rights is the development of standards limiting the period of detention on remand. Article 5, paragraph 3 grants a suspect the right "to trial within a reasonable time or to release pending trial." The release may be conditioned by guarantees to appear for trial. Although the right to trial within a reasonable time is also guaranteed by article 6 to those

234 Winterwerp Case, Judgment of 24 Oct. 1979, Series A: Vol. 33, p. 24 (Pubs. of Eur. Ct. H.R., 1980).

235 *Id.* at 26 ff.

236 Case of X v. U.K., Judgment of 5 Nov. 1981, Series A: Vol. 46, p.25 (Pubs. of Eur. Ct. H.R., 1981).

who are not detained,[237] the Court has held from the very beginning that the "reasonableness" in article 5, paragraph 3 is to be established in relation to the deprivation of liberty.[238] It seems clear that a much stricter standard was thereby applied than had been customary in some jurisdictions. In Germany, for instance, the rule that pre-trial detention is limited to six months, and may be prolonged after six months only by a reasoned decision of a court was introduced only in 1964, as a consequence of the jurisprudence of the Commission and the Court.[239] It is of course impossible to lay down any absolute limits for a period of reasonable detention, but it would seem that the Convention system has brought about a growing awareness of the problems created by long periods of pre-trial detention. That is certainly true for countries like Germany and Austria. But several applications against Switzerland concerning the length of detention on remand show that the problem may be more widespread. Trechsel may be correct in suspecting that different attitudes to pre-trial detention in Britain and Ireland on the one hand, and on the Continent on the other, may be at the root of these problems.[240] The Court has certainly not accepted any of the national standards as its own. But it had to remind the Continental states that article 5, paragraph 3 is worded on the basis of a tradition that sets as its goal the protection of individual liberty to the greatest extent possible. The influence of this tradition on other legal systems is clearly detectable. Legal integration in this area has, to some extent, taken place.

[237] (1) In the determination of his civil rights and obligations or of any criminal charge against him, everyone is entitled to a fair and public hearing within a reasonable time by an independent and impartial tribunal established by law. Judgment shall be pronounced publicly but the press and public may be excluded from all or part of the trial in the interests of morals, public order or national security in a democratic society, where the interests of juveniles or the protection of the private life of the parties so require, or to the extent strictly necessary in the opinion of the court in special circumstances where publicity would prejudice the interests of justice.
(2) Everyone charged with a criminal offence shall be presumed innocent until proved guilty according to law.
(3) Everyone charged with a criminal offence has the following minimum rights:
(a) to be informed promptly, in a language which he understands and in detail, of the nature and cause of the accusation against him;
(b) to have adequate time and facilities for the preparation of his defence;
(c) to defend himself in person or through legal assistance of his own choosing or, if he has not sufficient means to pay for legal assistance, to be given it free when the interests of justice so require:
(d) to examine or have examined witnesses against him and to obtain the attendance and examination of witnesses on his behalf under the same conditions as witnesses against him;
(e) to have the free assistance of an interpreter if he cannot understand or speak the language used in court.
ECHR art. 6.

[238] Wemhoff Case, *supra* note 227.

[239] StPO § 121.

[240] *See* Treschel, *supra* note 229.

4. Criminal Process

It is particularly in its general approach to the criminal process as a whole that the views of the Commission seem to have had considerable influence. This is well exemplified by the notion of "equality of arms" between prosecution and defense, which is seen as a necessary element of a "fair" proceeding.[241] This notion has received considerable attention in many Convention countries.

a) *Pre-Trial Investigations*

The law on search and seizure has not played a prominent role in Convention jurisprudence so far. However, the *Klass Case*, concerning secret telephone surveillance, has emphasized clearly the need to restrict and control the use of those advanced surveillance techniques so dangerous to modern societies.[242] The Court has recently decided the case of *Malone v. The United Kingdom*, where surveillance took place without a clear statutory basis.[243]

Assistance of defence counsel at all stages of pre-trial investigation is not guaranteed in all Convention countries. The "*mise au secret*" practiced in some Swiss Cantons, where people detained may not see their lawyer, was briefly investigated by the Commission in one case.[244] It would seem that the decision to reject the application was very much influenced by the specific features of the case. The Commission noted expressly:

> Unlike other international instruments in the field of human rights or humanitarian law, notably Article 14 (3) (b) of the United Nations Covenant on Civil and Political Rights, Article 6 (3) of the Convention does not expressly secure the right of an accused person to communicate with the counsel of his choice.
>
> However, that right can be inferred from the above-mentioned provisions since Article 6 (3) (b) secures the right of an accused person to have adequate time and facilities for the preparation of his defence, while sub-paragraph 3 of that same provision secures the right to have the legal assistance of his own choosing: the opportunity for the accused to confer with his defence counsel is fundamental to the preparation of his defence.
>
> In the case in point, the applicant was able to confer with his counsel frequently and without impediment during a period of nine months, from 16 July 1976 until 16 April 1977, the date of the judgment. He therefore had sufficient time and contact with his defence counsel to prepare for his trial, at the end of which he was released, following the passing of a sentence equivalent to the duration of his detention on remand and its suspension.[245]

241 *See* Ofner v. Austria, App. No. 524/59, Dec. of 19 Dec. 1960, 1960 Y.B. Eur. Conv. H.R. 322; Hopfinger v. Austria, App. No. 617/59, Dec. of 19 Dec. 1960, 1960 Y.B. Eur. Conv. H.R. 370.

242 Case of Klass *et al.*, Judgment of 6 Sept. 1978, Series A: Vol. 28, p. 23 (Pubs. of Eur. Ct. H.R., 1979).

243 Malone Case, Judgment of 2 Aug. 1984, Series A: Vol. 82 (Pubs. Eur. Ct. H.R., 1984).

244 Bonzi v. Switzerland, App. No. 7854/77, Dec. of 12 July 1978, 12 Eur. Comm'n H.R., Decs. & Reps. 185.

245 *Id.* at 190.

Practices of "plea bargaining" and obtaining evidence by granting immunity to an accomplice have also been mentioned as concerns of the Commission for their potential to adversely influence the fairness of a proceeding.[246]

b) The Right to a Defense

Article 6, paragraph 3 guarantees several important rights to the defendant. Information on the charge, sufficient time to prepare the defense, the right to counsel and – under certain conditions – the right to free defense counsel are expressly mentioned. It is of great importance that both Commission and Court refuse to consider those rights to be mere formalities. In the *Artico Case*, the Court confirmed the Commission's view that the right under article 6, paragraph 3 (c) was violated where a legal aid counsel had been named, but had not at all acted in the case.[247] In the *Goddi Case*,[248] the Court found a violation of article 6, paragraph 3 (c) where a defense counsel had been appointed at the trial, without the accused (or his preferred counsel) being present. And finally, in the *Pakelli Case*,[249] the Court confirmed the earlier finding of the Commission in holding that article 6, paragraph 3 (c) includes the indigent's right to legal aid representation not only for the written procedures, but also for the rarely-held hearing at an advanced appeals stage of proceedings where only very technical points of law were to be discussed.

c) The Right to be Present at the Trial

Unlike the United Nations Covenant on Civil and Political Rights, the European Convention on Human Rights does not expressly guarantee the right of the accused to be present at the trial. Read literally, article 6, paragraph 3 (c) can even be seen as providing for alternative solutions to the presence of the accused, who may either defend himself in person or be defended by counsel without being present. This understanding can be seen underlying some decisions of the Commission.[250] In more recent times, however, the Commission has seemed to recognize that most of the guarantees in article 6, paragraph 3 indeed presuppose the presence of the accused at the trial.[251] A meaningful defense will be impossible without the participation of the accused. The problem will have to be tackled in two cases that have been declared admissible,

[246] X v. U.K., App. No. 5574/72, Dec. of 21 Mar. 1975, 3 Eur. Comm'n H.R., Decs. & Reps. 10; X v. U.K., App. No. 7306/75, Dec. of 6 Oct. 1976, 7 Eur. Comm'n H.R., Decs. & Reps. 115.

[247] Artico Case, Judgment of 13 May 1980, Series A: Vol. 37 (Pubs. of Eur. Ct. H.R., 1980).

[248] Goddi Case, Judgment of 9 Apr. 1984, Series A: Vol. 76 (Pubs. Eur. Ct. H.R., 1984).

[249] Judgment of 25 Apr. 1983, Series A: Vol. 64 (Pubs. of Eur. Ct. H.R., 1983).

[250] *See, e.g.*, X v. Norway, App. No. 5923/72, Dec. of 30 May 1975, 3 Eur. Comm'n H.R., Decs. & Reps. 43; X v. Austria, App. No. 7138/75, Dec. of 5 July 1977, 9 Eur. Comm'n H.R., Decs. & Reps. 50.

[251] *See, e.g.*, X v. Austria, App. No. 8289/78, Dec. of 5 Mar. 1980, 18 Eur. Comm'n H.R., Decs. & Reps. 160.

concerning Italian trials held while the accused is *in absentia*.[252] Under Italian law, proceedings of this sort are permissible. When the accused is later arrested, there are only very limited procedures for review, unlike the French procedure where the trial will be repeated if the person so wishes. The *Rubinat Case* is particularly telling: in this instance, a sailor who apparently knew nothing at all about his trial was convicted in his absence. It would not be surprising if the Convention organs reached the conclusion that proceedings held in the absence of the accused, where there are no specific remedies for reopening the trial, lack the element of fairness guaranteed by article 6. This does not mean, of course, that the accused may not be excluded if he continuously disturbs the trial, as some terrorists in Germany and Italy have done.[253]

It would seem that the Commission already basically recognized the right of the accused to be present at the proceedings when it declared admissible an application against Austria, where the Supreme Court had increased the sentence of a convicted person without hearing or seeing the person concerned.[254] A friendly settlement was reached in the case, by which Austria committed itself to a change in legislation.[255]

d) Impartiality of the Court

The right to be tried by an impartial tribunal is of fundamental importance for any accused, and essentially distinguishes systems of criminal justice safeguarding the rule of law from procedures that are merely arbitrary and oppressive. In general, the notion of impartiality would seem to be rather self-evident. Interestingly enough, several cases brought against Belgium have recently raised issues in this context. In the case concerning the application of *Piersack v. Belgium*, both organs, *i.e.* the Commission and the Court, unanimously found a violation of the principle of impartiality since a former prosecutor who had dealt with the case – although only as supervisor of the prosecutor immediately in charge – had later sat as president of the *Cour d'Assizes*.[256] In the case giving rise to the application *De Cubber v. Belgium*, decided by the Court on 26 October 1984, the investigating judge (*juge d'instruction*) had become a member of the trial court.[257] In all these cases, the old saying that justice must

252 Colozza and Rubinat v. Italy, App. Nos. 9024/80, 9317/80, Dec. of 9 July 1982 (Eur. Comm'n H.R., Strasbourg, 1982). Both cases are now pending before the Court, after the Commission in its report had unanimously found a violation.

253 Ensslin *et al.* v. Fed. Rep. of Ger., App. Nos. 7572/76, 7586/76, 7587/76, Dec. of 8 July 1978, 14 Eur. Comm'n H.R., Decs. & Reps. 64.

254 X v. Austria, App. No. 8289/78, *supra* note 251.

255 X v. Austria, App. No. 8289/78, Rep. of 13 Oct. 1981 (Eur. Comm'n H.R., Strasbourg, 1981).

256 Piersack v. Belgium, App. No. 8692/79, Rep. of 13 May 1981 (Eur. Comm'n H.R., Strasbourg, 1981); Piersack Case, Judgment of 1 Oct. 1982, Series A: Vol. 53 (Pubs. Eur. Ct. H.R., 1982).

257 DeCubber Case, Judgment of 26 Oct. 1984, Series A: Vol. 86 (Pubs. Eur. Ct. H.R., 1984).

also be seen to be done seems to be of fundamental importance. One may wonder whether the Court should not have taken that principle more seriously in the *Delcourt Case,* again against Belgium, where the applicant had challenged the presence of the *Procureur du Roi* at deliberations of the *Cour de Cassation;* no violation of article 6 was found.[258]

e) Presumption of Innocence

Article 6, paragraph 2 proclaims the principle of the presumption of innocence, which again is basic for any criminal proceeding respecting the rule of law. However, here again important differences in the various systems of criminal law may become important. Some countries know rules of evidence which might be viewed as putting that principle into doubt. The Commission has recognized that, for instance, a rule which places the burden on the owner of a car to prove that someone else has used it, is a permissible rule of evidence, and not in violation of article 6, paragraph 2.[259] Most cases involving the principle of the presumption of innocence so far have concerned proceedings in which a trial ended without either conviction or acquittal; the court in such cases did not find the accused guilty. Procedures of this sort exist in several Convention countries. The Commission and the Court have emphasized that article 6, paragraph 2 protects the accused against indirect findings of guilt in a decision without formal conviction.[260] Here again, it seems that standards are being harmonized through the application of the Convention.

5. Trial Within a Reasonable Time

Systems of criminal justice have different standards for determining the reasonable length of a criminal proceeding. Where the prosecuting authority is under a formal obligation to investigate all criminal behavior and, in principle, to bring charges in all cases, investigations will inevitably take longer than in those systems where the prosecutor is permitted to choose the most important cases to bring to trial. Article 6 guarantees some common standard of reasonableness for these practices. In 1982 the Court unanimously confirmed the unanimous holding of the Commission that the German criminal proceeding against the applicant Eckle, which had taken seventeen years, was in clear violation of article 6.[261] Indeed, the case was an example of what is possible where the principle of full and complete investigation of all criminal behavior is carried to extremes. It seems that some harmonizing effect of Convention

[258] Delcourt Case, Judgment of 17 Jan. 1970, Series A: Vol. 11 (Pubs. of Eur. Ct. H.R., 1970).

[259] Van den Noort v. Netherlands, App. No. 6170/73, Dec. of 26 May 1975 (Eur. Comm'n H.R., Strasbourg, 1975).

[260] Adolf Case, Judgment of 26 March 1982, Series A: Vol. 49 (Pubs. of Eur. Ct. H.R., 1982); Minelli Case, Judgment of 25 Mar. 1983, Series A: Vol. 67 (Pubs. Eur. Ct. H.R., 1983).

[261] Eckle Case, Judgment of 15 July 1982, Series A: Vol. 51 (Pubs. of Eur. Ct. H.R., 1982).

procedures can be detected here. At very least, it is possible to see a growing awareness of the need to shorten criminal proceedings in Germany and in several other Convention countries, such as Italy.

6. Conclusion

It is too early to say whether the Convention system will have a lasting effect on practices of criminal justice in even a handful of the Convention states. One can detect already, however, a growing tendency to apply the standards laid down by article 6 rather strictly, and not to refrain from finding violations in national criminal procedures. Understandably, this was not always the case. In the early years of the Commission there was a great reluctance to tackle difficult matters and to develop standards not in harmony with those applied by national courts. This situation has changed considerably. Although states are still formally free to withdraw the right to individual application under article 25 of the Convention, the possibility of such action does not feasibly exist today for most of the Western European states bound by the Convention. This seems to have given both the Commission and Court a greater confidence for developing new common standards of criminal justice. One would think that the results which can be achieved by developing these common European standards on the basis of the Convention are far from negligible.

D. Towards a Common Standard for Freedom of Speech and the Press

1. Early Developments

Important differences exist among the Convention states as far as guarantees of freedom of speech are concerned. Although all countries recognize the general principle of free expression, it is not always possible to attack legislation or even administrative decisions on the basis of a formal guarantee of this right. This is due to the fact that the internal protection of fundamental rights varies greatly in the different member countries. Britain does not have an internal Bill of Rights, and the Convention is not applicable in domestic law. In Switzerland, it is not possible to attack decisions of federal authorities with a constitutional complaint based on a violation of the right to freedom of expression. Even more important than the differences concerning formal guarantees and remedies may be those concerning traditions and attitudes. The "Little Red School-Book," which in Britain gave rise to the proceeding in the *Handyside Case*,[262] had circulated freely in the Scandinavian countries and in Germany. Libel statutes would seem to be applied in a manner much more restrictive of speech in the south of Europe than in the north.

It is not surprising that, given the comparatively short history of the Convention, its Commission and Court, there has as yet been no development towards common standards of free speech parallel to that which occurred in the United

[262] Judgment of 7 Dec. 1976, Series A: Vol. 24 (Pubs. of Eur. Ct. H.R., 1976).

States. However, we may point to some interesting examples which may show the potential impact of the Convention in this area.

It was not until 1976, with the *Handyside Case,* that the European Court of Human Rights could address itself to the problems of free speech. Up to this time the Commission had of course dealt with several applications alleging violations of article 10,[263] but most of these were decided in a summary manner because they did not raise substantial issues. There was one exception, however, in the first years of the Convention: in 1956 De Becker filed an application with the Commission against the operation of a provision of the Belgian penal code which banned from the publishing business certain people who had been convicted of treason on the basis of their behavior during the German occupation.[264] De Becker was deprived for life of the following rights:

- the right to have a proprietary interest in or to take part in any capacity whatsoever in the administration, editing, printing or distribution of a newspaper or any other publication;
- the right to take part in organising or managing any cultural, philanthropic or sporting activity or any public entertainment;
- the right to have a proprietary interest in or to be associated with the administration or any other aspect of the activity of any undertaking concerned with theatrical production, films or broadcasting.[265]

While the Commission found in its Report that it may be justifiable under article 10, paragraph 2 to impose on persons convicted of treason in time of war the penalty of a total ban for life on their right to publish their political opinions, it stated that this Belgian legislation went far beyond that standard. The Commission concluded that the Belgian restrictions were not "fully justifiable" under the Convention.[266] The case was brought before the Court, but a settlement was reached after Belgium changed its legislation and the Court struck the case off its list.[267]

Although the Commission went very far here in accepting restrictions on political expression, the case would seem to show rather that freedom of

[263] (1) Everyone has the right to freedom of expression. This right shall include freedom to hold opinions and to receive and impart information and ideas without interference by public authority and regardless of frontiers. This Article shall not prevent States from requiring the licensing of broadcasting, television or cinema enterprises.
(2) The exercise of these freedoms, since it carries with it duties and responsibilities, may be subject to such formalities, conditions, restrictions or penalties as are prescribed by law and are necessary in a democratic society, in the interests of national security, territorial integrity or public safety, for the prevention of disorder or crime, for the protection of health or morals, for the protection of the reputation or rights of others, for preventing the disclosure of information received in confidence, or for maintaining the authority and impartiality of the judiciary.
ECHR art. 10.

[264] *See* "De Becker" Case, Series B: Vol. 2 (Pubs. of Eur. Ct. H.R., 1962).

[265] De Becker v. Belgium, App. No. 214/56, Rep. of 8 Jan. 1960, in *id.* at p. 105.

[266] *Id.* at p. 127 ff.

[267] *See* EUR. COMM'N H.R., *supra* note 219, at 107.

expression was taken seriously from the very beginning of the Convention system as one of the cornerstones of democracy. One must not forget that the Convention was drafted after World War II, and as a clear reaction to violations of human rights in Germany and the occupied countries. It was a rather courageous act for the Commission, therefore, to declare admissible already in 1958 a complaint against a punishment imposed for collaboration with the occupation authorities.

In several other subsequent cases the Commission has upheld restrictions on political expression on the basis of the rationale developed in the *De Becker* report.[268]

2. The Approach of the European Court of Human Rights

In its first case dealing with the issue of freedom of expression the Court took the opportunity to dwell at some length on the function of this right.[269] It stated that freedom of expression constitutes one of the essential foundations of a democratic society, one of the basic conditions for its progress, and for the development of every individual. The Court stressed that article 10 is applicable not only to information or ideas that are favorably received or regarded either as inoffensive or with indifference, but also to those ideas that offend, shock or disturb the State or any sector of the population. Such are, in the view of the Court, the demands of that pluralism, tolerance and broadmindedness without which there is no "democratic society." The Court repeated this statement in the *Sunday Times Case* and underlined its particular importance as far as the press is concerned. It added that the public has a "right" to receive information and ideas concerning matters of public interest from the press.[270]

It is interesting to note that the function of this freedom as the essential basis of democracy was underlined by the German Federal Constitutional Court in its first important decision on freedom of expression in 1958. This Court chose to quote Justice Cardozo, who had described freedom of expression as "the matrix, the indispensable condition of nearly every other form of freedom."[271] One must not overlook the fact that statements of this sort do not by themselves change the differing conditions existing in the various countries of Europe. And there are indications that in some European countries, restrictions on freedom of expression may be extensive, particularly in the guise of criminal libel statutes. On the other hand, a general philosophical approach of this nature to questions of free speech is far from unimportant. A liberal attitude may, hopefully, influence developments in national court procedures. It may also create a heavy burden of proof for the State that would restrict freedom of expression.

[268] *See, e.g.*, X v. Belgium, App. No. 924/60, Dec. of 27 Mar. 1963, 1963 Y.B. Eur. Conv. H.R. 150; X v. Belgium, App. No. 764/60, Dec. of 28 Sept. 1964, 16 Eur. Comm'n H.R. Coll. Decs. 1, 8.

[269] Handyside Case, *supra* note 262, at p. 23.

[270] The Sunday Times Case, *supra* note 221, at pp.40–41.

[271] [1958] 7 BVerfGE 198 ("Lüth" case); *see also* [1956] 5 BVerfGE 85 ("KPD" case).

Article 10, paragraph 2 in its wording is rather broad in approving various legitimate restrictions on free expression. However, the Court has also drawn the conclusion from its general stance on free expression that any restriction on expression must be proportional to the legitimate aim pursued by the legislation.[272] In the *Sunday Times Case* the Court added simply that the exceptions in article 10, paragraph 2 must be narrowly interpreted.[273] The real test will be of course only the application of this qualification in a concrete case.

The first important requirement for any legitimate restriction of freedom of expression, as is true also for the other liberties guaranteed in articles 8–11[274] of the Convention, is that it must be "prescribed by law." This is indeed an essential consequence of the rule of law, under which the liberties of the individual can be restricted only on the basis of a law. In the *Sunday Times Case* it was argued that the principles of the Common Law concerning contempt of court were so vague that the restrictions could not be seen as being "prescribed by law." Both Commission and Court dealt with this problem and came to the conclusion, even if only reluctantly, that the requirement was fulfilled in this case.[275] The Court distinguished two consequences flowing from the expression "prescribed by law." First, the law must be accessible to the citizen. One would have expected that criterion to be self-evident. Much more important, however, was the second criterion. A norm cannot be regarded as a "law" unless it is formulated with sufficient precision to enable the citizen to regulate his conduct in conformance with it. The citizen must be able to foresee, to a reasonable degree in the circumstances – if need be, with appropriate legal advice – the consequences which a given action may entail. The Court recognized that absolute certainty is unattainable, but the principle is correctly stated.[276] The Court then explained that the applicants were able to foresee, to a degree that was reasonable in the circumstances, a risk that the draft article might come within the reach of contempt of court procedures. The Commission had used the same criterion of predictability as the Court, and has applied it again in a case concerning the British Incitement to Disaffection Act of 1934.[277]

In most cases, it will not be difficult to establish whether the aim pursued by the restrictive measure is one included in the catalogue of exceptions listed in article 10, paragraph 2 of the Convention. In the *Handyside Case* the Court had

[272] Handyside Case, *supra* note 262, at p. 23.

[273] The Sunday Times Case, *supra* note 221, at p. 41.

[274] Art. 8–11 contain fundamental guarantees of the right to respect for private and family life (art. 8); to freedom of thought, conscience and religion (art. 9); to freedom of expression (*see supra* note 263); and to freedom of peaceful assembly and association with others (art. 11).

[275] The Sunday Times Case, *supra* note 221, at pp. 30–33.

[276] *Id.* at p. 31.

[277] Times Newspapers, Ltd., *et al.* v. U.K., App. No. 6538/74, Report of 18 May 1977, Series B: Vol. 28, p. 11, 65–66 (paras. 200–205) (Pubs. of Eur. Ct. H.R., 1982); Arrowsmith v. U.K., App. No. 7050/75, Rep. of 12 Oct. 1978, 19 EUR. COMM'N H.R., DECS. & REPS. 5, 21 ff.

to deal with the argument that the protection of morals was in this instance only a pretext for the repression of information. The argument was rejected on the basis of the facts of the case.[278] The *Sunday Times* judgment had no difficulty establishing that the authority of the judiciary was to be protected by the rules and restrictions concerning contempt of court.[279] Therefore, the aim of the law was legitimate. The Commission discussed at some length in the *Arrowsmith Case* whether prosecution under the Incitement to Disaffection Act of 1934 served one of the legitimate purposes listed under article 10, paragraph 2. It found that the Act itself aimed at the protection of national security and at the prevention of disorder in the armed forces.[280] As to the particular distribution of leaflets which was the basis for the conviction in that case, the Commission found that it was not the expression of political opinion on the use of the army in Northern Ireland that was the crucial issue, but the fact that in the leaflets the applicant had encouraged individual soldiers to desert their posts, and had indicated specific means of assistance for them.[281] This would seem to indicate that criticism concerning the use of the army alone could never be restricted on national security grounds.

The most difficult problem is always that of determining whether a specific restriction is "necessary in a democratic society." It is clear from the jurisprudence of the Commission and the Court that it is up to the national authorities to make the first decision in this respect.[282] They may take into account the specific prevailing national or even local conditions.[283] This means that what is considered to be a "pressing social need" requiring some action may be regarded differently by diverse authorities. The Court has especially recognized this in the area of the protection of morals, where there is no uniform European conception.[284]

On the other hand, it is up to the Commission and the Court to review the decisions taken by the national organs.[285] The latter are permitted a certain "margin of appreciation" but the limits of this discretion will be controlled by the Convention organs.[286] It is clear, however, that these words can never wholly supplant the subjective decision by the members of the Commission or of the Court. In the *Sunday Times Case* this difficulty emerged rather clearly. The *Sunday Times* had been held in contempt of court, in a tort case brought by victims of a dangerous drug against the drug's manufacturers, for publishing an article about prior industry knowledge of the adverse effects of the drug. The bare majority of the Court which found a violation of the Convention shifted

[278] Handyside Case, *supra* note 262, at p. 35.
[279] The Sunday Times Case, *supra* note 221, at pp. 33–35.
[280] Arrowsmith v. U.K., App. No. 7050/75, *supra* note 277, at 22 ff.
[281] *Id.* at 23.
[282] Handyside Case, *supra* note 262, at p. 22.
[283] *Id.* at p. 26 ff.
[284] *Id.* at p. 22.
[285] *Id.*
[286] *Id.* at p. 23.

the burden of proof, stating that the families of the numerous victims of the drug had a vital interest in knowing all the facts about it and could be deprived of these facts, "only if it appeared absolutely certain that ... [the] diffusion of them would have presented a threat to the authority of the judiciary."[287] This threat certainly did not exist, but it is doubtful how its existence could ever be established. The minority of nine judges found that the House of Lords was "entitled to think" that publication of the article would have detrimental effects upon the due administration of justice.[288] They concluded that the interference did not overstep the limits of "what might be deemed necessary in a democratic society" for the maintenance of the authority and impartiality of the judiciary.[289]

It seems clear that the last formula is much less stringent and leaves a higher degree of flexibility to the competent national organs. The difference in attitude seems to be influenced by the interpretation of the notion of "authority of the judiciary." The majority saw a substantial measure of common responsibility in this area. Therefore, a more extensive European control corresponds, in the eyes of the majority, to a less discretionary margin of appreciation.[290] The minority did not accept that analysis. According to its opinion, the notion of "authority of the judiciary" cannot be determined in such a uniform manner.[291] The basic difference between the two approaches becomes clear when the minority states that European supervision is concerned,

> in the first place, with determining whether the national authorities have acted in good faith, with due care and in a reasonable manner when evaluating those facts and circumstances, as well as the danger that might thereby be occasioned for the interests listed in Art. 10 § 2; further and above all, it seeks to ensure that, in a society that means to remain democratic, the measures restricting freedom of expression are proportionate to the legitimate aim pursued.[292]

It may be said that legal integration in Europe with regard to standards for the restriction of freedom of expression will be brought about more easily if the Commission and the Court apply more or less uniform standards. But this evaluation is open to question. For a long time to come, there will be important social, institutional and legal differences between the countries of Europe. It would probably be too heavy a burden for the European human rights protection mechanism to bear to aim constantly at a uniform standard for freedom of expression. It may be sufficient to review the motives of the national authorities and their investigations of the facts to conclude whether "they were entitled to think" that a particular restriction on expression was necessary.

[287] The Sunday Times Case, *supra* note 221, at p. 41 ff.

[288] *Id.* at p. 51.

[289] *Id.* at p. 56.

[290] *Id.* at p. 36 ff.

[291] *Id.* at p. 52.

[292] *Id.* at p. 50.

3. Towards a More Activist Attitude?

The Commission has recently adopted its report in the case of *Barthold v. The Federal Republic of Germany*, in which a veterinary surgeon has complained about restrictions placed on his right to publish material about the need to create emergency services for animals injured at night.[293] The restrictions were based on rules of the profession which forbid any kind of advertising. While final resolution of this case is still pending, when compared to the earlier cases it would appear that the Commission is looking much more critically at the need for restrictions on expression today than it was some years ago. This change in attitude may also be seen in two decisions, in which applications were declared inadmissible, but where the rationales show that the Commission went deeply into the questions at hand.

The first application, the case of *Lingens and Leitgeb v. Austria*,[294] raised difficult issues of interpretation of article 10, in connection with the law of libel. The applicants had called a politician a liar in a newspaper article; the politician brought libel proceedings against them, but refused to appear as a witness although ordered to do so by the courts. The court orders could not be enforced by reason of the parliamentary immunity enjoyed by the politician, and the applicants were convicted. The Commission stressed that the restrictions on free expression must be necessary in the particular case:

> In view of the fundamental importance which this freedom has in the field of political discussion it is of the utmost importance that these restrictive regulations should only be applied where it is really necessary in the particular case. They should under no circumstances be used to curb legitimate criticism in the press of the behaviour and statements of a politician since it is the very function of the press in a democratic society to participate in the political process by checking on the development of the debate of public issues carried on by political office-holders. A politician must in principle be prepared to accept even harsh criticism of his public activities and statements, and such criticism may not be understood as defamatory unless it throws a considerable degree of doubt on his personal character and good reputation.[295]

The Commission noted that there is no general obligation for the press to publish only what can be proven to be true, but that the rule applies only where allegations have an objectively defamatory character. One may wonder whether this decision was not mainly influenced by the use of language which clearly went beyond what may be considered as acceptable in even the most direct and open public debate. To call someone a "liar" would seem to bring the case right outside any normal expression of political or other opinions.

The case of *Gay News Ltd. and Lemon v. The United Kingdom*[296] concerned the Common Law crime of blasphemous libel. The homosexual magazine *Gay News* had printed a poem referring to homosexual acts committed with the body of Christ. The Commission went at length into the question whether the crime was "prescribed by law" in the sense of the *Sunday Times* judgment,

293 App. No. 8734/79, Dec. of 13 Oct. 1981 (Eur. Comm'n H.R., Strasbourg, 1981).
294 App. No. 8803/79, Dec. of 11 Dec. 1981 (Eur. Comm'n H.R., Strasbourg, 1981).
295 *Id.* at 27. *Cf.* now the case of Lingens v. Austria, pending before the Court.
296 App. No. 8710/79, Dec. of 7 May 1982 (Eur. Comm'n H.R., Strasbourg, 1982).

although it had not been settled as a question of law if an intent to blaspheme was necessary to commit the crime under the Common Law. The Commission found that, nevertheless, the applicants could have reasonably foreseen, with the assistance of appropriate legal advice, that a specific intent to blaspheme was not required by the law. As for the necessity of the restriction on expression, it was the opinion of the Commission that not only the legislation as such, but also its application in the given case could both be considered as necessary.[297]

Given the specific nature of this case, one could well imagine that some years ago the application would have been rejected in a summary manner. The approach of the Commission may have been influenced by the fact that the Law Commission in England had criticized the state of the law of blasphemous libel in particular with regard to its lack of clarity. This criticism was noted expressly in the Commission's decision. It may well be that the Strasbourg organs react, to some extent, to demands formulated in the national forum even if these demands are not directly related to the application pending in Strasbourg.

Although it is by far too early to judge whether the decisions of the Convention organs in the area of free speech may attain importance for harmonizing standards in Europe comparable to the role played in the United States by the jurisprudence of the U.S. Supreme Court, one can note at least a growing awareness of the fundamental nature of the right to freedom of expression.

E. Some Other Rights Examined

1. Basic Human Rights

The protection of the right to life and freedom from torture or inhuman treatment form very basic guarantees of human rights. There exists, of course, a common standard recognizing these guarantees in the legal orders of all Convention countries. One may wonder, therefore, if any sort of legal integration can be brought about by the system of protections laid down in the Convention.

In the case of *Cyprus v. Turkey* the Commission had to investigate alleged violations of article 2,[298] protecting the right to life, in connection with the occu-

[297] *Id.* at 16 ff.

[298] (1) Everyone's right to life shall be protected by law. No one shall be deprived of his life intentionally save in the execution of a sentence of a court following his conviction of a crime for which this penalty is provided by law.
(2) Deprivation of life shall not be regarded as inflicted in contravention of this Article when it results from the use of force which is no more than absolutely necessary:
(a) in defence of any person from unlawful violence;
(b) in order to effect a lawful arrest or to prevent the escape of a person lawfully detained;
(c) in action lawfully taken for the purpose of quelling a riot or insurrection.
ECHR art. 2.

pation of parts of Cyprus by Turkey.[299] These constituted clear cases of tragic violations of human rights but the findings of the Commission could not lead to anything which may be called legal integration. In most of these and similar instances the violation of fundamental human rights will be due to a failure on the part of the authorities to respect established standards of rights rather than to the application of particular national rules which have fallen below the European standard.

There are, however, different situations. The Commission has communicated a case raising the issue whether national legislation regulating the use of weapons by the police or security forces with the aim to kill is in line with the requirement that the use of deadly force must be "absolutely necessary" for an arrest, according to article 2, paragraph 2 (b).[300] The standard in the applicable national law seems to be that the use of force must be "reasonable in the circumstances." A case of this sort may clarify the legal standards established by the Convention and lead to a common European level of protection.

Article 3 prohibits torture as well as inhuman or degrading treatment or punishment.[301] Again, the standards laid down here are common to the legal systems of the Convention countries. That does not mean, however, that the interpretation of these standards will not raise difficult issues. The discussions concerning the characterization of judicial corporal punishment as "degrading treatment" by the Commission and the Court are a good example.[302] It seems also that in the area of the treatment of prisoners, especially those of a very dangerous nature – investigated by the Commission in several important cases – the Convention has at least contributed to the development of common European standards.[303]

This is also true for restrictions on the right to deport or extradite, which the Commission has drawn from article 3. Following some indications in national decisions, the Commission has developed the rule that a state is in violation of article 3 if it deports or extradites anyone to a country where he may be tortured or treated in an inhuman manner.[304] Only two cases on the point have been declared admissible; a friendly settlement was reached in the first, while the second was struck off the list after an arrangement was made preventing actual

299 Cyprus v. Turkey, Apps. Nos. 6780/74 and 6950/75, Rep. of 10 July 1976, Doc. No. 45.82306.2, pp. 110–119.

300 Farrell v. U.K., App. No. 9013/80, Dec. of 11 Dec. 1982 (Eur. Comm'n H.R., Strasbourg, 1982). The case was later settled.

301 "No one shall be subjected to torture or to inhuman or degrading treatment or punishment." ECHR art. 3.

302 Tyrer Case, *supra* note 205.

303 Ensslin, *et al.* v. Fed. Rep. of Ger., App. Nos. 7572/76, 7586/76, 7587/76, *supra* note 253, at 84 ff; McFeeley, *et al.* v. U.K., App. No. 8317/78, Dec. of 15 May 1980, 20 Eur. Comm'n H.R., Decs. & Reps. 44, 77 ff.

304 1962 Y.B. Eur. Conv. H.R. 256, 260; X v. Fed. Rep. of Ger., App. No. 7216/75, Dec. of 20 May 1976, 5 Eur. Comm'n H.R., Decs. & Reps. 137, 140.

extradition.[305] It would seem that the rule developed by this interpretation of the Convention is certainly a clarification of a common European standard.

2. Article 6 in Civil Procedure

Much less frequent than complaints in criminal cases are applications complaining about violations of article 6[306] in civil suits. The Court has made it clear that article 6 implies a right of access to the courts in civil matters.[307] The issue arose because of restrictions in British prisons on a prisoner's access to a solicitor. More important is the decision of the Court in the *Airey Case* where it was held that there must be an effective right of access to legal services, which may be violated by the high cost of proceedings or by the absence of any scheme for legal aid.[308] Although article 6 on its face only provides for legal aid in criminal cases, this interpretation of the article will, in practice, lead to the introduction of some sort of legal aid in civil cases as well. Indeed, this seems to be the only way to guarantee effective access to the courts in more complicated civil matters. Ireland has introduced a legal aid scheme for family law matters as a consequence of this judgment.

The length of civil proceedings was the major issue in the *Buchholz Case.*[309] A procedure that had lasted almost five years was still found to be reasonable, given the rather unusual circumstances of the case, and especially given the manner in which the applicant's lawyer had handled it.[310] One may wonder whether some general standard concerning the reasonableness of the time a civil procedure may last might be arrived at by comparing the practices in the various national systems. The difficulty with such a comparison lies in that the procedural systems are very different, and the length of civil proceedings can clearly be influenced by these differences.

3. Article 6 and Administrative Procedures

Article 6 does not expressly mention administrative procedures. However, as soon as one accepts the fact that civil rights may be at issue in administrative procedures, then access to an independent tribunal is also guaranteed by this article against state authorities where they interfere with the civil rights of the citizen. The Court has held that the revocation of a license to practice medicine and to run a private clinic is an act which affects civil rights.[311] Therefore, arti-

[305] Amekrane v. U.K., App. No. 5961/72, Dec. of 11 Oct. 1973, 1973 Y.B. Eur. Conv. H.R. 356, Rep. of 19 July 1974 (Eur. Comm'n H.R., Strasbourg, 1974); Brückmann v. Fed. Rep. of Ger., App. No. 6242/73, Dec. of 27 May 1974, 1974 Y.B. Eur. Conv. H.R. 458, Rep. of 14 July 1976, 6 Eur. Comm'n H.R., Decs. & Reps. 57.

[306] *See supra* note 237.

[307] Golder Case, Judgment of 21 Feb. 1975, Series A: Vol. 18 (Pubs. of Eur. Ct. H.R., 1975).

[308] Airey Case, *supra* note 225.

[309] Judgment of 6 May 1981, Series A: Vol. 42 (Pubs. of Eur. Ct. H.R., 1981).

[310] *Id.* at p. 15.

[311] König Case, Judgment of 28 June 1978, Series A: Vol. 27 (Pubs. of Eur. Ct. H.R., 1978).

cle 6 is applicable, and judicial review must be available. The *König Case*, in which this decision was made, concerned the Federal Republic of Germany which has a rather perfectionist system of administrative courts. Not all Convention countries have introduced administrative tribunals. Whether the remedies existing in British law can be considered sufficient under this interpretation is open to question. For disciplinary proceedings, the Court has held in *Le Compte* that the same reasoning applied in *König* applies where a medical doctor is suspended from practice even for a limited period of only several weeks.[312]

If the Court develops this jurisprudence further, it may result in an important step towards legal integration in Europe as far as the protection of the individual against public authorities is concerned.

4. Protection of Privacy and Family Life

The protection of privacy against state interference is certainly one of the most difficult challenges for legal systems in our time. The European Convention contains in article 8 the fundamental guarantee according to which everyone has the right to respect for his private and family life, his home and his correspondence.[313]

Again, with respect to these liberal rights to privacy protected by the Convention, it is undoubted that the principle expressed in article 8 is accepted by the legal orders of the member countries. Legal integration, therefore, may come about in those areas where there exist differences in important details, or where new developments in protection have taken place. In several important decisions the Court has had to deal with article 8 in these contexts.

In the *Klass Case* the German system of secret surveillance under particular conditions for the safeguarding of national security was at issue. Since these measures are by their very nature secret, the Court held that the possibility of their being used to create a "menace of surveillance," striking at freedom of communication between users of the postal and telecommunication services, constituted an interference with the exercise of the right to respect for private and family life and for correspondence.[314] The Court then examined the particulars of the German system and found that the legislation concerned was a justified interference with the right of privacy in the sense of article 8, paragraph 2.

312 Case of Le Compte, Van Leuven and De Meyere, Judgment of 23 June 1981, Series A: Vol. 43 (Pubs. of Eur. Ct. H.R., 1981).

313 (1) Everyone has the right to respect for his private and family life, his home and his correspondence.

(2) There shall be no interference by a public authority with the exercise of this right except such as is in accordance with the law and is necessary in a democratic society in the interests of national security, public safety or the economic well-being of the country, for the prevention of disorder or crime, for the protection of health or morals, or for the protection of the rights and freedoms of others.

ECHR art. 8.

314 Case of Klass *et al., supra* note 242.

The Court stressed that there must exist adequate and effective guarantees against abuse of such a system, to keep the measures within the limits of article 8.[315] Later the Commission and Court decided an application against the United Kingdom raising similar questions. They found that no comparable legislation articulating the possible justifications for surveillance exists in Great Britain. Neither is there any specific system of legal safeguards to prevent abuse.[316] It would seem already that the application by itself and the fact that the applicant had relied on the decision in the *Klass Case* in arguing before the British court is a good example of the process of legal integration through the transnational protection of fundamental rights in Europe.[317]

The second decision of the Court where article 8 was the main issue concerned the protection of family life. The Court found that there may be positive obligations on the part of the State inherent in an effective "respect" for family life. In this case, Belgian legislation which required a formal recognition of an illegitimate child was held to be in violation of article 8, paragraph 1.[318] Here, it was the existence of a rather unusual law which gave the Court the possibility of confirming the uniform rule in this matter expressed by the old maxim: "*mater semper certa est.*"[319]

Article 8 has also led the Court and Commission into even more sensitive areas dealing with privacy and family life. In the *Dudgeon Case* the Court found, as had the Commission, that legislation in Northern Ireland declaring homosexual relations between adults in private to be a crime constituted a violation of article 8.[320] Problems of abortion have been before the Commission twice. In a German case it was argued that the restrictions imposed on the availability of abortion were an interference with a woman's right to respect for her private life. The Commission held that this was not the case since other legal interests were at stake which might properly be protected by legislation.[321] The Commission relied in this respect on the fact that all member countries of the Convention have adopted legal rules concerning restrictions on abortion.[322] The various reforms and debates on the issue were mentioned, but the Commission saw no indication that a specific solution of the problem was required by article 8.[323] The case was not brought before the Court and the Committee of Ministers decided that there had been no violation of the Convention.[324] In the second case, the Commission had to decide on an application by a potential

315 *Id.* at p. 23.
316 Malone Case, *supra* note 243.
317 Malone v. Comm'r of Police of the Metropolis (No.2), [1979] 2 All ER 620.
318 Marckx Case, *supra* note 206, at p. 15.
319 *Id.* at p. 19.
320 Dudgeon Case, Judgment of 22 Oct. 1981, Series A: Vol. 45 (Pubs. of Eur. Ct. H.R., 1982).
321 Brüggemann v. Fed. Rep. of Ger., App. No. 6959/75, Rep. of 12 July 1977, 10 Eur. Comm'n H.R., Dec's & Rep's 100, 115 ff.
322 *Id.* at 116 ff.
323 *Id.* at 117 ff.
324 *Id.* at 121 ff.

father who had not agreed to the abortion undergone by his wife, who had left her husband.[325] The Commission discussed at length the question whether the right to life under article 2 protects the unborn, but left the question open. It held that even if this were so, the restrictions placed upon this right by the British legislation protecting the life and the health of the mother were in line with the Convention's implied limitations.[326] The Commission relied generally on the existing national legislation on the termination of pregnancy.[327]

It would seem that in this rather sensitive area, legal integration cannot be a simple matter. But it is of importance that even here European standards may slowly be developing and that this development may be influenced by Convention procedures.

5. The Protection of Property

The guarantee of property rights contained in article 1[328] of the First Protocol to the European Convention may become one of the more interesting examples of legal integration. The Commission has referred to the Court several cases concerning of the United Kingdom which raise the issue of compensation in case of expropriation.[329] Early decisions of the Commission seemed to show that a right to compensation in case of expropriation could only be claimed by foreigners, because the reference to "general principles of international law" in article 1, paragraph 1 could apply only to them.[330] More recent decisions seem to leave this question open.[331]

It would be a most remarkable example of legal integration through the influence of the European Convention on Human Rights if the right to compensation in case of expropriation – which exists in most, but not in all Convention countries – were established as a fundamental right under the Convention. The European Court of Justice has not settled finally the question whether this right should be accepted as part of the common constitutional traditions of the

325 X v. U.K., App. No. 8416/79, Dec. of 13 May 1980, 19 EUR. COMM'N H.R. DECS. & REPS. 244.

326 *Id.* at 253.

327 *Id.* at 252.

328 (1) Every natural or legal person is entitled to the peaceful enjoyment of his possessions. No one shall be deprived of his possessions except in the public interest and subject to the conditions provided for by law and by the general principles of international law.

(2) The preceding provisions shall not, however, in any way impair the right of a State to enforce such laws as it deems necessary to control the use of property in accordance with the general interest or to secure the payment of taxes or other contributions or penalties.

ECHR, 1st Protocol, art. 1.

329 *See* Reports of the Commission of 7 Mar. 1984 (noted in 2/84 FORUM 16-17).

330 Gudmundsson v. Iceland, App. No. 511/59, Dec. of 20 Dec. 1960, Y.B. EUR. CONV. H.R. 394, 422 ff.

331 Company X v. Austria, App. No. 7987/77, Dec. of 13 Dec. 1979, 18 EUR. COMM'N H.R. DECS. & REPS. 31, 64.

Member States of the European Community, and therefore applied as a fundamental right in the Community.[332] The Advocate General, however, has taken the opportunity to state his opinion that the right to compensation must be seen as part of Community law.[333]

Article 1 of the First Protocol to the Convention, protecting the right to property, has been and will be a matter of discussion before the organs of the Convention also where the problem of expropriation does not arise. The Court had to deal with restrictions on the use of property in two cases. The first concerned the seizure, and later confiscation, of a book on the basis of provisions for the protection of morals. The Court had no difficulty accepting the confiscation as a measure "in accordance with the general interest."[334] For the confiscation question the Court relied on the common principle applied by the Contracting States, whereunder items whose use has been lawfully adjudged illicit and dangerous to the general interest must be forfeited with a view to destruction.[335] The Court made some rather important remarks in the judgment on the extent of its supervisory role under article 1 of the First Protocol. From the wording of paragraph 2, according to which these provisions shall not impair "the right of a State to enforce such laws as it deems necessary to control the use of property in accordance with the general interest," the Court concluded that this paragraph "sets the Contracting States up as sole judges of the 'necessity' for an interference."[336] The Court saw itself restricted to supervising the lawfulness and the purpose of the restriction in question. In the later *Marckx* judgment, the Court was more specific and stated that the Contracting States were set up as sole judges of the necessity "for such a law."[337] This seemed to imply that the concrete measure based on the law may well be reviewed for its conformity with the Convention guarantees.

F. The Impact of the Convention

It is certainly too early to draw any definite conclusions as to the potential of the European Convention on Human Rights to bring about some sort of legal integration by the protection of human rights and fundamental freedoms. Not yet thirty years have elapsed since Commission and Court have begun their work, and only in recent years has the jurisprudence grown considerably. But one may say that in some areas the impact of the Convention system has already been felt by the member countries. In some cases this has even led to changes in national legislation, in areas as diverse as the protection of freedom of expression (the *De Becker Case*, in Belgium), guarantees against overly long

[332] Case 44/79, Hauer v. Rheinland-Pfalz, [1979] ECR 3727, 3746.
[333] *Id.* at 3761.
[334] Handyside Case, *supra* note 262, at p. 29 ff.
[335] *Id.* at p. 30.
[336] *Id.* at p. 29.
[337] Marckx Case, *supra* note 206, at p. 28.

periods of detention on remand (as in Germany) and access to legal aid for family law matters (in Ireland).

It is also notable that courts of several member countries quote decisions of the European Court of Human Rights or the Commission when they apply the Convention as part of municipal law. This is true especially for Austria and Switzerland, but there are a number of other examples. Even in countries where the Convention is not internally applicable, as in Great Britain or in the Scandinavian States, courts have sometimes referred to the Convention and to the jurisprudence of the Convention organs. Since in many jurisdictions there exists a well-accepted principle according to which national law must be interpreted in line with international law, including treaties ratified by the State in question, such an approach should not be surprising.

At a time when a global discussion on the meaning of human rights and fundamental freedoms is taking place it would seem to be of increasing importance that the European States have developed a common system for the protection of human rights. This may influence practices in other States, but it may also bring about and articulate a common standard for those European States where such a standard does not yet exist.

G. The Interaction Between the European Convention on Human Rights and European Community Law

1. The Separate Legal Systems

The European Convention on Human Rights and the EC system are different legal orders. Altogether twenty-one states are adherents to the European Convention on Human Rights, while today only ten of those twenty-one belong to the European Community. Unlike former times, all the members of the EC are at the present time bound by the European Convention on Human Rights. This had not always been the case. France ratified the European Convention on Human Rights only in 1974. Until then, the two separate legal orders did not completely overlap. Today, the Convention system can be seen as the broader one, within which the EC system is completely covered.

The fact that the two legal orders are separate and distinct means that, legally speaking, there is no formal relationship between the two systems. Of course, in those signatory countries of the European Convention on Human Rights which have granted the Convention the force of municipal law, the same relationship that exists generally between Community law and municipal law will also apply for the relationship between Community law and the Convention, insofar as the latter is considered to be municipal law. This does not mean, however, that a formal connection exists between the two treaty systems.

On the other hand, it is very clear that both treaty systems are based on the same values. The EEC Treaty has created a legal order in which the principle of the rule of law occupies a very high position, as the European Court of Justice has frequently emphasized.[338] It is hardly surprising, therefore, that during recent years the issue of fundamental rights has become increasingly more important within the Community legal order. The issue had been underestimated at first, and there are consequently no provisions in the Treaty which concern human rights and fundamental freedoms.

However, the European Court of Justice has since recognized several general principles of law as binding rules for the Community organs – such as the principle of proportionality, the protection of individuals acting in good faith against retroactive changes of law or administrative policy, and the principle of legal certainty in general.[339] In a doctrinal development by now well established, the Court has recognized that the fundamental rights protected by the Constitutions of the Member States form an integral part of Community law.[340] The Court has also expressly stated that international treaties for the protection of human rights which are binding on the Member States of the Community are considered to furnish guidelines for the standards to be adopted in Community law.[341] In the famous decision *Hauer v. Rheinland-Pfalz* the Court analyzed for the first time a specific legal problem on the basis of article 1 of the First Protocol to the European Convention on Human Rights, which protects the right to property.

The question of the protection of fundamental rights in the Community system became especially serious when the Federal Constitutional Court of Germany held that Community law would be inapplicable within the Federal Republic if the law violated basic rights guaranteed by the Federal Constitution.[342] Although the holding of this decision has since been qualified, and would doubtless not be applicable today, it seems clear that, together with some more prudent hints in decisions of the Italian Constitutional Court, this surprising development inspired a considerable degree of activity by the Community at the time in the area of fundamental rights.[343] Not only have the

[338] The following is in part taken from my Memorandum, *Human Rights in International Law and Community Law*, published in HOUSE OF LORDS SELECT COMMITTEE ON THE EUROPEAN COMMUNITIES, HUMAN RIGHTS, 1979–80 SESSION, 71ST REPORT 73 ff (London, H.M.S.O., 1980).

[339] Case 10/56, Meroni v. High Authority, [1958] ECR 157; Case 1/73, Westzucker GmbH v. Einfuhr- und Vorratsstelle für Zucker, [1973] ECR 723; Case 78/74, Deuka v. Einfuhr- und Vorratsstelle für Getreide und Futtermittel, [1975] ECR 421.

[340] Case 29/69, Stauder v. City of Ulm, [1969] ECR 419; Case 11/70, Internationale Handelsgesellschaft mbH v. Einfuhr- und Vorratsstelle für Getreide und Futtermittel, [1970] ECR 1125; Case 36/75, Rutili v. Minister for the Interior, [1975] ECR 1219.

[341] Case 44/79, [1979] ECR 3727, 3746.

[342] Judgment of 29 May 1974, 37 BVerfGE 271 (1974); [1974] 2 C.M.L.R. 540. For further discussion of this case, its impact and aftermath, *see* Cappelletti & Golay, *supra* note 6, text accompanying note 298.

[343] *See* the Commission's clear statement, in COMMISSION OF THE EC, EIGHTH GENERAL REPORT ON THE ACTIVITIES OF THE EUROPEAN COMMUNITIES IN 1974, at 268–70 (Luxembourg, Office for Official Pubs. of EC, 1975).

political organs of the Community formally subscribed to the binding force of fundamental rights guarantees, including those protected by the European Convention of Human Rights,[344] but the Commission has also come forward with a Memorandum on the possible accession of the Communities to the European Convention on Human Rights and Fundamental Freedoms.[345] This Memorandum clearly poses the question of the extent to which the European Convention on Human Rights could be an efficient standard of protection within the Community system. This also raises the problem of the integrative value of the protection of fundamental rights within the Community.

2. The European Convention on Human Rights and the Community

Different opinions have been expressed as to the suitability of the Convention for application in the internal legal order of the Community. The Community has, of course, no jurisdiction to put people into jail or to use the police power to interfere with the right of assembly or of association. But this certainly is not the complete answer. With the further development of the Community, its activities may become more likely to touch upon areas protected by fundamental rights included in the Convention. Experience already shows that this may occur in a hitherto unexpected manner.

Not too long ago one could conceive of the applicability of article 1 of the First Protocol,[346] guaranteeing the right to the peaceful enjoyment of possessions, only in relation to Community regulations concerning cautionary payments or similar contributions. When the Administrative Court of Neustadt an der Weinstrasse referred a Community regulation prohibiting the planting of new vineyards to the Court of Justice,[347] it became suddenly apparent that Community law restricting the use of property had already developed much further than that. The restrictive clause in paragraph 2 of article 1 of the First Protocol[348] was to be of crucial relevance in judging the legality of this Community regulation.

This is by no means the only right guaranteed under the Convention which may be encroached upon by Community action. The Commission's Memorandum correctly stresses that articles 6, 7, 8, 10 and 11 of the Convention, articles 1 and 2 of the First Protocol, and articles of the Fourth Protocol relating to the free movement of persons are of possible relevance to the jurisdiction of the Community.[349] Article 8 of the European Convention establishes

[344] Joint Declaration by the European Parliament, the Council and the Commission of 5 Apr. 1977, OJ No. C 103, 27 Apr. 1977, p. 1.

[345] *Accession of the European Communities to the European Convention on Human Rights – Commission Memorandum of 4 April 1979*, Bull. EC, Supp. 2/79 [hereinafter cited as *Commission Memorandum*].

[346] *See supra* note 328.

[347] VerwG Neustadt a/d Weinstrasse, 2nd Chamber, Order of 14 Dec. 1978, 6 EuGRZ 341 (1979).

[348] *See supra* note 328.

[349] *See Commission Memorandum, supra* note 345, at p. 13; *see also supra* notes 237, 274, 313; *infra* note 380.

that everyone has the right to respect for his private and family life, for his home and his correspondence. This guarantee has been held also to apply if a person has been expelled or extradited and members of his or her family are thereby affected.[350] That does not mean that the expulsion or extradition becomes illegal, but rather that it must be justified as a legitimate interference under paragraph 2 of article 8.[351] Community legislation concerning the rights of migrant workers and their families may in theory raise problems under article 8 of the Convention.[352] The application of such legislation by Member States may be even more likely to come into conflict with article 8 in specific cases.[353]

The right to education protected by article 2 of the First Protocol could have been considered in several cases which have come before the Court of Justice.[354] The *Prais* case is an example which shows that even the freedom of religion may be involved in some matters within the Community jurisdiction.[355] These different cases show that the Commission is correct in stressing the relevance of the Convention provisions for Community law.[356]

People sometimes wonder about the necessity of making the restrictive clauses in the Convention more specifically applicable to the Community system. The Community is, of course, not a state. But if one accepts that the Convention may be applied to protect people against acts of the Community, then it seems likely that the restrictive clauses must work in favor of the Community *mutatis mutandis* in the same way as for a state.[357] Whether the Community formally becomes a member of the Convention or not, an amendment of the restrictive clauses should not be seen as being really essential.[358] True, some of the alternatives in the restrictive clauses may be less likely to be invoked by the Community. State security will probably come into consideration as a basis for interference only in special cases, because so far the Community has not generally been involved in the area of state security. But within the jurisdiction of Euratom cases of that sort would not be exceptional.[359] The economic well-being of the country, the protection of health and the protection of the rights and freedom of others, all of which are mentioned as legitimate reasons for restric-

[350] *Cf.* X v. Fed. Rep. of Ger., App. No. 8041/77, Dec. of 15 Dec. 1977, 12 EUR. COMM'N H.R. DECS. & REPS. 197, with further references.

[351] *Id.*

[352] Frowein, *Die Europäische Menschenrechtskonvention und das Europäische Gemeinschaftsrecht,* in DIE GRUNDRECHTE IN DER EUROPÄISCHEN GEMEINSCHAFT 47, 53 ff (J. Frowein, M. Hilf & K. Meessen eds., Nomos, Baden-Baden, 1978).

[353] *Id.*

[354] *Id.* at p. 54 ff. *See, e.g.,* Case 9/74, Casagrande v. Landeshauptstadt München, [1974] ECR 773.

[355] Case 130/75, Prais v. Council, [1976] ECR 1589.

[356] *See Commission Memorandum, supra* note 345, at p. 12 ff.

[357] This could be expressly stated in one article of the necessary Protocol to the Convention providing for the accession of the EC.

[358] *See Commission Memorandum, supra* note 345, at p. 13 ff.

[359] Euratom Treaty art. 24 ff.

tions on freedoms in the Convention, can be the basis for Community action much as they are for state action.

When discussing a possible relationship between Community law and the European Convention on Human Rights, it seems necessary to take into account a different sort of link between the two legal orders which already exists. The Convention may currently be invoked against states acting on the basis of Community law or in the sphere of Community activities. In cases of that sort the Convention can furnish additional protections for the individual. The European Commission of Human Rights has declared admissible the application of an EC "citizen" who claims to have had no court remedy against the deprivation of liberty pending deportation from the U.K. on the basis of both British and Community law.[360] Community law does not guarantee access to a court in this case, but article 5, paragraph 4 of the Convention does.[361] Other cases in which the Convention had to be applied to Community acitivities arose in conjunction with the European elections in June 1979. Applications were brought in this instance against the United Kingdom and Belgium. Applicants from Northern Ireland claimed that the U.K. had violated their rights under article 3 of the First Protocol because a different electoral system was to be applied in Northern Ireland than in the rest of the U.K.[362] Article 3 guarantees the right to free elections at reasonable intervals by secret ballot, under conditions which will ensure the free expression of the opinion of the people in the choice of the legislature. The European Commission of Human Rights rejected the application but did not rule out the applicability of article 3, First Protocol, to the European Parliament.[363] Cases against Belgium were of a similar nature, with the applicants claiming that their right under article 3 was violated because they were foreigners in Belgium who were not entitled to vote, or Belgians living in a foreign country who also had no possibility of voting in Belgium or in the foreign country. The applications were likewise rejected without excluding the applicability of article 3, First Protocol, to the European Parliament.[364]

These examples again show that, already today, there are more links between the legal orders of the Community and the European Convention on Human Rights than may be apparent at first glance.

3. The Jurisdiction of Convention Organs Over the Community at Present

In the only case brought before the European Commission of Human Rights which was directed against one of the three Communities, (in this case the Coal

[360] Caprino v. U.K., App. No. 6871/75, Dec. of 3 Mar. 1978, 12 EUR. COMM'N H.R., DECS. & REPS. 14.

[361] *See supra* note 226.

[362] Lindsay *et al.* v. U.K., App. No. 8364/78, Dec. of 8 Mar. 1979, 15 EUR. COMM'N H.R., DECS. & REPS. 247.

[363] *Id.*

[364] Alliance des Belges de la Communauté Européenne v. Belgium, App. No. 8612/79, Dec. of 10 May 1979, 15 EUR. COMM'N H.R., DECS. & REPS. 259.

and Steel Community), the Commission found that it had no jurisdiction.[365] Inasmuch as the application was directed against only the European Coal and Steel Community, this result could hardly be surprising. If Alkema criticizes the statement made by the European Commission on Human Rights in its rejection of the petition – that the act in question concerned only the internal organization of the European Community – his criticism may be due to a misunderstanding.[366] He stresses that the composition of the Consultative Committee affected private professional organizations and their functioning as well. This is certainly correct. But this is no argument against the rationale of the Commission. When reference was made in the Commission opinion to the internal organization of the Community, the issue was clearly the competence of the Community to provide a proper system of Consultative Committees within the limits of the Treaty.[367] In this area only the Community can have jurisdiction over the subject matter. That must mean – and this is the sense of the statement in the Commission's decision – that there are no other legal subjects whose direct responsibility for the acts in question could be invoked. But the application in this case was also directed against the Member States of the Community jointly, and against each of the Member States individually. The first of these alternatives was rejected because the Member States "jointly" are nothing else but the Council.[368] One may add here also that, since France had not recognized the right of individual application under article 25 of the European Convention on Human Rights, an application against all Member States was bound to fail.

As for the application directed against the Member States individually, the Commission left open the question if, under certain conditions, the individual responsibility of a Member State could be engaged by an act of the Community.[369] Since the applicant in question was a French trade union, the Commission had to look first to France. But here the Commission had no competence, because of France's refusal to recognize the right of individual application. As for the other Member States, the Commission decided that they could not be found responsible. Alkema criticizes this finding by comparing the case with an earlier one, concerning the Allied prison at Spandau, in Berlin.[370] He may not have recalled, however, that the position of France in this case made any other decision virtually impossible. France ratified the European Convention on Human Rights only long after the treaty establishing the European Coal and

[365] Confédération Française Démocratique du Travail (CFDT) v. EC, alternatively: their Member States, (a) jointly and (b) severally, App. No. 8030/77, Dec. of 10 July 1978, 13 Eur. Comm'n H.R., Decs. & Reps. 231.

[366] E.A. Alkema, The EC and the European Convention of Human Rights – Immunity and Impunity for the Community?, p. 2 (Colloquium paper presented at the British Institute of International and Comparative Law, London, June 21–23, 1979).

[367] ECSC Treaty art. 18.

[368] *CFDT v. EC, et al., supra* note 365, at 235.

[369] *Id.* at 236.

[370] Alkema, *supra* note 366, at p. 3 ff.

Steel Community. Therefore, in the case of France, there could be no question of having transferred powers to the Community which in this respect were already subject to the obligations of the Convention. Now, could one really argue that the other Member States of the Convention, and the Community itself are under an obligation to guarantee the compatibility of acts of the Community with the Convention in areas where the state most directly concerned would not itself be so bound? May one say that this would bring the matter under the jurisdiction of the other Member States in the sense of article 1 of the European Convention on Human Rights?

In the case concerning the Spandau prison, the Commission had held that the joint authority of the Four Powers for the prison could not be divided up into four separate jurisdictions, and therefore the acts in question were not within the sole jurisdiction of the U.K.[371] This clearly must also be true for the Community. But the Commission added one very important sentence to its opinion in the Spandau prison case. It expressed the opinion that the conclusion of an agreement such as the one in question would raise a justiciable issue if entered into after the ratification of the Convention by the State against which the application was brought.[372] This principle was certainly not overruled by the decision concerning the Coal and Steel Community.[373] But again, for France the issue could not arise, and the other Member States were, at least, fairly removed from the matter concerning the French trade union.

One may conclude that the European Community is, at present, not subject to the control of the supervisory organs set up by the European Convention on Human Rights. The responsibility of individual Member States under the Convention for acts of the European Community could be engaged only in rather exceptional cases. It does not seem likely that this gap could be bridged by the jurisprudence of the European Commission of Human Rights.

4. Accession of the Community to the Convention and Alternatives

The Memorandum drafted by the Commission of the European Communities clearly shows that considerable difficulties will have to be overcome before an accession of the Community to the Convention can take place.[374] The process will take quite some time. One may ask, therefore, what the various alternatives are.

The Community could go one step further than the position established by the common declaration of 5 April 1977.[375] It could adopt a Community regulation incorporating the substantive articles of the European Convention on Human Rights into Community law. This regulation would not have any

371 Hess v. U.K., App. No. 6231/73, Dec. of 28 May 1975, 2 Eur. Comm'n H.R., Decs. & Reps. 72–74.

372 *Id.* at p. 74.

373 The last paragraphs of the decision expressly leave open the question under which circumstances the individual responsibility of the Member States could be engaged.

374 *Commission Memorandum, supra* note 345, at p. 17 ff.

375 *See supra* note 344.

higher rank than a normal regulation under EEC Treaty article 189 and the comparable provisions in the other Community Treaties. But this fact would not preclude review of Community legislation on the basis of this internal Bill of Rights. The Court of Justice could, and one may add should, interpret later regulations on the basis of the rights mentioned in the Convention. But it should also declare regulations invalid if they contradict those existing general principles which would be restated in this form (as a Community regulation) only for the sake of clarity. The binding force of such a regulation, given the existing jurisprudence of the Court, could not be in doubt.[376]

Another alternative would be to draft a new catalogue of fundamental rights for the Community. It seems likely that the European Parliament will endeavor to elaborate such a catalogue in any case, even if a process of accession of the Community to the Convention should begin.[377] One may reasonably ask whether a meaningful catalogue of fundamental rights is likely to be acceptable to all those who would be involved in this process today. But this is a political question which cannot be investigated in this context.

5. The Problem of Social Rights

One problem should be discussed, however, which may influence the debate on the question of a new catalogue of fundamental rights. This is the question of social rights. It is true that the European Convention on Human Rights protects mainly what may be called traditional liberal rights. The European Social Charter is concerned with the social dimension of human rights and therefore refers to rights which very often have the character of a program for economic and social policy.[378] It is not surprising that the promulgation of the Social Charter was not accompanied by the introduction of a system of judicial protection similar to that of the European Convention on Human Rights. The character of the social rights laid down by the Social Charter lends itself much less readily to this sort of judicial protection. A Committee of Independent Experts may discuss the implementation of the Social Charter, but cannot decide specific cases.[379]

But it is not true that the European Convention on Human Rights is completely silent on the social dimension of human rights. Article 11 guarantees freedom of association, "including the right to form and to join trade unions for the protection of ... [workers'] interests."[380] The European Court of Human

[376] The problem of how best to "entrench" the ECHR in the Community legal system raises an interesting parallel to the status of EC law in the U.K. *Cf.* Cappelletti & Golay, *supra* note 6, at § V.A.2.b.

[377] European Parliament Resolution of 27 Apr. 1979, OJ No. C 127, 21 May 1979, p. 69.

[378] European Social Charter of 18 Oct. 1961, published in [1961] EUR. Y.B./ANNUAIRE EUROPÉEN 247 (The Hague, Martinus Nijhoff, 1962).

[379] European Social Charter art. 25.

[380] (1) Everyone has the right to freedom of peaceful assembly and to freedom of association with others, including the right to form and to join trade unions for the protection of his interests.

Rights has held that article 11 implies the right of trade unions to make their voice heard by employers in a procedure of collective bargaining.[381] The Court has declared as did the Commission, that article 11 was violated where closed-shop agreements had interfered with the applicants' right to join trade unions of their choice.[382] Another question which may show the relationship of the Convention to social rights is that of article 1 of the First Protocol.[383] The Commission has held in several cases that social security rights may, under certain circumstances, come under the protection made applicable to "possessions" by this article.[384] The making of compulsory contributions to a pension fund may, according to this holding, create a property right in a portion of such fund. In the *Müller Case,* however, the Commission adopted a cautious position as to the scope of such a right. In the view of the Commission, article 1 of the First Protocol guarantees not a right to the payment of a specific sum of money, but only the right to participate in and to derive benefit from the system.[385] Any other solution would, of course, make it impossible to run a social security system, which is by its very nature influenced by economic development in general. Social security has been called a "contract between the generations," which means, of course, that you do not necessarily get back what you have paid earlier, but only a portion of what people earn today.

One may also ask whether articles 3 and 8[386] of the Convention do not include a guarantee of a minimum standard of social security. The European Court of Human Rights has already found that article 8 creates obligations for the member countries to take positive action for the protection of family life.[387] It may well be that a minimum right to social security flows as a natural consequence from the guarantee that no one shall be subjected to inhuman treatment. The old liberal assumption according to which the state has no obligation to protect the individual against the consequences of his own economic fail-

> (2) No restrictions shall be placed on the exercise of these rights other than such as are prescribed by law and are necessary in a democratic society in the interests of national security or public safety, for the prevention of disorder or crime, for the protection of health or morals or for the protection of the rights and freedoms of others. This Article shall not prevent the imposition of lawful restrictions on the exercise of these rights by members of the armed forces, of the police or of the administration of the State.

ECHR art. 11.

381 Swedish Engine Drivers' Union Case, Judgment of 6 Feb. 1976, Series A: Vol. 20 (Pubs. of Eur. Ct. H.R., 1976).

382 Young and James v. U.K., App. No. 7601/76, Dec. of 11 July 1977, 9 EUR. COMM'N H.R., DECS. & REPS. 126; Webster v. U.K., App. No. 7806/77, Dec. of 3 Mar. 1978, 12 EUR. COMM'N H.R., DECS. & REPS. 168; Case of Young, James and Webster, Judgment of 13 Aug. 1981, Series A: Vol. 44 (Pubs. of Eur. Ct. H.R., 1981).

383 *See supra* note 328.

384 *See, e.g.,* Müller v. Austria, App. No. 5849/72, Rep. of 1 Oct. 1975, p. 10 (Eur. Comm'n H.R., Strasbourg, 1976).

385 *Id.*

386 *See supra* notes 301 and 313.

387 Marckx Case, *supra* note 206, at p. 10.

ure, is clearly no longer valid. Letting people starve in the streets is as inhuman a treatment as torture or murder. All European states recognize the obligation to extend minimum social protection to their citizens and to those living within their borders. But it seems important to realize that the Convention may also have an impact on these matters.

This social dimension of the European Convention on Human Rights would acquire special importance if the Community should join the Convention. Since it will be difficult to draft anew a meaningful catalogue of social rights for the Community, one should not underestimate this aspect of the European Convention.

6. The Accession of the Community and Internal Applicability of the Convention

It is well known that the European Convention on Human Rights is internally applicable only in those Member States which have transformed it into municipal law, or in those which have constitutional provisions mandating the internal application of treaties.[388] Unfortunately, the Convention is not applicable as internal law in Britain, Ireland and Denmark.[389] Were the Community to become a party to the Convention, difficulties might arise in this respect. As soon as all organs of the three Communities were formally bound by the Convention, this treaty would be internally applicable in the system of Community law.[390] The Court of Justice would then have the task of interpreting the Convention in the framework of the legal order of the Community. The European Commission and Court of Human Rights would exercise their supervisory functions over the Court of Justice just as they would for a state.[391]

One special problem could arise. The municipal courts of those Member States where the Convention is not internally applicable would be required to apply it wherever they made a decision on the basis of Community law. In theory, the distinction is quite clear, and therefore should not pose any difficulties for the courts. Only where a question of Community law was at issue would they be under an obligation to apply the European Convention on Human Rights directly. But undoubtedly lawyers in countries where the Convention is not otherwise applied by national courts might feel at a certain disadvantage. The best solution would of course be to make the Convention internally applicable by itself in those states.[392] Hopefully a fresh light will be shed on this

[388] This does not prevent judges from referring to the ECHR when they interpret municipal law. This happens in Britain. *See* Mann, *Britain's Bill of Rights,* 94 L.Q.R. 512 (1978).

[389] This is also true for Norway, Sweden, Malta, and Cyprus, countries which are not members of the EC but are signatories of the ECHR.

[390] *See Commission Memorandum, supra* note 345, at p. 20.

[391] The Commission stresses the necessity of accepting the right of individual application; *see Commission Memorandum, supra* note 345, at p. 16.

[392] *See* Mann, *supra* note 388, at note 57.

problem following the current activities on the relationship between the Community and the Convention. One should not overlook the fact that the European Court of Human Rights has expressly found that the Convention by its very nature requires internal application. The Court interpreted the change in the wording of article 1 from the draft "undertake to secure" to the final "shall secure" (in the French text, from "*s'engagent à reconnaître*" to "*reconnaissent*") as an indication that the drafters wished to make clear that the rights should be "directly secured" to anyone within the jurisdiction of the Contracting States. But the Court added one very significant sentence: "That intention finds a particularly faithful reflection in those instances where the Convention has been incorporated into domestic law."[393] It is difficult to comprehend why States that apply Community law internally should feel unable to make the same decision for the European Convention on Human Rights. This may take some time. One may hope, however, that the eventual accession of the Community to the Convention will not be postponed until this internal constitutional problem of some Community Member States has been solved.

7. Only Transformation?

The formal accession of the EC to the Convention poses difficult technical problems. Besides the complicated ratification procedure it would be necessary to amend the European Convention as far as the composition of its organs, the Commission and the Court, is concerned. It may well be that these difficulties will prove to be insurmountable. It is therefore necessary to investigate what alternatives may exist to formal accession.

One possibility would be the transformation of the substantive guarantees in the European Convention on Human Rights into Community law. This could be done by means of a regulation based on EEC Treaty article 235. This would give the European Court's use of the Convention a clear legal basis. It would seem that such a procedure could in fact lead to the establishment of the Convention provisions at a higher rank in EC law. Although a regulation promulgated under article 235 in theory has only the rank of a normal regulation, it should not be difficult for the Court to establish a principle according to which such a regulation could not be derogated from except by a clearly expressed provision of a new regulation.

One may of course still pose the question whether it is at all necessary to improve the position of fundamental rights in the Community legal system.

The real advantage of a Bill of Rights for the constitutional development of a country may be seen in two respects. A constitutional guarantee of fundamental rights is first of all a protection of the individual against the legislature. This will in most cases not be an important feature, because usually the legislature would only interfere with fundamental rights in a premeditated way. Today, however, the typical interference with fundamental rights may be

393 Case of Ireland v. U.K., Judgment of 18 Jan. 1978, Series A: Vol. 25, p. 91 (Pubs. of Eur. Ct. H.R., 1978).

a wholly unforeseen consequence of hasty legislation. Here, judicial review on the basis of a Bill of Rights can become an efficient protection of the individual. This may be even more true in the Community legal order, where legislation is not always discussed publicly and may be of a very technical character.

The second great advantage of a Bill of Rights seems to be its function of helping the law keep pace with social developments. The European Court of Human Rights has stressed that the law must be able to keep pace with changing circumstances. The general principles contained in Bills of Rights are particularly well suited for the translation of social developments into the legal sphere. In Community law these general standards have already proved to be very effective. For reasons developed earlier, one may hope that fresh discussion on the question of a Bill of Rights for Britain will be a consequence of the Community's activities with regard to the possibility of Community accession to the European Convention on Human Rights.

The potential of the Convention as a tool for integration – in fact, the potential for integration by making the substantive provisions of the European Convention on Human Rights directly applicable to the Community – should not be underestimated. Bills of Rights influence considerably the minds of people. It would give the European Community a new legitimacy to be formally connected to the European Convention on Human Rights, even if this were to be accomplished only by an act of Community legislation. In addition, it should not be forgotten that the real goal of European integration remains a far wider one, compared to the limited membership of the Community. Switzerland and Austria will probably never become members of the Community. They should, however, be seen as important parts of Europe for the important goal of preserving European identity. Integration between the wider circle of Convention countries and the smaller circle of Community countries would only be strengthened by some sort of link of the Communities to the Convention.

V. Conclusion

To a great degree, the introduction to this study is also its conclusion. The body of the paper offers two relatively detailed accounts of specific developments first in American constitutional law on human rights, and second in a more general survey of the European materials in order to support the general propositions put forward in the Introduction. Nevertheless, some brief concluding remarks seem in order.

Most generally, we must conclude that the tempo of judicial development of the law of fundamental human rights remains something of a mystery. The United States Supreme Court was slow to move toward trans-state or national standards for human rights law, and particularly slow where it confronted highly-developed bodies of state law. In those areas where the states had developed an extensive jurisprudence, the Court has tended to preserve very large areas of state autonomy. The European Court of Human Rights has shown similar tendencies. When a trans-state or transnational court embarks on a period of enunciating trans-state or transnational rights, it is often difficult to explain the causes of the particular outbreak. Such episodes fall at the intersection of two potential channels of political sentiment, one concerned with integration per se and the other concerned a priori with human rights. In U.S. history it is clear that, in a number of instances, standards of national rights were promoted by judicial or extra-judicial forces that had no particular concern for trans-state legal integration, but very great concern for the particular human rights involved. Similar tendencies can be seen in Europe, particularly in the case of U.K. litigation before the European Commission and Court of Human Rights. Human rights advocates are likely to enter whatever forum they can find that appears to give them some chance of success. In the process they may influence structures and theories of federalism and/or integration without themselves caring one way or the other about legal or political integration.

We have seen that in both the United States and Europe, however, trans-state and transnational human rights law is not always the product of "forum shopping" by human rights groups or lawyers. In the right-to-counsel and exclusionary rule cases in the United States, the Supreme Court seemed to reach out without any particular prodding from specialized groups to promote a national standard of rights. It may well be that even in *Gitlow*, the Justices in the majority were more motivated by their own desires to supersede state regulation of speech of business corporations than they were by the pleas of the A.C.L.U.

Thus not only the push of litigation, but also the pull of their own commitments either to rights, or to integration, or both, may move the judges of high courts to the pronouncement of trans-state or transnational standards of rights. It then follows that the tempo of integration will in part be determined by the accident of which judges, with what kinds of human rights temperaments and views on legal integration, are appointed to these high courts.

Even an active court can, of course, maintain a great deal of integrational "slack," allowing considerable local variation while yet setting trans-state or transnational standards. Such general doctrines as the "margin of appreciation" and "deference to state legislatures," and such particular doctrines as "ad hoc balancing" in freedom of speech and "fundamental fairness" and "voluntariness" in rights-of-the-accused cases, preserve a considerable degree of discretion for the member states. They do so, however, at the cost of creating considerable uncertainty and vagueness in the extent of legal protections for human rights. Tighter standards such as the "public forum" doctrine, the bans on content-based discrimination and on prior restraint, the absolute right to counsel in criminal cases, and the exclusionary rule, all grant higher, because more precise, protection to human rights, but cut deeply into local "margins of appreciation." It is this basic tension, experienced in both Europe and the U.S., that injects a basically integrationist theme into the human rights movement. To the extent that human rights groups, lawyers and judges press a trans-state or transnational court to impose greater protections for human rights, they become proponents of increased legal integration and of decreased margins of appreciation, at least at the "low end."

By the "low end" we mean the establishment of *minimum standards.* Both the European and the U.S. experiences suggest that a high court can impose more or less rigid minimum standards for human rights on the constituent states without limiting their discretion to provide higher standards if they wish to. "Constitutional," trans-state courts may possess a peculiar advantage in the setting of minimum standards that do not inhibit the creation of higher standards by others. Where a national legislature sets minimum standards by statute, they are also likely to become maximum standards – they are, after all, the law of the nation. Where a transnational, constitutional court sets a minimum standard by case decision, that standard becomes *a* law of *a* jurisdiction. There is no reason why the nation should not supplement such a law with its own higher standards for the protection of fundamental rights.

Yet the worry persists that negative consequences may still occur from this approach. A transnational, trans-state court, rightly concerned about excessively narrowing the margin of appreciation, may set rather modest human rights standards which it fully intends to be minimum standards. Yet individual state and national regimes and anti-human rights interests may then point to the minimum standards set by the highly esteemed court as the definition of what the full standards ought to be. In federal or quasi-federal systems, it is often difficult as a practical matter to get the citizens of a particular state to understand the difference between a federal court announcing a minimum standard out of deference to differences in the member states, and a high court announcing a complete standard of justice. The renewed enthusiasm for the death penalty in many states of the United States after the Supreme Court set minimum protections in this area is a clear example of the problem.

In assessing the applicability of this and other U.S. experiences to European problems, some similarities and differences between the European and the American situation should again be underlined.

It might be argued that the sense of trans-state political and moral community came first in the U.S., and the concern for nationalizing standards of human rights came afterward. It might be more accurate to say, however, that the sense of national community and the concern for human rights existed side by side from the very beginning, but that until about the 1930's the states were considered to be adequate guarantors of human rights. It would be far too simple to say that every American wanted every other American eventually to share in the same human rights because, and only because, every American saw every other American as a citizen of the same political community. Human rights sentiment in the U.S., as in Europe, has always had a universalist tinge. Both the American and the European experiences suggest that a shared concern for human rights may be a factor *contributing* to a sense of shared political community, as well as an *effect* of a sense of shared political community. We have seen that an important factor in some aspects of U.S. integration has been that the states and the Federal Government were often simultaneously building laws on the basis of common experiences and common beliefs. In Europe, the Convention on Human Rights and the human rights provisions of a number of post-war constitutions have appeared at the same time as products of a Europe-wide experience with governments that destroyed human rights. The existence of shared concerns and resulting simultaneous calls to action seem to be part of both U.S. and European human rights developments.

Of course we must not overemphasize these shared beliefs and concerns. The United States exhibits a far more integrated legal culture than Europe. All American lawyers speak the same language and share a common legal tradition, in spite of substantial variances in law from state to state. A European court experiences translation problems in the most literal sense that no U.S. court faces. Without minimizing these language barriers, however, we must point to translation problems in a broader sense as common to the U.S. Supreme Court and the various transnational European courts, particularly in the area of human rights. We have pointed out that ignorance of, and both overt and covert resistance to, Supreme Court rulings have been widespread in local criminal courts in the United States. Indeed, that very resistance has been part of the integrationist dynamic. The Supreme Court has been pushed to set more absolute, nationally uniform rules in part because of the difficulty it experienced in supervising local courts when it left them broad discretion.

Finally, we wish to return to the most obvious differences in this area between Europe and the United States. The status enjoyed by the Constitution of the United States is fundamentally different from that enjoyed by the European Convention on Human Rights, the former being both a national constitution and the supreme law of the land, and the latter simply a treaty within the domain of public international law. The U.S. Supreme Court and the Strasbourg and Luxembourg courts also enjoy fundamentally different institutional statuses, the former as one of the three coequal branches of a federal nation-state, and the latter two embedded in unique transnational governing arrangements.

We have seen, for instance, that the Supreme Court took the step of applying first amendment free speech rights against the states on the basis of having exercised a supervisory role, long regarded as legitimate, over the states in the area of fourteenth amendment property rights. In short, integration in the field of human rights was imposed by the Court as part of a movement of trans-state economic integration, backed by powerful trans-state political and economic forces. Of course, the Supreme Court's innovations in the jurisprudence of rights of accused persons came long after it had largely withdrawn its supervision of state regulation of business. Nonetheless, it embarked on this supervision of state criminal law against the doctrinal background of over a hundred-year history of imposing national standards on the states in a variety of other areas.

The European Court of Human Rights enjoys no such long history of legitimate intervention in the affairs of its member countries. Its legal foundation is a treaty rather than a constitution with a supremacy clause. While the point cannot be proven by direct evidence, there seems to be little doubt that, at least in their early years, both Commission and Court were inclined to be cautious in their pronouncements, given the existence of periodic renewal provisions that allowed member countries to withdraw from the Convention. The existence of two courts, one for human rights and one for essentially economic matters, may also reduce the judicial power in Europe as compared to the United States. In Europe, the judicial legitimacy acquired by judges who have done essential work in attaining a desired level of economic integration cannot readily be "borrowed" by judges who seek transnational human rights standards. They are not the same judges. No doubt this is why so many observers are interested in the hints of a human rights jurisprudence offered by the Court of the European Communities. The Court of Justice may have the potential to emulate the U.S. Supreme Court to some degree, by using a highly successful record of judicial activity in the realm of economic integration as a base of legitimacy for a more active judicial role in the establishment of transnational human rights. It is even more speculative, however, to propose that the successes of the Court of Justice may instill in European legal culture such a high level of legitimacy for transnational judicial activism that this legitimacy will "rub off" onto the Court of Human Rights. In any event, the tempo of activity undertaken by the Commission and the Court of Human Rights has increased markedly in recent years. The significance of the temporary membership arrangements subject to renewal has decreased as continuity of membership in the Convention has been sustained over time. The activities of both European Courts in human rights areas suggest that, over time, their role in the process of the vindication of human rights is likely to become more, rather than less like that played by the U.S. Supreme Court in the course of United States history.

Legal Education and Legal Integration: European Hopes and American Experience

LAWRENCE M. FRIEDMAN* and GUNTHER TEUBNER**

I. Introduction

Law is dependent on politics, and, thus, legal unification, in the strict sense, is tied up with the progress of political unification. This point seems obvious, even trivial, but the consequences are not trivial at all. In Europe today the ideal of political unification is dim, and progress has slowed down to a crawl. It is easy to point the finger of blame at power politics or regionalism and to call for a stronger commitment to European unity, backed up by political power. But the problems run deeper. Technology, science, economics, communications and culture are all much less tied to regional and national boundaries than politics; and indeed the life-blood of modern politics – democratic principles, participation, and legitimacy – depends on these boundaries.[1] The so-called functional approach to political integration,[2] which assumes a European polity as a more or less necessary spill-over from economic and technological integration, has been, alas, refuted by harsh reality.[3] If legal integration really does depend on political integration, then the chances for legal unification in Europe are slender.

But does legal unification depend so utterly on politics? Is there another way? Some jurists feel that there is. They look to the legal profession and legal science as ways to promote legal unity, independent of political integration. Many

* Marion Rice Kirkwood Professor of Law, Stanford University, Stanford, Cal.
** Professor of Law, University of Bremen, European University Institute, Florence.

1 On the "backwardness of politics" (and law) in general, *see* Luhmann, *Die Weltgesellschaft*, 57 ARSP 1 (1971); N. LUHMANN, RECHTSSOZIOLOGIE 333 ff (Reinbek, Rowohlt, 1972).

2 For a brief account *see* Behrens, *Integrationstheorie*, 45 RABELSZ 8 (1981); *see also* Elazar & Greilsammer, *The Federal Democracy: The U.S.A. and Europe Compared – A Political Science Perspective, supra* this vol., Bk. 1, at § II.A.3.b.

3 *See generally* Häckel, *Neue Entwicklungen von Integrationstheorien*, [79-3] INTEGRATION 86 (1979).

comparative lawyers nourish hopes for a revitalized *jus commune.*[4] These hopes are based, in the end, on the idea of a legal profession which transcends national boundaries in its training, techniques and ideology.[5] In addition they invoke the idea of a legal science based on principles which lay claim to universal validity and thus are international almost by definition. Obviously, it is in the universities that scientific and professional training flourish. Thus we find there a bubbling spring of legal unification, which can transcend political boundaries. Hence our question takes on special importance: Can legal education help promote European integration – and should it? What do we know about the possible integrating functions of legal education? Are there aspects of legal education which are universalistic enough to serve as tools of international integration?

René David, in an argument for legal unification, identified a number of "obstacles" to the process. Interestingly enough, these obstacles are less political, legal and institutional, than social and educational: They lie in the attitudes, orientations and knowledge of legal professionals.[6] "The spirit of routine," he argues, is the first and main obstacle to the international unification of law. "People are used to certain ways of thinking, to certain rules, and are afraid of any change which attacks their peace of mind and necessitates alterations of their patterns of behavior."[7] In the second place, the ideology of lawyers binds them to pure exegesis of legislation (or, he adds, "of case law"); this hinders needed reform and renovation.[8] Thirdly, David accuses lawyers of inability (or unwillingness?) to come to grips with the "diversity of nations with their divergent economic, social and political structures, and divergent ideas of justice."[9] Still another obstacle to unification lies in the variety of techniques lawyers learn to use in handling their national legal traditions.[10] The "conceptual approach" to law blinds lawyers to the possibility of a "functional" approach which would reduce diversity, lead them to see commonalities in legal problems and teach them to use common techniques for coping with these problems.

If these obstacles are real, then reform of legal education might indeed be a crucial step toward unification. David's account suggests some counterbalancing goals for legal education: (1) It could try to train students to be more flexible in dealing with legal problems; (2) it could train lawyers in problem-ori-

[4] *See, e.g.,* David, *The International Unification of Private Law,* II INT'L ENC. COMP. L., ch.5, at 3, 4 (1969); 1 K. ZWEIGERT & H. KÖTZ, EINFÜHRUNG IN DIE RECHTSVERGLEICHUNG AUF DEM GEBIETE DES PRIVATRECHTS § 1 (Tübingen, Mohr (Siebeck), 1971); Kötz, *Gemeineuropäisches Zivilrecht,* in FESTSCHRIFT FÜR KONRAD ZWEIGERT 481, 481–500 (H. Bernstein, U. Drobnig & H. Kötz eds., Tübingen, Mohr (Siebeck), 1981).

[5] *See* Puttfarken, *Droit commun législatif und die Einheit der Profession: Eine ketzerische Reflexion zur Rechtsvereinheitlichung,* 45 RABELSZ 91 (1981).

[6] *See* David, *supra* note 4, at 23 ff.

[7] *Id.* at 33.

[8] *Id.* at 24.

[9] *Id.* at 27.

[10] *Id.* at 30 ff.

ented thinking, weaning them away from pure exegesis; (3) it could train lawyers to be sensitive to legal pluralism, to confront different social and economic national orders; and, (4) it could train them to think about legal methods which avoid the fallacies of conceptualism. Remarks such as David's can serve as guidelines, but we hope to go beyond them in suggesting ways in which legal education can play an integrative role.

In this paper we will examine, from a social, legal and historical standpoint, the question of legal education and integration. Basically, in Europe an "integrationist" legal education could work on three levels. The first would be that of teaching concrete *legal norms.* Lawyers could be trained thoroughly in international and comparative law and particularly in the law of European (primarily Community) institutions. This would mean a fundamental reworking of the curricula of law schools of the Member States, in the direction of more "international" or "transnational" courses. *Doctrinal abstraction* represents a second level. It might be possible to revitalize the Roman law tradition and the old idea of a European *jus commune;* students could be trained in conceptual tools and doctrinal constructs which could be applied across the board, in the different European countries. The third level would be that of *methodology.* The student could be trained in methods and theories which transcend national diversities in legal norms and doctrines. Yet the methods and theories would at the same time help the student to understand and deal with diversity.

The central point of this essay is that the first two levels – norms and doctrine – have to be discarded in the search for tools for European integration. The normative and doctrinal approaches are based on misconceptions of law, and are incapable of producing the changes in attitudes and training which are thought to be necessary for unification. We will use the experience of the United States as a springboard for examining the possibilities of legal unification through law schools which have aims and methods beyond the merely parochial. We will ask: (1) In what concrete ways did American legal education contribute to national legal unity? (2) Is there a way to translate the American experience into the European context? And, (3) do we *want* to?

In the United States as well as in Europe, there is, we think, a long-term trend toward injecting an interdisciplinary outlook into the study of law. It is this methodological approach, the third level described above, which, in our opinion, could serve as a way to internationalize the legal profession. Thus, we propose a social science approach to a common European legal education. We suggest something more than mere form and dogma, and advocate an approach which would take social forces into account. The key concepts of this approach are: "legal construction of social reality," "problem-centered inquiry" and "legal policy analysis."[11] This framework would transform traditional forms of legal reasoning, and thus would serve both the practical and intellectual legal needs of the European Community.

[11] *See infra* notes 102–03 and accompanying text.

In short, our thesis is that a genuine "European" education cannot come out of the study of a "common law" that does not exist and never did. Unification of this type would be artificial and purely conceptual. Nor can we achieve transnational goals by straining for a level of abstraction that ignores what is actually happening in the market-places of law in various countries. Rather, we propose an approach which takes account of cultural and economic diversity, a social science approach. This may indeed lay the basis for transnational legal education.

II. The Analytical Framework

Before we turn to discuss American legal education and its implications for Europe, a few general comments are in order. The problem before us is unification of law within a plural legal system. Legal pluralism can be (roughly) defined as "the existence of distinct legal systems or cultures within a single political community."[12] There are many kinds of pluralism. Pluralism can be cultural (two ethnic groups share a single country, for example); or it can be purely political (characteristic of the United States, for the most part, but also true of sections of other federal countries, such as Canada and Switzerland). As these last two examples show, the various kinds of pluralism can also exist side by side. "Unification" means reducing or limiting legal pluralism.

A. Methods of Unification

There are essentially three ways to unify a plural legal system.

1. Imposition

The first is through imposition or command, that is, a direct order from above insisting that the quarreling legal dialects must speak with a single tongue. "Imposition" is one of the hallmarks of colonialism,[13] but there are other forms of command as well. In the American context, federalism itself is one of the best examples. The American constitutional system is a system of divided powers; there are sovereign states, but there is also a federal government, and the Federal Government is supreme in its sphere.[14] Under the Constitution of

[12] L. M. FRIEDMAN, THE LEGAL SYSTEM – A SOCIAL SCIENCE PERSPECTIVE 196 (New York, The Russell Sage Foundation, 1975).

[13] *See generally* THE IMPOSITION of LAW (S.B. Burman & B.E. Harrell-Bond eds., New York, Academic Press, 1979).

[14] Although we are using American examples in this section, similar examples can also be found, *mutatis mutandis,* for Europe. For European examples, *see generally* Jacobs & Karst, *The "Federal" Legal Order: The U.S.A. and Europe Compared – A Juridical Perspective, supra* this vol., Bk. 1; Stein, *Towards a European Foreign Policy? The European Foreign Affairs System from the Perspective of the United States Constitution, supra* this book.

1787, for example, Congress was given power to create a uniform bankruptcy law.[15] Actually, in the event, for various political reasons, Congress did not make much use of this power, and, aside from a couple of short-lived statutes, a permanent federal bankruptcy law dates only from 1898. Meanwhile, the states went ahead on their own; each had its separate, quite distinct law of insolvency.[16] After 1898, the babel of state tongues largely ended, and a single unified system of bankruptcy law was imposed on the states. This, then, was command. But it is interesting to note that the command had to wait for more than a century after the time when it was first authorized. "Unification" was delayed, not by an absence of formal power, but by unwillingness of subordinate units to submit to command.

2. Planned Parallelism

A second source of unification is what we might call planned parallelism. There are good examples of this, too, in the American experience. Some of the best for our purposes lie in the field of commercial law. The framers of the American Constitution could not see the future, any more than other mortals. They did not anticipate an internal market of continental size. The Constitution gave the Federal Government, as we have seen, power to impose uniform bankruptcy laws on the states and power to deal with admiralty law;[17] all other commercial matters were left to the states to handle as they more or less saw fit. There was no easy way for the Federal Government to impose uniform commercial laws on New York, Idaho, Alabama, and the other states of the federal Union.

By the late nineteenth century, however, there was a strong feeling that a modern society needed uniformity in commercial law; that uniformity was essential to a developed economy.[18] A movement arose – strongly supported by jurists in the universities – to draft so-called "uniform" laws. Gradually, the states were coaxed into enacting these laws. The process was neither easy nor even, but it had considerable success. Most states adopted a Uniform Sales Act and a Uniform Negotiable Instruments law, to mention two prominent instances.[19] In the twentieth century, a Uniform Commercial Code was drafted.[20]

15 U.S. CONST. art. I, § 8, cl. 4.

16 For a capsule history of American bankruptcy law, *see* C. WARREN, BANKRUPTCY IN UNITED STATES HISTORY (1935 ed. reprinted, New York, Da Capo, 1972). On the various state insolvency laws *see generally* P.J. COLEMAN, DEBTORS AND CREDITORS IN AMERICA (Madison, State Hist. Soc. Wis., 1974).

17 U.S. CONST. art. I, § 8, cl. 18; art. III, § 2, cl. 1.

18 *See generally* Heller & Pelkmans, *The Federal Economy: Law and Economic Integration and the Positive State – The U.S.A. and Europe Compared in an Economic Perspective, supra* this vol., Bk. 1, at § II (by Heller).

19 For a brief account of this process *see* C.W. CORMAN, COMMERCIAL LAW – CASES & MATERIALS 6–7 (Boston, Little Brown & Co., 1976).

20 *See generally* Schnader, *A Short History of the Preparation and Enactment of the Uniform Commercial Code,* 22 U. MIAMI L. REV. 1 (1967).

After a slow start, the draftsmen of the Code have been amazingly successful in selling their product to the states. We will return to this theme later.[21]

3. Unplanned Parallelism

The third method is what we might call ***unplanned parallelism.*** The laws of the constituent units proceed more or less on their own tracks; but they tend to converge. In other words, the laws tend to unify themselves. This is in fact quite a striking phenomenon in American law.

We can take as an example the law of products liability. Here, unlike the situation in commercial law, there are no "uniform" laws. Tort law remains largely a common law province, that is, a creation of the judges, and under the control of individual states. But there have been dramatic developments in the twentieth century, and the states have tended to move along markedly similar lines.

The modern law of products liability was not born overnight. One convenient marker is the great decision of New York Judge Benjamin Cardozo in *MacPherson v. Buick Motor Company.*[22] In this famous case, the wheel of a car was defective; the driver was injured, and he sued the manufacturer. Even though he had no contractual relationship with the manufacturer, the court allowed the action. The case made a great stir in the legal world. It was followed quickly and eagerly in some states; more hesitatingly in others.

Strictly speaking, of course, the *MacPherson* case was law only in New York. No court of any other state was bound by it. It had no power whatsoever beyond the Hudson River. Exactly how and why it exerted "influence" is not an easy question to answer. One point of view is that it exerted no "influence" at all; it simply gave other states a convenient citation, an excuse to move in the same general direction. In any event, there has been a great deal of parallel movement in state law on products liability; and the parallel movement is unplanned, whatever its ultimate source.[23]

These, then, are the three methods of unification. It is probably a good idea to keep them analytically distinct, although in practice they blur together quite a bit. "Unplanned" parallelism means movement directed by social forces. But these forces also operate on the central government; and they also lie behind the busy hands trying to weave together planned parallelism. Planned and unplanned parallelism are thus clearly connected.[24]

[21] *See infra* notes 25, 46–52, 91–92 and accompanying text.

[22] 217 N.Y. 382 (1916).

[23] For further elaboration of this point, *see generally* M.A. FRANKLIN, TORT LAW AND ALTERNATIVES: INJURIES AND REMEDIES (Mineola, N.Y., Foundation Press, 1971).

[24] G. Edward White, commenting on Cardozo as a torts judge, argues that Cardozo was a judge at a time when "judges were regarded as important sources of doctrinal change; and when a symbiotic relationship between the appellate judiciary and a community of legal scholars had developed, personified by such institutions as the American Law Institute." G.E. WHITE, TORT LAW IN AMERICA: AN INTELLECTUAL HISTORY 124 (Oxford, O.U.P., 1980).

B. The Unification and Unifying Potential of Legal Education

Our subject, of course, is legal education. Here too we can describe three forms of unification – imposition, planned parallelism and unplanned parallelism. That is, if legal education itself in the United States is basically national (or "unified"), this may have come about in the same three ways. In the American context, however, unified legal education, to the extent it does exist, has nothing directly to do with command. There is no federal legal education. The Federal Government plays no role in training lawyers and jurists. Uniformities of legal education are the result of planned or unplanned parallelism. But legal education may play a role in the drama of *creating* parallelism. At least that is a hypothesis we want to explore.

Academia has obviously busied itself with what we have called planned parallelism. The "uniform laws" were, by and large, conceived and drafted by law professors. Practicing lawyers and judges helped as advisers, and occasionally did a bit more; but generally speaking they were not the leading spirits in this movement. The dominant figure in drafting the Uniform Commercial Code was a scholar and professor, Karl Llewellyn. Often enough, Llewellyn spoke – or claimed he spoke – in the name of the commercial bar; he drafted a code which gave commercial lawyers (he felt) what they needed. But in general the wants of lawyers and businessmen were recognized only in so far as they were filtered through the minds of Llewellyn and his colleagues.[25]

It is harder to come to any firm conclusions about the role of legal education in unplanned parallelism. We will have to take a brief look at the history of American legal education, and say something about its general nature. The hypothesis to be tested runs something as follows: American legal education is "national," that is, in general it ignores local law, and stresses what is common to the law of the fifty states. Lawyers all over the country receive much the same training. There is little or no difference in the way law is taught and learned in Florida, Alaska or New York. The curriculum is the same, the methods are the same. Schools do differ, to be sure, but not in ways that reflect geography at all. Lawyers receive a common – and powerful – socialization experience. Their training becomes absorbed into their bloodstreams, and forms a part of their legal culture. This training fosters a national, general view of the law; and thus helps, in turn, to create a national legal culture. It helps to override, in other words, the very striking, very powerful forces of provincialism and parochialism that are also at work in the internal legal culture.

The question is, to what extent does this experience help explain unplanned parallelism in American law. A moment's thought is enough to tell us that this question cannot really be answered. This becomes even clearer if we rephrase the question: How much *less* parallelism would there be in the law of the various

[25] On Llewellyn's career *see generally* W.L. Twining, Karl Llewellyn and the Realist Movement (London, Weidenfeld, 1973) (chs. 11 & 12 deal specifically with the U.C.C.).

states, if the United States had a different, less "national" system of legal education? Would the striking changes in (say) products liability have been of a different order? To put the matter in still another way, if we are trying to explain the precise form taken by products liability in the twentieth century, how much explanatory weight should we give to general socio-economic forces, and how much to peculiarities of American legal education? If we put the question this way, the answer seems obvious: It *must* be the case that socio-economic forces play the dominant role. We can prove this (if "prove" is the appropriate word) by pointing to other countries with very different systems of education, which have nonetheless undergone rather similar developments in products liability. On the other hand, legal education may play *some* role in unifying law.

This role, however, might be different in different areas of law. There is no reason, theoretical or practical, to expect that the impact of legal education on parallelism, planned or unplanned, must be the same in every branch of law. Indeed, there is evidence that points in the opposite direction. Consider, for example, the success of the Uniform Commercial Code. It has been due, at least in part, to the feeling that a unified country must have a unified body of commercial law. For all we know, there is no basis whatsoever for this belief; but it is enough to know that people think so. No movement of corresponding strength exists for tort law, or family law, or for criminal justice.

In short, the impact of legal education on the unity (and disunity) of American law is probably *marginal* at best. This does not mean we can dismiss it out of hand. The road to unification – if we decide we want to take it – is long and difficult. We may need all the help we can get, marginal or otherwise.

III. The American Experience and Its Lessons for Europe

A. The American Approach to Uniform Legal Education

1. Provincialism in American Law

An outstanding feature of American legal culture is its localism. Each state controls its own bar, and admits its own lawyers to practice. A person who is a member of the bar of Maine has no legal right to practice law in next-door New Hampshire, let alone in California. From the standpoint of New Hampshire, a member of the Maine bar is just another layman. Some states in the past were even more parochial; a lawyer admitted to practice in one county was not automatically entitled to practice in another. This extreme localism is dead, and under certain conditions some states will allow out-of-state lawyers to practice in their state. Other states are stickier on this point, and it is very rare for a lawyer to practice, or have the right to practice, in more than two or three states. *Most* lawyers are members of a single bar only.

The bench is if anything more parochial. There is no separate career line for judges in the United States. A judge is, basically, a lawyer sitting on the bench. Usually he or she is a lawyer with good policital connections – one who has managed to get an appointment to office, or to be put on the slate of some political party for election. The road to the bench passes through the jungles of local politics; hence judges are not, by and large, drawn from the upper strata of the bar, or from the large firms in the big cities. Rather, they come from the smaller firms, or from the ranks of solo practitioners, and they tend to be identified fairly intensively with the politics of their county, town or state. Moreover, a judge stays put. A Kansas judge will always be a Kansas judge. He cannot transfer to another state. Lower-court judges will not move from their district or their town.[26] The federal judge who sits in Kansas is also a Kansas man. There is no movement from place to place, no system of transfers. All of this means that local peculiarities, once they get started, are difficult to root out. Procedures tend to be local, especially the little quirks and habits. These "customs" are likely to cling stubbornly to life. The jurisdictions are, in a way, sealed off hermetically from each other.

All this promotes what one might call legal dialects. The analogy to language is, on the whole, a fair one. If people who speak a common language move to a new place and settle down, dispersed (let us say) in small, isolated valleys, the original language will split up over time into dialects that grow further and further apart. In a sense, the English Common Law was a kind of "mother tongue" of the people who settled the United States.[27] Since the states have legal sovereignty, and since American legal culture has been quite provincial, individual colonies (and then states) split into dialects of the Common Law from a very early period. The result is what we see today: great variation in what Thomas Church, Jr., has called "local legal culture."[28] Church used the term to explain what he found in a study of delay in trials courts. He had posed the question: Why do some courts work so slowly, while others work much faster? None of the usual explanations seemed to fit the facts. Church felt he had to fall back on "the centrality of informal court system attitudes, concerns and practices,"[29] in short, on the local legal culture. But why do these cultures survive? They can only survive in isolation.

Against these localizing tendencies are others that tend to counterbalance them. Legal provincialism is, on the whole, small potatoes – matters of procedure, or little doctrines on the margin of significance, clinging to life like primitive organisms that resist extinction in some highly specialized niche. Not all

26 At an early period in American history, judges did "ride circuit," in districts of greater or lesser size. *See* L.M. FRIEDMAN, A HISTORY OF AMERICAN LAW 123 (New York, Simon & Schuster, 1973). This is no longer done.

27 Of course, the Civil Law has been influential and has left important traces in such states as Texas, California and, most strikingly, Louisiana.

28 T. CHURCH, JR., A. CARLSON, J. LEE & T. TAM, JUSTICE DELAYED – THE PACE OF LITIGATION IN URBAN TRIAL COURTS (Williamsburg, Nat'l Center for State Courts, 1978).

29 *Id.* at 83. On the local *appellate* court culture *see* Kagan, Cartwright, Friedman & Wheeler, *The Evolution of State Supreme Courts*, 76 MICH. L. REV. 961 (1978); Friedman, Kagan, Cartwright & Wheeler, *State Supreme Courts: A Century of Style and Citation*, 33 STAN. L. REV. 733 (1981).

localisms are trivial – courtroom dispatch and delay is an important topic, after all – but most of them are. Meanwhile, strong forces are at work driving the law toward a central tendency. The most significant of these forces are social and economic. Provincialism thrives on isolation; but telephone, telegraph, radio, and TV bind the country together in a manner undreamt of a hundred years ago. Internal migration has been another great counterbalance. A tide of human beings swept across the country in the nineteenth century, and lawyers were among them. One account in the nineteenth century speaks about "enormous numbers" of lawyers, "heading west to practice law, looking for 'better pasture.' "[30] The Western states were settled by people who came from the Eastern states; they brought their legal culture with them along with their other baggage. The West also lacked the time or skill to invent a fresh legal system. It borrowed, as it had to, from the East. This helps explain the Western appetite for codes. The famous Field codes of the mid-nineteenth century were mostly repudiated or ignored in the East; but they were eagerly adopted by some of the Western states.[31]

Thus it does not surprise us that the provincialism of American legal culture is somewhat on the wane in recent years. After all, the United States is now a single country in a way that was never true in the nineteenth century. It takes less than six hours to fly from coast to coast; television, for all practical purposes, reaches everywhere instantaneously. On the whole, lawyers and judges remain isolated in little occupational communities. But there are at least national organizations of lawyers and judges, and national legal magazines and newspapers. Also, in recent years, there has emerged a trend toward interstate lawyering. In the past, only a few of the very largest firms had any branches at all – in Washington D.C., perhaps, or in New York, if the firm was located elsewhere. Multiple branching has suddenly become more common. Lawyers have a long way to go before they match the record of MacDonald's hamburgers, or the various fried chicken chains, but the first bold steps have at least been taken.

The need is there. Client corporations are themselves sprawled out across the states; and the law of the Federal Government (tax law, defense contracting, regulation of business, etc.) has become vastly more important to these clients. This means that lawyers in all parts of the country share, for the first time, aspects of practice which are not simply *similar* to that of lawyers in other states, but absolutely *identical*, because they are federal: The Internal Revenue Code is the same in the frozen villages of Alaska as in the mangrove swamps of southern Florida.

There are stirrings, too, of national feeling and intercommunication among state judges. A National Center for State Courts has been set up, in Williamsburg, Virginia; a National Judicial College, in Reno, Nevada, runs training programs. The isolation of judges is lessening; at national meetings, judges

[30] 1 THE LAW STUDENT'S HELPER 144, 164 (Detroit, Mich., The Collector Pub. Co., 1893).

[31] L.M. FRIEDMAN, *supra* note 27, at 343–44.

from different places meet and talk to each other, at least more so than before. Still, it is probably true that American legal education is a major source of unity in legal culture. To this subject we now turn.

2. Legal Education in the United States

Legal education has a long and complex history in the United States.[32] The details do not concern us, but the main outlines are instructive. One central theme has been the war between two methods of training: Apprenticeship, and university (or school) training. In 1800 apprenticeship was almost universal; today, school training is, practically speaking, the only real path to the bar. In other words, school training has won out completely. But what kind of school? And what kind of training?

Law school training has varied over the years. The earliest American law school was founded by Judge Tapping Reeve, in Litchfield, Connecticut. It flourished in the late eighteenth and early nineteenth centuries. This school was in many ways, a glorified, concentrated form of apprenticeship. Educationally, it was fairly primitive. Yet, even so, the Litchfield school was quite "national," in the sense that its students came from many different states. The first law school with a University connection was Harvard, which opened its doors around 1817.[33] It, too, was educationally primitive, yet "national" in the same general sense.

The most important date in the history of American legal education, by common consent, is 1870. That was the year in which a new Dean, Christopher Columbus Langdell, introduced the case method of legal education at Harvard.[34] The basic principles of this system are well-known. Langdell announced boldly that law was a "science," and that it had to be studied scientifically, that is, through the examination of reported cases. These, he claimed, were the primary sources for studying legal principles. Langdell made war on older methods of teaching. He used cases and cases only, and taught by the Socratic method. It was Langdell who put together the first case-book, on *Contracts,* in 1870. Other teachers and case-books followed. Professor William A. Keener, for example, one of Langdell's disciples, compiled a *Selection of Cases on Quasi-Contracts* in 1888.[35] The student, said Keener in his preface, "must look upon law as a science," made up of "a body of principles to be found in the

[32] There is a huge literature on the subject of legal education in America. Worthy of special mention is Stevens, *Two Cheers for 1870: The American Law School,* in 5 LAW IN AMERICAN HISTORY – PERSPECTIVES IN AMERICAN HISTORY 405 (D. Fleming & B. Bailyn eds., Boston, Little, Brown & Co., 1971). *See also* A.Z. REED, TRAINING FOR THE PUBLIC PROFESSION OF THE LAW (1921 ed. reprinted, New York, Arno Press, 1976).

[33] A fair number of histories of particular law schools have been written; quite a few deal with Harvard. *See, e.g.,* A.E. SUTHERLAND, THE LAW AT HARVARD: A HISTORY OF MEN AND IDEAS, 1817–1967 (Cambridge, Harv. U.P., 1967).

[34] *See* Stevens, *supra* note 32.

[35] W.A. KEENER, A SELECTION OF CASES ON QUASI-CONTRACTS (New York, Baker, Voorhis & Co., 1888–9).

adjudged cases"; the case is to the student "what the specimen is to the geologist."[36]

Under this general conception of law, the Common Law is indeed a unity. Its apparent diversity, in a union of sovereign states, drops away into minor importance. Law, or at least the Common Law, is a single entity, a "science." It has an underlying, unified core, a body of principles or doctrines, and it is this core which forms the proper object of study. This notion was of course by no means peculiar to the United States. As many scholars have pointed out, Langdell's notion of legal science owed a great deal to European theories of legal science. In Europe, too, legal scholars struggled with a paradox. Legislative supremacy meant that law was completely bound to a particular country or sovereignty. Yet in Europe too – or especially there – the sense was strong that the "science" of law transcended national boundaries.[37]

The case-method had a shaky beginning at Harvard; attendance dropped off, and for a while, the future of the experiment was in doubt. But Langdell stuck to his guns. His method gradually conquered, first Harvard, then, slowly, the whole world of American legal education. Some schools resisted or fought back – indeed, the law school at Boston University was founded in 1872 as a reaction against the Harvard madness – but history proved to be on Langdell's side. Harvard proselytized vigorously, but that explains very little of its success. What seems clear is that it had a product that other law schools ultimately wanted to buy.[38]

The case-method was, in some ways, a sharp break with the past. In other ways, it was not quite so radical. Law schools continued to be "national." The more prestigious schools, like Harvard, drew their students from all over the country. These schools were also "national" in the sense that they ignored local peculiarities in their curriculum and in their course-materials. What they taught was the general common law of the United States – a thing which, in an important sense, never really existed.[39] The general Common Law of the United States was purely an intellectual construct; yet it had a certain practical value. Young lawyers-to-be (and young lawyers) as often as not were destined to practice far away from their home communities. Lawyers were as rootless, as shift-

[36] *Id.* at iv.

[37] *See infra* § IV.B., especially at text accompanying notes 75–77.

[38] For an account of how the case-method conquered the University of Wisconsin *see* W.R. JOHNSON, SCHOOLED LAWYERS: A STUDY IN THE CLASH OF PROFESSIONAL CULTURES 114–15, 121–27 (New York, N.Y.U.P.; 1978); for an account of the adoption of the Harvard method at the University of Chicago *see* F.L. ELLSWORTH, LAW ON THE MIDWAY: THE FOUNDING OF THE UNIVERSITY OF CHICAGO LAW SCHOOL (Chicago, U. Chi. P., 1977).

[39] Except, of course, insofar as cases like Swift v. Tyson, 41 U.S. (16 Pet.) 1 (1842), created what was in effect a "federal common law." But *Swift v. Tyson* was repudiated in the 1930's. *See* T. FREYER, HARMONY & DISSONANCE: THE *Swift* & *Erie* CASES IN AMERICAN FEDERALISM (New York, N.Y.U.P., 1981). *See* Jacobs & Karst, *supra* note 14, at § III.A.2.a.iii; P. HAY & R. ROTUNDA, THE UNITED STATES FEDERAL SYSTEM: LEGAL INTEGRATION IN THE AMERICAN EXPERIENCE 245–50 (Milan, Giuffrè, 1982).

less, as apt to drift West, as members of other occupations, perhaps more so. The young lawyer would take root permanently at some point, but who could know where that would be? He was like a barnacle, which begins life free-floating, then settles on a rock and stays there for life. It made no sense for the young lawyer to cram into his head the quirks and foibles of local law. A school with students *from* all sorts of places, heading *for* all sorts of places, was bound to want to teach more general materials and skills.

Langdell provided a *theory* to justify this trait of legal education. There had always been a feeling that "the Common Law," though it owed a great deal to its English heritage, transcended that heritage; that it was the foundation on which the laws of all states (except Louisiana) rested. Jurists also assumed that Common Law systems had a great deal in common, legally speaking. Dozens of treatises on the "American law" of this or that subject were written before 1870, even though, strictly speaking, there was no such thing as "American law"; there was only the New York law of contracts, the Pennsylvania law of contracts, and so on. The local dialects were close enough to each other so that a generalizing approach made sense.

We must recall, too, that, in 1870, certain practical considerations were becoming more compelling. As the country urbanized and industrialized, there was more need to learn the *general* shape of the law, or at least how to approach it. It was not only that the dialects of law were mutually intelligible; an age of big business, of railroads, telephone and telegraph, and an age of rapid (and constant) travel, was bound to emphasize the unity (real or desired) of the law of the country.

Yet it would be wrong to stress the practical side of Langdell's revolution too much. Langdell's case method emphasized the Common Law in its purest form. It focussed on those pieces and branches of the Common Law – and hence of legal culture – which were most likely to be similar in various parts of the country. One of the most striking peculiarities of Langdell's system was its fixation on appellate cases. No one denies that case-law is important in a Common Law country. But what is surprising is the almost total neglect of other sources of law. Langdell disdained statutes. He even banished constitutional law from his curriculum. (Its sin, of course, was its dependence on a written text.) Nothing enacted was part of Langdell's original curriculum.[40] It is instructive to look at the early case-books, especially Langdell's. Langdell's case-book on contracts[41] contained mostly English cases; the American cases came from a handful of states, notably Massachusetts and New York. Langdell paid no attention to innovations outside of the East Coast; he also had no particular interest in keeping up to date. Nor was he interested in reforms, statutory or

40 In his casebook on contracts, Langdell did present some cases on the Statute of Frauds, an English law of 1677 which was so old, and so encrusted with judicial glosses, that it was almost part of the Common Law. And indeed, every state had adopted the Statute of Frauds in one form or another. *See generally* C.W. CORMAN, *supra* note 19.

41 *Supra* note 34.

otherwise. What he wanted was to present the "science" of law, pure and simple. This point is worth stressing, because it shows how high a price was paid for "uniformity" in legal education.

Of course, the case-method never lacked for critics, even in its hour of triumph. It is interesting, for example, to re-read the Redlich Report.[42] Redlich was a Viennese scholar, invited by the Carnegie Foundation to take a look at American legal education, especially the case-method. Redlich's report came out in 1914. He found much to praise in the case-method: It had "unrivaled" power to train students in "independent thought," and it evoked "the keenest powers of legal reasoning." But he noted that the case-method concerned itself "only with the knowledge of that law which may be designated as the general common law of America," that is, with "principles of the whole common law which are more or less current in all the separate states of the union." It thus neglected "those not inconsiderable variations in the law which are due in part to the legislation of individual states, in part to deviations made by the courts in certain fields from the general norm or standard of the common law." These "local divergences" did not "lend themselves to scientific instruction." Redlich felt, however, that these "divergences" would "sooner or later tend to disappear, because of the well-known strong tendency of the American judiciary to maintain in all important points the legal unity of the common law."[43]

Whether there was such a "tendency" is an open question. This much is clear: The curriculum of American law schools (whatever the state of American *law*) has remained amazingly uniform. It is still substantially impervious to the local *as such.* The modern case-book, to be sure, has come a long way from Langdell. It is full of material about divergencies, majority and minority rules, and the like. Still, in essence, the case-books used in the "best" schools are as "general" as possible. They emphatically do *not* teach the law of the state in which the law school sits. To suggest that Harvard should teach Massachusetts law, exclusively or predominantly, or that Yale should turn its elegant attention to the law of Connecticut, would be greeted with horror or derision; one might as well ask these schools to teach students how to send out their monthly bills, or how to pick the best secretary. No, indeed. The materials must be national. Indeed, the word "national" is misleading here; what the law schools teach is legal principle – a body of matter that is not tied to one particular (American) place.

Attitudes toward written texts have, of course, changed a great deal since 1870. Constitutional law, for example, survived Langdell's purge and sits on a throne of honor at every law school today. The leading case-books in this field, we note, consist *exclusively* of federal materials. They are basically about the United States Supreme Court. There are fifty states, with fifty constitutions, and fifty high courts, but no one pays attention to them in the law schools. It is

[42] J. Redlich, The Case Method in American Law Schools (New York, Carnegie Found. for Advancement of Teaching, 1914).

[43] *Id.* at 52–53.

unlikely that a single case from any *state* court can be found in any leading case-book in constitutional law. The California Constitution is supreme law in its sphere for an empire of more than 20,000,000 people; the California Supreme Court is its oracle. But no major California law school teaches state constitutional law, and most never mention it at all.

Statutory courses have indeed entered the curriculum. They claim a good deal of the student's time. They too are mostly federal. For them also the emphasis is somewhat lop-sided. The federal income tax generates billions of dollars, and more law than any other modern statute. It deserves pride of place in legal education; but surely state and local tax laws merit *some* word or two. They get none, typically. Local procedure is in a little better shape. But by and large, the bias toward the general, the national, is as strong as ever – at the expense of the real world of legal practice and legal behavior. Law school professors look down on local variations in the law; they sneer at schools which emphasize the training of local lawyers, and call them "bar cram" schools. That there is some middle ground between a cram course and the cloud-cuckoo land of concepts has escaped most of the jurists.

Legal education, in Langdell's scheme, stresses method, not content. Langdell was not interested in teaching law; his field was "legal science." Nobody believes in legal science any more, at least not in the same sense; but law schools still shy away from teaching law as brute, naked subject matter. They are interested only in teaching "how to think like a lawyer," or "legal skills," or "fundamental principles." All this makes it still possible to ignore the actual law of the land, and most especially local variations. It is good to keep this trait of legal education in mind, as we turn now to the role of legal education in fostering legal uniformity.

B. Legal Education and Its Influence on Unification

1. The Role of Legal Education in Unification by Imposition

Of the three paths to uniformity, legal education would have least to do, it would seem, with unification through command. Yet a case could be made out that the centralization of American law – the expansion of federal power – owes a great deal to the lawyers. Certainly, lawyers are all over Washington, in great packs and swarms; they are found on all sides of every public issue. On the one hand, lawyers are the bureaucrats, the regulators; on the other hand, lawyers go into the ring to battle *against* regulation, on behalf of the great corporations. Lawyers sit in the Senate and the House; they dominate the various boards, commissions, agencies, and departments; sometimes they occupy the White House itself. Lawyers have always been overrepresented in Washington, but they became particularly common during the 1930's, during the New Deal of Franklin D. Roosevelt. The New Deal, in Jerold Auerbach's phrase, was "a lawyer's deal." It "institutionalized the modern liberal activist state." Lawyers were people "trained to govern"; they had "direct access" to "critical levers of power and monopolized the instruments of governance."[44] These lawyers came from the "high citadel," Harvard, and from the other schools that trained "national" lawyers.

The presence of lawyers in Washington is, of course, a hard, rock-like fact. What is less clear is how or if the training of men and women *as* lawyers makes a difference to the *kind* of government the United States has, or what the government tries to do or not to do. That lawyers matter is by no means clear.[45] Nor is it obvious that centralization of the country would have gone on slower or faster – or different in any way – without these lawyers. In any event, it is hard to see how one could prove the matter either way. It is even less clear that the centralized state owes much to the fact that the training at Harvard and other law schools was "national" in method and scope.

2. The Role of Legal Education in Unification by Planned Parallelism

We are on firmer ground when we consider the role of law schools in the development of *planned* parallelism. There has been, as we noted, a strong, successful movement to draft uniform and model laws, and to talk the states into enacting them.[46] Both the organized bar and the professional jurists were active in the movement. The organized bar probably played the smaller role. Practicing lawyers do not, generally speaking, have the time or patience to draft codes of law. Still, the American Bar Association did push to establish a Conference of Commissioners on Uniform State Laws, which popped into life in 1892. The Conference was made up of "commissioners," appointed in each state by the governor. Commissioners served without pay. The Conference sponsored a series of uniform laws, starting with the Negotiable Instruments Law (1896), adopted by forty-eight states, and the Uniform Sales Act (1906), which gained thirty-four converts.[47] The draftsmen of the Uniform Laws were by and large professors of law. Samuel Williston of Harvard, for example, was the genius (if that is the word) behind the Sales Act.

The American Law Institute (ALI) sprang more directly from the world of legal education. It was the brainchild of the Association of American Law

[44] J.S. AUERBACH, UNEQUAL JUSTICE – LAWYERS AND SOCIAL CHANGE IN MODERN AMERICA 226 (Oxford, O.U.P., 1976).

[45] *See, e.g.,* H. EULAU & J.D. SPRAGUE, LAWYERS IN POLITICS: A STUDY IN PROFESSIONAL CONVERGENCE (Indianapolis, Bobbs-Merrill, 1964); Green, Schmidhauser, Berg & Brady, *Lawyers in Congress: A New Look at Some Old Assumptions,* 26 WESTERN POL. Q. 440 (1973).

[46] *See supra* notes 18–21, 25, and accompanying text.

[47] *See* C.W. CORMAN, *supra* note 19. By 1925, fifty-one jurisdictions had adopted the Negotiable Instruments Law, forty-eight the Warehouse Receipts Act, twenty-seven the Sales Act, twenty-six the Bill of Lading Act. But a Uniform Workmen's Compensation Act had gotten only three adoptions, an Occupational Diseases Act none at all. These figures are from a presidential address by Nathan W. MacChesney to the 35th annual National Conference of Commissioners on Uniform State Laws, *Uniform State Laws: Their Effectiveness and Vital Function as an Aid to Constitutional Government* (Delivered at the Hotel Statler, Detroit, Mich., 25 Aug. 1925).

Schools, trade-group of the law professors. The main work of the Institute was to prepare the famous *Restatements* of the law. As Twining has put it, the Restatements were supposed to do two things: first, where the law was "clear," to set out "in clear and simple terms a statement of principles"; and, second, "where the law was unclear or lacking in uniformity," to propose a "solution." Twining also remarks, very aptly, that the Restatements had a kind of hybrid nature: they were mostly descriptive, but they were also (though in much smaller doses) prescriptive.[48]

The Restatements restated "the law"; but the law they restated was primarily the plain Common Law. There is a Restatement of contracts, torts, and property; but there is no Restatement of anti-trust law, or the law of business regulation. (There were some attempts to restate tax law, but these ultimately came to nothing.) The philosophy underlying the Restatements was not unlike Langdell's. The Restatements, too, searched for the essence of the Common Law, the principles behind it. Uniformity was always an important goal of the Restatements – not reform of the law in any fundamental sense, nothing that would or could change the balance of power, even in tiny ways, or alter social structure; the goals were technical and esthetic – rationality, system, order, method. The Restatements were meant to even out the bumps and warts which disfigured the Common Law.[49] By using the Restatements, a judge could find out the general or preferred rule on some particular issue. If his own state (or state of mind) deviated from the norm, the judge would tend (so the theory went) to rethink the issue. He might well decide to join the majority, or adhere to the sound sense of the draftsmen.

Were the Restatements successful? They were the product of much back-breaking work. Courts cited them frequently. The ALI proudly kept track of how often courts referred to the Restatements as "authority." Judges usually agreed with the Restatements. In 1935 it was reported that courts deviated from the Restatement rule only 2% of the time.[50] This may mean that there was less disunity to begin with than anybody expected; or, perhaps, that the Restatement made quite an impact on the judges. On the other hand, these figures may be rather misleading. We do not know exactly what "disagreed with" means. Many "rules" of the Restatements were vague, abstract, windy formulations which nobody could really disagree with; the real question is how they were interpreted or applied. But the "rules" of the Restatements did try to convince judges to conform their work to a more or less national standard. The Restatements thus labored to overcome the disintegrative forces of localism and legal dialect. They were in partnership with the "uniform laws" and model codes. Legal scholars created all of these, and taught them to their students.

48 W.L. Twining, *supra* note 25, at 274. *See also* J.W. Johnson, American Legal Culture 1908–1940, at 58–61, 67–68 (Westport, Ct., Greenwood Press, 1981); Crystal, *Codification and the Rise of the Restatement Movement*, 54 Wash. L. Rev. 239 (1979).

49 *See* Friedman, *Law Reform in Historical Perspective*, 13 St. Louis U.L.J. 341 (1969).

50 *Noted in* J.W. Johnson, supra note 48, at 61.

3. The Role of Legal Education in Unification by Unplanned Parallelism

This brings us to unplanned parallelism: What role can we assign to the uniform (or almost uniform) legal culture, which American legal education helps bring about? The uniformity – one might even say monotony – of legal education is a simple matter of fact. The curriculum hardly varies at all from state to state, from school to school. The first year, in particular, is much the same everywhere, with only tiny variations. Law teachers themselves seem to come from the same general mold. Almost all of them (at the "better" schools) are graduates of a handful of top law schools (Harvard has the lion's share); many serve as clerks for justices of the Supreme Court or other federal judges before they enter teaching; all did well in law school, and, typically, served on their school's Law Review. Among American law teachers, it is possible to find radicals and conservatives; but the great mass fall in the middle, leaning perhaps a bit toward the conservative side. Certainly, on educational matters, law teachers honor traditional ways.

Once again, we raise the question of consequences: does this similarity in background and training contribute to similarities in the practice of law, and in the behavior of law? Does the parallelism in legal education produce parallelism in legal life? To be sure, uniformity in American legal education means that lawyers all over the country have no trouble talking with each other. They have a common vocabulary, and they share a common learning experience. In some sense, they recognize each other as brothers and sisters. How much this contributes to commonalities in behavior; and how this affects the legal system itself, is, and has to be, guesswork. There is some research on what legal education does to the hearts and minds of law students,[51] but the results are not overwhelming. It is extremely hard to know how much of this impact stays with lawyers in the real world, and how much dribbles away under the pressures of making a living.

C. Two Lessons from America: The Potential of Autonomous Legal Integration

What do we learn from this history, or, more exactly, what do we learn that would be useful in the context of European unification? As everyone who contributes to the Florence Research Project will agree, there are tremendous differences between the two sides of the Atlantic; we hesitate to draw conclusions from one shore to the other. What we learn from American experience is,

[51] Among the few surveys of law students is Stevens, *Law Schools and Law Students*, 59 VA. L. REV. 551 (1973). *See also* Erlanger & Klegon, *Socialization Effects of Professional School: The Law School Experience and Student Orientations to Public Interest Concerns*, 13 LAW & SOC'Y REV. 11 (1978); A. HELDRICH & G. SCHMIDTCHEN, GERECHTIGKEIT ALS BERUF: REPRÄSENTATIVUMFRAGE UNTER JUNGEN JURISTEN (Munich, C. H. Beck, 1982) (study conducted in Germany); on law teachers, *see* E. KLAUSA, DEUTSCHE UND AMERIKANISCHE RECHTSLEHRER (Baden-Baden, Nomos, 1981).

arguably, neither concrete nor precise enough to permit clear-cut recommendations. Legal education in the United States may have contributed to legal unity in that country. We were unable to weigh or measure that contribution, to say whether legal education made a heavy contribution, or a light one, or to compare its contribution with that of other social or economic factors. Still, on a certain level of abstraction, we can learn some lessons from the American experience.

American experience demonstrates, for example, that at least some modest forms of legal integration can be achieved independently of political processes. The American states were, are, and will be "sovereign" in some legal spheres; yet they have drawn together in certain fields of law.[52] Autonomous legal integration, as far as it goes, probably owes something to the training provided by the law schools. We ask, then: First, what are the integrative functions of legal education? And second, what structures *within* legal education permit or foster this integration?

1. Lesson I: Integrative Functions of Legal Education

Traditionally, "unification" has been looked upon as a territorial, political matter. After all, what determines territorial boundaries is essentially a political process.[53] Political systems, and only political systems, fit neatly inside territorial boundaries. The economy, the culture, the language, the religion – all these are likely to spill over the political boundaries, or stop short of them.[54] To put it another way, social subsystems define their borders in terms of their own logic and tradition, independent of the political definition of local, regional, or national boundaries (though of course these boundaries often exert a certain influence). Each subsystem can be more or less integrated or uniform; a country can strive for cultural uniformity, religious uniformity, linguistic uniformity. From the standpoint of economic, cultural, linguistic, or scientific integration, politics appears as a kind of obstacle. Politics concerns itself with power, and legitimation of power; it is more dependent on local forces and behavior than, say, technology or the economic system.

European law defines legal boundaries in a strictly political way – it equates them with the boundaries of the nation-state. In the era of the sovereign, independent nation-state, strictly national systems of law displaced, at least in part, the old idea of *jus commune*. Codification meant that the main (legitimate) source of law was legislation – enactments of national political bodies. Democratic theory meant that parliamentary procedures legitimated legal norms and

[52] Thus although much of modern *economic* law does not lend itself to parallel development so long as legal units are sovereign and, therefore, not subject to command, yet some parts of the so-called private law may be otherwise.

[53] For an overview of different theories of integration in political science, especially the so-called federalist approach (C. J. Friedrich, Amitai Etzioni), and the pluralist approach (Karl W. Deutsch), *see* Behrens, *supra* note 2, at 19 ff. *See also* Elazar & Greilsammer, *supra* note 2, at § II.A.3.b.

[54] *See* Luhmann, *supra* note 1, at 5 ff.

principles. In this context, it was natural to conclude that law could not be "internationalized" unless politics was – or, as we said above, that legal unification depends entirely on political unification.[55]

The American experience at least suggests that this point goes too far. The legal system *can* define boundaries independently of political boundaries. In the American tradition, the Common Law is a *social* phenomenon, as well as a political one. American jurists are used to thinking about the "Common Law" as an entity in society, separate from the state. This makes it possible for Common Law to transcend state borders. American legal theory rejected the idea of a federal Common Law;[56] still, lawyers always felt the Common Law was a reality, and in some form and manner separate from the common law of Vermont, Alabama and Texas. The principles of this Common Law were the subject of "legal science." Langdell's Harvard taught law in such a way as to ignore political boundary lines or political process. Legal education was universalistic even though legal *practice* was local. Law schools taught lawyers to think of themselves as masters of a universalistic body of principles, principles that transcended state boundaries. In this way, legal education, in the national law schools, struck a blow for legal unification; the material taught was relatively free of localism and regionalism, and of American politics itself.

2. Lesson II: Universalistic Structures in Legal Education

Exactly what was it in American legal education that conveyed the universalistic message? We can isolate two structural characteristics; first, the curriculum itself; second, the cognitive flexibility of the "legal skills" taught. As our brief account of American legal education has shown, American law schools foster universalistic thinking about law, with regard to norms, doctrines, and methods. As to norms, there is the "benign neglect" of local, regional and state law; American law schools mainly teach federal and "common" law. European law schools draw heavily on the laws of the country in which the schools sit; they leave European Community and international law more or less to specialists. The same is true of legal doctrine. Despite the common tradition of Roman law and the *jus commune,* European lawyers are trained primarily in doctrines and conceptual tools specific to their own nations. Again, this contrasts with American training, which stresses "principles" of the one Common Law. European legal education even tends to stress national differences in methods and in legal reasoning, despite the fact that these are supposed to be universal subjects. In American legal education the same "legal skills," the same approaches to "thinking like a lawyer," are found from the Atlantic to the Pacific.[57]

[55] David, *supra* note 4, at 30 ff.

[56] *See supra* note 39.

[57] A thorough account of comparative legal methods can be found in 2 W. FIKENTSCHER, METHODEN DES RECHTS IN VERGLEICHENDER DARSTELLUNG (Tübingen, Mohr (Siebeck), 1975). On the openness of the American legal system to social science contributions *see*

The second point is this. If lawyers are to be internationally-minded, they must be trained to be open and flexible in their ways of thinking about law. Again, we can point to the habits of American legal education. American legal thought is weak in philosophy, in system, in Weberian formal rationality; it neglects questions of method and concept that are at the core of European legal thought. But (compared to Europe, at any rate) it is more open to ideas from economics and other social sciences, and from the outside world in general. American lawyers learn that judge-made law changes with the times; they avoid the sense of fixity in the legal system which is natural in systems where (as in Europe) the code is the law, the whole law, and remains law until the legislature changes it. None of this means that American law or legal education is "better" than the European equivalents; it simply means that, in at least one or two regards, it is more receptive to diversity and legal pluralism. (As we pointed out, American legal education is in other ways quite inimical to diversity and pluralism.)

In short, there *are* lessons we can learn from the American experience. The question is, can we translate them (if we wish to) into concrete suggestions? Does it make sense to develop a special European curriculum? What are the chances for doctrinal uniformity – a new European *jus commune?* Or should one rather try to reform legal education, to make it more suitable for training flexible, internationally-minded and open-minded lawyers?

IV. European Hopes and Experience

A. Imposition of a Uniform Curriculum and the Limitations of the Normative Approach

Comparative lawyers, actively engaged in the movement for legal unification, often complain that law schools in Europe neglect international law and, more particularly, the law of the European Community.[58] European law schools' curricula generally rely heavily on national legal materials, often banishing international law and Community law into marginal introductory courses, or pushing them off into specialized seminars. These subjects do not, on the

Collins, *The Use of Social Research in the Courts,* in KNOWLEDGE AND POLITICS: THE UNCERTAIN CONNECTION 147 ff (L.E. Lynn, Jr. ed., Wash. Nat'l Research Council, 1978).

58 *See generally* B. AUBIN & K. ZWEIGERT, RECHTSVERGLEICHUNG IM DEUTSCHEN HOCHSCHULUNTERRICHT (Tübingen, Mohr (Siebeck), 1952); Kahn-Freund, *Comparative Law as an Academic Subject,* 82 L.Q.R. 40 (1966); M. CAPPELLETTI, *Il diritto comparato e il suo insegnamento in rapporto ai bisogni della società moderna,* in L'EDUCAZIONE DEL GIURISTA E LA RIFORMA DELL'UNIVERSITÀ 179 (Milan, Giuffrè, 1974); Neumayer, *Rechtsvergleichender Unterricht auf internationaler Grundlage,* 32 RABELS Z 405 (1968); Zweigert & Puttfarken, *Die Bedeutung der Rechtsvergleichung in der Juristenausbildung der Bundesrepublik Deutschland,* 75–76 ZVR 125 (1975).

whole, shape the intellectual climate of legal education. Consequently, comparativists call for a more "European" legal education – for giving higher priority to studies with an international and transnational flavor. Karl Neumayer, for example, feels that such studies are vital "not only for ... legal culture," but also for "professional, that is, 'practical' education"; and that they therefore deserve "*first place* among the fundamental subjects of academic instruction," a place which they do not now occupy.[59]

To be sure, in recent years there has been a good deal of progress in developing broader curricula of the type advocated by the comparativists in Europe. In the Member States of the European Community the increasing importance of Community law has been recognized and is reflected in the syllabuses of the law faculties of many of the national universities.[60] Interest in international and comparative law is also growing throughout the EC domain,[61] sometimes involving exchange programs with foreign universities,[62] and a new factor is the development of multinational institutions which have links with

[59] Neumayer, *Rechtsvergleichung als Unterrichtsfach an deutschen Universitäten*, in FESTSCHRIFT FÜR KONRAD ZWEIGERT, *supra* note 4, at 507.

[60] In Germany, for instance, this has been particularly noticeable since 1960. There are now compulsory courses in Hesse, Hannover and Augsburg, while other schools offer electives in the subject. *See* Oppermann & Thomas, *Das Europarecht in der deutschen Juristenausbildung*, in DEUTSCHE GESELLSCHAFT FÜR VÖLKERRECHT, DAS INTERNATIONALE RECHT IN DER JURISTENAUSBILDUNG 25, 29 (R. Bernhardt ed., Heidelberg/Karlsruhe, Müller, 1981) [hereinafter cited as DAS INTERNATIONALE RECHT].

[61] For example, in Germany comparative law is heavily emphasized at some universities (*e.g.*, Bremen) both as a teaching subject and as a vehicle for research. In France, international and comparative law are recognized fields of study, although separated from the study of law itself. Various law faculties offer work in international law (*e.g.*, Strasbourg offers lectures in the history of international relations and politics in the first two years of study). *See* Jonathan, *L'enseignement du droit international dans les Universités en France*, in DAS INTERNATIONALE RECHT, *supra* note 60, at 113–14. In England, at least fifteen universities offer courses in comparative law, sometimes in cooperation with foreign universities. Electives in international and EC law are also offered by most law faculties. *See* Collier, *International Law in the University Education of Lawyers in the United Kingdom*, in DAS INTERNATIONALE RECHT, *supra* note 60, at 123, 126. Students in the Benelux countries, Denmark, Ireland, and Italy also have opportunities in these and similar fields.

[62] Various law schools in the Community have such cooperative research projects or studies, which may conceivably serve as a first step toward a European curriculum. One of the most interesting is the link between the University of London (King's College) and the University of Paris I (Pantheon-Sorbonne). The project is called "English law and French law." Students may follow a course of study divided between London and Paris. After a four-year program, they may earn the right to qualify to practice law in both countries. As an example of a research project of European concern, we may cite the activities of ZERP (*Zentrum für Europäische Rechtspolitik*), founded in Bremen in 1982. ZERP concerns itself with European legal policy. *See* A. SMITH, JOINT PROGRAMMES OF STUDY – AN INSTRUMENT OF EUROPEAN COOPERATION IN HIGHER EDUCATION (Collection Studies – Education Series, EC Commission, Luxembourg, Office for Official Pubs. of EC, 1979).

several schools of different nationalities or which have broken free of bondage to a particular country.[63]

But notwithstanding all these recent efforts, it is hard not to agree that international and European legal materials deserve a still greater role in legal education. The demand for "first place," however, may be rather unrealistic. On the whole, it seems unlikely that a common European curriculum will evolve in such a way as to displace the narrower national courses. And, as far as the goal of legal integration is concerned, the quest for such a curriculum seems beside the point.

The first and most important factor that inhibits the development of a common curriculum is the fact that national legal systems *do* play the dominant role in European legal life, and they will probably go on doing so far into the future. In this regard, Europe and America differ drastically. In our account of American legal education, we pointed out how social and economic factors in the United States helped foster legal unity. We also noted the growing dominance of *federal* law. Europe is a different story. There are many high barriers between countries – barriers of culture, politics, economics, language. Legal education cannot cope with such barriers, cannot achieve the unity missing in these other domains. The *amount* of transnational law useful *inside* countries is growing, but is still very small. No European law school could take its job of professional training seriously if it yielded to the comparativists and gave pride of place to Community, comparative or international materials.

A second inhibiting factor is that in any event Community, international and comparative materials are themselves too concrete to contribute much to inter-

[63] A good example is the European University Institute. The Messina Conference of Foreign Ministers of the six original EC Member States first broached the subject of a European institute of higher education and research in 1955 but the European University Institute opened its doors only in 1976. A post-graduate institution, it has four departments – History and Civilization, Economics, Law, and Political and Social Sciences. In the Law Department, there are, at present, five professors, one assistant and a number of postdoctoral researchers and research fellows. Study and research is transnational: Projects currently in progress include one on "Methods, tools, and potential for European legal integration in the light of the American federal experience," of which this volume is a part; another is on "Regional problems in Europe," (dealing with the emergence of the regional problem within the various states of Western Europe); a third is "Alternatives to de-legalization," dealing with the use of law as an instrument of economic policy; and, finally, there is a fourth dealing with industrial democracy, public policy, and the corporation. *See* EUI, Prospectus – Academic Year 1984–85, at 7 (available from Academic Service of the EUI, Florence, Italy) and EUI, Sixth Report of Activities – Academic Year 1981–82, at 28 (1982) (available from Academic Service of the EUI, Florence, Italy).

Another good example is provided by The College of Europe (Bruges), founded in 1949, and the oldest institution of European studies. It offers to holders of university degrees one year of "complementary studies" on problems of the unity and integration of Europe. Law is one of the subjects covered at Bruges. *See* COMMISSION OF THE EEC, HIGHER EDUCATION IN THE EUROPEAN COMMUNITY – A HANDBOOK FOR STUDENTS 241 (Luxembourg, Office for Official Pubs. of EC, 1979).

national thinking and cognitive flexibility. For if legal education were to concentrate on the law of the European Community, let us say, it would soon run into a dilemma. The rather narrow, technical aspects of Community law could be stressed, which would be fine for producing experts in European affairs – but that is all. Or broader legal problems, in different fields of law, could be considered but from a comparative perspective, breaking loose from the bounds of the local (national) law. But this approach would overburden legal education with all the minutiae of the legal systems of Europe. It would multiply the problems of standard legal education by two, four, or ten. This is the general dilemma of comparative law, and comparative lawyers have hardly been able to solve it.[64] Neither the over-specialized Eurocrat, nor the splintered comparativist, suits our goals or our needs.

There is, in fact, increasing emphasis on European matters in European law schools; but this is probably a reaction to the increased importance of "European" law in national life, rather than the result of a policy to train lawyers for mobility across national borders. In America, lawyers *were* mobile, across state lines, and law schools took this fact into account. For a Californian to go to law school in Massachusetts and eventually practice in Illinois is an everyday affair. But in Europe the legal community is static. Of course, within the Community some measure of free movement of lawyers is guaranteed by Community law.[65]

[64] *See, e.g.*, Schmidt, *The Need for a Multi-Axial Method in Comparative Law*, in FESTSCHRIFT FÜR KONRAD ZWEIGERT, *supra* note 4, at 525 *et passim*. To be sure, other comparativists think that the role of comparative analysis is one of going beyond the minutiae of the various legal systems – of locating *common societal problems and needs* (political, economic, etc.) and of evaluating the legal *solutions* given by various systems to such problems and needs, analyzing the *reasons* (historical, technical, organizational, and again also political, economic, social, etc.) for such solutions as well as their impact, and explaining the *trends*, parallel, diverging, converging, which emerge from such solutions. *See, e.g.*, M. CAPPELLETTI, *Il diritto comparato, supra* note 58; Cappelletti, *Vindicating the Public Interest Through the Courts: A Comparativist's Contribution*, 25 BUFFALO L. REV. 643, esp. at 645–648 (1976); Cappelletti, *Who Watches the Watchmen? A Comparative Study on Judicial Responsibility*, 31 AM. J. COMP. L. 1, esp. 2–17 (1983). Needless to say, this conception has many significant contacts with the methodological approach suggested by us *infra* at § C.

[65] On the free movement of lawyers in the Community, *see generally* Varano, *La libera circolazione degli avvocati nella Cee e l'ordinamento italiano: problemi e prospettive*, in L'INFLUENZA DEL DIRITTO EUROPEO SUL DIRITTO ITALIANO 477 (M. Cappelletti & A. Pizzorusso eds., Milan, Guiffrè, 1982) and references cited therein.

The European Court of Justice has on several occasions upheld the application of the free movement principles to lawyers. *See, e.g.*, Case 2/74, Reyners v. Belgium, [1974] ECR 631; Case 33/74, Van Binsbergen v. Bestuur van de Bedrijfsvereniging voor de Metaalnijverheid, [1974] ECR 1299; and Case 71/76, Thieffry v. Conseil de l'ordre des avocats à la Cour de Paris, [1977] ECR 765; Case 107/83, l'Ordre des avocats au Barreau de Paris v. Klopp, Judgment of 12 July 1984 (not yet reported), 9 EUR. L. REV. 439 (1984). *See also* Council Directive (EEC) No. 249/77 of 22 March 1977, to facilitate the effective exercise by lawyers of freedom to provide services, OJ No. L 78, 26 March 1977, p. 17.

But it would be most unusual, to say the least, for a German to train in England, and end up practicing in Holland. The idea that the free movement principle applies to lawyers has only recently come to the fore.[66] Certain barriers to the free circulation of lawyers have been removed.[67] Yet no mass movement of lawyers has occurred or is likely to occur.

This brings us to what seems to be a curious paradox: in the United States, with a single language and (essentially) one culture, lawyers generally cannot practice law, outside of their home state; while in the EEC, a hopeless melange of languages and cultures, lawyers, like waiters or shoe salesmen, have at least *some* rights in theory to set up shop throughout the Community.[68] In fact, this is no paradox at all. A New York lawyer would actually find it rather easy to get the hang of legal practice in California, with a little brushing-up and a bit of cramming. That is precisely why California is so anxious to keep him out. The typical English barrister, on the other hand, would be as helpless as a baby in a Danish or Italian court, whatever his theoretical rights.

But this is another way of restating one brute and inescapable fact. The "lessons" from America do not easily fit the European situation. These lessons presuppose a system of education that somehow transcends borders. Harvard is a "national" law school, not a school for Massachusetts law. But what would a European version of Harvard look or act like? To take the very simplest point: what language would it use in the classroom? (The choice would no doubt have to be English, which would offend the French, among others; this time with good reason.) What norms would this school teach? What curriculum would it follow? It is not only language that divides the countries; it is also tradition, legal history, and the very structure of the bar. Would the school train (for example) both barristers and solicitors?

Of course, schools could teach their subjects comparatively or multi-nationally, and this approach would enhance (in theory) the mobility of lawyers. A curriculum that taught both French and English law might enable a person to qualify to practice in France and England. After a while, these dual-purpose lawyers would carry ideas from place to place, which might lead to unplanned parallelism, as it did in America. But nobody would be able to master more than two or three legal systems at most. The substantive barriers, added to cultural and linguistic barriers, make any attempt to teach in this way out of the question for the Community as a whole.

In America, the mobility of lawyers was only feasible because the legal systems of the states were similar enough to permit it. The uniformity of legal education can be analyzed as a response to the needs of lawyers and law students, within a federal union. In Europe, the demand comes from above, not below; from policy-makers, not practitioners. There is no tradition of transfrontier

66 The first leading case dates only from 1974. The draft directive was first presented by the Commission to the Council in 1975.

67 *See* Varano, *supra* note 65, at 488 ff. Varano reports that only France, Denmark, Great Britain and Ireland have fully implemented the Council Directive.

68 Lawyer's rights of establishment in the EEC are described in Varano, *supra* note 65.

mobility. Indeed, integrationist legal education would have to teach lawyers to be mobile. This cannot be done if the subject-matter of law schools is the law of one, two, or many countries. But is there another way – through doctrinal abstraction?

B. Planned Parallelism and the Limits of Doctrinal Abstraction: The Revival of the Doctrine of a Jus Commune?

This is, however, another forlorn hope. Some scholars have argued that a common European legal culture may exist on a more abstract level than norms, cases and materials. These hopes are nourished by European history itself,[69] and in particular focus on the medieval *jus commune* doctrine and on the nineteenth century codification movement. The revival of Roman law which began in Bologna in the twelfth century and later spread throughout Europe is not without interest for our purposes; not only was the "reception" of Roman law in Continental legal systems a driving force that created a transregional legal culture, but it also appears that education had a role to play in that development.[70] Later codification was also a unifying experience on the Continent, although its impact was probably greater in the national than in the international context.[71] On the level of doctrinal abstraction it would no doubt be possible to find some common ground for the Continental Civil Law systems.

German legal history provides a striking example of the potential unifying effects of such an approach to legal education. The "historical school" laid the conceptual groundwork for a uniform system of legal education. This system overrode the territorial and political boundaries inside the German-speaking world and the *Pandektenwissenschaft* generally taught at German universities formed the intellectual basis for a kind of legal unity. Franz Wieacker ascribes to it a "national-political mission." It provided a certain amount of "unity of legal doctrine," despite the "continuing legal particularism of the German Federation and of the early Bismarckian empire." It "anticipated the legal unity of the Civil Code."[72]

[69] *See* F. Wieacker, Privatrechtsgeschichte der Neuzeit unter besonderer Berücksichtigung der deutschen Entwicklung §§ 6 ff, 20 ff (Göttingen, Vandenhoeck & Ruprecht, 1967).

[70] *See supra* note 4 and accompanying text; *see generally* Coing, *European Common Law: Historical Foundations*, in New Perspectives for a Common Law of Europe/Nouvelles perspectives d'un droit commun de l'Europe 31 (M. Cappelletti ed., Leyden/Brussels/Stuttgart/Florence, Sijthoff/Bruylant/Klett-Cotta/Le Monnier, 1978) [hereinafter New Perspectives]; Gorla, *La "Communis opinio totius orbis" et la réception jurisprudentielle du droit au cours des XVIe, XVIIe et XVIIIe siècles dans la "Civil Law" et la "Common Law," id.* at 45. *See also* Cappelletti, *Introduction, id.* at 1, 3–4, 6.

[71] *See generally* F. Wieacker, *supra* note 69.

[72] *Id.* at 443.

The integrative aspects of *Pandektenwissenschaft* were rooted in the concept of "legal science," and, more particularly, in the prominent role assigned to legal doctrine. Doctrinal thinking, as Wieacker puts it, looks on the legal order as a "closed system of institutions and norms, independent of social reality." It is possible, in principle, "to decide any legal case correctly, solely by a logical operation which subsumes the case under the hypothetical judgment that is contained in a general doctrinal theorem (and implicitly in legal concepts as well)."[73] Modern legal thought generally rejects this kind of "legal science," although the idea of *some* "legal science" is still strong. The autonomy and independence of law from society is (alas) still taken for granted, and classificatory concepts and analytical systems still play a crucial role in the work of legal scholars.[74]

Theories of "legal science" in nineteenth century Europe have an obvious kinship to Langdell's idea of "legal science."[75] Langdell's notions contributed in their own way to unification of legal education (and legal culture) in the United States. Hence some are quite tempted by the notion of a modern *jus commune* in Europe, based on "legal science," which would define common, transnational legal concepts, and construct a tissue of common, transnational doctrines.[76] Helmut Coing, for example, thinks the historical experience of the *jus commune* might well be revived, or mined to yield a "common tradition of thinking" which could be given "uniform application."[77] Coing's program is based explicitly on a historical paradigm of legal unification in Europe in which universities played a dominant role. This paradigm would replace the *legislative* model of unification which dominates the European scene today. Law schools would teach fundamental concepts and institutions, common to the various countries of Europe.

Kötz, in a recent article, has presented a more detailed program for a European *jus commune civile* ("*Gemeineuropäisches Zivilrecht*").[78] His goal is to foment international consensus over general legal rules in contract and tort. He looks to the development of a genuinely European system: "European concepts" would guide uniform definitions of legal rules on formation and validity of contracts, their forms and interpretation, contracts of adhesion, damages and so on. Interestingly, Kötz refers specifically to the American experience: like David and Lando, he proposes a "Restatement of European Law," to

[73] *Id.* at 433.

[74] For a sophisticated discussion of the functions of legal doctrine today *see* N. LUHMANN, RECHTSSYSTEM UND RECHTSDOGMATIK 24 ff (Stuttgart/Berlin/Cologne, Kohlhammer, 1974).

[75] *See supra* note 37 and accompanying text.

[76] *See* David, *supra* note 4, at 4.

[77] Coing, *Jus commune, nationale Kodifikation und internationale Abkommen: Drei historische Formen der Rechtsvereinheitlichung*, in LE NUOVE FRONTIERE DEL DIRITTO E IL PROBLEMA DELL'UNIFICAZIONE 171, 198 (Milan, Giuffrè, 1979) (Atti del Congresso internazionale, Univ. of Bari, April 1975).

[78] Kötz, *supra* note 4, at 481 ff.

guide jurists, after the manner of the American Restatements. Law schools, quite naturally, figure prominently in his program.

There are good reasons, however, to reject this kind of "unification through legal doctrine." There are some – Kahn-Freund for example – who flatly deny the practical need to harmonize fundamental principles of private law.[79] Mertens has pointed out that there is bound to be strong political resistance to any legal unification which goes beyond traditional private law principles, and which touches on social and economic policy. Yet these policies are deeply embedded in modern doctrines of private law.[80] But even if we put these considerations to one side, it would be no easy matter to construct a common doctrine that could serve as the basis of a unified legal curriculum. This is true for Civil Law countries; and, of course, the technical problems multiply enormously if Common Law systems are also taken into account. In America, the general Common Law is part of American legal culture. Europe has much less legal unity, and to find some sort of common denominator would require a level of abstraction way up in the stratosphere.

This is the fundamental objection. It would be a mistake to try to resurrect the conceptual world of the nineteenth century; and in any event it would be impossible.[81] A word or two about that world is in order. The conceptual architecture of *Pandektenwissenschaft* was a form of what Weber called formal rationality.[82] Law is formally rational to the extent that it is conceptual, deductive, and rule-oriented in its structure and reasoning. Weber tried to explain formal rationality in terms of its social function.[83] Formal rationality, in its highly-developed European form, was (he believed) useful to a market economy. It facilitated the private ordering of social action.

[79] Kahn-Freund, *Common Law and Civil Law: Imaginary and Real Obstacles to Assimilation,* in NEW PERSPECTIVES, *supra* note 70, at 137, 141.

[80] *See* Mertens, *Rechtsvereinheitlichung rechtspolitisch betrachtet,* in RECHT UND WIRTSCHAFT IN GESCHICHTE UND GEGENWART: FESTSCHRIFT FÜR JOHANNES BÄRMANN ZUM 70. GEBURTSTAG 651 ff (M. Lutter, H. Kollhosser & W. Trusen eds., Munich, Beck, 1975). Conceptual and analytical problems of dogmatic legal unification are discussed in the dissertation on techniques of legal assimilation: W. SCHMID, PRIVATRECHTSANGLEICHUNG IN DEN EUROPÄISCHEN GEMEINSCHAFTEN 36 (Frankfurt, Metzner, 1975).

[81] *See* L.M. FRIEDMAN, *supra* note 11, at 283; R.M. UNGER, LAW IN Modern SOCIETY 47, 192 (New York, Free Press, 1976); P. NONET & P. SELZNICK, LAW AND SOCIETY IN TRANSITION: TOWARD RESPONSIVE LAW (New York, Octagon Books, 1978). For Germany *see* F. WIEACKER, *Das Sozialmodell der klassischen Privatrechtsgesetzbücher und die Entwicklung der modernen Gesellschaft,* in INDUSTRIEGESELLSCHAFT UND PRIVATRECHTSORDNUNG 29 (Frankfurt, Athenäum, 1974). On the modern status of legal rationality *see* Eder, *Zur Rationalisierungsproblematik des modernen Rechts,* [1978] 29 SOZIALE WELT 247; Schelsky, *Die juridische Rationalität,* in DIE SOZIOLOGEN UND DAS RECHT 34 (Opladen, Westdeutscher Verlag, 1980).

[82] M. WEBER, WIRTSCHAFT UND GESELLSCHAFT 468 ff, 503 ff (Tübingen, Mohr (Siebeck), 1972).

[83] *See* Trubek, *Max Weber on Law and the Rise of Capitalism,* 1972 WIS. L. REV. 720; Friedman, *On Legalistic Reasoning: A Footnote to Weber,* 1966 WIS. L. REV. 148, 149–50.

Weber also pointed out certain "anti-formal" tendencies in modern European law, tendencies which threatened to destroy formal rationality. Legal doctrine, in his view, would inevitably decline, if the "materialization" of law became dominant. The "juristic precision" of judicial opinions would be seriously impaired, "if sociological, economic, or ethical argument were to take the place of legal concepts."[84] But contemporary legal theorists do indeed see a growing trend toward "materialization of formal law."[85] To be sure, theorists – men like Habermas or Luhmann – differ greatly among themselves on the causes and effects of this trend.[86] But they, and others, agree on the *phenomenon:* the decline of formal rationality, and, with it, of legal doctrine.[87] The new, substantive orientation of law is associated with the rise of the welfare state, with greater intervention in market structures. This, of course, is a fundamental historical process; we observe it in all European countries, and in North America as well.

The style and structure of law, in other words, is no longer dominated by sheer rules (if it ever was); more and more, considerations of *policy* supplement or replace a conceptual orientation. Jurists no longer see their job as strict logical application of precisely-defined rules; on the one hand, they confront vague general clauses, on the other hand, highly-detailed regulations. Especially in new fields of law – labor and business regulation, consumer and environmental law, tax law – the work of the jurist moves away from traditional methods of reasoning (deriving definite consequences from "legal facts") to a style more openly influenced by "policy." This style demands different cognitive orientations, different methods, different forms of argument.[88] This development has grave consequences for the conceptual structure of legal systems and – to return to our theme – for the transnational potential of legal doctrine in the traditional sense.

Under the hypnotic spell of formal rationality, the jurist could at least dream of the unity of legal systems. If the scholar could analyze legal concepts closely enough, and cleverly enough, he would discover a higher unity, a level of abstraction which would tie together fundamental concepts in different systems of law. The modern world – the world of substantive rationality – is

[84] MAX WEBER ON LAW IN ECONOMY AND SOCIETY 320 (M. Rheinstein ed., Cambridge, Harv. U. P., 1954).

[85] For further discussion *see, e.g.*, Teubner, *Substantive and Reflexive Elements in Modern Law,* 17 LAW & SOC'Y REV. 2 (1982).

[86] *See, e.g.*, Habermas, *Überlegungen zum evolutionären Stellenwert des modernen Rechts,* in ZUR REKONSTRUKTION DES HISTORISCHEN MATERIALISMUS 260 (Frankfurt, Suhrkamp, 1976); 1 N. LUHMANN, *supra* note 1, at 132.

[87] For a discussion of the "materialization" of law from different theoretical perspectives, *see* WIRTSCHAFTSRECHT ALS KRITIK: BEITRÄGE ZUR WIRTSCHAFTSTHEORIE (H.D. Assmann, G. Brüggemeier, D. Hart & D. Joerges eds., Königstein, Athenäum, 1979).

[88] *See* Wiethölter, *Entwicklung des Rechtsbegriffs,* 8 JAHRBUCH FÜR RECHTSSOZIOLOGIE UND RECHTSTHEORIE (RECHTSFORMEN DER VERFLECHTUNG VON STAAT UND WIRTSCHAFT) 38 (G. Winter & V. Gessner eds., 1982); Schmidt, *Von der Privat- zur Sozialautonomie,* 35 JZ 153 (1980).

cruelly unkind to these dreams. "Doctrine," in the nineteenth century sense, has become a dead end. Hence, efforts to unify through legislation succeed only in framing extremely vague and abstract rules, and then only in traditional fields of private law, since matters that touch on social or economic policy have to be systematically excluded.[89]

The politicians, of course, resist these and other schemes for unity. But political resistance is only a symptom of an underlying problem: social and economic structures in the modern world are so various and complex that they cannot be harmonized across borders through abstract legal rules.[90] How can we expect a transnational legal system to coordinate different or even contradictory policies? After all, the source of the differences does not stem from some little quirk or error of legal thought, but in fundamental national policies. It is of no help to take up a doomed, hopeless hunt for lost doctrines, and to rouse the old concepts from their graves.

We suggest a different approach. We would begin with a thoughtful use of social science insights and techniques. The goal is to develop flexible and responsive ideas about law, and to study how to contrive procedures that help coordination among nations.[91] The two central elements of classical legal doctrine – "scientific" autonomy, and classificatory abstraction – must be replaced by interdisciplinary analysis and a problem-oriented, functional style of legal thought.[92]

C. Unplanned Parallelism and a Methodological Approach to Unification: A Social Science Reorientation

Up to now we have assumed that legal education can and should contribute to legal uniformity, though whether it can and should contribute much or a little was hard to say. We have also assumed that uniformity is "a good thing" in a legal system. Neither of these assumption, however, is necessarily correct.

First, it can be at least argued that the American form of legal education has in some ways *contributed* to disunity. Its dogged generality ignored local legal cultures, and helped allow stubborn pockets of diversity to thrive in their dark little corners, unexposed to the light of scholarship and criticism. The overwhelming emphasis on *appellate* case-law strengthens this tendency.

In the second place, it is not clear that the United States, or Europe, really *need* "uniformity," in the sense of the American Restatements, uniform acts, and the Commercial Code – or of the proposals put forth for unifying European law. The Uniform Commercial Code makes perhaps the strongest case; even here, it is not clear why all fifty states have to lie in the same bed. The draftsmen

[89] Mertens, *supra* note 80, at 651.

[90] C. Joerges, *Vorüberlegungen zu einer Theorie des internationalen Wirtschaftsrechts*, 43 RabelsZ 7, 47 (1979).

[91] *See id.* at 51.

[92] *See* N. Luhmann, *supra* note 73, rejecting direct cooperation between law and the social sciences, and putting forward a new version of sociological jurisprudence.

of the Code convinced the American states that the Code was useful. And a uniform law is, of course, rather convenient for interstate business. But local conditions *might* justify local "deviations"; and the cost *might* be worthwhile in terms of social justice or furtherance of some state policy. The benefits of non-uniformity have never been really examined. In Europe, where differences in culture and traditions among nation-states are much greater than is true among American states, the question is even more serious. Is nothing *lost* when law becomes unified?

From the scholarly or scientific point of view, what was clearly bad about the "national" aspects of American legal education was its disdain for local law. We say this not because of any romantic attachment to local traditions. Rather, the search for "general principles" reinforced one of the most dubious aspects of legal education – its refusal to confront the relationship between law and society, its deliberate blindness to the social functions of law. Langdell insisted that law was a "science." This implied that somehow law stood apart from the hurly-burly of the market-place, the push and pull of partisan forces, class struggle, interest group jockeying and so on. In legislatures, city halls, and in national Parliaments, it is impossible to ignore politics and economics. But if we shut our eyes tightly enough, we can pretend that the "principles" of case-law have some sort of cold, objective reality in themselves, however false or foolish this notion may be.

Legal education which stressed law *in* society – the social realities of legal process – would be profoundly different from legal education as it is today in the United States or in Europe. A sophisticated system of legal education would confront uniformity and diversity in the context of their social meaning. And this, we feel, would be a system worthy of, and appropriate for, a new European society. Creating interdisciplinary legal education in Europe would be without question an ambitious program. But it is not Utopian. On the contrary, it can build on a tradition in legal thought, on both sides of the Atlantic, which has never been dominant, but has made a definite mark.

This is not the place to retell the story of the long, rocky romance between jurists and social scientists. The story goes back, of course, to Max Weber and even earlier. At the famous "*Congrès international de droit comparé*" of 1900, in Paris, Gabriel Tarde insisted that comparative legal research was, consciously or unconsciously, a form of sociology.[93] This idea has been repeated ever since among comparativists,[94] though actual research hardly

[93] *See* 1 CONGRÈS INTERNATIONAL DE DROIT COMPARÉ, PROCÈS-VERBAUX DES SÉANCES ET DOCUMENTS 437 ff (Congrès international de droit comparé tenu à Paris du 31 juillet au 4 août 1900, Paris, vol. 1: 1905, vol. 2: 1907). Tarde's speech is also reproduced, in a German translation, in RECHTSSOZIOLOGIE UND RECHTSVERGLEICHUNG 11 (U. Drobnig & M. Rehbinder eds., Berlin, Duncker & Humblot, 1977).

[94] *See, e.g.*, various contributions in RECHTSSOZIOLOGIE UND RECHTSVERGLEICHUNG, *supra* note 93; Ziegert, *Juristische und soziologische Empirie des Rechts, Genese und Zukunft der Rechtsvergleichung als wissenschaftliches Problem des europäischen Rechts,* 45 RABELSZ 51 (1981).

bears it out. But scholars concede that legal institutions can be sensibly compared only if we treat them in social context; this is the heart of the so-called "functional approach" to comparative law. This approach asks not whether country A and country B share a particular doctrine, but how legal system A attacks this or that social problem, as compared with legal system B.[95] In recent years, there have been some beginnings of a sociology of comparative law, quantitative and rigorous. Occasional studies have analyzed the social effects of legal norms in different societies and social contexts.[96]

The relationship between legal education in the United States and the social sciences has been jagged and uneven. Bursts of enthusiasm have been followed by periods of let-down and disillusionment. Yet on the whole, if we ignore the zigs and the zags, the *use* of social science in legal education has grown steadily, even if, over-all, the impact has been modest. Some people connect the rise of the law-and-society movement with legal realism and "sociological jurisprudence." Others believe that the movement's roots lie more in the growing sophistication of the social sciences themselves, their increasing interest in studying the legal system as an important subsystem in society – the feeling among some social scientists that legal phenomena are too important to be left to the lawyers. In Europe, too, there has been a great increase in research and theory on the relationship between law and society. The tradition, of course, goes back to Weber, Eugen Ehrlich, and others, and although it all but died out in the early twentieth century, it shared in the health and growth of the social sciences after World War II.

The union of social science and legal education has been talked about for decades, but usually with more talk than action. Still, there are a few active experiments worth mentioning. There is, for example, the graduate program in jurisprudence and social policy (JSP) at the University of California (Berkeley). The program unites many disciplines: law, sociology, history, economics and philosophy. Students may work toward an M.A. or a Ph.D. degree. It is important to note that the JSP program has a commitment to a problem-centered approach, in contrast to traditional ways of approaching the sociology or philosophy of law.[97] For examples of other relevant programs we may turn to Germany, where in the 1970's, on the basis of article 5b of the *Deutsches Richter-*

[95] J. Esser, Grundsatz und Norm in der richterlichen Fortbildung des Privatrechts 327 (Tübingen, Mohr, 1956); K. Zweigert & H. Kötz, *supra* note 4, at 27 *et passim. See also supra* note 64.

[96] Falke, Gessner & Höland, *Sozialwissenschaftliche Forschung als Vorstufe internationaler Rechtsvereinheitlichung am Beispiel des Arbeitsrechts,* 45 RabelsZ 268 (1981). For an example of quantitative comparative law, *see* Law and Social Change in Mediterranean Europe and Latin America (J.H. Merryman, D. Clark & L.M. Friedman eds., Dobbs Ferry, N.Y., Oceana, 1979). *See also generally* Volkmar Gessner, Methoden und Probleme Vergleichender Rechtssoziologie (ZERP Diskussionspapier No. 2/83, Bremen, U. of Bremen, 1983).

[97] *See* Selznick, *Jurisprudence and Social Policy: Aspirations and Perspectives,* 68 Cal. L. Rev. 206, 207 (1980); Kadish, *The JSP Program in Perspective,* The Transcript (Spring, 1978).

gesetz (1971), which authorized reform of legal education within the individual German states (*Länder*),[98] a number of law schools introduced experimental programs. Unfortunately, with the end of the reformist wave, most of these experiments are now being phased out. For our purposes, one of the most interesting programs was that of the University of Bremen. Students of the schools of law, economics and social science all followed a so-called "*Integriertes sozialwissenschaftliches Eingangsstudium*" in their first year. Law students covered basic fields of law in the next three years, but with attention to sociological and economic aspects and issues. In the last two years of legal education, the student specialized in a "project study," *i.e.*, in problem-oriented research in labor, economic, or administrative law, or in other fields.[99] Finally, one might turn to England and mention the programs at the University of Sussex, where there is no faculty of law, but courses in law are included within other programs, for example, in the School of European Studies. The student can major in law, taking courses in English law, and European Community law, in the context of a richer study of European politics, sociology and economics.[100]

There is, then, some concrete basis, some experience, which points the way to a new kind of legal education. Clearly, we do not propose replacing legal concepts with sociological concepts, nor do we claim that law is or ought to be itself a social science (whatever that would mean). We do not even claim that lawyers must be trained in sociological methods and theories (or psychological, anthropological and economic methods and theories). We merely suggest using social science as a guide, a way to approach transnational law more realistically. How can law take account of social problems? How can it cope with differences in economies and cultures? With different legal languages and traditions? The answer is, surely, only through channeling legal method away from doctrine, classification and abstraction, toward a problem-oriented, functional approach.[101]

The goal is to train European lawyers by teaching them to understand law, not as a network of concepts, but as a machine for solving problems. The various countries of Europe, no matter how diverse their legal languages, do in fact face common problems, and have common traditions. A functional approach would permit study of how to "compare the consequences of

98 BGBl 1972, I, § 713 (and with the latest 1980 modifications in BGBl 1980, I, § 1451).

99 Rinken, *Das Juristenausbildungsgesetz: Grundriß und Rahmen einer Reform als Planungs- und Lernprozeß*, in DER NEUE JURIST: MATERIALIEN Z. REFORMIERTEN JURISTENAUSBILDUNG IN BREMEN 11, 20 ff (A. Rinken ed., Neuwied, Luchterhand, 1973); Joerges, *Die Rolle der Sozialwissenschaften und die Bedeutung des Schwerpunktkonzepts für die Ausbildung*, 15 ZRP 96 (1982); EINSTUFIGE JURISTENAUSBILDUNG IN BREMEN. 10 JAHRE BREMER MODELL (R. Francke, D. Hart, R. Lautmann & P. Thoss eds., Neuwied, Luchterhand, 1982).

100 The research program of the European University Institute (*see supra* note 63) is also interdisciplinary. The Research Projects currently in progress in the Law Department involve lawyers, sociologists, political scientists and economists.

101 *See* N. LUHMANN, *supra* note 74, at 53.

different solutions to problems," how to "accumulate critical experience," how to compare "experiences from different fields."[102] Philip Selznick stresses two elements, vital to policy-oriented study of law: "problem-centered inquiry," that is, empirical research, guided by policy aims; and "social policy analysis," that is, the study of law's social consequences.[103] These would be at the heart of the functional approach.

Every legal system has its own internal models or pictures of social reality.[104] By carefully observing patterns of legal thought one can reconstruct the theories of social reality which underlie the legal norms, appellate opinions, and doctrines. These patterns and models serve to guide and orient legal decision-makers. There are models of contract, of business associations, of the relationships between state and society. Often, legal perceptions and constructions differ greatly from everyday understanding – public perceptions – as well as from the models that underlie sociological or economic theories. The law creates its own world, its own reality.

Ultimately, the legal pictures of life are derived from those of life in society; but the legal system distorts and bends them under the institutional necessities of resolving conflicts, and under the influence of specific legal cultures.[105] It is generally true that legal models of reality tend to neglect – on the surface at least – political, economic, or socially "relevant" elements.[106] In other words, three clusters of factors determine the nature of legal models of reality: first, the socio-economic forces in a given society; second, the functions and operational needs of a modern legal system; third, the specific legal traditions of the society. The first two tend to converge in Europe. The Member States of the Community are all more-or-less welfare states, with parliamentary systems. The third is more variable; but it can be cut down to size by a more general, more "European" form of legal education.

Law and legal education can leap over narrow boundaries, can become more transnational, more universal, by studying legal models of reality, and by emphasizing empirical research, and the effects of legal actions on society. Functional analysis is almost inherently transnational since it looks at norms or institutions and asks what their functional equivalents are in other societies.[107]

[102] N. LUHMANN, *Die Evolution des Rechts*, in 1 RECHTSTHEORIE 19 (Berlin, Duncker & Humblot, 1970).

[103] Selznick, *Jurisprudence and Social Policy: Aspirations and Perspectives*, in LAW AND SOCIETY IN TRANSITION, *supra* note 81, at 78.

[104] On the model theory in general, *see* THE USE OF MODELS IN SOCIAL SCIENCES (L. Collins ed., London, Tavistock, 1976); H. STACHOWIAK, ALLGEMEINE MODELLTHEORIE (Vienna, Springer, 1973). In legal theory, *see* Reale, *Pour une théorie des modèles juridiques*, [1970] V ACTS OF THE 4TH INT'L CONG. for PHIL. 144 ff; Teubner, *Generalklauseln als sozio-normative Modelle*, in GENERALKLAUSELN ALS GEGENSTAND DER SOZIALWISSENSCHAFTEN 13 ff (K. Lüderssen ed., Baden-Baden, Nomos, 1978).

[105] On the selectivity of legal models, *see* Teubner, *supra* note 104, at 30 ff.

[106] *See* H. STACHOWIAK, *supra* note 104, at 269 ff.

[107] For a functional analysis in law generally, *see* Luhmann, *Funktionale Methode und juristische Entscheidung*, 94 AöR 1 (1969).

Policy research is research that looks at legal reality and those aspects of social reality which bear on the choice between competing policies and norms. Impact analysis is also important. Traditionally, norms were dealt with as if they existed in a kind of vacuum; legislatures or courts proclaimed laws which were assumed to be magically self-executing. Even where this was patently false, the problems of effectiveness, side effects, functions and dysfunctions were ignored. They were no concern either of the lawyer or the scholar.[108]

One should reject, of course, any naive, technocratic view of what social science (or science in general) can do for a legal system, or for society. To begin with, the social sciences are themselves often weak and inconsistent in methods and theories. This must be conceded. Second the social science orientation does not solve the decision-making problems of lawyers (or jurists, judges and legislators). Indeed, it may make them at least *seem* more difficult. There is absolutely no way in which "facts," or social science, or policy analysis, can dictate choices between competing values. Legal models of reality correspond in complex ways to social models and social science models. It is useful to explore these relationships; but the discovery of interrelationships does *not* produce "answers" to policy dilemmas.

For example, we might explore the relationship between the market economy, and the norms of contract law, or of business associations. What we find would explain a lot about how law works; but it could not tell us whether the free market is better than a mixed or socialized economy. We would find that classical economic theories of competition, and political theories of parliamentary democracy and the rule of law, influence the legal construction of reality. They affect definitions of the social functions of law, and how people feel about the free market system and its rivals.[109] Similarly, economic theories about a mixed economy, and political theories of the interventionist state, point to different policies, hence to different norms and doctrines.[110] Competing approaches imply different selections of what to study empirically, and what consequences are worth looking for (and how to recognize them when we find them). The differences have consequences for legal method too; and for the ways in which legal unification ought to proceed.[111] A social science approach is a neutral tool, not a guide to ultimate values.

108 On the relationship between politics and the social sciences in general, *see* C.E. LINDBLOM & D.K. COHEN, USABLE KNOWLEDGE: SOCIAL SCIENCE AND SOCIAL PROBLEM-SOLVING (New Haven, Yale, U.P., 1979).

109 Mestmäcker, *Macht – Recht – Wirtschaftsverfassung*, in DIE SICHTBARE HAND DES RECHTS 7 (Baden-Baden, Nomos, 1978); Mestmäcker, *Multinationale Unternehmen im nationalen und internationalen Wirtschaftsrecht*, in *id.* at 63.

110 Wiethölter, *Begriffs- oder Interessenjurispudenz – falsche Fronten im IPR und Wirtschaftsverfassungsrecht*, in INTERNATIONALES PRIVATRECHT UND RECHTSVERGLEICHUNG IM AUSGANG DES 20. JAHRHUNDERTS – BEWAHRUNG ODER WENDE? FESTSCHRIFT FÜR GERHARD KEGEL 213 (A. Lüderitz & J. Schröder eds., Frankfurt, Metzner, 1977); Joerges, *supra* note 90, at 6.

111 *See* Joerges, *supra* note 90, at 43.

Still, it would be fruitful in the long-run to think in the directions suggested – and practical, too. The traditional approach to legal doctrine is either dead, or at best ineffective in explaining how legal systems actually behave. The social sciences may not have satisfactory answers; but at least they do sometimes ask the right questions. For example, although anthropology, the study of culture, deals with the *diversity* of human arrangements, this has not prevented general theories from arising within the discipline. In other words, anthropology is a *general* subject, even though its raw materials are the shifting and incredibly diverse faces of social order. This is the model for what we propose: an approach to legal study that focusses directly and rigorously on legal diversities and commonalities. This orientation might create a common language for the definition, study, and solution of legal problems. If so, it might better serve the intellectual and practical needs of the European legal profession.

Practically speaking, what would a curriculum oriented toward social science look like? It would include introductory courses in the sociology, history, and philosophy of law; in law and economics; and in the sociology of the legal profession. In each country, perhaps, the material would draw most heavily on *local* examples; but always in a comparative perspective. Only after this kind of foundation had been laid, would the student approach the substantive law, both national and European. And (ideally) each subject course would build on foundations laid down in the beginning. Of course all this is the merest sketch; and there are obvious difficulties standing in the way. Legal scholars typically show all the stubbornness of an endangered elite. They do not care to recycle themselves; and who can blame them? Our suggested "European" form of education, moreover, does not bridge the real gaps between the various countries in the EC. How could it? The curriculum would not teach French to an Englishman, or Dutch to an Italian. It could not equip lawyers to practice ordinary law in some foreign country. But such a curriculum would (we feel) hold out at least some hope of a more flexible profession, less hidebound, less old-fashioned in its thinking, certainly less provincial. It would be more united in background and in habits of mind; ready for Europe, if Europe would only arrive.

Cumulative Index

(Roman numerals refer to the Book number, arabic numerals refer to the page number)

Please note that this index is simply a modified key word index and not an analytical index. In addition, the most frequently recurrent words have not been listed (*e.g.* Congress, Commission, Council, and the names of the Member States comprising the EC).
The Cumulative Tables of Treaty Provisions, Constitutional Provisions and Cases are to be found at the beginning of Book 1: references in the Index to the EEC Treaty, the European Convention on Human Rights, the Australian, Canadian and US Constitutions and to the Grundgesetz of the Federal Republic of Germany refer to these Tables.

Integration Through Law

Europe and the American Federal Experience

A Series under the General Editorship of

Mauro Cappelletti · Monica Seccombe · Joseph Weiler

Part One

Volume 1

Methods, Tools and Institutions

edited by Mauro Cappelletti, Monica Seccombe & Joseph Weiler

Book 1: A Political, Legal and Economic Overview
Book 2: Political Organs, Integration Techniques and Judicial Process
Book 3: Forces and Potential for a European Identity

Part Two

Integration Policies in Selected Areas

Volumes 2—6

Volume 2: Environmental Protection Policy
by
Eckard Rehbinder & Richard Stewart

Volume 3: Consumer Law, Common Markets and Federalism in Europe and the United States
by
Thierry Bourgoignie & David Trubek (with Louise Trubek & Denis Stingl)

Volume 4: Legal Harmonization and the Business Enterprise: Corporate Law and Capital Market Harmonization Policy in Europe and the U.S.A.
by
Richard Buxbaum & Klaus J. Hopt

Volume 5: The Legal Integration of Energy Markets
by
Terence Daintith & Stephen Williams

Volume 6: Regionalism and Federalism: The Challenge of Regions in National and Transnational Polities
by
Yves Mény, Bruno De Witte & Jerry Webman

Kolibri 360 GmbH
Ferdinand-Jühlke-Straße 7
99095 Erfurt, Deutschland
produktsicherheit@kolibri360.de